CUBAN LITERATURE

GARLAND REFERENCE LIBRARY
OF THE HUMANITIES
(VOL. 511)

CUBAN LITERATURE
A Research Guide

David William Foster

GARLAND PUBLISHING, INC. • NEW YORK & LONDON
1985

Library of Congress Cataloging in Publication Data

Foster, David William.
Cuban literature.

(Garland reference library of the humanities ;
vol. 511)
Includes index.
1. Cuban literature—History and criticism—
Bibliography. I. Title. II. Series: Garland reference
library of the humanities ; v. 511.
Z1521.F694 1985 016.86′09′97291 84-48099
[PQ7371]
ISBN 0-8240-8903-0 (alk. paper)

Printed on acid-free, 250-year-life paper
Manufactured in the United States of America

CONTENTS

BIBLIOGRAPHY OF CRITICISM

General References

84-7340

Authors

viii   *Contents*

INTRODUCTION

Cuban Literature is the last—for the time being—in a series of bibliographic guides on various national Latin American literatures and special topics. It complements volumes published on Argentina, Mexico, Chile, Peru, and Puerto Rico, on the twentieth-century Spanish American novel, the so-called "new Spanish American novel," general references sources in Hispanic literature, and a comprehensive annotated primary and secondary bibliography of Jorge Luis Borges. The range of Latin American literature is enormous, and much work remains to be done. However, with *Cuban Literature* the compiler has accomplished his goal of providing Latin American literary studies with guides to many of its most essential aspects.

In a certain sense, *Cuban Literature* was the most difficult of all of these compilations. Although Cuban writers enjoy a position of high prestige in the overall literary panorama of Latin America, there are few major research collections of Cuban literature in the U.S. that the bibliographer can draw upon (see, however, the University of Miami's Cuban collection, represented by item A.10). The intellectual and general sociocultural dialogue between the United States and Cuba has been interrupted for over twenty years, and the consequences have been regrettable for the continuity of research on Cuba in the United States. But the thorniest aspect has been the fratricidal cleavage between writers in Cuba and writers who for one reason or another have left the island. Both groups feel themselves to be the legitimate heirs of the Cuban cultural tradition, and the differences between them are too great for foreseeable reconciliation. Although there are many Latin American writers in exile—and often they are the key figures of concern to the literary critic—Cuba presents the unfortunate circumstances (perhaps it is yet one more variety in Latin America of the Lévi-Strauss hypothesis of the *tristes tropi-*

ques) of two virtually antagonistic literary traditions since the Castro Revolution. My solution to this problem, in view of my belief that it is the bibliographer's responsibility neither to interpret nor to judge such complex issues, has been simply to ignore it: for purposes of this compilation, Cuban writers are those who were born and raised in Cuba and who write in Spanish. Where their books are published and by whom, where they reside, and what their interpretation of Cuba's sociohistory may be are all aspects that are irrelevant to the decision to include particular authors in this compilation. Other reference tools have chosen to adopt a different criterion; the criterion of this compilation reflects the simple fact that the primary audience contemplated, that of American research scholars, has a comprehensive need for information relating to all aspects of Latin American culture, regardless of ideological persuasion. The one significant exception is María Mercedes Santa Cruz, the Condesa de Merlín (1789–1852). Although born in Cuba, where she spent her early years, Santa Cruz wrote about Cuba in French. I have included criticism on her writings because of their historical importance (she has been called the author of the first Cuban novel), because of my desire to provide a comprehensive representation of Cuba's many important women authors and because of the large body of criticism on her in Spanish. By contrast, Cuba's other famous French-language author, José María de Heredia (1842–1905), the author of *Les trophées* and a relative of the José María Heredia included in this compilation, is not customarily considered a "Cuban" author, nor is there a significant body of criticism on his writing in Spanish.

As a consequence, the overriding principle has been to include those authors who have attracted a measurable degree of criticism of interest to research scholars in literature (this criterion is amplified below). Such authors include not only the key names in Cuba's literary history from the time of the Spanish conquest but also those newer writers who have earned the sort of attention that augurs well for their emerging importance. Neither the consecration of an inventory of new names nor an Olympus of monumentalized figures, the list of authors represented by *Cuban Literature* strives simply for an accurate and balanced representation.

The guiding criterion has been to list those items considered useful to serious scholarly research and opinion—articles in all types of scholarly journals and the most important cultural ones, and all monographic studies—and those likely to be easily accessible in Latin American and the United States, a criterion that accounts for my not attempting to take every cultural publication into account. The distinction is undoubtedly difficult to sustain between "useful" and "nonuseful," "important" and "trivial," items, and I have been inclined to be overinclusive, a circumstance reflected in the coverage for José Martí, on whom so much has been published. Certainly, it is not the bibliographer's task to distinguish between competent and incompetent criticism nor to restrict a compilation to essays representing a certain trend or range of trends.

Yet, in the case of authors like Martí or Alejo Carpentier, it would not be practical—and would constitute a misunderstanding of the task of the literary bibliographer—to list all known references, especially those in general-audience magazines and newspapers. I have, accordingly, attempted the difficult task of distinguishing academic and "cultural" criticism from "journalistic" presentations and have excluded the latter. Thus, materials appearing in newspapers and mass-circulation publications are not represented. References in *Bohemia,* which combines the goals of a magazine and a cultural review, are one notable exception to this policy.

In the case of each author and the general references, my objective has been to serve the interests, as I understand them, of the academic literary scholar. Items in magazines, dailies, and literary supplements have, as a consequence, been omitted, since they rarely meet the twofold criterion of abiding interest and accessibility. However, those items that have been reprinted in collected essays have been listed, not only because such collections are more readily available but because reprinting in this format attests to some degree to the intrinsic importance of the essay and the stature of the critic involved. All known criticism and review articles in scholarly and cultural journals have, of course, been listed.

A word about the distinction between reviews and review articles is in order. By the former, I understand a relatively brief notice, ranging from the 250–500-word review published in *World literature today*, to the two- or three-page presentation of more specialized journals like *La palabra y el hombre, Plural, Revista iberoamericana, Revista de crítica literaria latinoamericana,* or *Chasqui*. Typically, the review is untitled and is identified by the book's pertinent bibliographic information; it is usually "signed" with the name of the reviewer at the foot of the review, although initials may be used in the case of staff reviewers. When I have cited reviews for works by authors whom I deem important but for whom there is scant criticism, I have given as the title of the review a shortened form of the heading, enclosed in brackets. Clearly, any reasonable criterion of selection based on the relative merit and depth of critical notes would, in the case of authors like Carpentier, rank reviews very low in importance. An exception might be unusually noteworthy contributions—say, the reviews by famous writers on his early works in the 1930s.

To be sure, a complete bibliography for any author would aim to present all such pertinent material (for example, the bibliographies that *Revista iberoamericana* has been publishing for the last ten years). Nevertheless, only the scholar concerned with the minutiae of the development of a writer's career could find reviews important when placed alongside extensive, in-depth critical studies meeting well-defined standards of academic methodology. Given this circumstance and the fact that to include reviews would have at least doubled the number of entries, I feel that to exclude them for the majority of authors does not seriously misrepresent the criticism available on their writings of interest to the modern literary scholar. On the other hand, reviews may be sought by referring to the specialized bibliographies listed for each major author and to available cumulative indexes for Latin American publications that register reviews.

Although I do not list references that are included without distinguishing headings in general treatises of Latin American literature and monographs on specific aspects of genres and movements, the scholar should always consult such works and discover pertinent passages through an index or table of contents. Latin American bibliographies have often listed such references as though they were monographic articles or chapters simply because there has never been a general and well-organized bibliography of general treatises on Spanish American literature and various national literatures, movements, periods, genres; such a bibliography is an outstanding desideratum. However, since references in this guide are arranged hierarchically, beginning with a hierarchically subdivided section of general topics, followed by sections of specific authors, references of a general nature that include comments on specific authors have not been repeated in the sections on the latter. If one is researching references on, say, Heredia's romantic poetry, he should, in addition to consulting the specific references in the section on Heredia, consult the section on the Nineteenth Century Poetry.

In general, the bibliographic formats followed are those of the U.S. Library of Congress and the Modern Language Association of America. All names of critics have been standardized to one form. It should be noted that the volume and number information may vary from one entry to another—i.e., *Atenea* may be cited by volume number in one reference but by consecutive number in another. Since either number is sufficient to locate the item, I have not tried to establish rigid conformity. Hence, items must be sought on the basis of both volume/issue number and date. Any residual errors are the combined responsibility of the compiler and the lamentably long-lived tradition in Hispanic bibliography of incomplete, confusing, and inaccurate references. I hope, however, that this compilation represents a step toward the sort of bibliographic control the several national literatures so clearly deserve.

Sources like Rela's *Guía bibliográfica de la literatura hispanoamericana*, Flores's *Bibliografía de escritores hispanoamericanos 1609–1974*, and UNESCO's *Bibliografía general de la literatura hispanoamericana* provided basic points of departure for gathering references, both monographs and articles. Sources tend to complement each other rather than to overlap, and the amount of contradictory information is frequently startling. But one can at least assemble a nucleus, if only partial and unreliable, of citations.

Special sources on individual authors or topics remain monographic studies and their footnotes and/or bibliographies of references. All major monographs—and most minor ones—on Cuban literature were combed for citations. Again, I found inconsistencies, inaccuracies, and contradictions that had to be checked against library catalogs (primarily the National Union Catalog and the Latin American Collection of the University of Texas) or, as often as possible, against the journals and books themselves.

I found the growing number of specialized bibliographies on Latin American literature extremely valuable; the bibliographies that have appeared in *Revista iberoamericana* in recent years are especially valuable. My goal was to double-check the data on each reference against the item itself, and this was possible for virtually all monographs and for articles in major journals. However, if one compares the list of journals from which items are cited against the entries in the volumes for Cuba in Quintero Mesa's union catalog, *Latin American serial documents: a holdings list,* it will be quickly discovered that many of the journals are either unavailable in U.S. libraries or are represented by incomplete holdings. References in these journals are necessarily less reliable because they have been difficult to actually see. Yet, the fact that they are cited in several sources with consistent imprint data has led me to believe they are worth including nevertheless.

Of course, the MLA's *International bibliography* continues to be a good source of citations, and the *Hispanic American periodical index* has become a major reference source as it continues to expand coverage. On the other hand, I found the *Index to Latin American periodical literature 1929–1960* extremely unreliable and incomplete, although the supplement volumes published through the late sixties were more comprehensive. The *Handbook of Latin American studies,* while it served to verify some difficult references, was surprisingly not very useful: its value appears to be the annotations of items that are given, rather than the scope of journals it covers (*HLAS,* I note, also lists monographs).

There continues to be a large gap, in Latin American literary bibliography, between major journals, easily consulted in the U.S. and for which there are printed cumulative indexes (see the items in section Z) and journals that, although they are well known, seem somehow to get lost in the shuffle. Needless to say, the lack of cumulative indexes makes it all the more difficult to verify citations in them.

One final important source needs mentioning: bibliographies of criticism included as an ancillary item in an author's complete or selected works and bibliographies of criticism included in appendices to collections of critical essays on an author. The latter is a growing phenomenon in Latin American literature—one recalls the useful collections on Paz, Neruda, Vallejo, Quiroga assembled by Angel Flores—and provides an excellent opportunity for a conscientious compiler to commission such a listing.

A few miscellaneous observations concerning bibliographical standards employed:

1. American doctoral dissertations are cited in two fashions: if the reference in *Dissertation abstracts/Dissertation abstracts international* is known, American titles have been listed in terms of their abstract. The reason for this is that this reference is necessary in order to obtain the order number for the dissertation, should the researcher wish to locate a copy. For dissertations written prior to the *DA/DAI* listings or at those few institutions that do not participate in the listing, I have cited the studies as unpublished manuscripts.

2. All title citations of creative works have been made uniform, despite the manner in the actual article or monograph. Thus, poems, short stories, and individual essays are cited with quotation marks; titles of novels, monographs, and long poems are italicized. By the same token, capitalization has been made uniform in all references, in accord with the dominant practice of Spanish. In general, the criterion for capitalization follows the rules of the Library of Congress, which explains the use of lower case with English-language titles also.

3. Sections of monographs dealing with specific authors have been listed separately only if the appropriate section is autonomous in title and content. Thus, as a general rule, sections of literary histories and other panoramic studies have not been listed separately.

4. Because of the difficulty of obtaining references to recent publications in Latin America and because of the general delay in bibliographic communications, the general cut-off date for references in this compilation was 1982–1983. No bibliography can ever be completely current, and, in any case, the principal value of such a compilation like this one lies in the inclusion, with

accurate bibliographic data, of references not easily accessible through current and cumulative indexes.

Many individuals have contributed extensively to making this compilation possible. My research assistants Luis Peña, Magdalena Maiz, and Justa Zoila Gamero Abarca de Tovar provided unflagging support. The Interlibrary Loan staff of Arizona State University's Hayden Library has, as always, been a model of professional assistance. Finally, I am especially grateful to the administration of Arizona State University for the numerous ways in which it has supported my entire research program over the years.

ABBREVIATIONS AND JOURNALS

A. *CITIES*

BA   Buenos Aires
H   La Habana
M   México, D.F.
NY   New York

Cities in Cuba are listed as places of publication without designation "Cuba," with the exception of Santiago, in order to distinguish it from Santiago, Chile.

B. *JOURNALS*

AA   Alacrán azul. Miami, 1970–1971.
AAHC   Anales de la Academia de la Historia de Cuba. H, 1919–1948.
AANAL   Anales de la Academia Nacional de Artes y Letras. H, 1916–.
AAntr   Anales de antropología. M, 1964–.
Abdala.   H, 1959–.
Abraxas.   NY, 1970–1972.
Abside.   M, 1937–.
AC   Alma cubana. H, 1923–?
ACACA   Anales de ciencias, agricultura, comercio y artes. H, 1827–1830.
ACh   Araucaria de Chile. Madrid, 1978–.
Actual.   Mérida, Venezuela, 1968–.
Actualidades.   Caracas, 1967?–.
Adelante.   H, 1935–1939?
AdF   Arbol de fuego. Caracas, 1968?–.
AdL   Arbol de letras. Santiago, Cuba, 1959–.
AdUA   Annales de l'Université d'Abidjan. Abidjan, Ivory Coast, 1965–.

AFC   Archivos del folklore cubano. H, 1924–1930.
Aidai.   Boston, 1945–.
AION-SR   Annali, Istituto Universitario, Napoli: Sezione Romanza. Napoli, Italy, 1959–.
AJM   Archivo José Martí. H. 1940–.
ALat   América latina. Moscow, 1974–.
El álbum.   H, 1838–1839.
Alero.   Guatemala, 1973–.
ALetM   Anuario de letras. M, 1961–.
ALHisp   Anales de literatura hispanoamericana. Madrid, 1972–.
ALit   Acta litteraria Academiae Scientiarum Hungaricae. Budapest, 1957–.
AMart   Anuario martiano. H, 1969–1976.
Amaru.   Lima, 1967–1971.
AmerI   América indígena. M, 1941–.
América   H, 1907–?, 1939–1958.
AméricaQ   América. Quito, 1925–?
The Americas.   NY, 1945–.
Anales.   Trujillo, Dominican Republic, 1937–.
AnBC   Anuario bibliográfico cubano. H, 1938–1966.
AnBret   Annales de Bretagne et des Pays de L'Ouest. Rennes, France, 1886–.
AnuarioF   Anuario de filología. Maracaibo, Venezuela, 1962–.
Aportes.   Paris, 1966–1972.
Araisa.   Caracas, 1975–.
L'Arc   Aix-en-Provence, France, 1958–.
Archipiélago.   Santiago, Cuba, 1928–1930?
Arco.   Bogotá, 1959–.
Areito.   NY, 1975–.
Ars.   San Salvador, 1951–.
ASGHG   Anales de la Sociedad de Geografía e Historia de Guatemala. Guatemala, 1924–.
Asomante.   San Juan, P.R., 1945–1972?
Atenea.   Santiago, Chile, 1924–?
Ateneo.   San Salvador, 1912–.
AtP   Ateneo puertorriqueño. San Juan, P.R., 1935–1940.
AUC   Anales de la Universidad de Chile. Santiago, Chile, 1843–.
AUCC   Anales de la Universidad Central de Caracas. Caracas, 1900–1939?
AUCE   Anales de la Universidad Central de Ecuador. Quito, 1883–.
Aurora.   Santiago, Chile, 1954–? 2a época, 1964–.
Avance.   Revista de avance. H, 1927–1930.
Azor.   Barcelona, 1961?–.

Azul.   Revista azul. M, 1894–1896.
BA   Books abroad. Norman, Okla., 1927–1976. Continued as *WLT*, q.v.
BAAL   Boletín de la Academia Argentina de Letras. BA, 1933–.
BACL   Boletín de la Academia Cubana de la Lengua. H, 1952–.
BACPS   Boletín de la Academia de Ciencias Políticas y Sociales. Caracas, 1936–.
BAHL   Boletín de la Academia Hondureña de la Lengua. Tegucigalpa, Honduras, 1955–.
BAN   Boletín del Archivo Nacional. H, 1902–1963.
BANLE   Boletín de la Academia Norteamericana de la Lengua Española. NY, 1976–.
BAVC   Boletín de la Academia Venezolana Correspondiente a la Española. Caracas, 1934–.
BBDI   Bulletin of bibliography and dramatic index. Boston, 1897–. Title varies, also *Bulletin of bibliography.*
BBib   Boletín bibliográfico. M, 1938–.
BBIBA   Boletín de la Biblioteca Americana y de Bellas Artes. M, 1938–.
BBMP   Boletín de la Biblioteca Menéndez Pelayo. Santander, Spain, 1919–1938, 1945–.
BCA   Capilla Alfonsina. Boletín. M, 1965–.
BCB   Boletín cultural y bibliográfico. Bogotá, 1958–.
BEG   Boletín de estudios germánicos. Mendoza, Argentina, 1942–.
Belén.   H, 1926–?
Belfagor.   Firenze, Italy, 1946–.
BFLS   Bulletin de la Faculté des Lettres de Strasbourg. Strasbourg, France, 1922–.
BH   Bulletin hispanique. Bordeaux, France, 1899–.
BHist   Boletín histórico. Caracas, 1962–.
BHS   Bulletin of Hispanic studies. Liverpool, 1923–.
Bibliotecas.   H, 1963–.
BILL   Boletín del Instituto de Literatura y Lingüística. H, 1967–.
BlackW   Black world. Chicago, 1970–.
BLM   Bonniers litterära magasin. Stockholm, 1932–.
BlS   Black scholar. San Francisco, 1969–.
Bohemia.   H, 1911–.
Bolívar.   Bogotá, 1951–.
BolP   Boletín del poeta. Santiago, Cuba, 1971–.
Boreal.   Hearst, Ontario, 1974–1978.
BöV   Böckernas Värld. Stockholm, 1969?–.
BR/RB   The bilingual review/La revista bilingüe. Jamaica, NY, etc., 1974–.

BRAH   Boletín de la Real Academia de la Historia. Madrid, 1877–. Title varies.

Brecha.   San José, Costa Rica, 1956–.

BrechaM   Brecha. Montevideo, 1968.

BRP   Beiträge zur romanischen Philologie. Berlin, 1961–.

BSUF   Ball State Univerity forum. Muncie, Ind., 1960–.

BUP   Boletín de la Unión Panamericana. Washington, D.C., 1911–1948. Continued as *Américas,* q.v.

CA   Cuadernos americanos. M, 1942–.

CAL   Cahiers des Amériques latines; série arts et littérature. Paris, 1967–.

CAm   Casa de las Américas. H, 1960–.

CAmer   El curioso americano. H, 1892–1920.

CAn   Correo de los Andes. Bogotá, 1979–.

CanF   The Canadian forum. Toronto, 1920–.

CAP   Cuadernos de arte y poesía. Quito, 1952?–.

Caravelle; cahiers du monde hispanique et luso-brésilien. Toulouse, 1966–.

Caribe.   Honolulu, 1976–1980?

CarQ   Caribbean quarterly. Mona, Jamaica, 1949–.

CarR   Caribbean review. Hato Rey, P.R., 1969–.

Carrell.   The carrell. Coral Gables, Fla., 1960–.

CarS   Caribbean studies. Río Piedras, P.R., 1961–.

Carteles.   H, 1919–1939.

CB   Caimán barbudo. H, 1966–.

CBib   Cuba bibliotecológica. H, 1953–1955. 2a serie, 1956–1960?

CC   Cine cubano. H, 1960–.

CCLC   Cuadernos del Congreso por la Libertad de la Cultura. Paris, 1953–1966.

CCont   Cuba contemporánea. H, 1913–1927.

CCSN   Center for Cuban Studies newsletter. NY, 1973–.

CdA   Camp de l'arpa; revista de literatura. Barcelona, 1972–.

CdG   Cauadernos del Guayás. Guayaquil, Ecuador, 1948–.

Ceiba.   Ponce, P.R., 1972/1973–.

CEm   El corno emplumado. M, 1962–.

Centro.   NY, 1965–.

Centroamericana.   M, 1954–1960.

CER   Cahiers d'études romanes: C.E.R. Toulouse, 1979–.

Cervantes.   H, 1925–1946.

CFil   Cuadernos de filología. Santiago, Chile, 1968–.

CH   Crítica hispánica. Johnson City, Tenn. 1979–.

CHA   Cuadernos hispanoamericanos. Madrid, 1948–.

Chasqui.   Madison, Wisc., etc., 1972–.

CHH   Cuadernos de historia habanera. H, 1935–.

CHL Cuadernos del hombre libre. Miami, 1966–.
ChU The Christian union. NY, 1870–1935.
Ciclón. H, 1955–1957
CILH Cuadernos para investigación de la literatura hispánica. Madrid, 1978–.
CimR Cimarron review. Stillwater, Okla., 1967–.
CInt Cuba intelectual. H, 1909–1926.
Círculo. NY, 1970?–.
CJItS Canadian journal of Italian studies. Hamilton, Ontario, 1977–.
CLAS College Language Association journal. Baltimore. 1957–.
Claridad. BA, 1926–1941.
CLEB Comunidad Latinoamericana de Escritores. Boletín. M, 1968–.
CLS Comparative literature studies. Urbana, Ill., 1963–.
CMB Caribbean monthly bulletin. Río Piedras, P.R., 1963–.
ČMF Časopis pro moderní filologii. Prague, 1911–.
Comentario. BA, 1953–1968.
Comunidad. M, 1966–.
Conjunto. H, 1964–.
Cordillera. La Paz, 1956.
Coromán. Santiago, Chile, 1970–?
CpD Cuadernos para el diálogo. Madrid, 1963–.
CPro Cuba profesional. H, 1952?–.
CRB Cahiers de la Compagnie Madeleine Renaud-Barrault. Paris, 1953–.
Crisis. BA, 1973–1976.
Critique. Paris, 1946–.
Crónica. H, 1949–.
CS Cuban studies/Estudios cubanos. Pittsburgh, 1975–. Continues *CSN,* q.v.
CSeg Carte segrete. Roma, 1967–.
CSí Cuba sí. Paris, ca. 1965–?
CSN Cuban studies newsletter. Pittsburgh, 1970–.
CSoc Cuba socialista. H, 1961–1967.
CSov Cultura soviética. M, 1944–1954?
CUA Cuadernos de la Universidad del Aire. H, 1933?–?
Cuba. H, 1961–1969.
CubaI Cuba internacional. H, 1969–.
CubaL Cuba literaria. H, 1861–1862.
CubaN Cuba nueva. Coral Gables, Fla., 1962–1963?
CubaR Cuba review. NY, 1971?–.
El cuento; revista de imaginación. M, 1964–.

CUG   Cuadernos universitarios. Guatemala, 1979–.

Cultura.   Santiago, Cuba, 1964–.

CulturaSS.   Cultura. San Salvador, 1955–.

CUn   Cultura universitaria. Caracas, 1947–.

CUNESCO   Cuba en la UNESCO. H, 1960–. Title varies; also *Boletín de la Comisión Cubana de la UNESCO.*

CyA   Cuba y América. NY, 1897–1912, 1913–1917.

CyC   Cursos y conferencias. BA, 1931–?

CyE   Cuba y España. H, 1941–.

CyF   Contabilidad y finanzas. H, 1928–1932, 1934–.

DA   Dissertation abstracts. Ann Arbor, Mich., 1952–1969. Continued as *DAI*, q.v.

Daedalus.   Cambridge, Mass., 1958–.

DAI   Dissertation abstracts international. Ann Arbor, Mich., 1969–. Continues *DA*, q.v.

Destino.   Barcelona, 1939?–.

DHR   Duquesne Hispanic review. Pittsburgh, 1962–?

Diacritics.   Syracuse, N.Y., 1970–.

Dialéctica.   H, 1942–.

Diálogos.   M, 1964–.

Dieciocho.   Ithaca, N.Y., 1978–.

Difusión.   La Paz, 1971–.

Dispositio.   Ann Arbor, Mich., 1976–.

EAf   Estudios afrocubanos. H, 1937–.

EAm   Estudios americanos. Seville, 1948–.

Eco   Bogotá, 1960–.

Educación.   San Juan, P.R., 1951–.

EducaciónH   Educación. H. 1971–.

EducaciónM   Educación. Managua. Nicaragua, 1957–.

EFil   Estudios filológicos. Valdivia, Chile, 1965–.

EIA   Estudios ibero-americanos. Pôrto Alegre, Brazil, 1975–.

ELic   Las entregas de la Licorne. Montevideo, 1953–1961.

ELWIU   Essays in literature. Macomb, Ill., 1974–.

Los ensayistas.   Athens, Geor., 1976–.

Envíos.   Hoboken, N.J., 1971–.

Escandalar.   Elmhurst, N.Y., 1978–.

Escena.   Caracas, ca. 1975–.

Escritura.   Caracas, 1976–.

EsP   Espuela de plata. H, 1939–1941.

EspN   España nueva. H, 1921–1926?

ESPSL   O Estado de São Paulo. Suplemento literário. São Paulo, 1956?–.

Estaciones.   M, 1956–1960.

EstLit   Estafeta literaria. Madrid, 1944–1977.
EstudiosD   Estudios; revista de cultura hispánica. Pittsburgh 1951–1954.
Et caetera.   Guadalajara, México, 1966–.
Europe.   Paris, 1923–.
Exilio.   NY, 1965–.
ExTL   Explicación de textos literarios. Sacramento, 1972–.
EyD   Economía y desarrollo. H, 1970–.
EyF   Etnología y folklore. H, 1966–.
FA   Folklore americano. Lima, 1953–.
FedE   El federado escolar. H, 1943–1954.
FigL   Le Figaro littéraire. Paris, 1946–.
Finlay.   H, 1941–.
FK   Filológiai kozlony/Philological review. Budapest, 1955–.
FMLS   Forum for modern language studies. St. Andrews, Scotland, 1975–.
Folio.   Brockport, N.Y., 1978–.
FrN   France nouvelle. Paris, 1945–.
FurmS   Furman studies. Greenville, S.C., 1912–.
GdC   Gaceta de Cuba. H, 1962–.
Germinal.   Cárdenas, 1921–.
GLit   Gaceta literaria. M, 1927–1932.
GLite   Guión literario. San Salvador, 1956–
GLR   García Lorca review. NY, 1973–.
Goya.   Madrid, 1954–.
Grafos.   H, 1933?–?
GSLA   Graduate studies on Latin America at the University of Kansas. Lawrence, Kan., 1973–?
Guadalupe.   Revista Guadalupe. Madrid, 1933–.
El habanero.   Miami, 1969–.
HAHR   Hispanic American historical review. Baltimore, etc., 1918–.
HBA   Historiografía y bibliografía americanistas. Seville, 1955–.
HdP   Hora de poesía. Barcelona, 1978–.
HeM   Hommes et mondes. Paris, 1946–1956.
Hero.   Sancti-Spiritus, 1907–.
Hispamérica.   Takoma Park, Md., 1972–.
Hispania.   Baltimore, etc., 1917–.
HLit   Hojas literarias. H, 1893–?
Horizontes.   M, 1958–1967.
HP   El hijo pródigo. M, 1943–1946.
HR   Hispanic review. Philadelphia, 1933–.
Humanismo.   H, 1952–1961.
Humanist.   NY, 1941–.

Humboldt.   Hamburg, 1960–.
HumM   Humanitas. Monterrey, México, 1960–.
HumT   Humanitas. Tucumán, Argentina, 1953–?
I&L   Ideologies and literature. Minneapolis, 1976/1977–.
IAA   Ibero-amerikanisches Archiv. Berlin, 1924–1944, 1975–.
IAL   Indice de artes y letras. Madrid, 1945–1955.
IAP   Ibero-americana pragensia. Prague, 1967–.
Iberoamericana.   Frankfurt am Main, 1977–.
ICub   La ilustración cubana. Barcelona, 1885–1888?
Ideas.   H, 1929–?
IFR   International fiction review. Fredericton, New Brunswick, 1974–.
Imagen.   Caracas, 1967–.
InC   Informaciones culturales. H, 1947–.
IndH   Indian horizons. New Delhi, 1952–.
Indice.   Madrid, 1945–.
IndiceH   Indice. H, 1936–1937?
INRA.   H, 1960–.
Insula.   Madrid, 1946–.
InsulaH   Insula. H, 1957–.
Inter-América.   NY, 1917–1926.
Inti.   Storrs, Conn., 1974–.
IPNA   Instituto Cultural Peruano-Norteamericano. Lima, 1944–1958.
Islas.   Santa Clara, 1958–.
JACL   Journal of African and comparative literature. Ibadan, Nigeria, 1981–.
JCS   Journal of Caribbean studies. Coral Gables, Fla., 1980–.
JdP   Le journal des poètes. Bruxelles, 1931–1935; 1946–.
JIAS   Journal of Inter-American studies. Coral Gables, Fla., 1959–.
JJ   Jamaica journal. Kingston, Jamaica, 1967–.
JNH   Journal of Negro history. Washington, D.C., 1916–.
José   Rio de Janeiro, 1976–.
JSL   Journal of the School of Languages. New Delhi, 1973–.
JSSTC   Journal of Spanish Studies: twentieth century. Manhattan, Kan., etc., 1973–.
Kañina.   San José, Costa Rica, 1977–.
KFLQ   Kentucky Foreign language quarterly. Lexington, Ken., 1954–1967. Continued as *KRQ,* q.v.
Knji   Književnost. Belgrade, 1955.
KRQ   Kentucky Romance quarterly. Lexington, Ken., 1967–. Continues *KFLQ,* q.v.
L&I   Literature and ideology. Montreal, 1969–.

L/L   H, 1967–. Title varies; also *Anuario L/L*
LALR   Latin American literary review. Pittsburgh, 1972–.
LangQ   The USF language quarterly. Tampa, 1962–.
LanM   Les langues modernes. Lavausseau, France, 1903–.
LARR   Latin American research review. Chapel Hill, N.C., etc., 1965–.
LatA   Latinskaia Amerika. Moscow, 1969–.
Lateinamerika.   Berlin, 1920?–.
LatH   Lateinamerika heute. München, 1970?–.
Latinoamérica.   M, 1968–.
LATR   Latin American theatre review. Lawrence, Kan., 1967–.
LB   The liberty bell. Boston, 1839–1858.
LCub   Libros cubanos. H, 1940–1942.
LetE   Letras del Ecuador. Quito, 1945–.
LetF   Lettres françaises. Paris, 1942–1944, 1944–.
LetN   Lettres nouvelles. Paris, 1953–.
LetNa   Letras nacionales. Bogotá, 1965–.
Letras.   H, 1905–1914, 1918
LetrasC   Letras. Caracas, 1967–.
LFem   Letras femeninas. Boulder, Col., etc., 1975–.
LH   Liceo de la Habana. H, 1857–1886.
Liberalis.   BA, 1949–?
Libre.   Paris, 1971–?
Los libros.   BA, 1969–1976?
Literatura.   Rio de Janeiro, 1946–1948?
LitS   Literatura soviética. Moscow, 1942–.
LJ   Library journal. NY, 1876–.
LLM   Linden Lane magazine. Millburn, N.J., 1982?–.
LNL   Les langues néo-latines. Paris, 1947–.
LO   Literaturnoe obozrenie. Moscow, 1973–.
Lotería.   Panamá, 1958–.
LsNs   Letras nuevas. M, 1957–.
LSt   Le lingue straniere. Roma, 1952–.
La lucha.   H, 1883–?
Lyceum.   H, 1939–.
LyL   Lanzas y letras. Guatemala, 1958–.
LyP   El libro y el pueblo. M, 1922–.
MAHC   Memoria de Alfonso Hernández Catá. H, 1953–?
Maize.   San Diego, 1977–.
MALHC   Mensuario de arte, literatura, historia y crítica. H, 1949–.
Mapocho.   Santiago, Chile, 1963–.
Marcha.   Montevideo, 1939–1973?
Máscara.   BA, 1941–.

MD   Modern drama. Toronto, 1959–.

MEC   El monitor de la educación común. BA, 1881–?

Medicina.   H, 1943–.

Mediodía.   H, 1936–?

Mensaje.   Santiago, Chile, 1952–.

Mester.   Los Angeles, 1970–.

MGSL   Minas Garais. Suplemento literário. Belo Horizonte, Brazil, 1966–.

MHisp   Mundo hispánico. Madrid, 1948–.

MIHC   Mensajes de la Institución Hispanocubana de Cultura. H, 1928–?

MLJ   Modern language journal. NY, etc. 1916–.

MLN   MLN; modern language notes. Baltimore, 1886–.

MLR   Modern language review. Edinburgh, 1918–.

MNu   Mundo nuevo. Paris/Buenos Aires, 1966–1971.

MPer   Mercurio peruano. Lima, 1918–.

MRev   Monthly review. NY, 1965–.

Mujeres.   H, 1960–.

Museo.   Matanzas, 1960–.

Nation.   NY, 1965–.

NCent   New century. Washington, D.C., 1886–.

NConL   Notes on contemporary literature. Carrollton, Geor., 1971–.

NCRMM   La nouvelle critique, revue de marxisme militant. Paris, 1949–. Title varies; also *La nouvelle critique, politique, marxisme, culture.*

ND   Nueva democracia. NY, 1920–1963.

NE   Nueva estafeta. Madrid, 1978–. Continues *EstLit,* q.v.

NewS   New scholar. La Jolla, Calif., 1969–.

Ngam.   Yaounde, Cameroun, 1977–.

NHB   Negro history bulletin. Washington, D.C., 1937–.

Nivel.   M, 1959–1962, 1963–.

NL   Les nouvelles littéraires. Paris, 1922–.

NNH   Nueva narrativa hispanoamericana. Garden City, N.Y., 1971–1975.

Noéma.   Xalapa, México, 1955–.

Nosotros.   BA, 1907–1934, 1936–1943.

Noverim.   H, 1954–1958.

NRC   Nueva revista cubana. H, 1959–1961/1962.

NRFH   Nueva revista de filología hispánica. M, 1947–.

NRRP   Nueva revista del Río de la Plata. San Isidro, Argentina, 1952–1953.

NS/N   NS/Northsouth; Canadian journal of Latin American studies. Ottawa, 1976–.

NSa   La nueva sangre. NY, 1968?–.
NTiem   Nuestro tiempo. H, 1959?–.
Número.   Montevideo, 1949–?
NYRB   New York review of books. N.Y., 1963–.
OB   Ord och bild. Stockholm, 1891–.
Odyssey.   Brooklyn, N.Y., 1961–1963,
Orbe.   H, 1931–1938.
Orientación.   H, 1942–?
Orígenes.   H, 1944–1954.
Orto.   Manzanilla, 1912–?
PA   Présence africaine. Paris, 1947–.
Phaedrus.   Madison, N.J., 1973–.
PHisp   Poesía hispánica. Madrid, 1952–.
Phylon.   Atlanta, 1940–.
Plamăk.   Sofia, Bulgaria, 1957–.
PLit   Prensa literaria. San Juan, P.R., 1963–.
Plural.   M. 1971–.
PMLA; publications of the Modern Language Association of America. NY, 1884/1885–.
PolI   Política internacional. H, 1963–.
Política.   Caracas, 1959–.
PolíticaH   Política. H, 1943–.
Ponte.   Firenze, Italy, 1945–.
PP   Philologica pragensia. Prague, 1958–.
PPNWCFL   Proceedings of the Pacific Northwest Conference on Foreign Languages. Seattle, etc., 1949–.
PR   Partisan review. Boston, 1932–.
PrA   Primer acto. Madrid, 1957–.
Presencia.   H, 1957–?
PajP   La pajarita de papel. Tegucigalpa, Honduras, 1949–?
PalL   El palenque literario. H, 1880–1883?
PAm   Pan American. NY, 1940–?
Panorama.   H, 1953–?
Papeles.   Caracas, 1966–.
Parnassus.   NY, 1972–.
Partisans.   Paris, 1961–.
PCL   Perspectives on contemporary literature. Louisville, Ken., 1975–.
PCLS   Proceedings of the Comparative Literature Symposium. Lubbock, Tex., 1970–.
PCr   Pensamiento crítico. H, 1967–1971.
PdP   Punto de partida. M, 1966–.
PE   Punta Europa. Madrid, 1956–1967.

PenP   Pensamiento político. M, 1969–.
PEsp   Poesía española. Madrid, 1952–1970.
PH   La palabra y el hombre. Xalapa, México, 1957–.
Prisma. Panamá, 1971–.
Prohemio.   Madrid, 1970–.
PRom   Papers in Romance. Seattle, 1979–.
Prometeo.   H, 1947–1950?
PSA   Papeles de Son Armadans. Madrid, 1956–1979?
PU   El pequeño universo. Santo Domingo, Dominican Republic, 1971–.
Pueblo.   NY, 1977?–.
PyC   Pueblo y cultura. H, 1961–1965?
QIA   Quaderni ibero-americani. Torino, Italy, 1946–.
QIG   Quaderni dell'Istituto di Glottologia. Bologna, 1955/56–1965.
QL   La quinzaine littéraire. Paris, 1966–.
RABA   Revista americana de Buenos Aires. BA, 1924–?
RABM   Revista de archivos, bibliotecas y museos. Madrid 1871–1878, 1883, 1897–1931, 1947–1952, 1953–.
RAm   Repertorio americano. San José, Costa Rica, 1919–1959.
RAmer   Repertorio americano. Heredia, Costa Rica, 1974–.
RANCR   Revista de los Archivos Nacionales de Costa Rica. San José, Costa Rica, 1936–.
RBA   Revista de Bellas Artes. M, 1971–.
RBAC   Resumen bimestral de arte y cultura. Miami, 1966–?
RBAM   Revista de la Biblioteca, Archivo y Museo del Ayuntamiento de Madrid. Madrid, 1924–1935.
RBC   Revista bimestre cubana. H, 1831–.
RBibC   Revista bibliográfica cubana. H, 1936–.
RBJM   Revista bibliográfica José Martí. H, 1958?–.
RBNC   Revista de la Biblioteca Nacional. H, 1909–1912. 2a serie, 1949–1958. Continued as *RBNJM*, q.v.
RBNJM   Revista de la Biblioteca Nacional "José Martí." H, 1959–. 3a serie; continues *RBNC*, q.v.
RCEH   Revista canadiense de estudios hispánicos. Toronto, 1976–.
RCF   Revista cubana de filosofía. H, 1949–.
RCHG   Revista chilena de historia y geografía. Santiago, Chile, 1911–.
RChL   Revista chilena de literatura. Santiago, Chile, 1970–.
RCLL   Revista de crítica literaria latinoamericana. Lima, 1975–.
RCub   Revista cubana. H, 1885–1895. Continued as *RdC*, q.v.
RdAm   Revista de América. Bogotá, 1945–1951.
RDC   Revista dominicana de cultura. Ciudad Trujillo, Dominican Republic, 1955–1956.
RdC   Revista de Cuba. H, 1877–1884. Continues *RCub*, q.v.
RdL   Revista do livro. Rio de Janeiro, 1956–1970.

Realidad.   BA, 1947–?

REAM   Revista española de ambos mundos. Madrid, 1853–.

RECIFS   Recherches et études comparatistes ibéro-françaises de la Sorbonne. Paris, 1979–.

Reflexión.   Ottawa, 1968–1971, 1972–1975? Continued as *RCEH*, q.v.

REH   Revista de estudios hispánicos. University, Ala., 1967–.

REH-PR   Revista de estudios hispánicos. Río Piedras, P.R., 1928–1930, 1971–.

RepAm   El repertorio americano. London, 1826–1827.

REsp   Revista de España. Madrid, 1868–1895.

REU   Revista de estudios universitarios. M, 1940.

RevAm   Revista de América. Paris, 1912–1914.

RevC   Revista cubana. H, 1935–1957.

RevCu   Revista cubana. NY, 1968–?

RevE   Revista de educación. H, 1924–.

RevEG   Revista de educación. Guatemala, 1931–.

RevG   Revista de Guatemala. Guatemala, 1945–.

RevH   Revista de la Habana. H, 1930–?

RevI   Revista de Indias. Madrid, 1940–.

Review   [Center for Inter-American Relations]. NY, 1968–.

RevL   Revista de letras. Mayagüez, P.R., 1969–?

Revolución.   H, 1959–1965.

RevP   Revista del Pacífico. Valparaíso, Chile, 1964–.

RFD   Revista de la Federación de Doctores en Ciencias y en Filosofía y Letras. H, 1940–.

RFE   Revista de filología española. Pamplona, Spain, 1914–.

RFEV   Revista de la Federación de Estudiantes de Venezuela. Caracas, 1937?–.

RFH   Revista de filosofía hispánica. BA, 1939–1946.

RFLC   Revista de la Facultad de Letras y Ciencias de la Universidad de la Habana. H, 1905–1930.

RFUCR   Revista de filosofía de la Universidad de Costa Rica. San José, Costa Rica, 1957–.

RHA   Revista de historia de América. M, 1938–.

RHab   Revista habanera. H, 1861–1862, 1913–?

RHCB   Revista histórica crítica y bibliográfica de la literatura cubana. Matanzas, 1916–1917?

RHM   Revista hispánica moderna. NY, 1934–.

RI   Revista iberoamericana. México, D.F., etc., 1939–.

RIB   Revista interamericana de bibliografía/Inter-American review of bibliography. Washington, D.C., 1951–.

RICP   Revista del Instituto de Cultura Puertorriqueña. San Juan, P.R., 1958–.

RIE   Revista de ideas estéticas. Madrid, 1943–.

RIL   Revista iberoamericana de literatura. Montevideo, 1959–1970.
RInter   Revista/Review interamericana. Hato Rey, P.R., 1971–.
RJ   Romanistisches Jahrbuch. Hamburg, 1947–.
RLAE   Reseña de literatura, arte y espectáculo. Madrid, 1964–.
RLati   Repertorio latinoamericano. BA, 1975–.
RLC   Revue de littérature comparée. Tours-Cedex, France, 1926–.
RLet   Revista de letras. Assis, Brazil, 1960–.
RLR   Revue des langues romanes. Alès, France, 1870–.
RMC   Revista médica cubana. H, 1901–.
RMS   Revista mexicana de sociología. M, 1939–.
RNC   Revista nacional de cultura. Caracas, 1938–.
RNM   Revista nacional. Montevideo, 1938–1954, 1956–.
RNT   Revista nacional de teatro. H, 1961–.
RO   Revista de Occidente. Madrid, 1923–1936, 1963–1974?, 1975–1977, 1980–.
RoLit   Romània literară. Bucarest, 1968–.
Romance.   M, 1940–1941.
Románica.   NY, 1975–.
Romboid.   Bratislava, Czechoslovakia, 1966?–.
RomN   Romance notes. Chapel Hill, N.C., 1959–.
RP   Río Piedras, P.R., 1972–.
RPA   Revista Pan-América. Tegucigalpa, Honduras, 1944–.
RPL   El revisor político y literario. H, 1823.
RR   Romanic review. NY, 1909–.
RRev   Revista de revistas. H, 1910–.
RSBV   Revista de la Sociedad Bolivariana de Venezuela. Caracas, 1939–.
RSFB   Revista de Santa Fé y Bogotá. Bogotá, ca. 1890.
RUCR   Revista de la Universidad de Costa Rica. San José, Costa Rica, 1945–.
Rueca.   M, 1941–1948.
RUM   Revista de la Universidad de México. M, 1959–. Continues *UM*, q.v.
RUMa   Revista de la Universidad de Madrid. Madrid, 1952–.
RUT   Revista de la Universidad. Tegucigalpa, Honduras, 1909–.
RUY   Revista de la Universidad de Yucatán. Mérida, México, 1959–.
RUZ   Revista de la Universidad de Zulia. Maracaibo, Venezuela, 1947–.
RyC   Revolución y cultura. H, 1972–.
RyF   Razón y fe. Madrid, 1901–.
RyFa   Razón y fábula. Bogotá, 1967–.
SAB   South Atlantic bulletin. University, Ala., 1935–.
SAm   Sembradores de amistad. Monterrey, México, 194?–?

Santiago. Santiago, Cuba, 1970–.
Sarmiento. Tucumán, Argentina, 1949–?
Savacou. Kingston, Jamaica, 1970–.
SCRI Suplemento de Cuadernos de Ruedo Ibérico. Paris, 1966–.
SECOLASA Southeastern Council on Latin American Studies. Annals. Carrollton, Geor., 1970–.
Selecta. Corvalis, Ore., 1980–.
SeN Seara nova. Lisboa, 1921–.
Shell. Revista Shell. Caracas, 1952–1962.
SIC; revista venezolana de orientación. Caracas, 1938–.
Signos. H, 1969–.
SinN Sin nombre. Santurce, P.R., 1970–.
Síntesis. Ciego de Avila, 1941–?
SLI Studi di litteratura ispano-americana. Milano, Italy, 1976–.
Social. H, 1916–1938?
Sphinx. Lima, 1937–.
SSF Studies in short fiction. Newberry, S.C., 1963–.
SuF Sinn und Form. Berlin, 1949–.
Sur. BA, 1931–.
SXX Secolul 20. Bucarest, 1961–.
Symposium. Syracuse, N.Y., 1946–.
Synthèses. Bruxelles, 1946–?
TAH The American Hispanist. Clear Creek, Ind., 1975–?
Taller. M, 1938–1941.
TallerC Taller. Santiago, Cuba, 1973?–.
Tapia. Tunapuno, Trinidad, 1969–.
TC Texto crítico. Xalapa, México, 1975–.
TDR The drama review. NY, 1955–.
TelQ Tel quel. Paris, 1960–?
Término. Cincinnati, 1982–.
ThA Theatre arts. NY, 1916–.
Theater. New Haven, Conn., 1977–.
Thesaurus. Bogotá, 1945–.
TLit Taller literario. H, 1966–1973? Continued as *TallerC*, q.v.
TLS Times literary supplement. London, 1902–.
TMC Tribuna médica. H, 1927–.
La torre. Río Piedras, P.R., 1953–.
TQ Texas quarterly. Austin, Tex., 1958–.
Tricontinental. H, 1967–.
Trimestre. H, 1947–1950.
Triunfo (prensa periódica). Madrid, ?–.
Tw Twórczós. Warszawa, Poland, 1945–.
UAnt Universidad de Antioquia. Medellín, Colombia, 1935–.

UCB	Universidad Católica Bolivariana. Medellín, Colombia, 1937–.
UH	La última hora. H, 1951?–?
ULH	Universidad de la Habana. H, 1934–.
Ultra.	H, 1936–1947.
UM	Universidad de México. M, 1930–1933, 1946–1959. Continued as *RUM*, q.v.
Unión.	H, 1962–.
Universidad.	Monterrey, México, 1942–.
UPC	Unión de Periodistas de Cuba. H, 1968?–.
El urogallo.	Madrid, 1970–.
USC	Universidad de San Carlos. Guatemala, 1945–.
USF	Universidad. Santa Fe, Argentina, 1935–.
UTQ	University of Toronto quarterly. Toronto, 1931–.
VAmer	Voces de América. Cartagena, Colombia, 1944–?
Verbum	H, 1937.
Vértice.	Coimbra, Portugal, 1942–.
VidaL	Vida literaria. M, 1965–.
Vinduet.	Oslo, 1947–.
VLit	Vida literaria. BA, 1928–1931.
VO	Verde olivo. H, 1960–.
Vórtice.	Stanford, Calif., 1974–.
La voz.	NY, 1956?–?
VP	Visión del Perú. Lima, 1964?–.
Vsesvit.	Kiev, U.S.S.R., 1925–.
VU	Vida universitaria. H, 1950–.
Vuelta.	M, 1976–.
VUM	Vida universitaria. Monterrey, México, 1970–.
WB	Weimarer Beiträge. Berlin, 1955–.
WTh	World theatre. Paris, 1950–1968.
WZUB	Wissenschaftliche Zeitschrift der Humboldt-Universität zu Berlin. Berlin, 1976–.
WZUR	Wissenschaftliche Zeitschrift der Wilhelm-Pieck-Universität Rostock. Rostock, East Germany, 1951–.
Xilote.	M, 1967–.
Yelmo.	Madrid, 1971–.
ZF	Zona franca. Caracas, 1976–.
ZS	Zeitschrift für Slawistik. Berlin, 1956–.

General References

A. BIBLIOGRAPHIES

(Note: For a listing of periodical indexes, see section AA.)

A.1　Abella, Rosa. "Bibliografía de la novela publicada en Cuba y en el extranjero por cubanos desde 1959 hasta 1965." RI, No. 62 (1966), 307-318.

A.2　Antuña, María Luisa, and Josefina García Carranza. "Bibliografía de teatro cubano." RBNJM, 3a serie, 13, 3 (1971), 87-154.

A.3　Anuario bibliográfico cubano; bibliografía cubana. H/Gainesville, Fla., 1937-1963?

A.4　Batista Villarreal, Teresita, Josefina García Carranza, and Miguelina Ponte. Catálogo de publicaciones periódicas cubanas de los siglos XVIII y XIX. H: Biblioteca Nacional José Martí, Departamento Colección Cubana, 1965.

A.5　Bibliografía cubana. H: Biblioteca Nacional, 1967-.

A.6　Bibliografía de la poesía cubana en el siglo XIX. H: Departamento de Publicaciones de la Biblioteca Nacional José Martí, 1965.

A.7　C., C. "11 autores cubanos." PrA, No. 108 (1969), 31-32.

A.8　Casal, Lourdes. "A bibliography of Cuban creative literature: 1958-1971." CSN, 2, 2 (1972), 2-29.

A.9　_____. "The Cuban novel, 1959-1969: an annotated bibliography." Abraxas, 1, 1 (1970), 77-92.

A.10　Catalog of the Cuban and Caribbean Library of the University of Miami. Boston: G. K. Hall, 1977.

A.11　Dihigo y Mestre, Juan Miguel. Bibliografía de la Universidad de la Habana. H: Imprenta, Librería y Papelería "La Propagandista", 1936.

A.12　Engber, Marjorie. Caribbean fiction and poetry. NY: Center for Inter-American Relations, 1970.

A.13　Figarola-Caneda, Domingo. Diccionario cubano de seudónimos. H: El Siglo XX, 1922.

A.14   Ford, Jeremiah D. M., and Maxwell I. Raphael. A bibliography of
       Cuban belles-lettres. Cambridge, Mass.: Harvard University
       Press, 1933. Reprint, NY: Russell and Russell, 1970.

A.15   Fort, Gilberto V. "Fiction and poetry." In The Cuban revolution
       of Fidel Castro viewed from abroad (Lawrence, Kan.: Univer-
       sity of Kansas Libraries, 1969), Section 14.

A.16   Hernández-Miyares, Julio. "The Cuban short story in exile: a
       selected bibliography." Hispania, 54 (1971), 384-385. Also
       as "Cuentos cubanos en el destierro: una lista bibliográfi-
       ca." Círculo, 2 (1970), 189-191.

A.17   Los incunables en la Biblioteca Nacional José Martí. H: Consejo
       Nacional de Cultura, 1974.

A.18   Inerárity Romero, Zayda. "Ensayo de una bibliografía para un es-
       tudio del teatro cubano hasta el siglo XIX." Islas, No. 36
       (1970), 151-171.

A.19   Le Riverand, Julio. "Notas para una bibliografía cubana de los
       siglos XVII y XVIII." ULH, Nos. 88-90 (1950), 128-231.

A.20   Leal, Rine. "Acerca de una bibliografía de teatro cubano."
       RBNJM, 3a serie, 14, 2 (1972), 164-172. Review of item
       no. A.2.

A.21   Lewis, Horacio D. A guide to publications on Latinos at Indiana
       University Library. Pueblo Latino. Volume III: The Cubans.
       Bloomington, Ind.: Indiana University, 1975.

A.22   Librería Martí, booksellers, Havana. Catálogo de libros, anti-
       guos y modernos, impresos en Cuba o que tratan de Cuba de
       venta en la Librería Martí. H, 1945. Appendixes dated
       1949, 1950, 1951, and 1952.

A.23   El libro en Cienfuegos; catálogo de las obras relacionadas con
       Cienfuegos que se exhiben en la Biblioteca Nacional como
       homenaje al libro cubano. H: Biblioteca Nacional José Mar-
       tí, 1954.

A.24   Libros cubanos; boletín de bibliografía cubana. H, 1940-42.

A.25   Lozano, Eduardo. Cuban periodicals in the University of Pitts-
       burgh Libraries, 3. ed. Pittsburgh: University of Pitts-
       burgh Libraries, 1981.

A.26   Medina, José Toribio. La imprenta en la Habana (1707-1810). No-
       tas bibliográficas. Santiago de Chile: Elzeviriana, 1904.
       Also, Amsterdam: N. Israel, 1964.

A.27   No item.

A.28 Menton, Seymour. "Bibliography." In his Prose fiction of the Cuban revolution (Austin: University of Texas Press, 1975), pp. 287-317.

A.29 _____. La novela y el cuento de la revolución cubana, 1959-1969: bibliografía. Cuernavaca, Méx.: Centro Intercultural de Documentación, 1969.

A.30 Montes Huidobro, Matías, and Yara González. Bibliografía crítica de la poesía cubana (exilio: 1959-1971). Madrid: Playor, 1973.

A.31 Mota, Francisco. "Algunas fuentes bibliográficas sobre la narrativa cubana." L/L, No. 5 (1974), 161-199.

A.32 _____. "Ensayo de una bibliografía cubana de y sobre Rubén Darío." BILL, No. 2 (1967), 279-303.

A.33 _____, and Célida Cejudo. "El teatro en Cuba colonial: apuntes para una bibliografía." L/L, Nos. 7-8 (1976-1977), 308-347.

A.34 Movimiento editorial en Cuba, 1959-60; exposición de libros, folletos y revistas. H: Biblioteca Nacional José Martí, 1961.

A.35 Palls, Terry L. "Annotated bibliographical guide to the study of Cuban theatre after 1959." MD, 22 (1979), 391-408.

A.36 Peavler, Terry J. "Prose fiction criticism and theory in Cuban journals: an annotated bibliography." CS, 7, 1 (1977), 58-118.

A.37 Peraza Sarausa, Fermín. Bibliografía cubana; complementos: 1937-1961. Gainesville, Fla.: University of Florida Libraries, 1966.

A.38 _____. Bibliografía cubano-uruguaya. H: Anuario Bibliográfico Cubano, 1956.

A.39 _____. Bibliografías cubanas. Washington, D.C.: Library of Congress, Hispanic Foundation, 1945.

A.40 _____. Directorio de bibliotecas de Cuba, 1968. Gainesville, Fla.: Biblioteca del Bibliotecario, 1968.

A.41 _____. Directorio de revistas y periódicos de Cuba. Gainesville, Fla.: Biblioteca del Bibliotecario, 1968.

A.42 Pérez Beato, Manuel. Bibliografía comentada sobre los escritos publicados en la isla de Cuba relativos al Quijote. H, 1905.

A.43 _____. Cervantes en Cuba; estudio bibliográfico. H: F. Verdugo, 1929.

A.44 Perrier, Joseph Louis. Bibliografía dramática cubana, incluye
      a Puerto Rico y Santo Domingo. NY: Phos, 1926.

A.45 "Relación de las nuevas revistas cubanas publicadas desde 1950
      hasta 1955, existentes en la Biblioteca Nacional." RBNJM,
      2a serie, 9, 1 (1958), 297-302.

A.46 Revista bibliográfica cubana. H: Cultura, 1936-1939.

A.47 Revolutionary Cuba: a bibliographical guide. Miami: University
      of Miami, Research Institute for Cuba and the Caribbean
      Center for Advanced International Studies, 1966-1968.

A.48 Rivero Muñiz, José. Bibliografía del teatro cubano. H: Biblio-
      teca Nacional, 1957.

A.49 Sánchez, Julio C. "Bibliografía de la novela cubana." Islas,
      3, 1 (1960), 321-356.

A.50 Schulman, Ivan A., and Erica Miles. "A guide to the location
      of nineteenth-century Cuban magazines." LARR, 12, 2
      (1977), 69-102.

A.51 Skinner, Eugene R. "Research guide to post-revolutionary Cuban
      drama." LATR, 7, 2 (1974), 59-68.

A.52 Trelles Govín, Carlos Manuel. Bibliografía cubana de los siglos
      XVII y XVIII; 2. ed. H: Imprenta del Ejército, 1927. See
      item no. A.59.

A.53 ____. Bibliografía cubana del siglo XIX. Matanzas: Quirós y
      Estrada, 1911-1915.

A.54 ____. Bibliografía cubana del siglo XX. Matanzas: Quirós y
      Estrada, 1916-1917.

A.55 ____. "Bibliografía de autores de la raza de color, en Cuba."
      CCont, 43 (1927), 30-78.

A.56 ____. "Bibliografía de la prensa cubana de 1764 a 1900."
      RBibC, 2 (1938), 7-40, 81-114, 145-168, 206-268; 3 (1939),
      5-34, 67-100.

A.57 ____. Bibliografía de la Universidad de la Habana. H: Rambla,
      Bouza, 1938.

A.58 ____. Biblioteca histórica cubana. Matanzas: J. F. Oliver,
      1922-1926.

A.59 ____. Ensayo de bibliografía cubana de los siglos XVII y XVIII
      seguido de unos apuntes para la bibliografía dominicana y
      portorriqueña. Matanzas: "El Escritorio", 1907. Suple-
      mento, 1908. First edition of item no. A.52.

A.60 Valdés, Nelson P., and Edwin Lieuwen. The Cuban revolution, a research-study guide (1959-1969). Albuquerque: University of New Mexico Press, 1971.

A.61 Valdés Domínguez, Eusebio. "Bibliografía cubana." RCub, 5 (1879), 368-369, 581-592; 6 (1879), 85-89.

A.62 Villa Buceta, María. "Guías de la bibliografía cubana." LCub, 1, 2 (1940), 1-4; 1, 3 (1940), 9.

A.63 Zubatsky, David S. "Annotated bibliography of Latin American author bibliographies. Part II: Central America and the Caribbean." Chasqui, 6, 2 (1977), 41-72.

A.64 ____. "United States doctoral dissertations on Cuban studies." CSN, 4, 2 (1974), 33-55.

B. GENERAL LITERARY HISTORIES

B.1 Armas y Cárdenas, José de. Historia y literatura. H: Jesús Montero, 1915.

B.2 Ayala Duarte, Crispín. "Historia de la literatura cubana." AAUC, 24 (1935), 154-183, 195-216.

B.3 Bachiller y Morales, Antonio. Apuntes para la historia de las letras y de la instrucción pública en Cuba. H: Tiempo, 1959-1961. 2. ed., H: Cultural, 1936-1937. Also H: Academia de Ciencias de Cuba, Instituto de Literatura y Lingüística, 1965-.

B.4 Belic, Oldrich. O kubánské literatura. Praha: Nakl. Politické Literatura, 1964.

B.5 Bernal, Emilia. Cuestiones cubanas para América. Madrid: Hernández y Galo Sáez, 1928.

B.6 Boza Masvidal, Aurelio A. "Ensayo de historia de la literatura cubana." RFLC, 36, 3-4 (1926), 289-294; 37, 1-2 (1927), 62-96.

B.7 _____. El problema de la originalidad de la literatura cubana. H: "La Propagandista", 1924.

B.8 Bueno, Salvador. Historia de la literatura cubana; 3. ed. H: Ministerio de Educación, 1963. Also H: Minerva, 1954. Orig. as Historia de la literatura cubana (1902-1952). H: Edición del Cincuentenario, 1953.

B.9 Calcagno, Francisco. Diccionario biográfico cubano. NY: N. Ponce de León, 1878-1886.

B.10 Carbonell y Rivero, José Manuel. Evolución de la cultura cubana (1608-1927). H: El Siglo XX, 1928.

B.11 Carbonell y Rivero, Miguel Angel. Las generaciones literarias; 3. ed. H: Guáimaro, 1940.

B.12 Chacón y Calvo, José María. Literatura cubana; ensayo crítico. Madrid: Saturnino Calleja, 1922.

B.13 _____. "Literatura de Cuba." In Historia universal de la literatura (BA: Uteha, Unión Tipográfica Editorial Hispanoamericana, 1941-1942), XI, 466-481; XII, 11-76.

B.14 Diccionario de la literatura cubana. H: Letras Cubanas, 1980-.
At head of title: Instituto de Literatura y Lingüística de
la Academia de Ciencias de Cuba.

B.15 Domínguez Roldán, Guillermo. "La literatura cubana: necesidad
de su enseñanza." RFLC, 20, 2 (1915), 164-182.

B.16 Esténger, Rafael. Caracteres constantes en las letras cubanas;
apuntes para la revisión de los valores literarios. H:
"Alfa", 1954?

B.17 Fernández Carvajal Bello, Juan. "Literatura cubana." In Historia general de las literaturas hispánicas (Barcelona: Barna,
1949-1958), V, 439-486.

B.18 Fernández de Castro, José Antonio. Esquema histórico de las letras en Cuba (1548-1902). H: Universidad de la Habana, Departamento de Intercambio Cultural, 1949.

B.19 Fernández de la Vega, Oscar, and Juan Fernández Carvajal Bello.
Español Cuarto Curso. II. Literatura cubana. H: Selecta,
1946. 8. ed., 1961.

B.20 Gay-Calbó, Enrique. Orígenes de la literatura cubana; ensayo de
interpretación. H: "Cultural", 1939. Orig. AANAL, 18
(1936-1937), 268-302. Also ULH, Nos. 20-21 (1938), 199-237.

B.21 Grismer, Raymond L., and Manuel Rodríguez Saavedra. Vida y obras
de autores cubanos. H: "Alfa", 1940-. Only v. I ever published.

B.22 Henríquez Ureña, Max. La enseñanza de la literatura cubana. H,
1915.

B.23 _____. Panorama histórico de la literatura cubana. San Juan?,
P.R.: Mirador, 1963. Also NY: Las Américas, 1963.

B.24 _____. Tablas cronológicas de la literatura cubana. Santiago
de Cuba: "Archipiélago", 1929. Orig. as "Literatura cubana: bosquejo histórico." Archipiélago, No. 11 (1929), 188;
No. 12 (1929), 204; No. 13 (1929), 220; No. 14 (1929), 246-
247.

B.25 Herdeck, Donald E. Caribbean writers; a biobibliographical-
critical encyclopedia. Washington, D.C.: Three Continents
Press, 1979.

B.26 Lazo, Raimundo. Historia de la literatura cubana; 2. ed. M:
Universidad Nacional Autónoma de México, Dirección General
de Publicaciones, 1974. Orig. H: Universitaria, 1967.

B.27 _____. La literatura cubana; esquema histórico desde sus orígenes hasta 1964. M: Universidad Nacional Autónoma de México,
1965. Also H: Universitaria, 1967.

B.28 _____. Reseña de historia literaria y cultural de Cuba. BA:
W. M. Jackson, 1945.

B.29 _____. La teoría de las generaciones y su aplicación al estudio
histórico de la literatura cubana; ensayo. H: Universidad
de la Habana, 1954. Orig. as "La teoría de las generaciones
y su aplicación al estudio histórico de la literatura cubana." ULH, Nos. 112-113 (1954), 40-82.

B.30 Lizaso y González, Félix. Panorama de la cultura cubana. M:
Fondo de Cultura Económica, 1949.

B.31 Mañach, Jorge. La crisis de la alta cultura cubana. H: La Universal, 1925.

B.32 Martín, Juan Luis. Elementos históricos de la cultura cubana.
H, 1948.

B.33 Mitjáns, Aurelio. Estudio sobre el movimiento científico y literario de Cuba. H: A. Alvarez, 1890. Also Madrid: América,
1918. Also H: Consejo Nacional de Cultura, 1963.

B.34 _____. Historia de la literatura cubana. Del Monte. Heredia.
Milanés. Saco. Gertrudis Gómez de Avellaneda. Zenea,
etc., etc. M: América, 1918.

B.35 Olivera, Otto. Breve historia de la literatura antillana. M:
de Andrea, 1957.

B.36 Ortiz, Fernando. "La literatura cubana. Resumen de su evolución." In Biblioteca internacional de obras famosas (London: Sociedad Internacional, 1900-?), XXVII, i-xx.

B.37 Panorama de la literatura cubana; conferencias. H: Universidad
de la Habana, Centro de Estudios Cubanos, 1970.

B.38 Piedra-Bueno, Andrés de. Literatura cubana; síntesis histórico.
H: América, 1945.

B.39 Pogolotti, Marcelo. La República de Cuba a través de sus escritores. H: Lex, 1958.

B.40 Portuondo, José Antonio. Bosquejo histórico de las letras cubanas. H: Ministerio de Relaciones Exteriores, Departamento
de Asuntos Culturales, División de Publicaciones, 1960.
Also H: Editora Nacional de Cuba, 1962. Also as Panorama
historique des lettres cubaines. H: Ministère des Affaires
Estrangers, 1961.

B.41 _____. El contenido social de la literatura cubana. M: El Colegio de México, 1944.

B.42 _____. "Corrientes literarias en Cuba." CA, No. 153 (1967),
193-213.

B.43   ____. "Introducción a Cuba: literatura." In his Crítica de la
        época y otros ensayos (Santa Clara?: Universidad Central de
        Las Villas, 1965), pp. 136-163.

B.44   ____. "Proyección americana de las letras cubanas." In his
        Crítica de la época y otros ensayos (Santa Clara?: Univer-
        sidad Central de Las Villas, 1965), pp. 164-187.

B.45   ____. "Temas literarios del Caribe." CA, No. 57 (1951), 217-
        230.

B.46   Ramos i Duarte, Félix. Diccionario de observaciones crítica so-
        bre el lenguaje de los escritores cubanos. M: Guerra, 1912.

B.47   Remos y Rubio, Juan Nepomuceno José. Curso de historia de la
        literatura cubana. H: Cárdenas, 1945.

B.48   ____. Historia de la literatura cubana. H: J. Abela, 1925.
        Also Miami: Mnemosyne, 1963.

B.49   ____. "Orientaciones sobre las lecturas literarias, a través
        de los géneros." In his Micrófono (H: Molina, 1937), pp.
        11-127.

B.50   ____. Proceso histórico de las letras cubanas. Madrid: Guada-
        rrama, 1958.

B.51   ____. Resumen de historia de la literatura cubana. Para el
        uso de institutos y escuelas normales. H: Molina, 1930.
        2. ed. corr., 1945.

B.52   Rodríguez, Ileana, and Marc Zimmerman, eds. Process of unity in
        Caribbean society: ideologies and literature. Minneapolis:
        Institute for the Study of Ideologies and Literatures, 1983.

B.53   Saíz de la Mora, Jesús. Nociones de la literatura histórica cu-
        bana. H: La Propagandista, 1925.

B.54   Salazar y Roig, Salvador. Historia de la literatura cubana. H:
        Avisador Comercial, 1929.

B.55   ____. "Literatura cubana." In his Curso de literatura caste-
        llana (histórica) (H: La Moderna Poesía, 1926), II, 247-
        455.

B.56   Sánchez de Bustamante y Montoro, Antonio. Las generaciones li-
        terarias. H: Molina, 1937. Followed by a response by Mi-
        guel Angel Carbonell y Rivero. Orig. ULH, No. 13 (1937),
        124-142. Also in his Ironía y generación (H, 1937), pp.
        39-70.

B.57   Trelles, Carlos M. "Los ciento cincuenta libros más notables
        que los cubanos han escrito." In José Manguel Carbonell y
        Rivero, Las bellas artes en Cuba (H: "El Siglo XX", 1928),
        pp. 80-96. Also H: "El Siglo XX", de Aurelio Miranda, 1914.

B.58   Valdés Codina, Carlos A. Apuntes de literatura histórica cubana.
       Pinar del Río: "Villalba", 1921.

B.59   _____. Literatura histórica cubana, apuntes biográficos, arre-
       glados para los estudiantes de 2ª enseñanza. H: L. V. Co-
       dina, 1911. 2. ed., Pinar del Río: Villalba, 1921.

B.60   Valdivia, Humberto. Nuevo curso de literatura hispanocubana.
       H: El Score, 1938.

B.61   Vitier, Medardo. Las ideas y la filosofía en Cuba. H: Ciencias
       Sociales, 1970. Las ideas en Cuba, orig. H: Trópico, 1938.
       Also Miami: Mnemosyne, 1969. La filosofía en Cuba, orig.
       M: Fondo de Cultura Económica, 1948.

C. COLLECTED ESSAYS

C.1 Ardura, Ernesto. Prédica ingenua; ensayos y comentarios de interpretación nacional. H: Ucar García, 1954.

C.2 Arias, Salvador. Búsqueda y análisis; ensayos críticos sobre literatura cubana. H: Unión, 1974.

C.3 Arrom, José Juan. Estudios de literatura hispanoamericana. H, 1950.

C.4 Baeza Flores, Alberto. Cuba, el laurel y la palma; ensayos literarios. Miami: Universal, 1977.

C.5 Bedriñana, Francisco C. Papel de china; tres ensayos. H: Antena, 1941.

C.6 Bielsa Vives, Manuel. Cosas de ayer (colección de artículos políticos y literarios). H: La Correspondencia, 1906.

C.7 Bueno, Salvador. Temas y personajes de la literatura cubana. H: Unión, 1964.

C.8 Castellanos, Jesús. Colección póstuma. H: El Siglo XX de A. Miranda, 1914-1916.

C.9 Chacón y Calvo, José María. Ensayos de literatura cubana. Madrid: "Saturnino Calleja", 1932. Orig. 1922.

C.10 Cruz, Manuel de la. Literatura cubana. Madrid: Calleja, 1924. Orig. BA: Lagomaggiore, 1890.

C.11 Entralgo, Elías José. Perfiles (apuntes críticos sobre literatura cubana contemporánea). H: "Hermes", 1923.

C.12 Feijóo, Samuel. Azar de lecturas. Crítica. Santa Clara: Universidad Central de Las Villas, 1961.

C.13 Fernández Retamar, Roberto. Ensayo de otro mundo. Santiago de Chile: Universitaria, 1969. Orig. H: Instituto del Libro, 1967.

C.14 _____. Papelería. Santa Clara: Universidad Central de Las Villas, Dirección de Publicaciones, 1962.

C.15 Fornet, Ambrosio. En tres y dos. H: R, 1964.

C.16 González Echevarría, Roberto. Relecturas: estudios de literatura cubana. Caracas: Monte Ávila, 1976.

C.17 Guillén, Nicolás. Prosa de prisa; crónicas. Santa Clara: Universidad Central de Las Villas, Dirección de Publicaciones, 1962.

C.18 ____. Prosa de prisa, 1929-1972. H: Arte y Literatura, 1975-1976.

C.19 Iraizoz y de Villar, Antonio. Lecturas cubanas; 2. ed. H: "Hermes", 1939.

C.20 ____. Libros y autores cubanos. Santa María de Rosario: Rosareña, 1956.

C.21 Leante, César. El espacio real. H: Unión de Escritores y Artistas de Cuba, 1975.

C.22 Lezama Lima, José. La cantidad hechizada. Madrid: Júcar, 1974.

C.23 Lles, Fernando. Conferencias. Matanzas: Casas y Mercado, 1944.

C.24 Marinello, Juan. Contemporáneos. H: Contemporáneos, 1975.

C.25 ____. Contemporáneos: noticia y memoria. Santa Clara: Universidad Central de Las Villas, Consejo Nacional de Universidades, 1964.

C.26 Márquez Sterling, Manuel. Quisicosas; sátiras y críticas. M: F. Hoeck, 1895.

C.27 Pogolotti, Marcelo. La república de Cuba al través de sus escritores. H: Lex, 1958.

C.28 Portuondo, José Antonio. Crítica de la época y otros ensayos. Santa Clara?: Universidad Central de Las Villas, 1965.

C.29 Remos y Rubio, Juan Nepomuceno José. Micrófono. H: Molina, 1937.

C.30 Roa, Ramón. Con la pluma y el machete. H: Academia de la Historia de Cuba, 1950.

C.31 Rodríguez Feo, José. Notas críticas (primera serie). H: Unión, 1962.

C.32 Rodríguez y Expósito, César. Apuntes bibliográficos; entre libros. H: "Selecta", 1947.

C.33 Sánchez de Bustamante y Montoro, Antonio de. Ironía y generación; ensayos. H, 1937. Signed Antonio de Bustamante y Montoro.

C.34 Sanguily y Garritte, Manuel. Juicios literarios. H: Molina, 1930. His Obras, VII.

C.35 Torre, Miguel Angel de la. Prosas varias. H: Universidad de la Habana, 1966.

C.36   Varona y Pera, Enrique José.   Artículos y discursos (literatura
          --política--sociología).   H: Alvarez, 1891.

C.37   Vitier, Cintio.   Crítica sucesiva.   H: Contemporáneos, UNEAC,
          1971.

C.38   _____.   Estudios críticos.   H: Biblioteca Nacional José Martí,
          1964.

C.39   _____.   Estudios, notas, efigies cubanas.   H: Minerva, 1944.

C.40   Vitier, Medardo.   Apuntaciones literarias.   H: Minerva, 1935.

D. LITERARY CRITICISM, REVIEWS, AND JOURNALS

D.1   Alba-Buffill, Elio. "Impresionismo y positivismo en la crítica
       literaria de Manuel Sanguily." Círculo, 10 (1981), 47-55.

D.2   Armas, Mirta. "Búsqueda y valorización de la literatura cubana
       [Salvador Bueno]." RyC, No. 63 (1977), 84-86.

D.3   Arrufat, Antón. "Función de la crítica literaria." CAm, Nos.
       17-18 (1963), 78-80.

D.4   Avila, Leopoldo. "Sobre algunas corrientes de la crítica y la
       literatura en Cuba." VO, No. 47 (1968), 14-18. Also in
       Lourdes Casal, El caso Padilla: literatura y revolución en
       Cuba; documentos (Miami: Universal; NY: Nueva Atlántida,
       n.d.), pp. 34-41. Also as "Di alcune correnti della critica
       e della letteratura cubane." In his Cuba: letteratura e ri-
       voluzione (Milano: Libreria Feltrinelli, 1969), pp. 22-37.

D.5   Azize, Yamila. "Dos revista literarias de la década del treinta:
       la Revista bimestre cubana y la revista Ateneo puertorrique-
       ño." DAI, 41 (1980), 549A.

D.6   Barradas, Efraín. "La revista Orígenes (1944-1956)." DAI, 39
       (1978), 2310A.

D.7   Benedetti, Mario. "De un reportaje a Bohemia." In his Cuaderno
       cubano; 2. ed. aum. (Montevideo: Arca, 1971), pp. 35-38.

D.8   _____. "Reportaje a la revista Cuba." In his Cuaderno cubano;
       2. ed. aum. (Montevideo: Arca, 1971), pp. 51-54.

D.9   Brower, Gary, and Raymond D. Souza. "Ciclón: índice e introduc-
       ción." Et caetera, No. 13 (1969), 105-125.

D.10   Bueno, Salvador. La crítica literaria cubana del siglo XIX.
       H: Letras Cubanas, 1979.

D.11   _____. "Periodismo literario: de El fígaro a Social." In his
       Temas y personajes de la literatura cubana (H: Unión, 1964),
       pp. 115-134.

D.12   _____. "Periodismo literario. La Revista habanera (1861-1862)."
       In his Temas y personajes de la literatura cubana (H: Unión,
       1964), pp. 97-114.

D.13   _____. "Periodismo literario: publicaciones menores hasta 1868."
       In his Temas y personajes de la literatura cubana (H: Unión,
       1964), pp. 75-95.

D.14 _____. "La revista Cuba y América (1897-1917)." In his Temas y personajes de la literatura cubana (H: Unión, 1964), pp. 135-153.

D.15 _____. "La Revista habanera." RBNC, 2a serie, 8, 3 (1957), 139-158.

D.16 _____. "Surgimiento de la crítica literaria en Cuba." CHA, Nos. 224-225 (1968), 552-564. Also Unión, 4, 3 (1965), 121-134.

D.17 Campuzano, Luisa. "¿Un nuevo estilo? Una nueva revista: Pensamiento crítico." RBNJM, 3a serie, 9, 2 (1967), 103-105.

D.18 Carbonell y Rivero, José Manuel. La crítica en la literatura cubana. H: Avisador Comercial, 1930.

D.19 Casanovas, Martí. Orbita de la revista Avance. H: UNEAC, 1965. 2. ed., 1972.

D.20 Castro de Morales, Lilia. "La prensa cubana en Estados Unidos durante el siglo XIX." RBNC, 2a serie, 1, 2 (1950), 37-50.

D.21 Cepero Bonilla, Raúl. El siglo, 1862-68; un periódico en lucha contra la censura. H, 1957. Also in his Obras históricas (H: Instituto de Historia, 1963), pp. 245-302.

D.22 Chacón y Calvo, José María. "El almendras." RBNC, 2a serie, 7, 2 (1956), 91-112.

D.23 _____. "Manuel de la Cruz." In Manuel de la Cruz, Estudios literarios (Madrid, 1924), pp. 9-41. His Obras completas, I.

D.24 _____. "La obra literaria y histórica del Dr. Juan J. Remos." In Juan Nepomuceno José Remos y Rubio, Discursos leídos en la recepción pública (H: "El Siglo XX" Muñiz, 1949), pp. 143-172.

D.25 "Criticar a la crítica." GdC, No. 75 (1969), 25-27.

D.26 Febres Cordero G., Julio. "[Revista cubana]." RBNC, 2a serie, 2, 1 (1951), 272-277.

D.27 Fernández Arrondo, Ernesto. "Conferencia sobre la Revista de la Habana." RBNC, 2a serie, 7, 1 (1956), 91-123.

D.28 Fernández Carvajal Bello, Juan. "A través de La Habana elegante." RBNC, 2a serie, 8, 2 (1957), 39-67. Signed Juan F. Carvajal y Bello.

D.29 Fernández Retamar, Roberto. "La Nueva revista cubana y el primer año de la revolución." In his Papelería (Santa Clara: Universidad Central de Las Villas, Dirección de Publicaciones, 1962), pp. 240-247.

D.30   _____. "Sobre el Primer Congreso Nacional de Escritores y Artis-
        tas." In his Papelería (Santa Clara: Universidad Central de
        Las Villas, Dirección de Publicaciones, 1962), pp. 275-278.

D.31   Fernández Santana, Isabel. "La restauración del Papel periódico
        de la Habana." L/L, Nos. 7-8 (1976-1977), 294-300.

D.32   Figueroa-Amaral, Esperanza. "Inicios del periodismo en Cuba (en
        el 150° aniversario del Papel periódico)." RBC, No. 49
        (1942), 39-68.

D.33   Fornet, Ambrosio. "La crítica contemporánea." In Panorama de
        la literatura cubana; conferencias (H: Universidad de la
        Habana, Centro de Estudios Cubanos, 1970), pp. 173-181.

D.34   _____. "La crítica literaria aquí y ahora." In his En tres y
        dos (H: R, 1964), pp. 13-43.

D.35   Gay-Calbó, Enrique. "Los redactores del Papel periódico." RBC,
        No. 46 (1940), 467-471.

D.36   _____. "El Revisor político y literario." RBNC, 2a serie, 6, 4
        (1955), 65-94.

D.37   González Echevarría, Roberto. "Criticism and literature in rev-
        olutionary Cuba." CS, 11, 1 (1981), 1-17.

D.38   Guerrero, María Luisa. "El Lyceum de la Habana: 1929-1968."
        RevC, 1, 2 (1968), 467-470.

D.39   Guiral Moreno, Mario. "Cuba contemporánea. Su origen, su exis-
        tencia y su significación." In Fermín Peraza Sarausa, In-
        dice de Cuba contemporánea (H: Municipio de la Habana, De-
        paratmento de Cultura, 1940), pp. 9-36.

D.40   _____. "La Revista de Cuba." RBNC, 2a serie, 7, 4 (1956), 33-
        67.

D.41   Gutiérrez de la Solana, Alberto. "La crítica y la investigación
        literaria de la diáspora cubana." In Instituto Internacio-
        nal de Literatura Iberoamericana, Otros mundos otros fuegos:
        fantasía y realismo mágico en Iberoamérica (East Lansing,
        Mich.: Michigan State University, Latin American Studies
        Center, 1975), pp. 239-244.

D.42   Hollingsworth, Charles. The development of literary theory in
        Cuba, 1959-1968. Unpublished Ph.D. dissertation, Univer-
        sity of California at Berkeley, 1972.

D.43   Iraizoz y de Villar, Antonio. La crítica en la literatura cuba-
        na. H: "Avisador Comercial", 1930.

D.44   _____. "Justificación de las tertulias y salones literarios:
        conferencia." AANAL, 23, 20 (1938), 204-223.

D.45   Lazo, Raimundo. "La Revista cubana." ULH, No. 177 (1966), 91-114.

D.46   ———. "El sesquicentenario del Papel periódico de la Habana." RI, No. 5 (1941), 117-121.

D.47   Lizaso y González, Félix. "La Revista de avance." BACL, 10, 3-4 (1961), 19-43.

D.48   Llaverías y Martínez, Joaquín. Contribución a la historia de la prensa periódica. H: Archivo Nacional de Cuba, 1957-1959.

D.49   Marinello, Juan. "Sobre nuestra crítica literaria." VUM, No. 219 (1970), 43-48.

D.50   Menocal Villalón, Feliciana. "La piragua y el siboneyismo." RBNJM, 3a serie, 6, 2 (1964), 5-13.

D.51   Monte, Ricardo del. "La Revista de Cuba, su vida y su influencia." In Fermín Peraza Sarausa, Indice de la Revista de Cuba (H: Municipio de la Habana, Departamento de Cultura, 1938), pp. 9-33.

D.52   Montes Huidobro, Matías. "Nueva generación." Chasqui, 9, 1 (1979), 39-74.

D.53   Pérez Cabrera, José Manuel. "El álbum." RBNC, 2a serie, 7, 3 (1956), 63-85.

D.54   Pérez de la Riva, Juan. "En nuestro sexagésimo aniversario." RBNJM, 3a serie, 11, 3 (1969), 161-169.

D.55   "Periodismo cubano. Primer periódico de Santiago de Cuba." RBNC, 2, 1-2 (1909), 13-16.

D.56   Piedra, Armando J. "La revista cubana Orígenes (1944-1956): portavoz generacional." DAI, 38 (1977), 3535A.

D.57   Pogolotti, Marcelo. "Cuba contemporánea." In his La república de Cuba al través de sus escritores (H: Lex, 1958), pp. 41-48.

D.58   ———. "La Revista de avance." In his La república de Cuba al través de sus escritores (H: Lex, 1958), pp. 101-107.

D.59   ———. "La revista Social." In his La república de Cuba al través de sus escritores (H: Lex, 1958), pp. 66-72.

D.60   Portuondo, José Antonio. "El ensayo y la crítica en Cuba revolucionaria." In Instituto Internacional de Literatura Iberoamericana, El ensayo y la crítica en Iberoamérica (Toronto: Universidad de Toronto, 1970), pp. 215-220.

D.61   "Relación de periódicos cubanos editados en los Estados Unidos en el siglo XIX, existentes en la Biblioteca Nacional." RBNC, 2a serie, 1, 2 (1950), 51-58.

D.62 Remos y Rubio, Juan Nepomuceno José. "Los oradores de La Claridad del Cerro." In his Micrófano (H: Molina, 1937), pp.
200-209.

D.63 ____. "Las revistas cubanas más representativas del siglo XIX."
In his Micrófano (H: Molina, 1937), pp. 221-227.

D.64 "Revista cubana. Instituto Nacional de Cultura. (Ministerio de
Educación.) La Habana, octubre-diciembre 1956." RBNC, 2a
serie, 7, 3 (1956), 201-202.

D.65 Rexach, Rosario. "La Revista de avance publicada en la Habana."
CarS, 3, 3 (1963), 3-16.

D.66 Ripoll, Carlos. Archivo José Martí: repertorio crítico, medio
siglo de estudios martianos. Eastchester, N.Y.: Eliseo
Torres, 1972.

D.67 ____. Patria: el periódico de José Martí; registro general
(1892-1895). NY: Eliseo Torres, 1971.

D.68 ____. La Revista de avance (1927-1930): episodio de la literatura cubana. NY: Las Américas, 1969.

D.69 ____. "La Revista de avance (1927-1930): vocero de vanguardismo
y pórtico de revolución." RI, No. 58 (1964), 261-282.

D.70 Rivero Muñiz, José. "Los orígenes de la prensa obrera en Cuba."
RBNJM, 3a serie, 2, 1-4 (1960), 67-89.

D.71 Roig de Leuchsenring, Emilio. "Los periódicos." In his La li-
teratura costumbrista cubana de los siglos XVIII y XIX (H:
Oficina del Historiador de la Ciudad de la Habana, 1962-),
I-II.

D.72 Saco, José Antonio. Justa defensa de la Academia Cubana de Literatura contra los violentos ataques que se le han dado
en el Diario de la Habana. New Orleans: St. Romes, 1834.

D.73 Sánchez, Reinaldo. "Don Junípero: vehículo del costumbrismo en
Cuba." Caribe, 2, 2 (1977), 55-67.

D.74 Sánchez Roig, Mario. "El Nuevo regañón de la Habana." RBNC,
2a serie, 8, 4 (1957), 133-147.

D.75 Sarusky, Jaime. "La revista Casa de las Américas." Bohemia,
69, 4 (1977), 26-27.

D.76 Schwartz, Kessel. "Ciclón and Cuban culture." CarS, 14, 4
(1974), 151-161. Also in his Studies on twentieth-century
Spanish and Spanish American literature (Lanham, Md.: University Press of America, 1983), pp. 245-256.

D.77 ____. "Ciclón and the Castro revolution." Hispania, 58
(1975), 926-928. Also in his Studies on twentieth-century

Spanish and Spanish American literature (Lanham, Md.: University Press of America, 1983), pp. 257-261.

D.78 _____. "Verbum and Spanish culture." CarS, 15, 2 (1975), 153-155. Also in his Studies on twentieth-century Spanish and Spanish American literature (Lanham, Md.: University Press of America, 1983), pp. 241-244.

D.79 Sosa de Quesada, Arístides. "Album cubano de lo bueno y lo bello." RBNC, 2a serie, 8, 1 (1957), 103-119.

D.80 Tro Pérez, Rodolfo. "Orígenes. Revista de arte y literatura, año VIII, no. 27, La Habana, 1951." RBNC, 2a serie, 2, 4 (1951), 259.

D.81 Vérez de Peraza, Elena Luisa. Publicaciones de las instituciones culturales cubanas; 2. ed. H: Anuario Bibliográfico Cubano, 1954.

D.82 Vitier, Cintio. "Prólogo." In his La crítica literaria y estética en el siglo XIX cubano (H: Biblioteca Nacional José Martí, Departamento Colección Cubana, 1968), I, 7-46; II, 7-59.

D.83 Weiss, Judith A. Casa de las Américas: an intellectual review in the Cuban revolution. Chapel Hill, N.C.: Estudios de Hispanófila, 1977.

E. LITERATURE AND OTHER SUBJECTS

E.1   Borden, Caroline. "Ideology and culture in Cuba." L&I, 7 (1970), 73-80.

E.2   Campuzano, Luis. "Casa No. 40: desde la revolución veinte escritores escriben..." RBNJM, 3a serie, 9, 1 (1967), 111-14.

E.3   Carpentier, Alejo. "Papel social del novelista." CAm, No. 53 (1969), 8-18.

E.4   Casal, Lourdes. El caso Padilla: literatura y revolución en Cuba; documentos. Miami: Universal; NY: Nueva Atlántida, n.d.

E.5   _____. "Literature and society." In Revolutionary change in Cuba (Pittsburgh: University of Pittsburgh Press, 1971), pp. 447-469.

E.6   Coulthard, Gabriel R. "Cuban literature and politics." CMB, 6, 5 (1969), 5-8.

E.7   Dalton, Roque et al. "Diez años de revolución: el intelectual y la sociedad." CAm, No. 56 (1969), 7-52. Also as El intelectual y la sociedad. M: Siglo XXI, 1969.

E.8   "Literatura y revolución." CAm, Nos. 51-52 (1968-1969), 179-200.

E.9   "Literatura y revolución (encuestas): los autores." CAm, Nos. 51-52 (1968-1969), 119-174.

E.10   Masó, Fausto. "Los escritores cubanos y el castrismo." Política, No. 29 (1963), 49-57.

E.11   _____. "Literatura y revolución en Cuba." MNu, No. 32 (1969), 50-54.

E.12   Otero, Lisandro. "El escritor en la revolución cubana." CAm, Nos. 36-37 (1966), 203-209.

E.13   Portuondo, José Antonio. "Los intelectuales y la revolución." CSoc, No. 34 (1964), 51-64.

E.14   Torriente, Loló de la. "El compromiso y los escritores cubanos." CA, No. 178 (1971), 7-17.

E.15   _____. "La política cultural y los escritores y artistas cubanos." CA, No. 130 (1963), 78-89.

F. RELATIONS WITH FOREIGN LITERATURES

F.1 Arrom, José Juan. "Voltaire y la literatura dramática cubana." RR, 34 (1943), 228-234. Also Prometeo, 1, 4 (1948), 13-15.

F.2 Augier, Angel I. "Cuba y Rubén Darío." L/L, No. 2 (1967), 87-278.

F.3 ____. "Lenin en las letras cubanas (1918-1934)." L/L, No. 1 (1970), 224-226.

F.4 Caballero, Juan. "García Lorca y Cuba: algunas rectificaciones." GLR, 6, 1-2 (1978), 43-54.

F.5 Clinkscales, Orline. "Bécquer's influence in Cuba and the other Antilles." In his Bécquer in Mexico, Central America, and the Caribbean countries (Madrid: Hispanoamericana, 1970), pp. 51-106.

F.6 Godoy, Armando. "Influencia de la cultura francesa en Cuba." ND, 37 (1957), 96-97.

F.7 Henríquez Ureña, Max. "Poetas cubanos de expresión francesa." RI, No. 6 (1941), 301-344.

F.8 Iraizoz y de Villar, Antonio. "Edmundo Goncourt y los cubanos." In his Libros y autores cubanos (Santa María de Rosario: Rosareña, 1956), pp. 52-54.

F.9 ____. "Espronceda en Cuba." In his Libros y autores cubanos (Santa María de Rosario: Rosareña, 1956), pp. 21-23.

F.10 Kuteischikova, Vera N., and Inna Terterian. "Literatura cubana editada en la Unión Soviética." CAm, No. 112 (1979), 65-68.

F.11 Marinello, Juan. "Federico [García Lorca] en Cuba." In his Contemporáneos; noticia y memoria (H: Universidad Central de Las Villas, 1964), pp. 203-226.

F.12 ____. García Lorca en Cuba. H: Ediciones Especiales, 1965.

F.13 Müller-Bergh, Klaus. "Unamuno y Cuba (dos contribuciones unamunianas poco conocidas a la Revista de avance)." CA, No. 166 (1969), 201-211.

G. WOMEN AUTHORS

G.1 Aparicio Laurencio, Angel. "Introducción." In Cinco poetisas cubanas 1935-1969: Mercedes García Tudurí--Pura del Prado --Teresa María Rojas--Rita Geada--Ana Rosa Núñez (Miami: Universal, 1970), pp. 7-12.

G.2 García de Coronado, Domitila. Album poético-fotográfico de escritoras y poetisas cubanas escrito en 1868 para la señora doña Gertrudis Gómez de Avellaneda. H: El Fígaro, 1926.

G.3 Harrison, Polly F. "Images and exile: the Cuban woman and her poetry." RInter, 4 (1974), 184-219.

G.4 Ibarzábal, Federico de. "Mujeres cuentistas." In his Cuentos contemporáneos (H: Trópico, 1937), pp. 195-197.

G.5 Jiménez, Reynaldo L. "Cuban women writers and the revolution: toward an assessment of their literary contribution." Folio, 11 (1978), 75-95.

G.6 Macías de Cartaya, Graziella. "Seis poetisas cubanas del siglo XX." Horizontes, 9, 18 (1966), 15-29.

G.7 Waldman, Gloria Feiman. "Affirmation and resistence: women poets from the Caribbean." In Contemporary women authors of Latin America; introductory essays (Brooklyn, NY: Brooklyn College Press, 1983), pp. 33-57.

H. SPECIAL TOPICS

(General studies on black culture in Cuba are included here; see also
the sections on Special Topics in Poetry, Drama, and Prose Fiction.
Because of the large number of references on Afro-Latin American literature available, included here are only those studies dealing spe-
cifically with Cuba and the Caribbean. For a list of comprehensive
studies, see Richard L. Jackson, The Afro-Spanish American author; an
annotated bibliography of criticism [NY: Garland, 1980].)

H.1   Amor, Rosa Teresa. "Afro-Cuban folklore tales as incorporated
           into the literary tradition of Cuba." DAI, 30 (1969),
           2517A.

H.2   Arrom, José Juan. "Mitos taínos en las letras de Cuba, Santo Do-
           mingo y México." CA, No. 168 (1970), 110-123. Also in his
           Certidumbre de América; 2. ed. ampl. (Madrid: Gredos, 1971),
           pp. 59-76.

H.3   Brathwaite, Edward Kamau. "The African presence in the Carib-
           bean literature." Daedalus, 103 (1904), 73-109. Also as
           "Presencia africana en la literatura del Caribe." In Afri-
           ca en América Latina (M: Siglo XXI; Paris: UNESCO, 1977),
           pp. 152-184.

H.4   Bueno, Salvador. "'La canción del bongó': sobre la cultura mula-
           ta de Cuba." CA, No. 206 (1976), 89-106.

H.5   _____. "París en la literatura cubana." RBNC, 2a serie, 3, 2
           (1952), 68-92. Also in his Temas y personajes de la lite-
           ratura cubana (H: Unión, 1964), pp. 173-188.

H.6   Carbonell y Rivero, José Manuel. "La oratoria en Cuba." In his
           La oratoria en Cuba (H: Montalvo y Cárdenas, 1928), I, v-
           xxi.

H.7   Cartey, Wilfred. Black images. NY: Columbia University, Teach-
           ers College Press, 1970.

H.8   Coulthard, Gabriel R. "El afrocubanismo." In his Raza y color
           en la literatura antillana (Sevilla: Escuela de Estudios
           Hispano-Americanos de Sevilla, 1958), pp. 39-62.

H.9   _____. "Antecedentes de la negritud en la literatura hispanoa-
           mericana." MNu, No. 11 (1967), 73-77.

H.10   Cuesta, Leonel-Antonio de la. "Introducción." In Alvaro de la
           Iglesia, Tradiciones cubanas (Montevideo: Gémenis; Madrid:
           Centro Cubano de España, 1974), pp. 19-31.

H.11   Dathrone, O. R. "Afro-new world movements: Harlem renaissance, negrista, and négritude." In his Dark ancester; the literature of the black man in the Caribbean (Baton Rouge: Louisiana State University Press, 1981), pp. 172-209.

H.12   Deschamps Chapeaux, Pedro. El negro en el periodismo cubano en el siglo XIX; ensayo bibliográfico. H: R, 1963.

H.13   Dihigo, Juan Manuel. "El habla popular al través de la literatura cubana." RFLC, 20, 1 (1915), 53-110.

H.14   Elizagaray, Alga Marina. "Floraison cubaine." Europe, Nos. 607-608 (1979), 44-54. On children's literature in Cuba.

H.15   _____. "La literatura para niños y jóvenes de la revolución cubana." CAm, No. 116 (1979), 22-32.

H.16   _____. "A survey of literature for children and adolescents in socialist Cuba." Phaedrus, 5, 2 (1978), 25-30.

H.17   Feijóo, Samuel. "El cocuyo en la literatura cubana." Islas, 6, 2 (1964), 91-107.

H.18   _____. El negro en la literatura folklórica cubana. H: Letras Cubanas, 1980.

H.19   Fernández de Castro, José Antonio. "El aporte negro en las letras de Cuba en el siglo XIX." RBC, 38 (1936), 46-66.

H.20   _____. "La literatura negra actual de Cuba (1902-1934). Datos para un estudio." EAf, 4 (1940), 3-22.

H.21   _____. Tema negro en las letras de Cuba (1608-1935). H: Mirador, 1943.

H.22   Fornet, Ambrosio. "El ajuste de cuentas del panfleto autonomista a la literatura de campaña." CAm, No. 100 (1977), 49-57.

H.23   Fure, Rogelio M. "Patakin: littérature sacrée de Cuba." PA, 77 (1971), 267-285.

H.24   García Barrio, Constance S. de. "The black in post-revolutionary Cuban literature." RInter, 8 (1978), 263-270.

H.25   García Pérez, Severo. "Nacionalismo y costumbrismo." In José Manuel Carbonell y Rivero, Evolución de la cultura cubana (H: El Siglo XX, 1928), XII, 187-189.

H.26   García Tudurí, Mercedes. "Influencia del medio en el carácter cubano." RBC, 40 (1937), 5-26.

H.27   Gordils, Janice Doris. "La herencia africana en la literatura cubana de hoy." DAI, 37 (1977), 5865A.

H.28   Iraizoz y del Villar, Antonio. "La oratoria sagrada en Cuba."
       In his Lecturas cubanas; 2. ed. (H: "Hermes", 1939), pp.
       137-168.

H.29   Johnson, Lemuel A. "Cuba and Afro-Latin radicalism: context and
       literature in a paradigm." JCS, 1 (1980), 74-103.

H.30   Labraña, José M. "La prensa en Cuba." In Cuba en la mano; en-
       ciclopedia popular ilustrada (H: Ucar, García, 1940), pp.
       649-786.

H.31   Lachataneré, Rómulo. "Las religiones negras y el folklore cu-
       bano." RHM, 9 (1943), 138-143.

H.32   León, Julio A. "Los cabildos afro-cubanos y su tradición cultu-
       ral." Caribe, 2, 2 (1977), 121-130.

H.33   Mañach, Jorge. Indagación del choteo. H: "Revista de Avance",
       1928. 2. ed., H: La Verónica, 1940.

H.34   Méndez Capote, Renée. Oratoria cubana; ensayos. H: "Hermes",
       1927.

H.35   Ojo-Ade, Femi. "De origen africano, soy cubano: African ele-
       ments in the literature of Cuba." ALT, 9 (1978), 47-57.
       Also in his African literature today: Africa, America and
       the Caribbean (NY: Africana, 1978), pp. 47-57.

H.36   Ortiz, Fernando. "La cubanidad y los negros." EAf, 3 (1939),
       3-15.

H.37   La palabra forjada de nuestra nacionalidad, academia literaria
       sobre oratoria cubana; homenaje a la patria cubana en el
       cincuentenario de su independencia. H: Pérez Sierra, 1955.

H.38   Piedra-Bueno, Andrés de. La Virgen María en la literatura cuba-
       na. H: A. Rodríguez, 1955.

H.39   Portell Vilá, Herminio. "El criollismo: su aparición y su des-
       arrollo en Cuba." In Libro jubilar de homenaje al Dr. J.
       M. Dihigo y Mestre (H: Revista de la Universidad de la Ha-
       bana, 1941), pp. 351-371.

H.40   Portuondo, José Antonio. "El negro, el héroe, bufón y persona
       en la literatura cubana colonial (1608-1896)." EyF, No. 7
       (1969), 63-68.

H.41   Rodríguez, Luis Felipe. "El sentido del paisaje vernáculo."
       RevC, Nos. 16-18 (1936), 14-33.

H.42   San Martín, Hernán. "La santería cubana: notas sobre folklore
       de la isla." AUC, No. 124 (1962), 150-156.

H.43   Sanguily y Garritte, Manuel. Oradores de Cuba. H: Revista Ha-
       banera, 1886. Also H: A. Dorrbecker, 1926.

H.44   Schulman, Ivan A. "Reflections on Cuba and its antislavery lit-
       erature." SECOLASA, 7 (1976), 59-67.

H.45   Torre, Guillermo de. "Literatura de color." RBC, 38 (1936), 5-
       11. Also in his La aventura y el orden (BA: Losada, 1943),
       pp. 305-314.

H.46   Valdés-Cruz, Rosa E. "Huella africana en la literatura cubana."
       In Actes du VIIe Congrès de l'Association Internationale
       de Littérature Comparée (Stuttgart: Bieber, 1979), pp. 323-
       326.

I. GENERAL STUDIES ON COLONIAL LITERATURE

I.1 Arrom, Juan José. "Letras en Cuba antes de 1608." RevC, 18 (1944), 67-85. Also in his Estudios de literatura hispano-americana (H, 1950), pp. 11-31.

I.2 Coronado, Francisco de Paula. "Frutos coloniales." RBNC, 2a serie, 7, 3 (1956), 9-101. Signed César de Madrid.

I.3 Le Riverend, Julio. "Síntesis histórica de la cubanidad en el siglo XVIII." RBC, 46 (1940), 178-197.

I.4 Olivera, Otto. "La cubanidad en el siglo XVI." RBNC, 2a serie, 4, 3 (1953), 96-127.

I.5 _____. "Siglo XVI: espíritu local y literatura cubana." RBNC, 2a serie, 1, 4 (1951), 57-62.

I.6 Portell Vilá, Herminio. "Sobre el ideario político cubano del siglo XVIII." RBC, 27 (1931), 358-361.

I.7 Portuondo, José Antonio. "Los comienzos de la literatura cubana (1510-1790)." In Panorama de la literatura cubana; conferencias (H: Universidad de la Habana, Centro de Estudios Cubanos, 1970), pp. 5-41.

I.8 Roig de Leuschsenring, Emilio. La literatura costumbrista cubana de los siglos XVIIIy XIX. H: Oficina del Historiador de la Ciudad, 1962-.

J. GENERAL STUDIES ON 19TH CENTURY LITERATURE

J.1 Andeuza, J. M. de. "Literatura cubana." In Isla de Cuba pinto-
resca (Madrid: Boix, 1841), pp. 48-102.

J.2 Blanco García, Francisco. "La isla de Cuba." In his La literatura española en el siglo XIX; 3. ed. (Madrid: Sáenz de
Jubera, 1909-1912), III, 267-279.

J.3 Bueno, Salvador. Contorno del modernismo en Cuba. H: Lex, 1950.
Orig. RevI, No. 116 (1950), 155-163. Also CHA, Nos. 212-
213 (1967), 481-489.

J.4 ____. Figuras cubanas del siglo XIX. H: Unión de Escritores
y Artistas, 1980.

J.5 Campa, Román V. de la. "El romanticismo en la literatura cubana." Círculo, 2 (1970), 9-17.

J.6 Cruz, Manuel de la. Cromitos cubanos. H: Arte y Literatura,
1975. Orig. H: La Lucha, 1892. Also Madrid: Saturnino
Calleja, 1926.

J.7 ____. "Reseña histórica del movimiento literario en la isla
de Cuba (1790-1890)." In his Literatura cubana (Madrid:
Calleja, 1924), pp. 7-95.

J.8 Díaz Martínez, Manuel. "El modernismo en Cuba." In Panorama de
la literatura cubana; conferencias (H: Universidad de la
Habana, Centro de Estudios Cubanos, 1970), pp. 129-141.

J.9 Flouret, Michèle. "Le thème de l'étranger dans la littérature
cubaine du XIXème siècle." In Nationalisme et cosmopoli-
tisme dans les littératures ibériques au XIXème siècle
(Lille: Université de Lille; Paris: Editions Universitaires, 1975), pp. 199-212.

J.10 Forest, Michèle. "Les écrivains cubains de la première moitié
du XIXe siècle face au régime colonial." In Culture et
société en Espagne et en Amérique latine au XIXe siècle
(Lille: Centre d'Etudes Ibériques et Ibéro-Américaines
de l'Université de Lille III, 1980), pp. 121-134.

J.11 Fornet, Ambrosio. "Criollismo, cubanía y producción editorial
(1855-1885)." Santiago, No. 17 (1975), 109-121.

J.12 González del Valle, José Zacarías. La vida literaria en Cuba
(1836-1840). H: Secretaría de Educación, Dirección de
Cultura, 1938.

J.13 Henríquez Ureña, Max. "Cuba." In his <u>Breve historia del moder-</u>
<u>nismo</u>; 2. ed. (M/BA: Fondo de Cultura Económica, 1962),
pp. 418-447. Orig. 1954.

J.14 Heredia, Nicolás. "Siluetas cubanas." In Cintio Vitier, <u>La crí-</u>
<u>tica literaria y estética en el siglo XIX cubano</u> (H: <u>Biblio-</u>
<u>teca Nacional "José Martí"</u>, Departamento Colección Cubana,
1968), III, 252-267.

J.15 Lamar Schweyer, Alberto. <u>Los contemporáneos (ensayos sobre li-</u>
<u>teratura cubana del siglo)</u>. H: "Los Rayos X", 1912.

J.16 Montalvo, José Rafael. "Disertación acerca de la vida intelectual de la isla de Cuba." <u>RBNC</u>, 2a serie, 5, 4 (1954), 7-
19.

J.17 Nuiry, Nuria. "El romanticismo y Cuba." In <u>Panorama de la li-</u>
<u>teratura cubana; conferencias</u> (H: Universidad de la Habana,
Centro de Estudios Cubanos, 1970), pp. 43-55.

J.18 Remos y Rubio, Juan Nepomuceno José. "Los albores del modernismo en Cuba." In his <u>Micrófano</u> (H: Molina, 1937), pp. 236-
244.

J.19 _____. "La reacción del buen gusto en el romanticismo cubano."
In his <u>Micrófano</u> (H: Molina, 1937), pp. 155-160.

J.20 Rodríguez Demorizi, Emilio. "El romanticismo en Cuba, un apunte
y una sugerencia." <u>RBNC</u>, 2a serie, 6, 3 (1955), 63-88.

J.21 Zamora, Juan Clemente. "La inédita antología cubana del centenario." <u>Hispania</u>, 51 (1968), 528-532.

K. GENERAL STUDIES ON 20TH CENTURY LITERATURE

K.1   Alvarez Bravo, Armando. "Temas y personajes de la literatura cubana." Unión, 3, 4 (1964), 170-172.

K.2   Anuario cultural de Cuba, 1943. H: Dirección General de Relaciones Culturales, 1944.

K.3   Arias, Salvador. "Literatura cubana, 1959-1975." CAm, No. 113 (1979), 14-26.

K.4   Avila, Leopoldo. Cuba: letteratua e rivoluzione. Le correnti della critica e della letteratura cubana. Milano: Libreria Feltrinelli, 1969.

K.5   Bahner, Werner. "Revolution und revolutionäres Bewusstsein in der kubanischen Literatur der Gegenwart." In Revolution und Literatur (Leipzig: Reclam, 1971), pp. 355-376.

K.6   Baquero, Gastón. "Tendencias de nuestra literatura." In Anuario cultural de Cuba, 1943, q.v., pp. 261-287.

K.7   Barrera, Ernesto M. "Philosophical transformations in contemporary Cuban literature." NewS, 5 (1975), 109-112.

K.8   Bueno, Salvador. "Diez años de literatura y revolución en Cuba." RBNJM, 3a serie, 11, 1 (1969), 161-194.

K.9   _____. "La literatura cubana en el siglo XX." In Panorama das literaturas das Américas (Nova Lisboa: Edição do Município de Nova Lisboa, 1958), II, 435-464.

K.10   _____. Medio siglo de literatura cubana, 1902-1952. H: Comisión Nacional Cubana de la UNESCO, 1953.

K.11   _____. "Panorama da literatura cubana." SeN, 48 (1970), 297-303.

K.12   _____. "Panorama de la literatura cubana contemporánea." Ars, No. 8 (1957), 3-10.

K.13   Carpentier, Alejo. "La actualidad cultural de Cuba." Sur, No. 293 (1965), 61-67.

K.14   Casaus, Víctor. "La historia de la guerra." Unión, 3, 1 (1964), 161-163.

K.15 Coulthard, Gabriel R. "Cuban literary prizes for 1963." CarS, 4, 4 (1965), 3-10, 48-55.

K.16 _____. "The situation of the writer in contemporary Cuba." CarS, 7, 1 (1967), 23-35.

K.17 _____. "The writer and the revolution: literary development in Russia and Cuba since their respective revolutions." CarS, 15, 2 (1975), 163-168.

K.18 Desnoes, Edmundo. "No es prólogo para cubanos." In Los dispositivos de la flor; Cuba: literatura desde la revolución (Hanover, N.H.: Ediciones del Norte, 1981), pp. xv-xxv.

K.19 Dey, Susnigdha, and Sujan Singh Pannu. "Casa de las Américas prize." JSL, 4, 2 (1976-1977), 39-53.

K.20 Díaz, Filiberto. "Cuba y su literatura." MNu, Nos. 39-40 (1969), 83-86.

K.21 Dill, Hans-Otto. "Dies Herausbildung der sozialistischen Nationalliteratur Kubas." ZS, 20 (1975), 587-593.

K.22 Ecrivains de Cuba. Paris: Denoël, 1967. Special issue of LetN, déc.1967-jan. 1968. Pertinent items are listed separately.

K.23 Ehnmark, Anders. "Återblick och fjärrsyn: kubansk litteratur under revolutionen." BLM, 32 (1963), 41-50.

K.24 Ellis, Keith. "La literatura cubana y la revolución." CanF, No. 576 (1969), 224-226.

K.25 "Encuesta generacional." GdC, No. 50 (1966), 8-9.

K.26 "Encuesta: ¿qué ha significado para ti la revolución cubana?" CA, No. 111 (1960), entire issue.

K.27 Entralgo, Elías. Perfiles (apuntes críticos sobre literatura cubana contemporánea). H: "Hermes", 1923.

K.28 "Entrevistas." CAm, Nos. 22-23 (1964), 139-149.

K.29 Fernández, Alvaro. "Primer Congreso Nacional de Cultura." Cuba, 2, 10 (1963), 74-81.

K.30 Fernández Retamar, Roberto. "Algunas nociones sobre la cultura en la Cuba revolucionaria." Plural, No. 78 (1978), 10-15.

K.31 _____. "Apuntes sobre revolución y literatura en Cuba." Reflexión, 2, 2-4 (1973), 113-122. Also in his Para una teoría de la literatura hispanoamericana; 2. ed. (M: Nuestro Tiempo, 1977), pp. 159-176.

K.32 _____. "Hacia una intelectualidad revolucionaria en Cuba." In his Ensayo de otro mundo (Santiago de Chile: Universitaria, 1969), pp. 141-163.

K.33 _____. "Les intellectuels et la révolution." In Ecrivains de
      Cuba, q.v., pp. 40-61.

K.34 _____. "1961: cultura cubana en Marcha." In his Papelería
      (Santa Clara: Universidad Central de Las Villas, Dirección
      de Publicaciones, 1962), pp. 283-294.

K.35 Franco, Jean. "Literature in the revolution." TCent, Nos.
      1039-1040 (1968-1969), 64-66.

K.36 "La Gaceta pregunta." GdC, No. 19 (1963), 2-7.

K.37 Gallagher, David P. "The literary life in Cuba." NYRB, 23-V-
      1968, pp. 37-41.

K.38 Gay-Calbó, Enrique. "Nuestra literatura (cubana)." RBC, 30
      (1932), 59-61, 181-198, 440-449.

K.39 Gončarova, Tat'jana. "Prizvany revoluciej: zametki o kubanskoj
      literatura 70-x godov." LO, 7 (1979), 24-28.

K.40 González, Manuel Pedro. "La vida literaria en Cuba." REH-PR,
      2, 1 (1929), 75-82.

K.41 Guiral Moreno, Mario. Auge y decadencia del vanguardismo lite-
      rario en México. H: Molina, 1942. Orig. AANAL, 23 (1941),
      200-218.

K.42 Gutiérrez de la Solana, Alberto. "[J. M. Cohen, Writers in the
      new Cuba]." RevC, 1, 2 (1968), 457-480.

K.43 Hasse, Federico. "Filiberto [Díaz] o el último compilador."
      MNu, No. 46 (1970), 63-74. See item no. K.20.

K.44 Henríquez Ureña, Camila. "La literatura cubana en la revolu-
      ción." In Panorama de la literatura cubana; conferencias
      (H: Universidad de la Habana, Centro de Estudios Cubanos,
      1970), pp. 209-239.

K.45 Lamar Schweyer, Alberto. Los contemporáneos (ensayos sobre li-
      teratura cubana del siglo). H: "Los Rayos X", 1912.

K.46 Leante, César. "Esbozo de la literatura cubana actual." GdC,
      No. 13 (1963), 6-7.

K.47 Literatura y arte nuevo en Cuba. Barcelona: Estela, 1971.

K.48 "Literatura y revolución (encuestas): los autores." CAm, Nos.
      51-52 (1968-1969), 119-174.

K.49 Llopis, Rogelio. "Puntos de vista acerca de la nueva literatura
      cubana." GdC, No. 40 (1964), 10-11.

K.50 López Segrera, Francisco. "Psicoanálisis de una generación
      (1940-1959)." RBNJM, 3a serie, 11, 3 (1969), 99-120; 12,
      1 (1970), 93-125; 12, 2 (1970), 101-152.

K.51 Low, Mary. "El Grupo H." Orígenes, No. 40 (1956), 69-75.

K.52 Luca, Gemma R. del. "Creativity and revolution: cultural dimen-
sion of the new Cuba." In Cuba, Castro and revolution (Coral Gables: University of Miami Press, 1972), pp. 94-118.

K.53 Madrigal Ecay, Roberto. "Literatura cómplice." Término, 1, 4
(1983), 15-16.

K.54 Mañach, Jorge. "Diálogo sobre el año prosaico." Social, 14, 1
(1929), 12-13.

K.55 Marinello, Juan. "Congreso de Escritores y Artistas." In his
Contemporáneos; noticia y memoria (H: Universidad Central
de Las Villas, 1964), pp. 227-229.

K.56 Martí, Agenor. "De frente, la cultura." CubaI, No. 30 (1972),
50-57.

K.57 Martí, Jorge Luis. "The Cuban society as reflected in its literature (1900-1930)." SECOLASA, 4 (1973), 80-93.

K.58 Martínez Laínez, Fernando. Palabra cubana. Madrid: Akal, 1975.

K.59 Masó, Fausto. "Los escritores cubanos y el castrismo." Política, No. 29 (1963), 49-57.

K.60 Miranda, Julio E. Nueva literatura cubana. Madrid: Taurus,
1971.

K.61 _____. "El nuevo pensamiento cubano." El urogallo, No. 8
(1971), 84-93.

K.62 Novás Calvo, Lino. "Cuba literaria." GLit, No. 116 (1931), 9-
10; No. 118 (1931), 1-4.

K.63 Núñez y Domínguez, José de Jesús. "Nuevo movimiento literario
de Cuba." RRev, No. 768 (1925), 32.

K.64 Orlando, Felipe. Panorámica actual de la literatura cubana.
M: Machado, 1956.

K.65 Otero, Lisandro et al. "Conversación sobre arte y literatura."
CAm, Nos. 22-23 (1964), 130-138.

K.66 Paulo, Rogério. Um actor em viagem, Cuba, 1970 e 1972. Lisboa:
Seará Nova, 1972. 2. ed., 1976.

K.67 Piñera, Virgilio. "Cuba y la literatura." Ciclón, 1, 2 (1955),
51-55.

K.68 _____. "Notas sobre la vieja y la nueva generación." GdC, No.
2 (1962), 2-3.

K.69 Portuondo, José Antonio. "Ideas estéticas de la revolución cubana." L/L, No. 6 (1975), 3-12.

K.70 _____. "Las letras cubanas durante la República." Humanismo,
Nos. 58-59 (1959-1960), 99-105.

K.71 _____. "Literatura de la emancipación de la literatura." L/L,
No. 2 (1971), 3-8.

K.72 _____. "Tarjetero: Cuba literaria (1941)." RBC, 50 (1942), 98-
109, 251-260, 421-433; 51 (1943), 71-81; 52 (1943), 275-
281; 53 (1944), 153-173.

K.73 Pou, Angel Neovildo. Presencia de una nueva generación literaria: tres artículos periodísticos. H: Renuevo, 1957.

K.74 Remos y Rubio, Juan Nepomuceno, José. "Movimiento literario de
Cuba desde 1902." In José Manuel Carbonell y Rivero, Las
bellas artes en Cuba (H: "El Siglo XX", 1928), pp. 13-50.

K.75 _____. Panorama literario de Cuba en nuestro siglo. H: Cárdenas, 1942.

K.76 Ripoll, Carlos. "Coacción y creación en la literatura cubana
actual." ZF, No. 62 (1968), 38-41.

K.77 _____. The Cuban scene: censors & dissenters. Washington, D.C.:
The Cuban-American National Foundation, 1982. Orig. PR, 48
(1981), 574-587.

K.78 _____. La generación del 23 en Cuba y otros apuntes sobre el
vanguardismo. NY: Las Américas, 1968.

K.79 Rodríguez Alemán, Francisco. "La narrativa cubana del siglo XX
hasta el año 1929." Islas, No. 57 (1977), 25-49.

K.80 Rodríguez Feo, José. "Littérature à Cuba." In Ecrivains de
Cuba, q.v., pp. 88-94.

K.81 Rodríguez Sosa, Fernando. "Temas de la narrativa cubana actual."
ULH, No. 207 (1978), 203-210.

K.82 Rodríguez y Expósito, César. Los mejores libros cubanos de 1900-
1950, según la encuesta iniciada el 19 de julio de 1950.
H: Biblioteca Nacional, 1952.

K.83 S., I. "Cuba, ¿fin de una tregua?" MNu, No. 32 (1969), 80-84.

K.84 Salkey, Andrew. "Introduction." In his Writing in Cuba since
the revolution; an anthology (London: Bogle-L'Ouverture,
1977), pp. 11-14.

K.85 Salper, Roberta. "Literature and revolution in Cuba." MRev,
22, 5 (1970), 15-30.

K.86 Sánchez-Boudy, José. Historia de la literatura cubana (en el
exilio). Miami: Universal, 1975-.

K.87 Schiffrin, André. "Report from Cuba." LJ, 93, 9 (1968), 1865-
        1867.

K.88 Valle, Rafael Heliodoro. "Cuban authors and thinkers." HAHR,
        3 (1920), 634-638.

K.89 Walsh, Rodolfo. "Cuba escribe." In Crónicas de Cuba (BA: Jorge
        Alvarez, 1969), pp. 9-15.

L. GENERAL STUDIES ON POETRY

L.1 Augier, Angel I. "Tres siglos de poesía cubana." Unión, 5, 2 (1966), 168-169.

L.2 Carbonell y Rivero, José Manuel. "Breve reseña de la poesía lírica en Cuba desde 1608 hasta nuestros días." In his Evolución de la cultura cubana (H: El Siglo XX, 1928), I, 7-146.

L.3 Chabás, Juan. Poetas de todos los tiempos: hispanos, hispanoamericanos, cubanos. H: Cultural, 195?

L.4 Chacón y Calvo, José María. "Los orígenes de la poesía en Cuba." CCont, 2 (1913), 167-174, 238-252, 308-319; 3 (1913), 67-88, 151-176. Also H: "Siglo XX", 1913. Also in his Ensayos de literatura cubana (Madrid: "Saturnino Calleja", 1932), pp. 11-82.

L.5 _____. "La poesía desde los orígenes hasta fines del siglo XX." In El libro de Cuba (H: Molina, 1925), pp. 571-572.

L.6 Esténger, Rafael. "Trayecto de la poesía cubana." In his Cien de las mejores poesías cubanas; 3. ed. aum. (H: Mirador, 1948), pp. 7-59. Orig. 1943.

L.7 Fernández Retamar, Roberto. "Algo semejante a los monstruos antediluvianos." RBNJM, 64, 2 (1973), 45-69.

L.8 _____. "La poesía cubana nuevamente contada." Santiago, No. 9 (1972), 7-26.

L.9 Florit, Eugenio. "Notas sobre la poesía cubana." In his Poesía casi siempre (ensayos literarios) (Madrid/NY: Mensaje, 1978), pp. 63-69.

L.10 Jiménez, Juan Ramón. Prólogo a la poesía cubana. H: P. Fernández, 1937.

L.11 Lezama Lima, José. "Después de lo raro la extrañeza." Orígenes, No. 6 (1945), 51-55.

L.12 _____. "Prólogo." In his Antología de la poesía cubana (H: Consejo Nacional de Cultura, 1965), I, 7-46. Also in his La cantidad hechizada (Madrid: Júcar, 1974), pp. 83-133.

L.13 López, César. "Atisbos en la poesía de Cuba." Unión, 4, 3 (1965), 168-174.

L.14 Mañach, Jorge. "La natividad poética de Cuba." In Studia philologica: homenaje ofrecido a Dámaso Alonso (Madrid: Gredos, 1960), II, 423-434.

L.15 Marinello, Juan. Poética; ensayos en entusiasmo. Madrid: Espasa-Calpe, 1933.

L.16 Olivera, Otto. Cuba en su poesía. M: de Andrea, 1965.

L.17 Ripoll, Carlos. "Prólogo." In Naturaleza y alma de Cuba; dos siglos de poesía cubana (1760-1960) (NY: Anaya-Las Américas, 1974), pp. 7-12.

L.18 Salazar y Roig, Salvador. El dolor en la lírica cubana. H: "El Siglo XX", 1925.

L.19 Vitier, Cintio. "Nemósine (datos para una poética)." Orígenes, No. 20 (1948), 29-41.

L.20 _____. "La rebelión de la poesía." RevC, 27 (1950), 23-41.

L.21 _____. "Recuento de la poesía lírica en Cuba. De Heredia a nuestros días." RevC, 30 (1956), 53-96.

L.22 _____, and Fina García Marruz. "Flor oculta de la poesía cubana." RBNJM, 3a serie, 19, 1 (1977), 95-139.

L.23 Zambrana, Ramón. "Diferentes épocas de la poesía en Cuba." In José Manuel Carbonell y Rivero, La poesía lírica en Cuba (H: El Siglo XX, 1928), I, 235-290.

M. COLONIAL AND 19TH CENTURY POETRY

M.1 Carbonell y Rivero, José Manuel. Los poetas de "El laúd del desterrado". H: "Avisador Comercial", 1930.

M.2 Del Monte y Aponte, Domingo. "Del destino de la poesía en el siglo XIX." El álbum, 3 (1838), 5-19.

M.3 Escoto, José Augusto. "Albores de la poesía cubana en el siglo XVI." RHCB, 1, 2 (1916), 113-135.

M.4 Feijóo, Samuel. "Poetas cubanos del siglo XIX." In his Azar de lecturas. Crítica (Santa Clara: Universidad Central de Las Villas, 1961), pp. 9-83.

M.5 _____. "Sobre los movimientos por una poesía cubana hasta 1856." RevC, 25 (1949), 64-176. Also as Sobre los movimientos por una poesía cubana hasta 1856 (1947-49); 2. ed. Santa Clara: Universidad Central de Las Villas, 1961.

M.6 Florit, Eugenio. "Menéndez Pelayo y la poesía cubana del romanticismo." In his Poesía, casi siempre (ensayos literarios) (Madrid/NY: Mensaje, 1978), pp. 81-90.

M.7 González del Valle y Carbajal, Emilio Martín. La poesía lírica en Cuba; apuntes para un libro de biografía y de crítica. Barcelona: Luis Tasso, 1900. Orig. Oviedo: Vallina, 1882.

M.8 Guiteras, Pedro José. Vidas de poetas cubanos. H, 1875.

M.9 Henríquez Ureña, Pedro. "El modernismo en la poesía cubana." In his Ensayos críticos (H: Esteban Fernández, 1905), pp. 33-42. Also in his Obra crítica (M: Fondo de Cultura Económica, 1960), pp. 17-22.

M.10 Kostia, Conde. "Prólogo." In Arpas cubanas (poetas contemporáneas) (H: Rampla y Bouza, 1904(, pp. v-xi.

M.11 Languasco, Nardo. La poesía romántica cubana. Toulouse: Edouard Privat; Paris: Henri Didier, 1930.

M.12 López Prieto, Antonio. "Introducción a la poesía en Cuba." In his Parnaso cubano (H: Miguel de Villa, 1881), pp. v-lxxxi.

M.13 Pichardo Moya, Felipe. "La cubanidad de nuestra poesía anterior a Heredia." RevH, 20 (1943), 70-77.

M.14 Piñeyro, Enrique. "Poetas líricos cubanos." In his Estudios y conferencias de historia y literatura (NY: Thompson y Moreau, 1880), pp. 197-215.

M.15 Ponce de León, Néstor. "Los primeros poetas de Cuba." RCub, 15 (1892), 385-399.

M.16 Remos y Rubio, Juan Nepomuceno José. "Los albores del modernismo en Cuba." In his Micrófano (H: Molina, 1937), pp. 236-244.

M.17 ____. "Los cantores del 27 de noviembre [1871]." In his Micrófano (H: Molina, 1937), pp. 228-235.

M.18 ____. Los poetas de "Arpas amigas". H: Cárdenas, 1943.

M.19 Ricardo, Yolanda. "Valoraciones en torno a la poesía naturalista." Bohemia, 69, 41 (1977), 10-15.

M.20 Rivero González, Juana Luisa. El sentimiento patriótico-revolucionario en la lírica cubana desde Heredia hasta Martí. Pinar del Río: Pinareño, 1947.

M.21 Santos Fuentes y Betancourt, Emilio de los. Aparición y desarrollo de la poesía en Cuba. Lima: "La Opinión Nacional", 1877.

M.22 Vitier, Cintio. "Introducción." In his Los grandes románticos cubanos; antología (H: Tercer Festival del Libro Cubano, 1960?), pp. 5-15. Also H: Consejo Nacional de Cultura, 1962; pp. 5-10.

M.23 ____. Poetas cubanos del siglo XIX; semblanzas. H: Unión, 1969.

N. 20TH CENTURY POETRY

N.1 Alvarez, Federico. "Cuba hoy: poesía." Insula, Nos. 260-261 (1968), 1, 23.

N.2 Arrom, José Juan. "Cuba: polaridades de su imagen poética." ALit, 17 (1975), 3-41.

N.3 Báez, Paulino G. "Nota preliminar." In his Poetas jóvenes cubanos (Barcelona: Maucci, 1922?), pp. 5-13.

N.4 Boti, Regino Eladio. "La nueva poesía." CCont, 54 (1927), 55-71.

N.5 _____. La nueva poesía en Cuba. H: El Siglo XX, 1927.

N.6 _____. "Tres temas sobre la nueva poesía." Avance, No. 19 (1928), 50-51, 63; No. 21 (1928), 91-93; No. 22 (1928), 127-129, 136.

N.7 Branly, Roberto. "Panorama de la joven poesía revolucionaria cubana (1959-1963)." L/L, No. 1 (1967), 79-105.

N.8 Cardenal, Ernesto. "Presentación." In Poesía cubana de la revolución (M: Extemporáneos, 1976), pp. 11-19.

N.9 Chrisman, Robert. "Impressions of Cuba: revolutionaries and poets." BlS, 11, 3 (1980), 12-25.

N.10 Cohen, J. M. En tiempos difíciles; la poesía cubana de la revolución. Barcelona: Tusquets, 1970.

N.11 Cruz-Alvarez, Félix L. "Los poetas del grupo de Orígenes." DAI, 40 (1979), 2084A.

N.12 Cúneo, Dardo. "Sobre la poesía cubana." In his Esquemas americanos (BA: Instituto Cultural Joaquín B. González, 1942), pp. 93-101.

N.13 Feijóo, Samuel. "Poética cubana de los sonidos en el siglo XX." NRC, 2, 1 (1960), 53-76.

N.14 _____. "Prólogo a la edición cubana. Poesía moderna en Cuba: panorama." Islas, 9, 4 (1967), 9-11.

N.15 Fernández Retamar, Roberto. "Para presentar Poesía joven de Cuba." In his Papelería (Santa Clara: Universidad Central de Las Villas, Dirección de Publicaciones, 1962), pp. 217-222.

N.16 _____. La poesía contemporánea en Cuba (1927-1953). H: Orígenes, 1954.

N.17 _____. "La poesía cubana nuevamente contada." PP, 16 (1973),
38-47.

N.18 _____. "La poesía vanguardista en Cuba." In Oscar Collazos,
Los vanguardismos en América Latina (Barcelona: Península,
1977), pp. 191-210.

N.19 _____. "Sobre poesía y revolución en Cuba." In his Ensayo de
otro mundo (Santiago de Chile: Universitaria, 1969), pp.
70-81.

N.20 Godoy, Gustavo J. "La generación cubana de poetas posmodernis-
tas." DA, 28 (1968), 2682A-2683A.

N.21 González Jiménez, Omar. "Poesía joven y realidad en Cuba." CB,
No. 128 (1978), 7-9.

N.22 Goytisolo, José Agustín. "Estudio preliminar." In his Nueva
poesía cubana; antología poética (Barcelona: Península,
1970, c1969), pp. 5-36.

N.23 Herrera Ysla, Nelson. "Nota de presentación." In Poesía por la
victoria (H: Letras Cubanas, 1981), pp. 5-7.

N.24 Jimenes Grullón, Juan Isidro. Seis poetas cubanos (ensayos apologéticos). H: "Cromos", 1954.

N.25 Jiménez, José Olivio. Estudios sobre poesía cubana contemporánea. NY: Las Américas, 1967.

N.26 _____. "Hacia la poesía pura en Cuba." Hispania, 45 (1962),
428-435.

N.27 _____. Panorama de la lírica cubana contemporánea. Unpublished
doctoral dissertation, Universidad de Madrid, 1955.

N.28 Jiménez, Juan Ramón. "Estado poético cubano." In his La poesía
cubana en 1936 (colección) (H: Institución Hispanocubana de
Cultura, 1937), pp. xii-xxx [anthology comes between pages
xxi and xxiii].

N.29 Lezama Lima, José. "Alrededores de una antología." Orígenes,
No. 31 (1952), 63-68.

N.30 Linares Pérez, Marta. La poesía pura en Cuba y su evolución.
Madrid: Playor, 1975.

N.31 López, César. "En torno a la poesía cubana actual." Unión, 6,
4 (1967), 186-198.

N.32 López Morales, Humberto. "[Introducción]." In his Poesía cubana
contemporánea; un ensayo de antología (NY: Las Américas,
1967), pp. 5-18.

N.33 Luis, Raúl. "Prólogo." In Poemas David 69 (H: Unión de Escritores y Artistas de Cuba, 1970), pp. 7-10.

N.34 Lukin, Boris V. "Testimonios sobre la poesía popular cubana del segundo tercio del siglo XIX." Santiago, No. 31 (1978), 61-80.

N.35 Marinello, Juan. "Sobre el vanguardismo en Cuba y en la América Latina." In Oscar Collazos, Los vanguardismos en la América Latina (Barcelona: Península, 1977), pp. 211-224.

N.36 _____. "Veinticinco años de poesía cubana. Derrotero provisional." RBC, 39 (1937), 236-239, 366-388.

N.37 Mario, José. "Novísima poesía cubana." MNu, No. 38 (1969), 63-69.

N.38 Marrast, Robert. "Poesía contemporánea cubana." GdC, No. 37 (1964), 9.

N.39 Martínez Bello, Antonio. "Orientaciones de la nueva lírica." RBC, 38 (1936), 169-183.

N.40 Melon, Alfred. "Sobre poesía cubana: realidad, poesía e ideología." In his Realidad: poesía e ideología (H: Unión, 1973?), pp. 5-24.

N.41 Ortiz de Montellano, Bernardo. "Poesía nueva en Cuba." Avance, No. 10 (1927), 249.

N.42 Pita Rodríguez, Félix. "Los poetas cubanos y la revolución." GdC, No. 44 (1965), 33.

N.43 Prats Sariol, José. "La más reciente poesía cubana." CB, No. 107 (1976), 6-7; No. 110 (1977), 9-10; No. 111 (1977), 21-22; No. 113 (1977), 18-26; No. 114 (1977), 26.

N.44 Raggi, Carlos M. "Tangentes y paralelas en la poética cubana de hoy." Círculo, 3 (1971), 65-76.

N.45 Randall, Margaret. "Introduction." In Estos cantos habitados. These living songs: fifteen new Cuban poets (Fort Collins, Colo.: Colorado State Review Press, 1978), pp. i-xxv. Colorado State review, n.s., 6, 1.

N.46 Rodríguez Padrón, Jorge. "Nueva poesía cubana." CHA, No. 273 (1973), 616-623.

N.47 Rodríguez Rivera, Guillermo. "En torno a la joven poesía cubana." Unión, 17, 2 (1978), 63-80.

N.48 Rodríguez Sardiñas, Orlando. "Cuba: poesía entre revolución y exilio." RInter, 4 (1974), 359-369.

N.49 ____. "Prólogo." In his La última poesía cubana; antología reunida, 1959-73 (Madrid: Hispanova, 1973), pp. 7-39.

N.50 Ruprecht, Hans-George. "De la poésie cubaine dans la révolution." In Littérature latino-américaine d'aujourd'hui: Colloque de Cerisy (Paris: Union Génerale d'Editions, 1980), pp. 390-406.

N.51 Saldaña, Excilia. "Vanguardia y vanguardismo." CB, No. 47 (1971), 6-9; No. 48 (1971), 4-9.

N.52 Sánchez-Boudy, José. "Poesía cubana del exilio." Círculo, 2 (1970), 103-108.

N.53 Sender, Ramón. "Genio poético y desesperanza." In Escrito en Cuba: cinco poetas disidentes (Madrid: Playor, 1978), pp. 5-9.

N.54 Suárez Solís, Rafael. "La poesía cubana en 1936." RevC, Nos. 25-27 (1937), 230.

N.55 ____. "La rebelion de la poesía." RevC, 28 (1950), 23-41.

N.56 Vegas Garcia, Irene. "Nueva conciencia, nueva expresión: seis poetas en la revolución cubana." RCLL, No. 17 (1983), 213-229.

N.57 Vitier, Cintio. "El Pen Club y los 'Diez poetas cubanos'." Orígenes, No. 19 (1948), 41-43.

N.58 Worthley Underwood, Edna. "A los poetas cubanos." RevC, 5 (1936), 357.

0. SPECIAL TOPICS IN POETRY

(Note: See the note in Section H. concerning comprehensive studies on Afro-Latin American topics.)

0.1 Arrom, José Juan. "El negro en la poesía folklórica americana." In Miscelánea de estudios dedicados a Fernando Ortiz por sus discípulos, colegas y amigos (H, 1955), pp. 81-106.

0.2 ____. "La poesía afrocubana." RI, No. 8 (1942), 379-411. Also in his Estudios de literatura hispanoamericana (H: Ucar, García, 1950), pp. 109-145.

0.3 ____. "Polaridades líricas de la imagen de Cuba (desde los inicios hasta fines de la dominación española)." CHA, Nos. 280-282 (1973), 710-730.

0.4 Ballagas, Emilio. "Poesía afro-cubana." In Iniciación a la poesía afro-americana (Miami: Universal, 1973), pp. 78-87. Orig. RBNC, 2a serie, 2, 4 (1951), 6-18.

0.5 ____. "Situación de la poesía afrocubana." RevC, 21 (1946), 5-60.

0.6 Baquero, Gastón. "La poesía afroantillana y el asturiano Alfonso Camin." PE, No. 127 (1967), 12-21.

0.7 ____. "Sobre la falsa poesía negra: tres notas polémicas." In his Darío, Cernuda y otros temas poéticos (Madrid: Nacional), pp. 209-218.

0.8 Barradas, Efraín. "Nota sobre la poesía pura en Cuba." CHA, Nos. 326-327 (1977), 468-481.

0.9 Bedriñana, Francisco C. "La luna en la poesía negra." RBC, 38 (1936), 12-16. Also in his Papel de China; tres ensayos (H: Antena, 1941), pp. 75-86.

0.10 Calcagno, Francisco. Poetas de color. H: Soler, 1878.

0.11 Canfield, Marta L. "Los precursores de la poesía negra." RyFa, No. 21 (1970), 13-26.

0.12 Carbonell y Rivero, José Manuel. "Los poetas cubanos y el ideal de independencia." In his La poesía revolucionaria en Cuba (H: "El Siglo XX", 1928), pp. 13-32. See also his "Introducción," pp. 5-11.

0.13 Chacón y Calvo, José María. "Romance tradicionales; contribución
      al estudio del folk-lore cubano." In his Ensayos de litera-
      tura cubana (Madrid: "Saturnino Calleja", 1932), pp. 83-186.
      Also as Romances tradicionales en Cuba (contribución al es-
      tudio del "folk-lore" cubano). H: "El Siglo XX" de Aurelio
      Miranda, 1914.

0.14 Coulthard, Gabriel R. "Emergence of Afro-Cuban poetry." CarQ,
      2, 3 (1962), 14-17.

0.15 Cúneo, Dardo. "Tiempos de la poesía negra." In his Esquemas
      americanos (BA: Instituto Cultural Joaquín V. González,
      1942), pp. 19-27.

0.16 DeCosta, Miriam. "Social lyricism and the Caribbean poet/rebel."
      CLAJ, 14 (1972), 441-451. Also in her Blacks in Hispanic
      literature (Port Washington, N.Y.: Kennikat Press, 1977),
      pp. 114-122.

0.17 Domínguez, Ivo. "En torno a la poesía afro-hispanoamericana."
      CHA, No. 319 (1977), 125-131.

0.18 Duvalier, Vauquelin. "La poesía negra de Cuba." Atenea, No.
      145 (1937), 28-36.

0.19 Farray, Nicolás. "Romances y cantares españoles en la tradición
      cubana." In Actas del Tercer Congreso Internacional de His-
      panistas (M: El Colegio de México, 1970), pp. 331-344.

0.20 Feijóo, Samuel. "Buscando el símbolo de Cuba." Signos, No. 20
      (1977), 61-71.

0.21 _____. "Nuevas formas en la décima moderna." Signos, No. 21
      (1978), 382-390.

0.22 _____. "Poesía del humor en Cuba." Signos, No. 21 (1978), 404-
      450.

0.23 _____. "Prólogo." In his Sabiduría guajira (H: Universitaria,
      1965), pp. 7-12.

0.24 Fernández Retamar, Roberto. "Poesía y revolución." In his Pa-
      pelería (Santa Clara: Universidad Central de Las Villas,
      Dirección de Publicaciones, 1962), pp. 223-233.

0.25 García Prada, Carlos. "Nuestros hai-kais." Islas, 4, 1 (1961),
      123-128.

0.26 González, Manuel Pedro. "A propósito de 'lo cubano en la poe-
      sía'." RHM, 27 (1961), 143-149.

0.27 González López, Waldo. "La nueva décima." Bohemia, 70, 52
      (1978), 10-13.

0.28   González-Pérez, Armando. Poesía afrocubana última. Milwaukee:
       University of Wisconsin, Center for Latin America, 1975.

0.29   ____. "Tres momentos en la poesía afrocubana." QIA, Nos. 51-
       52 (1978-1979), 153-163.

0.30   González y Contreras, Gilberto. "La poesía negra." RBC, 37
       (1937), 40-45.

0.31   Guerra Castañeda, Armando. "La mujer vueltabajera en la poesía
       cubana." RBC, 37 (1937), 249-267. Also H: Molina, 1941.

0.32   ____. "Presencia negra en la poesía popular cubana del siglo
       XIX." In Iniciación a la poesía afro-americana (Miami:
       Universal, 1973), pp. 119-131. Orig. EAf, 3, 1-4 (1939),
       16-27.

0.33   Guirao, Ramón. "Orbita de la poesía afro-cubana." In Iniciación
       a la poesía afro-americana (Miami: Universal, 1973), pp. 92-
       104.

0.34   ____. Orbita de la poesía afrocubana (1928-1937). H: Ucar,
       García, 1938.

0.35   Gutiérrez de la Solana, Alberto. "En torno al siboneyismo y la
       poesía cubana alusiva a la emancipación." In Instituto In-
       ternacional de Literatura Iberoamericana, Literatura de la
       emancipación hispanoamericana y otros ensayos (Lima: Univer-
       sidad de San Marcos, 1972), pp. 66-74.

0.36   Harth, Dorothy Feldman. "La poesía afrocubana, sus raíces e in-
       fluencias." In Miscelánea de estudios dedicados a Fernando
       Ortiz por sus discípulos, colegas y amigos (H, 1955), pp.
       789-815.

0.37   Hernández Franco, Tomás Rafael. Apuntes sobre poesía popular y
       poesía negra en las Antillas. San Salvador: Ateneo de El
       Salvador, 1942.

0.38   Herrera Rodríguez, Roberto. "En torno a la poesía afro-cubana."
       Círculo, 2 (1970), 164-170.

0.39   ____. "La poesía afrocubana." In his Charlas literarias (Mia-
       mi: Universal, 1972), pp. 19-32.

0.40   ____. "La poesía de la guerra en Cuba." Círculo, 6 (1977),
       113-120.

0.41   Iraizoz y de Villar, Antonio. "La décima cubana." In his Lec-
       turas cubanas; 2. ed. (H: "Hermes", 1939), pp. 7-29.

0.42   ____. "La décima cubana en la poesía popular." AFC, 6 (1929),
       133-152.

0.43 _____. "El poema de la emigración revolucionaria." In his Pnys [sic] (Madrid: Mundo Latino, 1926), pp. 141-149.

0.44 _____. "La poesía civil en Cuba." In his Lecturas cubanas; 2. ed. (H: "Hermes", 1939), pp. 67-88. Also H: Club Cubano de Bellas Artes, 1928.

0.45 León, Julio A. "Los cabildos afro-cubanos y su poesía." ExTL, 7, 2 (1978-1979), 171-176.

0.46 López Morales, Humberto. "Observaciones fonéticas sobre la lengua de la poesía afrocubana." In his Estudios sobre el español de Cuba (Long Island City, N.Y.: Las Américas, 1971), pp. 106-113.

0.47 Lukin, Boris. "Acerca de las raíces del decimario popular en Cuba." Santiago, No. 28 (1977), 117-138.

0.48 Mansour, Mónica. La poesía negrista. M: Era, 1973.

0.49 Martín Llorente, Francisco. La mujer vuelta-bajera en la poesía cubana. H: Molina, 1941.

0.50 _____. Presencia negra en la poesía popular cubana del siglo XIX. H: "Alfa", 1938.

0.51 Méndez, Manuel Isidro. "Prólogo." In Constantino Suárez, Floresta patriótica (Barcelona: B. Bauza, 1926), I, v-xiv.

0.52 Moreno Frangináls, Manuel. "El problema negro en la poesía cubana." In Iniciación a la poesía afro-cubana (Miami: Universal, 1973), pp. 147-148. Orig. CHA, No. 3 (1948), 519-530.

0.53 Olchyk, Marta K. "Historical approach to Afro-Cuban poetry." DAI, 33 (1972), 2265A.

0.54 Olivera, Otto. "La poesía del Papel periódico de la Habana." RI, No. 22 (1946), 259-272.

0.55 Orovio, Helio. "La muerte en la poesía cubana." Unión, 11, 1 (1972), 196-216.

0.56 Orta Ruiz, Jesús. "Prólogo." In Poesía criollista y siboneísta (H: Arte y Literatura, 1976), pp. 11-29.

0.57 Ortiz, Fernando. "Más acerca de la poesía mulata." RBC, 37 (1936), 23-39, 218-227, 439-443.

0.58 _____. "La poesía mulata." RBC, 34 (1934), 205-213.

0.59 _____. "La religión en la poesía mulata." EAf, 1, 1 (1937), 15-62.

0.60 _____. "Los últimos versos mulatos." RBC, 35 (1935), 321-336.

0.61 Pagés Larraya, Antonio. "Poesía negra del Caribe hispanoameri-
      cano." In Libro de homenaje a Luis Alberto Sánchez (Lima:
      Universidad Nacional Mayor San Marcos, 1967), pp. 389-421.

0.62 Palma, Ramón de. "Cantares de Cuba." In José Manuel Carbonell
      y Rivero, La poesía lírica en Cuba (H: El Siglo XX, 1928),
      I, 291-323. Also in Cinio Vitier, La crítica literaria y
      estética en el siglo XIX cubano (H: Biblioteca Nacional
      "José Martí", Departamento Colección Cubana, 1968), I, 194-
      229.

0.63 Perdomo, Omar. "El poeta cubano que en 1917 cantó a la Revolu-
      ción de Octubre." Bohemia, 69, 20 (1977), 28.

0.64 Pereda Valdés, Ildefonso. Lo negro y lo mulato en la poesía cu-
      bana. Montevideo?: Ciudadela, 1970?

0.65 Piedra-Bueno, Andrés de. El epigrama en Cuba. H: Villegas,
      1937.

0.66 Poncet y de Cárdenas, Carolina. El romance en Cuba. H: A. Mi-
      randa, 1914.

0.67 Redondo de Feldman, Susana. "Romances viejos en la tradición
      popular cubana." RHM, 31 (1965), 365-372.

0.68 Remos y Rubio, Juan Nepomuceno José. La bandera en la emoción
      de nuestros poetas. H: "El Siglo XX", Muñiz, 1950.

0.69 ____. "El sentido de la naturaleza en la lírica cubana." In
      his Micrófono (H: Molina, 1937), pp. 245-268.

0.70 Rodríguez Embil, Luis. La poesía negra en Cuba. Santiago de
      Chile: Universidad de Chile, 1939.

0.71 Salazar y Roig, Salvador. El elemento patriótico en la lírica
      cubana. H: Molina, 1935.

0.72 Sánchez, Emilia. "Indagación folklórica y literaria de la impro-
      visación popular. La décima." Islas, No. 42 (1972), 85-
      122.

0.73 Sánchez de Fuentes y Peláez, Eduardo. Viejos ritmos cubanos; la
      letra en nuestras canciones. H: Molina, 1937.

0.74 Smart, Ian I. "The Cuban son: one of Africa's contributions to
      contemporary Caribbean poeticas." JACL, 1 (1981), 14-29.

0.75 Valbuena Briones, Angel. "El tema negro en la poesía antillana."
      In his Literatura hispanoamericana (Barcelona: Gustavo Gili,
      1962), pp. 413-431.

0.76 Valdés-Cruz, Rosa E. "La poesía negroide en Cuba." In her La
      poesía negroide en América (NY: Las Américas, 1970), pp.
      51-132.

0.77 _____. "Tres poemas representativos de la poesía afroantillana."
Hispania, 54 (1971), 39-45.

0.78 Varela, José Luis. Ensayos de poesía indígena en Cuba. Madrid?:
Cultura Hispánica, 1951.

0.79 Vitier, Cintio. Lo cubano en la poesía. Santa Clara: Universidad Central de Las Villas, Departamento de Relaciones Culturales, 1958. Also H: Instituto del Libro, 1970.

0.80 Zayas y Alfonso, Alfredo. La poesía patriótica en Cuba hasta
1868. H: Molina, 1931. Orig. AANAL, 14 (1930), 105-147.

P.   GENERAL STUDIES ON DRAMA

P.1   Arrom, José Juan. Bosquejo histórico del teatro en Cuba. Un-
      published Ph.D. dissertation, Yale University, 1941.

P.2   ____. "En torno a la historia de la literatura dramática cuba-
      na." AANAL, 25 (1944), 8-23.

P.3   ____. Historia de la literatura dramática cubana. New Haven:
      Yale University Press; London: H. Milford, Oxford University
      Press, 1944. Also NY: AMS Press, 1973.

P.4   Colón, Edwin Teurbe, and José Antonio González. Historia del
      teatro en la Habana. Santa Clara: Universidad Central de
      Las Villas, 1961-.

P.5   Díaz, Ignacio Gutiérrez. "History and theatre." In Theatre and
      social reality (Berlin: GDR Centre of the International
      Theatre Institute, 1977), pp. 29-31.

P.6   González, Jorge Antonio. "Repertorio teatro cubano (con anota-
      ciones bibliográficas correspondientes a nuestra Biblioteca
      Nacional)." RBNC, 2a serie, 2, 4 (1951), 69-184.

P.7   González Curquejo, Antonio. Breve ojeada sobre el teatro cubano
      al través de un siglo (1820-1920). H: "La Universal",
      1923.

P.8   González Freire, Natividad. "Desarrollo del teatro en Cuba."
      RNT, 1 (1961), no pagination.

P.9   ____. "En busca del teatro cubano." NTiem, No. 25 (1968), 6-7.

P.10 Jones, Willis Knapp. "Cuban drama." In his Behind Spanish Amer-
      ican footlights (Austin: University of Texas Press, 1966),
      pp. 392-414.

P.11 Leal, Rine. Breve historia del teatro cubano. H: Letras Cuba-
      nas, 1980.

P.12 ____. Introducción a Cuba. El teatro. H: Instituto del Li-
      bro, Cuadernos Populares, 1968. Also as Introdução ao te-
      tro cubano. Lisboa: Cadernos Seará Nova, 1971.

P.13 ____. "El teatro de un acto en Cuba." Unión, 5, 6 (1963), 52-
      75.

P.14 ____. "El teatro en Cuba." Cuba, No. 30 (1964), 64-73.

P.15 Manet, Eduardo. "Movimiento teatral cubano desde sus orígenes hasta 1955." <u>PrA</u>, No. 108 (1969), 14-21.

P.16 Marquina, Rafael. <u>Teatro cubano de selección (reseña y crítica)</u>. H: Publicaciones de la Secretaría de Educación, Dirección de Cultura, 1938.

P.17 Matas, Julio. "Teatro cubano en un acto." <u>Unión</u>, 3, 1 (1964), 168-170.

P.18 Palls, Terry L. "El teatro del absurdo en Cuba: el compromiso artístico frente al compromiso político." <u>LATR</u>, 11, 2 (1978), 25-32.

P.19 Ratto Valera, T. O. "El teatro en la cultura cubana." <u>Máscara</u>, No. 94 (1948), 12-14.

P.20 Robreño, Eduardo. <u>Historia del teatro popular cubano</u>. H: Oficina del Historiador de la Ciudad de la Habana, 1961.

P.21 Salazar y Roig, Salvador. "El teatro cubano." In José Manuel Carbonell y Rivero, <u>Las bellas artes en Cuba</u> (H: "El Siglo XX", 1928), pp. 53-77.

P.22 Sánchez Galarraga, Gustavo. <u>El arte teatral en Cuba</u>. H: Instituto de Artes Gráficas, 1918.

P.23 <u>Teatro cubano</u>. H: Sociedad Teatro Cubano, 1919-.

P.24 <u>El teatro, panorama general</u>. H: CTC-R, 1964.

Q. COLONIAL AND 19TH CENTURY DRAMA

Q.1 Aguirre, Yolanda. Apuntes sobre el teatro colonial (1790-1833). H: Universidad de la Habana, 1968.

Q.2 Arrom, José Juan. "Primeras manifestaciones dramáticas en Cuba, 1512-1776." RBC, 48 (1941), 274-284.

Q.3 _____. "Representaciones teatrales en Cuba a fines del siglo XVIII." HR, 11 (1943), 64-71.

Q.4 García Marruz, Fina. "Obras de teatro representadas en la Habana en la última década del siglo XVIII, según el Papel periódico." RBNJM, 3a serie, 14, 2 (1972), 92-125.

Q.5 González Freire, Natividad. "Prólogo." In Teatro cubano del siglo XIX; antología (H: Arte y Literatura, 1975), I, 9-23.

Q.6 _____. "Teatro dramático cubano del siglo XIX." Bohemia, 67, 10 (1975), 12-13.

Q.7 Leal, Rine. "Prólogo: la chancleta y el coturno." In Teatro bufo, siglo XIX (H: Arte y Literatura, 1975), I, 13-46.

Q.8 Montes Huidobro, Matías. "La reacción antijerárquica en el teatro cubano colonial." CHA, No. 334 (1978), 5-19.

Q.9 Parajón, Mario. "El teatro cubano del siglo XIX." In Panorama de la literatura cubana; conferencias (H: Universidad de la Habana, Centro de Estudios Cubanos, 1970), pp. 143-156.

Q.10 Pérez Beato, Manuel. "Los primeros días del teatro cubano." CAmer, 6, 1 (1927), 26-29.

Q.11 Tobar García, Francisco. "Nuestro teatro en la segunda mitad del siglo XIX." Carteles, 2-I-1949, pp. 40-41.

Q.12 _____. "La vida teatral de la Habana de 1790 a 1846." Carteles, 1-II-1948, pp. 30-31.

R. 20TH CENTURY DRAMA

R.1   Abdo, Ada. "Seis meses de teatro habanero." CAm, Nos. 17-18 (1963), 89-92.

R.2   Agüero, Luis. "Paseo por un festival." Cuba, No. 69 (1968), 23-24.

R.3   _____ et al. "Lo que ve la Habana." Cuba, No. 22 (1964), 52-57.

R.4   Alonso, Eduardo H. "Nuestra larga crisis teatral." InC, 1, 2 (1947), 29-30.

R.5   Arrufat, Antón. "An interview on the theater in Cuba and in Latin America." Odyssey, 2, 4 (1962), 248-263. Orig. as "Charla sobre teatro." CAm, No. 9 (1961), 88-102.

R.6   Badía, Nora. "Notes: Cuba." WTh, 14, 1 (1965), 60.

R.7   Beltrán, Alejo. "Estrenos en la Habana, 3 de teatro, 1 de cine." Cuba, No. 11 (1963), 20-27.

R.8   _____. "Nuestra escena." Cuba, No. 1 (1962), 26-29.

R.9   _____. "Sexto festival de teatro." Unión, 6, 1 (1967), 166-172.

R.10 Bloy, Red. "El teatro gesticula, baila, canta, ríe, llora." INRA, No. 3 (1960), 12-21.

R.11 Boudet, Rosa Ileana. "En Cuba: los jóvenes y el teatro." Unión, 17, 2 (1978), 15-22.

R.12 _____. "Nuestro teatro cubano." Unión, 17, 1 (1978), 34-49.

R.13 _____. "Teatro nuevo en Cuba." Bohemia, 69, 51 (1977), 10-12.

R.14 Cano, Carlos José. "El tiempo cíclico y el teatro cubano desde la revolución." In Instituto Internacional de Literatura Iberoamericana, XVII Congreso (Madrid: Cultura Hispánica del Centro Iberoamericano de Cooperación, 1978), pp. 1273-1283.

R.15 Carpio, Antonio. "Cuba: panorama teatral." Cuba, No. 9 (1963), 66-71.

R.16 _____. "Un montoncito de luces y un teatro." INRA, No. 2 (1961), 4-7.

R.17   Casey, Calvert. "Teatro/61." CAm, No. 9 (1961), 103-111.

R.18   Castillo, Bertha del. "Las relaciones: un teatro genuinamente
        popular." Santiago, No. 25 (1977), 211-232.

R.19   Chacón y Calvo, José María. "Teatro cubano." RevC, 15 (1941),
        261-266.

R.20   Cid Pérez, José. "Cincuenta años de teatro cubano." Carteles,
        33, 20 (1952), 110-13, 188-189.

R.21   ____. "El teatro en Cuba republicana." In Teatro cubano con-
        temporáneo; 2. ed. (Madrid: Aguilar, 1962), pp. 13-38.

R.22   Cuba. Ministerio de Educación. Teatro (1956-1957). H: Palacio
        de Bellas Artes, 1957.

R.23   Dauster, Frank N. "Cuban drama today." MD, 9, 2 (1966), 153-164.

R.24   Diego, Eliseo. "En teatro como en todo." CubaI, No. 96 (1977),
        20-25.

R.25   Espinosa Domínguez, Carlos. "Nueva dramaturgia cubana: tres en-
        trevistas." LATR, 15, 1 (1981), 59-66.

R.26   ____. "El teatro en Cuba, problemas y perspectivas." RyC, No.
        58 (1977), 78-81.

R.27   Felipe, Carlos. "Los pretextos y el nonato teatro cubano."
        Islas, 2, 1 (1959), 79-81.

R.28   Goldsmith, Margaret Poynter. "Playwrights of the Cuban revolu-
        tion." DAI, 36 (1975), 2489A-2490A.

R.29   González Freire, Natividad. "Cuba, un resumen del año teatral."
        Conjunto, No. 6 (1968), 85-89.

R.30   ____. "La nueva generación teatral cubana." NTiem, No. 17
        (1957), 10-11.

R.31   ____. "Sobre dramas y dramaturgos." Unión, 6, 4 (1967), 232-
        242.

R.32   ____. Teatro cubano contemporáneo (1928-1957). H: Sociedad
        Colombista Panamericana, 1958. 2. ed. as Teatro cubano
        contemporáneo (1927-1961). H: Ministerio de Relaciones
        Exteriores, 1961.

R.33   Hart Dávalos, Armando. "El teatro cubano." Bohemia, 69, 9
        (1977), 10-14.

R.34   Leal, Rine. "Actuales corrientes en el teatro cubano." NRC,
        1, 1 (1959), 163-170.

R.35 _____. "Algunas consideraciones sobre el teatro cubano." Insula, Nos. 260-261 (1968), 9.

R.36 _____. En primera persona, 1954-1966. H: Instituto del Libro, 1967.

R.37 _____. "El nuevo rostro del teatro cubano." GdC, No. 193 (1963), 10-16.

R.38 _____. "Seis meses de teatro en pocas palabras." CAm, Nos. 11-12 (1962), 46-50.

R.39 _____. "Siete días de entreacto [I Seminario Nacional de Teatro]." Cuba, No. 69 (1968), 24-25.

R.40 _____. "Viaje de un largo siglo hacia el teatro." Islas, No. 35 (1970), 59-77.

R.41 Manet, Eduardo. "Où en est le théâtre cubain." In Ecrivains de Cuba (Paris: Denoël, 1967), pp. 286-291. Special issue of LetN, déc. 1967-jan. 1968.

R.42 Manet, Julio E. "El nuevo teatro cubano." EstLit, No. 364 (1967), 33-34.

R.43 Matas, Julio. "Theater and cinematography." In Revolutionary change in Cuba (Pittsburgh: University of Pittsburgh Press, 1971), pp. 427-445.

R.44 Méndez, Graziella. "El pueblo en escena, Primer Festival de Aficionados." Cuba, No. 7 (1962), 74-77.

R.45 Miranda, Julio E. "El nuevo teatro cubano." LsNs, No. 8 (1971), 16-17.

R.46 _____. "El nuevo teatro cubano." EstLit, No. 364 (1967), 33-34.

R.47 _____. "El nuevo teatro cubano." RO, No. 105 (1971), 336-346.

R.48 Montes Huidobro, Matías. Persona, vida y máscara en el teatro cubana. Miami: Universal, 1973.

R.49 Muguerencia, Magaly. "En Cuba: el teatro." ULH, Nos. 186-188 (1967), 71-76.

R.50 Núñez, Carlos. "Un mes de teatro." INRA, 2, 3 (1961), 32-35.

R.51 _____. "El pueblo en escena, Festival del Teatro." INRA, 2, 4 (1961), 86-91.

R.52 Padrón, Carlos. "Conjunto dramático de Oriente." RyC, No. 64 (1977), 64-72.

R.53 Palls, Terry L. "El carácter del teatro cubano contemporáneo." LATR, 13, 2 suppl. (1980), 51-58.

R.54 _____. "Myth in Cuban revolutionary theatre." In Tradition, change, and revolution in the Caribbean (Coral Gables: Association of Caribbean Studies, 1983), pp. 52-53. Abstract only.

R.55 _____. "The theatre in revolutionary Cuba: 1959-1969." DAI, 36 (1976), 4532A.

R.56 _____. "The theatre of the absurd in Cuba after 1959." LALR, No. 7 (1975), 67-72.

R.57 Panelo, Antonio, and Isabel Herrera. "Hacia una dramaturgia nacional y un teatro internacional." CB, No. 34 (1969), 16-19.

R.58 "Panorama del teatro cubano." CUNESCO, 6 (1965), 3-175.

R.59 Parajón, Mario. "El teatro que queremos para Cuba." Islas, 2, 1 (1959), 69-77.

R.60 Parreño, Desiderio. "Havana meets the twentieth century." ThA, 31 (1947), 52-54.

R.61 Peña Gutiérrez, Isaías. "Compermiso, maestro Vidales (o introducción a La obreriada)." CAm, No. 107 (1978), 37-42.

R.62 Piñera, Virgilio. "Notas sobre el teatro cubano." Unión, 6, 2 (1967), 130-142. Also as "Notes sur le théâtre cubain." CRB, No. 75 (1971), 27-42.

R.63 _____. "El teatro actual." CAm, Nos. 22-23 (1964), 95-107.

R.64 Quinto, José María de. "Teatro cubano actual." Insula, Nos. 260-261 (1968), 3, 24-26.

R.65 Rizk, Beatriz J. "I Taller Internacional del Nuevo Teatro (Cuba 1983)." LATR, 16, 2 (1983), 73-80.

R.66 Rodríguez Sardiñas, Orlando. "El teatro cubano: un teatro para revolución." Escena, No. 3 (1975), 30-32.

R.67 _____. "Texto del teatro cubano contemporáneo en el contexto revolucionario." In Festschrift José Cid Pérez (NY: Senda Nueva, 1981), pp. 125-127.

R.68 Sfeir, Dahd. "Ocho días en el nuevo teatro de la revolución." Crisis, No. 6 (1973), 49-55.

R.69 Skinner, Eugene R. "Education and theater in post-revolutionary Cuba." In Popular theater for social change in Latin America (Los Angeles: University of California, Latin American Center, 1978), pp. 71-76.

R.70 Sóbolveda, I. V. "Dramaturgia cubana en el camino de la revolución." ALat, No. 4 (1971), 139-152.

R.71 Suárez Radillo, Carlos Miguel. "Apuntes incompletos para una historia del teatro cubano en el siglo XX." Guadalupe, No. 6 (1958), 3-7.

R.72 "El teatro actual." CAm, Nos. 22-23 (1964), 95-107.

R.73 Teatro cubano. H: Sociedad Teatro Cubano, 1919-1920.

R.74 "Teatro cubano." GdC, No. 19 (1964), entire issue.

R.75 "Transforming theatre." CubaR, 7, 4 (1977), entire issue.

R.76 Tunberg, Karl A. "The new Cuban theatre: a report." TDR, 14, 2 (1970), 43-55.

R.77 Valdés Rodríguez, José Manuel. "Algo sobre el teatro en Cuba." ULH, No. 170 (1964), 47-63.

R.78 Vieta, Ezequiel. "Cuba: dramaturgia y revolución." PrA, No. 108 (1969), 22-30. Also as "Dramaturgia y revolución." ULH, Nos. 186-188 (1967), 59-70.

R.79 Vitier, Cintio. "Eros en el infierno." RBNJM, 3a serie, 10, 2 (1968), 168-175.

R.80 Warren, Virgil A. "Status of modern Cuban theater." Hispania, 24 (1941), 205-210.

R.81 Watson-Espener, Maida Isabel. "Observaciones sobre el teatro chicano, nuyorriqueño y cubano en los Estados Unidos." BR/RB, 5, 1-2 (1978), 117-125.

R.82 Weiss, Judith A. "Cuba's Teatro Nuevo: first national festival." LATR, 13, 1 (1979), 87-92. Also as "Teatro Nuevo: Primer Festival Nacional en Cuba." Areito, Nos. 19-20 (1979), 39-41.

R.83 Woodyard, George W. "Perspectives on Cuban theater." RInter, 9 (1979), 42-49.

S. SPECIAL TOPICS IN DRAMA

S.1   Alonso, Alejandro G. "Y que las masas sean creadoras." <u>Conjunto</u>, No. 21 (1974), 113-115.

S.2   Arrufat, Antón. "El teatro bufo." <u>Unión</u>, 1, 3-4 (1962), 61-72.

S.3   Artiles, Freddy. "Teatro popular: nuevo héroe, nuevo conflicto." <u>Conjunto</u>, No. 17 (1973), 3-7.

S.4   B., R. "El Teatro Nacional de la Habana a Santiago." <u>INRA</u>, 1, 5 (1960), 66-69.

S.5   Barletta, Leónidas. "Sobre un teatro del pueblo." <u>CAm</u>, No. 10 (1962), 87-107.

S.6   Beltrán, Alejo. "Muñecos y algo más que muñecos." <u>Unión</u>, 5, 2 (1966), 187-188.

S.7   _____. "Nuevo teatro profesional en el interior." <u>Unión</u>, 4, 3 (1965), 164-168.

S.8   "Las brigas de teatro de la Coordinación Provincial de Cultura de la Habana." <u>Conjunto</u>, No. 2 (1964), 59-64.

S.9   Camejo, Carucha. "El teatro de títeres en Cuba." <u>Conjunto</u>, No. 2 (1964), 3-6.

S.10 Camps, David. "Puppets in Cuba." <u>WTh</u>, No. 14 (1965), 458-459.

S.11 Conte, Antonio. "Escambray: el teatro va a la montaña." <u>CubaI</u>, 3, 20 (1971), 62-66.

S.12 Corrieri, Sergio. "Al pie de la letra [Teatro Escambray]." <u>CAm</u>, No. 68 (1971), 189-192.

S.13 _____. "Escambray: un teatro de la revolución." <u>CB</u>, No. 46 (1971), 22-25.

S.14 _____. "El Grupo Teatro Escambray: una experiencia de la revolución." <u>Conjunto</u>, No. 18 (1973), 2-6. Also in <u>Popular theater for social change in Latin America</u> (Los Angeles: University of California, Latin American Center, 1978), pp. 363-369.

S.15 Cruz, José Raúl. "Cuba/Brecht en Teatro Estudio: una aplicación consecuente." <u>Conjunto</u>, No. 21 (1974), 130-131.

S.16 Cruz-Luis, Adolfo. "El movimiento teatral cubano en la revolución." CAm, No. 113 (1979), 40-50.

S.17 Dorr, Nicolás. "Teatro y revolución." VU, Nos. 216-217 (1969), 18.

S.18 Edwards, Flora Mancuso. "The theater of the black diaspora: a comparative study of black drama in Brazil, Cuba and the United States." DAI, 36 (1975), 3222A.

S.19 "En la búsqueda de un teatro nacional [Grupo Yarabey]." Conjunto, No. 19 (1974), 113-114.

S.20 Garzón Céspedes, Francisco. "Hemos creado inquietudes de actores, de directores, de público [Grupo Teatro Escambray]." Conjunto, No. 18 (1973), 7-16.

S.21 _____. "Un teatro de creación colectiva." Unión, 16, 1 (1977), 40-43.

S.22 _____. "Teatro de la creación colectiva de la humanidad." Conjunto, No. 30 (1976), 44-69.

S.23 _____. "La Teatrova: dar, inventar y reinventar el teatro." Conjunto, No. 31 (1977), 91-102.

S.24 González Freire, Natividad. "Conjunto dramático de Camagüey." Bohemia, 69, 43 (1977), 31.

S.25 _____. "El Teatro Velasco." Bohemia, 70, 18 (1978), 28.

S.26 Gutkin, Adolfo. "Amerindias, una experiencia de creación colectiva [Conjunto Dramático de Oriente]." Conjunto, No. 16 (1973), 37-39.

S.27 Lavardi, Cecilia. "Anotaciones sobre Brecht en Cuba." CAm, Nos. 15-16 (1963), 77-90; Nos. 17-18 (1963), 92-98.

S.28 Lázaro, Angel. "Sobre un teatro en el Palacio de Bellas Artes." ICult, 1, 3 (1947), 3-4.

S.29 Leal, Rine. "Diario de Escambray." Conjunto, No. 28 (1976), 114-132.

S.30 Martí de Cid, Dolores. "El negro y lo negro en el teatro cubano." In Homenaje a Lydia Cabrera (Miami: Universal, 1978), pp. 285-291.

S.31 Martin, Eleanor Jean. "Dos viejos pánicos: a political interpretation of the Cuban theater of the absurd." RInter, 9, 1 (1979), 50-56.

S.32 Miranda, Nilda. "Escambray: un teatro de la revolución." CB, No. 47 (1971), 28-31.

S.33 Ortiz, Fernando. Los bailes y el teatro de los negros en el folklore de Cuba. H, 1951.

S.34 _____. "El teatro de los negros." RBC, 64 (1949), 87-194.

S.35 Padrón, Carlos. "Cine con gente de verdad; los primeros once años del Conjunto Dramático de Oriente." Conjunto, No. 14 (1972), 102-110.

S.36 Petit, Anne. "Teatro y sociedad en Cuba: El Grupo Teatro Escambray." LATR, 12, 1 (1978), 71-76.

S.37 Revuelta, Vicente. "Un théâtre d'imprécation." CRB, No. 75 (no date), 3-8.

S.38 Rodríguez, Antonio Orlando. "Children's theater: a Cuban experience." Theater, 12, 1 (1980), 26-29.

S.39 Rodríguez Sosa, Fernando. "En los 15 del Teatro Lírico de Holguín." Bohemia, 69, 36 (1977), 27.

S.40 _____. "Extensión teatral." Bohemia, 69, 41 (1977), 26.

S.41 Sarusky, Jaime. "Teatrova." Bohemia, 69, 12 (1977), 26.

S.42 Sedley, Marian. "Theater as revolutionary activity: the Escambray." In Cuba: the second decade (London: Writers & Readers, 1979), pp. 189-193.

S.43 Sejourné, Larette. Teatro Escambray: una experiencia. H: Ciencias Sociales, 1977.

S.44 "Teatro de muñecos." CubaI, No. 19 (1971), 68-74.

S.45 El Teatro Nacional de Guignol: Cuba. H: Consejo Nacional de Cultura, 1966.

S.46 Tobar García, Francisco. "El teatro vernáculo cubano." Carteles, No. 43 (1950), 52-53; No. 49 (1950), 50-51; No. 53 (1950), 74-75.

S.47 Toro, Aída de. "Notas para el estudio de la trayectoria del teatro remediano." Islas, No. 41 (1972), 99-115.

S.48 Valenzuela, Lídice. "Teatro de relaciones." CubaI, No. 94 (1977), 26-29.

S.49 Villabella, Manuel. "Teatro del Camagüey." CB, No. 29 (1969), 13-15.

T. GENERAL STUDIES ON PROSE FICTION

T.1 Agostini, Víctor. "Fuerza y debilidad del cuento." RBNC, 2a serie, 5, 4 (1954), 43-53.

T.2 Alvarez García, Imeldo. "La prehistoria del cuento en Cuba." GdC, No. 103 (1972), 13-15.

T.3 Boydston, Jo Ann Harrison. The Cuban novel: a study of its range and characteristics. Unpublished Ph.D. dissertation, Columbia University, 1950 [i.e., 1951].

T.4 Bueno, Salvador. "Recuento del cuento cubano." CubaI, No. 60 (1974), 56-58.

T.5 ____. "Los temas de la novela cubana." Asomante, 16, 4 (1961), 39-48. Also as "Temas y personajes de la novela cubana." In his Temas y personajes de la literatura cubana (H: Unión, 1964), pp. 277-289. Also Bohemia, 53, 11 (1961), 102-104, 114.

T.6 ____. "Trayectoria del cuento y la narración corta en Cuba." In Arturo Alfonso Roselló, Libro de Cuba (H: Publicaciones Unidas, 1954), pp. 602-606.

T.7 Carricarte, Arturo. "La novela en Cuba. I. Los orígenes." América, 1, 2 (1907), 42-53.

T.8 Catalá, Ramón A. "Divagaciones sobre la novela." In Carlos Loveira, Un gran ensayista cubano: Fernando Llés (H: El Siglo XX, 1926), pp. 23-56.

T.9 Chaple, Sergio. "El cuento en Cuba." L/L, No. 5 (1974), 91-100.

T.10 Coll, Edna. "Novelistas cubanos." In her Indice informativo de la novela hispanoamericana (San Juan, P.R.: Editorial Universitaria, Universidad de Puerto Rico, 1974-), I, 223-413.

T.11 Eligio de la Puente, Antonio. "Introducción." In Ramón de Palma, Cuentos cubanos (H: Cultural, 1928), pp. v-xliv.

T.12 Espinosa, Ciro. Indagación y crítica; novelistas cubanos. H: Cultural, 1940.

T.13 Fernández Cabrera, Carlos. "La novela y el cuento en Cuba." In Album del Cincuentenario de la Asociación de Repórters de la Habana, 1902-1952 (H: Lex, 1953), pp. 217-222.

T.14   Havana. Consejo Provincial de Cultura de la Habana. El cuento, panorama general. H: CTC-R, 1964.

T.15   _____. La novela, panorama general. H: CTC-R, 1964.

T.16   Kirby, Marjorie T. "A literary history of the Cuban short story (1797-1959)." DAI, 32 (1972), 5233A.

T.17   Lazo, Raimundo. Personajes de la novela cubana. H: Universidad de la Habana, 1947-1948.

T.18   Llerena, Mario. "Ausencia del héroe en la novela cubana." América, 38, 1 (1966), 60-66.

T.19   _____. "Función del personaje en la novela cubana." RHM, 16 (1950), 113-122.

T.20   Meléndez, Concha. "El cuento en Cuba y Puerto Rico: estudio sobre dos antologías." RHM, 24 (1958), 201-212.

T.21   Montori, Arturo. "La novela." In El libro de Cuba (H: Molina, 1925), pp. 584-587.

T.22   Mota, Francisco. "Ensayo de una cronología de la novela en Cuba." Islas, 8, 3 (1966), 441-466.

T.23   Novás Calvo, Lino. "Novela por hacer." RNC, No. 23 (1940), 81-94. Also RBC, 47 (1941), 348-359.

T.24   Remos y Rubio, Juan Nepomuceno José. "El cuento y la novela." In his Micrófano (H: Molina, 1937), pp. 100-112.

T.25   _____. Tendencias de la narración imaginativa en Cuba. H: La Casa Montalvo-Cárdenas, 1935.

T.26   Rodríguez Feo, José. "Breve recuento de la narrativa cubana." Unión, 6, 4 (1967), 131-136.

T.27   Salazar y Roig, Salvador. La novela en Cuba: sus manifestaciones, ideales y posibilidades. H: Molina, 1934.

T.28   Serpa, Enrique. "Fichas de la novela cubana." In Libro de Cuba; edición conmemorativa (H: Publicaciones Unidas, 1954), pp. 595-601.

T.29   Torriente, Loló de la. "Los caminos de la novela cubana." CA, No. 67 (1953), 264-284; No. 69 (1953), 243-262.

T.30   Valdés, Bernardo J. Panorama del cuento cubano. Miami: Universal, 1976.

U. 19TH CENTURY PROSE FICTION

U.1 Alvarez García, Imeldo. "Noveletas cubanas del siglo XIX." GdC, No. 128 (1974), 29-31.

U.2 Ara, Guillermo. "Cuba." In his La novela naturalista hispanoamericana (BA: EUDEBA, 1965), pp. 63-69.

U.3 Benítez Rojo, Antonio. "Los precursores del cuento en Cuba." Unión, 11, 1 (1972), 6-13.

U.4 Bueno, Salvador. "Costumbristas cubanos del siglo XIX." In his Temas y personajes de la literatura cubana (H: Unión, 1964), pp. 51-73.

U.5 ____. "Cuentos cubanos del siglo XIX." Unión, 13, 4 (1974), 132-152.

U.6 ____. Policromía y sabor de los costumbristas cubanos. Santiago de Cuba: Universidad de Oriente, 1953.

U.7 ____. "La primitiva narración antiesclavista en Cuba (1835-1839)." ULH, No. 207 (1978), 143-165.

U.8 ____. "Prólogo." In Cuentos cubanos del siglo XIX (H: Arte y Literatura, 1977), pp. 7-41.

U.9 Céspedes, José M. "La novela en Cuba." In Teodoro Guerrero, La Habana por fuera; 2. ed. (H: El Iris, 1866), pp. iii-xii.

U.10 Corbitt, Roberta Day. "A survey of Cuban costumbrismo." Hispania, 33 (1950), 41-45. Also RBC, 73 (1957), 257-264.

U.11 Friol, Roberto. "Los cuentos del Papel periódico." RBNJM, 3a serie, 65, 1 (1974), 111-133.

U.12 ____. "La novela cubana en el siglo XIX." Unión, 6, 4 (1968), 178-207.

U.13 García-Barrio, Constance S. de. "The abolitionist novel in nineteenth century Cuba." CLAJ, 21 (1977), 224-237.

U.14 Hernández de Norman, Isabel. La novela romántica en las Antillas. NY: Ateneo Puertorriqueño, 1969. Orig. DAI, 27 (1966), 2539A.

U.15 Iznaga, Alcides. "Novelas cubanas del ochocientos." Islas, 8, 3 (1966), 419-439. Also Bohemia, 64, 47 (1972), 8-15.

U.16 López Barrero, Olga L. "Cronología de la novela cubana: 1850-
      1900." Islas, No. 48 (1974), 187-212.

U.17 Mota, Francisco. "Ensayo de una cronología de la novela en Cuba
      durante el siglo XIX." Islas, 8, 3 (1966), 441-466.

U.18 Nieves, Dolores. "Caracteres generales de la narrativa cubana
      en el siglo XIX." In Panorama de la literatura cubana; con-
      ferencias (H: Universidad de la Habana, Centro de Estudios
      Cubanos, 1970), pp. 87-106.

U.19 Obaya Martínez, Alicia. "El costumbrismo en el siglo XIX. An-
      tecedentes. Costumbres y costumbristas. Trascendencia."
      In Panorama de la literatura cubana; conferencias (H: Uni-
      versidad de la Habana, Centro de Estudios Cubanos, 1970),
      pp. 157-171.

U.20 Pérez de la Riva, Francisco. "Bibliografía cafetalera cubana."
      RBNC, 2a serie, 3, 4 (1952), 99-321.

U.21 Remos y Rubio, Juan Nepomuceno José. "Los costumbristas cubanos
      del siglo XIX." In his Micrófono (H: Molina, 1937), pp.
      191-199.

U.22 Rodríguez, Iraida. "Prólogo." In Artículos de costumbres cuba-
      nos del siglo XIX; antología (H: Arte y Literatura, 1974),
      pp. 9-18.

U.23 Roig de Leuschsenring, Emilio. La literatura costumbrista cuba-
      na de los siglos XVIII y XIX. H: Oficina del Historiador
      de la Ciudad, 1962-. A fragment appeared as "Prefacio."
      In Artículos de costumbres cubanos del siglo XIX; antología
      (H: Arte y Literatura, 1974), pp. 19-24.

U.24 _____. "La literatura de costumbres: los articulistas." In El
      libro de Cuba (H: Molina, 1925), pp. 581-583.

U.25 Ruiz del Vizo, Hortensia. "El costumbrismo." In Antología del
      costumbrismo en Cuba, prosa y verso (Miami: Universal,
      1975), pp. 9-16.

U.26 Sosa, Enrique. La economía en la novela cubana del siglo XIX.
      H: Letras Cubanas, 1978. Orig. H: Unión, 13, 3 (1974), 75-
      95.

U.27 _____. "La esclavitud en la novelística cubana del XIX."
      RBNJM, 3a serie, 67, 3 (1976), 53-92.

U.28 Suárez-Murias, Marguerite. "Cuba." In her La novela romántica
      en Hispanoamérica (NY: Hispanic Institute in the United
      States, 1963), pp. 20-40.

U.29 _____. "La novela en Cuba en el siglo XIX." RIB, 11, 2 (1961),
      125-136. Also in her Essays on Hispanic literature; ensa-
      yos de literatura hispana; a bilingual anthology (Washing-
      ton, D.C.: University Press of America, 1982), pp. 29-49.

U.30 Toro González, Aida Julia. "Algunos aspectos de la novela en la
      década de 1830-1840." <u>Islas</u>, No. 48 (1974), 213-237.

V. 20TH CENTURY PROSE FICTION

V.1   Abella, Rosa. "Cinco años de la novela cubana." CLH, No. 1
      (1966), 9-14. Also as "Five years of the Cuban novel."
      Carrell, 7, 1 (1966), 17-21.

V.2   Abreu Gómez, Ermilo. "Cuentos de Cuba." Unión, 3, 4 (1964),
      152-158.

V.3   Agüero, Luis. "La novela de la revolución." CAm, Nos. 22-23
      (1964), 60-67.

V.4   Alfonso, María Rosa. "Novela y revolución del 30." Bohemia, 69,
      39 (1977), 10-13. Also Islas, No. 59 (1978), 51-109.

V.5   Alvarez García, Imeldo. "La novela en la revolución cubana."
      CA, No. 227 (1979), 45-64.

V.6   _____. "Nuevos narradores cubanos." CB, No. 91 (1975), 6.

V.7   Barnet, Miguel. "La novela testimonio: socio-literatura." In
      his La canción de Rachel (Barcelona: Estela, 1970), pp.
      125-150. Orig. as "La novela documental." Unión, 9, 4
      (1970), 160-167. Also as "The documentary novel." CS, 11,
      1 (1981), 19-32.

V.8   Branciková, Zdenka. "K problematice vývoje kubánské povídky."
      CMF, 52 (1970), 85-93.

V.9   Bueno, Salvador. "Costumbristas cubanos del siglo XX." In his
      Temas y personajes de la literatura cubana (H: Unión, 1964),
      pp. 51-73.

V.10 _____. "Cuba hoy: novela." Insula, Nos. 260-261 (1968), 1, 21,
      24.

V.11 _____. "El cuento cubano contemporáneo." HP, No. 42 (1946),
      141-147.

V.12 _____. "Cuentos cubanos del siglo XX." Unión, 14, 2 (1975),
      84-96.

V.13 _____. "Introducción al cuento cubano contemporáneo." RevI,
      No. 36 (1950), 217-218.

V.14 _____. "La nueva cuentística cubana (1959-1963)." In his Temas
      y personajes de la literatura cubana (H: Unión, 1964), pp.
      291-299. Orig. GdC, No. 27 (1963), 10-12.

V.15 _____. "La nueva (y actual) novela cubana." In Francisco Fer-
nández-Santos, and José Martínez, Cuba: una revolución en
marcha (Paris: Ruedo Ibérico, 1967), pp. 401-407.

V.16 _____. "Prólogo." In Cuentos cubanos del siglo XX; antología
(H: Arte y Literatura, 1975), pp. 11-30.

V.17 Caballero Bonald, J. M. "Introducción." In Narrativa cubana
de la revolución; 2. ed. (Madrid: Alianza, 1969), pp. 7-
23. Orig. 1968; 3. ed., 1971.

V.18 Cabrera Infante, Guillermo. "[Reseña de] Antología del cuento
en Cuba (1902-1952)." Ciclón, 1, 2 (1955), 55-58.

V.19 Campos, Jorge. "Diez años de cuentos: una reciente antología
cubana." Insula, No. 177 (1962), 11. See item no. V.55.

V.20 _____. "Fantasía y realidad en los cuentos cubanos." Insula,
No. 268 (1969), 11.

V.21 Casal, Lourdes. "Images of Cuban society among pre- and post-
revolutionary novelists." DAI, 37 (1976), 1482B.

V.22 _____. "La novela en Cuba 1959-1967: una introducción." Exilio,
3, 3-4 (1969), 185-216; 4, 1 (1970), 184-217.

V.23 Codina, Iverna. "Cuba: novela y revolución." Plural, No. 86
(1978), 59-60.

V.24 Cortina, Alvaro. "La novela cubana de la 'flecha de oro'."
Exilio, 6, 3 (1972), 27-34.

V.25 Ejsner, Aleksej. "Korotkij put'-- krutoj pod'em." LO, 4
(1980), 92-95.

V.26 Fernández, José B. "Salient themes in Cuban-American narrative."
Chasqui, 6, 3 (1977), 76-83.

V.27 Fernández, Roberto G. "El cuento cubano del exilio: un enfoque."
DAI, 38 (1978), 5507A-5508A.

V.28 Fernández Vázquez, Antonio A. La novelística cubana de la revolución (testimonio y evocación en las novelas cubanas es-
critas fuera de Cuba: 1959-1975). Miami: Universal, 1980.
Orig. as "La novela de la revolución cubana escrita fuera
de Cuba: 1959-1975." DAI, 39 (1978), 3612A.

V.29 Fornet, Ambrosio. "El cuento." CAm, Nos. 22-23 (1964), 3-10.

V.30 _____. En blanco y negro. H: Instituto del Libro, 1967.

V.31 _____. "Introducción." In Antología del cuento cubano contemporáneo (M: Era, 1967), pp. 9-46.

V.32 ____. "Introducción." In Cuentos de la revolución cubana (Santiago de Chile: Universitaria, 1969?), pp. 9-17.

V.33 ____. "La nueva narrativa y sus antecedentes." CAm, Nos. 22-23 (1964), 2-9.

V.34 Garcés Larrea, Cristóbal. "Narradores cubanos contemporáneos." In Narradores cubanos contemporáneos (Guayaquil: Ariel, 1973), pp. 7-12.

V.35 García Alzola, Ernesto. "La novela cubana en el siglo XX." In Panorama de la literatura cubana; conferencias (H: Universidad de la Habana, Centro de Estudios Cubanos, 1970), pp. 183-207.

V.36 Gómez Valdés, Amada. La novela social cubana durante el primer cuarto del siglo XX. Unpublished thesis, Universidad de la Habana, 1943.

V.37 Goodyear, Russell Howard. "A critical anthology of contemporary Cuban short stories in translation." DAI, 39 (1978), 3563A.

V.38 Gutiérrez de la Solana, Alberto. "La novela cubana escrita fuera de Cuba." ALHisp, Nos. 203 (1973-1974), 167-189.

V.39 Hernández-Miyares, Julio E. "Introducción." In Narradores cubanos de hoy (Miami: Universal, 1975), pp. 5-11.

V.40 Ibarzábal, Federico de. "[Prólogo]." In Cuentos contemporáneos (H: Trópico, 1937), pp. 9-14.

V.41 Iriarte, Helena. "Nuevos cuentistas cubanos." CAm, No. 9 (1961), 155-156.

V.42 Kapcia, Antoni. "La novela cubana a partir de 1959, ¿revolución literaria o literatura revolucionaria?" CA, No. 225 (1979), 33-45.

V.43 Kejzlarová, Inge. "Algunos apuntes sobre la temática de la novela cubana de hoy." PP, 9 (1966), 275-281.

V.44 Lax, Judith Heckelman. "Themes and techniques in the socially oriented Cuban novel 1933-1952." DA, 22 (1961), 4350.

V.45 Lazo, Raimundo. La novela cubana contemporánea. H: Universidad de la Habana, 1950-1951.

V.46 Leante, César. "La otra oreja de Menton." CAm, No. 31 (1965), 99-101. See item no. V.63.

V.47 Lipp, Solomon. "The anti-Castro novel." Hispania, 58 (1975), 284-296.

V.48 Llopis, Rogelio. "Recuento fantástico." CAm, No. 42 (1967), 148-155.

V.49 Lucyga, Christine. "Die Autor-Leser-Beziehung im modernen kubanischen Roman." WZUR, 28 (1979), 155-158.

V.50 _____. "Kommunikationsbeziehungen im modernen kubanischen Roman." Lateinamerika, Spring 1979, pp. 69-78.

V.51 _____. "Zur Darstellung con Geschichte und Gegenwart im neuen kubanischen Roman." Lateinamerika, Fall 1978, pp. 5-24.

V.52 Mario, José. "La narrativa cubana de la revolución." MNu, No. 41 (1969), 75-79.

V.53 Marquina, Rafael. "Los caminos de la novela cubana contemporánea." RevC, 2a época, Nos. 34-36 (1938), 68-90.

V.54 Martí de Cid, Dolores. "La novela y el cuento durante la República." Carteles, 33, 20 (1952), 138-141.

V.55 Masó, Fausto, and Antón Arrufat. "Prólogo." In Nuevos cuentistas cubanos (H: Casa de las Américas, 1961), pp. 9-12.

V.56 Méndez, Adriana. "The historical image in the novel of the Cuban revolution: realism and neo-Baroque." DAI, 40 (1980), 5069A-5070A.

V.57 Méndez y Soto, Ernesto. Panorama de la novela cubana de la revolución (1959-1970). Miami: Universal, 1977. Orig. DAI, 34 (1974), 6598A-6599A.

V.58 Menton, Seymour. "The Cuban novel of the revolution: a decade of growing national consciousness." In The cry of home: cultural nationalism and the modern writer (Knoxville: University of Tennessee Press, 1972), pp. 320-333.

V.59 _____. "El cuento de la revolución cubana: una visión antológica y algo más." In El cuento hispanoamericano ante la crítica (Madrid: Castalia, 1973), pp. 338-355.

V.60 _____. "Four stages in the Cuban novel of the revolution." In Contemporary Latin American literature (Houston: University of Houston, Office of International Affairs, 1973), pp. 48-59.

V.61 _____. "Models for the epic of the Cuban revolution." In In honor of Boyd G. Carter (Laramie: University of Wyoming, Department of Modern and Classical Languages, 1981), pp. 49-58.

V.62 _____. "La narrativa extranjera de la revolución cubana." In Instituto Internacional de Literatura Iberoamericana, Literatura de la emancipación hispanoamericana y otros ensayos (Lima: Universidad de San Marcos, 1972), pp. 275-280.

V.63 _____. "La novela de la revolución cubana." CA, No. 123 (1964), 231-241. Also CAm, Nos. 22-23 (1964), 150-156.

V.64 ____. "Periodization of typology of the novel of the Cuban rev-
       olution." PCLS, 10 (1978), 87-99.

V.65 ____. Prose fiction of the Cuban revolution. Austin: Univer-
       sity of Texas Press, 1975. Also as La narrativa de la re-
       volución cubana. Madrid: Playor, 1978.

V.66 ____. "The short story of the Cuban revolution, 1959-1969."
       SSF, 8 (1971), 32-43.

V.67 Miranda, Julio E. "Sobre la nueva narrativa cubana." CHA, No.
       246 (1970), 641-654.

V.68 Noack, Rudolf. "Geschichtsbewusstein und Realismus in der revo-
       lutionären kubanischen Epik." WB, 24, 12 (1978), 49-71.

V.69 Novás Calvo, Lino. "Novela por hacer." RNC, No. 23 (1940), 81-
       94.

V.70 Ortega, Julio. "Sobre narrativa cubana actual." NNH, 2, 1
       (1972), 65-87.

V.71 Portuondo, José Antonio. "Prólogo." In Cuentos cubanos contem-
       poráneos (M: Leyenda, 1946), pp. 7-11.

V.72 Pozo, Orlando del. "Tres cuentistas jóvenes." Unión, 4, 2
       (1965), 169-173. Nelson Rodríguez, David Camps, José Ma-
       nuel Fernández.

V.73 Raggi, Carlos M. "Tendencias epistemológicas en la nueva nove-
       lística cubana." Círculo, 2 (1970), 175-184.

V.74 Rodríguez Feo, José. "Breve recuento de la narrativa cubana."
       Unión, 6, 4 (1967), no pagination.

V.75 ____. "Prólogo." In Aquí once cubanos cuentan (Montevideo:
       Arca, 1967), pp. 7-12.

V.76 Rodríguez Monegal, Emir. "La nueva novela vista desde Cuba."
       RI, Nos. 92-93 (1975), 647-662.

V.77 Sánchez-Boudy, José. "El cuento cubano en el extranjero: inno-
       vación y perspectiva." In The contemporary Latin-American
       short story (NY: Senda Nueva, 1979), pp. 88-92.

V.78 ____. "La novela cubana del exilio: análisis a vuelo de pája-
       ro." Círculo, 7 (1978), 63-70.

V.79 Schwartz, Kessel. "Social and esthetic concerns of the twentieth
       century Cuban novel." REH, 6 (1972), 19-35.

V.80 Siemens, William L. "Recent developments in the Cuban novel."
       RInter, 8 (1978), 305-308.

V.81   Sorel, Andrés. "A manera de introducción." In <u>Cuentos de Cuba</u>
       <u>socialista</u> (Bilbao: Zero, 1976), pp. 5-21.

V.82   Souza, Raymond D. "La imaginación y la magia en la narrativa
       cubana (1932-33)." <u>Caribe</u>, 2, 2 (1977), 86-96.

V.83   ____. Major Cuban novelists; innovation and tradition. Colum-
       bia: University of Missouri Press, 1976.

V.84   Suardíaz, Luis. "Los días de nuestra angustia." <u>Unión</u>, 2, 5-6
       (1963), 119-123.

V.85   Subercaseaux, Bernardo. "¿Qué entendemos por joven narrativa
       cubana?" In <u>Narrativa de la joven Cuba; antología</u> (Santia-
       go de Chile: Nascimento, 1971), pp. 7-23.

V.86   Valdés, Bernardo J. <u>Panorama del cuento cubano</u>. Miami: Univer-
       sal, 1976. Orig. as "El cuento cubano en la República
       (1902-1959)." <u>DAI</u>, 35 (1974), 420A-421A.

V.87   Véguez, Roberto Andrés. "Estudio histórico-crítico del cuento
       cubano revolucionario." <u>DAI</u>, 36 (1975), 2872A-2873A.

W. SPECIAL TOPICS IN PROSE FICTION

W.1   Barreda-Tomás, Pedro M. The black protagonist in the Cuban novel. Amherst: University of Massachussets Press, 1979. Orig. as "La caracterización del protagonista negro en la novela cubana." DAI, 31 (1970), 1788A.

W.2   Bueno, Salvador. "Presencia negra en la narrativa cubana." Indice, 24 (15-III-1969), 31-32.

W.3   Chevalier, Maxime. "De los cuentos populares cubanos a los cuentos folklóricos del siglo de oro." In Hommage des hispanistes français à Noël Salomon (Barcelona: LAIA, 1979), pp. 155-168.

W.4   Del Monte y Aponte, Domingo. "Sobre la novela histórica." In his Escritos (H: Cultural, 1929), pp. 217-230.

W.5   Drake, Sandra E. "The uses of history in the Caribbean novel." DAI, 37 (1977), 7734A.

W.6   Febres Cordero G., Julio. "Balance del indigenismo en Cuba." RBNC, 2a serie, 1, 4 (1950), 61-204.

W.7   García, Calixto. "El negro en la narrativa cubana." DAI, 34 (1973), 1908A.

W.8   Garzón Céspedes, Francisco. "Cuba: el papel del género policíaco en la lucha ideológica." CAm, No. 89 (1975), 159-162.

W.9   Jiménez, Onilda. "Un nuevo fenómeno de la literatura cubana: la novela policial." Círculo, 9 (1980), 93-100.

W.10   Llopis, Rogelio. "Prólogo." In Cuentos cubanos de lo fantástico y lo extraordinario (San Sebastián, Spain: Equipo, 1968), pp. 11-28. Orig. as "Recuento fantástico." CAm, No. 42 (1967), 148-155.

W.11   Luis, William. "La novela antiesclavista: texto, contexto y escritura." CA, No. 236 (1981), 103-116.

W.12   _____. "La novela antiesclavista y el concepto de modernidad." CS, 11, 1 (1981), 33-47.

W.13   Nieves, Dolores. "Juan Criollo y la novela picaresca." Bohemia, 66, 22 (1974), 10-13.

W.14   Ordóñez, Roger. "La literatura policiaca en Cuba." Areito, Nos. 19-20 (1979), 64-65.

W.15 Ortiz Aponte, Sally. "Cuba." In her La esoteria en la narrativa hispanoamericana (Río Piedras, P.R.?: Editorial Universitaria, Universidad de Puerto Rico, 1977), pp. 65-81.

W.16 Remos y Rubio, Juan Nepomuceno José. Tendencias de la narración imaginativa en Cuba. H: La Casa Montalvo-Cárdenas, 1935.

W.17 Schulman, Ivan A. "The portrait of the slave: ideology and aesthetics in the Cuban antislavery novel." In Comparative perspectives on slavery in New World plantation societies (NY: New York Academy of Sciences, 1977), pp. 356-367.

X.   GENERAL STUDIES ON THE ESSAY

X.1   Bueno, Salvador. "Figuras y tendencias del ensayismo en Cuba."
      In Los mejores ensayistas cubanos (H: Organización Continen-
      tal de los Festivales del Libro, 1959), pp. 7-12.

X.2   ____. "La prosa reflexiva en el siglo XIX." In Panorama de la
      literatura cubana; conferencias (H: Univeridad de la Habana,
      Centro de Estudios Cubanos, 1970), pp. 107-127.

X.3   Lizaso, Félix. Ensayistas contemporáneos, 1900-1920. H: Trópico,
      1938.

X.4   Portuondo, José Antonio. "El ensayo y la crítica en Cuba revolu-
      cionaria." In Instituto Internacional de Literatura Iberoa-
      mericana, El ensayo y la crítica en Iberoamérica (Toronto:
      Universidad de Toronto, 1970), pp. 215-220.

X.5   Rosell, Raúl Gonzalo. "El ensayo de la generación de 1924 en Cu-
      ba." DAI, 34 (1974), 7779A.

X.6   Suárez-Murias, Marguerite. "Cuba painted by Cubans: the nine-
      teenth century journalistic essay." RIB, 30 (1980), 375-
      386. Also in her Essays on Hispanic literature; ensayos de
      literatura hispana; a bilingual anthology (Washington, D.C.:
      University Press of America, 1982), pp. 47-66.

X.7   Yero Pérez, Luis. "El tema de la esclavitud en la narrativa cu-
      bana." Islas, No. 49 (1974), 63-94.

Y. REGIONAL AND LOCAL LITERATURE

Y.1 Bulit, Ilse. "Poetas de Camajuaní." Bohemia, 69, 4 (1977), 27-28.

Y.2 Dollero, Adolfo. Cultura cubana: la provincia de Matanzas y su evolución cultural. H: Seoane y Fernández, 1919.

Y.3 Espinosa Domínguez, Carlos. "Introducción al teatro en Santiago de Cuba." Conjunto, No. 31 (1977), 57-62.

Y.4 "Estructuras poéticas en la regional Caibarién." Signos, 4, 2 (1973), 292-298.

Y.5 Fuentes y Matons, Laureano. Las artes en Santiago de Cuba; apuntes históricos. Santiago de Cuba: Juan E. Ravelo, 1893.

Y.6 García Garófalo y Mesa, Manuel. "Exposición histórica." In his Diccionario de seudónimos de escritores, poetas y periodistas villaclareños (H, 1926), pp. 7-15.

Y.7 Martínez-Moles, Manuel. Periodismo y periódicos espirituanos. H: "El Siglo XX", 1930.

Y.8 Piedra-Bueno, Andrés de. Matanzas y sus poetas; conferencia. H: P. Fernández, 1939.

Y.9 Rosales, Antonio. "Apuntes para la historia de las letras villaclareñas." CyA, No. 105 (1901), 463-466.

Y.10 Trelles y Govín, Carlos Manuel. :Matanceros notables. Los novelistas." CyA, 12, 14 (1913), 12-13.

Z. PERIODICAL INDEXES

(See section A. for bibliographies of periodical publications; see section D. for critical studies on periodical publications.)

Z.1   Alfonso Quintero, Rubén. Indice de la Revista cubana (1935-1957). H: Instituto Nacional de Cultura, Ministerio de Educación, 1958? Orig. as Indice general de la Revista cubana, 1935-1952. Marianao: Biblioteca Municipal, 1957.

Z.2   _____. Indice general de la revista Universidad de la Habana, 1934-1956. Marianao: Biblioteca Municipal, 1959.

Z.3   Becerra Bonet, Berta. Indice de la Revista de la Facultad de Letras y Ciencias de la Universidad de la Habana. H: Sociedad Económica de Amigos del País, 1955.

Z.4   Brower, Gary, and Raymond D. Souza. "Ciclón: índice e introducción." Et caetera, 2a época, No. 13 (1969), 105-125.

Z.5   Domínguez Alfonso, Aleida, and Luz Berta Marín. Indice de la revista Casa de las Américas 1960-1967. H: Biblioteca Nacional José Martí, 1969.

Z.6   _____ et al. Indices de las revistas cubanas. H: Biblioteca Nacional José Martí, 1969.

Z.7   Feito, Francisco E., and Elio Alba-Buffill. Indice de El pensamiento (Cuba 1879-1880). NY: Senda Nueva, 1977.

Z.8   García-Carranza, Araceli. Indice analítico de La gaceta de Cuba. H: Instituto Cubano del Libro; Organismos, 1974.

Z.9   _____. Indice analítico de la Revista bimestre cubana. H: Biblioteca Nacional José Martí, Departamento Colección Cubana, 1968.

Z.10   _____. Indice de la Revista de la Biblioteca Nacional José Martí: 1909-1969. H: Biblioteca Nacional José Martí, Departamento Colección Cubana, 1975.

Z.11   _____. Indices de revistas cubanas siglo XIX. H: Biblioteca Nacional José Martí, 1970.

Z.12   Giráldez, Elena. Unión-UNEAC índice, 1962-1967. H: Hemeroteca, Información de Humanidades, Biblioteca Nacional José Martí, 1969.

Z.13 Havana. Biblioteca Nacional José Martí. Indice de la revista
      El Siglo XIX. H, 196?

Z.14 _____. _____. Indice de la revista La mariposa. H, 196?

Z.15 _____. Consejo Nacional de Cultura. Prosas cubanas. H: Edito-
      rial Nacional de Cuba, 1962-1964.

Z.16 _____. Universidad. Departamento de Intercambio Universitario.
      Indice general de Universidad de la Habana. H: La Verónica,
      1942.

Z.17 Indice, 1906-1913 [de Letras; revista universal ilustrada]. H?,
      n.d.

Z.18 Indice general de publicaciones periódicas cubanas. H: Consejo
      Nacional de Cultura, 1970-.

Z.19 Marín, Luz Berta. Indice de la revista Islas. H: Biblioteca
      Nacional José Martí, Departamento de Hemeroteca e Informa-
      ción de Humanidades, 1974.

Z.20 Menocal Villalón, Feliciana. "Indice de la revista La piragua."
      RBNJM, 3a serie, 6, 2 (1964), 14-26.

Z.21 _____. "Indice general de El colibrí." RBNJM, 3a serie, 5, 1-4
      (1963), 78-103.

Z.22 _____. "Indice general de El plantel." RBNJM, 3a serie, 3, 1-4
      (1961), 160-172.

Z.23 _____. "Indice general de La cartera cubana." RBNJM, 3a serie,
      4, 1-4 (1962), 48-71.

Z.24 _____, and Araceli García-Carranza. Indices analíticos de El
      almendares, El cesto de flores, Flores del siglo, Floresta
      cubana, La guirnalda cubana, Miscelánea de útil y agradable
      recreo, La piragua, Revista de la Habana, El rocío y Semi-
      nario cubano. H: Biblioteca Nacional José Martí, Departa-
      mento de la Colección Cubana, 1964.

Z.25 Peraza Sarausa, Fermín. Indice de Cuba contemporánea. H: Muni-
      cipio de la Habana, 1940.

Z.26 _____. Indice de El asno (1805-1808). H: Anuario Bibliográfico
      Cubano, 1944.

Z.27 _____. Indice de El fígaro. H: Anuario Bibliográfico Cubano,
      1945-1948.

Z.28 _____. Indice de la Revista cubana. H: Municipio de la Habana,
      Departamento de Cultura, 1939.

Z.29 _____. Indice de la Revista de Cuba. H: Municipio de la Habana,
      Departamento de Cultura, 1938.

Z.30 _____. Indice del Aviso de la Habana (1809-1810). H: Anuario
Bibliográfico Cubano, 1944.

Z.31 _____. "Indice del Papel periódico de la Habana." RBC, 51
(1942), 134-136, 287-289, 450-456; 52 (1943), 137-145, 304-
313, 468-470; 53 (1944), 80-84, 174-178, 271-279; 54 (1944),
82-84, 180-185; 55 (1945), 90-94, 167-179, 279-282; 56
(1945), 66-71, 180-183, 260-269; 57 (1945), 71-76, 175-182;
58 (1946), 88-91, 187-190; 59 (1947), 273-282; 60 (1947),
281-284; 61 (1948), 279-282; 62 (1948), 262-268; 64 (1949),
280-284; 65 (1950), 274-283; 66 (1950), 277-284; 67 (1951),
90-92, 189-191.

Z.32 Ripoll, Carlos. Archivo José Martí: repertorio crítico, medio
siglo de estudios martianos. Eastchester, N.Y.: Eliseo Torres, 1972.

Z.33 _____. Indice de la Revista de avance (Cuba, 1927-1930). NY:
Las Américas, 1969.

Z.34 _____. Patria: el periódico de José Martí; registro general
(1892-1895). NY: Eliseo Torres, 1971.

Z.35 Rodríguez, Amalia. Indice de La siempreviva. H: Universidad de
la Habana, Escuela de Bibliotecarios, 1961.

Z.36 Valle, Adrián del. Indices de las Memorias de la Sociedad Económica de Amigos del País, 1793-1896. H: Molina, 1938.

Authors

1. ACOSTA, AGUSTIN (1886-   )

Critical Monographs and Dissertations

1.1   Forés, Aldo R. La poesía de Agustín Acosta, poeta nacional de Cuba. Miami: Universal, 1976. Orig. DAI, 37 (1977), 6527A.

Critical Essays

1.2   Aparicio Laurencio, Angel. "Agustín Acosta, poeta nacional de Cuba." Arco, No. 92 (1968), 466-472.

1.3   Buesa, José Angel. "Preámbulo." In Agustín Acosta, Sus mejores poesías (Barcelona: Bruguera, 1955), pagination unknown.

1.4   Camín, Alfonso. "Agustín Acosta." In his Hombres de España y de América (H: Militar, 1925), pp. 283-287.

1.5   Chacón y Calvo, José María. "El poema 'Jesús' de Agustín Acosta." BACL, 7, 1-2 (1958), 179-182.

1.6   _____. "Un poeta nacional." RevC, 8 (1937), 214-217.

1.7   Duarte, Julio M. "Las cartas de un poeta: Agustín Acosta." Círculo, 10 (1981), 77-84.

1.8   Entralgo, José. "[La zafra]." CCont, 43 (1927), 369-370.

1.9   Fernández, Jesse. "La obra poética de Agustín Acosta." Envíos, 2, 3-4 (1972), 5-11.

1.10   Fernández de la Vega, Oscar. "[Jesús]." Envíos, 2, 3-4 (1972), 20.

1.11   Guerra Flores, José. "[Jesús]." RBNC, 2a serie, 8, 4 (1957), 203-205.

1.12   Jiménez, José Olivio. "En torno a un poema de Agustín Acosta ['Mediodía en el campo']." Noverim, No. 7 (1957), 73-94.

1.13   Labrador Ruiz, Enrique. "[Jesús]." RevC, 31, 2 (1957), 144-148.

1.14   Lamar Schweyer, Alberto. "Agustín Acosta." In his Los contemporáneos; ensayos sobre la literatura cubana del siglo (H: "Los Rayos X", 1921), pp. 25-42.

1.15   Mañach, Jorge. "Carta a Agustín Acosta (en el cincuentenario de sus primeros versos)." Bohemia, 46, 49 (1954), 38, 95-96.

1.16 Marinello, Juan. "Agustín Acosta." CCont, No. 150 (1925), 164-166.

1.17 ____. "Cincuenta años de poesía cubana: tres hombres encadenados." RBC, No. 39 (1937), 366-388.

1.18 Martínez Villena, Rubén. "Hermanita de Agustín Acosta." In his En un nombre y otras prosas (H: Ucar, García, 1940), pp. 99-103. Also RBNC, 2a serie, 6, 4 (1955), 179.

1.19 Mella, Julio Antonio. "Un comentario a La zafra de Agustín Acosta." Bohemia, 55, 32 (1963), 70-71, 79.

1.20 Ortiz, Fernando. "El poema de La zafra," RBC, 22 (1957), 5-22. Also as "Sobre La zafra." CCont, 43 (1927), 369-370.

1.21 Poveda, Héctor. "Cierto poeta..." Avance, No. 18 (1928), 7.

1.22 Santovenia y Echaide, Emeterio Santiago. "Agustín Acosta." In his Vidas humanas (H: Librería Martí, 1956), pp. 533-537.

1.23 Suarée, Octavio de la. "Mensaje romántico de Agustín Acosta a Dulce María Barrero." Envíos, 2, 3-4 (1972), 12-19.

1.24 Torriente, Loló de la. "Agustín Acosta: coloquio del poeta y la poesía. Charla con Loló de la Torriente." Bohemia, 60, 21 (1968), 32-35.

1.25 Vitier, Medardo. "Agustín Acosta." In his Apuntaciones literarias (H: Minerva, 1935), pp. 145-154.

1.26 ____. "Agustín Acosta y Los camellos distantes." Lyceum, Nos. 11-12 (1938), 21-25.

1.27 ____. "Un canto de Agustín Acosta." Letras, 2a época, No. 24 (1913), 509.

2. ALFONSO, PACO (1906-)

Critical Essays

2.1   Boudet, Rosa Ileana. "Paco Alfonso habla sobre Cañaveral."
      RyC, 2a época, No. 23 (1974), 47-48.

2.2   Cruz-Luis, Adolfo. "Paco Alfonso: la solidaridad con la patria
      de Lenin." Conjunto, No. 34 (1977), 52-55.

2.3   "Entrevista con Paco Alfonso." PyC, No. 7 (1962), 7.

2.4   González Freire, Natividad. "De Paco Alfonso, por cañaveral."
      Bohemia, 66, 21 (1974), 25.

2.5   _____. "Paco Alfonso, un teatro partidista." Bohemia, 69, 24
      (1977), 10-13.

2.6   Leal, Rine. "Ya me dueles, luna; Cañaveral; realismo socialis-
      ta." In his En primera persona (1954-1966) (H: Instituto
      del Libro, 1967), pp. 57-59, 67-73, 88-89.

2.7   Méndez, Graziella. "Cañaveral en los bateyes." INRA, 2, 5
      (1961), 64-67.

2.8   "Paco Alfonso y el teatro popular." RyC, 2a época, No. 6
      (1972), 54-59.

2.9   "Rafael. Cañaveral." VO, 16, 20 (1974), 60-61.

2.10 Vera Estrada, Ana. "Teatro Popular en la tribuna." RyC, No.
      74 (1978), 70-73.

3. ALONSO, DORA (1910-   )

Critical Essays

3.1 Alonso, Dora. "Encuesta." GdC, No. 164 (1978), 8.

3.2 Alzola, Concepción Teresa. "Cuentística de Dora Alzola." Unión, 1, 2 (1962), 89-106.

3.3 Bueno, Salvador. "[Tierra inerme]." ULH, No. 173 (1965), 179-181.

3.4 Elizagaray, Alga Marina. "Dora Alonso: por el reino de la fantasía." Bohemia, 68, 37 (1976), 10-13.

3.5 González, Omar. "La alegría es lo primero." CB, No. 131 (1978), 20-21, 29, 31.

3.6 González López, Waldo. "[Aventuras de Guille]." Bohemia, 67, 43 (1975), 25.

3.7 _____. "[Cuentos]." ULH, No. 207 (1978), 223-236.

3.8 Martínez, Mayra A. "La experiencia comunicada." CB, No. 110 (1977), 16.

3.9 Pereira, Manuel. "Un primer paso." CubaI, No. 65 (1975), 42-43.

3.10 Ramos, SIdroc. "[Tierra inerme]." CAm, No. 9 (1961), 167-168.

3.11 Repilado, Ricardo. "Cuentos de dos primaveras." TLit, No. 20 (1969), 30-33.

3.12 Rivero, Angel. "Las tres lámparas de Dora Alonso." RyC, No. 72 (1978), 67-71.

3.13 Toural, Eduardo. "Análisis del cuento 'Once caballos'." Santiago, No. 12 (1973), 195-208.

4. ALVAREZ BARAGAÑO, JOSE (1932-1962)

Critical Essays

4.1 Alcides Pérez, Rafael. "Ante una tumba sin razón." Unión, 1, 3-4 (1962), 59-60.

4.2 Arcocha, José Antonio. "Rescate de Baragaño." AA, 1, 2 (1971), 84-85.

4.3 Branly, Roberto. "Baragaño: Himno a las milicias." GdC, No. 6-7 (1962), 21-22.

4.4 _____. "Canta hacia Baragaño." GdC, No. 25 (1963), 13.

4.5 Casaus, Víctor. "Un poco de Baragaño [Poemas escogidos]." Unión, 4, 1 (1965), 152-154.

4.6 Díaz Martínez, Manuel. "Baragaño." Bohemia, 57, 7 (1965), 24-25.

4.7 _____. "Baragaño tal como lo vi." In José Alvárez Baragaño, Poemas escogidos (H: Unión de Escritores y Artistas de Cuba, 1964), pp. 8-18. Orig. Unión, 1, 3-4 (1962), 54-58.

4.8 Fernández, Pablo Armando. "Sima del agua." Unión, 1, 3-4 (1962), 45-46.

4.9 Jamís, Fayad. "El poeta a los veinte años." Unión, 1, 3-4 (1962), 47-50.

4.10 Jiménez, Vicente. "Mi amigo Baragaño." AA, 1, 2 (1971), 78-80.

4.11 López, César. "José A. Baragaño: Poesía, revolución del ser." CAm, No. 4 (1961), 76-78.

4.12 Oráa, Pedro de. "Dualidad de la poesía." NRC, 1962, pp. 255-258.

4.13 _____. "Tus enemigos, Baragaño." Unión, 1, 3-4 (1962), 51-53.

4.14 Piñera, Virgilio. "El amor original [de] José A. Baragaño." Ciclón, 1, 6 (1955), 75-76.

4.15 _____. "El caso Baragaño." GdC, Nos. 6-7 (1962), 21.

5. APARICIO, RAUL (1913-1970)

Critical Essays

5.1 Abreu Gómez, Ermilo. "[Cuentos de Cuba]." Unión, 3, 4 (1964), 157-158.

5.2 Bernal del Riesgo, Alfonso. "Biografía y tanatografía." Unión, 6, 3 (1967), 120-124.

5.3 Bueno, Salvador. "En la muerte de Raúl Aparicio." RBNJM, 3a serie, 12, 1 (1970), 147-150.

5.4 _____. "Hijos de nuestro tiempo." Bohemia, 56, 21 (1964), 30.

5.5 Cabrera Alvarez, Guillermo. "Con Aparicio en el tiempo." GdC, No. 81 (1970), 5.

5.6 Díaz Martínez, Manuel. "[Espejos de alinde]." GdC, No. 69 (1969), 29-30.

5.7 Franco, José Luciano. "Aparicio." GdC, No. 81 (1970), 3.

5.8 Guillén, Nicolás. "Hombradía de Raúl Aparicio." GdC, No. 81 (1970), 2.

5.9 Iznaga, Alcides. "Raúl Aparicio: hombre de bien y de letras." Bohemia, 69, 13 (1977), 10-13.

5.10 Llanos, Marcos. "[Hombradía de Antonio Maceo]." CAm, No. 47 (1968), 140-141.

5.11 Luis, Raúl. "Lo más puro de su labor creadora." GdC, No. 81 (1970), 3.

5.12 "Premio de Biografía [entrevista]." GdC, No. 53 (1966), 3.

5.13 Rodríguez Herrera, Mariano. "Trabajar con Raúl Aparicio." GdC, No. 81 (1970), 4.

5.14 Selva, Mauricio de la. "[Hijos del tiempo]." CAm, Nos. 28-29 (1965), 148-150.

5.15 Torriente, Loló de la. "Interpretación de Antonio Maceo [Hombradía de Antonio Maceo]." GdC, No. 58 (1967), 4, 13.

6. ARENAS, REINALDO (1943-   )

Critical Monographs and Dissertations

6.1   Stewart, Janet Louise Beckwith. "The concept of 'lyrical novel'
       as seen in three Spanish American novels." DAI, 40 (1980),
       4071A. Arenas inter alios.

6.2   Zaldívar, Gladys. Novelística cubana de los años 60: Paradiso,
       El mundo alucinante. Miami: Universal, 1977.

Critical Essays

6.3   Alomá, Orlando. "Arenas antes del alba." Cuba, No. 65 (1967),
       37.

6.4   Arcocha, José M. "El mundo alucinante de Reynaldo Arenas." AA,
       1, 1 (1970), 69.

6.5   Arenas, Reinaldo. "Celestino y yo." Unión, 6, 3 (1967), 119.

6.6   _____. "Fray Servando: víctima infatigable." In Rose S. Minc,
       Literature and popular culture in the Hispanic world; a
       symposium (Gaithersburg, Md.: Hispamérica; Upper Montclair,
       N.J.: Montclair State College, 1981), pp. 15-18.

6.7   Barnet, Miguel. "Celestino antes y después del alba." GdC, No.
       60 (1967), 21.

6.8   Borinsky, Alicia. "Re-escribir y escribir: Arenas, Menard, Bor-
       ges, Cervantes, Fray Servando." RI, Nos. 92-93 (1975),
       605-616. Also as "Rewriting and writings." Diacritics,
       4, 4 (1974), 22-28.

6.9   Bovi-Guerra, Pedro. "El mundo alucinante: ecos de Orlando y
       otros ecos." Románica, 15 (1978-1979), 97-107.

6.10   Diego, Eliseo. "Sobre Celestino antes del alba." CAm, No. 45
       (1967), 162-166.

6.11   Fell, Claude. "Un neobarroco del desequilibrio: El mundo alu-
       cinante de Reinaldo Arenas." In Instituto Internacional
       de Literatura Iberoamericana, XVII Congreso (Madrid: Cul-
       tura Hispánica del Centro Iberoamericano de Cooperación,
       1978), pp. 725-731.

6.12   Fernández Guerra, Angel Luis. "Recurrencias obsesivas y varian-
       tes alucinantes en la obra de Reinaldo Arenas." Caravelle,
       No. 16 (1970), 133-140.

6.13   González, Eduardo G. "A razón de santo: últimos lances de Fray
       Servando." RI, Nos. 92-93 (1975), 593-603.

6.14   Gordon, Amrbose, Jr. "Rippling ribaldry and pouncing puns: the
       two lives of Friar Servando." Review, No. 8 (1973), 40-44.

6.15   Jara, René. "Aspectos de la intertextualidad en El mundo aluci-
       nante." TC, No. 13 (1979), 219-235.

6.16   Koch, Dolores. "[Termina el desfile]." ExTL, 12 (1983-1984),
       88-90.

6.17   Libertella, Héctor. "Reynaldo Arenas: El mundo alucinante." In
       his Nueva escritura en Latinoamérica (Caracas: Monte Avila,
       1977), pp. 89-92.

6.18   Morley, Mónica, and Enrico-Mario Santí. "Reinaldo Arenas y su
       mundo alucinante: una entrevista." Hispania, 66 (1983),
       114-118.

6.19   Ortega, Julio. "El mundo alucinante de Reynaldo Arenas." Ima-
       gen, No. 18, 2° cuerpo (1971), 3, 16-23. Also RUM, 26, 4
       (1971), 25-27. Also in his Relato de la utopía (Barcelona:
       La Gaya Ciencia, 1973), pp. 217-226. Also as "The dazzling
       world of Friar Servando." Review, No. 8 (1973), 45-48.

6.20   Rivera, Carlos. "Tres escrituras: Cobra, El mundo alucinante y
       Sebregondi retrocede." Románica, 12 (1975), 55-62.

6.21   Rodríguez Monegal, Emir. "The labyrinthine world of Reinaldo
       Arenas." LALR, No. 16 (1980), 126-131.

6.22   Rozencvaig, Perla. "Reinaldo Arenas." Hispamérica, No. 28
       (1981), 41-48.

6.23   Shaw, Donald L. "Reynaldo Arenas." In his Nueva narrativa his-
       panoamericana (Madrid: Cátedra, 1981), pp. 179-182.

6.24   Tamargo, María Isabel. "Celestino antes del alba: la violencia
       y el lenguaje infantil." In J. Cruz Mendizábal, Hispanic
       literatures (Indiana, Penn.: Indiana University of Pennsyl-
       vania, 1978), pp. 89-96.

6.25   Tobin, Patricia. "The author as escape artist." Review, No. 8
       (1976), 86-87.

6.26   Velázquez, Jaime G. "Vida de muertos [El palacio de las blan-
       quísimas mofetas]." RUM, 36, 4 (1981), 47-48.

6.27   Vesterman, William. "Going no place with Arenas." Review, No.
       8 (1973), 49-51.

6.28 Waller, Claudia Joan. "Reynaldo Arenas' El mundo alucinante: aesthetic and thematic focal points." KRQ, 19 (1972), 41-50.

7. ARMAS, AUGUSTO DE (1869-1893)

Critical Essays

7.1 Darío, Rubén. "Augusto de Armas." In his Los raros (Barcelona: Maucci, n.d.), pp. 129-132. Various other editions.

7.2 Martí, José. "Augusto de Armas." In his Obras completas (H: Editora Nacional de Cuba, 1963), V, 217. Various other editions.

7.3 ____. "Un soneto de Augusto de Armas." In his Obras completas (H: Editora Nacional de Cuba, 1963), V, 217. Various other editions.

7.4 Reyes, Alfonso. "Sobre las Rimas bizantinas de Augusto de Armas." In his Cuestiones estéticas (Paris: P. Ollendorff, 1919), pp. 165-186.

7.5 Tejera, Diego Vicente. "Augusto de Armas." In his Prosa literaria (H: Rambla, Bouza, 1936), II, 191-196.

7.6 ____. "Rimes byzantines." In his Prosa literaria (H: Rambla, Bouza, 1936), II. 135-140.

8. ARMAS Y CARDENAS, JOSE DE ("Justo de Lara," 1866-1919)

Bibliographies

8.1 Soler Mirabent, Antonia. "Bibliografía de José de Armas y Cárdenas (1909-1915)." L/L, No. 1 (1967), 63-76.

Critical Monographs and Dissertations

8.2 Ateneo de la Habana. Ofrenda floral a Justo de Lara. H, 1942?

8.3 Chacón y Calvo, José María. Evocación de Justo de Lara. H: Revista de la Habana, 1943.

8.4 Valverde y Maruri, Antonio L. Elogio del Lic. José de Armas y Cárdenas (Justo de Lara) individuo de número. H: "El Siglo XX", 1923.

Critical Essays

8.5 "Algunas opiniones sobre José de Armas y Cárdenas." In José de Armas y Cárdenas, 35 trabajos periodísticos (H: Cultural, 1935), pp. 241-250.

8.6 Baig Baños, Aurelio. "Importancia del epistolario que trascribimos." In José de Armas y Cárdenas, Epistolario de don José de Armas (Madrid: "Revista de Archivos", 1926), pp. 5-13.

8.7 Bueno, Salvador. "Algunos apuntes sobre Justo de Lara con motivo de su centenario." ULH, No. 182 (1966), 57-67.

8.8 Díaz Martínez, Manuel. "José de Armas y Cárdenas (Justo de Lara)." L/L, No. 1 (1967), 6-15.

8.9 Figarola-Caneda, Domingo. "Cervantes y el duque de Sessa. Nuevas observaciones sobre el Quijote de Avellaneda y su autor." RBNC, 1, 2 (1909), 47-50.

8.10 Iraizoz y de Villar, Antonio. "En la tumba de Justo de Lara." In his Pnys [sic, for Pnyx] (Madrid: Mundo Latino, 1926), pp. 195-202.

8.11 "José de Armas y Cárdenas (Justo de Lara)." BILL, 1, 1 (1967), 5-76.

8.12 Ramos, José Antonio. "José de Armas y Cárdenas (Justo de Lara)."
      In his Brega de libertad (H: Ministerio de Educación, Direc-
      ción de Cultura, 1950), pp. 99-108.

8.13 ____. "La personalidad de Justo de Lara." L/L, No. 1 (1967),
      16-32.

8.14 Salazar y Roig, Salvador. "Justo de Lara." CCont, 23 (1920),
      349-358.

8.15 Sanguily y Garritte, Manuel. "Un folleto sobre El Quijote de
      Avellaneda (noticia bibliográfica)." In his Juicios lite-
      rarios (H: Molina, 1930), pp. 29-33.

9. ARRUFAT, ANTON (1935-   )

Critical Monographs and Dissertations

9.1 Flynn, Susan Kingston. "The alienated hero in contemporary
     Spanish American drama." DAI, 38 (1977), 299A. Arrufat
     inter alios.

Critical Essays

9.2 Arreola, Juan José. "Antón Arrufat: El vivo al pollo." CAm,
     No. 9 (1961), 157.

9.3 Avila, Leopoldo. "Antón se va a la guerra." VO, No. 47 (1968),
     16-18. Also in his Cuba: letteratura e rivoluzione. Le
     correnti della critica e della letteratura cubana (Milano:
     Libreria Feltrinelli, 1969), pp. 15-21.

9.4 Bejel, Emilio F. "La dirección del conjuro en Los siete contra
     Tebas de Antón Arrufat." PH, nueva época, No. 30 (1979),
     40-46.

9.5 _____. "El mito de la casa de Layos en Los siete contra Tebas,
     de Antón Arrufat." Hispamérica, No. 20 (1978), 110-114.

9.6 Dalton, Roque. "En claro de Antón Arrufat." CAm, Nos. 17-18
     (1963), 63-64.

9.7 Dauster, Frank N. "The theater of Antón Arrufat." In Dramatists
     in revolt; the new Latin American theater (Austin: Universi-
     ty of Texas Press, 1976), pp. 3-18.

9.8 Desnoes, Edmundo. "Para estos libros que esperan." Unión, 3,
     2 (1964), 195-198.

9.9 Díaz Martínez, Manuel. "Repaso final." Bohemia, 57, 38 (1965),
     23.

9.10 Galich, Manuel. "Arrufat en el Teatro Experimental." GdC, No.
     29 (1963), 15.

9.11 Leal, Rine. "Dos farsas cubanas del absurdo." Ciclón, 3, 2
     (1957), 65-67. Virgilio Piñera, Falsa alarma; Antón Arru-
     fat, El caso se investiga.

9.12 Llopis, Rogelio. "Antón Arrufat, escritor versátil." GdC, No.
     35 (1964), 20-21.

9.13 Muguerencia, Magaly. "Por que jamás ocurra en días laborales
      [Todos los domingos]." CB, No. 5 (1966), 22.

9.14 Piñera, Virgilio. "Tres en uno a una." GdC, No. 15 (1963), 11-
      12.

9.15 Reading, Rodney Karl. "Final del repaso." Unión, 4, 3 (1965),
      145-149.

9.16 _____. "The renewal of traditional myth and form in the works
      of Antón Arrufat." RInter, 10 (1980), 357-377.

9.17 Triana, José. "Apuntes sobre un libro de Arrufat." GdC, No. 18
      (1963), 12-13.

10. BALBOA TROYA Y QUESADA, SILVESTRE DE (1563-1624)

Critical Monographs and Dissertations

10.1 Chacón y Calvo, José María. El primer poema escrito en Cuba. Documentos inéditos referentes al obispo fray Juan de las Cabezas. H: Maza, Arroyo y Caso, 1922.

10.2 Sainz, Enrique. Silvestre de Balboa y la literatura cubana. H: Letras Cubanas, 1982.

Critical Essays

10.3 Aparicio Laurencio, Angel. "El Espejo de paciencia, primer po- ema épico-histórico de las letras cubanas." In Silvestre Balboa Troya y Quesada, Espejo de paciencia (Miami: Univer- sal, 1970), pp. 7-38. Orig. CHA, No. 228 (1968), 707-730.

10.4 Chacón y Calvo, José María. "El Espejo de paciencia. Una nueva edición del más antiguo poema escrito en Cuba." RevC, 17 (1943), 119-122.

10.5 _____. "Orígenes de la poesía cubana." In his Ensayos de li- teratura cubana (Madrid: "Saturnino Calleja", 1922), pp. 27-34.

10.6 _____. "El primer poema escrito en Cuba." RFE, 8 (1921), 170- 175.

10.7 Fernández, Clara. "Las alusiones cultas en el poema Espejo de la paciencia de Silvestre Balboa." TLit, No. 14 (1967), 22-23.

10.8 Fernández Carvajal y Bello, E. "Algunas consideraciones sobre las fuentes del Espejo de la paciencia." BACL, 8 (1959), 1-4.

10.9 García del Pino, César. "El obispo Cabezas, Silvestre de Bal- boa y los contrabandistas de Manzanillo." RBNJM, 3a serie, 17, 2 (1975), 13-54.

10.10 Pichardo Moya, Felipe. "Estudio crítico." In Silvestre de Balboa Troya y Quesada, Espejo de paciencia (H: Escuela del Instituto Cívico Militar, 1941), pp. 3-48.

10.11 _____. "Estudio crítico." In Silvestre de Balboa Troya y Quesada, Espejo de paciencia (H: Comisión Nacional Cuba- na de la UNESCO, 1962), pp. 27-40.

10.12   Ponce de León, Néstor. "Los primeros poetas de Cuba." RCub,
        15 (1892), 385-399.

10.13   Sainz, Enrique. "En torno a la autenticidad del Espejo de pa-
        ciencia." RBNJM, 3a serie, 20, 3 (1978), 83-109.

10.14   Vitier, Cintio. "Prólogo." In Silvestre de Balboa Troya y Que-
        sada, Espejo de paciencia (H: Comisión Nacional Cubana de
        la UNESCO, 1962), pp. 9-23.

10.15   _____. "Prólogo y advertencia." In Silvestre de Balboa Troya
        y Quesada, Espejo de paciencia (Santa Clara: Universidad
        de Las Villas, Departamento de Estudios Hispánicos, 1960),
        pp. 5-38.

11. BALLAGAS, EMILIO (1908-1954)

Critical Monographs and Dissertations

11.1 Boulware-Miller, Patricia Kay. "Nature in three 'negrista' poets: Nicolás Guillén, Emilio Ballagas, and Luis Palés Matos." DAI, 39 (1979), 5186A-5187A.

11.2 Bueno, Salvador. La poesía de Emilio Ballagas. H: Unión, 1964.

11.3 Cartey, Wilfred. "The Antillian poets: Emilio Ballagas, Luis Palés Matos, and Nicolás Guillén: literary development of Negro theme in relation to the making of modern Afro-Antillian poetry in the historic evolution of the Negro." DAI, 28 (1967), 2203A.

11.4 Collins, María Castellanos. "Brull, Florit, Ballagas, y el vanguardismo en Cuba." DAI, 37 (1976), 3664A-3665A.

11.5 Emilio Ballagas: el autor y su obra. H: Dirección Nacional de Educación General, 1973.

11.6 Pallas, Rosa. La poesía de Emilio Ballagas. Madrid: Playor, 1973.

11.7 Pryor Rice, Argyll. Emilio Ballagas, poeta o poesía. M: de Andrea, 1966.

11.8 Torre, Rogelio de la. La obra poética de Emilio Ballagas. Miami: Universal, 1977. Orig. as "Emilio Ballagas, poeta de su tiempo." DAI, 34 (1974), 7744A.

Critical Essays

11.9 Antuña, Rosario. "Sobre Emilio Ballagas." Unión, 4, 1 (1965), 123-142.

11.10 Augier, Angel I. "Prólogo." In Emilio Ballagas, Orbita de Emilio Ballagas; 2. ed. (H: Instituto Cubano del Libro, 1972), pp. 7-18. Orig. 1965.

11.11 Bueno, Salvador. "Apuntes sobre la poesía de Emilio Ballagas." IAL, No. 84 (1955), 6-7.

11.12 _____. "Emilio Ballagas ante la muerte." Humanismo, No. 28 (1955), 71-77.

11.13 ____. "La poesía de Emilio Ballagas." In his Temas y perso-
      najes de la literatura cubana (H: Unión, 1964), pp. 237-
      250.

11.14 Casaus, Víctor. "[Orbita de Emilio Ballagas]." Unión, 4, 3
      (1965), 149-152.

11.15 Castañeda, León T. "Guillén y Ballagas." RAm, 25 (1932), 68-
      69.

11.16 Collins, María Castellanos. "Emilio Ballagas y la jitanjáfora."
      In Twenty-Seventh Annual Mountain Interstate Foreign Lan-
      guage Conference (Johnson City, Tenn.: East Tennessee
      State University, Research Council, 1978), pp. 178-185.

11.17 Feijóo, Samuel. "Una añeja entrevista inédita a Emilio Balla-
      gas, en 1938." In his Azar de lecturas; crítica (Santa
      Clara: Universidad Central de Las Villas, Departamento de
      Estudios Hispánicos, 1961), pp. 194-203, 224-225.

11.18 Fernández de la Vega, Oscar, and Alberto N. Pamies. "Emilio
      Ballagas: biografía y bibliografía." In their Iniciación
      a la poesía afro-americana (Miami: Universal, 1973), pp.
      32-36.

11.19 Fernández Retamar, Roberto. "Emilio Ballags." In his La poe-
      sía contemporánea en Cuba (1927-1953) (H: Orígenes, 1954),
      pp. 39-43, 54-56.

11.20 ____. "Recuerdo a Emilio Ballagas." In his Papelería (Santa
      Clara: Universidad Central de Las Villas, Dirección de Pu-
      blicaciones, 1962), pp. 195-204.

11.21 Giner de los Ríos, Francisco. "Forma y color de Emilio Balla-
      gas [Sabor eterno]." Romance, 1, 3 (1940), 18.

11.22 González del Valle, Luis. "Un poema desconocido de Emilio Ba-
      llagas ['Despedida del viernes']." Chasqui, 7, 1 (1977),
      63-66.

11.23 Herrera, Roberto. "La poesía mulata de Emilio Ballagas." Cír-
      culo, 10 (1981), 93-103.

11.24 Linares Pérez, Marta. "Emilio Ballagas, el poeta niño." In
      her La poesía pura en Cuba y su evolución (Madrid: Playor,
      1975), pp. 83-121.

11.25 Marinello, Juan. "Inicial angélica." In his Poética; ensayos
      en entusiasmo (Madrid: Espasa-Calpe, 1933), pp. 49-61.
      Also in his Orbita de Juan Marinello (H: Colección Orbita,
      1968), pp. 63-66.

11.26 ____. "Poesía negra; apuntes desde Guillén y Ballagas." In
      his Poética; ensayos en entusiasmo (Madrid: Espasa-Calpe,
      1933), pp. 99-143.

11.27   Nandino, Elías. "Estudio y pequeña antología poética de Emilio
        Ballagas." Estaciones, 1, 2 (1956), 202-237.

11.28   Paz, Octavio. "Sabor eterno de Emilio Ballagas." Taller, No.
        10 (1940), 52-53.

11.29   Pérez, Ricardo. "Datos para una biografía de Emilio Ballagas."
        Hispania, 48 (1965), 585-586.

11.30   Piñera, Virgilio. "Ballagas en persona." Ciclón, 1, 5 (1955),
        41-50.

11.31   ____. "Dos poetas, dos poemas, dos modos de poesía." EsP, No.
        H (1941), 16-18.

11.32   Polit, Carlos E. "Imagen inocente del negro en cuatro poetas
        antillanos." SinN, 5, 2 (1975), 43-60. Ballagas inter
        alios.

11.33   Pryor Rice, Argyll. "Júbilo y fuga de Emilio Ballagas." RI,
        No. 62 (1966), 167-175.

11.34   Rodríguez Rivera, Guillermo. "Visión de la isla. Emilio Balla-
        gas." Bohemia, 57, 7 (1965), 30-32.

11.35   Sánchez, Luis Alberto. "Emilio Ballagas. 7 noviembre, 1908-11
        setiembre, 1954." Sphinx, No. 15 (1962), 1-8. Also as
        "Emilio Ballagas." In his Escritores representativos de
        América; segunda serie (Madrid: Gredos, 1972), III, 235-
        245.

11.36   Suárez Solís, Rafael. "Nota bibliográfica a Cuaderno de poesía
        negra." RevC, 16 (1941), 155-156.

11.37   Valdés-Cruz, Rosa E. "Emilio Ballagas." In her La poesía ne-
        groide en América (NY: Las Américas, 1970), pp. 77-82.

11.38   Vitier, Cintio. "La poesía de Emilio Ballagas." Lyceum, No.
        40 (1955), 5-34. Also in Emilio Ballagas, Obra poética
        (H: Ucar, García, 1955), pp. v-xli. Also Miami: Mnemosyne,
        1969.

12. BARNET, MIGUEL (1940-   )

Critical Essays

12.1   Angvik, Birger. "Innenfra/utenfra. Et spørsmål om autentisitet i den spansk-amerikanske roman." Vinduet, 26, 3 (1973), 46-50. Barnet inter alios.

12.2   Barnet, Miguel. "La novela documental [Canción de Rachel]." Unión, 9, 4 (1970), 160-167. Also as "La novela testimonio: socio-literatura." In his La canción de Rachel (Barcelona: Estela, 1970), pp. 125-150. Also as "The documentary novel." CS, 11, 1 (1981), 19-32.

12.3   Baycroft, Bernardo. "Miguel Barnet charla con los editores de Vórtice." Vórtice, 2, 2-3 (1979), 1-10.

12.4   Bejel, Emilio F. "Miguel Barnet." Hispamérica, No. 29 (1981), 41-52.

12.5   Campuzano, Luisa. "Al cabo de un siglo de silencio, biografía de un cimarrón." CB, No. 8 (1966), 20-21.

12.6   Casaus, Víctor. "Inventario de cólera y amor." CAm, No. 48 (1968), 143-144.

12.7   Chang-Rodríguez, Raquel. "Sobre La canción de Rachel, novela-testimonio." RI, Nos. 102-103 (1978), 133-138.

12.8   Colina, José de la. "[La piedrafina y el pavorreal]." Bohemia, 56, 14 (1964), 23.

12.9   Collazos, Oscar. "[Canción de Rachel]." CAm, No. 59 (1970), 190-192.

12.10   Morejón, Nancy. "Mi libro es ante todo una venganza [La sagrada familia]." GdC, No. 55 (1967), 6, 14.

12.11   Moreno Fraginéls, Manuel. "[Biografía de un cimarrón]." CAm, No. 40 (1967), 131-132.

12.12   Rigali, Rolando. "Otra vez la poesía." GdC, No. 41 (1964), 23.

12.13   Rodríguez Rivera, Guillermo. "El origen de la familia [La sagrada familia]." Unión, 6, 2 (1968), 152-155.

12.14   Selva, Mauricio de la. "[La sagrada familia]." CA, No. 156 (1968), 277-279.

12.15 Triana, José. "Biografía de un cimarrón: ¿un relato etnográfi-
co como confiesa su autor o una novela?" GdC, No. 52
(1966), 12.

13. BENITEZ ROJO, ANTONIO (1931-   )

Critical Essays

13.1   Acosta, Leonardo. "Benítez gana la partida [Tute de reyes]."
       CAm, No. 45 (1967), 166-169.

13.2   Alvarez Alvarez, Luis. "Faena naciente de Antonio Benítez Ro-
       jo." CAm, No. 111 (1978), 148-150.

13.3   _____. "El mar de lentejas: historia, acción y personajes."
       CAm, No. 116 (1979), 150-155.

13.4   Alvarez García, Imeldo. "La cálida ternura de Antonio Benítez
       Rojo." GdC, No. 160 (1977), 22-23.

13.5   Arenas, Reinaldo. "Benítez en el juego." Unión, 6, 2 (1968),
       146-152.

13.6   Ayala, Delia. "En torno a Tute de reyes." CUn, Nos. 98-99
       (1968), 30-35.

13.7   Chang-Rodríguez, Raquel. "La experiencia revolucionaria en la
       cuentística cubana actual: Los años duros [Jesús Díaz Ro-
       dríguez] y Tute de reyes [Benítez Rojo]." CA, No. 222
       (1979), 59-75.

13.8   _____. "[Heroica]." RCLL, Nos. 7-8 (1978), 221-224.

13.9   Chió, Evangelina. "Hacia el hombre que cabalga." RyC, No. 71
       (1978), 69-75.

13.10 Llopis, Rogelio. "[El escudo de hojas secas]." CAm, No. 62
       (1970), 199-201.

13.11 Luis, César. "Mi tema: el individuo vs. el medio social. Entre-
       vista con Antonio Benítez Rojo (Premio Cuento Casa de las
       Américas 1967)." GdC, No. 55 (1967), 5, 14.

13.12 Martínez Laínez, Fernando. "Entrevista con Antonio Benítez Ro-
       jo." In his Palabra cubana (Madrid: Akal, 1975), pp. 107-
       125.

13.13 Ortega, Julio. "Cuentos, de Antonio Benítez." In his Relato
       de la utopía (Barcelona: La Gaya Ciencia, 1973), pp. 173-
       190.

13.14 Prada Oropeza, Renato. "Cuba: literatura y revolución. Diálo-
       go con Antonio Benítez." Difusión, 1, 2 (1971), 6-7.

13.15 Saldaña, Excilia. "Benítez Rojo: el destructor de mitos." CB,
       2a época, No. 42 (1970), 26-28.

13.16 Sánchez, María Teresa. "¿Qué edita ahora? [La victoria sobre
       los Esterlines]." RyC, No. 63 (1977), 73.

14. BETANCOURT, JOSE RAMON DE (1823-1890)

Critical Essays

14.1 Bernal, Calixto. "Biografía del excmo. señor d. José R. de Betancourt." In José Ramón de Betancourt, Discursos y mani-
fiestos políticos (Madrid: Felipe Pinto, 1887), pp. i-xvii.

14.2 Casal, Julián del. "José Ramón Betancourt." In his Prosas (H:
Consejo Nacional de Cultura, 1963), II, 167-169.

14.3 Franch, Javier. "[Una feria de la caridad en 183 ...]." LH, 2a
serie, 1, 10 (1859), 75-76; 1, 11 (1859), 82-84.

14.4 González de Cascorro, Raúl. "Prólogo." In José Ramón de Betancourt, Una feria de la caridad en 183 ... (H: Letras Cubanas, 1978), pp. 7-14.

14.5 Hernández de Norman, Isabel. "José Ramón de Betancourt (1823-
1890)." In her La novela romántica en las Antillas (NY:
Ateneo Puertorriqueño de Nueva York, 1969), pp. 187-191.

14.6 _____. "José Ramón de Betancourt (1823-1890)." In her La novela
criolla en las Antillas (NY: Plus Ultra, 1977), pp. 187-191.

14.7 Luaces, Joaquín Lorenzo. "[Una feria de la caridad en 183 ...]."
LH, 1, 15 (1859), 115-116; 1, 16 (1859), 124-128.

14.8 Roig de Leuchsenring, Emilio. "José Ramón Betancourt." In his
La literatura costumbrista cubana de los siglos XVIII y XIX
(H: Oficina del Historiador de la Ciudad de la Habana,
1962-), III, 139-148.

14.9 Villaverde, Cirilo. "Juicio crítico." In José Ramón de Betancourt, Una feria de la caridad en 183- (Barcelona: L. Tasso
Serra, 1885), pagination unknown.

15. BETANCOURT, LUIS VICTORIANO (1813-1875)

Critical Monographs and Dissertations

15.1 Córdoba, Federico de. Luis Victoriano Betancourt (1843-1885). H: "El Siglo XX", 1943.

15.2 Rodríguez Cuétara, Eva. Luis Victoriano Betancourt: vida y o- bra. H: Centro de Estudios Políticos y Sociales de Cuba, 1949.

15.3 Santovenia y Echaide, Emeterio Santiago. José Victoriano Be- tancourt, estudio biográfico. H: "La Universal" de Ruiz, 1912.

Critical Essays

15.4 Fidelio. "El Club de Matanzas." RCub, 6 (1879), 73-77.

15.5 González Curquejo, Antonio. "Luis Victoriano Betancourt." CyA, No. 116 (1902), 353-358.

15.6 Iraizoz y de Villar, Antonio. "Luis Victoriano Betancourt." In his Libros y autores cubanos (Santa María de Rosario: Rosareña, 1956), pp. 40-43.

15.7 Remos y Rubio, Juan Nepomuceno José. "...Luis Victoriano Betan- court." In his Los poetas de "Armas amigas" (H: Cárdenas, 1943), pp. 45-81.

15.8 Roa, Ramón. "Luis Victoriano Betancourt." In his Con la pluma y el machete (H: Academia de la Historia de Cuba, 1950), I, 304-305.

15.9 Roig de Leuchsenring, Emilio. "Luis Victoriano Betancourt." In his La literatura costumbrista cubana de los siglos XVIII y XIX (H: Oficina del Historiador de la Ciudad de la Habana, 1962), IV, 229-236.

15.10 Santovenia y Echaide, Emeterio Santiago. "Introducción." In Luis Victoriano Betancourt, Artículos de costumbre (H: Cultural, 1929), pp. v-li.

15.11 _____. "Luis Victoriano Betancourt y los derechos de la mujer." Carteles, 13, 2 (1929), 47.

15.12 Suárez-Murias, Marguerite C. "Cuba painted by Cubans: the nineteenth century." RIB, 30 (1980), 375-386.

16. BOBADILLA, EMILIO ("Fray Candil," 1862-1921)

Critical Monographs and Dissertations

16.1   Barinaga y Ponce de León, Graziella. Estudio crítico biográfico de Emilio Bobadilla (Fray Candil). H: Carasa, 1926.

16.2   Entralgo, Elías José. La cubanía de Fray Candil. H: "El Siglo XX", 1957.

16.3   _____. Una vocación y un temperamento: desde Emilio Bobadilla hasta después de Fray Candil. H: Universidad de la Habana, 1958.

16.4   Ledesma de los Reyes, Pedro Pablo. "Spanish civilization in the works of Emilio Bobadilla." DAI, 38 (1977), 308A.

Critical Essays

16.5   Alas, Leopoldo. "Prólogo." In Emilio Bobadilla, Escaramuzas (sátiras y críticas) (Madrid: Librería de Fernando Fé, 1888), pp. vii-xxix. Signed Clarín.

16.6   Bazil, Osvaldo. "Fray Candil o las antipatías." In his Cabezas de América (H: Molina, 1933), pp. 37-43.

16.7   Bueno, Salvador. "Fray Candil, crítico iconoclasta." In his Figuras cubanas del siglo XIX (H: Unión de Escritores y Artistas, 1980), pp. 305-316. Orig. Bohemia, 55, 19 (1963), 86-87.

16.8   _____. "'Fray Candil' en una novela." In Emilio Bobadilla, A fuego lento (H: Editorial de la Universidad de la Habana, 1965), pp. ix-xl.

16.9   _____. "Rehabilitación de Fray Candil." CUNESCO, 1, 3 (1962), 26-27.

16.10 Castellanos, Jesús. "Emilio Bobadilla." In his Los optimistas (H: Academia de Artes y Letras, 1914), pp. 279-284. Also in his Colección póstuma (H: El Siglo XX de A. Miranda, 1914-1916), I, 279-284.

16.11 Cruz, Manuel de la. "De 'Fray Candil' (cartas abiertas)." In his Literatura cubana (Madrid: Calleja, 1924), pp. 377-389.

16.12 García Pons, César. "Un gran escritor olvidado, Emilio Bobadilla." RBC, 68 (1946), 91-102.

16.13 González Serrano, U. "Prólogo." In Emilio Bobadilla, Solfeo (crítica y sátira) (Madrid: M. Tello, 1893), pp. v-xxii.

16.14 Heredia, José María de. "[Carta-prólogo]." In Emilio Bobadilla, Vórtice; 4. ed. (Madrid: V. Suárez, 1902), pp. vii-xii.

16.15 Labrador Ruiz, Enrique. "Emilio Bobadilla." In his El pan de los muertos (Santa Clara: Universidad Central de Las Villas, 1958), pp. 33-40.

16.16 Martí, José. "Piedad Zenea y Emilio Bobadilla." In his Obras completas (H: Editorial Nacional de Cuba, 1963), V, 456.

16.17 Martínez Ruiz, José. "Un libro de Fray Candil." In his Los valores literarios (Madrid: Caro-Raggio, 1921), pp. 57-62.

16.18 Mesa y Surama, Domingo. "Prólogo." In Emilio Bobadilla, Artículos periodísticos (H: Ediciones del Cincuentenario, 1952), pp. 7-31.

16.19 Pogolotti, Marcelo. "El bilioso Bobadilla." In his La república de Cuba al través de sus escritores (H: Lex, 1958), pp. 17-22.

16.20 Rodríguez, Emilio Gaspar. "Emilio Bobadilla." Social, 6, 2 (1921), 19.

16.21 Sanguily y Garritte, Manuel. "Otro libro de Emilio Bobadilla: Escaramuzas." RCub, 8 (1888), 43-59, 136-150. Also in his Juicios literarios (H: Molina, 1930), I, 41-92. His Obras, VII.

16.22 Varona y Pera, Enrique José. "Reflejos de Fray Candil, por Emilio Bobadilla." RCub, 5 (1887), 365-375.

17. BORRERO, JUANA (1877-1896)

Critical Monographs and Dissertations

17.1 Augier, Angel I. *Juana Borrero, la adolescente atormentada.* H: Molina, 1938.

17.2 González, Manuel Pedro. *Amor y mito en Juana Borrero.* Montevideo: Centro de Estudios Latinoamericanos, 1973, c1972.

Critical Essays

17.3 Augier, Angel I. "En torno al epistolario de Juana Borrero y los 'escolios' a este libro por Manuel Pedro González." *L/L*, No. 1 (1970), 155-165. See item no. 17.12.

17.4 Borrero, Dulce María. "Evocación de Juana Borrero." *RevC*, 20 (1945), 5-63.

17.5 Bueno, Salvador. "Epistolario de una escritora cubana." *Unión*, 5, 3 (1966), 172-175.

17.6 _____. "Juana Borrero, la poetisa adolescente." In his *Figuras cubanas del siglo XIX* (H: Unión de Escritores y Artistas, 1980), pp. 371-375.

17.7 Carricarte, Arturo R. de. "Juana Borrero." *Bohemia*, 3, 47 (1912), 561-562.

17.8 Casal, Julián del. "Juana Borrero." In his *Bustos y rimas* (H: Molina, 1938), pp. 75-91.

17.9 Cuza Malé, Belkis. "El clavel y la rosa." *GdC*, No. 155 (1977), 8-9.

17.10 Darío, Rubén. "Juana Borrero." In José María Monner Sans, *Julián del Casal y el modernismo hispanoamericano* (M: El Colegio de México, 1952), pp. 250-254.

17.11 Dobuen, Alvaro S. "Juana Borrero, la poetisa adolescente." *Carteles*, 34, 22 (1953), 58.

17.12 González, Manuel Pedro. "Escolios al *Epistolario* de Juana Borrero." *L/L*, No. 1 (1970), 103-150. See also items 17.3 and 17.18.

17.13 González López, Waldo. "Juana Borrero." *Bohemia*, 69, 22 (1977), 29.

17.14 Núñez, Ana Rosa. "Juana Borrero: portrait of a poetess." Carrell, 16 (1976), 1-21.

17.15 "Para el epistolario de Juana Borrero." L/L, No. 6 (1975), 197-
205.

17.16 Vitier, Cintio. "Las cartas de amor de Juana Borrero." CAL,
No. 2 (1969), 20-40. Also in his Crítica sucesiva (H:
Contemporáneos, UNEAC, 1971), pp. 365-407.

17.17 _____. "En el centenario de Juana Borrero." Bohemia, 69, 23
(1977), 10-13.

17.18 _____. "Notas sobre los 'Escolios al epistolario de Juana Borrero' por Manuel Pedro González." L/L, No. 1 (1970),
151-154. See item no. 17.12.

18. BOTI, REGINO ELADIO (1878-1958)

Critical Monographs and Dissertations

18.1 Suarée, Octavio de la, Jr. La obra literaria de Regino E. Boti. NY: Senda Nueva, 1977. Orig. as "The literary works of Regino E. Boti." DAI, 37 (1976), 1588A.

Critical Essays

18.2 Acosta, Agustín. "Elegía en la muerte de Regino Boti." BACL, 7, 3-4 (1958), 246.

18.3 Aparicio Laurencio, Angel. "Guantánamo en la obra de Regino E. Boti." BACL, 7, 3-4 (1958), 247-272.

18.4 _____. "Regino E. Boti, miembro de la Academia Cubana de la Lengua." BACL, 7, 3-4 (1958), 217-219.

18.5 "Centenario de Regino E. Boti." GdC, No. 166 (1978), 23.

18.6 Chacón y Calvo, José María. "Homenaje a Regino E. Boti." BACL, 7, 3-4 (1958), 223-226.

18.7 Chaple, Sergio. "El epistolario de Boti-Poveda." L/L, No. 6 (1975), 89-113.

18.8 Duchesne, Concepción. "Boti: cien años de su natalicio." Bohemia, 70, 9 (1978), 25.

18.9 Fernández Retamar, Roberto. "En los 80 años de Regino Boti." Islas, 1, 2 (1959), 311-329. Also in his Papelería (H: Universidad Central de Las Villas, Dirección de Publicaciones, 1962), pp. 39-69.

18.10 Gay Calbó, Enrique. "Regino E. Boti, el árbol del Rey David." CCont, 27 (1921), 82-86.

18.11 _____. "Regino E. Boti, hipsipilas." CCont, 25 (1921), 429-433.

18.12 Jimenes Grullón, Juan Isidro. "Regino E. Boti." In his Seis poetas cubanos (ensayos apologéticos) (H: "Cromos", 1954), pp. 11-31.

18.13 Jiménez, José Olivio. "La poesía de Regino E. Boti en su momento." BACL, 7, 3-4 (1958), 227-245. Also in his Estudios sobre poesía cubana contemporánea (NY: Las Américas, 1967), pp. 7-27.

18.14 Lizaso y González, Félix. "Regino E. Boti." In his Ensayistas contemporáneos, 1900-1920 (H: Trópico, 1938), pp. 64-67.

18.15 López Morales, Eduardo E. "La palabra y la poética de Regino E. Boti." ULH, Nos. 184-185 (1967), 107-126.

18.16 Mañach, Jorge. "[La nueva poesía en Cuba]." Avance, No. 14 (1927), 53.

18.17 Marinello, Juan. "Notas acerca de José Manuel Poveda, por Regino E. Boti y Héctor Poveda." Avance, No. 23 (1928), 160.

18.18 Martínez, Miguel A. "Criolloismo y humorismo en la obra de Regino E. Boti." REH, 11 (1977), 347-364.

18.19 Medrano, Higinio J. "Prosas del norte. Regino E. Boti." Bohemia, 3, 35 (1912), 418.

18.20 Orta Ruiz, Jesús. "Revalorización patriótica y social de 'El cucalambé'." Bohemia, 66, 27 (1974), 12-19.

18.21 Portuondo, José Antonio. "Regino Eladio Boti." NTiem, 5, 26 (1958), 8-9.

18.22 Poveda, Héctor. "Cierto poeta..." Avance, No. 18 (1928), 7.

18.23 _____. "El resplandor de la patología sobre el arte." CCont, 43 (1927), 151.

18.24 Poveda, José Manuel. "Regino E. Boti y la lírica actual." CyA, 18, 3 (1913), 141-143. Also in his José Manuel Poveda (H: Instituto de Literatura y Lingüística de la Academia de Ciencias de Cuba, 1975), pp. 305-315.

18.25 Suarée, Octavio de la, Jr. "Del modernismo a la vanguardia: las ideas estéticas de Regino E. Boti." In Estudios críticos sobre la prosa modenista hispanoamericana (NY: Eliseo Torres, 1975), pp. 281-291.

18.26 _____. "La variedad estética del vanguardismo en la obra de Regino E. Boti." CH, 1 (1979), 15-23.

18.27 Torre, Miguel Angel de la. "Arabescos mentales, de Regino E. Boti." Bohemia, 4, 41 (1913), 482.

18.28 Torriente, Loló de la. "Boti y Poveda: el provincialismo literario." GdC, No. 173 (1978), 26-27.

18.29 Vasconcelos, Ramón. "Regino E. Boti, poeta de su aldea." Bohemia, 38, 43 (1946), 35, 56.

19. BRULL, MARIANO (1891-1956)

Critical Monographs and Dissertations

19.1 Collins, María Castellanos. "Brull, Florit, Ballagas, y el vanguardismo en Cuba." DAI, 37 (1976), 3664A-3665A.

Critical Essays

19.2 Baquero, Gastón. "En la muerte de Mariano Brull." RBNC, 2a serie, 7, 2 (1956), 173-178. Also CUNESCO, 5, 7 (1956), 4-7.

19.3 Chacón y Calvo, José María. "En la muerte de un amigo: Mariano Brull." BACL, 5, 1-4 (1956), 203-205.

19.4 Fello, Jaime. "Poetas contemporáneos de América: Mariano Brull." RevAm, 11 (1947), 39-43.

19.5 Fernández Retamar, Roberto. "Mariano Brull." In his La poesía contemporánea en Cuba (1927-1935) (H: Orígenes, 1954), pp. 33-34.

19.6 Florit, Eugenio. "Mariano Brull y la poesía cubana de vanguardia." In Instituto Internacional de Literatura Iberoamericana, XI Congreso (M, 1965), pp. 55-63. Also in his Poesía, casi siempre (ensayos literarios) (Madrid/NY: Mensaje, 1978), pp. 149-157.

19.7 _____. "[Poemas en menguante]." Avance, No. 30 (1929), 25.

19.8 No item.

19.9 Henríquez Ureña, Max. "Tránsito y poesía de Mariano Brull." BACL, 7, 1-2 (1958), 49-69.

19.10 Jérez Villarreal, Jean[?]. "Mariano Brull y Caballero. Ríen que..." América, 44, 3 (1954), 96.

19.11 Jiménez, José Olivio. "Destino humano de la rosa." Brecha, 5, 12 (1961), pagination unknown.

19.12 Linares Pérez, Marta. "Mariano Brull, el iniciador." In his La poesía pura en Cuba y su evolución (Madrid: Playor, 1975), pp. 55-82.

19.13 "Mariano Brull. Solo de rosa." América, 20, 1-2 (1943), 90.

19.14 Matas, Julio. "Mariano Brull y la poesía pura en Cuba." NRC, 1, 3 (1959), 60-77.

19.15 Posada, Rafael. "La jitjanjáfora revisitada." ALHisp, Nos. 2-3 (1973-1974), 55-82.

19.16 Reyes, Alfonso. "Alcance a las jitjanjáforas." Avance, No. 46 (1930), 133-134.

19.17 Rodríguez-Luis, Julio. "Recuerdo de Mariano Brull." Ciclón, 2, 5 (1956), 3-6.

19.18 Russell, Dora Isella. "Personalidad y obra poética de Mariano Brull." América, 50, 1-3 (1956), 42-43.

19.19 Valéry, Paul. "Prefacio a los poemas de Mariano Brull." EsP, Nos. E-F (1940), 3.

19.20 Valle, Rafael Heliodoro. "Diálogo con Mariano Brull." UM, No. 14 (1947), 1-4.

19.21 Vitier, Cintio. "Mariano Brull, una traducción de La jeune parque." RevC, 28 (1951), 176-185. Also as "Una traducción de La jeune parque." In his Crítica sucesiva (H: Instituto del Libro, 1971), pp. 57-66.

20. BUZZI, DAVID (1933-   )

Critical Essays

20.1   Aparicio, Raúl. "Acotación a Los desnudos." Unión, 6, 3 (1967), 124-131.

20.2   Arenas, Reinaldo. "Mariana entre los hombres [Mariana]." GdC, No. 86 (1970), 28-29.

20.3   Buzzi, David. "Encuesta." GdC, No. 164 (1978), 9-10.

20.4   Chang-Rodríguez, Raquel. "Sobre el realismo socialista y Los desnudos de David Buzzi." RyFa, No. 36 (1974), 3-15.

20.5   Correal, José A. "[Sol de los talleres]." RI, Nos. 112-113 (1980), 657-659.

20.6   "El creador y su obra." GdC, No. 86 (1970), 19.

20.7   Cuza Malé, Belkis. "Una novela al desnudo [Los desnudos]." GdC, No. 60 (1967), 19.

20.8   Fernández, Pablo Armando. "Buzzi y el sueño compartido [Mariana]." Unión, 9, 4 (1970), 153-156.

20.9   Heras León, Eduardo. "Los elefantes al desnudo [La religión de los elefantes]." Unión, 6, 2 (1969), 144-149.

20.10 Oráa, Pedro de. "Todos los desheredados." GdC, No. 75 (1969), 28-29.

20.11 Sáez, Luis M. "Cinco preguntas a cinco menciones." Bohemia, 58, 11 (1966), 24-25. Buzzi inter alios.

21. BYRNE, BONIFACIO (1861-1936)

Bibliographies

21.1 Moliner, Israel M. Indice bio-bibliográfico de Bonifacio Byrne. Matanzas: Carreño, 1943.

Critical Monographs and Dissertations

21.2 Piedra-Bueno, Andrés de. Evocación de Byrne y Martí americanista. H: Escuela Tipográfica de la Institución Inclán, 1942.

Critical Essays

21.3 Blanco Cabrera, Gladys. "Bonifacio Byrne. El poeta cubano que escribió sobre los soviets rusos." VO, 17, 15 (1975), 30-33.

21.4 _____. "En versos inéditos: la rebeldía estudiantil universitaria." Romance, 41, 3 (1978), 14-16.

21.5 _____. "La inédita poesía antiimperialista de Bonifacio Byrne." Bohemia, 69, 3 (1977), 10-13.

21.6 Bueno, Salvador. "Bonifacio Byrne: poeta de la bandera." In his Figuras cubanas del siglo XIX (H: Unión de Escritores y Artistas, 1980), pp. 183-188. Orig. Bohemia, 64, 11 (1972), 98-101.

21.7 Carbonell y Rivero, José Manuel. "Lira y espada." CyA, No. 103 (1901), 321-323.

21.8 Casal, Julián del. "Bonifacio Byrne." In his Bustos y rimas (H: La Moderna, 1893), pp. 93-103.

21.9 "Homenaje a Bonifacio Byrne." Museo, 1, 9-10 (1961), entire issue.

21.10 Iznaga, Alcides. "Byrne, poeta de la guerra." Bohemia, 69, 37 (1977), 29.

21.11 Lazo, Raimundo. "Bonifacio Byrne a los cien años." ULH, Nos. 151-153 (1961), 105-121.

21.12 Medrano, Higinio J. "Un libro de Byrne." Letras, 2a época, 10, 21 (1914), 245.

21.13   Salazar y Roig, Salvador. "Antologías de poetas cubanos contem-
        poráneos. Bonifacio Byrne." A̲C̲, 2, 5 (1924), 186-188.

21.14   Salom, Diwaldo. "Sobre un poema socialista. Divagaciones."
        Letras, 2a época, 2, 14 (1906), no pagination; 2, 15
        (1906), no pagination; 2, 16 (1906), no pagination; 2, 17
        (1906), no pagination.

21.15   Zamora Céspedes, Vladimir, and Arturo Arango Arias. "Un poeta
        de la guerra." C̲B̲, 2a época, No. 93 (1975), 7-8.

22. CABALLERO Y RODRIGUEZ, JOSE AGUSTIN (1762-1835)

Bibliographies

22.1 González del Valle y Ramírez, Francisco, and Emilio Roig de Leuchsenring. "Bibliografía de José Agustín Caballero y Rodríguez." RevC, 1 (1935), 62-67. Also in Homenaje al ilustre habanero, q.v., pp. 23-27.

22.2 ____. "Bibliografía [de y sobre] José Agustín Caballero y Rodríguez." RBC, 35 (1935), 177-183.

Critical Monographs and Dissertations

22.3 Agramonte y Pichardo, Roberto. José Agustín Caballero y los orígenes de la conciencia cubana. H: Ucar y García, 1952.

22.4 Castro y Bachiller, Raimundo de. A la memoria de un maestro en el centenario de su muerte: presbítero José Agustín Caballero. H: Molina, 1937.

22.5 González del Valle y Ramírez, Francisco. Dos orientadores de la enseñanza. El padre José Agustín Caballero y José de la Luz y Caballero. H: Molina, 1935.

22.6 Homenaje al ilustre habanero pbro. Dr. José Agustín Caballero y Rodríguez en el centenario de su muerte, 1835-1935. H: Municipio de la Habana, 1935. Pertinent items are listed separately.

22.7 Méndez, Manuel Isidro. Notas para el estudio de las ideas éticas en Cuba (siglo XIX: José A. Caballero, Félix Varela y José de la Luz y Caballero). H: Lex, 1947.

Critical Essays

22.8 Agramonte y Pichardo. "José Agustín Caballero, filósofo del criollismo." CA, No. 59 (1951), 98-116.

22.9 ____. "José Agustín Caballero y la reforma filosófica cubana." ULH, Nos. 52-54 (1944), 7-49.

22.10 Castro y Bachiller, Raimundo de. "Presbítero José Agustín Caballero." RBC, 39 (1937), 5-27.

22.11 "Documentos referentes a José Agustín Caballero y Rodríguez,
       conservados en el archivo del doctor F. de P. Coronado."
       RBC, 35 (1935), 184-189.

22.12 Escoto, José Augusto. "José Agustín Caballero reformador de
       los estudios históricos en Cuba." RHCB, 1, 2 (1916), 150-
       156.

22.13 González del Valle y Ramírez, Francisco. "El padre José Agustín
       Caballero." RevC, 1, 4-6 (1936), 32-52.

22.14 _____. "Páginas para la historia de Cuba: documentos para la
       biografía del padre José Agustín Caballero." CCont, 29
       (1922), 73-85.

22.15 Luz y Caballero, José de la. "A la memoria del doctor don José
       Agustín Caballero." In his Escritos literarios (H: Univer-
       sidad de la Habana, 1946), pp. 178-197.

22.16 _____. "Filósofos cubanos. El presbítero don José Agustín Ca-
       ballero." RdC, 3 (1878), 481-491.

22.17 Menocal, Raimundo. "El presbítero José Agustín Caballero y el
       padre Félix Varela." In his Origen y desarrollo del pen-
       samiento cubano (H: Lex, 1945), I, 159-204.

22.18 Monal, Isabel. "Tres filósofos del centenario." ULH, No. 192
       (1968), 111-129. Caballero inter alios.

22.19 Prat Puig, Francisco. "El pbro. José Agustín Caballero y el
       obispo de Trespalacios." RBC, 46 (1940), 245-255.

22.20 Quiroz Martínez, Olga. "José Agustín Caballero y el eclecti-
       cismo del siglo XVIII." ULH, Nos. 73-75 (1947), 58-84.

22.21 Rexach, Rosario. "El padre José Agustín Caballero y la forma-
       ción de la conciencia cubana." CUA, No. 43 (1952), 23-40.

22.22 Roig de Leuchsenring, Emilio. "El centenario de la muerte de
       José Agustín Caballero y Rodríguez." In Homenaje al ilus-
       tre habanero, q.v., pp. 7-22. Also RBC, 35 (1935), 161-
       176.

22.23 Vallejos, Miguel A. Raúl. "José Agustín Caballero o el eclec-
       ticismo sistemático." RBNC, 2a serie, 4, 2 (1955), 95-101.

22.24 Vitier, Medardo. "La enseñanza del padre José Agustín Caballe-
       ro." In his La filosofía en Cuba (M: Fondo de Cultura Eco-
       nómica, 1948), pp. 49-59. Also in his Las ideas y la filo-
       sofía en Cuba (H: Ciencias Sociales, 1970), pp. 329-338.

22.25 _____. "José Agustín Caballero." In his Estudios, notas, efi-
       gies cubanas (M: Minerva, 1944), pp. 205-207.

22.26 _____. "El P. José Agustín Caballero." ULH, Nos. 50-51 (1943),
       78-89.

22.27 Zayas y Alfonso, Alfredo. "El presbítero don José Agustín Ca-
       ballero." <u>RCub</u>, 14 (1891), 5-28.

23. CABRERA, LYDIA (1899-   )

Critical Monographs and Dissertations

23.1   Homenaje a Lydia Cabrera. Miami: Universal, 1978. Pertinent
        items are listed separately.

23.2   Inclán, Josefina. Ayapá y otras otán iyebiyé de Lydia Cabrera.
        Miami: Universal, 1976.

23.3   Perera Soto, Hilda. Idapo, el sincretismo en los Cuentos ne-
        gros de Lydia Cabrera. Miami: Universal, 1971.

23.4   Valdés-Cruz, Rosa E. Lo ancestral africano en la narrativa de
        Lydia Cabrera. Barcelona: Vosgos, 1974.

Critical Essays

23.5   Arcocha, José Antonio. "Vislumbración de Lydia Cabrera." AA,
        1, 1 (1970), 6-7.

23.6   Ben-Ur, Lorraine Elena. "Diálogo con Lydia Cabrera." Caribe,
        .2, 2 (1971), 131-137.

23.7   Carpentier, Alejo. "Los cuentos de Lydia Cabrera." Carteles,
        28, 41 (1936), 40.

23.8   González, Manuel Pedro. "Cuentos y recuentos de Lydia Cabrera."
        NRC, 1, 2 (1959), 153-161.

23.9   Gordo-Guarinos, Francisco. "El negrismo de Lydia Cabrera visto
        con perspectiva de España." In Homenaje a Lydia Cabrera,
        q.v., pp. 25-30.

23.10   Guzmán, Cristina. "Diálogo con Lydia Cabrera." ZF, No. 24
        (1981), 34-38.

23.11   Hiriart, Rosario. "En torno al mundo negro de Lydia Cabrera."
        CHA, No. 359 (1980), 433-440. Also Américas, 32, 3 (1980),
        40-42. Also as "Lydia Cabrera and the world of Cuba's
        blacks." Américas [English edition], 32, 3 (1980), 40-42.

23.12   _____. "La expresión viva en la ficción: Lydia Cabrera e Hilda
        Perera." Círculo, 8 (1979), 125-131.

23.13   _____. "El tiempo y los símbolos en Cuentos negros de Cuba."
        In Homenaje a Lydia Cabrera, q.v., pp. 31-34.

23.14 Irizarry, Estelle. "Lydia Cabrera, fabuladora surrealista." In Rose S. Minc, The contemporary Latin American short story (NY: Senda Nueva, 1979), pp. 105-111.

23.15 Josephs, Allen. "Lydia and Federico [García Lorca]: towards a historical approach to Lorca studies." JSSTC, 6 (1978), 123-130.

23.16 León, Argeliers. "El monte, de Lydia Cabrera." NTiem, 2, 7 (1955), 15-16.

23.17 Lezama Lima, José. "El nombre de Lydia Cabrera." In his Tratados de la Habana (H: Universidad Central de Las Villas, Departamento de Relaciones Culturales, 1958), pp. 144-148.

23.18 Madrigal, José A. "El mito paradisíaco y la poesía afrocubana contemporánea." In Homenaje a Lydia Cabrera, q.v., pp. 35-39.

23.19 Miomandre, Francis de. "Introduction." In Lydia Cabrera, Contes negres de Cuba (Paris: Gallimard, 1936), pp. 9-15.

23.20 ____. "Sobre El monte, de Lydia Cabrera." Orígenes, No. 39 (1955), 75-78.

23.21 Montes Huidobro, Matías. "Itinerario del ebó." Círculo, 8 (1979), 105-114.

23.22 ____. "Lydia Cabrera: observaciones estructurales sobre su narrativa." In Homenaje a Lydia Cabrera, q.v., pp. 41-50.

23.23 Novás Calvo, Lino. "Los cuentos de Lydia Cabrera." Exilio, 3, 2 (1969), 17-20.

23.24 ____. "El monte." PSA, No. 150 (1968), 298-304.

23.25 Ortiz, Fernando. "Dos nuevos libros del folklore afrocubano." RBC, 42 (1938), 307-319.

23.26 ____. "Lydia Cabrera, una cubana afroamericanista." Crónica, 1, 3 (1949), 7-8.

23.27 ____. "Prólogo." In Lydia Cabrera, Cuentos negros de Cuba (H: Nuevo Mundo, 1961), pp. 9-12.

23.28 Ortiz Aponte, Sally. "La virtud del árbol Dagame, de Lydia Cabrera." In her La esoteria en la narrativa hispanoamericana (Río Piedras, P.R.?: Editorial Universitaria, Universidad de Puerto Rico, 1977), pp. 231-238.

23.29 Perera Soto, Hilda. "El aché de Lydia Cabrera." In Homenaje a Lydia Cabrera, q.v., pp. 51-59.

23.30 R. B. "Los negros en Cuba." IAL, No. 127 (1959), 24. Cabrera inter alios.

23.31   Rodríguez-Florida, Jorge J. "Función del doble en los Cuentos
        negros y en Por qué..." In Homenaje a Lydia Cabrera, q.v.,
        pp. 61-71.

23.32   Ruiz del Vizo, Hortensia. "La función del monte en la obra de
        Lydia Cabrera." In Homenaje a Lydia Cabrera, q.v., pp.
        73-82.

23.33   Sánchez-Boudy, José. "La armonía universal en la obra de Lydia
        Cabrera." In Homenaje a Lydia Cabrera, q.v., pp. 83-92.

23.34   Torre, Guillermo de. "Literatura de color." RBC, 38 (1936),
        5-11. Lydia Cabrera inter alios.

23.35   Valdés-Cruz, Rosa E. "African heritage in folktales." In Actes
        du VIIe Congrès de l'Association Internationale de Littéra-
        ture Comparée (Stuttgart: Bieber, 1979), pp. 327-330.

23.36   _____. "Los cuentos de Lydia Cabrera: ¿transposiciones o crea-
        ciones?" In Homenaje a Lydia Cabrera, q.v., pp. 93-99.

23.37   _____. "Mitos africanos conservados en Cuba y su tratamiento
        literario por Lydia Cabrera." Chasqui, 3, 1 (1973), 31-36.

23.38   _____. "El realismo mágico en los Cuentos negros de Lydia Ca-
        brera." In Instituto Internacional de Literatura Iberoa-
        mericana, Otros mundos otros fuegos: fantasía y realismo
        mágico en Iberoamérica (East Lansing, Mich.: Michigan
        State University, Latin American Studies Center, 1975),
        pp. 206-209.

23.39   _____. "The short stories of Lydia Cabrera: transpositions or
        creations?" In Latin American women writers: yesterday
        and today (Pittsburgh: Latin American Literary Review,
        1977), pp. 148-154.

23.40   Viera, Ricardo. "Arte visual y la palabra de Lydia Cabrera."
        In Homenaje a Lydia Cabrera, q.v., pp. 101-108.

23.41   Zambrano, María. "Lydia Cabrera, poeta de la metamorfosis."
        Orígenes, No. 25 (1950), 11-15.

24. CABRERA INFANTE, GUILLERMO (1929-)

Bibliographies

24.1 Foster, David William. "A bibliography of the fiction of Carpentier, Cabrera Infante, and Lezama Lima." Abraxas, 1, 3 (1971), 305-310.

Critical Monographs and Dissertations

24.2 Alvarez-Borland, Isabel D. "Modes of writing in the prose of Guillermo Cabrera Infante." DAI, 41 (1980), 270A.

24.3 Carpenter, Jane French. "The ontological prision: paradoxes of perception in the contemporary Latin American novel." DAI, 36 (1975), 918A.

24.4 Guillermo Cabrera Infante. Madrid: Espiral/Fundamentos, 1974. Pertinent items are listed separately.

24.5 Hayworth, Karen Lyn Getty. "Language as technique in Tres tristes tigres and El recurso del método." DAI, 40 (1979), 3333A.

24.6 Jiménez, Reynaldo L. Guillermo Cabrera Infante y Tres tristes tigres. Miami: Universal, 1976. Orig. DAI, 35 (1975), 7907A.

24.7 Merrim, Stephanie. Logos and the word: the novel of language and linguistic motivation in Grande sertão: veredas [by João Guimarães Rosa] and Tres tristes tigres. NY: Verlag Peter Lang, 1983. Orig. as "Logos and the word: the role of language in Grande sertão: veredas and Tres tristes tigres." DAI, 40 (1979), 286A-287A.

24.8 Mickelsen, Vicki Gillespie. "Games novelists play: technical experiments in La muerte de Artemio Cruz [by Carlos Fuentes], La casa verde [by Mario Vargas Llosa], Tres tristes tigres, and Rayuela [by Julio Cortázar]." DAI, 35 (1974), 4537A.

24.9 Nelson, Ardis L. Cabrera Infante and the Menippean tradition. Newark, Del.: Juan de la Cuesta, 1982. Orig. as "Characterization and Menippean satire in the major works of Guillermo Cabrera Infante." DAI, 41 (1981), 4052A.

24.10 Older, Dora Vázquez. "El juego contradictorio en Cabrera Infante." DAI, 38 (1978), 4862A-4863A.

24.11   Pereda, Rosa María. Guillermo Cabrera Infante. Madrid: EDAF,
        1978.

24.12   Sánchez-Boudy, José. La nueva novela hispanoamericana y Tres
        tristes tigres. Miami: Universal, 1971.

24.13   Siemens, William L. "Guillermo Cabrera Infante: language and
        creativity." DAI, 32 (1972), 5807A.

Critical Essays

24.14   Acosta-Belén, Edna. "The literary exorcisms of Guillermo Ca-
        brera Infante." CH, 3, 2 (1981), 99-110.

24.15   Alvarez-Borland, Isabel D. "El cine documental y las viñetas
        de G. Cabrera Infante." ExTL, 11 (1982-1983), 3-10.

24.16   _____. "Viaje verbal a La Habana, ¡Ah Vana! Entrevista de Isa-
        bel Alvarez Borland con G. Cabrera Infante, arquitecto de
        una ciudad de palabras erigida en el tiempo." Hispamérica,
        No. 31 (1982), 51-68.

24.17   Arcocha, José Antonio. "Dicotomías: Lezama Lima y Cabrera In-
        fante." Aportes, No. 11 (1969), 59-65.

24.18   Armengol Ríos, Armando. "Tres tristes tigres en tesis." RUM,
        33, 8 (1979), 53. See item no. 24.6.

24.19   Arrufat, Antón. "Vista del autor fuera del trópico." Cuba,
        No. 37 (1965), 27-29.

24.20   "Ataque de Cabrera Infante a la revolución y respuesta de inte-
        lectuales argentinos." GdC, No. 67 (1968), 8-10.

24.21   Avila, Leopoldo. "Respuesta de Caín." VO, No. 44 (1968), 17-
        48.

24.22   Ben-Ur, Lorraine Elena. "Hacia la novela del Caribe: Guillermo
        Cabrera Infante y Luis Rafael Sánchez." REH-PR, 5 (1978),
        129-138.

24.23   Benítez Villabla, Jesús. "[O]." ALHisp, No. 4 (1975), 331-334.

24.24   Bensoussan, Albert. "Entrevistas: Guillermo Cabrera Infante."
        Insula, No. 286 (1970), 4. Also as "Trois tristes tigres:
        entretien avec G. Cabrera Infante." LanM, 64 (1970), 297-
        301.

24.25   _____. "Tres tristes tigres de G. Cabrera Infante et la censu-
        re espagnole: restitution du texte original." LNL, No.
        207 (1973), 81-85.

24.26   Bilder, J. Raben. "Tres tristes tigres." CarR, 4, 3 (1972),
        28-30.

24.27 Block de Behar, Lisa. "Una lectura diferente: el juego como nuevo recurso anagógico." In her Análisis de un lenguaje en crisis (Montevideo: Nuestra Tierra, 1969), pp. 95-103.

24.28 Borges, Beatriz, and Flora Süssekind. "Tres triste tigres: um blasfemo jogo de espelhos." José, 1, 2 (1976), 39-44.

24.29 Cabrera, Vicente. "La destrucción de la creación de Tres tristes tigres." RI, Nos. 96-97 (1976), 553-559.

24.30 ____. "Diálogo de Tres tristes tigres y una Cobra con Cervantes y Góngora." CA, No. 228 (1980), 114-123.

24.31 Cabrera Infante, Guillermo. "(C)ave attempotor! A chronology of GCI (after Laurence Sterne's)." Review, Nos. 4-5 (1972), 5-9.

24.32 ____. "Epilogue for late(nt) readers." Review, Nos. 4-5 (1972), 23-32.

24.33 ____. "El presentador presentado." Vuelta, No. 38 (1980), 10-11.

24.34 ____. "30 respuestas para Alex Zisman." Plural, No. 31 (1974), 57-60.

24.35 Castro Arenas, Mario. "Guerrilleros de la novela." CLEB, 6 (1969), 26-34. Cabrera Infante inter alios.

24.36 Coddou, Marcelo. "Tres tristes tigres de Cabrera Infante." Atenea, No. 424 (1970), 83-86.

24.37 Colina, José de la. "[Exorcismos de esti(1)o]." Vuelta, No. 2 (1977), 41-42.

24.38 Corrales Egea, José. "Diálogo con Guillermo Cabrera Infante." CAm, Nos. 17-18 (1963), 49-62.

24.39 ____. "Tres escritores hispanoamericanos en París: con Guillermo Cabrera Infante." Insula, No 195 (1963), 7.

24.40 Cozarinsky, Edgardo. "[Páginas del libro de la noche: Arcadia todas las noches]." Escandalar, 3, 1 (1980), 91-92.

24.41 Fornet, Ambrosio. "Las caras de la violencia [Así en la paz como en la guerra]." In his En tres y dos (H: R, 1964), pp. 43-52.

24.42 Foster, David William. "Hacia una caracterización de la escritura de Vista del amanecer en el trópico, por Guillermo Cabrera Infante." Caribe, 2, 1 (1977), 5-17. Also as "Guillermo Cabrera Infante's Vista del amanecer en el trópico and the generic ambiguity of narrative." In his Studies in the contemporary Spanish-American short story (Columbia: University of Missouri Press, 1979), pp. 110-120.

24.43   Frederick, Bonnie K. "Tres tristes tigres: the lost city."
        Mester, 7, 1-2 (1978), 21-31.

24.44   Gallagher, David P. "Guillermo Cabrera Infante." In his Modern
        Latin American literature (NY: Oxford University Press,
        1973), pp. 164-185. Also, in Spanish, as "Guillermo Cabre-
        ra Infante (Cuba, 1929-)." In Guillermo Cabrera Infante,
        q.v., pp. 47-79.

24.45   García, Eligio. "Conversación con Guillermo Cabrera Infante."
        Eco, No. 207 (1979), 242-268.

24.46   ____. "Los relatos de Cabrera Infante." Imagen, 2a época,
        No. 61, 2° cuerpo (1972), 4-5.

24.47   GdC, No. 43 (1965), entire issue.

24.48   Giordano, Jaime. "Función estructural del bilingüismo en algu-
        nos textos contemporáneos (Cabrera Infante, Luis R. Sán-
        chez)," In Rose S. Minc, Literatures in transition: the
        many voices of the Caribbean area (Gaithersburg, Md.: His-
        pamérica, 1982), pp. 161-175.

24.49   González, Eloy R., and Barbara Sanborn. "Universal symbolism
        in Tres tristes tigres: the spiral and the circle." Se-
        lecta, 1 (1980), 98-101.

24.50   Goytisolo, Juan. "Lectura cervantina de Tres tristes tigres."
        RI, No. 94 (1976), 1-18.

24.51   ____. "Prólogo [a Así en la paz como en la guerra]." GdC,
        Nos. 11-12 (1963), 28.

24.52   Gregorich, Luis. "Tres tristes tigres, obra abierta." In Jorge
        Lafforgue, Nueva novela latinoamericana (BA: Paidós, 1969-
        1972), I, 241-261. Also in Guillermo Cabrera Infante, q.
        v., pp. 129-155.

24.53   Guibert, Rita. "Guillermo Cabrera Infante: conversación sobre
        Tres tristes tigres. Una entrevista." RI, Nos. 76-77
        (1971), 537-554. Also as "The tongue-twisted tiger: an
        interview with Cabrera Infante." Review, Nos. 4-5 (1972),
        10-16. Also as "Guillermo Cabrera Infante." In her Seven
        voices (NY: Alfred A. Knopf, 1973), pp. 338-436.

24.54   Guillermo, Edenia, and Juana A. Hernández. "Tres tristes ti-
        gres." PSA, No. 193 (1972), 25-48.

24.55   Hernández, Cruz. "Oh, you sexy kid you [La Habana para un in-
        fante difunto]." CarR, 9, 4 (1980), 40-41.

24.56   Hussey, Barbara L. "Mirror images in Three trapped tigers."
        IFR, 2 (1975), 165-168.

24.57   Johansson, Kjell A. "Una entrevista con Cabrera Infante." AA,
        1, 1 (1970), 12-17.

24.58 Joucla-Ruau, André. "Sur une publication récente de Guillermo Cabrera Infante." BFLS, 41, 8 (1963), 537-542.

24.59 Kadir, Djelal. "Stalking the oxen of the sun and felling the sacred cows: Joyce's Ulysses and Cabrera Infante's Three trapped tigers." LALR, No. 8 (1976), 15-22.

24.60 Kennedy, William Jerald. "Island of luminous artifact [Vista del amanecer en el trópico]." Review, Nos. 25-26 (1980), 136-137.

24.61 Leal, Rine. "El oficio de Caín [Un oficio del siglo veinte]." Unión, 2, 7 (1963), 86-92.

24.62 Lértora, Juan Carlos. "[O y Exorcismos de esti(1)o]." SinN, 8, 2 (1977), 77-79.

24.63 Levine, Suzanne Jill. "La escritura como traducción: Tres tristes tigres y una Cobra." RI, Nos. 92-93 (1976), 557-567. Also as "Writing as translation: Three trapped tigers and a Cobra." MLN, 90 (1975), 265-277.

24.64 Lipski, John M. "Paradigmatic overlapping in Tres tristes tigres." Dispositio, No. 1 (1976), 33-45.

24.65 Little, William T. "Notas acerca de Tres tristes tigres de G. Cabrera Infante." RI, No. 73 (1970), 635-642.

24.66 Llopis, Rogelio. "Algunos tics de T.T.T. [Tres tristes tigres]." Término, 1, 4 (1983), 16-18.

24.67 _____. "Así en la paz como en la guerra." GdC, No. 43 (1965), 7-8.

24.68 López, César. "[Así en la paz como en la guerra]." CAm, No. 4 (1961), 78-79.

24.69 Ludmer, Josefina. "Tres tristes tigres: órdenes literarios y jerarquías sociales." RI, Nos. 108-109 (1979), 493-512.

24.70 Mac Adam, Alfred J. "Guillermo Cabrera Infante, the vast fragment." In his Modern Latin America narratives; the dreams of reason (Chicago: University of Chicago Press, 1977), pp. 61-68. Also as "Tres tristes tigres: el vasto fragmento." RI, Nos. 92-93 (1975), 549-556.

24.71 Magnarelli, Sharon. "The 'writerly' in Tres tristes tigres." In The analysis of Hispanic texts; current trends in methodology (Jamaica, N.Y.: Bilingual Press/York College, 1976), pp. 320-325.

24.72 Malcuzynski, M.-Pirette. "Tres tristes tigres, or the treacherous play on carnival." I&L, No. 15 (1981), 33-56.

24.73 Martínez, Tomás Eloy. "América: los novelistas exilados." In
       Lourdes Casal, El caso Padilla (Miami: Universal; NY: Nueva
       Atlántida, n.d.), pp. 11-19.

24.74 Matas, Julio. "Orden y visión de Tres tristes tigres." RI, No.
       86 (1974), 87-104. Also in Guillermo Cabrera Infante, q.
       v., pp. 157-186.

24.75 Mejía, Eduardo. "Decadencia y caída [Exorcismos de esti(l)o]."
       Plural, No. 74 (1977), 77-79.

24.76 Merrim, Stephanie. "[Exorcismos de esti(l)o]." RI, Nos. 102-
       103 (1978), 276-279.

24.77 _____. "La Habana para un infante difunto y su teoría topográ-
       fica de las formas." RI, Nos. 118-119 (1982), 403-413.

24.78 _____. "A secret idiom: the grammar and role of language in
       Tres tristes tigres." LALR, No. 16 (1980), 96-117.

24.79 Mestas, Juan E. "Realidad, lenguaje, literatura: Tres tristes
       tigres." SinN, 5, 1 (1974), 62-70.

24.80 Mitchell, Phyllis. "The reel against the real: cinema in the
       novels of Guillermo Cabrera Infante and Manuel Puig."
       LALR, No. 11 (1978), 22-29.

24.81 Monte, Esteban de. "Trotes tras Tres tristes tigres." MNu, No.
       21 (1968), 69-70.

24.82 Montes Huidobro, Matías. "[La Habana para un infante difunto]."
       Chasqui, 8, 3 (1979), 90-91.

24.83 Nelson, Ardis L. "Betrayal in Tres tristes tigres and Petro-
       nius' Satyricon." In Rose S. Minc, Latin American fiction
       today (Takoma Park, Md.: Hispamérica; Upper Montclair,
       N.J.: Montclair State College, 1980), pp. 153-162.

24.84 _____. "El doble, el recuerdo y la muerte: elementos de fuga-
       cidad en la narrativa de Guillermo Cabrera Infante." RI,
       Nos. 123-124 (1983), 509-521.

24.85 _____. "La Habana para un infante difunto: Cabrera Infante's
       'continuous showing'." RCEH, 5, 2 (1981), 216-218.

24.86 Nieto, Jorge. "Cabrera Infante habla de su obra." RyFa, Nos.
       33-34 (1973), 64-83.

24.87 Ordóñez, Montserrat. "Tres tristes tigres y La traición de Rita
       Hayworth: teoría y práctica del discurso narrativo." Eco,
       No. 173 (1975), 516-529.

24.88 Ortega, Julio. "Cabrera Infante." In Guillermo Cabrera Infan-
       te, q.v., pp. 187-207.

24.89 ____. "Una novela abierta." MNu, No. 25 (1968), 88-92. Also as "Cabrera Infante." In his Relato de la utopía (Barcelona: La Gaya Ciencia, 1973), pp. 141-151. Also as "An open novel." Review, Nos. 4-5 (1972), 17-21.

24.90 ____. "Tres tristes tigres." In his La contemplación y la fiesta (Caracas: Monte Avila, 1969), pp. 171-182.

24.91 Padro, Mateo. "Bad art and good intentions [Vista del amanecer en el trópico]." Nation, 227 (1978), 477-478.

24.92 Peavler, Terry J. "Guillermo Cabrera Infante's debt to Ernest Hemingway." Hispania, 62 (1979), 289-296.

24.93 Pereira, Armando. "O: la torre de Babel de Guillermo Cabrera Infante." RUM, 30, 3 (1975), 44-45.

24.94 Pérez Perdomo, Francisco. "Cabrera Infante y el signo de lo trágico." Imagen, No. 32 (1968), 24.

24.95 Resnick, Clauda Cairo. "The use of jokes in Cabrera Infante's Tres tristes tigres (Three trapped tigers)." LALR, No. 9 (1976), 14-21.

24.96 Riccio, Alessandro. "Guillermo Cabrera Infante." Belfagor, 34 (1972), 513-525.

24.97 Rivero, Eliana. "Hacia un análisis feminista de Tres tristes tigres." In Theory and practice of feminist literary criticism (Ypsilanti, Mich.: Bilingual Press/Editorial Bilingüe, 1982), pp. 279-291.

24.98 Rivers, Elias L. "Cabrera Infante's dialogue with language." MLN, 92 (1977), 331-335.

24.99 Rodríguez-Luis, Julio. "Dos versiones de subdesarrollo: Tres tristes tigres, de Cabrera Infante, y Temporada de duendes, de Pedro Juan Soto." SinN, 12, 1 (1981), 39-45.

24.100 Rodríguez Monegal, Emir. "Cabrera Infante: la novela como autobiografía total." RI, Nos. 116-117 (1981), 265-271. Also as "La novela como autobiografía total." RUM, 36, 1 (1981), 34-36.

24.101 ____. "Cuba: la escritura de su historia [Vista del amanecer en el trópico]." Plural, 4, 8 (1975), 66-70.

24.102 ____. "Estructura y significación de Tres tristes tigres." Sur, No. 320 (1969), 38-51. Also in his Narradores de esta América; 2. ed. (Montevideo: Alfa, 1969-1974), II, 331-364. Also in Guillermo Cabrera Infante, q.v., pp. 81-127. Also as "Structure and meaning of Three trapped tigers." LALR, No. 2 (1973), 19-35.

24.103 _____. "Las fuentes de la narración." MNu, No. 25 (1968),
       41-58. Also in his El arte de narrar; diálogos (Caracas:
       Monte Avila, 1968), pp. 48-80.

24.104 Rosa, Nicolás. "Cabrera Infante: una patología del lenguaje."
       In his Crítica y significación (BA: Galerna, 1970), pp.
       175-224.

24.105 Sarris, Andrew. "Rerunning Puig and Cabrera Infante." Review,
       No. 9 (1973), 46-48.

24.106 Schraibman, Joseph. "Cabrera Infante tras la búsqueda del len-
       guaje." Insula, No. 286 (1970), 1, 15-16.

24.107 Schwartz, Ronald. "Cabrera Infante: Cuban lyricism." In his
       Nomads, exiles, and emigrés: the rebirth of the Latin
       American narrative, 1960-80 (Metuchen, N.J.: Scarecrow
       1980), pp. 60-69.

24.108 Shaw, Donald L. "Guillermo Cabrera Infante." In his Nueva na-
       rrativa hispanoamericana (Madrid: Cátedra, 1981), pp. 156-
       159.

24.109 Siemens, William L. "The devouring female in four Latin Ameri-
       can novels." ELWIU, 1 (1974), 118-129. Cabrera Infante
       inter alios.

24.110 _____. "Guillermo Cabrera Infante: man of three islands."
       Review, No. 28 (1981), 8-11.

24.111 _____. "Guillermo Cabrera Infante's Tres tristes tigres."
       GSLA, 1 (1973), 75-85.

24.112 _____. "Heilsgeschichte and the structure of Tres tristes ti-
       gres." KRQ, 22 (1975), 77-90.

24.113 _____. "Mirrors and metamorphosis: Lewis Carroll's presence
       in Tres tristes tigres." Hispania, 62 (1979), 297-303.

24.114 _____. "Women as cosmic phenomena in Tres tristes tigres."
       JSSTC, 3 (1975), 199-209.

24.115 Souza, Raymond D. "Cabrera Infante: creation in progress."
       In his Major Cuban novelists; innovation and tradition
       (Columbia: University of Missouri Press, 1976), pp. 80-
       108.

24.116 _____. "Language versus structure in the contemporary Spanish
       American novel." Hispania, 52 (1969), 833-839. Cabrera
       Infante inter alios.

24.117 Tittler, Jonathan. "Intertextual distances in Tres tristes
       tigres." MLN, 93 (1978), 285-296.

24.118 Torres Fierro, Danubio. "Entrevista a Guillermo Cabrera Infante: Así en la paz como en la guerra." Vuelta, No. 11 (1977), 18-27.

24.119 _____. "El eterno retorno de lo mismo [Vista del amanecer en el trópico]." Escandalar, 1, 3 (1978), 73-75.

24.120 _____. "Guillermo Cabrera Infante: algunas (biográficas) revelaciones." Escandalar, 1, 1 (1978), 60-68.

24.121 _____. "[La Habana para un infante difunto]." Vuelta, No. 42 (1980), 37-39.

24.122 _____. "Uso y abuso del wit [O]." Plural, No. 48 (1975), 64-65.

24.123 Vargas, Aura Rosa. "Al margen de 'Un rato de tenmeallá'." Káñina, 3, 1 (1979), 7-18.

24.124 Volek, Emil. "Tres tristes tigres en la jaula verbal: las antinomias dialécticas y la tentativa de lo absoluto en la novela de Guillermo Cabrera Infante." RI, Nos. 116-117 (1981), 175-183.

24.125 Walker, John. "Havana in slow motion [La Habana para un infante difunto]." Américas, 32, 11-12 (1980), 47-48. Also as "La Habana a cámara lenta." Américas [Spanish edition]." 32, 11-12 (1980), 47-48.

24.126 Walsh, Rodolfo. "Documentos." LetNa, No. 20 (1968), 71-74.

25. CARDOSO, ONELIO JORGE (1914-   )

Bibliographies

25.1   Arias, Salvador. "Sorbe Onelio Jorge Cardoso. En su sesenta
       aniversario. Bibliografía pasiva (1946-1974)." L/L, No.
       5 (1974), 158-160.

Critical Essays

25.2   Agostini, Víctor. "Cómo se hace un cuento." GdC, No. 18
       (1963), 7.

25.3   Alomá, Orlando. "El sople de los cincuenta." Cultura, 1, 10
       (1964), 14.

25.4   Alvarez Conesa, Sigifredo. "Cuentos de camino." GdC, No. 123
       (1974), 3-4.

25.5   Aparicio, Raúl. "[El caballo de coral]." CAm, No. 9 (1961),
       165-167.

25.6   _____. "Prólogo." In Onelio Jorge Cardoso, Cuentos completos
       (H: Unión, 1965), pp. vii-xii.

25.7   Arenas, Reinaldo. "Con los ojos abiertos [Abrir y cerrar los
       ojos]." GdC, No. 81 (1970), 10-11.

25.8   Arias, Salvador. "Análisis de un cuento de Onelio Jorge Cardo-
       so ['Niño']." In his Búsqueda y análisis; ensayos críti-
       cos sobre literatura cubana (H: Unión, 1974), pp. 89-112.
       Orig. CAm, No. 71 (1972), 55-68.

25.9   Augier, Angel I. "[Gente de pueblo]." ULH, No. 163 (1963),
       205.

25.10 Azucena, Isabel. "El hilo y la cuerda." Bohemia, 66, 30
       (1974), 37.

25.11 Benítez Rojo, Antonio. "[Abrir y cerrar los ojos]." CAm, No.
       61 (1970), 171-173.

25.12 Bogach, Inna. "Amistad entre los pueblos, amistad entre las
       literaturas [Francisca y la muerte]." Santiago, No. 28
       (1977), 63-71.

25.13 Bueno, Salvador. "Onelio Jorge Cardoso: un cuentista casi des-
       conocido." Bohemia, 66, 48 (1974), 10-11.

25.14 Buzzi, David. "Entre el lenguaje directo y la poesía." RyC, No. 10 (1973), 48-54.

25.15 Chaple, Sergio. "En torno a un cuento de Onelio Jorge Cardoso ['Hierro viejo']." L/L, No. 1 (1970), 196-207.

25.16 Díaz, Jesús. "Onelio, el cuentero." CB, No. 3 (1966), 23.

25.17 Díaz Martínez, Manuel. "¿Análisis de un cuento ['Abrir y cerrar los ojos']?" Cuba, No. 73 (1969), 23-24.

25.18 Diego, Eliseo. "[Abrir y cerrar los ojos]." Unión, 9, 3 (1970), 196-198.

25.19 ____. "Tres cuentos para niños de Onelio Jorge Cardoso." Unión, 6, 3 (1968), 144-150.

25.20 Elizagaray, Alga Marina. "Un caballito blanco para los niños cubanos." Bohemia, 67, 14 (1975), 26.

25.21 García, Esther. "Con Onelio." TLit, No. 14 (1967), 1-2, 24.

25.22 García Ronda, Denia. "Los setenta años del cuentero." GdC, No. 123 (1974), 2-3.

25.23 Gavilán, Angelina. "Introducción." In Onelio Jorge Cardoso, Onelio Jorge Cardoso (H: MINED, Dirección de Educación General, 1973), pp. 3-12.

25.24 González, Eliseo. "[El hilo y la cuerda]." CB, No. 82 (1974), 29-30.

25.25 González, Reinaldo. "A qué huele el criollismo." GdC, No. 71 (1969), 2-4.

25.26 ____. "El hombre siempre tiene dos hambres." GdC, No. 26 (1963), 2-3.

25.27 "Habla Onelio Jorge Cardoso/escritor cubano." Cultura, No. 7 (1964), 10.

25.28 Hernández Novo, Corina. "Camino de las lomas." TallerC, No. 25 (1973), 29-31.

25.29 Huete, Angel. "Un solitario: Onelio Jorge Cardoso." NRC, 1, 1 (1959), 147-151.

25.30 Jorge, Elena. "Cultura, antes. Onelio Jorge Carodoso habla sobre su paso por el radio." GdC, No. 123 (1974), 4-5.

25.31 López-Nussa, Leonel. "Onelio Jorge Cardoso. Un señor cuentero." Cuba, No. 18 (1963), 56-59.

25.32 Marinello, Juan. "Algunas opiniones sobre Onelio Jorge Cardoso." Cuba, No. 22 (1971), 43.

25.33 Martí, Agenor. "Onelio: se toma o se deja." CubaI, No. 22
       (1971), 38-43.

25.34 Martínez, Laínez, Fernando. "Entrevista con Onelio Jorge Cardo-
       so." In his Palabra cubana (Madrid: Akal, 1975), pp. 257-
       280.

25.35 Navarro, Noel. "[Sobre la huella del pulgar]." CAm, No. 73
       (1972), 137-138.

25.36 "Onelio, claridad y audacia." CAm, No. 89 (1975), 176-177.

25.37 Orozco Sierra, Guillermo. "Algunos cuentos más leídos: 'En la
       caja del cuerpo'." Santiago, No. 30 (1978), 77-84.

25.38 _____. "Apuntes para un estudio de la caracterización en la
       cuentística de Onelio Jorge Cardoso." TLit, No. 18 (1968),
       5-7.

25.39 Ortega, Julio. "Cuentos, de Onelio Jorge Cardoso." In his Re-
       lato de la utopía (Barcelona: La Gaya Ciencia, 1973), pp.
       115-125.

25.40 Paporov, Yuri. "La literatura cubana en el mundo. A los hom-
       bres los guían las ciencias y los sueños." GdC, No. 152
       (1977), 16-17.

25.41 Pereira, Manuel. "Onelio: de canto a canto." CubaI, No. 94
       (1977), 20-23.

25.42 Pi, Agustín. "Conversación con Onelio Jorge Cardoso." GdC, No.
       111 (1973), 13.

25.43 Rodríguez Feo, José. "Onelio Jorge Cardoso: el cuentero." GdC,
       No. 2 (1962), 10. Also as "Onelio Jorge Cardoso." In his
       Notas críticas (primera serie) (H: Unión, 1962), pp. 141-
       144.

25.44 Royero, Maida. "Teatro en extensión." RyC, No. 65 (1978), 18-
       25.

25.45 S. A. "Sobre Onelio Jorge Cardoso. En su sesenta aniversario."
       L/L, No. 5 (1974), 158-160.

26. CARPENTIER, ALEJO (1904-1980)

Bibliographies

26.1 Alejo Carpentier: 45 años de trabajo intelectual. H: Biblioteca Nacional José Martí, 1966.

26.2 Foster, David William. "A bibliography of the fiction of Carpentier, Cabrera Infante, and Lezama Lima: works and criticism." Abraxas, 1, 3 (1971), 305-310.

26.3 García Carranza, Araceli. "Bibliografía de una exposición." RBNJM, 3a serie, 17, 1 (1975), 45-87.

26.4 González Echevarría, Roberto, and Klaus Müller-Bergh. Alejo Carpentier: bibliographical guide/guía bibliográfica. Westport, Conn.: Greenwood Press, 1983.

Critical Monographs and Dissertations

26.5 Acosta, Leonardo. Música y épica en la novela de Alejo Carpentier. H: Letras Cubanas, 1981.

26.6 Alexander, Roberta May. "The fictional portrayal of popular movements." DAI, 40 (1980), 5431A. Carpentier inter alios.

26.7 Alonso, Juan M. "The search for identity in Alejo Carpentier's contemporary urban novels: an analysis of Los pasos perdidos and El acoso." DAI, 28 (1968), 3173A.

26.8 Assardo, M. Roberto. "La técnica narrativa en la obra de Alejo Carpentier; énfasis: el tiempo." DAI, 29 (1968), 1889A.

26.9 Barroso, Juan. Realismo mágico y lo real maravilloso en El reino de este mundo y El siglo de las luces. Miami: Universal, 1977. Orig. DAI, 36 (1976), 4530A.

26.10 Bush, Roland Edward. "The art of la fuga: mythic and musical modes in relation to the theme of identity in Alejo Carpentier's Los pasos perdidos." DAI, 41 (1981), 5116A.

26.11 Cano, Carlos José. "Tres momentos significativos en la novelística hispanoamericana contemporánea." DAI, 34 (1973), 1897A.

26.12 Cheuse, Alan. "Memories of the future: a critical biography of
       Alejo Carpentier." DAI, 35 (1975), 6659A-6660A.

26.13 Colavita, Federica Domínguez. "El sentido de la historia en la
       obra de Alejo Carpentier." DAI, 35 (1975), 6132A-6133A.

26.14 Díaz, Ramón. "El simbolismo en cuatro obras de Alejo Carpen-
       tier." DAI, 40 (1970), 2085A.

26.15 Fernández, Ricardo R. "La novelística de Alejo Carpentier."
       DAI, 31 (1970), 1796A.

26.16 Flores, Julio et al. El realismo mágico de Alejo Carpentier.
       Valparaíso, Chile: Orellana, 1971.

26.17 Floyd, Jo Ann. "The journey home: the intellectual's search
       for identity in five Spanish-American novels." DAI, 40
       (1979), 4927A. Carpentier's Los pasos perdidos inter a-
       lias.

26.18 García-Castro, Ramón. "Perspectivas temporales en la obra de
       Alejo Carpentier." DAI, 34 (1973), 313A.

26.19 Gerhold, Kathryn Marie. "The aesthetic use of the epigraph in
       the works of Alejo Carpentier." DAI, 42 (1981), 2150A.

26.20 Giacoman, Helmy F. Homenaje a Alejo Carpentier; variaciones in-
       terpretativas en torno a su obra. NY: Las Américas, 1970.
       Pertinent items are listed separately.

26.21 Gómez Mango, Edmundo. Construcción y lenguaje en Alejo Carpen-
       tier (de Los pasos perdidos a El siglo de las luces).
       Montevideo: Fundación Cultura Universitaria, 1968.

26.22 González, Eduardo G. Alejo Carpentier: el tiempo del hombre.
       Caracas: Monte Avila, 1978. Orig. as "El tiempo del hom-
       bre: huella y labor de origen en cuatro obras de Alejo
       Carpentier." DAI, 36 (1975), 923A-924A.

26.23 González Echevarría, Roberto. Alejo Carpentier: the pilgrim at
       home. Ithaca, N.Y.: Cornell University Press, 1977.

26.24 González León, Adriano. Gotas de lectura sobre novelas y rela-
       tos breves de Alejo Carpentier. H: Consejo Nacional de
       Cultura, Dirección General de Literatura y Publicaciones,
       1975.

26.25 Green, George K. "The early writings of Alejo Carpentier."
       DAI, 37 (1976), 3665A.

26.26 Hayworth, Karen Lyn Getty. "Language as technique in Tres tris-
       tes tigres and El recurso del método." DAI, 40 (1979),
       3333A.

26.27 Hidalgo-Martín, Jorge. "El tiempo y las formas en tres obras de Alejo Carpentier." DAI, 35 (1975), 5406A-5407A.

26.28 Historia y mito en la obra de Alejo Carpentier. BA: Fernando García Cambeiro, 1972. Pertinent items are listed separately.

26.29 Janney, Frank. Alejo Carpentier and his early works. London: Tamesis, 1981. Orig. as Regression in the early works of Alejo Carpentier. Unpublished Ph.D. dissertation, Harvard University, 1972.

26.30 Kilmer-Tchalekian, Mary A. "Synthesis as process and vision in El siglo de las luces and Cien años de soledad." DAI, 35 (1975), 5411A.

26.31 Márquez Rodríguez, Alexis. Lo barroco y lo real-maravilloso en la obra de Alejo Carpentier. M: Siglo XXI, 1982.

26.32 _____. La obra narrativa de Alejo Carpentier. Caracas: Universidad Central de Venezuela, Biblioteca, 1970.

26.33 Martocq, Bernard. Las dimensiones de la historia en El siglo de las luces. Aix-en-Provence: Faculté de Lettres d'Aix-en-Provence, 1964.

26.34 Mocega-González, Esther P. La narrativa de Alejo Carpentier: el concepto del tiempo como tema fundamental (ensayo de interpretación y análisis). NY: Eliseo Torres, 1975.

26.35 Montero, Janina J. "La perspectiva histórica en Augusto Roa Bastos, Alejo Carpentier y Gabriel García Márquez." DAI, 34 (1973), 1924A.

26.36 Müller-Bergh, Klaus. Alejo Carpentier, estudio biográfico crítico. Long Island City, N.Y.: Las Américas, 1972.

26.37 _____. Asedios a Carpentier: once ensayos críticos sobre el novelista cubano. Santiago de Chile: Universitaria, 1972. Pertinent items are listed separately.

26.38 _____. "La prosa narrativa de Alejo Carpeniter en Los pasos perdidos." DAI, 27 (1967), 2537A-2538A.

26.39 Narváez, Jorge. El idealismo en El siglo de las luces. Santiago de Chile: Universidad de Concepción, Instituto Central de Lenguas, 1972.

26.40 Ortiz, Nora Mijares. "Alejo Carpentier: un estudio de Los pasos perdidos." DAI, 39 (1978), 3614A-3615A.

26.41 Pacheco, José Ignacio. "La obra narrativa de Alejo Carpentier." DAI, 34 (1974), 6652A.

26.42 Pérez-Reilly, Elizabeth Kranz. "'Lo real-maravilloso' in the
       prose fiction of Alejo Carpentier: a critical study."
       DAI, 36 (1957), 4532A.

26.43 Pickerhayn, Jorge Oscar. Para leer a Alejo Carpentier. BA:
       Plus Ultra, 1978.

26.44 Quinze études autour de El siglo de las luces de Alejo Carpen-
       tier. Paris: L'Harmatan, 1983. Pertinent items are listed
       separately.

26.45 Ramírez Molas, Pedro. Tiempo y narración: enfoques de la tempo-
       ralidad de Borges, Carpentier, Cortázar y García Márquez.
       Madrid: Gredos, 1978.

26.46 Raventós de Marín, Nury. Haití a horcajadas en su independencia
       en la visión de Alejo Carpentier. Ciudad Universitaria Ro-
       drigo Facia, Costa Rica: Universidad de Costa Rica, 1973.

26.47 Rein, Mercedes. Cortázar y Carpentier. BA: Crisis, 1974.

26.48 Rodríguez, Ileana. "La política de la producción literaria en
       dos de las principales novelas de Carpentier." DAI, 37
       (1976), 2215A.

26.49 Salomon, Noël. Sobre dos fuentes antillanas y su elaboración
       en El siglo de las luces de Alejo Carpentier. Talance,
       France: Université de Bordeaux, Institut d'Etudes Ibériques
       et Ibéro-Américaines, 1972.

26.50 Sánchez, Marta Ester. "Three Latin-American novelists in search
       of lo americano: a productive failure." DAI, 38 (1977),
       819A.

26.51 Sánchez, Napoleón Neptali. "El surrealismo: fermento transfor-
       mador en la obra novelística de Alejo Carpentier." DAI,
       38 (1977), 301A.

26.52 Sánchez-Boudy, José. La temática novelística de Alejo Carpen-
       tier. Miami: Universal, 1969.

26.53 Skinner, Eugene R. "Archetypal patterns in four novels of Alejo
       Carpentier." DAI, 30 (1970), 3023A.

26.54 Sokoloff, Naomi Beryl. "Spatial form in the social novel: John
       Dos Passos, Alejo Carpentier, and S. Y. Agnon." DAI, 41
       (1980), 2593A.

26.55 Solano Salvatierra de Chase, Cida. Correlación entre algunos
       procedimientos estilísticos y la temática en la ficción
       extensa de Alejo Carpentier hasta El siglo de las luces.
       San José, Costa Rica: Texto, 1980. Orig. DAI, 37 (1977),
       5159A-5160A.

26.56 Speratti-Piñero, Emma Susana. Pasos hallados en El reino de
       este mundo. M: El Colegio de México, 1981.

26.57 St. Omer, Garth. "The colonial novel: studies in the novels of
       Albert Camus, V. S. Naipaul and Alejo Carpentier." DAI, 37
       (1975), 1534A.

26.58 Taliela, Isabel. "La función del lenguaje en El siglo de las
       luces de Alejo Carpentier." DAI, 39 (1978), 2964A-2965A.

26.59 Vila Selma, José. El "último" Carpentier. Las Palmas: Excelen-
       tísima Mancomunidad de Cabildos, 1978.

26.60 Worth, Fabienne André. "Historical modes of narrative in four
       twentieth century novels: Marcel Proust's A la recherche du
       temps perdu, Alejo Carpentier's Los pasos perdidos, Virgin-
       ia Woolf's Between the acts, Günter Grass's Die Blechtrom-
       mel." DAI, 41 (1980), 239A.

26.61 Young, Richard A. Carpentier: El reino de este mundo. A crit-
       ical guide. London: Grant and Cutler, 1983.

26.62 Zabala, Mercedes. "Alejo Carpentier: un mundo en metamorfosis
       (estudio estilístico)." DAI, 34 (1974), 4297A.

Critical Essays

26.63 "A cierre..." RyC, No. 28 (1974), 74-83.

26.64 Acevedo, Federico. "Estructura temporal e historia en la obra
       de Carpentier." SinN, 12, 2 (1981), 39-59.

26.65 Acosta, Leonardo. "El almirante, según don Alejo [El arpa y la
       sombra]." CAm, No. 121 (1980), 26-40.

26.66 _____. "El 'barroco americano' y la ideología colonialista."
       Unión, 11, 2-3 (1972), 51-57.

26.67 _____. "El doctor Fausto se interna en la selva." CAm, No.
       109 (1978), 93-112.

26.68 Adams, M. Ian. "Alejo Carpentier: alienation, culture, and
       myth." In his Three authors of alienation (Austin: Uni-
       versity of Texas Press, 1975), pp. 81-105.

26.69 Adams, Rolstan P. "The search for the indigenous: an evaluation
       of the literary vision of Alejo Carpentier and Miguel Angel
       Asturias." In The analysis of Hispanic texts: current
       trends in methodology (Jamaica, N.Y.: Bilingual Press/York
       College, 1976), pp. 74-88.

26.70 Adoum, Jorge Enrique. "Mi última visita a Alejo." CAm, No.
       121 (1980), 15-16.

26.71   Albertocchi, Giovanni. "La figura del dittatore in alcuni ro-
        manzi latinoamericani." Ponte, 33 (1977), 616-625. Car-
        pentier inter alios.

26.72   Alegría, Fernando. "Alejo Carpentier: realismo mágico." HumM,
        1 (1960), 345-372. Also in his Literatura y revolución
        (M: Fondo de Cultura Económica, 1971), pp. 92-125. Also
        in Helmy F. Giacoman, Homenaje, q.v., pp. 33-69.

26.73   "Alejo Carpentier: 75 aniversario; exposición homenaje de la
        Biblioteca Nacional José Martí." RBNJM, 3a serie, 22, 1
        (1980), 189-194.

26.74   Alonso, Carlos J. "'Viaje a la semilla'; historia de una ente-
        lequía." MLN, 94 (1979), 386-393.

26.75   Alvarez Alvarez, Luis. "[Crónicas, II]." ULH, No. 207 (1978),
        241-243.

26.76   Amorós, Andrés. "Alejo Carpentier." In his Introducción a la
        novela hispanoamericana actual (Salamanca: Anaya, 1971),
        pp. 56-75.

26.77   Aponte, Barbara Bockus. "El arpa y la sombra: the novel as por-
        trait." HispJ, 3, 1 (1981), 93-105.

26.78   _____. "La creación del espacio literario en El recurso del mé-
        todo." RI, Nos. 96-97 (1976), 567-572.

26.79   Arango L., Manuel Antonio. "Correlación social e histórica y
        'lo real maravilloso' en El reino de este mundo de Alejo
        Carpentier." Thesaurus, 33 (1978), 317-325.

26.80   _____. "Correlación surrealista y social en dos novelas: El
        reino de este mundo, de Alejo Carpentier, y Hombres de
        maíz de Miguel Angel Asturias." ExTL, 7, 1 (1978), 23-30.

26.81   _____. "Perspectivas estructurales en la obra de Alejo Carpen-
        tier." BCA, No. 21 (1971), 25-29.

26.82   _____. "Relación social e histórica afro-espiritual y el 'rea-
        lismo mágico' en ¡Ecué-yamba-ó!, de Alejo Carpentier."
        CA, No. 234 (1981), 84-91.

26.83   Arias, Salvador. "Carpentier periodista [Letra y solfa]." CAm,
        No. 95 (1976), 128-130.

26.84   _____. "Preludio y variaciones [Tientos y diferencias]." CB,
        No. 3 (1966), 22.

26.85   Armbruster, Claudius. "Alejo Carpentiers La consagración de la
        primavera: Geschichte der Revolution zur Musik eines Bal-
        lets." Iberoamericana, 4, 10 (1980), 54-65.

26.86 Arrigoitía, Luis de. "[El reino de este mundo]." La torre, No. 58 (1967), 244-250.

26.87 Arrom, José Juan. "Congrí: apostilla lexicográfica a un cuento de Carpentier." BANLE, Nos. 2-3 (1977-1978), 85-87.

26.88 Arturo, Héctor de. "¡Gracias, Alejo!" VO, 19, 16 (1978), 58-59.

26.89 Assardo, M. Roberto. "El concepto del tiempo circular en la relato 'El camino de Santiago' de Alejo Carpentier." La torre, No. 72 (1971), 123-128.

26.90 _____. "El concepto temporal y la técnica cinematográfica en el relato 'Viaje a la semilla'." ExTL, 5 (1976), 39-47.

26.91 _____. "El efecto de la disgragación temporal en El acoso de Alejo Carpentier." RevL, 6 (1974), 74-86.

26.92 _____. "'Semejante a la noche' o la contemporalidad del hombre." CA, No. 163 (1969), 263-271. Also in Helmy F. Giacoman, Homenaje, q.v., pp. 209-225.

26.93 Augier, Angel I. "Alejo Carpentier." Bohemia, 55, 52 (1963), 10-11.

26.94 _____. "[Guerra del tiempo]." ULH, No. 164 (1963), 195-196.

26.95 Ayora, Jorge. "La alienación marxista en Los pasos perdidos de Carpentier." Hispania, 57 (1974), 886-892.

26.96 Baldran, Jacqueline. "Esteban ou l'épiphanie sans roi..." In Quinze études, q.v., pp. 207-216.

26.97 Barbero, Teresa. "Alejo Carpentier: El derecho de asilo." EstLit, No. 492 (1972), 946.

26.98 Bareiro Saguier, Rubén. "El dictador latinoamericano visto por Alejo Carpentier y por Augusto Roa Bastos." In La letteratura latino-americana e la sua problematica europea (Roma: Istituto Italiano-Latino Americano, 1978), pp. 455-467.

26.99 Barnet, Miguel. "Alejo." Areito, No. 23 (1980), 51-52.

26.100 Barón Palma, Emilio. "Tiempos paralelos en la novelística de Alejo Carpentier." ALHisp, No. 5 (1976), 241-251.

26.101 Barradas, Efraín. "Cigarro, Colón: ciclón: ciclo: nota para una relectura de ¡Ecué-yamba-ó!" SinN, 12, 2 (1981), 81-95.

26.102 Barreda-Tomás, Pedro M. "Alejo Carpentier: dos visiones del negro, dos conceptos de la novela." Hispania, 55 (1972), 34-44.

26.103 Barrera, Ernesto M. "El vodú y el sacrificio del tótem en El
        reino de este mundo." CA, No. 211 (1977), 148-157.

26.104 Barrera Vidal, A. "Estructuras narrativas de Alejo Carpen-
        tier." In Studi di letteratura ispano-americana (Milano:
        Cisalpino-Goliardica, 1967-1972), III, 87-99.

26.105 Barthélémy, Françoise. "Alejo Carpentier ou le métier de ré-
        véler." NCRMM, 90 (1976), 50-55.

26.106 Bell, Steven M. "Carpentier's El reino de este mundo in a new
        light: toward a theory of the fantastic." JSSTC, 8
        (1980), 29-43.

26.107 Benedetti, Mario. "Alejo Carpentier: un anuncio de la vida."
        CAm, No. 122 (1980), 96-98.

26.108 _____. "Homenaje a Alejo Carpentier." CA, No. 231 (1980), 53-
        61.

26.109 _____. "El recurso del supremo patriarca." CAm, No. 98
        (1976), 12-23. Also RCLL, No. 3 (1976), 55-67.

26.110 _____. "Sobre paisajes y personas." In his Crítica cómplice
        (H: Instituto Cubano del Libro, 1971), pp. 29-32.

26.111 Benítez Rojo, Antonio. "'El camino de Santiago', de Alejo Car-
        pentier, y el Canon perpetuus, de Juan Sebastián Bach: pa-
        ralelismo estructural." RI, Nos. 123-124 (1983), 293-322.

26.112 Benítez Villalba, Jesús. "Notas sobre la naturaleza en El si-
        glo de las luces." ALHisp, No. 9 (1980), 39-47.

26.113 Bianchi Ross, Ciro. "Carpentier a cuatro tiempos." CubaI,
        No. 64 (1974), 50-53.

26.114 Blanch, Antonio. "Alejo·Carpentier, de la historia a la mito-
        logía." RLAE, No. 37 (1970), 387-400.

26.115 Blanzat, Jean. "[Prologue]." In Alejo Carpentier, Le siècle
        des lumières (Paris: Gallimard, 1962), pp. 3-8.

26.116 Bonnett de Segura, Piedad. "Alejo Carpentier: su vida y su
        amor." CAn, 2, 3 (1980), 25-26.

26.117 Bosch, Rafael. "Análisis objetivo (o material) del primer
        Carpentier, 1933-1962." RCLL, No. 4 (1976), 81-102.

26.118 Boskho, Oleksandr. "Alekho Karpent'ier: krnologiia zhyttis
        i tvorchosti." Vsesvit, 1 (1981), 167-172.

26.119 Brotherston, Gordon. "The genesis of America: Alejo Carpen-
        tier." In his The emergence of the Latin American novel
        (Cambridge: Cambridge University Press, 1977), pp. 45-59.

26.120 Brushwood, John S. "El criollismo 'de esencias' en Don Goyo
[de Demetrio Aguilera Malta] y Ecue-yamba-o." In Estudios
de literatura hispanoamericana en honor a José J. Arrom
(Chapel Hill: University of North Carolina, Department of
Romance Languages, 1974), pp. 215-225.

26.121 Bueno, Salvador. "Alejo Carpentier, novelista antillano y universal." In his La letra como testigo (Santa Clara: Universidad Central de Las Villas, 1957), pp. 153-179.

26.122 _____. "Alejo Carpentier y su concepto de la historia." Indice, Nos. 272-273 (1970), 44-46. Also in Instituto
Internacional de Literatura Iberoamericana, El ensayo y
la crítica literaria en Iberoamérica (Toronto: University
of Toronto, 1970), pp. 257-263.

26.123 _____. "Carpentier en la maestría de sus novelas y relatos."
Unión, 13, 1 (1974), 102-121.

26.124 _____. "El criollismo alucinante de Alejo Carpentier." Mapocho, 22 (1960), 90-101.

26.125 _____. "En charla con Alejo Carpentier." Carteles, 34, 17
(1953), 36.

26.126 _____. "Ensayos de Carpentier." ULH, No. 177 (1966), 247-249.

26.127 _____. "Homenaje a Alejo Carpentier con motivo de su septuagésimo aniversario." RBNJM, 3a serie, 17, 1 (1975), 31-37.

26.128 _____. "Lo que me dijo Alejo Carpentier." Carteles, 40, 26
(1959), 36-37.

26.129 _____. "Notas para un estudio sobre la concepción de la historia en Alejo Carpentier." ALit, 11 (1969), 237-251. Also
ULH, No. 195 (1972), 122-138.

26.130 _____. "Nuevos relatos en Guerra del tiempo." GdC, No. 96
(1971), 32.

26.131 _____. "La obra periodística de Alejo Carpentier." CHA, No.
360 (1980), 707-710.

26.132 _____. "Reflexiones de un novelista [Tientos y diferencias]."
Bohemia, 58, 21 (1966), 9.

26.133 _____. "[El siglo de las luces]." ULH, No. 164 (1963), 188-190.

26.134 Burgos, Fernando. "Conexiones: barroco y modernidad [Concierto
barroco]." Escritura, No. 11 (1981), 153-162.

26.135 Bush, Roland Edward. "Musical form in Carpentier's Los pasos
perdidos." In Tradition, change, and revolution in the

Caribbean (Coral Gables, Fla.: Association of Caribbean Studies, 1983), p. 31. Abstract.

26.136 Caballero Ríos, Norberto. "El reino de este mundo: lo maravilloso llevado al plano de lo objetivo." TLit, 5, 11-12 (1975), 23-25.

26.137 Callejas, Bernardo. "Introducción." In Alejo Carpentier, El autor y su obra. Alejo Carpentier (H: MINED: Dirección Nacional de Educación General, 1973), pp. 3-7.

26.138 Campbell, Stephanie. "The artist in bourgeois society, as seen in Carpentier's La consagración de la primavera." Maize, 3, 3-4 (1980), 6-16.

26.139 Campos, Jorge. "Alejo Carpentier y sus pasos hallados." Insula, No. 118 (1955), 4.

26.140 _____. "La Antilla de A. Carpentier [El siglo de las luces]." Insula, No. 240 (1966), 11, 15.

26.141 _____. "El arpa y la sombra, de Alejo Carpentier." Insula, No. 394 (1979), 11.

26.142 _____. "El derecho de asilo. Un relato de Carpentier." Insula, No. 307 (1972), 11.

26.143 _____. "Fantasía y realidad en los cuentos cubanos." Insula, No. 268 (1961), 1.

26.144 _____. "Klaus Müller-Bergh y el asedio a Alejo Carpentier." Insula, No. 330 (1974), 11. See item no. 26.37.

26.145 _____. "[La música en Cuba]." RevC, 23 (1948), 318-322.

26.146 Campos, Julieta. "Carpentier: el estilo de nuestro mundo." In her La imagen en el espejo (M: Universidad Nacional Autónoma de México, 1965), pp. 135-139.

26.147 _____. "El realismo subjetivo de Alejo Carpentier." RUM, 13, 11 (1959), 17-19. Also as "Realidad y fantasía de Alejo Carpentier." In her La imagen en el espejo (M: Universidad Nacional Autónoma de México, 1965), pp. 127-134.

26.148 Carlos, Alberto J. "El anti-héroe en El acoso." CA, No. 168 (1970), 193-204. Also in Helmy F. Giacoman, Homenaje, q.v., pp. 365-384.

26.149 Carpentier, Alejo. "Autobiografía de urgencia." Insula, No. 218 (1965), 3, 13.

26.150 _____. "Mundo y ambiente de El siglo de las luces." Cuba, No. 24 (1964), 22-29.

26.151 "Carpentier en la Habana." RBNJM, 3a serie, 17, 1 (1975), 39-40.

26.152 "Carpentier en la Universidad de Yale." Areito, Nos. 19-20 (1979), 62.

26.153 Carr, Bill. "Carpentier and the Caribbean." CarS, 11, 3 (1971), 75-82.

26.154 Carreras González, Olga. "Tres fechas, tres novelas y un tema, estudio comparativo de La vorágine [de José Eustacio Rivera], Canaima [de Rómulo Gallegos] y Los pasos perdidos." ExTL, 2, 2 (1974), 169-178.

26.155 Cartagena Portalín, Aída. "Las Ginés de Santiago de los Caballeros en textos de Alejo Carpentier y Pedro Henríquez Ureña." PU, No. 2 (1971), 27-35.

26.156 Cartano, Tony. "Le roman de Christophe Colomb." QL, No. 310 (1979), 13-14.

26.157 Castillo, Fernando. "La consagración de la maestría [La consagración de la primavera]." RUM, 33, 8 (1979), 51-52.

26.158 Castro, Fidel. "Cable ... a Alejo Carpentier." CAm, No. 109 (1978), 92. Also Bohemia, 70, 19 (1978), 54.

26.159 Castro López, Octavio. "En torno a Guerra del tiempo, de Alejo Carpentier." Noéma, No. 32 (1961), 19-26. Also Islas, 4, 2 (1962), 327-335.

26.160 Catalá, Rafael. "La crisis de la reconciliación y de la trascendencia en Los pasos perdidos." In Cinco aproximaciones a la narrativa hispanoamericana (Madrid: Playor, 1977), pp. 83-107.

26.161 Celorio, Gonzalo. "Yo conocí a Alejo Carpentier." Diálogos, No. 94 (1980), 15-17.

26.162 Cerzo, María del C. "Del Discurso al Recurso del método: Descartes y Carpentier." SinN, 12, 2 (1981), 96-106.

26.163 Cheuse, Alain. "Hamlet in Haiti: style in Carpentier's The kingdom of this world." CarQ, 21, 4 (1975), 13-29.

26.164 _____. "The lost books." Review, No. 18 (1976), 14-19.

26.165 Chiampi Cortez, Irlemar. "Alejo Carpentier y el surrealismo." RUM, 37, 5 (1981), 2-10.

26.166 _____. "In search of Latin American writing." Diacritics, 8, 4 (1978), 2-15.

26.167 _____. "La reescritura de Carpentier según Roberto González Echevarría." RI, Nos. 102-103 (1978), 157-164. See item no. 26.23.

26.168 Ciplijauskaité, Biruté. "Laiko ir erdvés svytuoklé Alejo Carpentier kúryboje." Aidai, 4 (1981), 235-242.

26.169 Clevenger, Darnell H. "The frontier process: Carpentier's Los
        pasos perdidos." TAH, No. 1 (1975), 11-13.

26.170 Colavita, Federica. "Dos relatos de Alejo Carpentier ['Viaje
        a la semilla' y 'Semejante a la noche']." Eco, Nos. 131-
        132 (1971), 593-603.

26.171 Conte, Rafael. "Alejo Carpentier o la historia." In his Len-
        guaje y violencia (Madrid: Al-Borak, 1972), pp. 107-113.

26.172 Cortés Larrieu, Norman. "Idea de América en la narrativa de
        Alejo Carpentier." In Ricardo Vergara, Novela hispanoa-
        mericana (Valparaíso, Chile: Ediciones Universitarias de
        Valparaíso, 1973), pp. 95-145.

26.173 Couffon, Claude. "Alejo Carpentier." In his Hispanoamérica
        en su nueva literatura (Santander: La Isla de los Ratones,
        1962), pp. 41-46.

26.174 "Cronología de Alejo Carpentier." RBNJM, 3a serie, 17, 1
        (1975), 41-43.

26.175 Cros, Edmond. "L'univers fantastique de Alejo Carpentier."
        Caravelle, No. 9 (1967), 75-84.

26.176 Cruz-Luis, Adolfo. "Latinoamérica en Carpentier: génesis de
        lo real maravilloso." CAm, No. 87 (1974), 48-59.

26.177 _____. "Mundonovismo y surrealidad en Alejo Carpentier." CB,
        2a época, No. 41 (1970), 9-12.

26.178 Cudjoe, Selwyn Reginald. "Revolutionary struggle and the nov-
        el." CarQ, 25, 4 (1979), 1-30.

26.179 Cvitanovic, Dinko. "Duplicidad y fascinación del pasado en
        tres cuentos de Carpentier." Criterio, No. 1712 (1975),
        142-145.

26.180 _____. "Lo barroco, clave de confluencias en la obra de Alejo
        Carpentier." RInter, 4 (1974), 370-384.

26.181 Dallal, Alberto. "[El siglo de las luces]." RUM, 17, 10
        (1963), 31.

26.182 Danielson, J. David. "Alejo Carpentier and the United States:
        notes on the Recurso del método." IFR, 4 (1977), 137-145.

26.183 De Armas, Frederick A. "Lope de Vega and Carpentier." In Ac-
        tas del Simposio Internacional de Estudios Hispánicos
        (Budapest: Akademiai Kiadó, 1978), pp. 363-373.

26.184 _____. "Metamorphosis as revolt: Cervantes' Persiles y Sigis-
        munda and Carpentier's El reino de este mundo." HR, 49
        (1981), 297-316.

26.185 Debray, Régis. "Alejo Carpentier et le réalisme [El siglo de las luces]." <u>Partisans</u>, No. 8 (1963), 200-205.

26.186 Delay, Florence. "La fabrication de <u>Siècle</u>." In <u>Quinze études</u>, q.v., pp. 11-19.

26.187 Dellepiane, Angela B. "Tres novelas de la dictadura: <u>El recurso del método, El otoño del patriarca</u> [de Gabriel García Márquez], <u>Yo el Supremo</u> [de Augusto Roa Bastos]." <u>Caravelle</u>, No. 29 (1977), 65-87.

26.188 Depestre, René. "Pequeña biografía de un capitán de la guerra en el tiempo." <u>CAm</u>, No. 87 (1974), 5-6.

26.189 Desnoes, Edmundo. "El sentido de este mundo [El reino de este mundo]." <u>Unión</u>, 3, 4 (1964), 153-156.

26.190 _____. "[El siglo de las luces]." <u>CAm</u>, No. 26 (1964), 100-109. Also in Helmy F. Giacoman, <u>Homenaje</u>, q.v., pp. 293-313.

26.191 Díaz Seijas, Pedro. "De la realidad al mito en <u>El siglo de las luces</u>." <u>LetrasC</u>, Nos. 32-33 (1976), 87-112. Also in his <u>La gran narrativa hispanoamericana</u> (Caracas: Nuevo Siglo, 1976), pp. 123-164.

26.192 Diego, Luis de. "[El reino de este mundo]." <u>SIC</u>, No. 302 (1968), 87-88.

26.193 Díez, Luis Alfonso. "Carpentier y Rulfo: dos largas ausencias." <u>CHA</u>, No. 272 (1973), 338-349.

26.194 Donahue, Francis James. "Alejo Carpentier: la preocupación del tiempo." <u>CHA</u>, No. 202 (1966), 133-151.

26.195 Dorfman, Ariel. "Entre Proust y la momia americana: siete notas y un epílogo sobre <u>El recurso del método</u>." <u>RI</u>, Nos. 114-115 (1981), 95-128.

26.196 _____. "El sentido de la historia en la obra de Alejo Carpentier." In his <u>Imaginación y violencia en América</u> (Santiago de Chile: Universitaria, 1970), pp. 93-137.

26.197 Drake, Sandra E. "Los pasos perdidos." <u>Escritura</u>, No. 7 (1979), 93-109.

26.198 Dubcová, Viera. "K struktúre sujetu Carpentierovho románu Stratené kroky a k jej konkretitácii." In <u>O interpretácii umeleckého textu 2</u> (Bratislava: Slovenské Pedagogické Nakladateľstvo, 1970), pp. 217-231.

26.199 _____. "Zápas o naplnenie casu." In Alejo Carpentier, <u>Stratené kroky</u> (Bratislava: Nakladatelstvo Pravda, 1971), pp. 281-289.

26.200 Dumas, Claude. "El siglo de las luces, de Alejo Carpentier."
        CA, No. 147 (1966), 187-200. Also in Helmy F. Giacoman,
        Homenaje, q.v., pp. 325-363.

26.201 Durán, Manuel. "'Viaje a la semilla', el cómo y el por qué de
        una pequeña obra maestra." In Klaus Müller-Bergh, Asedios
        a Carpentier, q.v., pp. 63-87.

26.202 Durán Luzio, Juan. "Nuestra América, el gran propósito de Ale-
        jo Carpentier." CA, No. 233 (1980), 22-34.

26.203 Džadžić, Petar. "Banket u Blitvi na juznoamericki nacin."
        Knji, 66 (1978), 1299-1310.

26.204 Epple, Juan Armando. "El punto de vista en Concierto barroco
        de Alejo Carpentier." PH, n.s., No. 25 (1978), 74-77.

26.205 Escrivá de Romaní, Manuel M. "Alejo Carpentier recurre a René
        Descartes." CdA, Nos. 17-18 (1975), 49-51.

26.206 _____. "Componiendo barroco, sin excusas [Concierto barroco]."
        CdA, No. 19 (1975), 25-27.

26.207 Esquinazi Mayo, Roberto. "Los pasos perdidos." In his Ensayos
        y apuntes (H: Selecta, 1956), pp. 117-119.

26.208 Eyzaguirre, Luis B. "Sobre tiranía y 'métodos' de 'supremos'
        y 'patriarcas'." Inti, No. 3 (1976), 64-74.

26.209 Fama, Antonio. "La magia como perspectiva en la novela hispa-
        noamericana contemporánea." Actas del Sexto Congreso In-
        ternacional de Hispanistas (Toronto: University of Toron-
        to, Department of Spanish and Portuguese, 1980), pp. 229-
        231.

26.210 _____. "Proceso de individuación y concepto de ánima junguia-
        na en Los pasos perdidos de Alejo Carpentier." RCEH, 3,
        3 (1979), 183-188.

26.211 _____. "Structural parallelisms in Vittorini's In Sicily and
        Carpentier's The lost steps." CJItS, 4 (1980-1981), 104-
        117.

26.212 Faris, Wendy B. "Alejo Carpentier à la recherche du temps
        perdu." CLS, 17 (1980), 133-154.

26.213 _____. "El arpa y la sombra by Alejo Carpentier: 'prima della
        revoluzione'." RInter, 10 (1980), 200-204.

26.214 Fell, Calude. "Recontre avec Alejo Carpentier." LanM, 59, 3
        (1965), 101-108.

26.215 Fernández, Gastón J. "El Primer Magistrado en El recurso del
        método de Carpentier y el olvidado Primer Ministro."
        Círculo, 7 (1978), 71-80.

26.216 Fernández, Sergio. "El destino de los dioses fuertes." Diá-
        logos, No. 85 (1979), 3-9.

26.217 Fernández, Sinesio. "El mito de Sísifo en El siglo de las lu-
        ces." In Festschrift José Cid Pérez (NY: Senda Nueva,
        1981), pp. 243-246.

26.218 Fernández-Marcané, Leonardo. "Un episodio negro en dos nove-
        las hispanoamericanas [María de Jorge Isaacs y El reino
        de este mundo]." In Homenaje a Lydia Cabrera (Miami: Uni-
        versal, 1978), pp. 191-199.

26.219 Fernández Retamar, Roberto. "Alegría por el regreso de Alejo
        Carpentier." In his Papelería (H: Universidad Central de
        Las Villas, Dirección de Publicaciones, 1962), pp. 160-
        164.

26.220 Fisher, Sofía. "Notas sobre el tiempo en Alejo Carpentier."
        Insula, Nos. 260-261 (1968), 5, 8. Also in Helmy F. Gia-
        coman, Homenaje, q.v., pp. 261-273.

26.221 Forgues, Roland. "El arpa y la sombra de Alejo Carpentier:
        ¿desmitificación o mixtificación?" RCLL, No. 14 (1981),
        87-102.

26.222 Foster, David William. "The Everyman theme in Carpentier's
        'El camino de Santiago'." Symposium, 18 (1964), 229-240.

26.223 Fouques, Bernard. "La autopsia del poder según Roa Bastos,
        Carpentier y García Márquez." CA, No. 222 (1979), 83-111.

26.224 _____. "Aux confins de l'utopie et de l'histoire." In Quinze
        études, q.v., pp. 233-245.

26.225 Francés-Benítez, María Elena. "Arquetipos y mitos en ¡Ecué-
        yamba-ó! de Alejo Carpentier." Mester, 8, 2 (1979), 41-
        47.

26.226 Friedmann de Goldberg, Florinda. "Estudio preliminar." In
        Alejo Carpentier, El reino de este mundo (BA: Librería
        del Colegio, 1975), pp. 9-48.

26.227 Fry, Gloria M. "El problema de la voluntad y el acto en 'El
        camino de Santiago'." REH, 3 (1969), 129-144.

26.228 Fuentes, Carlos. "Alejo Carpentier." In Alejo Carpentier,
        El siglo de las luces (Caracas: Biblioteca Ayacucho,
        1979), pp. ix-xix.

26.229 _____. "Carpentier o la doble adivinación." Diálogos, 3, 4
        (1967), 9-11. Also in his La nueva novela hispanoameri-
        cana (M: Joaquín Mortiz, 1969), pp. 48-58.

26.230 Galeano, Eduardo H. "A don Alejo Carpentier." CAm, No. 99
        (1976), 74-75.

26.231 Gálvez Acero, Marina. "Estructura musical del Concierto barro-
        co de Carpentier." In Instituto Internacional de Litera-
        tura Iberoamericana, XVII Congreso (Madrid: Cultura Hispá-
        nica del Centro Iberoamericano de Cooperación, 1978), pp.
        539-553.

26.232 García Bacca, Juan David. "Lied mit worten." Orígenes, No.
        14 (1947), 20-22.

26.233 García-Castro, Ramón. "Dos nuevos cuentos de Alejo Carpen-
        tier: 'Los elegidos' y 'El derecho de asilo'." In Ins-
        tituto Internacional de Literatura Iberoamericana, Otros
        mundos otros fuegos: fantasía y realismo mágico en Ibero-
        América (East Lansing: Michigan State University, Latin
        American Studies Center, 1975), pp. 217-220.

26.234 _____. "Notas sobre la pintura en tres obras de Alejo Car-
        pentier: Los convidados de plata, Concierto barroco y
        El recurso del método." RI, Nos. 110-111 (1980), 67-
        84.

26.235 García-Suárez, Pedro. "Alejo Carpentier." Bohemia, 55, 21
        (1963), 67-69.

26.236 Garscha, Karsten. "[El arpa y la sombra]." Iberoamericana,
        No. 10 (1980), 66-69.

26.237 Giacoman, Helmy F. "La estructura musical en la novelística
        de Alejo Carpentier." Hispanófila, No. 33 (1968), 49-57.

26.238 _____. "La relación músicoliteraria entre la tercera sinfonía
        'Eroica' de Beethoven y la novela El acoso de Alejo Car-
        pentier." CA, No. 158 (1968), 113-129. Also in his Ho-
        menaje, q.v., pp. 439-465. Also as "The use of music in
        literature: El ocoso [sic] by Alejo Carpentier and Sym-
        phony No. 3 (Eroica) by Beethoven." SSF, 8, 1 (1971),
        103-111.

26.239 Giordano, Jaime. "Unidad estructural en Alejo Carpentier."
        RI, No. 75 (1971), 391-401.

26.240 Gleaves, Robert M. "Los pasos perdidos, Pedro Páramo [by Juan
        Rulfo] and the 'classic' novel in Spanish America."
        LangQ, 8, 1-2 (1969), 5-8.

26.241 Glissant, Edouard. "Alejo Carpentier et 'l'autre Amérique'."
        Critique, No. 105 (1956), 113-119.

26.242 Gnutzmann, Rita. "Alejo Carpentier [La consagración de la pri-
        mavera]." Humboldt, No. 70 (1979), 60-62.

26.243 _____. "Alejo Carpentier, lector." CILH, No. 5 (1983), 5-18.

26.244 _____. "Lo picaresco y el punto de vista en El recurso del
        método, de Alejo Carpentier." In La picaresca: orígenes,

textos y estructuras (Madrid: Fundación Universitaria Española, 1979), pp. 1151-1158.

26.245 _____. "Sobre la función del comienzo en la novela: un análisis de las novelas Las lanzas coloradas [de Arturo Uslar Pietri] y El reino de este mundo a través de sus comienzos." CHA, No. 302 (1975), 416-431.

26.246 González, Eduardo H. "El acoso: lectura, escritura e historia." In Enrique Pupo-Walker, El cuento hispanoamericano ante la crítica (Madrid: Castalia, 1973), pp. 126-149.

26.247 _____. "Baroque endings: Carpentier, Sarduy and some textual contingencies." MLN, 92 (1977), 269-295.

26.248 _____. "Los pasos perdidos, el azar y la aventura." RI, No. 81 (1972), 585-613.

26.249 _____. "'Viaje a la semilla' y El siglo de las luces: conjugación de dos textos." RI, Nos. 92-93 (1975), 423-443.

26.250 González, Reinaldo. "Alejo Carpentier: el quehacer de un desmitificador." Areito, No. 23 (1980), 46-50.

26.251 González Bermejo, Ernesto. "Alejo Carpentier: 'Para mí terminaron los tiempos de la soledad'." Crisis, No. 30 (1975), 40-48.

26.252 González Bolaños, Aimée. "Alejo Carpentier y lo real-maravilloso americano." Islas, No. 36 (1970), 92-99.

26.253 González Echevarría, Roberto. "Alejo Carpentier." In Narrativa y crítica de nuestra América (Madrid: Castalia, 1978), pp. 127-160.

26.254 _____. "Borges, Carpentier y Ortega." RI, Nos. 100-101 (1977), 697-704.

26.255 _____. "Carpentier, crítico de la literatura hispanoamericana: Asturias y Borges." SinN, 12, 2 (1981), 7-27.

26.256 _____. "Carpentier y el realismo mágico." In Instituto Internacional de Literatura Iberoamericana, Otros mundos otros fuegos: fantasía y realismo mágico en Iberoamérica (East Lansing: Michigan State Unviersity, Latin American Studies Center, 1975), pp. 221-231.

26.257 _____. "Carpentier's chronos-logic." Review, No. 18 (1976), 9-14.

26.258 _____. "The dictatorship of rhetoric/the rhetoric of dictatorship: Carpentier, García Márquez, and Roa Bastos." LARR, 15, 3 (1980), 205-228.

26.259 _____. "Historia y alegoría en la narrativa de Carpentier."
CA, No. 228 (1980), 200-220.

26.260 _____. "Ironía narrativa y estilo en Los pasos perdidos, de
Alejo Carpentier." NNH, 1, 1 (1971), 117-125. Also as
"Ironía y estilo en Los pasos perdidos, de Alejo Carpentier." In Klaus Müller-Bergh, Asedios a Carpentier, q.
v., pp. 134-145. Also in his Relecturas: estudios de literatura cubana (Caracas: Monte Avila, 1976), pp. 37-51.

26.261 _____. "Isla a su vuelo fugitiva: Carpentier y el realismo mágico." RI, No. 86 (1974), 9-63.

26.262 _____. "Modernidad, modernismo y nueva narrativa: El recurso
del método." RIB, 30 (1980), 157-163.

26.263 _____. "Notas para una cronología de la obra narrativa de Alejo Carpentier, 1944-1954." In Estudios de literatura hispanoamericana en honor a José A. Arrom (Chapel Hill: University of North Carolina, Department of Romance Languages, 1974), pp. 201-214.

26.264 _____. "On Reasons of state." Review, No. 18 (1976), 25-29.

26.265 _____. "The parting of the waters." Diacritics, 4, 4 (1974),
8-17.

26.266 _____. "'Semejante a la noche', de Alejo Carpentier: historia/
ficción." MLN, 87 (1972), 272-285. Also in Klaus Müller-
Bergh, Asedios a Carpentier, q.v., pp. 178-190.

26.267 Gowland de Gallo, María. "Baroque music and new world reality
[Concierto barroco]." Américas, 27, 9 (1975), 37-38. Also as "Música barroca y la realidad del nuevo mundo." A-
méricas [Spanish edition], 27, 9 (1975), 37-38.

26.268 Gribanov, Alexandr. "El nombre como factor constructivo en
las novelas de Alejo Carpentier." ALat, No. 2 (1980),
84-104.

26.269 Gullón, Germán. "El narrador y la narración en Los pasos perdidos." CHA, Nos. 263-264 (1972), 501-509.

26.270 Harss, Luis. "Alejo Carpentier, o el eterno retorno." In his
Los nuestros (BA: Sudamericana, 1966), pp. 51-86. Also,
with Barbara Dohmann, as "Alejo Carpentier, or the eternal
return." In their Into the mainstream (NY: Harper and
Row, 1967), pp. 37-67.

26.271 Hart Dávalos, Armando. "Despedida de duelo." CAm, No. 121
(1980), 8-12.

26.272 Hidalgo-Martín, Jorge. "Estructura de la acción e implicacio-
nes ideológicas en un relato de Alejo Carpentier." RCEH,
3, 3 (1979), 247-258.

26.273 _____. "Utopía y frustración en 'El camino de Santiago' de
Alejo Carpentier." In Actas del Sexto Congreso Interna-
cional de Hispanistas (Toronto: University of Toronto,
Department of Spanish and Portuguese, 1980), pp. 386-390.

26.274 Hodousek, Eduard. "Einige Bemerkungen zur Personlichkeit und
zum literarischen Schaffen von Alejo Carpentier." WZUR,
14 (1965), 41-47.

26.275 "Impresiones." CAm, No. 121 (1980), 13-23.

26.276 Ionescu, Andrei. "In căutarea identităţii culturale." SXX,
Nos. 186-187 (1976), 42-50.

26.277 Iragorri, Delia. "Un Carpentier menos retórico [El derecho de
asilo]." Imagen, No. 62 (1972), 12.

26.278 Irish, G. "Alejo Carpentier: regionalist or universalist."
CarQ, 18, 4 (1972), 57-66.

26.279 Irish, James. "El reino de este mundo by Alejo Carpentier: a
Cuban criollo and the Afro-Haitian world." Savacou, 1
(1970), 98-107.

26.280 Iznaga, Alcides. "Carpentier: su mejor recompensa." Bohemia,
70, 1 (1978), 24-25.

26.281 Janney, Frank. "Apuntes sobre un cuento de Alejo Carpentier."
In Klaus Müller-Bergh, Asedios a Carpentier, q.v., pp.
89-100.

26.282 Jansen, André. "Alejo Carpentier (1905)." In his La novela
hispanoamericana actual y sus antecedentes (Barcelona:
Labor, 1973), pp. 65-73.

26.283 Jiménez-Fajardo, Salvador. "Carpentier's El derecho de asilo:
a game theory." JSSTC, 6 (1978), 193-206.

26.284 _____. "The redeedming quest: patterns of unification in Carpentier, Fuentes and Cortázar." REH, 11 (1977), 91-117.

26.285 Jitrik, Noé. "Blanco, negro, ¿mulato? Una lectura de El reino
de este mundo de Alejo Carpentier." TC, No. 1 (1975), 32-
60. Also Araisa, 1975, pp. 167-205.

26.286 Kapschutschenko, Ludmila. "Alejo Carpentier: búsqueda de lo
perdido en el tiempo." In her El laberinto en la narrativa hispanoamericana (London: Tamesis, 1981), pp. 56-71.

26.287 Kilmer-Tchalekian, Mary A. "Ambiguity in El siglo de las luces." LALR, No. 8 (1976), 47-55.

26.288 King, Lloyd. "A note on the rhetorical structure of Los pasos
perdidos." Reflexión, 2nd series, 1, 1 (1972), 147-152.

26.289 _____. "Souls of Afro-Caribbean folk." Tapia, No. 22 (1973), 6-7.

26.290 Kirk, John M. "Concientización: keystone to the novels of Alejo Carpentier." IFR, 8, 2 (1981), 106-113.

26.291 _____. "Magic realism and voodoo: Alejo Carpentier's The kingdom of this world." PCL, 5 (1979), 124-130.

26.292 Korsi, Demetrio. "El estreno de La pasión negra. Un triunfo de Alejo Carpentier." Carteles, 18, 32 (1932), 16, 53, 60.

26.293 Koui, Théophile. "La problématique de l'échec dans El reino de este mundo d'Alejo Carpentier." AdUA, 12D (1979), 245-260.

26.294 Kuteischikova, Vera N. "Carpentier ha muerto." CAm, No. 122 (1980), 93-95.

26.295 _____. "El concepto del barroco en Alejo Carpentier y la nueva visión artístico-ideológica en la novela contemporánea de América latina." Araisa, 1975, pp. 121-128.

26.296 _____. "Versión al ruso de Los pasos perdidos de Alejo Carpentier." LitS, No. 11 (1965), 197-200.

26.297 Labanyi, J. "Nature and the historical process in Carpentier's El siglo de las luces." BHS, 57 (1980), 55-66.

26.298 Labastida, Jaime. "Alejo Carpentier: realidad y conocimiento estético [El recurso del método]." CAm, No. 87 (1974), 21-31.

26.299 _____. "Nadie puede saltar su sombra [La consagración de la primavera]." Plural, No. 79 (1979), 64-65.

26.300 Labrador Ruiz, Enrique. "El acoso, por Alejo Carpentier." RevC, 31, 3-4 (1957), 159-161.

26.301 Ladra, Luis Antonio. "Alejo Carpentier: 'Viaje a la semilla'." Orígenes, No. 3 (1944), 45-46.

26.302 LaFollette Milla, Martha. "La angustia en tres novelas contemporáneas latinoamericanas." JSSTC, 2 (1974), 137-153.

26.303 Lafourcade, Enrique. "Carpentier, Lezama Lima: la revolución puesta a prueba." Imagen, No. 90 (1971), 16-19.

26.304 Lamb, Ruth S. "El exhuberante barroquismo de Alejo Carpentier." In Instituto Internacional de Literatura Iberoamericana, XVII Congreso (Madrid: Cultura Hispánica del Centro Iberoamericano de Cooperación, 1978), pp. 489-498.

26.305 Langowski, Gerald J. "Los pasos perdidos: concepto surrealista de le merveilleux." In Instituto Internacional de Literatura Iberoamericana, Otros mundos otros fuegos: fantasía y realismo mágico en Iberoamérica (East Lansing: Michigan State University, Latin American Studies Center, 1975), pp. 211-215.

26.306 Láscaris Comneno, Constantino. "El método del recurso del método." RFUCR, No. 42 (1977), 381.

26.307 Lastra, Pedro. "Aproximaciones a ¡Ecué-yamba-ó!" Eco, Nos. 133-134 (1971), 50-67. Also RChL, No. 4 (1971), 79-89. Also in Klaus Müller-Bergh, Asedios a Carpentier, q.v., pp. 40-51.

26.308 _____. "Notas sobre la narrativa de Alejo Carpentier." AUC, No. 125 (1962), 94-101.

26.309 Leante, César. "Confesiones sencillas de un escritor barroco." CubaI, No. 24 (1964), 30-33. Also in Helmy F. Giacoman, Homenaje, q.v., pp. 11-31.

26.310 _____. "Cuba en dos obras iniciales de Carpentier." CA, No. 240 (1980), 55-59.

26.311 _____. "Un reto a la novela moderna [El siglo de las luces]." In his El espacio real (H: Unión de Escritores y Artistas de Cuba, 1975), pp. 79-94. Orig. Unión, 3, 2 (1964), 184-190.

26.312 Lemus, Sylvia. "Carpentier: nuevas obras." CAm, No. 81 (1973), 148-149.

26.313 León, María Teresa. "La música en Cuba por Alejo Carpentier." RevC, 22 (1947), 216-217.

26.314 Levine, Suzanne Jill. "Lo real maravilloso de Carpentier a García Márquez." Eco, No. 120 (1970), 563-576.

26.315 Libertella, Héctor. "[El arpa y la sombra]." Vuelta, No. 41 (1980), 36-37.

26.316 _____. "Por Alejo Carpentier." Vuelta, No. 43 (1980), 48-49.

26.317 Liscano, Juan. "Alejo Carpentier, intérprete de mitos necesarios." Trimestre, 3, 4 (1949), 473-479.

26.318 López, Ana María. "Fracaso y rehabilitación en el protagonista de Los pasos perdidos, de Alejo Carpentier." ALHisp, No. 8 (1979), 127-136.

26.319 López Morales, Eduardo E. "Una conciencia crítica en la encrucijada cultural [Los pasos perdidos]." RyC, No. 28 (1974), 56-65.

26.320 López-Nussa, Leonel. "Goya en El siglo de las luces." GdC,
        No. 35 (1964), 4.

26.321 Lorentzen, Eva. "Alejo Carpentier--en kulturens talsmann på
        Cuba." In Stemmer fra den tredje verden (Oslo: Gyldenal
        Norsk Verlag, 1970), pp. 144-155.

26.322 Loveluck, Juan. "Los pasos perdidos; Jasón y el nuevo velloci-
        no." Atenea, No. 399 (1963), 120-134. Also CHA, No. 165
        (1963), 414-426. Also in his Diez conferencias (Santiago
        de Chile: Universidad de Concepción, Facultad de Filosofía
        y Letras, 1963), pp. 286-305.

26.323 Luna, Norman. "The barbaric dictator and the enlightened ty-
        rant in El otoño del patriarca [by Gabriel García Márquez]
        and El recurso del método." LALR, No. 15 (1979), 25-32.

26.324 _____. "Paradiso [de José Lezama Lima] y El siglo de las lu-
        ces: en torno a la dialéctica mitopoética." REH, 14, 1
        (1980), 121-130.

26.325 Macdonald, Ian R. "Magical eclecticism: Los pasos perdidos
        and Jean-Paul Sartre." FMLS, 15 (1979), 97-113. Also
        in Contemporary Latin American fiction (Edinburgh: Scot-
        tish Academic Press, 1980), pp. 1-17.

26.326 Macé, Marie-Anne. "Le siècle des lumières ou les turbulences
        baroques." In Quinze études, q.v., pp. 187-204.

26.327 Macías de Cartaya, Graziella. "Lo real-maravilloso en la no-
        vela El siglo de las luces." Horizontes, No. 25 (1969),
        5-17.

26.328 Magnerelli, Sharon. "'El camino de Santiago' de Alejo Carpen-
        tier." RI, No. 86 (1974), 65-86.

26.329 Maldonado-Denis, Manuel. "Alejo Carpentier y El reino de este
        mundo." Marcha, No. 1285 (1965), 31.

26.330 Mansau, Andrée. "Le siècle des lumières: histoire de l'escla-
        vage en forme de rêve visionnaire et naïf." In Quinze
        études, q.v., pp. 101-112.

26.331 Marco, Joaquim. "Un gran maestro de la narrativa latinoameri-
        cana: Alejo Carpentier [El reino de este mundo]." In his
        Ejercicios literarios (Barcelona: Taber, 1969), pp. 317-
        323.

26.332 Marinello, Juan. "Homenaje a Alejo Carpentier." RBNJM, 3a
        serie, 17, 1 (1975), 9-17.

26.333 _____. "Homenaje a Alejo Carpentier." GdC, No. 129 (1974),
        10-12.

26.334 _____. "Un hombre excepcional." Bohemia, 56, 32 (1964), 94-
        95.

26.335 _____. "Una novela cubana [¡Ecué-yamba-ó!]." In his Literatura hispanoamericana: hombres-meditaciones (M: Universidad de México, 1937), pp. 167-178.

26.336 _____. "Sobre el asunto en la novela [El acoso]." In his Meditación americana (BA: Procyón, 1959), pp. 57-77.

26.337 Márquez Rodríguez, Alexis. "La adjetivación en la escritura barroca de Alejo Carpentier." SinN, 12, 2 (1981), 28-38.

26.338 _____. "Dos dilucidaciones en torno a Alejo Carpentier." CAm, No. 87 (1974), 35-44.

26.339 _____. "La labor periodística de Alejo Carpentier en Venezuela." In Alejo Carpentier, Letra y solfa (BA: Nemont, 1976), pp. 9-18.

26.340 _____. "Tres vertientes en la crisis de un perseguido en la novela El acoso, de Alejo Carpentier." Actual, 2, 3-4 (1968-1969), 218-223.

26.341 Martí, Agenor. "Alejo Carpentier." CubaI, No. 107 (1978), 14.

26.342 Martínez, Iván César. "Con los pasos en la tierra [El reino de este mundo]." RyC, No. 28 (1974), 46-49.

26.343 Martínez Gómez, Juana et al. "Tiempo y discurso en la consagración de la primavera de Alejo Carpentier." In Organizaciones textuales (textos hispánicos): actas del III Simposio del Séminaire d'Etudes Littéraires de l'Université de Toulouse-Le Mirail (Toulous: Université de Toulouse-Le Mirail, 1981), pp. 53-74.

26.344 Martínez-Palacio, Javier. "Los anti-héroes de Alejo Carpentier." Insula, No. 226 (1965), 1, 14.

26.345 Mas, José L. "El mito de Sísifo en Los pasos perdidos de A. Carpentier." ExTL, 6, 2 (1978), 175-181.

26.346 Mason, Patricia E. "Indetermination in Alejo Carpentier's El derecho de asilo." KRQ, 28 (1981), 383-390.

26.347 Maturo, Graciela. "Religiosidad y liberación en ¡Ecué-yamba-ó! y El reino de este mundo." In Historia y mito, q.v., pp. 53-86.

26.348 _____. "El simbolismo de la cruz en El siglo de las luces." SinN, 8, 2 (1977), 46-53.

26.349 Medina, Ramón Felipe. "La vorágine [de José Eustacio Rivera] y Los pasos perdidos: apuntes para la confrontación de una deuda superada." RP, No. 2 (1973), 117-135.

26.350 Mejía Duque, Jaime. "Los recursos de Alejo Carpentier [El recurso del método]." CAm, No. 89 (1975), 155-158

26.351 Méndez Capote, Renée. "Ese Alejo Carpentier." GdC, No. 165
        (1978), 11.

26.352 Méndez y Soto, E. "La trayectoria revolucionaria de El siglo
        de las luces." ExTL, 5, 2 (1976), 221-226.

26.353 Menton, Seymour. "Asturias, Carpentier y Yáñez: paralelismos
        y divergencias." RI, No. 67 (1969), 31-52.

26.354 _____. "Lo nuevo y lo viejo en el nuevo neobarroco de Alejo
        Carpentier." In Instituto Internacional de Literatura
        Iberoamericana, XVII Congreso (Madrid: Cultura Hispánica
        del Centro Iberoamericano de Cooperación, 1978), pp. 481-
        487.

26.355 _____. "Models for the epic novel of the Cuban revolution
        [La consagración de la primavera]." In honor of Boyd G.
        Carter (Laramie: University of Wyoming, Department of
        Modern and Classical Languages, 1981), pp. 49-58.

26.356 Merino Reyes, Luis. "Presencia en Chile de Alejo Carpentier."
        Atenea, No. 396 (1962), 141-144.

26.357 Micha, René. "Alejo Carpentier, un homeride du nouveau monde."
        L'arc, No. 23 (1963), 65-75.

26.358 Miliani, Domingo. "El dictador, objeto narrativo en dos nove-
        las hispanoamericanas: Yo el supremo [de Augusto Roa Bas-
        tos] y El recurso del método." In Actas del Simposio In-
        ternacional de Estudios Hispánicos (Budapest: Akademiai
        Kiadó, 1978), pp. 463-490.

26.359 _____. "El dictador, objeto narrativo en El recurso del méto-
        do." RI, Nos. 114-115 (1981), 189-225.

26.360 Mimoso-Ruiz, Duarte. "Du référant iconique à la symbolisation
        des personnages." In Quinze études, q.v., pp. 165-186.

26.361 Mínguez S., José Miguel. "Günter Grass (Die Blechtrommel) y
        Julio Cortázar (Rayuela), Heinrich Böll (Opiniones de un
        payaso) y Alejo Carpentier (El reino de este mundo): no-
        tas sobre el realismo mágico y las nuevas actitudes del
        novelista ante su obra." BEG, 9 (1972), 273-290.

26.362 Miomandre, Francis de. "La magie et la foi [El reino de este
        mundo]." NL, 20-X-1949, p. 9.

26.363 _____. "[Los pasos perdidos]." HeM, No. 92 (1954), 602-605.

26.364 Miranda, Julio E. "Cuando el invitado abre su equipaje [En
        torno a razón de ser]." CHA, No. 324 (1977), 597-602.

26.365 Mocega-González, Esther P. "La circularidad temporal en 'Via-
        je a la semilla'." Chasqui, 3, 2 (1974), 5-11.

26.366 ____. "Los pasos perdidos: a propósito de la estructura mística del viaje." TC, No. 9 (1978), 71-82.

26.367 ____. "El recurso del método: una interpretación." Chasqui, 5, 3 (1976), 5-17.

26.368 ____. "El reino de este mundo, de Alejo Carpentier." CHA, Nos. 322-323 (1977), 219-239.

26.369 ____. "La simbología religiosa en El acoso de Alejo Carpentier." ALHisp, Nos. 2-3 (1973-1974), 521-532.

26.370 ____. "El trasfondo hispánico en la narrativa carpentieriana." ALHisp, No. 5 (1976), 253-273.

26.371 Molho, Maurice. "Alejo Carpentier ou le refoulement de l'histoire (analyse d'un trait d'écriture)." In Quinze études, q.v., pp. 37-43.

26.372 Moody, Michael. "Georg Lukács, the historical novel, and El siglo de las luces." REH, 13 (1979), 45-63.

26.373 Morán, Fernando. "De lo real maravilloso y de la historia: Alejo Carpentier." In his Novela y semidesarrollo (una interpretación de la novela hispanoamericana y española) (Madrid: Taurus, 1971), pp. 300-307.

26.374 Morell-Chardon, Hortensia R. "Contextos musicales en Concierto barroco." RI, Nos. 123-124 (1983), 335-350.

26.375 ____. "Funcionalidad del motivo 'moro' en la composición de Concierto barroco de Alejo Carpentier." SinN, 12, 2 (1981), 60-66.

26.376 Moreno, Fernando, and Carlos Santander. "Alejo Carpentier: la verídica (y maravillosa) imagen de América latina." ACh, No. 11 (1980), 75-84.

26.377 Moretić, Yerko. "El siglo de las luces, la más reciente novela de Carpentier." Aurora, 2a época, 1, 1 (1964), 64-77.

26.378 Müller-Bergh, Klaus. "Alejo Carpentier: autor y obra en su época." RI, No. 63 (1967), 9-43. Also in Historia y mito, q.v., pp. 7-42.

26.379 ____. "Alejo Carpentier, 1974: una charla con el novelista cubano." SinN, 12, 2 (1981), 117-123.

26.380 ____. "Concierto color barroco de Alejo Carpentier." In Instituto Internacional de Literatura Iberoamericana, XVII Congreso (Madrid: Cultura Hispánica del Centro Iberoamericano de Cooperación, 1978), pp. 529-538.

26.381 ____. "Corrientes vanguardistas y surrealismo en la obra de Alejo Carpentier." RHM, 35 (1969), 323-340. Also in his Asedios a Carpentier, q.v., pp. 13-38.

26.382 _____. "De Alejo Carpentier." José, No. 7 (1977), 2.

26.383 _____. "En torno al estilo de Alejo Carpentier en Los pasos perdidos." CHA, No. 219 (1968), 554-569. Also in Helmy F. Giacoman, Homenaje, q.v., pp. 179-207.

26.384 _____. "Entrevista con Alejo Carpentier." CA, No. 165 (1969), 141-144.

26.385 _____. "Mito y realidad en Los advertidos." In Estudios de literatura hispanoamericana en honor a José J. Arrom (Chapel Hill: University of North Carolina, Department of Romance Languages, 1974), pp. 239-256.

26.386 _____. "Notas sobre Alejo Carpentier." RO, 2a época, No. 48 (1967), 378-381.

26.387 _____. "Oficio de tinieblas de Alejo Carpentier." In Instituto Internacional de Literatura Iberoamericana, El ensayo y la crítica en Iberoamérica (Toronto: Universidad de Toronto, 1970), pp. 249-255. Also in his Asedios a Carpentier, q.v., pp. 53-61.

26.388 _____. "The persistence of the marvelous." Review, No. 28 (1981), 25-26.

26.389 _____. "Reflexiones sobre los mitos en Alejo Carpentier." Insula, Nos. 260-261 (1968), 5, 22-23. Also in Helmy F. Giacoman, Homenaje, q.v., pp. 275-291.

26.390 _____. "Sentido y color de Concierto barroco." RI, Nos. 92-93 (1975), 445-464.

26.391 _____. "Talking to Carpentier." Review, No. 18 (1976), 20-24.

26.392 _____. "Vida y hechos de un tirano ilustrado [El recurso del método]." RCEH, 3, 2 (1979), 189-195.

26.393 Muñiz, Mirta. "También escritor de radio." RyC, No. 28 (1974), 20-25.

26.394 Murcia, Claude. "Histoire et création romanesque." In Quinze études, q.v., pp. 47-57.

26.395 Nadereau Maceo, Efraín. "Sobre El recurso del método, de Alejo Carpentier." GdC, No. 132 (1975), 28-29.

26.396 Narváez, Jorge. "D. Alejo y el fusil del comandante." CAm, No. 121 (1980), 24-25.

26.397 Navarro, Noel. "Acoso en la ciudad de las columnas [El acoso]." RyC, No. 28 (1974), 35-45.

26.398 Navarro Salazar, María Teresa. "Alejo Carpentier o la modernidad de Dante." NE, 20 (1980), 80-83.

26.399 "'La novela, invención totalmente española': Alejo Carpentier recibe el Premio Cervantes de Literatura." LyF, 60 (1978), 1-3.

26.400 Nuiry, Nuria. "Alejo Carpentier, una biografía a través de siete décadas." Bohemia, 66, 52 (1974), 10-13, 24.

26.401 _____. "[El recurso del método]." Bohemia, 66, 52 (1974), 24.

26.402 Oelker, Dieter. "Morfología de un relato de Alejo Carpentier ['Semejante a la noche']." RChL, No. 12 (1978), 71-89.

26.403 Ojo, Patchechole Poindexter. "Nature in three Caribbean novels." JCSt, 2 (1981), 85-107. Carpentier, George Lemming, and Jacques Roumain.

26.404 Oleríny, Vladimír. "Le 'réalisme magique' de d'Alejo Carpentier." PP, 23 (1980), 112-113.

26.405 "On his seventieth birthday Alejo Carpentier answers seven questions." CarQ, 21, 1-2 (1975), 88-90.

26.406 O'Neill, Joseph F. "Cyclones and vortices: Alejo Carpentier's Reasons of state as Cartesian discourse." StTCL, 2 (1978), 159-174.

26.407 Oquendo, Abelardo. "[Concierto barroco]." Eco, No. 175 (1975), 108-112.

26.408 Oramas, Ada. "Diálogo con Alejo Carpentier." Mujeres, 5, 10 (1965), 14-17.

26.409 Orénoque, Haut. "[Los pasos perdidos]." LetN, No. 2 (1955), 650-674.

26.410 Orozco, Rudolfo. "Sobre las huellas de los pasos perdidos de Alejo Carpentier." Abside, 42 (1978), 243-267.

26.411 Orozco Sierra, Guillermo. "El siglo de las luces a través de la teoría de los 'contextos' de su propio autor." Taller, No. 22 (1971), 13-18.

26.412 Ortega, Julio. "Sobre El siglo de las luces." In his Relato de la utopía (Barcelona: La Gaya Ciencia, 1973), pp. 31-49. Also in Klaus Müller-Bergh, Asedios a Carpentier, q.v., pp. 191-206.

26.413 Ortiz Aponte, Sally. "[Carpentier]." In her La esoteria en la narrativa hispanoamericana (Río Piedras, P.R.: Editorial Universitaria, Universidad de Puerto Rico, 1977), pp. 189-209.

26.414 Osorio Cáceres, Miguel. "Carpentier: de la soledad a la solidaridad." Plural, No. 64 (1977), 34-41.

26.415   Ospovat, Lev. "El hombre y la historia en la obra de Alejo
         Carpentier." CAm, No. 87 (1974), 9-17. Also Islas, No.
         51 (1975), 181-197.

26.416   Otero Silva, Miguel. "Sobre Alejo Carpentier." CAm, No. 122
         (1980), 99-101.

26.417   Ovares, Flora Eugenia. "Aproximación a El reino de este mun-
         do." RAmer, 5, 2 (1979), 29-32.

26.418   Oviedo, José Miguel. "Un grabado preciosista de Carpentier
         [El recurso del método]." RI, Nos, 92-93 (1975), 665-667.

26.419   _____. "Para las fuentes de El acoso y El recurso del método:
         un artículo desconocido de Carpentier." Eco, No. 206
         (1978), 155-168.

26.420   Pacheco, José Emilio. "Vous êtes tous des sauvages! El recur-
         so del método." Plural, 3, 9 (1974), 74-76.

26.421   Pageaux, Daniel-Henri. "Visages et métamorphoses de l'enfer:
         notes sur la IVe partie." In Quinze études, q.v., pp.
         217-231.

26.422   Palermo, Zulma. "Aproximación a Los pasos perdidos." In His-
         toria y mito, q.v., pp. 87-119.

26.423   Pancorbo, Luis. "Tres triste tiranos." RO, 3a época, No. 19
         (1977), 12-16.

26.424   "Para Alejo Carpentier." CAm, No. 121 (1980), 7.

26.425   Pavón Tamayo, Luis. "[Discurso]." RBNJM, 3a serie, 17, 1
         (1975), 5-8.

26.426   _____. "Notas en torno al Recurso del método." RyC, 2a época,
         No. 28 (1974), 50-55. Also VO, 17, 5 (1975), 18-23.

26.427   _____. "Septuagésimo aniversario de Alejo Carpentier: un ca-
         mino de medio siglo." RBNJM, 3a serie, 17, 1 (1975), 5-8.

26.428   Peavler, Terry J. "Alejo Carpentier and the humanization of
         Spanish American fiction." Hispanófila, No. 74 (1982),
         61-78.

26.429   _____. "A new novel by Alejo Carpentier [El recurso del méto-
         do]." LALR, No. 6 (1975), 31-36.

26.430   _____. "The source for the archetype in Los pasos perdidos."
         RomN, 15 (1974), 581-587.

26.431   Pelegrin, Benito. "La harpe et l'ombre d'Alejo Carpentier ou
         l'espace de la parole." CER, 6 (1980), 145-170.

26.432 _____. "Sur le style d'Alejo Carpentier." CER, 6 (1980), 209-219.

26.433 Peña, Rafael Esteban. "Lo real maravilloso en El reino de este mundo." TLit, 5, 11-12 (1975), 7-9.

26.434 Pennington, Eric. "Cutting through the jungle: examining Carpentier's ironic style in Los pasos perdidos." NConL, 11, 2 (1981), 10-12.

26.435 Pereira, Manuel. "Carta desde Nicaragua." Areito, No. 23 (1980), 53.

26.436 Pérez de Francisco, César. "Sobre Alejo Carpentier." Medicina, No. 1056 (1969), 43-46.

26.437 Pérez González, Lilia. "El relato 'Los fugitivos' de Alejo Carpentier." PSA, No. 223 (1974), 41-54.

26.438 Pérez Minik, Domingo. "La guillotina de Alejo Carpentier: en torno a El siglo de las luces." Insula, No. 233 (1966), 3. Also in Helmy F. Giacoman, Homenaje, q.v., pp. 315-323.

26.439 Pérez-Venero, Danièle. "El siglo de las luces: análisis literario." Lotería, Nos. 296-297 (1980), 61-72.

26.440 Perioso, Graciela. "Los pasos perdidos: olvido y reminiscencia." In Historia y mito, q.v., pp. 121-138.

26.441 Phelps, Anthony. "Carta sobre Alejo Carpentier." CAm, No. 122 (1980), 102-103.

26.442 Pi, Agustín. "In praise of Carpentier." CarQ, 21, 1-2 (1975), 86-88.

26.443 Pichardo Gómez, Manuel. "En torno a Carpentier." RUCR, 41 (1975), 213-221.

26.444 Pineda, Rafael. "Alejo Carpentier en la ciudad de las maquetas." RAmer, No. 15 (1976), 1, 6-7.

26.445 _____. "Despedida a Alejo Carpentier." Islas, 2, 2-3 (1960), 413-416.

26.446 Piñeiro, Abelardo. "La Bienal de São Paulo y El siglo de las luces. Entrevista a Alejo Carpentier." PyC, No. 19 (1964), 16-21.

26.447 Pogolotti, Graziella. "Alejo Carpentier ensaya [Tientos y diferencias]." CAm, No. 31 (1965), 94-96.

26.448 _____. "Carpentier renovado." CAm, No. 86 (1974), 127-129.

26.449 _____. "La primavera de un consagrado." CAm, No. 116 (1979), 141-143.

26.450 _____. "El reino de este mundo. Alejo Carpentier en su 70 aniversario." RyC, 2a época, No. 20 (1974), 50-53.

26.451 Pogolotti, Marcelo. "El acoso." In his La república de Cuba al través de sus escritores (H: Lex, 1958), pp. 123-125.

26.452 Poniatowska, Elena. "El hijo pródigo." In her Palabras cruzadas (M: Era, 1961), pp. 216-230.

26.453 Pontiero, Giovanni. "The human comedy in El reino de este mundo." JIAS, 12 (1970), 528-538. Also as "A comédia humana em El reino de este mundo." ESPSL, 19-IX-1971, p. 1.

26.454 Porcel, Balthasar. "Alejo Carpentier, desdeñoso y barroco." Destino, 2a época, No. 1684 (1970), no pagination.

26.455 Portuondo, José Antonio. "Alejo Carpentier: creador y teórico de la literatura." L/L, No. 5 (1974), 3-15.

26.456 _____. "José Soler Puig y la novela de la revolución cubana [El siglo de las luces]." In his Crítica de la época y otros ensayos (H: Consejo Nacional de Universidades, Universidad Central de Las Vilass, 1965), pp. 197-199.

26.457 _____. "El retorno literario de Alejo Carpentier [El acoso]." NTiem, 4, 18 (1957), 6.

26.458 Poujol, Susana. "Palabra y creación en Los pasos perdidos." In Historia y mito, q.v., pp. 139-149.

26.459 Priestly, J. B. "Introduction." In Alejo Carpentier, The lost steps (NY: Knopf, 1967), pp. v-xiii.

26.460 Puisset, Georges. "Rationalisme, irrationnel, 'rationalité': aspects de ce ternaire et polarité dans El recurso del método d'Alejo Carpentier." In Hommage à Jean-Louis Flecniakoska par ces collègues (Montpellier: Université Paul Valéry, 1980), pp. 321-344.

26.461 Quesada, Luis Manuel. "Desarrollo evolutivo del elemento negro en tres de las primeras narraciones de Alejo Carpentier." In Instituto Internacional de Literatura Iberoamericana, Literatura de la emancipación hispanoamericana y otros ensayos (Lima: Universidad Nacional de San Marcos, 1972), pp. 217-223.

26.462 _____. "'Semejante a la noche': análisis evaluativo." In Helmy F. Giacoman, Homenaje, q.v., pp. 227-241.

26.463 Rabassa, Clementine. "The creative function of black characters in Alejo Carpentier's Reasons of state." LALR, No. 12 (1978), 26-37.

26.464 Rama, Angel. "Los adioses de Alejo Carpentier." <u>Eco</u>, Nos.
        224-226 (1980), 130-154.

26.465 _____. "El primer cuento de Alejo Carpentier." <u>Hispamérica</u>,
        No. 9 (1975), 83-86.

26.466 _____. "Los productivos años de Alejo Carpentier (1904-1980)."
        <u>LARR</u>, 16, 2 (1981), 224-245.

26.467 _____. "El siglo de las luces: coronación de Carpentier."
        <u>Marcha</u>, No. 1206 (1964), 1-4.

26.468 Rexach, Rosario. "El siglo de las luces: biografía de una
        ilusión." In Instituto Internacional de Literatura Ibero-
        americana, <u>XVII Congreso</u> (Madrid: Cultura Hispánica del
        Centro Iberoamericano de Cooperación, 1978), pp. 511-528.

26.469 Rey del Corral, José A. "Los pasos perdidos de Alejo Carpen-
        tier." <u>BCB</u>, 10, 4 (1967), 857-863.

26.470 Richard, Renaud. "Réflexions sur 'Voyage à la semence' d'Alejo
        Carpentier." <u>AnBret</u>, 82 (1975), 201-212.

26.471 _____. "Sur quelques aspects musicaux de la composition dans
        Le siècle des lumières: autour de la quartième séquence
        du roman." In <u>Quinze études</u>, q.v., pp. 59-84.

26.472 Rincón, Carlos. "Sobre Alejo Carpentier y la poética de lo
        real maravilloso americano." <u>CAm</u>, No. 89 (1975), 40-65.

26.473 _____. "Sobre 'Capítuo de novela' y 'Luis Garrafita': textos
        desconocidos de Alejo Carpentier y Miguel Angel Asturias."
        <u>Actualidades</u>, 2 (1977), 95-105.

26.474 Ríos, Roberto E. "Los pasos perdidos de Alejo Carpentier."
        In his <u>La novela y el hombre hispanoamericano</u> (BA: Nueva
        Imagen, 1969), pp. 84-91.

26.475 Rivera, Francisco. "[La consagración de la primavera]."
        <u>Vuelta</u>, No. 32 (1979), 35-37.

26.476 Roa, Miguel F. "Alejo Carpentier. El recurso a Descartes."
        <u>CubaI</u>, No. 59 (1974), 45-51.

26.477 Rodríguez, Ana María de. "[Razón de ser; conferencias]." Ac-
        tualidades, No. 2 (1977), 176-179.

26.478 Rodríguez, Ileana. "En busca de una expresión antillana: lo
        real maravilloso en Carpentier y Alexis." <u>I&L</u>, No. 10
        (1979), 56-68.

26.479 _____. "La esposa, la amante, la mujer ideal: tres tipos de
        relación formularia en Los pasos perdidos." <u>RAmer</u>, 4, 2
        (1978), 5-12.

26.480 _____. "Historia y alegoría en Alejo Carpentier." Hispamérica, No. 17 (1977), 24-45.

26.481 Rodríguez-Alcalá, Hugo. "Sobre 'El camino de Santiago' de Alejo Carpentier." In Helmy F. Giacoman, Homenaje, q.v., pp.
243-259. Also in his Narrativa hispanoamericana (Madrid:
Gredos, 1973), pp. 22-35. Orig. HumM, No. 5 (1964), 245-
254. Also in Klaus Müller-Bergh, Asedios a Carpentier,
q.v., pp. 165-176.

26.482 Rodríguez Almedóvar, Antonio. "La estructura narrativa de Alejo Carpentier." In his La estructura de la novela burguesa (Madrid: Betancer, 1976), pp. 123-219.

26.483 Rodríguez Monegal, Emir. "Dos novelas de Alejo Carpentier."
In his Narradores de esta América (Montevideo: Alfa,
1963?), pp. 147-153.

26.484 _____. "Lo real y lo maravilloso en El reino de este mundo."
RI, Nos. 76-77 (1971), 619-649. Also in Klaus Müller-
Bergh, Asedios a Carpentier, q.v., pp. 101-132. Also in
his Narradores de esta América; 2. ed. (Montevideo: Alfa,
1969-1974), II, 64-98.

26.485 _____. "Trayectoria de Alejo Carpentier." In his Narradores
de esta América; 2. ed. (Montevideo: Alfa, 1969-1974),
I, 270-287.

26.486 Rodríguez-Puértolas, Carmen C. de. "Alejo Carpentier, teoría
y práctica." Eco, No. 98 (1968), 171-201.

26.487 Ross, Waldo. "Alejo Carpentier o sobre la metamorfosis del
tiempo." UAnt, No. 171 (1968), 133-146. Also in Actas
del Tercer Congreso Internacional de Hispanistas (M: El
Colegio de México, 1970), pp. 753-764.

26.488 Rubén, José. "[Tientos y diferencias]." Eco, No. 65 (1965),
540-543.

26.489 Ruffinelli, Jorge. "Descubriendo a América [Tientos y diferen-
cias]." Marcha, No. 1384 (1976), 29.

26.490 Saad, Gabriel. "L'histoire et la révolution dans Le siècle
des lumières." In Quinze études, q.v., pp. 113-122.

26.491 Salomon, Noël. "A Baszkföld Alejo Carpentier El siglo de las
luces c imü regényében." FK, 13 (1967), 119-127.

26.492 _____. "Les sources de l'évocation de Paramaribo et son éla-
boration littéraire dans El siglo de las luces d'Alejo
Carpentier." In Mélanges à la mémoire d'André Joucla-
Ruau (Aix-en-Provence: Université de Provence, 1978),
pp. 355-369.

26.493 _____. "Sur le 'pays basque' dans El siglo de las luces d'Alejo Carpentier." LNL, No. 176 (1966), 71-83.

26.494 Sánchez, José G. "Carpentier's Los pasos perdidos: a middle ground view." TQ, 18, 1 (1975), 32-48.

26.495 Sánchez, Modesto G. "El fondo histórico de El acoso." RI, Nos. 92-93 (1975), 397-422.

26.496 Sánchez, Napoleón Neptali. "Lo real maravilloso americano o la americanización del surrealismo." CA, No. 219 (1978), 69-95.

26.497 Santana, Joaquín G. "Muertes, resurrecciones, triunfos, agonías." Bohemia, 63, 13 (1971), 4-9.

26.498 _____. "Los pasos encontrados." CubaI, No. 17 (1970), 44-49.

26.499 Santander, Carlos. "Historicidad y alegoría en El siglo de las luces de Alejo Carpentier." In Instituto Internacional de Literatura Iberoamericana, XVII Congreso (Madrid: Cultura Hispánica del Centro Iberoamericano de Cooperación, 1978), pp. 499-510.

26.500 _____. "Lo maravilloso en la obra de Alejo Carpentier." Atenea, 159 (1965), 99-126. Also in Helmy F. Giacoman, Homenaje, q.v., pp. 99-144.

26.501 _____. "Prólogo." In Alejo Carpentier, Viaje a la semilla (Santiago de Chile: Nascimento, 1971), pp. 7-21.

26.502 _____. "El tiempo maravilloso en la obra de Alejo Carpentier." EFil, 4 (1968), 107-129.

26.503 Santos Moray, Mercedes. "Alejo Carpentier y el nouveau roman." CB, 2a época, No. 50 (1971), 24-26.

26.504 _____. "Notas para el estudio de la novela en Alejo Carpentier." Santiago, No. 9 (1972), 189-196.

26.505 Sarrias, Cristóbal. "Alejo Carpentier, Premio Miguel de Cervantes." RyF, No. 197 (1978), 186-190.

26.506 Schanzer, George. "Carpentier fallen from grace." Hispania, 51 (1968), 188.

26.507 Schnelle, Kurt. "Carpentier und die Suche nach dem Geschichtsbewusstein." In Alejo Carpentier, Hetzjagd (Leipzig: Philipp Reclam, 1966), pp. 97-206.

26.508 Scholz, László. "Alejo Carpentier (1904-1980)." FK, 26 (1980), 467-470.

26.509 Schwartz, Ronald. "Carpentier: Cuban cosmopolite, baroque stylist." In Nomads, exiles, and emigrés: the rebirth of the Latin American narrative, 1960-80 (Metuchen, N.J.: Scarecrow, 1980), pp. 1-13.

26.510 Segre, Roberto. "La dimensión ambiental en lo real maravilloso de Alejo Carpentier." CAm, No. 120 (1980), 18-33.

26.511 Selva, Mauricio de la. "Con pretexto de El recurso del método." CA, No. 196 (1974), 226-237.

26.512 Serra, Edelweis. "Estructura y estilo de la novela: El acoso, de Alejo Carpentier." Prohemio, 3, 1 (1972), 119-143. Also in Historia y mito, q.v., pp. 151-179.

26.513 "Los setenta años de Carpentier." CubaI, No. 66 (1975), 22.

26.514 Seymour, Arthur J. "El significado de la obra de Alejo Carpentier." CAm, No. 122 (1980), 114-115.

26.515 Shaw, Donald L. "Alejo Carpentier." In his Nueva narrativa hispanoamericana (Madrid: Cátedra, 1981), pp. 79-88.

26.516 Silva-Cáceres, Raúl. "Un desplazamiento metonímico como base de la teoría de la visión en El siglo de las luces." RI, Nos. 123-124 (1983), 487-496.

26.517 _____. "Mito y temporalidad en Los pasos perdidos, de Alejo Carpentier." In Angel Flores, and Raúl Silva Cáceres, La novela hispanoamericana actual (NY: Las Américas, 1971), pp. 21-38.

26.518 _____. "Una novela de Carpentier [Los pasos perdidos]." MNu, No. 17 (1967), 33-37.

26.519 _____. "Los sistemas expresivos en la obra de Alejo Carpentier." Amaru, No. 7 (1968), 75-78.

26.520 Silva de Sánchez, María Teresa. "Los pasos perdidos: una búsqueda de sí mismo a través del tiempo." BCB, 9 (1966), 507-510.

26.521 Sokoloff, Naomi Beryl. "Spatial form in the 'social novel': John Dos Passos' U.S.A. and Alejo Carpentier's El reino de este mundo." PRom, 2 suppl. (1980), 111-119.

26.522 Sommers, Joseph. "Ecué-yamba-ó: semillas del arte narrativo de Alejo Carpentier." In Estudios de literatura hispanoamericana en honor a José J. Arrom (Chapel Hill: University of North Carolina, Department of Romance Languages, 1974), pp. 227-238.

26.523 Sorel, Andrés. "En torno a El siglo de las luces de A. Carpentier." CpD, No. 32 (1966), 39.

26.524 _____. "El mundo novelístico de Alejo Carpentier." CHA, No. 182 (1965), 304-318. Also in Helmy F. Giacoman, Homenaje, q.v., pp. 71-98.

26.525 Soto-Duggan, Silvia. "El acoso: análisis de motivos y corre-
latos." CA, No. 217 (1978), 158-164.

26.526 Souza, Raymond D. "Alejo Carpentier's timeless history." In
his Major Cuban novelists; innovation and tradition (Columbia: University of Missouri Press, 1976), pp. 30-52.

26.527 Speratti-Piñero, Emma Susana. "Noviciado y apoteosis de Ti
Noel en El reino de este mundo de Alejo Carpentier."
BH, 80 (1978), 201-228.

26.528 Stimson, Frederick S. "Alejo Carpentier, Cuban novelist." BA,
33 (1959), 149.

26.529 Suardíaz, Luis. "Trabajar con Alejo Carpentier." Areito, No.
23 (1980), 54-55.

26.530 Sucre, Guillermo. "Alejo Carpentier: El siglo de las luces."
Imagen, 4 supl. (1967), 10-11.

26.531 Talvet, Jüri. "Algunos aspectos del tiempo y del espacio en
la novelística de Alejo Carpentier." CAm, No. 122 (1980),
104-113.

26.532 Taylor, Karen. "La creación musical en Los pasos perdidos."
NRFH, 26 (1977), 141-153.

26.533 Tijeras, Eduardo. "El siglo de las luces en su edición española." CHA, No. 208 (1967), 199-204.

26.534 Timossi, Jorge. "Alejo Carpentier: la identidad latinoamericana." CAm, No. 109 (1978), 86-90. Also CubaI, No. 104
(1978), 22-25.

26.535 Tizón, Héctor. "[El arpa y la sombra]." CHA, No. 357 (1980),
719-722.

26.536 Torres Fierro, Danubio. "El recurso del método de Carpentier
[Concierto barroco]." Plural, 4, 8 (1975), 71-73.

26.537 Treil-Labarre, Françoise. "Le voyage du jeune Esteban à tra-
vers la révolution." In Quinze études, q.v., pp. 123-146.

26.538 Troth, Eva. "Tradición e invención en la obra de Alejo Carpentier." In Actas del Simposio Internacional de Estudios
Hispánicos (Budapest: Akademiai Kiadó, 1978), pp. 359-362.

26.539 Townsend, Lindsay. "The image of art in Carpentier's Los pasos
perdidos and El acoso." RomN, 20 (1980), 304-309.

26.540 Trigo, Pedro. "Alejo Carpentier, pedagogo literario de la revolución. Entrevista: ¿Qué es la épica sino política?"
RLAE, No. 89 (1975), 2-5.

26.541 ____. "El derecho de asilo." RLAE, No. 59 (1972), 11-12.

26.542 No item.

26.543 Uria Santos, María Rosa. "El recurso del método: una exploración de la realidad hispanoamericana." AlHisp, No. 5 (1976), 387-394.

26.544 Uriarte, Fernando. "El criollismo alucinante de Alejo Carpentier." Mapocho, 5, 1 (1966), 90-101.

26.545 Usabiaga, Mario. "Alejo Carpentier y su primer magistrado." TC, No. 3 (1976), 128-140.

26.546 Valbuena Briones, Angel. "Una cala en el realismo mágico." CA, No. 166 (1969), 233-241.

26.547 Valdés Bernal, Sergio. "Caracterización lingüística del negro en la novela ¡Ecué-yamba-ó! de Alejo Carpentier." L/L, No. 2 (1971), 123-183.

26.548 Valdés-Cruz, Rosa. "En torno al poema 'Liturgia' de Alejo Carpentier." ExTL, 5, 1 (1976), 29-33.

26.549 Valle, Rafael del. "[Concierto barroco]." CAm, No. 94 (1976), 149-151.

26.550 Van Praag-Chantraine, Jacqueline. "El acoso de Alejo Carpentier." In Actas del Tercer Congreso de Americanistas (M: El Colegio de México, 1970), pp. 225-231.

26.551 ____. "Alejo Carpentier ou la guerre du temps." Synthèses, Nos. 254-255 (1967), 51-59.

26.552 "Variaciones sobre un tema: fragmentos, notas, de y sobre Alejo Carpentier." RyC, No. 28 (1974), 4-19.

26.553 Vasconcelos, Ramón. "El folklorista de Yamba O." In his Montparnase (H: Cultural, 1938), pp. 125-137.

26.554 Vásquez, Carmen. "Dans le sillage de Victor Hugues et de son temps." In Quinze études, q.v., pp. 85-97.

26.555 ____. "Mis años de trabajo con Alejo Carpentier." SinN, 12, 2 (1981), 107-116.

26.556 Vázquez Amaral, José. "The return of the native: Alejo Carpentier's The lost steps." In his The contemporary Latin American narrative (NY: Las Américas, 1970), pp. 95-119.

26.557 Vega, José L. "Tiempo, ritmo e historia en Concierto barroco." SinN, 12, 2 (1981), 67-80.

26.558 Verdeboye, Paul. "Las novelas de Alejo Carpentier y la reali-
        dad maravillosa." RI, Nos. 118-119 (1982), 317-320.

26.559 _____. "Le siècle des lumières et la réalité merveilleuse."
        In Quinze études, q.v., pp. 149-163.

26.560 Versazconi, Ray. "Juan and Sisyphus in Carpentier's 'El camino
        de Santiago'." Hispania, 48 (1965), 70-75. Also as "Juan
        y Sísifo en 'El camino de Santiago'." In Historia y mito,
        q.v., pp. 43-52.

26.561 Vidal, Hernán. "Arquetipificación e historicidad en Guerra del
        tiempo." NNH, 3, 2 (1973), 245-256.

26.562 Villares, Ricardo. "Entrevista con Alejo Carpentier." Bohe-
        mia, 66, 52 (1974), 58-61.

26.563 Volek, Emil. "Alejo Carpentier y la narrativa latinoamericana
        actual: dimensiones de un 'realismo mágico'." CHA, No.
        296 (1975), 319-342.

26.564 _____. "Algunas reflexiones sobre El siglo de las luces y el
        arte narrativo de Alejo Carpentier." CAm, No. 74 (1972),
        42-54.

26.565 _____. "Análisis del sistema de estructuras musicales e inter-
        pretación de El acoso de Alejo Carpentier." PP, 12
        (1969), 1-24. Also in Helmy F. Giacoman, Homenaje, q.v.,
        pp. 385-438.

26.566 _____. "Análisis e interpretación de El reino de este mundo
        y su lugar en la obra de Alejo Carpentier." Unión, 4, 1
        (1969), 98-118. Also as "Análisis e interpretación de
        El reino de este mundo de Alejo Carpentier." In Helmy
        F. Giacoman, Homenaje, q.v., pp. 145-178. Also IAP, 1
        (1967), 23-41.

26.567 _____. "Dos cuentos de Carpentier: dos caras del mismo método
        artístico ['Semejante a la noche' y 'El camino de Santia-
        go']." NNH, 1, 2 (1971), 7-19.

26.568 _____. "Los pasos perdidos." ULH, No. 189 (1968), 25-37.

26.569 Volkening, Ernesto. "Reconquista y pérdida de la América ar-
        caica en Los pasos perdidos de Alejo Carpentier." Eco,
        No. 82 (1967), 367-402.

26.570 Wagener, Françoise. "Una novela histórica de Alejo Carpen-
        tier: ¿fue Cristóbal Colón un santo? [El arpa y la som-
        bra]." CAn, 2, 1 (1980), 89-90.

26.571 Weber, Frances Wyers. "El acoso: Alejo Carpentier's war on
        time." PMLA, 78 (1963), 440-448. Also as "El acoso: la
        guerra del tiempo de Alejo Carpentier." In Klaus Müller-
        Bergh, Asedios a Carpentier, q.v., pp. 147-164.

26.572 _____. "Los contextos de El recurso del método, de Carpentier." RI, Nos. 123-124 (1983), 323-334.

26.573 West, Paul. "Despot-au-feu." Review, No. 18 (1976), 5-9.

26.574 Williams, Lorna V. "The image of King Christophe." CLAJ, 20 (1977), 333-340.

26.575 _____. "The utopian vision in Carpentier's El reino de este mundo." JCSt, 2 (1981), 129-139.

26.576 Zherdynivs'ka, Marharyta. "Pro Alekho Karpent'iera: latinoamerikans'ka symfoniia." Vsesvit, 1 (1981), 163-166.

26.577 Zimmerman, Marie-Claire. "La poétisation dans le roman: procédure et signification." In Quinze études, q.v., pp. 21-36.

27. CARRION, MIGUEL DE (1875-1929)

Bibliographies

27.1 "En el centenario de Miguel de Carrión. Bibliografía de su obra narrativa." L/L, No. 6 (1975), 190-196.

Critical Monographs and Dissertations

27.2 González, Mirza L. La novela y el cuento psicológicos de Miguel de Carrión. Miami: Universal, 1979. Orig. DAI, 35 (1974), 3739A-3740A.

Critical Essays

27.3 Bernal, Emilia. "A don Miguel de Carrión." Bohemia, 10, 30 (1919), 3-4.

27.4 Bianchi Ross, Ciro. "Cien años para Carrión." CubaI, No. 70 (1975), 71.

27.5 Bibliófilo, pseud. "Tinta fresca. Las honradas: novela por Miguel de Carrión." Bohemia, 10, 28 (1919), 4.

27.6 Bueno, Salvador. "Aproximaciones críticas a Miguel de Carrión." In his Temas y personajes de la literatura cubana (H: U-nión, 1964), pp. 189-207.

27.7 _____. "Una mujer en la sociedad burguesa [Las honradas]." Unión, 6, 2 (1967), 168-172.

27.8 Casey, Calvert. "Carrión a escena." GdC, No. 2 (1962), 15.

27.9 _____. "Carrión o la desnudez." LRev, No. 52 (1960), 15-17.

27.10 _____. "[La esfinge]." CAm, Nos. 11-12 (1962), 63-65.

27.11 "Dos novelas de Carrión." CCont, 19 (1919), 342.

27.12 Espinosa, Ciro. "Juicio sobre la novela Las honradas, de Miguel de Carrión." In his Indagación y crítica; novelistas cubanos (H: Cultural, 1940), pp. 121-175. See also "Datos biográficos de Miguel de Carrión," pp. 119-120.

27.13 Hermann, pseud. "Acotaciones literarias. Dos novelas de Carrión." Social, 4 (1919), 7.

27.14 "Homenaje a Miguel de Carrión." CUNESCO, 2, 3 (1961), entire
       issue.

27.15 Mañalich, Ramiro. "Miguel de Carrión y Cárdenas, como pedago-
       go." Ideas, 2, 2 (1929), 88-96.

27.16 Montori, Arturo. "La obra literaria de Miguel de Carrión."
       CCont, 21 (1919), 337-352.

27.17 "La muerte de Miguel de Carrión." Social, 14 (1929), 5.

27.18 "Las muertes cubanas: Miguel de Carrión." Avance, 4 (1929), 248.

27.19 Parajón, Mario. "Prólogo." In Miguel de Carrión, La esfinge
       (H: Comisión Nacional Cubana de la UNESCO, 1961), pp. 5-15.

27.20 Pogolotti, Marcelo. "El bovarismo criollo." In his La repúbli-
       ca de Cuba al través de sus escritores (H: Lex, 1958), pp.
       50-52.

27.21 _____. "La vida galante." In his La república de Cuba al tra-
       vés de sus escritores (H: Lex, 1958), pp. 56-58.

27.22 Remos y Rubio, Juan Nepomuceno José. "Miguel de Carrión."
       CCont, 8 (1915), 333-335.

27.23 _____. "La personalidad literaria de Miguel de Carrión." Ide-
       as, 2, 2 (1929), 97-107. Also in his Hombres de Cuba (H:
       Cárdenas, 1941), pp. 111-136.

27.24 "Revista de impresos. La última voluntad, por Miguel de Ca-
       rrión." CyA, No. 49 (1903), 748.

27.25 Rohan, L. de. "Carrión." In his Figuras del retablo (H: La
       Prueba, 1919), pp. 115-119.

27.26 Roig de Leuchsenring, E. "Las honradas de Miguel de Carrión."
       Social, 2 (1917), 14, 51.

27.27 "La segunda edición de Las honradas." CCont, 19 (1919), 343.

27.28 Torre, Miguel Angel de la. "Tras la última página [Las impu-
       ras]." In his Prosas varias (H: Editorial de la Universi-
       dad, 1966), pp. 321-324.

27.29 Valle, Adrián del. "El milagro." CyA, 14, 4 (1904), 108.

27.30 Varona y Pera, Enrique José. "Una novela nietzscheana [El mi-
       lagro]." In his Violetas y ortigas; notas críticas (Ma-
       drid: Editorial-América, n.d.), pp. 208-211.

37.31 Yedra, Elena. "La imagen de la mujer en la obra de Miguel de
       Carrión: Las honradas." Islas, No. 51 (1975), 121-152.

28. CASAL, JULIAN DEL (1863-1893)

Bibliographies

28.1 Duplessis, Gustavo. "Julián del Casal: bibliografía." RBC, 54 (1944), 283-286.

28.2 Figueroa Amaral, Esperanza. "Bibliografía cronológica de la obra de Julián del Casal." RI, No. 68 (1969), 385-399.

28.3 ____. "Bibliografía de y sobre Julián del Casal." BBC, 2, 3-4 (1942), 33-38.

28.4 Geada de Prulletti, Rita. "Bibliografía de y sobre Julián del Casal (1863-1893)." RI, No. 53 (1967), 133-139.

28.5 Pane, Remigio U. "Cuban poetry in English: a bibliography of English translations from Casal, Florit, Gómez de Avellaneda, Guillén, Heredia, Pedroso and 'Plácido'." BBDI, 18, 9 (1946), 199-201.

Critical Monographs and Dissertations

28.6 Clay Méndez, Luis Felipe. "Julián del Casal: estudio comparativo de prosa y poesía." DAI, 37 (1977), 5167A.

28.7 Duplessis, Gustavo. Julián del Casal. H: Molina, 1945.

28.8 Estudios críticos [sobre Julián del Casal]. H: Biblioteca Nacional, Departamento Colección Cubana, 1964-. Pertinent items are listed separately.

28.9 Gómez Cortés Quírino, Francisco Rubén. "Julián del Casal: el hombre y su poesía." DAI, 34 (1974), 6640A.

28.10 Hernández-Miyares, Julio E. "Julián del Casal, escritor." DAI, 33 (1973), 6312A.

28.11 Julián del Casal: estudios críticos sobre su obra. Miami: Universal, 1974. Pertinent items are listed separately.

28.12 Meza y Suárez, Ramón. Julián del Casal, estudio biográfico. H: Avisador Comercial, 1910.

28.13 Monner Sans, José María. Julián del Casal y el modernismo hispanoamericano. M: El Colegio de México, 1952.

28.14 Nunn, Marshall E. The life and works of Julián del Casal. Un-
       published Ph.D. dissertation, University of Illinois, 1939.

28.15 Portuondo, José Antonio. Angustia y evasión de Julián del Ca-
       sal. H: Molina, 1937. A fragment appeared as item no.
       28.122.

28.16 Rey-Barreau, José Luis. "El concepto de la muerte en cuatro
       poetas premodernistas." DAI, 32 (1971), 5803A. Casal
       inter alios.

28.17 Sos, Ciriaco. Julián del Casal o un falsario de la rima. H:
       "La Prensa", 1893. Signed César de Guanabacao.

Critical Essays

28.18 Acosta, Agustín. "Evocación de Julián del Casal." RevC, 19
       (1945), 5-15. Also BACL, 11, 1 (1964), 123-129.

28.19 Aguirre, J. M. "Pies/paloma: Casal, Vilé-Griffin, Valéry, Pe-
       mán." RI, No. 91 (1975), 257-261.

28.20 Armas y Cárdenas, José de. "Julián del Casal." In his Estudios
       y retratos (Madrid: V. Suárez, 1911), pp. 307-311.

28.21 Augier, Angel I. "Evocación de Julián del Casal." PolíticaH,
       No. 25 (1943), 4.

28.22 _____. "Julián del Casal." GdC, No. 40 (1964), 8-9.

28.23 _____. "Julián del Casal (noviembre 1863-octubre 1893)." ULH,
       Nos. 50-51 (1943), 133-144.

28.24 _____. "El periodista Julián del Casal." In Album del cincuen-
       tenario de la Asociación de Repórters de la Habana, 1902-
       1952 (H: Asociación de Repórters de la Habana, 1952), pp.
       63-64. Also GdC, No. 25 (1963), 6-7.

28.25 _____. "Prosa periodística y literaria de Julián del Casal."
       In Julián del Casal, Crónicas habaneras (Santa Clara: Uni-
       versidad Central de Las Villas, 1963), pp. 9-18.

28.26 _____. "6 notas sobre Julián del Casal." ULH, No. 164 (1963),
       161-170.

28.27 Avedaño, Fausto. "'En el campo'." In Francisco E. Porrata,
       and Jorge A. Santana, Antología comentada del modernismo
       (Sacramento: California State University, Department of
       Spanish and Portuguese, 1974), pp. 175-179. ExTL, Anexo I.

28.28 Balseiro, José A. "Cuatro enamorados de la muerte de la lírica
       hispanoamericana." In his Expresión de Hispanoamérica;
       primera serie (San Juan, P.R.: Instituto de Cultura Puer-
       torriqueña, 1960), I, 121-137. Casal inter alios.

28.29 Bar-Lewaw Mulstock, Itzhak. "La prosa de José Martí y de Julián del Casal." In his Temas literarios latinoamericanos (M: Costa-Amic, 1961), pp. 33-46.

28.30 Berger, Margaret Robinson. "The influence of Baudelaire on the poetry of Julián del Casal." RR, 37 (1946), 177-187.

28.31 Blanco-Aguinaga, Carlos. "Crítica marxista y poesía: lectura de un poema de Julián del Casal." In The analysis of Hispanic texts: current trends and methodology (Jamaica: Bilingual Press/York College, 1976), pp. 191-205.

28.32 _____. "Lectura de 'Neurosis' de Julián del Casal." CAm, No. 122 (1980), 48-56.

28.33 Borrero Echeverría, Esteban. "In memoriam." In Julián del Casal, Prosas (H: Consejo Nacional de Cultura, 1963), I, 37-39.

28.34 Bueno, Salvador. "Julián del Casal, precursor del modernismo." In his Figuras cubanas del siglo XIX (H: Unión de Escritores y Artistas, 1980), pp. 173-177.

28.35 _____. "Sentido del color en la poesía de Julián del Casal." GdC, No. 25 (1963), 3-4.

28.36 Cabrera, Rosa M. "Julián del Casal: vida y obra poética." In Julián del Casal, Vida y obra poética (NY: Las Américas, 1970), pp. 11-86.

28.37 _____. "'Kakemono'." In Francisco E. Porrata, and Jorge A. Santana, Antología comentada del modernismo (Sacramento: California State University, Department of Spanish and Portuguese, 1974), pp. 149-154. ExTL, Anexo I.

28.38 _____. "El sentido del color y del sonido en la poesía de Casal y Martí." PLit, No. 22 (1966), 16.

28.39 Cabrera Saqui, Mario. "Ensayo preliminar." In Julián del Casal, Poesías completas (H: Ministerio de Educación, Dirección de Cultura, 1945), pp. 7-40.

28.40 _____. "Julián del Casal y el modernismo." RBC, No. 57 (1946), 28-53.

28.41 Caillet-Bois, Julio. "Julián del Casal." Realidad, 1 (1947), 282-287.

28.42 Chacón y Calvo, José María. "En torno a un epistolario de Julián del Casal." BACL, 7, 3-4 (1958), 346-373.

28.43 Clay Méndez, Luis Felipe. "Una autopsia psicológica de Julián del Casal." CHA, No. 374 (1981), 270-286.

28.44 _____. "El descubrimiento de Julián del Casal a través de su prosa." CA, No. 219 (1978), 211-220.

28.45 _____. "Julián del Casal and the cult of artificiality: roots and functions." In Waiting for Pegasus: studies of the presence of symbolism and decadence in Hispanic letters (Macomb: Western Illinois University, 1979), pp. 155-168.

28.46 _____. "Julián del Casal: juicios críticos sobre el periodismo." ALHisp, No. 6 (1977), 87-96.

28.47 _____. "Julián del Casal: nuevas rectificaciones crítica." REH, 14, 1 (1980), 101-120.

28.48 Cruz, Manuel de la. "Julián del Casal." In his Cromitos cubanos (H: Arte y Literatura, 1975), pp. 223-236. Also in his Literatura cubana (Madrid: Calleja, 1924), pp. 425-428. Also in Cintio Vitier, La crítica literaria y estética en el siglo XIX cubano (H: Biblioteca Nacional "José Martí", Departamento Colección Cubana, 1968), III, 97-106. Also in Aurelio Mitjans, Estudio sobre el movimiento científico y literario de Cuba (H: A. Alvarez, 1890), pp. 299-321.

28.49 Cuza Malé, Belkis. "Ambitos desconocidos de Julián del Casal." GdC, No. 165 (1978), 13-15.

28.50 Darío, Rubén. "Julián del Casal." In Julián del Casal, Prosas (H: Consejo Nacional de Cultura, 1963), I, 31-35.

28.51 Duplessis, Gustavo. "Julián del Casal." RBC, No. 54 (1944), 140-170, 241-286. Also ULH, No. 164 (1963), 7-134. Same as item no. 28.7.

28.52 Durán-Cerda, Julio. "'Elena'." In Francisco E. Porrata, and Jorge A. Santana, Antología comentada del modernismo (Sacramento: California State University, Department of Spanish and Portuguese, 1974), pp. 138-145. ExTL, Anexo I.

28.53 Englekirk, John E. "Julián del Casal." In his Edgar Allan Poe in Hispanic literature (NY: Instituto de las Españas en los Estados Unidos, 1934), pp. 230-239.

28.54 Esténger, Rafael. "Con la hermana de Julián del Casal." Bohemia, 42, 19 (1950), 36-37, 106-107.

28.55 _____. "José A. Silva y Calibán sonríe (recuerdos de Casal)." CCont, 23 (1920), 31-44.

28.56 Federman, Joan. "La visión decadente del mundo en los cuentos y crónicas de Julián del Casal." In Estudios críticos sobre la prosa modernista hispanoamericana (NY: Eliseo Torres, 1975), pp. 122-134.

28.57 Feijóo, Samuel. "El tiempo aciago de Julián del Casal, centenario de un poeta." Bohemia, 55, 27 (1963), 32-35.

28.58 Fernández de Castro, José A. "Aniversario y revisión de Casal."
       RevH, 1 (1930), 51-56.

28.59 Figueroa de Amaral, Esperanza. "Apuntes sobre Julián del Ca-
       sal." RI, No. 14 (1944), 329-335.

28.60 _____. "Comentario biográfico y rectificaciones." In Julián
       del Casal: estudios críticos sobre su obra, q.v., pp. 9-
       31.

28.61 _____. "Julián del Casal y el modernismo." RI, No. 59 (1965),
       47-69.

28.62 _____. "Julián del Casal y Rubén Darío." RBC, 50 (1942), 191-
       208.

28.63 _____. "Luz y sombra en la poesía casaliana." In Julián del
       Casal: estudios críticos sobre su obra, q.v., pp. 33-46.

28.64 _____. "Revisión de Julián del Casal." In Primer Congreso de
       Historia (H, 1943), 251-255.

28.65 Fontanella, Lee. "Parnassian precept and a new way of seeing
       Casal's Museo ideal." CLS, 7 (1970), 450-479.

28.66 García Vega, Lorenzo. "La opereta cubana en Julián del Casal."
       Unión, 3, 2 (1964), 59-79.

28.67 Geada de Pruletti, Rita. "'Nostalgias'." In Francisco E. Po-
       rrata, and Jorge A. Santana, Antología comentada del mo-
       dernismo (Sacramento: California State University, Depart-
       ment of Spanish and Portuguese, 1974), pp. 138-145. ExTL,
       Anexo I.

28.68 _____. "El sentido de la evasión en la poesía de Julián del
       Casal." RI, No. 61 (1966), 101-108.

28.69 Geada y Fernández, Juan J. "Introducción." In Julián del Ca-
       sal, Selección de poesías (H: Cultural, 1931), pp. v-cxvii.

28.70 Gicovate, Bernardo. "Tradición y novedad en un poema de Julián
       del Casal ['Elena']." NRFH, 14 (1960), 119-125. Also in
       his Conceptos fundamentales de literatura comparada (San
       Juan, P.R.: Asomante, 1962), pp. 105-116.

28.71 Glickman, Robert Jay. "Julián del Casal: letters to Gustave
       Moreau." RHM, 37 (1972-1973), 101-103.

28.72 _____. "'Neurosis'." In Francisco E. Porrata, and Jorge A.
       Santana, Antología comentada del modernismo (Sacramento:
       California State University, Department of Spanish and
       Portuguese, 1974), pp. 171-175. ExTL, Anexo I.

28.73 _____. "'Vespertino'." In Francisco E. Porrata, and Jorge A.
       Santana, Antología comentada del modernismo (Sacramento:

California State University, Department of Spanish and
Portuguese, 1974), pp. 146-149. ExTL, Anexo I.

28.74 González, Manuel Pedro. "Un notable estudio argentino sobre
       Julián del Casal. Glosa de aniversario." RI, No. 38
       (1954), 253-260. See item no. 28.18.

28.75 González, Sandra. "Tres cartas desconocidas de Julián del Ca-
       sal." L/L, Nos. 7-8 (1976-1977), 276-293.

28.76 Goytisolo, José Agustín. "Sobre el modernismo y Julián del Ca-
       sal." CdA, 12 (1974), 20-23.

28.77 Guerra Flores, José. "La poesía de Julián del Casal." Abside,
       27, 3 (1963), 301-307.

28.78 Gutiérrez-Vega, Zenaida. "La deuda con Julián del Casal."
       ALHisp, No. 4 (1975), 267-268. Also Abside, 39 (1975),
       472-480.

28.79 Henríquez Ureña, Camila. "Julián del Casal, poeta de la muer-
       te." ULH, No. 164 (1963), 145-160.

28.80 Henríquez Ureña, Max. "Julián del Casal." In his Breve histo-
       ria del modernismo; 2. ed. (M: Fondo de Cultura Económica,
       1962), pp. 115-134.

28.81 Henríquez Ureña, Pedro. "Ante la tumba de Casal." In Julián
       del Casal, Prosas (H: Consejo Nacional de Cultura, 1963),
       I, 41-42.

28.82 Hernández-Miyares, Julio E. "Los cuentos modernistas de Casal:
       apuntes para un estudio." In Festschrift José Cid Pérez
       (NY: Senda Nueva, 1981), pp. 237-241.

28.83 _____. "Julián del Casal: decadentismo y modernismo." In Ins-
       tituto Internacional de Literatura Iberoamericana, XVII
       Congreso (Madrid: Cultura Hispánica del Centro Iberoameri-
       cano de Cooperación, 1978), pp. 735-744.

28.84 _____. "Julián del Casal: sus ideas y teorías sobre el arte y
       la literatura." In Julián del Casal: estudios críticos
       sobre su obra, q.v., pp. 47-80.

28.85 Jiménez, Luis A. "Elementos decadentes en la prosa castaliana."
       In Julián del Casal: estudios críticos sobre su obra, q.
       v., pp. 81-119.

28.86 "Julián del Casal visto por sus contemporáneos." GdC, No. 25
       (1963), 9-12.

28.87 Júlio, Sílvio. "Julián del Casal." In his Escritores antilha-
       nos (Rio de Janeiro: H. Antunes, 1944), pp. 146-178.

28.88   Lamothe, Louis. "Julián del Casal." In his Los mayores poetas
        latinoamericanos del 1850 a 1950 (M: Libro Mex, 1959), pp.
        49-54.

28.89   Lara, Justo de. "Julián del Casal." In Julián del Casal, Pro-
        sas (H: Consejo Nacional de Cultura, 1963), I, 35-37.

28.90   Lazo, Raimundo. "Julián del Casal y su poesía a los cien
        años." ULH, No. 164 (1963), 135-143.

28.91   Leslie, John K. "Casal's Salomé: the mystery of the missing
        prophet." MLN, 62 (1947), 402-404.

28.92   Lezama Lima, José. "Julián del Casal." In his Analecta del
        reloj; ensayos (H: Orígenes, 1953), pp. 62-97. Also in
        Julián del Casal, Prosas (H: Consejo Nacional de Cultura,
        1963), I, 69-90. A fragment appeared as "Esteticismo y
        dandyismo." GdC, No. 25 (1963), 5-6.

28.93   _____. "Oda a Julián del Casal." RBNJM, 3a época, 5, 1-4
        (1963), 5-10.

28.94   Lizaso y González, Félix, and José Antonio Fernández de Castro.
        "Julián del Casal." RAm, 9 (1924), 245-246.

28.95   Loynaz, Dulce María. "Ausencia y presencia de Julián del Ca-
        sal." BACL, 5 (1956), 5-26. Signed Dulce María Loynaz
        de Alvarez Cañas.

28.96   Márquez Sterling, Manuel. "El espíritu de Casal." In Julián
        del Casal, Prosas (H: Consejo Nacional de Cultura, 1963),
        I, 39-41.

28.97   _____. "Julián del Casal." In his Quisicosas (sátira y críti-
        ca) (M: F. Hoeck, 1895), pp. 98-104.

28.98   Martí, José. "Julián del Casal." In his Páginas selectas (BA:
        Angel Estrada, 1957), pp. 21-23. Also in his Obras com-
        pletas (H: Editorial Nacional de Cuba, 1963), V, 221-222.
        Also in Julián del Casal, Prosas (H: Consejo Nacional de
        Cultura, 1963), I, 25-26. Also in Cintio Vitier, La crí-
        ca literaria y estética en el siglo XIX cubano (H: Biblio-
        teca Nacional José Martí, Departamento Colección Cubana,
        1968), II, 480-481. Also in his Hombres de Cuba (H: Pu-
        blicaciones de la Secretaría de Educación, 1936), pp. 54-
        57.

28.99   Meza y Suárez Inclán, Ramón. "Julián del Casal." RFLC, 11
        (1940), 105-142.

28.100 Meza Fuentes, Roberto. "Un desterrado del mundo." In his De
        Díaz Mirón a Rubén Darío (Santiago de Cuba: Andrés Bello,
        1964), pp. 93-109.

28.101 Mocega-González, Esther P. "Tres momentos poéticos de Julián
        del Casal." CHA, No. 236 (1969), 473-483.

28.102 Monner Sans, José María. "Biografía y semblanza de Julián del
        Casal." BAAL, 16 (1947), 411-437.

28.103 ____. "La iniciación poética de Julián del Casal." Atenea,
        No. 273 (1948), 214-222.

28.104 ____. "Julián del Casal bajo el influjo parnasiano." BAAL,
        17 (1948), 75-85.

28.105 ____. "Los temas poéticos de Julián del Casal." CA, No. 49
        (1950), 246-260.

28.106 Mullen, Edward J. "'La reina de la sombra'." In Francisco E.
        Porrata, and Jorge A. Santana, Antología comentada del
        modernismo (Sacramento: California State University, De-
        partment of Spanish and Portuguese, 1974), pp. 161-165.
        ExTL, Anexo I.

28.107 Nunn, Marshall E. "Julián del Casal. First modernist poet."
        Hispania, 23 (1940), 73-80.

28.108 ____. "Preface." In Julián del Casal, Selected prose (Uni-
        versity: University of Alabama Press, 1949), pp. vii-xi.

28.109 ____. "Vida y obras de Julián del Casal." América, 4, 1
        (1939), 49-55.

28.110 Onís, Federico de. "Julián del Casal, 1863-1893." In his Es-
        paña en América (San Juan, P.R.: Ediciones de la Univer-
        sidad de Puerto Rico, 1955), pp. 194-195.

28.111 Ortal, Yolanda. "La muerte de Julián del Casal." PSA, No.
        159 (1969), 317-324.

28.112 Oyuela, Calixto. "Julián del Casal." In his Poetas hispanoa-
        mericanos (BA: Academia Argentina de Letras, 1949-1950),
        II, 57-60.

28.113 Pearsall, Priscilla. "Casal's translations of Beaudelaire and
        Maupassant: the failure of transcendent value." In Essays
        in honor of Jorge Guillén on the occasion of his 85th year
        (Cambridge, Mass.: Abedul, 1977), pp. 64-73.

28.114 ____. "Julián del Casal's portraits of women." In The anal-
        ysis of literary texts: current trends in methology;
        3rd and 4th York College Conference (Ypsilanti, Mich.:
        Bilingual Press, 1980), pp. 78-88.

28.115 ____. "Julián del Casal's Rimas: an unfinished work." CH,
        2 (1980), 143-147.

28.116 ____. "Neoplatonism and modernity in Julián del Casal."
        RCEH, 5 (1980), 106-109.

28.117   ____. "A new look at duality in Julián del Casal." Chasqui, 8, 3 (1979), 44-53.

28.118 Phillips, Allen W. "Una nota sobre el primer modernismo: Julián del Casal y algunos poetas mexicanos." In Estudios de literatura hispanoamericana en honor a José J. Arrom (Chapel Hill: University of North Carolina, Department of Romance Languages, 1974), pp. 109-123.

28.119 Plácido, A. D. "Supervivencia de Julián del Casal en la poesía." RNM, 10 (1965), 232-242.

28.120 Poncet, Carmen P. "Dualidad de Casal." RBC, 53 (1944), 193-212.

28.121 Porrata, Francisco E. "'Salomé'." In Francisco E. Porrata, and Jorge A. Santana, Antología comentada del modernismo (Sacramento: California State University, Department of Spanish and Portuguese, 1974), pp. 134-137. ExTL, Anexo I.

28.122 Portuondo, José Antonio. "Angustia y evasión de Julián del Casal." CHH, No. 13 (1937), 55-87. Also in Julián del Casal, Prosas (H: Consejo Nacional de Cultura, 1963), I, 42-68. A fragment of item no. 28.15. A fragment also appeared as "Retrato del poeta adolescente." GdC, No. 25 (1963), 2-3.

28.123 Poveda, José Manuel. "Para la lectura de las Rimas de Julián del Casal." In his José Manuel Poveda (H: Instituto de Literatura y Lingüística de la Academia de Ciencias de Cuba, 1975), pp. 287-289.

28.124 Quackenbush, Louis Howard. "'A la belleza'." In Francisco E. Porrata, and Jorge A. Santana, Antología comentada del modernismo (Sacramento: California State University, Department of Spanish and Portuguese, 1974), pp. 166-170. ExTL, Anexo I.

28.125 Roig de Leuchsenring, Emilio. "Julián del Casal." In his La literatura costumbrista cubana de los siglos XVIII y XIX (H: Oficina del Historiador de la Ciudad de la Habana, 1962), III, 251-261.

28.126 Ruprecht, Hans-George. "Aspects logiques de l'intertextualité: pour une approche sémiotique de la poésie de Julián del Casal." Dispositio, No. 4 (1977), 1-27.

28.127 ____. "L'intertextualité isotope: 'Horridum somnium', de Julián del Casal." NS/N, 2, 3-4 (1977), 223-249.

28.128 Sánchez, Luis Alberto. "Julián del Casal." In his Escritores representativos de América; segunda serie (Madrid: Gredos, 1972), I, 122-130.

28.129 Sanguily y Garritte, Manuel. "Corona fúnebre." In Julián del
        Casal, Prosas (H: Consejo Nacional de Cultura, 1963), I,
        29-31.

28.130 Schulman, Ivan A. "Casal's Cuban counterpoint of art and real-
        ity." LARR, 11, 2 (1976), 113-128.

28.131 ____. "Las estructuras polares en la obra de José Martí y
        Julián del Casal." RI, No. 56 (1963), 251-282. Also in
        his Génesis del modernismo (M: El Colegio de México,
        1966), pp. 153-187.

28.132 Smith, Mark I. "Julián del Casal y la violencia literaria."
        MFS, 10, 3 (1980), 71-75.

28.133 Suarée, Octavio de la, Jr. "La obsesión de la muerte, el uso
        de la máscara y la idea del suicidio: algunas observacio-
        nes sobre la prosa modernista de Julián del Casal." Cír-
        culo, 7 (1978), 45-54.

28.134 Torres-Ríoseco, Arturo. "A rebours [by Joris Karl Huysmans]
        and two sonnets of Julián del Casal." HR, 23 (1955), 295-
        297. Also in his Ensayos sobre literatura latinoamerica-
        na; segunda serie (M: Fondo de Cultura Económica, 1958),
        pp. 90-92.

28.135 ____. "En torno a seis poetas hispanoamericanos. ¿Es Julián
        del Casal precursor del modernismo o no?" In his Ensayos
        sobre literatura latinoamericana; segunda serie (M: Fondo
        de Cultura Económica, 1958), pp. 145-147.

28.136 ____. "Julián del Casal (1863-1893)." In his Precursores del
        modernismo (Madrid: Calpe, 1925), pp. 35-46. 2. ed., NY:
        Las Américas, 1963.

28.137 Urbina, Luis G. "Julián del Casal (fragmento)." Azul, 2
        (1895), 181-182.

28.138 Varona y Pera, Enrique José. "[Hojas al viento]." RCub, 11
        (1890), 473-477. Also in Julián del Casal, Prosas (H:
        Consejo Nacional de Cultura, 1963), I, 26-29.

28.139 ____. "[Nieve]." RCub, 16 (1892), 142-146.

28.140 ____. "Notas editoriales: Julián del Casal." RCub, 18
        (1893), 240-241.

28.141 Vian, Francesco. "Julián del Casal (1863-1893)." In his El
        "modernismo" nella poesia ispanica (Milano: La Goliardi-
        ca, 1955), pp. 113-125.

28.142 Villena, Luis Antonio de. "El camino simbolista de Julián del
        Casal." Inti, 7 (1978), 35-48.

28.143 Vitier, Cintio. "El artista." In his Poetas cubanos del siglo XIX; semblanzas (H: Unión, 1969), pp. 47-49.

28.144 _____. "Casal como antítesis de Martí. Hastío, forma, belleza, asimilación y originalidad. Nuevos rasgos de lo cubano." In his Lo cubano en la poesía (Santa Clara: Universidad Central de Las Villas, Departamento de Relaciones Culturales, 1958), pp. 242-268. Also in Julián del Casal, Prosas (H: Consejo Nacional de Cultura, 1963), I, 90-111.

28.145 _____. "Julián del Casal en su centenario." In Cintio Vitier, and Fina García Marruz, Estudios críticos (H: Biblioteca José Martí, Departamento Colección Cubana, 1964), pp. 5-42. Also in his Crítica sucesiva (H: Contemporáneos, UNEAC, 1971), pp. 276-325.

28.146 Zaldívar, Gladys. "Dos temas de búsqueda metafísica en Huysmans y Casal." In Julián del Casal: estudios críticos sobre su obra, q.v., pp. 135-144.

28.147 _____. "Significación de la nostalgia de otro mundo en la poesía de Julián del Casal." In Julián del Casal: estudios críticos sobre su obra, q.v., pp. 121-133.

29. CASTELLANOS, JESUS (1879-1912)

Critical Monographs and Dissertations

29.1   Domínguez y Roldán, Guillermo. Jesús Castellanos; el porvenir de la literatura. H: "Avisador Comercial", 1914.

29.2   Smith, Wilburn Philip. Jesús Castellanos. His life and works. Unpublished Ph.D. dissertation, University of North Carolina, 1935.

Critical Essays

29.3   Barros, Bernardo G. "Jesús Castellanos." CCont, 8 (1915), 333-335.

29.4   Bazil, Osvaldo. "La bondad de Jesús Castellanos." In his Cabezas de América (H: Molina, 1933), pp. 71-75.

29.5   Carbonell y Rivero, Miguel Angel. "Jesús Castellanos." In his Hombres de nuestra América (H: La Prueba, 1915), pp. 265-271.

29.6   Guerra Núñez, Juan. "La novela de Jesús Castellanos." CyA, 31, 3 (1910), 39-40.

29.7   Henríquez Ureña, Maz. "En el parque de Jesús del Monte. A propósito de La conjura." Letras, 2a época, 5, 20 (1909), 273-274.

29.8   _____. "La vida y las obras de Jesús Castellanos." RBC, 7, 3 (1912), 219-247; 8, 1 (1912), 60-91. Also as "Jesús Castellanos: su vida y su obra." In Jesús Castellanos, Colección póstuma (H: El Siglo XX de A. Miranda, 1914-1916), I, 9-70.

29.9   Iznaga, Alcides. "En torno a viejas novelas cubanas: La manigua sentimental." Islas, 2, 1 (1959), 304-305.

29.10 Lizazo y González, Félix. "Jesús Castellanos." In his Ensayistas contemporáneos, 1900-1920 (H: Trópico, 1938), pp. 15-18.

29.11 Pogolotti, Marcelo. "Un cubano en el umbral del siglo." In his La república al través de sus escritores (H: Lex, 1958), pp. 22-24.

29.12 Rodríguez-Embril, Luis. "Jesús Castellanos y su tiempo." AAHAL, 32 (1945-1946), 120-148.

29.13 Soto Morejón, Estrella. "Jesús Castellanos." ULH, No. 158
       (1962), 57-71.

29.14 Toledo Sande, Luis. "Jesús Castellanos: un escritor agonizan-
       te." ULH, No. 207 (1978), 175-184.

30. CHACON Y CALVO, JOSE MARIA (1893-1969)

Bibliographies

30.1 Gutiérrez-Vega, Zenaida. *Estudio bibliográfico de José María Chacón y Calvo*. Madrid: Cultura Hispánica, 1969.

Critical Monographs and Dissertations

30.2 Gutiérrez-Vega, Zenaida. *Epistolario Alfonso Reyes/José María Chacón*. Madrid: Fundación Universitaria Española, 1976.

30.3 _____. *José María Chacón y Calvo, hispanista cubano*. Madrid: Fundación Universitaria Española, 1976.

Critical Essays

30.4 Bisbé, Manuel. "Chacón y Calvo: hombre vario." RBC, 36 (1935), pagination unknown.

30.5 Bueno, Salvador. "En memoria de José María Chacón y Calvo." RBNJM, 3a serie, 12, 1 (1970), 144-147.

30.6 Conde, Carmen. "El historiador don José María Chacón y Calvo." MHisp, No. 262 (1970), 58-59.

30.7 Contreras y López de Ayala, Juan de. "Marqués de Lozoya: José María Chacón y Calvo, conde de Casa-Bayona." BRAH, 168, 1 (1971), 133-138.

30.8 D'Aquino, Hernando. "Chacón y Calvo." Abside, 35 (1971), 343-351.

30.9 Entralgo, Elías. "José M. Chacón y Calvo." In his *Perfiles* (H: "Hermes", 1923), pp. 93-127.

30.10 González, Manuel Pedro. "En torno a los nuevos." RBC, 25 (1930), 382-393. Chacón y Calvo inter alios.

30.11 Guerra Flores, José. "Mi última visita a Chacón y Calvo." Abside, 34 (1971), 85-87.

30.12 Gutiérrez-Vega, Zenaida. "Ideario de José María Chacón y Calvo." Círculo, 10 (1981), 19-27.

30.13 _____. "José María Chacón y Calvo en las letras hispánicas." CHA, No. 208 (1967), 115-134.

30.14 _____. "Pedro Henríquez Ureña, maestro continental: cartas a José María Chacón y Calvo, Francisco José Castellanos y Félix Lizaso, 1914-1919, 1935." RI, No. 94 (1976), 103-134.

30.15 Ichaso, Francisco. "[El documento y la reconstrucción histórica]." Avance, No. 39 (1929), 310-311.

30.16 _____. "[Ensayos de literatura española]." Avance, No. 23 (1928), 162.

30.17 Jiménez, José Olivio. "Los cincuenta años de vida literaria de José Ma. Chacón y Calvo." RI, No. 58 (1964), 305-312.

30.18 _____. "José María Chacón y Calvo." CHA, No. 241 (1970), 2.

30.19 Lazo, Raimundo. "Elogio a José María Chacón y Calvo." RevH, 8 (1946), pagination unknown.

30.20 Lizaso y González, Félix. "José María Chacón y Calvo." In his Ensayistas contemporénos, 1900-1920 (H: Trópico, 1938), pp. 183-188.

30.21 Mañach, Jorge. "[Los comienzos literarios de Zenea]." Avance, No. 9 (1927), 238. See item no. 98.3.

30.22 Novás Calvo, Lino. "José María Chacón y Calvo." RevC, 5 (1936), 257-277. RAm, 31 (1936), 260-262.

30.23 Sánchez de Bustamante y Montoro, Antonio. "Homenaje a José Ma. Chacón y Calvo." In his Ironías y generación; ensayos (H: Ucar, García, 1937), pp. 118-129.

30.24 Vitier, Medardo. "José M. Chacón y Calvo." In his Apuntaciones literarias (H: Minerva, 1935), pp. 155-158.

31. CHAPLE, SERGIO (1938-   )

<u>Critical Essays</u>

31.1 Augier, Angel I. "Indagación en Mendive [Rafael María Mendive; definición de un poeta]." <u>L/L</u>, Nos. 3-4 (1972-1973), 233-234.

31.2 Avila, Leopoldo. "La colección Pluma en ristre." <u>VO</u>, 10, 21 (1969), 17.

31.3 Casáus, Víctor. "Hera y Chaple: un paso más allá de la promesa." <u>PCr</u>, No. 31 (1969), 175-185.

31.4 Dubcová, Viera. "3.20 Popoludni." <u>Romboid</u>, 9, 1 (1974), 29.

31.5 Martínez Laínez, Fernando. "Entrevista a Sergio Chaple." In his <u>Palabra cubana</u> (Madrid: Akal, 1975), pp. 159-171.

31.6 Navarro, Noel. "[Hacia otra luz más pura]." <u>CB</u>, 2a época, No. 95 (1975), 29-30.

31.7 Rodríguez, Luis Enrique. "El estructuralismo y Rafael María Mendive [Rafael María Mendive; definición de un poeta]." <u>ULH</u>, Nos. 198-199 (1973), 207-210.

31.8 "Sergio Chaple hizo 3.20 p.m." <u>GdC</u>, No. 41 (1964), 2.

31.9 Suárez, Adolfo. "Por una crítica que no adultere los valores humanos." <u>CB</u>, 2a época, No. 94 (1975), 10-11.

32. CID PEREZ, JOSE (1906-   )

Critical Monographs and Dissertations

32.1   Davis, Michele Star. "Proyecciones estilísticas en los perso-
       najes femeninos de José Cid." <u>DAI</u>, 40 (1979), 3287A.

32.2   <u>Festschrift José Cid Pérez</u>. NY: Senda Nueva, 1981. Pertinent
       items are listed separately.

Critical Essays

32.3   Davis, Michele Star. "Del realismo a la vanguardia en tres
       dramaturgos hispano-americanos (Rodolfo Usigli, Vicente
       Martínez-Cuitiño y José Cid)." In <u>Festschrift</u>, q.v., pp.
       73-80.

32.4   Francovich, Guillermo. "José Cid Pérez." In <u>Festschrift</u>, q.v.,
       pp. 21-25.

32.5   Guardia, Alfredo de la. "El teatro de José Cid Pérez." In José
       Cid Pérez, <u>Un tríptico y dos comedias</u> (BA: Carro de Tespis,
       1972), pp. 11-25.

32.6   Herrera, Roberto. "El tema de la libertad en dos obras patrió-
       ticas de José Cid Pérez." In <u>Festschrift</u>, q.v., pp. 35-44.

32.7   Jackson, Mary H. "<u>Comedy of the dead</u> by José Cid Pérez." In
       <u>Festschrift</u>, q.v., pp. 51-56.

32.8   McKinney, James E. "José Cid y sus críticos: comentarios de al-
       gunas reseñas." In <u>Festschrift</u>, q.v., pp. 63-71.

32.9   _____. "El teatro de José Cid." <u>RABM</u>, 3a época, 77 (1974),
       327-334.

32.10 Piñera, Humberto. "Vida y dramaturgia." In <u>Festschrift</u>, q.v.,
       pp. 27-33.

32.11 Sánchez-Boudy, José. "Lo social en el teatro de José Cid-Pé-
       rez." In <u>Festschrift</u>, q.v., pp. 45-50.

32.12 Santalla, María Aurora. "Azucena: una nota infantil en el mun-
       do teatral de José Cid-Pérez." In <u>Festschrift</u>, q.v., pp.
       57-62.

33.   COFIÑO LOPEZ, MANUEL (1936-   )

Critical Essays

33.1   Arias, Salvador. "Manuel Cofiño. Tiempo de cambio." L/L, No.
       2 (1971), 205-206.

33.2   Armas, Mirta. "Cronista, juez y parte." RyC, No. 66 (1978),
       46-51.

33.3   Blanco Figueroa, Francisco. "Literatura y sociedad [La última
       mujer y el próximo combate]." Comunidad, No. 62 (1977-
       1978), 614-623.

33.4   Cofiño López, Manuel. "Encuesta." GdC, No. 164 (1978), 8-9.

33.5   Crespo, Francisco Julio. "Para leer siempre [Para leer maña-
       na]." CB, No. 113 (1977), 30.

33.6   Deschamps Chapeaux, Pedro. "[Cuando la sangre se parece al
       fuego]." No. 135 (1975), 4-5.

33.7   Díaz Martínez, Manuel. "[Tiempo de cambio]." GdC, No. 82
       (1970), 27.

33.8   Doblado, Raúl. "Manuel Cofiño: narrativa del cambio." CB, No.
       122 (1978), 5, 23, 26, 31.

33.9   Donoso Pareja, Miguel. "[La última mujer y el próximo combate]."
       No. 80 (1971), 483-484.

33.10 González Echevarría, Roberto. "[La última mujer y el próximo
       combate]." RI, Nos. 92-93 (1975), 669-670.

33.11 López Ruiz, Juvenal. "[La última mujer y el próximo combate]."
       RNC, No. 201 (1971), 147-148.

33.12 Lucyga, Christine. "Traditionsbeziehungen im modernen kuban-
       ischen Roman: Manuel Cofiño López und César Leante." WB,
       26, 9 (1980), 159-163.

33.13 "M. Kofin'io: pysaty pro te, shcho znaiesh." Vsevit, 11 (1981),
       232-233.

33.14 Menton, Seymour. "[La última mujer y el próximo combate]." RI,
       No. 79 (1972), 352-353.

33.15 Miyares, Eloína. "Algo sobre La última mujer y el próximo com-
       bate." Santiago, No. 8 (1972), 249-253.

33.16 Mocega-Gonález, Esther P. "[La última mujer y el próximo combate]." Chasqui, 4, 1 (1974), 80-81.

33.17 Muiños, René. "Análisis del cuento 'Tiempo de cambio'." Santiago, No. 12 (1973), 209-222.

33.18 Oleaga, Armando. "[La última mujer y el próximo combate]." CB, 2a época, No. 51 (1971), 28-29.

33.19 Portuondo, José Antonio. "Una novela revolucionaria [La última mujer y el próximo combate]." CAm, No. 71 (1972), 105-106.

33.20 "¿Qué escribe ahora." RyC, No. 63 (1977), 73.

33.21 Rodríguez Puértolas, Julio. "Manuel Cofiño, o la superación de lo real-maravilloso." I&L, No. 3 (1977), 73-80.

33.22 Rodríguez Sosa, Fernando. "Cofiño por debajo de Cofiño [Cuando la sangre se parece al fuego]." Bohemia, 67, 33 (1975), 24.

33.23 Rojas, Manuel. "[La última mujer y el próximo combate]." CAm, No. 67 (1971), 172-173. Also Caravelle, No. 17 (1971), 247.

33.24 Sosa, Ignacio. "La novela como ilustración y el ensayo como conciencia." RUM, 26, 6-7 (1972), 93.

33.25 "La última mujer y el próximo combate, una novela de la Revolución." VO, 13, 44 (1971), 62.

33.26 Walter, Monika. "Interview mit Manuel Cofiño López." WB, 26, 9 (1980), 104-112.

33.27 _____. "Notizen zum Interview mit Manuel Cofiño López." WB, 26, 9 (1980), 113-123.

34. CRUZ, MANUEL DE LA (1861-1896)

Critical Monographs and Dissertations

34.1 Chacón y Calvo, José María. Manuel de la Cruz (prólogo a sus obras completas). Madrid: Aldus, 1925.

34.2 Figueroa, Pedro Pablo. Un colorista cubano: Manuel de la Cruz; boceto literario. Lima: Gil, 1896.

34.3 Valverde y Maruri, Antonio L. Manuel de la Cruz, historiador y patriota cubano. H: "El Siglo XX", 1929.

Critical Essays

34.4 Bueno, Salvador. "Manuel de la Cruz." Bohemia, 64, 36 (1972), 92-98.

34.5 _____. "Manuel de la Cruz, el crítico." In his Figuras cubanas del siglo XIX (H: Unión de Escritores y Artistas, 1980), pp. 267-276.

34.6 _____. "Manuel de la Cruz, 'Mambí de las letras'." In Manuel de la Cruz, Cromitos cubanos (H: Arte y Literatura, 1975), pp. 11-36.

34.7 Capestany Meulener, Olga V. "Manuel de la Cruz, escritor y héroe civil." ULH, Nos. 151-153 (1961), 81-104.

34.8 Chacón y Calvo, José María. "Manuel de la Cruz." In Manuel de la Cruz, Obras (Madrid: Saturnino Calleja, 1924), I, 9-41. Orig. CCont, 36, 2 (1924), 173-195.

34.9 Figarola Caneda, Domingo. "Nota biográfica de Manuel de la Cruz." In Manuel de la Cruz, Episodios de la revolución cubana; 2. ed. (H: Miranda, 1911), pagination unknown.

34.10 Márquez Sterling, Manuel. "Prólogo." In Manuel de la Cruz, Episodios de la revolución cubana; 2. ed. (H: Miranda, 1911), pp. iii-xvi.

34.11 Martí, José. "Carta a Manuel de la Cruz." In his Obras completas (H: Editorial Nacional de Cuba, 1963), V, 179-181.

34.12 Piedra Bueno, Andrés de. "Dosel." In Manuel de la Cruz, Pasión de Cuba (H: Ministerio de Educación, 1947), pp. 5-16.

34.13 Roa, Raúl. "Manuel de la Cruz." In his Viento sur (H: Selecta, 1953), pp. 396-401.

34.14 Sanguily y Garritte, Manuel. "Cromitos cubanos." HLit, 1, 1 (1893), 17-63. Also in his Juicios literarios (H: Molina, 1930), I, 93-127. His Obras completas, VII. Also in Manuel de la Cruz, Cromitos cubanos (Madrid: Saturnino Calleja, 1926), pp. 7-33.

34.15 Varona y Pera, Enrique José. "[Episodios de la revolución cubana]." RCub, 11, 6 (1890), 379-382.

34.16 Vitier, Cintio. "Manuel de la Cruz como caso estilístico." RBNJM, 3a serie, 9, 2 (1967), 25-48. Also in his Crítica sucesiva (H: UNEAC, 1917), pp. 326-364.

35. DEL MONTE Y APONTE, DOMINGO (1804-1853)

Critical Monographs and Dissertations

35.1 Entralgo, Elías J. El mundo agraciado del enamoramiento en Domingo Delmonte. H, 1955.

35.2 Karras, Bill J. "The literary life of Domingo Delmonte y Aponte." DAI, 30 (1969), 2531A.

35.3 Soto Paz, Rafael. La falsa cubanidad de Saco, Luz y del Monte.
H: Alfa, 1941.

Critical Essays

35.4 Aldridge, A. Owen. "An early Cuban exponent of Inter-American
cultural relations: Domingo del Monte." Hispania, 54
(1971), 348-353.

35.5 Blanchet, Emilio. "Domingo del Monte como poeta y literato."
CCont, 6 (1914), 64-74.

35.6 Bueno, Salvador. "La compleja personalidad de Domingo Delmonte." In his Figuras cubanas del siglo XIX (H: Unión de
Escritores y Artistas, 1980), pp. 239-250.

35.7 _____. "Ideas literarias de Domingo del Monte." In his Temas
y personajes de la literatura cubana (H: Unión, 1964), pp.
9-28.

35.8 Coester, Alfred L. "Hallazgo de un regalo desconocido de Domingo del Monte a José María Heredia." RBC, 43 (1939), 354-
357.

35.9 Entralgo, Elías J. "Domingo del Monte." CCont, 30 (1922), 240-
257.

35.10 Fernández de Castro, José Antonio. "Tierras y hombres amados
por el sol." RBNC, 2a serie, 3, 3 (1952), 11-38.

35.11 García Marruz, Fina. "De estudios delmontinos." RBNJM, 3a serie, 19, 3 (1977), 17-40.

35.12 _____. "De Estudios delmontinos." RBNJM, 11, 3 (1969), 23-49.

35.13 _____. "Tres imágenes de Del Monte." RBNJM, 19, 2 (1977), 95-
112.

35.14	Pérez de Acevedo y Castillo, Luciano. "Domingo del Monte y el general Tacón." CCont, 1 (1913), 278-291.

35.15	Sánchez Martínez, Julio C. "Ubicación política de Domingo Delmonte." RBC, 59 (1974), 260-264.

35.16	Santovenia y Echaide, Emeterio Santiago. "Domingo del Monte." In his Vidas humanas (H: Librería Martí, 1956), pp. 477-480.

35.17	Vitier, Medardo. "Domingo Delmonte." In his Estudios, notas, efigies cubanas (H: Minerva, 1944), pp. 216-219.

36. DIAZ, JESUS (1939-   )

Critical Essays

36.1   Arias, Salvador. "Duros, pero inmensamente alentadores." CB, No. 7 (1966), 15.

36.2   Beltrán, Alejo (pseud. of Leonel López-Nussa). "[Unos hombres y otros]." Unión, 5, 4 (1966), 164-167.

36.3   Carrión, Ulises. "Un libro peligroso y admirable [Los años duros]." MNu, No. 13 (1967), 70-71.

36.4   Chang-Rodríguez, Raquel. "La experiencia revolucionaria en la cuentística cubana actual: Los años duros [Díaz] y Tute de reyes [Antonio Benítez Rojo]." CA, No. 222 (1979), 59-75.

36.5   Curreros Cuevas, Delio J. "Entrevista con el profesor Jesús Díaz." VU, Nos. 188-189 (1966), 31.

36.6   Espinosa Domínguez, Jesús. "Conversación con unos y otros." Conjunto, No. 39 (1979), 36-52.

36.7   Ortega, Julio. "Los años duros, de Jesús Díaz." CHA, No. 260 (1972), 391-399. Also in his Relato de la utopía (Barcelona: La Gaya Ciencia, 1973), pp. 127-139.

36.8   Otero, Lisandro. "[Los años duros]." CAm, No. 38 (1966), 116-117.

36.9   Pérez Ramírez, Nicolás. "[Los años duros]." PdP, No. 5 (1967?), 64-65.

36.10   Rodríguez Herrera, Mariano. "Premio Casa de las Américas 1966. Diálogo con Jesús Díaz." Bohemia, 58, 11 (1966), 20-21.

36.11   Simó, Ana María. "Encuesta generacional. (II) Respuesta de Jesús Díaz." GdC, No. 51 (1966), 4-5.

37. DIEGO, ELISEO (1920-   )

Bibliographies

37.1 García-Carranza, Araceli. Bibliografía de Eliseo Diego. H: Biblioteca Nacional "José Martí", 1970.

Critical Essays

37.2 Alomá, Orlando. "Un libro de la inocencia humana [El oscuro esplendor]." CAm, No. 42 (1967), 159-160.

37.3 Benedetti, Mario. "Eliseo Diego encuentra su Olimpo." Unión, 6, 2 (1968), 132-138.

37.4 _____. "Eliseo Diego y su brega contra el tiempo." In his Los poetas comunicantes (Montevideo: Biblioteca de Marcha, 1972), pp. 173-196.

37.5 Bragunskaia, Ella. "Nuestro amigo Eliseo Diego." LitS, No. 294 (1972), 164-165.

37.6 Bueno, Salvador. "Eliseo Diego: Nombrar las cosas." Bohemia, 66, 6 (1974), 14-15.

37.7 Campos, Julieta. "Una iluminación de relámpago [Divertimentos]." Plural, 5, 10 (1976), 66-67.

37.8 Contreras, Félix. "Diálogo con Eliseo Diego." Bohemia, 59, 5 (1967), 32.

37.9 Feria, Lina de. "Alquimia del siglo XX." CB, 2a época, No. 21 (1968), 26.

37.10 Fernández Retamar, Roberto. "Eliseo Diego." In his La poesía contemporánea en Cuba (1927-1953) (H: Orígenes, 1954), pp. 111-114.

37.11 Hernández Novás, Raúl. "Nombrar las cosas." CAm, No. 83 (1974), 166-169.

37.12 Ilin, Valeri. "Eliseo Diego: hombre que hace al mundo más sabio." ALat, No. 2 (1979), 206-214.

37.13 Labastida, Jaime. "Nombrar las cosas [Los días de tu vida]." CAm, No. 112 (1979), 162-165.

37.14 Lechuga, Lilliam. "Eliseo Diego." Bohemia, 61, 47 (1969), 12-
       17.

37.15 Lezama Lima, José. "Sobre Divertimentos de Eliseo Diego." Orí-
       genes, No. 10 (1946), 45-46.

37.16 Nadereau Maceo, Efraín. "El libro. Las Versiones de Eliseo
       Diego." BolP, 1, 2 (1971), 18-20.

37.17 "Nuevo libro de Eliseo Diego [Los días de tu vida]." GdC, No.
       172 (1978), 13-15.

37.18 Oráa, Francisco de. "Addenda al prólogo de Nombrar las cosas."
       Unión, 13, 1 (1974), 167-170.

37.19 Orovio, Helio. "Los tesoros de la caducidad." Unión, 6, 1
       (1967), 160-164.

37.20 Pérez Perdomo, Francisco. "Divertimentos y versions de Eliseo
       Diego." Imagen, No. 27 (1968), 4.

37.21 Pita Rodríguez, Félix. "Versión de versiones." Unión, 10, 3
       (1971), 144-146.

37.22 Prats Sariol, José. "Breve comentario de la poesía de Eliseo
       Diego." RyC, No. 24 (1974), 62-66.

37.23 Randall, Margaret. "El tiempo todo el tiempo [Los días de tu
       vida]." Bohemia, 70, 22 (1978), 26-27.

37.24 Sáinz, Enrique. "[Los días de tu vida]." CAm, No. 112 (1979),
       162-165.

37.25 _____. [Divertimentos]." Unión, 14, 3 (1975), 141-143.

37.26 Sologuren, Javier. "Dos libros de Eliseo Diego." Amaru, No. 9
       (1969), 89-90.

37.27 Teillier, Jorge. "[El oscuro esplendor]." AUC, Nos. 141-144
       (1967), 323-324.

37.28 Vitale, Ida. "Eliseo Diego." Marcha, No. 1350 (1967), 31.

37.29 _____. "Un poeta en verso y prosa." In Eliseo Diego, Diverti-
       mentos y Versiones (Montevideo: Arca, 1967), pp. 7-12.

37.30 Vitier, Cintio. "Divertimentos, de Eliseo Diego." RevC, 21
       (1946), 156-159.

37.31 _____. "[En la Calzada de Jesús del Monte]." Orígenes, No. 21
       (1949), 53-59.

37.32 Zaldívar, Gladys. "El arte narrativo de Eliseo Diego en Diver-
       timentos y Versiones." In Cinco aproximaciones a la na-
       rrativa hispanoamericana contemporánea (Madrid: Playor,
       1977), pp. 161-199.

38. DORR, NICOLAS (1947-   )

Critical Essays

38.1   Bueno, Salvador. "Sobre el teatro de Nicolás Dorr." Conjunto, No. 52 (1982), 145-147.

38.2   "Cinco tópicos con Nicolás Dorr." Conjunto, No. 16 (1973), 96-98.

38.3   Contreras, Félix. "Los desiertos y los premios." CB, No. 8 (1966), 16-18.

38.4   "Diálogo con Nicolás Dorr." Bohemia, 56, 47 (1964), 23.

38.5   Garzón Céspedes, Francisco. "La chacota se comunica con su público." Conjunto, No. 21 (1974), 115-117.

38.6   González Freire, Natividad. "El caso Dorr." Unión, 1, 2 (1962), 155-157.

38.7   _____. "La chacota." Bohemia, 66, 14 (1974), 29.

38.8   Leal, Rine. "Nicolás Dorr." In his Teatro cubano en un acto (H: Ediciones R, 1963), pp. 126-131.

38.9   _____. "[Nicolás Dorr]." In his En primera persona (1954-1966) (H: Instituto del Libro, 1967), pp. 139-140.

38.10 Montes Huidobro, Matías. "El caso Dorr: el autor en el vórtice del compromiso." LATR, 11, 1 (1977), 35-43.

38.11 Rigali, Rolando. "El teatro joven." GdC, No. 38 (1964), 21-22.

38.12 Vieta, Ezequiel. "Realidad y absurdo en el teatro de Nicolás Dorr." Unión, 4, 2 (1965), 157-160.

39. ESCARDO, ROLANDO (1925-1960)

Critical Essays

39.1 Agramonte, Elpidio. "Rolando Escardó." _Islas_, 3, 2 (1961), 186-187.

39.2 Alvarez Bravo, Armando. "Claves para Rolando Escardó." _GdC_, No. 96 (1971), 8-10.

39.3 Armas, Emilio de. "Donde se clava el diente de la nada: la poesía de Rolando Escardó." _RyC_, No. 32 (1975), 79-84.

39.4 Feijóo, Samuel. "En la muerte de Escardó." _Islas_, 3, 2 (1961), 172-173.

39.5 García Marruz, Fina. "Escardó." _Islas_, 3, 2 (1961), 174-181.

39.6 González López, Waldo. "La hermana poesía: su rostro verdadero." _Bohemia_, 67, 44 (1975), 27.

39.7 "Homenaje a Rolando Escardó." _Islas_, 3, 2 (1961), 165-218.

39.8 Iznaga, Alcides. "Ha muerto un poeta." _Islas_, 3, 2 (1961), 189-190.

39.9 Menéndez, Aldo. "Evocación de Rolando Escardó." _Islas_, 3, 2 (1961), 190-191.

39.10 Navarro, Noel. "Las páginas por Escardó." _Islas_, 3, 2 (1961), 184-186.

39.11 Núñez Jiménez, Antonia. "Rolando Escardó." _Islas_, 3, 2 (1961), 183.

39.12 Oráa, Pedro de. "[Libro de Rolando]." _CAm_, No. 9 (1961), 151-152.

39.13 Pita Rodríguez, Félix. "Escardó: el derrumbe de un mito." _CB_, 2a época, No. 91 (1975), 7.

39.14 Suardíaz, Luis. "Escardó: pasión y sueños." _Islas_, 3, 2 (1961), 181-183.

39.15 Triana, José. "[Las ráfagas]." _CAm_, No. 8 (1961), 177-178.

39.16 Vitier, Cintio. "Rolando Escardó in memoriam." In his _Crítica sucesiva_ (H: Contemporáneos, UNEAC, 1971), pp. 431-440.

40. ESTORINO, ABELARDO (1925-   )

Critical Essays

40.1 Abdo, Ada. "Teatro y revolución." GdC, No. 41 (1964), 21-22.

40.2 Arias, Salvador. "El 'machismo' en el teatro de Abelardo Estorino." CB, No. 9 (1966), 9-11.

40.3 Bejel, Emilio F. "La transferencia dialéctica en El robo del cochino de Estorino." Inti, No. 12 (1980), 65-71.

40.4 Bravo-Elizondo, Pedro. "El robo del cochino: la antesala de la revolución." In his Teatro hispanoamericano de crítica social (Madrid: Playor, 1975), pp. 72-82.

40.5 Casey, Calvet. "Los mangos de Estorino." Bohemia, 57, 36 (1965), 24.

40.6 Castagnino, Raúl H. "Teatro cubano. Abelardo Estorino: El robo del cochino." In his Semiótica, ideología y teatro hispanoamericano contemporáneo (BA: Nova, 1974), pp. 205-223.

40.7 "Diálogo con Estorino." Bohemia, 56, 44 (1964), 23.

40.8 Piñera, Virgilio. "Tres en uno tras una." GdC, No. 13 (1963), 11-12.

41.   FEIJOO, SAMUEL (1912-   )

Critical Essays

41.1   Bianchi Ross, Ciro. "Samuel Feijóo." CubaI, No. 64 (1974),
       32-33.

41.2   Boudet, Rosa Ileana et al. "Vivir en la punta de un güiro."
       RyC, No. 58 (1977), 51-62.

41.3   Dubuffet, Jean. "Carta a Feijóo." GdC, No. 125 (1974), 13.

41.4   Espinosa Domínguez, Carlos. "Un cuentacuentos llamado Feijóo."
       GdC, No. 165 (1978), 22.

41.5   ____. "[Juan Quinquín en Pueblo Mocho]." ULH, Nos. 203-204
       (1976), 199-200.

41.6   Fernández Retamar, Roberto. "Samuel Feijóo." In his La poesía
       contemporánea en Cuba (1927-1935) (H: Orígenes, 1954), pp.
       80-82.

41.7   ____. "Samuel Feijóo: entrada a su pinturería." GdC, No. 125
       (1974), 11. Also in his Papelería (Santa Clara: Universi-
       dad Central de Las Villas, Dirección de Publicaciones,
       1962), pp. 269-274. Also in Samuel Feijóo, Dibujos (H:
       Consejo Nacional de Cultura, 1961), no pagination.

41.8   García Espinosa, Julio. "A propósito de Aventuras de Juan Quin-
       quín." CC, No. 48 (1967), 12-15.

41.9   Iznaga, Alcides. "Feijóo en la poesía, la novela y el cuento."
       Bohemia, 62, 13 (1970), 4-13.

41.10 ____. "Viaje del poeta." Bohemia, 70, 16 (1978), 28.

41.11 Menéndez, Aldo. "Pleno día de Samuel Feijóo." Bohemia, 66, 30
       (1974), 36.

41.12 Navarro, Osvaldo. "Entrevista sobre la lírica nacional." Sig-
       nos, No. 20 (1977), 283-297.

41.13 Pereira, Manuel. "Alegrías de caballo copado [Cuentacuentos]."
       CB, No. 118 (1977), 27.

41.14 Piñera, Virgilio. "Samuel Feijóo: camarada celeste, poemas."
       Orígenes, No. 5 (1945), 50-51.

41.15 "[Pleno día]." GdC, No. 125 (1974), 29.

41.16 Rodríguez Núñez, Víctor. "Samuel Feijóo: su viaje de siempre [Viaje siempre]." CAm, No. 111 (1978), 142-147.

41.17 Santos Hernández, Alfonso de los. "Cuenta cuentos y Feijóo [Cuentacuentos]." Bohemia, 69, 15 (1977), 27-28.

41.18 Vidal, Manuel. "El mundo fabuloso de Samuel Feijóo." Unión, 11, 1 (1972), 138-149.

41.19 Vitier, Cintio. "Samuel Feijóo." In his Crítica sucesiva (H: Contemporáneos, UNEAC, 1971), pp. 243-251.

41.20 Zamora, Vladimir, and Arturo Arango Arias. "Pleno día a pleno sol [Pleno sol]." CB, No. 88 (1975), 19-20.

42. FELIPE, CARLOS (1914-1975)

Critical Essays

42.1   Abdo, Ada. "Teatro versus cine." GdC, No. 31 (1964), 15.

42.2   Alzola, Concepción Teresa. "Lectura de Yarini." In Fest-
       schrift José Cid Pérez (NY: Senda Nueva, 1981), pp. 111-
       117.

42.3   Beltrán, Alejo. "[Réquiem por Yarini]." Unión, 4, 2 (1965),
       173-178.

42.4   Beverido Duhalt, Francisco. "Teatro en el teatro: dos casos
       cubanos." TC, No. 10 (1978), 126-135. Felipe and José
       R. Brene.

42.5   Escarpanger, José A. "Réquiem por Yarini de Carlos Felipe:
       una tragedia cubana." In Festschrift José Cid Pérez (NY:
       Senda Nueva, 1981), pp. 103-109.

42.6   _____. "Sobre el teatro de Carlos Felipe." RevC, 2, 1 (1965),
       201-203.

42.7   _____. "El teatro de Carlos Felipe." RNT, No. 1 (1961), 26-27.

42.8   Garzón Céspedes, Francisco. "Prólogo. Carlos Felipe: una de
       las figuras claves de nuestra historia teatral." In Car-
       los Felipe, Teatro (H: Letras Cubanas, 1979), pp. 5-19.

42.9   González Freire, Natividad. "[Felipe]." In her Teatro cubano,
       1928-1961 (H: Ministerio de Relaciones Exteriores, 1961),
       pp. 114-118.

42.10 Leal, Rine. "Un Carlos llamado Felipe." GdC, No. 31 (1964),
       2-5. Also in his En primera persona (1954-1966) (H: Ins-
       tituto del Libro, 1967), pp. 189-201.

42.11 López-Nussa, Leonel. "Releyendo a Yarini." Unión, 1, 3-4
       (1962), 86-96.

42.12 Llana, María Elena. "De película [...]. Una entrevista, un
       reportaje." PyC, No. 19 (1964), 7-9.

42.13 Parrado, Gloria. "[Réquiem por Yarini]." GdC, No. 43 (1965),
       28-29.

42.14 _____. "[Teatro]." GdC, No. 43 (1965), 28-29.

42.15 Vieta, Ezequiel. "[De películas]." CAm, Nos. 28-29 (1965), 157.

42.16 Vitier, Cintio. "Eros en el infierno [Réquiem por Yarini]." RBNJM, 3a serie, 10, 2 (1968), 169-175.

43. FERNANDEZ, PABLO ARMANDO (1930   )

Critical Essays

43.1   Benedetti, Mario. "Nueve preguntas a Pablo Armando." In his
       Cuaderno cubano; 2. ed. aum. (Montevideo: Arca, 1971), pp.
       55-61. Orig. 1969.

43.2   _____. "Pablo Armando o el desafío subjetivo [Los niños se des-
       piden]." In his Crítica cómplice (H: Instituto Cubano del
       Libro, 1971), pp. 94-104.

43.3   Cardenal, Ernesto. "Pablo Armando." In his En Cuba (BA/M:
       Lohlé, 1972), pp. 98-101.

43.4   Díaz Martínez, Manuel. "[Libro de los héroes]." Unión, 4, 2
       (1965), 164-165.

43.5   Fernández, David. "[Libro de los héroes]." CAm, No. 32 (1965),
       105-107.

43.6   Font, Mauricio. "Entrevista a Pablo Armando Fernández."
       Areito, Nos. 19-20 (1979), 42-45.

43.7   González, Reinaldo. "El hombre y los libros. Pablo Armando
       Fernández. Amo las palabras desde niño." Cuba, No. 72
       (1968), 34-35.

43.8   _____. "La palabra, el mito, el mito de la palabra [Los niños
       se despiden]." CAm, No. 49 (1968), 147-154.

43.9   Larrázabal Henríquez, Osvaldo. "Pablo Armando Fernández. Los
       niños se despiden." CUn, Nos. 98-99 (1968), 286-287.

43.10 Martínez Estrada, Ezequiel. "[Toda la poesía]." GdC, No. 4
       (1962), 4.

43.11 Otero, José Manuel. "[Los niños se despiden]." VO, 9, 37
       (1968), 18.

43.12 Salazar Bondy, Sebastián. "[Toda la poesía]." CAm, No. 9
       (1961), 158-159.

44. FERNANDEZ RETAMAR, ROBERTO (1930-   )

Critical Monographs and Dissertations

44.1   Sánchez, Marta Ester. "Three Latin-American novelists in
       search of lo americano: a productive failure." DAI, 38
       (1977), 819A. Fernández Retamar in alios.

Critical Essays

44.2   Achúgar Ferrari, Hugo. "[Para una teoría de la literatura his-
       panoamericana]." RCLL, No. 5 (1977), 127-130.

44.3   Benedetti, Mario. "Fernández Retamar o las preocupaciones de
       un optimista." In his Los poetas comunicantes (Montevi-
       deo: Biblioteca Marcha, 1972), pp. 197-222.

44.4   ____. "Fernández Retamar: poesía desde el cráter." In his
       Crítica cómplice (H: Instituto del Libro, 1971), pp. 105-
       118.

44.5   ____. "Presentación de Roberto Fernández Retamar." RBNJM,
       3a serie, 64, 2 (1973), 41-43.

44.6   Bravet, Rogelio Luis. "[Con las mismas manos]." Bohemia, 55,
       10 (1963), 19.

44.7   Burke, Shirley Maynier. "The editor interviews Roberto Fernán-
       dez Retamar." JJ, 10, 2-4 (n.d. [ca. 1976]), 36-37.

44.8   Casar González, Eduardo. "Abstracción y concreción en la lite-
       ratura [Para una teoría de la literatura hispanoamerica-
       na]." Plural, No. 83 (1978), 67-68.

44.9   Cos Causse, Jesús. "En torno a circunstancias de poesía [Cir-
       cunstancias de poesía]." RyC, No. 68 (1978), 52.

44.10 Dalton, Roque. "[Con las mismas manos]." CAm, No. 19 (1963),
       56-57.

44.11 ____. "[Poesía reunida]." CAm, No. 41 (1967), 131-133.

44.12 "De la revolución y el amor." CB, No. 156 (1977), 15-17.

44.13 Debray, Régis. "Cartas a Roberto Fernández Retamar." CAm,
       Nos. 51-52 (1968-1969), 208-216.

44.14 Depestre, René. "Roberto Fernández Retamar o la poesía de ma-
       nos fértiles." GdC, No. 16 (1963), 13.

212   CUBAN LITERATURE

44.15 Diego, Eliseo. "Fernández Retamar." Cuba I, No. 72 (1975), 18-19.

44.16 Feijóo, Samuel. "Con las mismas manos." Islas, 6, 2 (1964), 301-304.

44.17 Fernández e Izaguirre, Antonio. "Vuelta a la antigua esperanza." LyL, noviembre-diciembre 1965, p. 8.

44.18 Fernández Retamar, Roberto. "Autocrítica de Fernández Retamar." Signos, No. 21 (1978), 52-55.

44.19 Fossey, Jean Michel. "Roberto Fernández Retamar." In his Galaxia latinoamericana (Las Palma de Gran Canaria: Inventarios Provisionales, 1973), pp. 267-292.

44.20 García Flores, Margarita. "Roberto Fernández Retamar." RUM, 22, 7 (1968), 21-23.

44.21 García Gómez, Jorge. "La poesía, la piadosa (introducción y apuntes a un poema de Roberto Fernández Retamar)." CHA, No. 241 (1970), 176-183.

44.22 González Echevarría, Roberto. "Entrevista con Roberto Fernández Retamar." SinN, 10, 2 (1979), 14-28. Also as "Interview." Diacritics, 8, 4 (1978), 76-88.

44.23 _____. "Roberto Fernández Retamar: an introduction." Diacritics, 8, 4 (1978), 70-75.

44.24 Håkansson, Maith. "Dikten i Havanna." BöV, 3, 6 (1969), 60-65.

44.25 Jiménez, José Olivio. "Sobre un poema de Roberto Fernández Retamar ['Palacio cotidiano']." DHR, 2, 1 (1963), 1-19. Also in his Estudios sobre poesía cubana contemporánea (NY: Las Américas, 1967), pp. 95-112.

44.26 Leante, César. "Amistad reunida." Unión, 5, 3 (1966), 175-176.

44.27 López Morales, Eduardo E. "La historia es para vivirla." Unión, 10, 1-2 (1971), 139-148.

44.28 Marinello, Juan. "Cartas a C. Roberto Fernández Retamar." CAm, No. 103 (1977), 114-121.

44.29 Marré, Luis. "Alabanzas de Fernández Retamar [Alabanzas, conversaciones]." Ciclón, 2, 4 (1956), 56-57.

44.30 Martínez Laínez, Fernando. "Entrevista con Roberto Fernández Retamar." In his Palabra cubana (Madrid: Akal, 1975), pp. 83-105.

44.31 Moro, Lilliam. "La historia nueva de Retamar [Historia antigua]." Bohemia, 57, 31 (1965), 27.

44.32 Navarro, Desiderio. "Un ejemplo de lucha contra el esquematismo
       eurocentrista en la ciencia literaria de la América latina
       y Europa." CAm, No. 122 (1980), 77-91.

44.33 Nuiry, Nuria. "[La poesía contemporánea en Cuba]." ULH, Nos.
       115-117 (1954), 243-246.

44.34 "[Patrias]." Germinal, No. 51 (1952), 27-28.

44.35 Plaza, Guillermo. "[Circunstancia de poesía]." CHA, No. 335
       (1978), 380-381.

44.36 Pogolotti, Graziella. "La poesía de R. Fernández Retamar."
       Unión, 2, 5-6 (1963), 111-117.

44.37 Prada Oropeza, Renato. "[Para una teoría de la literatura la-
       tinoamericana]." TC, No. 6 (1977), 229-231.

44.38 Prats Sariol, José. "Apuntes sobre la poesía de Retamar." CB,
       No. 121 (1977), 18-19.

44.39 Prieto, Abel E. "Trayectoria de una ensayística." CAm, No.
       120 (1980), 45-55.

44.40 Ramírez Rodríguez, Rómulo. "Fernández Retamar y su poesía co-
       municante." GdC, No. 152 (1977), 15-16.

44.41 Rodríguez Rivera, Guillermo. "Análisis de la historia." CAm,
       No. 33 (1965), 147-149.

44.42 Santos Moray, Mercedes. "Poesía de la descolonización: crítica
       descolonizada [El son de vuelo popular]." GdC, No. 141
       (1975), 25.

44.43 _____. "Tres poetas y una isla." CAm, No. 90 (1975), 138-141.

44.44 Selva, Mauricio de la. "[Con las mismas manos]." CA, No. 130
       (1963), 319-320.

44.45 Valle, Rafael de. "[Para una teoría de la literatura hispanoa-
       mericana]." CAm, No. 100 (1977), 197-199.

44.46 Vitier, Cintio. "Roberto Fernández Retamar." In his Crítica
       sucesiva (H: Contemporáneos, UNEAC, 1971), pp. 235-242.

44.47 Wong, Oscar. "Fernández Retamar y la conciencia crítica."
       Plural, No. 61 (1976), 61-63.

44.48 Yáñez, Mirta. "Cuatro ensayos en busca de Guillén." ULH,
       Nos. 196-197 (1972), 369-371.

45. FIGAROLA-CANEDA, DOMINGO (1852-1926)

Bibliographies

45.1 Dihigo, Juan M. "Bibliografía de Domingo Figarola-Caneda."
RBNC, 2a serie, 3, 1 (1952), 89-107.

Critical Monographs and Dissertations

45.2 Mesa Rodríguez, Manuel I. Don Domingo Figarola-Caneda (1852-1952). H: El Siglo XX, 1952.

Critical Essays

45.3 Castellanos García, Gerardo. "Cuba 24..." RBNC, 2a serie, 3,
1 (1952), 43-68.

45.4 Castro de Morales, Lilia. "Palabras pronunciadas en el homenaje
a la memoria de Domingo Figarola-Caneda." RBNC, 2a serie,
3, 2 (1952), 3-9.

45.5 García del Pino, César. "Los parientes vueltabajeros de Domingo
Figarola-Caneda." RBNJM, 3a serie, 19, 3 (1977), 53-60.

45.6 González del Valle y Ramírez, Francisco. "Domingo Figarola."
CCont, 40 (1926), 221-227.

45.7 _____. "Domingo Figarola-Caneda." RBC, 37 (1936), 371-387.

45.8 _____. "Domingo Figarola-Caneda." RBNC, 2a serie, 3, 1 (1952),
69-88.

45.9 Guerra Dabón, Ana. "Breve ensayo sobre don Domingo Figarola-Caneda." RBC, 73 (1957), 64-76.

45.10 Habana, Cristóbal de la. "Domingo Figarola-Caneda, fundador y
mecenas de la Biblioteca Nacional." Carteles, 33, 4
(1952), 54-55.

45.11 Mesa Rodríguez, Manuel I. "Introito." RBNC, 2a serie, 3, 1
(1952), 5-6.

45.12 Roig de Leuchsenring, Emilio. "Acotaciones literarias. Domingo Figarola-Caneda." Social, 8, 3 (1923), 45.

45.13 _____. "En el centenario del nacimiento de Domingo Figarola-Caneda." RBNC, 2a serie, 3, 1 (1952), 7-42.

45.14   Santovenia y Echaide, Emeterio Santiago. "El mejor homenaje a
        Figarola-Caneda." <u>RBNC</u>, 2a serie, 3, 1 (1952), 108-180.

46. FLORIT, EUGENIO (1903-   )

Bibliographies

46.1   Pane, Remigio U.   "Cuban poetry in English: a bibliography of
        English translations from Casal, Florit, Gómez de Avella-
        neda, Guillén, Heredia, Pedroso and 'Plácido'." BBDI, 18,
        9 (1946), 199-201.

46.2   Rosenbaum, Sidonia C.   "Eugenio Florit: bibliografía." RHM, 8
        (1943), 222-223. Also in Eugenio Florit, q.v., pp. 27-28.

Critical Monographs and Dissertations

46.3   Collins, María Castellanos.   "Brull, Florit, Ballagas, y el van-
        guardismo en Cuba." DAI, 37 (1976), 3664A-3665A.

46.4   ____. Tierra, mar y cielo en la poesía de Eugenio Florit.
        Miami: Universal, 1976.

46.5   Eugenio Florit; vida y obra--bibliografía--antología--obras iné-
        ditas. NY: Hispanic Institute in the United States, 1943.
        Pertinent items are listed separately.

46.6   Parajón, Mario.   Eugenio Florit y su poesía. Madrid, 1977.

46.7   Pollin, Alice M.   Concordancias en la obra poética de Eugenio
        Florit. NY: New York University Press; London: University
        of London Press, 1967.

46.8   Saa, Orlando E.   La serenidad en las obras de Eugenio Florit.
        Miami: Universal, 1973.

46.9   Servodidio, Mirella D'Ambrosio.   The quest for harmony: the
        dialectics of communication in the poetry of Eugenio Flo-
        rit. Lincoln, Neb.: Society of Spanish and Spanish-Ameri-
        can Studies, 1979.

46.10   Strathdee, Katherine Elizabeth.   "The four Greek elements in the
        poetry of Eugenio Florit." DAI, 40 (1979), 3335A.

Critical Essays

46.11   Andino, Alberto.   "¿Poetas y poesía?... ¿Por qué no Eugenio
        Florit." DHR, 5 (1966), 9-25.

46.12 Ardura, Ernesto. "Eugenio Florit, poet of the sea." Américas, 30, 10 (1978), 26-27. Also as "Eugenio Florit, poeta del mar." Américas [Spanish edition], 30, 10 (1978), 26-27.

46.13 Arrufat, Antón. "Acerca de Eugenio Florit [Asonante final y otros poemas]." Ciclón, 2, 4 (1956), 49-62.

46.14 Baeza Flores, Alberto. "Los reinos de la poesía de Eugenio Florit." In his Cuba, el laurel y la palma; ensayos literarios (Miami: Universal, 1977), pp. 143-161.

46.15 Bellini, Giuseppe. "Eugenio Florit." In his Poeti antillani (Milano: Cisalpino, 1957), pp. 65-80.

46.16 "Eugenio Florit. Doble acento." América, 3, 1 (1939), 95.

46.17 "Eugenio Florit. Reino." América, 20, 1-2 (1943), 91.

46.18 Fernández de la Vega, Oscar. "Florit y la evasión trascendente: el poeta conversa con Dios." Noverim, 2, 8 (1958), 61-65.

46.19 _____. "Hábito de esperanza." Insula, No. 232 (1966), 8-9.

46.20 Fernández Retamar, Roberto. "Eugenio Florit (1903)." In his La poesía contemporánea en Cuba (1927-1953) (H: Orígenes, 1954), pp. 34-39.

46.21 Figueroa-Amaral, Esperanza. "[Asonante final y otros poemas]." ND, 37, 1 (1957), 107-108.

46.22 Gonthier, Denys A. "Eugenio Florit: el poeta de la soledad." CHA, No. 96 (1957), 336-343.

46.23 _____. "Un homenaje a Florit." RevC, 23 (1948), 343-344.

46.24 González, Ana H. "Los autores y sus obras. Notas condensadas. Eugenio Florit, Rafael Esténger y Mercedes García Tudurí." Círculo, 3 (1971), 91-95.

46.25 González, Manuel Pedro. "[Asonante final y otros poemas]." CCLC, No. 21 (1956), 118-119.

46.26 Grismer, Raymond L., and Manuel Rodríguez Saavedra. "Eugenio Florit y Sánchez de Fuentes." In their Vida y orbas de autores cubanos (H: "Alfa", 1940-), I, 105-107.

46.27 Hiriart, Rosario. "La soledad en la poesía de Eugenio Florit." CHA, Nos. 322-323 (1977), 323-331.

46.28 "Un homenaje a Florit." RevC, 23 (1948), 343-344.

46.29 Iduarte, Andrés. "Prólogo." In Eugenio Florit, Antología poética (1930-1955) (M: de Andrea, 1956), pp. 11-24.

46.30 Jimenes Grullón, Juan Isidro. "Eugenio Florit." In his Seis
       poetas cubanos (ensayos apologéticos) (H: "Cromos", 1954),
       pp. 149-169.

46.31 Jiménez, José Olivio. "Eugenio Florit en sus setenta años (no-
       tas sobre su poesía última)." Insula, No. 325 (1973), 13.

46.32 _____. "[Hábatio de esperanza]." PH, No. 34 (1965), 313-316.

46.33 _____. "Introducción a la poesía de Eugenio Florit." Círculo,
       8 (1979), 7-26.

46.34 _____. "Un momento definitivo en la poesía de Eugenio Florit."
       BACL, 10, 3-4 (1961), 67-86. Also in his Estudios sobre
       poesía cubana (NY: Las Américas, 1967), pp. 51-72.

46.35 _____. "La poesía de Eugenio Florit." In Eugenio Florit, An-
       tología penúltima (Madrid: Plenitud, 1970), pp. 11-42.

46.36 _____. "La poesía última de Eugenio Florit. Sobre De tiempo
       y agonía." Exilio, 7, 4 (1974), 57-69.

46.37 Jiménez, Juan Ramón. "Eugenio Florit (1939)." In his Españo-
       les de tres mundos (BA: Losada, 1942), pp. 143-144.

46.38 _____. "Siluetas de hispanoamericanos: I. José Enrique Rodó,
       II. Alfonso Reyes, III. Eugenio Florit." RI, No. 4 (1940),
       353-357.

46.39 _____. "El único estilo de Eugenio Florit." RAm, 34 (1937),
       217-218. Also RevC, 8 (1937), 10-16. Also in his La co-
       rriente infinita: crítica y evocación (Madrid: Aguilar,
       1961), pp. 143-148.

46.40 Lazo, Raimundo. "[Cuatro poemas]." RI, No. 5 (1941), 222-225.

46.41 Linares Pérez, Marta. "Eugenio Florit: de la pureza a la tras-
       cendencia." In her La poesía pura en Cuba y su evolución
       (Madrid: Playor, 1975), pp. 123-180.

46.42 Lizaso y González, Félix. "Bibliografía de don Eugenio Florit."
       BACL, 2a época, 11, 1 (1964), 218-223. Florit's edition
       of José Martí's Versos.

46.43 _____. "Notas y comentarios: Eugenio Florit y la poesía en
       Martí." AJM, 2, 1 (1941), 99.

46.44 _____. "[Trópico]." Avance, No. 50 (1930), 283.

46.45 Marinello, Juan. "Verbo y alusión [Trópico]." In his Poética:
       ensayos en entusiasmo (Madrid: Espasa-Calpe, 1933), pp.
       17-48.

46.46 Nandino, Elías. "[Asonante final y otros poemas]." Estaciones,
       2, 5 (1957), 96-97.

46.47 Parajón, Mario. "Vida y poesía en Eugenio Florit." In Instituto Internacional de Literatura Iberoamericana, XVII Congreso (Madrid: Cultura Hispánica del Centro Iberoamericano de Cooperación, 1978), pp. 873-883.

46.48 "Poetas cubanos de hoy [Florit y Felipe Pichardo Mota]." InC, julio-agosto 1947, pp. 24-26; septiembre-diciembre 1947, pp. 45-47.

46.49 Prida, Dolores. "[Antología penúltima]." NSa, 3, 10 (1971), 13.

46.50 Rexach, Rosario. "[Antología penúltima]." RI, No. 75 (1971), 479-481.

46.51 Reyes, Alfonso. "Compás poético." Sur, No. 1 (1931), 64-73. Florit inter alios.

46.52 Río, Angel del. "Eugenio Florit." RHM, 8 (1943), 205-223. Also in Eugenio Florit, q.v., pp. 9-26. Also as "Eugenio Florit: vida y obra." In his Estudios sobre literatura contemporánea española (Madrid: Gredos, 1966), pp. 294-310.

46.53 Roggiano, Alfredo A. "[Antología poética]." RI, No. 46 (1958), 472-475.

46.54 Shuler, Esther E. "La poesía de Eugenio Florit." RI, No. 16 (1944), 301-324.

46.55 Tinnell, Roger D. "Conversation with Eugenio Florit." MLS, 8, 3 (1978), 77-85.

46.56 Valle, Rafael Heliodoro. "Diálogo con Eugenio Florit." UM, No. 52 (1951), 7-8.

46.57 Zardoya, Concha. "[Hábito de esperanza]." Asomante, 22, 2 (1966), 63-66.

47. FUENTES, NORBERTO (1943-   )

Critical Essays

47.1 Benedetti, Mario. "Diálogo con Norberto Fuentes." In his Cuaderno cubano; 2. ed. aum. (Montevideo: Arca, 1971), pp. 72-76. Orig. 1969.

47.2 Benítez Rojo, Antonio. "[Condenados de condado]." CAm, No. 49 (1968), 158-160.

47.3 "El hombre y los libros. Norberto Fuentes. Lo esencial es la honestidad." Cuba, No. 72 (1968), 24.

47.4 Larrázabal Henríquez, Osvaldo. "[Condenados de condado]." CUn, Nos. 98-99 (1968), 288-290.

47.5 Martí, Agenor. "Norberto Fuentes por un filtro." GdC, No. 63 (1968), 2.

47.6 Ortega, Julio. "[Cazabandido y Condenados de condado]." Libre, 2 (1971-1972), 146-151.

47.7 _____. "Relatos y crónicas, de Norberto Fuentes." In his Relato de la utopía (Barcelona: La Gaya Ciencia, 1973), pp. 203-215.

48. GOMEZ, JUAN GUALBERTO (1854-1933)

Critical Monographs and Dissertations

48.1   Edreira de Caballero, Angelina. Vida y obra de Juan Gualberto
       Gómez, 6 lecciones (en su centenario). H: Méndez, 1973.
       Orig. H: R. Méndez, 1954.

48.2   Sabourín Fornaris, Jesús. Juan Gualberto Gómez: símbolo del de-
       ber. Santiago de Cuba: Universidad de Oriente, Departa-
       mento de Extensión y Relaciones Culturales, 1954.

48.3   Torriente y Peraza, Cosme de la. Juan Gualberto Gómez. H:
       "El Siglo XX", 1954.

Critical Essays

48.4   Baquero, Gastón. "Nota sobre Juan Gualberto Gómez." RevH,
       marzo 1947, pp. 28-32.

48.5   Bilbao, Víctor. "Juan Gualberto Gómez, pluma de la revolución."
       RevH, agosto 1945, pp. 529-539.

48.6   Bueno, Salvador. "Juan Gualberto Gómez, héroe civil." In his
       Figuras cubanas del siglo XIX (H: Unión de Escritores y
       Artistas, 1980), pp. 71-83.

48.7   Castro de Morales, Lilia. "Palabras pronunciadas por la Sra.
       Lilia Castro, Directora de la Biblioteca Nacional en el
       homenaje rendido a Juan Gualberto Gómez." RBNC, 2a serie,
       5, 3 (1954), 259-260.

48.8   Caturla, Victoria de. "Trayectoria ideológica de Juan Gualberto
       Gómez." ULH, Nos. 130-132 (1957), 120-162.

48.9   Cervantes, Carlos A. "Del ideario político de Juan Gualberto
       Gómez." RevH, agosto 1945, pp. 540-542.

48.10 Costa, Octavio Román. "Juan Gualberto en la Asamblea del Ce-
       rro." Bohemia, 41, 27 (1949), 6-8, 140.

48.11 Duplessis, Gustavo. "Un hombre, sus ideas y un paraguas (evo-
       cación de Juan Gualberto Gómez y su ideario)." ULH, Nos.
       136-141 (1958-1959), 121-218.

48.12 Fernández Rodríguez, Lesbia Mirta. "Labor patriótica y socio-
       lógica de Juan Gualberto Gómez a través del periodismo."
       RUMa, No. 32 (1959), 635.

48.13 García Pons, César. "Juan Gualberto Gómez." <u>Lyceum</u>, No. 39
       (1954), 7-25.

48.14 Havia, Aurelio. "Juan Gualberto Gómez. Conferencia." <u>RevH</u>,
       octubre 1942, pp. 157-178.

48.15 Ichaso, Francisco. "Imagen de Juan Gualberto." <u>CUNESCO</u>, 3, 7
       (1954), 1-4.

48.16 Lara, María Julia de. "Junto a los restos de Juan Gualberto
       Gómez." <u>RevH</u>, agosto 1944, pp. 490-492.

48.17 Lizaso y González, Félix. "En la tumba de Juan Gualberto Gó-
       mez." <u>RevH</u>, marzo 1944, pp. 89-91.

48.18 Pando, Dalen. "Juan Gualberto Gómez, a Cuban portrait." <u>CarQ</u>,
       5, 2 (1958), 78-84.

48.19 Torriente y Peraza, Cosme de la. "Juan Gualberto Gómez."
       <u>RevH</u>, febrero 1947, pp. 439-445.

49. GOMEZ DE AVELLANEDA, GERTRUDIS (1814-1873)

Bibliographies

49.1 "Contribución a la bibliografía de Gertrudis Gómez de Avellaneda." L/L, Nos. 3-4 (1972-1973), 25-39.

49.2 García-Carranza, Araceli. "Esquema bibliográfico de la Avellaneda en su centenario (1814-1873)." RBNJM, 3a serie, 15, 3 (1973), 137-173.

49.3 Kelly, Edith L. "Bibliografía de la Avellaneda." RBC, 35 (1935), 107-139, 261-295.

49.4 Pane, Remigio U. "Cuban poetry in English: a bibliography of translations from Casal, Florit, Gómez de Avellaneda, Guillén, Heredia, Pedroso and 'Plácido'." BBDI, 18, 9 (1946), 199-201.

Critical Monographs and Dissertations

49.5 Alonso Cortés, Nicasio. La Avellaneda. Valladolid: Viejo y Nuevo, 1916.

49.6 Alzaga, Florinda. Las ansias de infinito en la Avellaneda. Miami: Universal, 1979.

49.7 ____, and Ana Rosa Núñez. Ensayo de diccionario del pensamiento vivo de la Avellaneda. Miami: Universal, 1975.

49.8 Aramburo y Machado, Mariano. Personalidad literaria de doña Gertrudis de Avellaneda. Madrid: Teresiana, 1898.

49.9 Ballesteros, Mercedes. Vida de la Avellaneda. Madrid: Cultura Hispánica, 1949.

49.10 Bravo-Villasante, Carmen. Una vida romántica: la Avellaneda. Barcelona: E.D.H.A.S.A., 1967.

49.11 ____ et al. Gertrudis Gómez de Avellaneda. Madrid: Fundación Universitaria Española, 1974. Three individually signed essays listed separately.

49.12 Castellá, Condesa de. Gertrudis Gómez de Avellaneda, gloria hispanoamericana. Madrid: El Liberal, 1914.

49.13   Castillo González, Aurelia. Biografía de Gertrudis Gómez de
        Avellaneda y juicio crítico de sus obras. H: Soler, Al-
        varez, 1887. Same as item no. 49.78.

49.14   Chacón y Calvo, José María. Gertrudis Gómez de Avellaneda.
        Las influencias castellanas: examen negativo. H: El Siglo
        XX, 1914.

49.15   Coronación de la Sra. Dª. Gertrudis Gómez de Avellaneda, acor-
        dada por el Liceo de la Habana. H: Imprenta Militar, 1860.

49.16   Cotarelo y Mori, Emilio. La Avellaneda y sus obras; ensayo
        biográfico y crítico. Madrid: Archivos, 1930.

49.17   Cuesta Jiménez, Valentín Bernardo. Sangre en los labios. Con-
        tribución al estudio de la vida de Gertrudis Gómez de Ave-
        llaneda. Güines: Tosco, 1943.

49.18   Escoto, José Augusto. Gertrudis Gómez de Avellaneda. Cartas
        inéditas y documentos relativos a su vida en Cuba de 1859
        a 1864. Matanzas, 1911. Also Madrid: Suárez, 1912.

49.19   Fernández del Campo, José P. Algunas cartas inéditas de Gertru-
        dis Gómez de Avellaneda existentes en el Museo del Ejérci-
        to. Madrid: Fundación Universitaria, 1975.

49.20   Figarola-Caneda, Domingo. Gertrudis Gómez de Avellaneda. Bio-
        grafía, bibliografía e iconografía. Madrid: Sociedad Ge-
        neral Española de Librería, 1929.

49.21   García, Juan C. L'oeuvre lyrique de la Avellaneda. Unpublished
        Ph.D. dissertation, Laval University, 1975.

49.22   Harter, Hugh A. Gertrudis Gómez de Avellaneda. Boston: Twayne,
        1981.

49.23   Homenaje a Gertrudis Gómez de Avellaneda: memorias del simposio
        en el centenario de su muerte. Miami: Universal, 1981.

49.24   Jiménez, R. S. Gertrudis Gómez de Avellaneda. Conferencia.
        H: "Avisador Comercial", 1914.

49.25   Lazcano, Antonio María. "Gertrudis Gómez de Avellaneda: ideas
        about Cuban society of her time in her prose." DAI, 39
        (1978), 909A.

49.26   Lazo, Raimundo. Gertrudis Gómez de Avellaneda. La mujer y la
        poetisa lírica. M: Porrúa, 1972.

49.27   Leal, Rine. El teatro de Gertrudis Gómez de Avellaneda. H:
        Consejo Nacional de Cultura, 1973.

49.28   León, José de la Luz. Fernán Caballero, "Tula" de Avellaneda.
        Paris: Le Cygne, 1949.

49.29 López Argüello, Alberto. La Avellaneda y sus versos. Santander, Spain: Boletín de la Biblioteca Menéndez y Pelayo, 1928.

49.30 Loynaz, Dulce María. La Avellaneda, una cubana universal. Camagüey, 1953.

49.31 Malo Rendón, Rina. Novelas y leyendas de la Avellaneda. H: Universidad de la Habana, 1944.

49.32 Marquina, Rafael. Gertrudis Gómez de Avellaneda, la peregrina. H: Trópico, 1939.

49.33 Martínez Bello, Antonio M. Dos musas cubanas: Gertrudis Gómez de Avellaneda, Luisa Pérez de Zambrana. H: P. Hernández, 1954.

49.34 Moore, Suzanne Shelton. "Themes and characterization in the dramatic works of Gertrudis Gómez de Avellaneda." DAI, 37 (1976), 1596A-1597A.

49.35 Piñera, Estela A. "El teatro romántico de Gertrudis Gómez de Avellaneda." DAI, 35 (1975), 4547A.

49.36 Rodríguez García, José Antonio. De la Avellaneda. H: Cuba Intelectual, 1914.

49.37 Roselló, Aurora Julia. "La poesía lírica de Gertrudis Gómez de Avellaneda." DAI, 33 (1973), 6883A.

49.38 Salazar y Roig, Salvador. Milanés, Luaces y la Avellaneda, como poetas dramáticos. H: Aurelio Miranda, 1916.

49.39 Valbuena, Segundo (pseud. of Arturo R. de Carricarte). Un centenario (injusticia patriótica y desastre político). Crítica de actualidad. H: Jesús Montero, 1914.

49.40 Williams, Edwin B. The life and dramatic works of Gertrudis Gómez de Avellaneda. Philadelphia: University of Pennsylvania Press, 1924.

Critical Essays

49.41 Adelstein, Miriam. "El amor en la vida y en la obra de Gertrudis Gómez de Avellaneda." Círculo, 9 (1980), 57-62.

49.42 Aguirre, Mirta. "Gertrudis Gómez de Avellaneda." In her Influencia de la mujer en Iberoamérica (H: Servicio Femenino para la Defensa Civil, 1948), pp. 20-26.

49.43 ____. "Una página de la Avellaneda." In her El romanticismo de Rousseau a Víctor Hugo (H: Instituto Cubano del Libro, 1973), pp. 348-353.

49.44 Alba-Buffill, Elio. "La Avellaneda a la luz de la crítica de
      Enrique José Varona." In Homenaje a Gertrudis Gómez de
      Avellaneda, q.v., pp. 213-223.

49.45 Altamirano, Ignacio Manuel. "Ensayo crítico sobre Baltasar."
      RCub, 7 (1880), 242-256, 365-380.

49.46 Alzaga, Florinda, and Ana Rosa Núñez. "Prólogo." In Gertrudis
      Gómez de Avellaneda, Antología de la poesía religiosa de
      la Avellaneda (Miami: Universal, 1975), pp. 7-9.

49.47 Alzola, Concepción T. "El personaje Sab." In Homenaje a Ger-
      trudis Gómez de Avellaneda, q.v., pp. 283-291.

49.48 Aramburo y Machado, Mariano. "[Discurso en acto conmemorativo
      del centenario de la Avellaneda]." CCont, 5 (1914), 94-99.

49.49 Arias, Salvador. "Algunas notas sobre la poesía lírica de la
      Avellaneda." Islas, No. 44 (1973), 43-90.

49.50 Armas y Cárdenas, José de. "La dicotomía amorosa de la vida de
      Gertrudis Gómez de Avellaneda." In Homenaje a Gertrudis
      Gómez de Avellaneda, q.v., pp. 224-235.

49.51 Artigas, M. "Dos promesas de la Avellaneda." BBMP, 1 (1919),
      69-71.

49.52 Ballagas, Emilio. "Mariposa insular." In Homenaje a Gertrudis
      Gómez de Avellaneda, q.v., pp. 145-152.

49.53 Baquero, Gastón. "Gertrudis Gómez de Avellaneda como prosista."
      In Carmen Bravo-Villasante et al., Gertrudis Gómez de Ave-
      llaneda, q.v., pp. 47-80.

49.54 _____. "Gertrudis Gómez de Avellaneda (1814-1873), la mariposa
      del romanticismo." MHisp, No. 299 (1973), 52-55.

49.55 Barbero, Teresa. "Gertrudis Gómez de Avellaneda, 'La Divina
      Tula'." EstLit, No. 533 (1974), 21-22.

49.56 Barreda-Tomás, Pedro M. "Abolicionismo y feminismo en la Ave-
      llaneda: lo negro como artificio narrativo en Sab." CHA,
      No. 342 (1978), 613-626.

49.57 Bernal, Emilia. "Gertrudis Gómez de Avellaneda: su vida y su
      obra." In her Cuestiones cubanas para América (Madrid:
      Hernández y Galo Sánz, 1928), pp. 273-316. Orig. CCont,
      37 (1925), 85-111.

49.58 Bielsa Vives, Manuel. "La Avellaneda y su poesía religiosa."
      In his Cosas de ayer (H: La Correspondencia, 1906), pp.
      59-73.

49.59 Blanchet, Emilio. "Gertrudis Gómez de Avellaneda como poetisa
      lírica y dramática." RFLC, 18, 2 (1914), 129-179.

Gómez de Avellaneda, Gertrudis   227

49.60 Boring, Phyllis Zatlin. "Una perspectiva feminista sobre la
       confesión de Avellaneda." In Homenaje a Gertrudis Gómez
       de Avellaneda, q.v., pp. 93-98.

49.61 Boti, Regino Eladio. "La Avellaneda como metrificadora."
       CCont, 3 (1913), 373-390.

49.62 Boyer, Mildred V. "Realidad y ficción en Sab." In Homenaje a
       Gómez de Avellaneda, q.v., pp. 292-300.

49.63 Bravo-Villasante, Carmen. "La Avellaneda: una mujer en sus
       cartas y en su poesía." In Carmen Bravo-Villasante et
       al., Gertrudis Gómez de Avellaneda, q.v., pp. 3-26.

49.64 _____. "Las corrientes sociales del romanticismo en la obra de
       la Avellaneda." CHA, No. 228 (1968), 771-775. Also in
       Actes du Ve Congrès de l'Association Internationale de
       Littérature Comparée (Belgrade: Université de Belgrade;
       Amsterdam: Swets & Zeitlinger, 1969), pp. 215-218.

49.65 _____. "Introducción." In Gertrudis Gómez de Avellaneda,
       Baltasar (Salamanca: Anaya, 1973), pp. 7-34.

49.66 _____. "Introducción." In Gertrudis Gómez de Avellaneda,
       Sab (Salamanca: Anaya, 1970), pp. 7-35.

49.67 Brushwood, John S. "Narrative transformation and amplification.
       Gertrudis Gómez de Avellaneda's Guatimozín." In his Gen-
       teel barbarism (Lincoln: University of Nebraska Press,
       1981), pp. 23-38.

49.68 Bueno, Salvador. "El epistolario amoroso de la Avellaneda."
       RevC, 31, 1 (1957), 87-98. Also in his Temas y personajes
       de la literatura cubana (H: Unión, 1964), pp. 29-40.

49.69 _____. "Gertrudis Gómez de Avellaneda, gran poetisa." In his
       Figuras cubanas del siglo XIX (H: Unión de Escritores y
       Artistas, 1980), pp. 363-368.

49.70 _____. "Un libro polémico: El viaje a la Habana de la Condesa
       Merlín." In Mélanges à la mémoire d'André Joucla-Ruau
       (Aix-en-Provence: Université de Provence, 1980), pp. 107-
       121.

49.71 _____. "Sesquicentenario. Gertrudis Gómez de Avellaneda."
       CUNESCO, 3, 8 (1964), 22-23.

49.72 Cárdenas, Izequiel. "La conciencia feminista en la prosa de
       Gertrudis Gómez de Avellaneda." LFem, 1, 2 (1975), 32-39.

49.73 Carlos, Alberto J. "La Avellaneda y la mujer." In Actas del
       Tercer Congreso Internacional de Hispanistas (M: El Cole-
       gio de México, 1970), pp. 187-193.

49.74 _____. "La conciencia feminista en dos ensayos: Sor Juana y la Avellaneda." In Instituto Internacional de Literatura Iberoamericana, El ensayo y la crítica en Iberoamérica (Toronto: Universidad de Toronto, 1970), pp. 33-41.

49.75 _____. "Un 'error' de Gertrudis Gómez de Avellaneda." BBMP, 45 (1969), 327-330. Also Thesaurus, 25 (1970), 287-290.

49.76 _____. "El mal du siècle en un soneto de la Avellaneda ['Mi mal']." RomN, 7 (1966), 134-138.

49.77 _____. "René, Werther y La nouvelle Héloïse en la primera novela de la Avellaneda." RI, No. 60 (1966), 223-239.

49.78 Castillo González, Aurelia. "Biografía de Gertrudis Gómez de Avellaneda y juicio de sus obras." RCub, 5, 1-6 (1887), 5-19, 143-152, 248-258, 334-346, 420-431, 529-546.

49.79 Castro y Calvo, José María. "Estudio preliminar: la vida y la obra." In Gertrudis Gómez de Avellaneda, Obras (Madrid: Atlas, 1974), pp. 7-233. Biblioteca de autores españoles, vol. 272.

49.80 "Centenario de la Avellaneda." BAN, 13, 2 (1914), 49-71.

49.81 Cervantes, Rodrigo. "El alma mística de la Avellaneda." Bohemia, 5, 12 (1914), 134-135.

49.82 Chacón y Calvo, José María. "Gertrudis Gómez de Avellaneda; las influencias castellanas: examen negativo." In his Ensayos de literatura cubana (Madrid: "Saturnino Calleja", 1932), pp. 187-219. Orig. CCont, 6 (1914), 273-294. Same as item no. 49.14.

49.83 Cid Pérez, José, and Dolores Martí de Cid. "Personalidad y personalidades del teatro colonial hispanoamericano." Círculo, 4 (1972), 62-72. Gómez de Avellaneda inter alios.

49.84 Claramunt, Laura. "Gertrudis Gómez de Avellaneda." Bohemia, 42, 12 (1950), 30-31, 130-131.

49.85 Clavijo, Uva A. "La Avellaneda." Américas, 25, 10 (1973), 2-6. Spanish and English editions.

49.86 Cotarelo y Mori, Emilio. "Una tragedia real de la Avellaneda." RBAM, 3 (1926), 133-157. Also CCont, 41 (1926), 316-342.

49.87 Cruz, Mary. "Comedias de la Avellaneda." In Gertrudis Gómez de Avellaneda, Errores del corazón y otras comedias (H: Arte y Literatura, 1977), pp. 11-35.

49.88 _____. "Gertrudis Gómez de Avellaneda y su novela Sab." Unión, 12, 1 (1973), 116-149.

49.89 _____. "¿Por qué Sab." GdC, No. 83 (1970), 9-10.

49.90 _____. "Prólogo." In Gertrudis Gómez de Avellaneda, Guatimozín (H: Letras Cubanas, 1979), pp. 9-39.

49.91 _____. "Sab, vigorosa protesta contra toda servidumbre." CB,
2a época, No. 60 (1972), 12-15.

49.92 Cruz de Fuentes, Lorenzo. "Prólogo de la primera edición."
In Gertrudis Gómez de Avellaneda, Autobiografía y cartas;
2. ed. corr. y aum. (Madrid: Helénica, 1914), pp. 23-35.

49.93 Cuza Malé, Belkis. "La Avellaneda: una mujer con importancia."
GdC, No. 74 (1969), 28-29.

49.94 _____. "Viaje a la Habana de Gertrudis Gómez de Avellaneda."
GdC, No. 167 (1978), 9-11.

49.95 Dávila Solera, Juan. "Mujeres de América: Gertrudis Gómez de
Avellaneda." RPA, No. 74 (1950), 11-12.

49.96 Del Monte, Ricardo. "Coronación de la Avellaneda." In his
Obras (H: Academia Nacional de Artes y Letras, 1929), pp.
51-59.

49.97 Delgado, Jaime. "El Guatimozín de Gertrudis Gómez de Avellaneda." In Instituto Internacional de Literatura Iberoamericana, XVII Congreso (Madrid: Cultura Hispánica del Centro
Iberoamericano de Cooperación, 1978), pp. 959-970.

49.98 Díaz del Gallego, Pascasio. "Noticias de la Avellaneda." Bohemia, 4, 32 (1913), 374.

49.99 Eguía Ruiz, C. "Cuatro cartas inéditas de la Avellaneda."
RyF, 52 (1918), 348-362.

49.100 Escarpanter, José A. "El teatro de la Avellaneda." In Carmen
Bravo-Villasante et al., Gertrudis Gómez de Avellaneda,
q.v., pp. 27-46.

49.101 Esténger, Rafael. "Heredia en la Avellaneda." América, 1, 4
(1939), 12-13.

49.102 "Expediente donde se decreta la retención y reembarque de dos
obras de Gertrudis Gómez de Avellaneda por contener doctrinas subversivas y contrarias a la moral." BAN, 40,
1-6 (1941), 103-108.

49.103 Fernández-Marcané, Leonardo. "El romanticismo europeo, preludio de Gertrudis Gómez de Avellaneda." In Homenaje a Gertrudis Gómez de Avellaneda, q.v., pp. 25-36.

49.104 Fernández Peláez, Julio. "Gertrudis Gómez de Avellaneda en la
Argentina." RBNC, 2a serie, 7, 4 (1956), 157-161.

49.105 Figarola-Caneda, Domingo. "Proemio." In Gertrudis Gómez de
Avellaneda, Memorias inéditas de la Avellaneda (H: Biblioteca Nacional, 1914), pp. v-vii.

49.106 Figueroa, Agustín de. "Gertrudis Gómez de Avellaneda." RBC, 37 (1936), 238-248.

49.107 Florit, Eugenio. "Algunas anticipaciones de la Avellaneda." In his Poesía, casi siempre (ensayos literarios) (Madrid/ NY: Mensaje, 1978), pp. 53-61.

49.108 Fontanella, Lee. "Mystical diction and imagery in Gómez de Avellaneda and Carolina Coronado." LALR, No. 19 (1981), 47-55.

49.109 Fox-Lockert, Lucía. "Gertrudiz [sic] Gómez de Avellaneda [Sab]." In her Women novelists in Spain and Spanish America (Metuchen, N.J.: Scarecrow Press, 1979), pp. 127-136.

49.110 Gacerán de Vall, Julio. "La Avellaneda y Cepeda: un tímido sexual." In Homenaje a Gertudis Gómez de Avellaneda, q.v., pp. 236-264.

49.111 García, Domitila. "Gertrudis Gómez de Avellaneda." In her Album poético-fotográfico de las escritoras cubanas (H: Soler, 1872), I, 1-19. Also as Album poético-fotográfico de escritoras y poetisas cubanas escrito en 1868 para la señora doña Gertrudis Gómez de Avellaneda (H: Fígaro, 1926), pp. 23-38. Signed Domitila García de Coronado.

49.112 García Pons, César. "Tres poetas: Heredia, Plácido y la Avellaneda." CUA, No. 20 (1950), 21-30.

49.113 "Gertrudis Gómez de Avellaneda." GdC, No. 118 (1973), 20-21.

49.114 "Gertrudis Gómez de Avellaneda." InC, marzo-abril 1947, pp. 12-15.

49.115 González Curquejo, Antonio. "Recuerdos de un sesentón de 1858 a 1867. La Avellaneda en Cuba." CyA, 2a época, 8, 1 (1917), 5-7.

49.116 González del Valle y Carbajal, Emilio Martín. "Gertudis Gómez de Avellaneda." In his La poesía lírica en Cuba; apuntes para un libro de biografía y de crítica (Barcelona: Luis Tasso, 1900), pp. 95-109.

49.117 Guillén, Nicolás. "La Avellaneda y don Juan Valera." CubaI, No. 91 (1977), 26-29.

49.118 Guiteras, Pedro José. "Poetisas cubanas. Gertrudis Gómez de Avellaneda." RCub, 2 (1877), 481-502.

49.119 Gullón, Ricardo. "Tula, la incomprendida." Insula, No. 62 (1951), 3.

49.120 Gutiérrez de la Solana, Alberto. "Sab y Francisco: paralelo y contraste." In Homenaje a Gertudis Gómez de Avellaneda, q.v., pp. 301-317. Anselmo Suárez y Romero's Francisco.

49.121 Hall, H. Gaston. "Gertrudis Gómez de Avellaneda's sonnet 'A Washington'." BSUF, 16, 2 (1975), 2-3.

49.122 Hernández de Norman, Isabel. "Gertrudis Gómez de Avellaneda (1814-1873)." In her La novela criolla en las Antillas (NY: Plus Ultra, 1977), pp. 139-165.

49.123 ____. "Gertrudis Gómez de Avellaneda (1814-1873)." In her La novela romántica en las Antillas (NY: Ateneo Puertorriqueño, 1969), pp. 139-165.

49.124 Hernández-Miyares, Julio. "Variación en un tema indianista de la Avellaneda: el epílogo de Guatimozín y Una anécdota de la vida de Cortés." In Homenaje a Gertrudis Gómez de Avellaneda, q.v., pp. 318-328.

49.125 Hiriart, Rosario. "Gertrudis Gómez de Avellaneda: 1873-1973." VUM, No. 1183 (1973), 1-4.

49.126 Ibarzábal, Federico de. "Casi crónicas. La Avellaneda." RHab, 1, 8 (1913), 5-6.

49.127 Inclán, Josefina. "La mujer en la mujer Avellaneda." In Homenaje a Gertrudis Gómez de Avellaneda, q.v., pp. 71-92.

49.128 Iraizoz y de Villar, Antonio. "Safo y la Avellaneda." In his Libros y autores cubanos (Santa María de Rosario: Rosareña, 1956), pp. 14-16.

49.129 Iznaga, Alcides. "La Avellaneda; cien años en las tres cubanas." Bohemia, 65, 5 (1973), 8-15.

49.130 Jackson, Shirley M. "Fact from fiction: another look at slavery in three Spanish-American novels." In Miriam De Costa, Blacks in Hispanic literature: critical essays (Port Washington, N.Y.: Kennikat, 1977), pp. 83-89.

49.131 Jones, Joseph R. "Two notes on Sterne: Spanish sources. The Hinde tradition." RLC, 46 (1972), 437-444.

49.132 Jones, Willis Knapp. "Women of the Americas. No. II--Cuba's greatest woman writer." PAm, November 1947, pp. 51-55.

49.133 Judicini, Joseph V. "The stylistic revision of La Avellaneda's Alfonso Munio." REH, 11 (1977), 451-466.

49.134 Kelly, Edith L. "La Avellaneda's Sab and the political situation in Cuba." The Americas, 1 (1945), 303-316.

49.135 ____. "La Avellaneda's sonnet to Washington." The Americas, 4 (1947), 235-242.

49.136 ____. "The banning of Sab in Cuba. Documents from the Archivo Nacional de Cuba." The Americas, 1 (1945), 350-353.

49.137 ____. "The centennial of a great sonnet ['Al partir']."
Hispania, 19 (1936), 337-344.

49.138 ____. "Lo que dicen los críticos acerca de la versificación
de la poesía lírica de la Avellaneda." RevC, 8 (1937),
120-133. Also as "Opiniones sobre la versificación en
la lírica de la Avellaneda." HR, 6 (1938), 337-344.
Also RBC, 43 (1939), 304-312.

49.139 ____. "The metamorphosis of a poet." BUP, 71 (1937), 546-
552.

49.140 ____. "Observaciones sobre algunas obras de la Avellaneda
publicadas en México." RI, No. 5 (1941), 123-132.

49.141 Laguerre, Enrique. "La mujer en las tragedias de Gertrudis
Gómez de Avellaneda." Alero, No. 15 (1975), 14-24. Also
in Homenaje a Gertrudis Gómez de Avellaneda, q.v., pp.
183-199.

49.142 Lazo, Raimundo. "El caso singular de Gertrudis Gómez de Avellaneda." In his El romanticismo; fijación sociológico-
social de su concepto (M: Porrúa, 1971), pp. 49-52.

49.143 Lichtblau, Myron I. "La leyenda de La velada del helecho: análisis de la técnica narrativa." In Homenaje a Gertrudis
Gómez de Avellaneda, q.v., pp. 329-377.

49.144 López Argüello, Alberto. "La Avellaneda y sus versos." BBMP,
8 (1926), 210-226, 298-315; 9 (1927), 15-24, 123-136.

49.145 Loynaz, Dulce María. "La Avellaneda." RevC, 31, 2 (1957),
7-28.

49.146 Mahieu, José A. "Abolicionismo y feminismo en la Avellaneda."
lo negro como artificio narrativo en Sab." CHA, No. 342
(1978), 613-626.

49.147 Marinello, Juan. "Centenario. Gertrudis Gómez de Avellaneda."
CUNESCO, No. 45 (1973), 2-4.

49.148 Marquina, Rafael. "La poesía religiosa de la Avellaneda."
RevC, 23 (1948), 193-221.

49.149 Martí, José. "[Avellaneda]." In his Obras completas (H: Editora Nacional de Cuba, 1963), VIII, 309-313.

49.150 Martí de Cid, Dolores, and José Cid Pérez. "Perennidad de la
Avellaneda." RABM, 76 (1973), 413-422.

49.151 Martínez, Luis. "El mundo dramático de Gertrudis Gómez de
Avellaneda." Islas, 1, 3 (1959), 585-591.

49.152 Martínez Arango, C. "El amor a Cuba en la poesía lírica de
la Avellaneda." Belén, No. 30 (1931), 54-58.

49.153 Martínez Bello, Antonio M. "La cubanidad de la Avellaneda." Carteles, 28, 35 (1947), 15-16; 28, 36 (1947), 21-22.

49.154 _____. "Reposarán en el suelo natal los restos de la Avellaneda." Carteles, 29, 23 (1948), 14-16.

49.155 Meléndez, Concha. "Las novelas indias de la Avellaneda." In her La novela indianista en Hispanoamérica (1832-1889) (Madrid: Hernando, 1934), pp. 73-79. Also in her Obras completas (San Juan, P.R.: Instituto de Cultura Puertorriqueña, 1970-), I, 161-167.

49.156 Méndez Bejarano, Mario. "Tassara erótico." In his Tassara; nueva biografía crítica (Madrid: J. Pérez, 1928), pp. 35-54.

49.157 Merchán, Rafael María. "La Avellaneda es nuestra." In his Patria y cultura (H: Ministerio de Educación, Dirección de Cultura, 1948), pp. 116-121.

49.158 Miller, Beth K. "Avellaneda, nineteenth century feminist." RInter, 4 (1974), 177-183.

49.159 _____. "The metamorphosis of Avellaneda's sonnet to Washington." Symposium, 33 (1979), 153-170.

49.160 _____, and Alan Deyermond. "On editing the poetry of Avellaneda." In Studia hispanica in honor of Rodolfo Cardona (Madrid: Cátedra, 1981), pp. 41-55.

49.161 Mitjans, Aurelio. "De la Avellaneda y sus obras." In his Estudios literarios (H: La Prueba, 1887), pp. 73-153.

49.162 Montoro, Rafael. "Discurso pronunciado en Puerto Príncipe el 3 de diciembre de 1886." In his Discursos políticos y parlamentarios, informaciones y disertaciones (Philadelphia: Levytype, 1894), pp. 96-97.   ·

49.163 Montoro, Santiago. "Dos mujeres apasionadas: la Avellaneda y la 'Fernán Caballero'." CPro, 3, 12 (1954), 43-95.

49.164 Montoya de Zayas, Ondina. "La Avellaneda en su tiempo." In Homenaje a Gertrudis Gómez de Avellaneda, q.v., pp. 111-131.

49.165 Nelken, Margarita. "La Corina española: Gertrudis Gómez de Avellaneda." In her Las escritoras españolas (Barcelona: Labor, 1930), pp. 185-198.

49.166 Novoa y Luis, Rosario. "Lírica cubana. Gertrudis Gómez de Avellaneda..." AC, 3, 8 (1925), 280-283.

49.167 Pardo Canalís, Enrique. "Gertrudis Gómez de Avellaneda." RIE, No. 87 (1964), 259-272.

49.168   ____. "El retrato de la Avellaneda por Federico Madrazo."
           Goya, No. 60 (1964), 434-437.

49.169 Peña, Margarita. "Tres aspectos de la obra de Gertrudis Gómez
        de Avellaneda." Diálogos, No. 83 (1978), 32-35.

49.170 Percas Ponsetti, Helena. "Sobre la Avellaneda y su novela
        Sab." RI, No. 54 (1962), 347-357.

49.171 Piñera, Virgilio. "Gertrudis Gómez de Avellaneda: revisión
        de su poesía." ULH, Nos. 101-103 (1952), 7-38.

49.172 Piñeyro, Enrique. "Gertrudis Gómez de Avellaneda." BH, 6
        (1904), 143-156. Also as "Sobre Gertrudis Gómez de Ave-
        llaneda." In his Bosquejos, retratos, recuerdos (Paris:
        Garnier, 1912), pp. 245-267.

49.173   ____. "Gertrudis Gómez de Avellaneda." In his El romanti-
           cismo en España (Paris: Garnier, 190?), pp. 233-253.

49.174   ____. "Poetas líricos cubanos. La muerte de la Avellaneda."
           In his Estudios y conferencias de historia y literatura
           (NY: Thompson y Moreau, 1880), pp. 213-215.

49.175 Portuondo, José Antonio. "La dramática neutralidad de Gertru-
        dis Gómez de Avellaneda." L/L, Nos. 3-4 (1972-1973), 3-
        24.

49.176 Raggi, Carlos M. "Influencias inglesas en la obra de Gertru-
        dis Gómez de Avellaneda." In Homenaje a Gertrudis Gómez
        de Avellaneda, q.v., pp. 37-51.

49.177   ____. "Raíces cubanas en Gertrudis Gómez de Avellaneda."
           Círculo, 4 (1972), 5-20.

49.178 Randolph, Donald Allen. "¿Un caso de arrepentimiento? Cañete
        contra la muerte de Avellaneda." La torre, No. 62 (1968),
        165-172.

49.179 Remos y Rubio, Juan Nepomuceno José. "El regreso de la Avella-
        neda." In his Micrófono (H: Molina, 1937), pp. 169-190.

49.180 Rexach, Rosario. "La Avellaneda como escritora romántica."
        ALHisp, Nos. 2-3 (1973-1974), 241-254.

49.181   ____. "Nostalgia de Cuba en la obra de la Avellaneda." In
           Homenaje a Gertrudis Gómez de Avellaneda, q.v., pp. 265-
           280.

49.182 Roberts, Graves Baxter. "Gertrudis Gómez de Avellaneda." In
        his The epithet in Spanish poetry of the romantic period
        (Iowa City: University of Iowa, 1936), pp. 132-142.

49.183 Rodríguez Embil, Luis. "La Avellaneda al través de sus cartas
        de amor." CyA, 2a época, 2, 1 (1914), 22-23.

49.184 Rodríguez Moñino, Antonio. "Epistolario inédito de doña Gertrudis Gómez de Avellaneda (1841-1871)." Hispanófila, No. 6 (1959), 1-52.

49.185 Roig de Leuchsenring, Emilio. "A propósito del traslado de unas cenizas. Glorifiquemos a Cuba glorificando a la Avellaneda." Carteles, 30, 14 (1949), 72-73.

49.186 _____. "Vida, obra y pasiones de la Avellaneda." Carteles, 29, 31 (1948), 1; 29, 34 (1948), 22; 29, 35 (1948), 29.

49.187 Roselló, Aurora J. "Naturaleza, ambiente y paisaje en la poesía lírica de la Avellaneda." In Homenaje a Gertrudis Gómez de Avellaneda, q.v., pp. 153-168.

49.188 Ruiz-Gaytán de San Vicente, Beatriz. "Gertrudis Gómez de Avellaneda y el pensamiento hispanoamericano de su tiempo." In Homenaje a Gertrudis Gómez de Avellaneda, q.v., pp. 52-68.

49.189 Sabat de Rivers, Georgina. "Sor Juana Inés de la Cruz y Gertrudis Gómez de Avellaneda: dos voces americanas en defensa de la mujer." In Homenaje a Gertrudis Gómez de Avellaneda, q.v., pp. 99-110.

49.190 Salgado, José. "El centenario de la Avellaneda." RHab, 2, 8 (1914), 72-73.

49.191 Salgado, María A. "El arte de la leyenda en Gertrudis Gómez de Avellaneda." In Homenaje a Gertrudis Gómez de Avellaneda, q.v., pp. 338-346.

49.192 Sánchez, J. "Date of the composition of Baltasar of Avellaneda." HR, 6 (1938), 79.

49.193 Santos, Nelly E. "Las ideas feministas de Gertrudis Gómez de Avellaneda." RInter, 5 (1975), 276-281. Also in Homenaje a Gertrudis Gómez de Avellaneda, q.v., pp. 132-141.

49.194 Schultz de Mantovani, Fryda. "Gertrudis Gómez de Avellaneda." ULH, Nos. 151-153 (1961), 147-163. Also CyC, Nos. 285-286 (1959), 148-162.

49.195 _____. "Pasión de la Avellaneda." CA, No. 90 (1956), 238-251.

49.196 Suárez-Galbán, Eugenio. "La angustia de una mujer indiana, o el epistolario de Gertrudis Gómez de Avellaneda." In L'autobiographie dans le monde hispanique (Aix-en-Provence: Université de Provence, 1980), pp. 281-296.

49.197 Valdés de la Paz, Osvaldo. "Dos iniciativas femeninas cubanas. EL monumento a la Avellaneda y la casa para la mujer americana." Carteles, 29, 39 (1948), 23-25.

49.198 ____. "Un natalicio glorioso. Otro aniversario de la Avellaneda." Carteles, 30, 13 (1949), 34-36.

49.199 Valenzuela, Víctor M. "Gertrudis Gómez de Avellaneda: Baltasar." In his Siete comediógrafas hispanoamericanas (Beth-
lehem, Penn.: Lehigh University, 1975), pp. 23-39.

49.200 Valera y Alcalá Galeano, Juan. "Gertrudis Gómez de Avellaneda." In his Obras completas (Madrid: Aguilar, 1961), pp.
1351-1354.

49.201 ____. "Observaciones sobre el drama Baltasar de la señora
doña Gertrudis Gómez de Avellaneda." In his Obras completas (Madrid: Aguilar, 1961), pp. 109-115.

49.202 ____. "Poesías líricas, de Gertrudis Gómez de Avellaneda."
In his Obras completas (Madrid: Aguilar, 1961), pp. 370-
382. Orig. as "Poesías líricas de la Sra. Da. Gertrudis
Gómez de Avellaneda." RBC, 9 (1914), 5-29.

49.203 Varela Jacomé, Benito. "Estudio preliminar." In Gertrudis
Gómez de Avellaneda, Poesías selectas (Barcelona: Bruguera, 1968), pp. 11-40.

49.204 Varona y Pera, Enrique José. "[Discurso en acto conmemorativo
del centenario de la Avellaneda]." CCont, 5 (1914), 99-
105.

49.205 ____. "Gertrudis Gómez de Avellaneda." La lucha, 1, 4
(1883), 6.

49.206 Villabella, Manuel. "Tula: provechosa sobra de crédito literario." Islas, No. 47 (1974), 51-69.

49.207 Villaverde, Luis G. "Gertrudis Gómez de Avellaneda, dramatur-
ga ecléctica." In Homenaje a Gertrudis Gómez de Avellaneda, q.v., pp. 200-209.

49.208 Virgillo, Carmelo. "El amor en la estética de Gertrudis Gómez
de Avellaneda." CA, No. 219 (1978), 244-258.

49.209 Vitier, Cintio. "La retórica." In his Poetas cubanos del siglo XIX; semblanzas (H: Unión, 1969), p. 24.

49.210 Ximénez de Sandoval, Felipe. "Tres poetisas americanas."
BBMP, 42 (1966), 305-385. Gómez de Avellaneda inter
alias.

49.211 Zaldívar, Gladys. "La noche mágica y otros temas afines en
un poema de la Avellaneda ['La noche de insomnio y el
alba']." In Homenaje a Gertrudis Gómez de Avellaneda,
q.v., pp. 174-179.

50. GUILLEN, NICOLAS (1902-   )

Bibliographies

50.1   Antuña, María Luisa, and Josefina García Carranza. Bibliografía de Nicolás Guillén. H: Biblioteca Nacional "José Martí", Instituto Nacional del Libro, 1975.

50.2   ____. "Bibliografía de Nicolás Guillén: suplemento, 1972-1977." RBNJM, 3a serie, 19, 3 (1977), 61-163.

50.3   Bibliografía de Nicolás Guillén. H: Orbe, 1975.

50.4   Havana. Biblioteca Nacional José Martí. Exposición homenaje a Nicolás Guillén en su 60 aniversario. H: Consejo Nacional de Cultura, 1962.

50.5   León, René. "Nicolás Guillén: bibliografía." ExTL, 7 (1978), 109-113.

50.6   Pane, Remigio U. "Cuban poetry in English: a bibliography of English translations from Casal, Florit, Gómez de Avellaneda, Guillén, Heredia, Pedroso and 'Plácido'." BBDI, 18, 9 (1946), 199-201.

50.7   "A short Guillén bibliography." CCSN, No. 2 (1974), 15-18.

Critical Monographs and Dissertations

50.8   Alderete Ramírez, Ana Nilda. El sonido y el ritmo en la poesía de Nicolás Guillén. La Banda, Arg.?, 1969.

50.9   Augier, Angel I. Nicolás Guillén. H: Instituto Cubano del Libro, 1971.

50.10   ____. Nicolás Guillén; notas para un estudio biográfico-crítico. H: Universidad Central de Las Villas, 1962-1964.

50.11   ____. La revolución cubana en la poesía de Nicolás Guillén. H: Letras Cubanas, 1979. Same as item no. 51.74.

50.12   Boulware-Miller, Patricia Kay. "Nature in three 'negrista' poets: Nicolás Guillén, Emilio Ballagas, and Luis Palés Matos." DAI, 39 (1979), 5186A-5187A

50.13   Boyd, Antonio Ortiz. "The concept of black esthetics as seen in selected works of three Latin American writers: Machado

237

de Assis, Nicolás Guillén and Adalberto Ortiz." DAI, 35 (1975), 7898A.

50.14 Cartey, Wilfred. "The Antillian poets: Emilio Ballagas, Luis Palés Matos, and Nicolás Guillén: literary development of the Negro theme in relation to the making of modern Afro-Antillian poetry in the historic evoluction of the Negro." DAI, 28 (1967), 2203A.

50.15 Castán de Pontrelli, Mary. "The criollo poetry of Nicolás Guillén." DAI, 29 (1969), 612A.

50.16 Cobb, Martha K. "The black experience in the poetry of Nicolás Guillén, Jacques Roumain, Langston Hughes." DAI, 35 (1975), 5392A-5393A.

50.17 Coin, Jeanette Bercovici. "Social aspects of black poetry in Luis Palés Matos, Nicolás Guillén and Manuel del Cabral." DAI, 37 (1976), 1581A.

50.18 Couffon, Claude. Nicolás Guillén; présentation, choix de textes, traduction. Paris: Seghers, 1964.

50.19 Davis, Stephanie Jo. "Development of poetic technique in the works of Nicolás Guillén (1927-1972)." DAI, 37 (1976), 1581A.

50.20 Ellis, Keith. Cuba's Nicolás Guillén: poetry and ideology. Toronto: University of Toronto Press, 1983.

50.21 Farrell, Joseph Richard. "Nicolás Guillén: poet in search of cubanidad." DAI, 29 (1969), 3133A-3134A.

50.22 Fernández Retamar, Roberto. El son del vuelo popular. H: UNEAC, 1972. Also H: Letras Cubanas, 1979.

50.23 Gaetani, Francis Marion. Nicolás Guillén: a study of the phonology and metrics in his poetry. Unpublished Ph.D. dissertation, Columbia University, 1940.

50.24 García-Barrio, Constance S. de. "The black in Cuban literature and the poetry of Nicolás Guillén." DAI, 36 (1975), 2806A.

50.25 González-Pérez, Armando. El sentimiento de la negritud en la poesía de Nicolás Guillén. Milwaukee: University of Wisconsin-Milwaukee, Center for Latin America, 1976.

50.26 Harth, Dorothy Feldman. Nicolás Guillén and Afro-Cuban poetry. Unpublished Ph.D. dissertation, Columbia University, 1948.

50.27 Levidova, I. M. Nicolás Guillén: bio-bibliografitseski akasatjel. Moscow, 1952.

50.28 Liddell, Janice Lee. "The whip's corolla: myth and politics in the literature of the black diaspora: Aimé Césaire,

Nicolás Guillén, Langston Hughes." DAI, 39 (1978), 3581A-3582A.

50.29 Lowery, Dellita Martin. "Selected poems of Nicolás Guillén and Langston Hughes: their use of Afro-Western folk music genres." DAI, 36 (1975), 1487A-1488A.

50.30 Marinello, Juan. Hazaña y triunfo americanos de Nicolás Guillén (1948-1951). H, 1962.

50.31 Martínez Estrada, Ezequiel. La poesía afrocubana de Nicolás Guillén. Montevideo: Arca, 1966. 3. ed., H: Unión, 1967. Also as La poesía de Nicolás Guillén. BA: Calicanto, 1977.

50.32 Milla Chapelli, Julio. Un criterio nuevo sobre un prejuicio viejo. Camagüey: Libertad, 1936.

50.33 Plavskin, Zacher Isaakovich. Nikolas Gil'en. Kritiko-biograficheski ocherk. Moscow/Leningrad: Izd. "Chudozhestyvennaia Literatura", 1965.

50.34 Recopilación de textos sobre Nicolás Guillén. H: Casa de las Américas, 1974. Pertinent items are listed separately.

50.35 Ruscalleda Bercedóniz, Jorge María. La poesía de Nicolás Guillén: cuatro elementos sustanciales. Río Piedras, P.R.: Editorial Universitaria, Universidad de Puerto Rico, 1975.

50.36 Salvioni, Giovanna. L'Affrica nera a Cuba; tradizione popolare e poesia di libertà di Nicolás Guillén. Milano: Vita e Pensiero, 1974.

50.37 Sardinha, Dennis. The poetry of Nicolás Guillén; an introduction. London: New Beacon Books, 1976.

50.38 Smart, Ian I. "The creative dialogue in the poetry of Nicolás Guillén: Europe and America." DAI, 36 (1976), 7457A.

50.39 Tous, Adriana. La poesía de Nicolás Guillén. Madrid: Cultura Hispánica, 1971.

50.40 White, Florence E. Poesía negra in the works of Jorge de Lima, Nicolás Guillén and Jacques Roumain. Unpublished Ph.D. dissertation, University of Wisconsin, 1952.

50.41 Williams, Lorna V. Self and society in the poetry of Nicolás Guillén. Baltimore: Johns Hopkins University Press, 1982.

Critical Essays

50.42 Agosti, Héctor P. "Adiós a Nicolás Guillén." In his Por una política de la cultura (BA: Procyón, 1956), pp. 134-137.

50.43   Aguirre, Mirta. "Discurso." RyC, No. 25 (1974), 46-49. Also
        Unión, 13, 4 (1974), 170-176.

50.44   ____. "En torno a la Elegía a Jesús Martínez." UH, 2, 23.
        (1952), 3-4. Also in Recopilación de textos, q.v., pp.
        293-302.

50.45   ____. "Guillén, maestro de la poesía." GdC, Nos. 8-9 (1962),
        16. Also in Recopilación de textos, q.v., pp. 159-170.

50.46   ____. "Otra vez Nicolás." GdC, No. 104 (1972), 8.

50.47   Aguirre, Sergio. "Proponemos canonización." GdC, No. 104
        (1972), 24.

50.48   Alemán, Luis. "Entrevista a Nicolás Guillén." PajP, Nos. 5-6
        (1950), 78-82.

50.49   Allen, Martha E. "Nicolás Guillén, poeta del pueblo." RI, No.
        29 (1949), 29-43.

50.50   Altolaguirre, Manuel. "[Sóngoro cosongo]." RO, No. 36 (1932),
        381-384.

50.51   Ardévol, José. "Nicolás Guillén (testimonio de un músico)."
        GdC, No. 104 (1972), 20.

50.52   Armas L., José. "Guillén habla de Guillén." VO, 14, 28 (1972),
        34-37.

50.53   ____. "Un homenaje al hombre, al poeta revolucionario." VO,
        14, 30 (1972), 52-53.

50.54   Arozarena, Marcelino. "El antillano domador de sones." Améri-
        ca, 17, 1-2 (1943), 37-42.

50.55   ____. "Más estudios sobre la obra de Nicolás Guillén." GdC,
        No. 122 (1974), 26.

50.56   ____. "Parroquiano del gran zoo." GdC, No. 104 (1972), 10-11.

50.57   ____. "Viaje a nuestras raíces culturales." GdC, No. 153
        (1977), 21.

50.58   Artel, Jorge. "Presentación de Nicolás Guillén." VAmer, 4
        (1946), 385-390.

50.59   Augier, Angel I. "La afirmación revolucionaria en las elegías."
        Bohemia, 64, 29 (1972), 46-53.

50.60   ____. "Alusiones africanas en la poesía de Nicolás Guillén."
        Islas, Nos. 39-40 (1971), 127-137. Also EyF, No. 7 (1969),
        69-73. Also Unión, 6, 4 (1968), 142-151.

50.61 _____. "La amarga poesía del azúcar." Bohemia, 53, 27 (1961), 62-64, 83.

50.62 _____. "La crítica extranjera ante la obra de Nicolás Guillén." GdC, No. 8-9 (1962), 4-6.

50.63 _____. "The Cuban poetry of Nicolás Guillén." Phylon, 12 (1952), 32-38.

50.64 _____. "Una denuncia poética en todas las lenguas." GdC, Nos. 8-9 (1962), 19-20.

50.65 _____. "En los 70 años de Nicolás Guillén: una poesía cubana y revolucionaria." VO, 14, 28 (1972), 32-33.

50.66 _____. "La metáfora objetiva de Nicolás Guillén." L/L, No. 2 (1971), 9-24.

50.67 _____. "Nicolás Guillén en la poesía cubana." GdC, No. 104 (1972), 21.

50.68 _____. "Nicolás Guillén. Poeta-profeta de la revolución cubana." Bohemia, 53, 29 (1961), 20-21, 102, 127; 53, 30 (1961), 40-43, 87-89.

50.69 _____. "Un poema desconocido ['El soldado Miguel Paz y el sargento José Inés']." GdC, No. 60 (1967), 12.

50.70 _____. "Poesía cubana y revolucionaria de Nicolás Guillén." CCSN, No. 2 (1973), 1-6. Also CubaI, No. 34 (1972), 8-13. Also in Nicolás Guillén, Cuba: amor y revolución; 2. ed. (Lima: Causachún, 1973), pp. 7-19.

50.71 _____. "Presencia cubana en la vida y la obra de Nicolás Guillén." ULH, No. 159 (1963), 13-26.

50.72 _____. "Prólogo." In Nicolás Guillén, Prosa de prisa 1929-1972 (H: Arte y Literatura, 1975), I, no pagination.

50.73 _____. "Prólogo: la poesía de Nicolás Guillén." In Nicolás Guillén, Obra poética 1920-1972 (H: Arte y Literatura, 1974), pp. x-lix.

50.74 _____. "La revolución cubana en la poesía de Nicolás Guillén." Plural, No. 59 (1976), 47-61. Also Unión, 12, 3-4 (1973), 23-48.

50.75 Ballagas, Emilio. "El mensaje inédito." In Recopilación de textos sobre Nicolás Guillén, q.v., pp. 259-261.

50.76 Bandeira, Manuel. "Discurso na Academia Brasileira de Letras." Literatura, 2, 6 (1974), 23-26.

50.77 Bellini, Giuseppe. "Nicolás Guillén." In his Poeti antillani (Milano: Cisalpino, 1957), pp. 9-32.

50.78 Bianchi Ross, Ciro. "Conversación hacia los 70." CubaI, No. 34 (1972), 14-21.

50.79 Boti, Regino Eladio. "La poesía cubana de Nicolás Guillén." RBC, 29 (1932), 343-353. Also in Recopilación de textos sobre Nicolás Guillén, q.v., pp. 81-90.

50.80 Bottiglieri, Nicola. "Considerazioni e appunti sul Gran zoo di Nicolás Guillén." AION-SR, 21 (1979), 439-453.

50.81 Boulware-Miller, Patricia Kay. "Nicolás Guillén's 'Balada del güije': an experiment in folklore." Vórtice, 2, 2-3 (1979), 206-217.

50.82 Branly, Roberto. "Guillén: vida y obra poética." GdC, No. 123 (1974), 28-29.

50.83 Bueno, Salvador. "'La canción del bongó': sobre la cultura mulata de Cuba." CA, No. 206 (1976), 89-106.

50.84 _____. "Guillén: por la liberación del hombre." GdC, No. 104 (1972), 25-27.

50.85 _____. "La obra poética de Nicolás Guillén." Bohemia, 66, 11 (1974), 16.

50.86 Buero Vallejo, Antonio. "Al poeta Nicolás Guillén en la Habana." GdC, No. 168 (1978), 22.

50.87 Campaña, Antonio. "Nicolás Guillén, sones y angustia." Atenea, 85 (1946), 444-458.

50.88 Campoamor, Fernando G. "[Prosa de prisa]." Unión, 1, 3-4 (1962), 97-99.

50.89 Carpentier, Alejo. "Como dice el poeta..." GdC, No. 104 (1972), 5.

50.90 Carrera Andrade, Jorge. "Nicolás Guillén, poeta del hombre común y mensajero del trópico." RIn, No. 90 (1946), 467-471.

50.91 Carrión, Ulises. "Un libro peligroso y admirable." MNu, No. 13 (1967), 70.

50.92 Cartey, Wilfred. "Cómo surge Nicolás Guillén en las Antillas." UAnt, No. 133 (1958), 257-274.

50.93 _____. "The 'son' in crescendo." In his Black images (NY: Teachers College Press, 1970), pp. 111-148.

50.94 Castañeda León, T. "Guillén y Ballagas." RAm, 14 (1932), 68-69.

50.95 Castellanos, Orlando. "Nicolás Guillén: tres veces veinticinco." CubaI, No. 95 (1977), 30-35.

50.96 Castellanos García, Gerardo. "Carta sobre Guillén." UH, 2, 23 (1952), 33.

50.97 Castilla, Belarmino. "En el 70 cumpleaños de Nicolás Guillén. Homenaje del PCC en el teatro de la CTC." GdC, No. 104 (1972), 213.

50.98 _____. "[Palabras]." RyC, 1, 5 (1972), 2-9.

50.99 _____. "Palabras en el homenaje a Nicolás Guillén." Unión, 11, 4 (1972), 181-189. Also in Recopilación de textos sobre Nicolás Guillén, q.v., pp. 63-70.

50.100 Castro, Julio. "Nicolás Guillén, poeta de América." Marcha, 14-III-1947, p. 16.

50.101 Chacón Nardi, Rafaela. "A Nicolás Guillén, en su 70 aniversario." GdC, No. 104 (1972), 13.

50.102 Cobb, Martha K. "Concepts of blackness in the poetry of Nicolás Guillén, Jacques Roumain and Langston Hughes." CLAJ, 18 (1974), 262-272.

50.103 _____. "Nicolás Guillén." In her Harlem, Havana, and Haiti (Washington, D.C.: Three Continents Press, 1979), pp. 103-131.

50.104 Contreras, Roberto. "Carta a Guillén." Unión, 13, 1 (1974), 122-123.

50.105 "Conversación con Nicolás Guillén." CAm, No. 73 (1972), 125-136.

50.106 Cossío, Adolfina. "Los recursos rítmicos en la poesía de Nicolás Guillén." Santiago, No. 5 (1971), 177-222.

50.107 Couffon, Claude. "En busca de una poesía popular de expresión nacional." GdC, No. 168 (1978), 19.

50.108 _____. "Guillén en París." Bohemia, 70, 19 (1978), 29.

50.109 _____. "Nicolás Guillén y la geografía sentimental." CAP, No. 6 (1955), 93-96. Also AUCE, No. 339 (1955), 122-125. Also as "Nicolás Guillén et la géographie sentimentale." LetF, 3-10-III-1955, p. 2.

50.110 Coulthard, Gabriel R. "Nicolás Guillén and West Indies négritude." CarQ, 16, 1 (1970), 52-57.

50.111 Cuéllar Vizcaíno, Manuel. "El Guillén que usted no conoce." GdC, No. 8-9 (1962), 7-8.

50.112 _____. "La historia de 'Laca'." GdC, No. 132 (1975), 9-10.

50.113 _____. "La leyenda de 'Sansemayá'." Adelante, No. 6 (1935), 15.

50.114 Davis, Paul A. "The black man and the Caribbean as seen by Nicolás Guillén and Luis Palés Matos." CarQ, 25, 1-2 (1979), 72-79.

50.115 Davis-Lett, Stephanie. "Literary games in the works of Nicolás Guillén." PCL, 6 (1980), 135-142.

50.116 ____. "Revisando a Nicolás Guillén." ExTL, 10 (1981), 87-94.

50.117 DeCosta, Miriam. "Nicolás Guillén and his poetry for Afro-Americans." BlackW, 22, 11 (1973), 12-16.

50.118 Depestre, René. "Nicolás Guillén. Orfeo negro de Cuba." GdC, No. 74 (1969), 10-11. Also as "Orfeo negro." In Recopilación de textos sobre Nicolás Guillén, q.v., pp. 121-125.

50.119 ____. "Paseo por el Gran zoo de Nicolás Guillén." In his Por la revolución, por la poesía (H: Instituto del Libro, 1969), pp. 160-164. Also Montevideo: Biblioteca de Marcha, 1970.

50.120 Díaz Usandivaras, Julio C. "Presencia y latitud de Nicolás Guillén." EstLit, No. 606 (1977), 4-5. Also as "Prezenţa şi latitudinea lui Nicolás Guillén." RoLit, 19 (1972), 27.

50.121 Diego, Eliseo. "Al joven Nicolás Guillén, con ocasión de cumplir sus setenta años." GdC, No. 104 (1972), 13.

50.122 ____. "Carta a Nicolás." Unión, 12, 304 (1973), 125-127.

50.123 ____. "Sobre un poeta casi anónimo de Nicolás Guillén." Unión, 17, 1 (1978), 59-63.

50.124 Dill, Hans-Otto. "De la exposición periodística a la representación artística." RBNJM, 3a serie, 14, 2 (1972), 65-80. Also as "De Übergang von publizistischer Darstellung zu künstlerischer Gestaltung bei Nicolás Guillén." WZUB, 18 (1969), 693-697. Also in Romanische Philologie heute; Festschrift Rita Schober (Berlin: Humboldt-Universität zu Berlin, 1969), pp. 693-697.

50.125 ____. "Methodenumbruch und kubanische Revolution im Werk Guilléns." WB, 24, 12 (1978), 171-176.

50.126 ____. "Zum Problem der Aktualität, de Agitation und des Publikumsbezuges. Die Bedeutung des publizistischen Schaffens für die Entwicklung des Lyrikers Nicolás Guillén." BRP, 8, 2 (1969), 256-281.

50.127 Dobos, Eva. "El reflejo de la transculturación en el West Indies Ltd. de Nicolás Guillén." In Actas del Simposio Internacional de Estudios Hispánicos (Budapest: Akademiai Kiadó, 1978), pp. 245-252.

50.128 Dromundo, Baltasar. "La poesía de Nicolás Guillén." Adelante, No. 12 (1936), 12.

50.129 Duque, Alfredo S. "Una pequeña antología de Nicolás Guillén." CA, No. 204 (1976), 155-180.

50.130 Ehremburg, Ilya. "La poesía de Nicolás Guillán." UH, 3, 6 (1953), 6.

50.131 _____. "Un poeta de gran corazón." UH, 2, 23 (1952), 9.

50.132 Ellis, Keith. "Cambio y continuidad en la poesía de Nicolás Guillén. In Actas del Simposio Internacional de Estudios Hispánicos (Budapest: Akademiai Kiadó, 1978), pp. 229-233.

50.133 _____. "Literary Americanism and the recent poetry of Nicolás Guillén." UTQ, 45 (1976), 1-18.

50.134 _____. "Nicolás Guillén at seventy." CarQ, 19, 1 (1973), 87-94.

50.135 Entralgo, Elías. "La poesía de Nicolás Guillén en miniatura." UH, 2, 23 (1952), 33.

50.136 Escarpenter, José A. "[La paloma de vuelo popular]." RBNJM, 3a serie, 1, 1-4 (1959), 96-98.

50.137 Esteban, José. "Unas preguntas a Nicolás Guillén." Insula, Nos. 224-225 (1965), 29.

50.138 Fabbiani Ruiz, José. "Comprensión de Nicolás Guillén." RFEV, 2 (1938), 19-21.

50.139 Feijóo, Samuel. "Guillén momentáneo." Signos, No. 21 (1978), 8-13.

50.140 _____. "Un paralelo satírico: Plácido y Nicolás Guillén." Unión, 16, 3 (1977), 150-155.

50.141 _____. "Visita de Nicolás Guillén en su trabajante sesentañía." Islas, 5, 1 (1962), 115-124.

50.142 Fernández Retamar, Roberto. "Nicolás Guillén." In his La poesía contemporánea en Cuba (1927-1935) (H: Orígenes, 1954), pp. 56-62, 69-74.

50.143 _____. "Sobre Guillén, poeta cubano." Islas, 5, 1 (1962), 127-132.

50.144 _____. "El son de vuelo popular." GdC, Nos. 8-9 (1962), 12-15. Also in Recopilación de textos sobre Nicolás Guillén, q.v., pp. 177-198.

50.145 Ferrand, Manuel. "Raíz española de la poesía de Nicolás Guillén." EAm, 8 (1954), 461-467.

50.146   Figueira, Gastón. "Dos poetas iberoamericanos de nuestro tiempo [Nicolás Guillén y Manuel del Cabral]." RI, No. 19 (1945), 107-117.

50.147   Fitz, Earl E. "The black poetry of Nicolás Guillén and Jorge de Lima: a comparative study." Inti, 4 (1976), 76-84.

50.148   Florit, Eugenio. "Nicolás Guillén." RHM, 8 (1942), 225.

50.149   _____. "Nicolás Guillén, poeta entero." RdAm, 13 (1948), 234-248. Also in his Poesía, casi siempre (ensayos literarios) (Madrid/NY: Mensaje, 1978), pp. 19-25.

50.150   Font, María Teresa. "Tres manifestaciones de espacialismo poético: Federico García Lorca, Nicolás Guillén y Jorge Luis Borges." RI, No. 73 (1970), 601-612.

50.151   Forné Farreres, José. "España en Nicolás Guillén." GdC, No. 104 (1972), 18-19.

50.152   Fossey, Jean Michel. "Nicolás Guillén." In his Galaxia latinoamericana (Las Palmas de Gran Canaria: Inventarios Provisionales, 1973), pp. 253-265.

50.153   Franco, José Luciano. "Prehistoria." GdC, No. 104 (1972), 9.

50.154   Franulic, Lenka. "Nicolás Guillén." In her Cien autores contemporáneos; 3. ed. (Santiago de Chile: Ercilla, 1952), pp. 363-370.

50.155   García-Barrio, Constance S. de. "The image of the black man in the poetry of Nicolás Guillén." In Miriam DeCosta, Blacks in Hispanic literature: critical essays (Port Washington, N.Y.: Kennikat, 1977), pp. 105-113.

50.156   García Veitía, Margarita. "Sobre El gran zoo (...el bestiario multifacético de Nicolás Guillén)." TLit, No. 21 (1970), 7-10. Also in Recopilación de textos sobre Nicolás Guillén, q.v., pp. 311-318.

50.157   Garzón Céspedes, Francisco. "Mi poesía ha sido siempre coherente consigo misma." CB, No. 89 (1975), 3-6.

50.158   González-Cruz, Luis F. "Nature and the black reality in three Caribbean poets: a new look at the concept of négritude." PCL, 5 (1979), 138-146.

50.159   González Freire, Natividad. "De las FAR a Nicolás Guillén." Bohemia, 64, 30 (1972), 32-33.

50.160   González López, Waldo. "Nicolás Guillén y el número 150 de la Gaceta." Bohemia, 69, 7 (1977), 26-27.

50.161   González-Pérez, Armando. "Raza y Eros en la poesía afrocubana de Nicolás Guillén." In Homenaje a Lydia Cabrera (Miami: Universal, 1978), pp. 149-164.

50.162 ____. "El sentimiento de la negritud en la poesía de Nicolás Guillén." Caribe, 2, 1 (1977), 47-58. Same as item no. 51.25.

50.163 González Tuñón, Raúl. "Guilléntero." Orientación, 4-VI-1947, p. 5.

50.164 Guillén, Nicolás. "Autocrítica de Guillén." Signos, No. 21 (1978), 15-27.

50.165 "Guillén en la Biblioteca." RBNJM, 3a serie, 3, 1-4 (1961), 173-177.

50.166 Hays, H. R. "Nicolás Guillén y la poesía afrocubana." In Recopilación de textos sobre Nicolás Guillén, q.v., pp. 91-99.

50.167 Hernández Catá, Sara. "Unas palabras sobre Nicolás Guillén." UH, 2, 23 (1952), 19.

50.168 Hernández Novás, Raúl. "La más reciente poesía de Nicolás Guillén." CAm, No. 75 (1972), 159-162.

50.169 "Homenaje a Guillén en Chile." RevC, 23 (1948), 344-348.

50.170 "Homenaje nacional a Nicolás Guillén." Bohemia, 64, 29 (1972), 50-53.

50.171 Hughes, Langston. "Sobre Guillén." The crisis, 55 (1948), 336.

50.172 Irish, J. A. George. "Nicolás Guillén's position on race: a reappraisal." RInter, 6 (1976), 335-347.

50.173 ____. "Notes on a historic visit: Nicolás Guillén in Jamaica." CarQ, 21, 1-2 (1975), 74-84.

50.174 ____. "The revolutionary focus of Guillén's journalism." CarQ, 22, 4 (1976), 68-78.

50.175 Iznaga, Alcides. "Guillén en su sexagésimo aniversario." Islas, 5, 2 (1962), 125-126.

50.176 ____. "Guillén entre nosotros." Bohemia, 69, 29 (1977), 26-27.

50.177 Jay, David. "La Cuba de Guillén." GdC, No. 114 (1973), 9.

50.178 Jimenes Grullón, Juan Isidro. "Nicolás Guillén." In his Seis poetas cubanos (H: Cromos, 1954), pp. 89-108.

50.179 Johnson, Harvey L. "Nicolás Guillén's portraits of blacks in Cuban society." In Homage to Irving A. Leonard (East Lansing: Michigan State University, Latin American Studies Center, 1977), pp. 197-207.

50.180 Johnson, Lemuel A. "Nicolás Guillén and Afro-Cubanism." In
his The devil, the gargoyle, and the buffoon; the Negro
as metaphor in Western literature (Port Washington, N.Y.:
Kennikat Press, 1969), pp. 136-155.

50.181 King, Lloyd. "Nicolás Guillén and afrocubanismo." In A cele-
bration of black and African writing (Oxford: Oxford University Press, 1975), pp. 30-45.

50.182 Knight, Franklin W. "Poet of the people." Review, No. 6
(1973), 67-69.

50.183 La Rosa, Lesmes. "A un soldado de la poesía." VO, 18, 20
(1977), 9.

50.184 Labarre, Roland. "Le poète national cubain Nicolás Guillén."
In his Eveil aux Amériques: Cuba (Paris: Editions Sociales, 1962), pp. 255-271.

50.185 Lavín, Pablo F. "Un gran hombre y un gran poeta." UH, 2, 25
(1952), 10.

50.186 Lázaro, Angel. "Poesía de Nicolás Guillén." Carteles, 23, 25
(1942), 9.

50.187 Lazo, Raimundo. "Con motivo de una biografía de Nicolás Guillén." ULH, No. 170 (1964), 7-21.

50.188 Le Bigot, Claude. "'Yanqui con soldado' de Nicolás Guillén
(essai d'analyse)." LanM, 71 (1977), 585-593.

50.189 Leante, César. "La historia como poesía." GdC, No. 106
(1972), 29-30. Also in his El espacio real (H: Unión
de Escritores y Artistas de Cuba, 1975), pp. 99-109.

50.190 León, María Teresa. "¡Adió, Nicolá!" GdC, Nos. 8-9 (1962), 3.

50.191 Lewis, Rupert. "El poeta nacional de Cuba." GdC, No. 124
(1974), 20-21.

50.192 López, César. "Guillén, los animales y el diluvio." GdC,
No. 55 (1967), 5. Signed C.L.

50.193 López del Amo, Rolando. "Un homenaje. (Notas sobre la temática de la poesía de Nicolás Guillén)." ULH, Nos. 196-
197 (1972), 320-326.

50.194 Lundkvist, Artur. "Expresionen i katedralen [Guillén y Carpen-
tier]." BLM, 32 (1963), 37-40.

50.195 McMurray, David Arthur. "Two black men in the New World: notes
on the 'Americanism' of Langston Hughes and the cubanía of
Nicolás Guillén." In Actes du VIIe Congrès de l'Association Internationale de Littérature Comparée (Stuttgart:
Bieber, 1979), pp. 359-366. Also as "Dos negros en el

nuevo mundo: notas sobre el 'americanismo' de Langston Hughes y la cubanía de Nicolás Guillén." CAm, No. 82 (1974), 122-128.

50.196 Madrigal, Luis Iñigo. "Las elegías de Nicolás Guillén: 'Elegía a Emmett Till'." CFil, No. 1 (1968), 47-58.

50.197 _____. "Introducción." In Nicolás Guillén, Summa poética (Madrid: Cátedra, 1976), pp. 13-57.

50.198 _____. "Introducción a la poesía de Nicolás Guillén." In Nicolás Guillén, Antología clave (Santiago de Chile: Nascimento, 1971), pp. 5-22.

50.199 _____. "Poesía última de Nicolás Guillén." RevP, 1, 1 (1964), 73-82.

50.200 Manjarrez, Froylán. "Cuba en la poesía de Nicolás Guillén." Bohemia, 55, 6 (1963), 7-9, 106.

50.201 Marinello, Juan. "Comentario en Cantos para soldados y sones para turistas." Mediodía, 2, 15 (1937), 8-9.

50.202 _____. "En los primeros setenta años de Nicolás Guillén. Idioma y mensaje." GdC, No. 104 (1972), 4-5. Also as "En los primeros setenta años de Nicolás Guillén." In his Contemporáneos (H: Contemporáneos, 1975), pp. 241-248.

50.203 _____. "En los sesenta años de Nicolás Guillén. El homenaje de la esperanza." In his Contemporáneos: noticia y memoria (Santa Clara: Universidad Central de Las Villas, Consejo Nacional de Universidades, 1964), pp. 277-288. Orig. ULH, No. 159 (1963), 7-12.

50.204 _____. "Hazaña y triunfo de Nicolás Guillén." In Nicolás Guillén, Cantos para soldados y sones para turistas (H: Masas, 1937), pp. 7-18. Also in his Orbita de Juan Marinello (H: Colección Orbita, 1968), pp. 102-113. Also in his Literatura hispanoamericana (M: Universidad Nacional Autónoma de México, 1937), pp. 79-90.

50.205 _____. "Negrismo y mulatismo." In his Orbita de Juan Marinello (H: Colección Orbita, 1968), pp. 67-81.

50.206 _____. "Poesía negra. Apuntes desde Guillén a Ballagas." In his Poética; ensayos de entusiasmo (Madrid: Espasa-Calpe, 1933), pp. 99-143.

50.207 _____. "Sobre Nicolás Guillén." UH, 2, 23 (1952), 11.

50.208 Márquez, Robert. "De rosa armado y de acero: la obra de Nicolás Guillén." SinN, 4, 2 (1973), 23-32.

50.209 _____. "Introduction." In Nicolás Guillén, ¡Patria o muerte!
The great zoo and other poems (NY: Monthly Review Press,
1972), pp. 13-29.

50.210 _____. "Introducción a Guillén." CAm, Nos. 65-66 (1971),
136-142. Also in Recopilación de textos sobre Nicolás
Guillén, q.v., pp. 127-138.

50.211 _____. "Racism, culture and revolution: ideology and politics
in the prose of Nicolás Guillén." LARR, 17, 1 (1982),
43-68. Also as "Racismo, cultura y revolución: ideología
y política en la prosa de Nicolás Guillén." Escritura,
No. 8 (1979), 213-239.

50.212 _____, and David Arthur McMurray. "Introduction." In Nicolás
Guillén, Manmaking words (Amherst: University of Massa-
chussetts Press, 1972), pp. ix-xx.

50.213 Marré, Luis. "Un acontecimiento editorial sin precedentes."
Unión, 13, 2 (1974), 182-186.

50.214 Martí-Fuentes, Adolfo. "España en cinco esperanzas (comentario a un poema de Nicolás Guillén)." RBNJM, 3a serie,
14, 2 (1972), 55-63.

50.215 Martin, Dellita L. "Afro-cubanidad as metaphor in the poetry
of Guillén." In Tradition, change, and revolution in the
Caribbean (Coral Gables, Fla.: Association of Caribbean
Studies, 1983), p. 34. Abstract.

50.216 _____. "West African and Hispanic elements in Nicolás Guillén's 'La canción del bongó'." SAB, 45, 1 (1980), 47-
53.

50.217 Martín, Edgardo. "Obras de música relacionadas con poemas de
Nicolás Guillén." GdC, No. 104 (1972), 28-30.

50.218 Martínez Estrada, Ezequiel. "Balada pascual para Nicolás Guillén, poeta de amor, dolor y valor." GdC, Nos. 8-9
(1962), 15.

50.219 _____. "La lengua de los vencidos." Unión, 2, 7 (1963), 43-
50.

50.220 _____. "Temas, motivos, diseños." Unión, 5, 3 (1966), 5-15.

50.221 Martínez Laínez, Fernando. "Entrevista con Nicolás Guillén."
In his Palabra cubana (Madrid: Akal, 1975), pp. 25-48.

50.222 Megenny, William W. "Las cualidades afrocubanas en la poesía
de Nicolás Guillén." La torre, No. 69 (1970), 127-138.

50.223 Melon, Alfred. "Guillén: poeta de la síntesis." Unión, 9, 4
(1970), 96-132. Also in his Realidad: poesía e ideología

(H: Unión, 1973?), pp. 25-61. Also in Recopilación de textos sobre Nicolás Guillén, q.v., pp. 199-242.

50.224 Michalski, André. "La 'Balada del güijé', de Nicolás Guillén: un poema garcilorquiano y magicorrealista." CHA, No. 274 (1973), 159-167.

50.225 Millan, Verna C. "Nicolás Guillén y la crítica yanki." Mediodía, No. 27 (1937), 20.

50.226 Miró, César. "[El son entero]." MPer, No. 242 (1947), 272-273.

50.227 Morejón, Nancy. "Guillén y los Estados Unidos: un comentario." GdC, No. 158 (1977), 4-5.

50.228 _____. "Oficio de Guillén." Bohemia, 69, 27 (1977), 8.

50.229 _____. "Poesía cantada de Nicolás Guillén." GdC, No. 126 (1974), 30.

50.230 _____ et al. "Conversación con Nicolás Guillén." In Recopilación de textos sobre Nicolás Guillén, q.v., pp. 31-61.

50.231 Mullen, Edward. "Langston Hughes y Nicolás Guillén: un documento y un comentario." Caribe, 1, 2 (1976), 39-48.

50.232 _____. "Nicolás Guillén and Carlos Pellicer: a case of literary parallels." LALR, No. 6 (1975), 77-78.

50.233 Nadereau Maceo, Efraín. "Nicolás Guillén, descubridor de nuestra esencia burlada." GdC, No. 104 (1972), 22-23.

50.234 _____. "Nicolás Guillén: poesía y tiempo, chéveres y navajas." GdC, No. 95 (1971), 28-29.

50.235 Navarro, Osvaldo. "Guillén: joven también." CB, No. 112 (1977), 12-13.

50.236 Navarro Luna, Manuel. "Un líder de la poesía revolucionaria." UH, 2, 26 (1952), 48, 50.

50.237 Navas-Ruiz, Ricardo. "Neruda y Guillén: un caso de relaciones literarias." RI, No. 60 (1965), 251-262.

50.238 Neruda, Pablo. "Discurso de despedida a Nicolás Guillén." UH, No. 23 (1952), 22.

50.239 _____. "Homenaje a Nicolás Guillén." RevC, 23 (1948), 344-347.

50.240 "Neruda y Guillén en Bohemia." Bohemia, 52, 51 (1960), 43-45.

50.241 "Nicolás Guillén." Crisis, No. 15 (1974), 40-47.

50.242   "Nicolás Guillén: poeta antillano." Watapana, 2, 7 (1970),
          6-7.

50.243   Nicolau, Ramón. "Capitán. Itinerario de una militancia."
          GdC, No. 104 (1972), 15.

50.244   Noble, Enrique. "Nicolás Guillén y Langston Hughes." NRC,
          1962, pp. 41-86.

50.245   Nogueras, Luis Rogelio, and Nelson Herrara Isla. "Nicolás
          Guillén: por el mar de las Antillas." Bohemia, 69, 42
          (1977), 24-25.

50.246   "Nota sobre Sóngoro cosongo y otros poemas." Dialéctica, 2,
          2 (1943), 207.

50.247   Olivera, Otto. "La mujer de color en la poesía de Nicolás
          Guillén." In Homenaje a Lydia Cabrera (Miami: Universal,
          1978), pp. 165-174.

50.248   Ortiz, Fernando. "Glosas a Motivos de son de Nicolás Guillén."
          AFC, 5 (1930), 222-238.

50.249   Otero, Lisandro. "Nicolás Guillén y la juventud." GdC, Nos.
          8-9 (1962), 16.

50.250   Otero Silva, Miguel. "Nicolás Guillén." UH, 2, 23 (1952), 9.

50.251   Pavón Tamayo, Luis. "Guillén 75." VO, 18, 28 (1977), 10-12.

50.252   Pedroso, Regino. "El poeta Guillén y yo." In his Regino Pe-
          droso (H: Unión de Escritores y Artistas de Cuba, 1975),
          pp. 353-359.

50.253   Peñalver Moral, Reinaldo. "Las FAR con Guillén por su 75 ani-
          versario." Bohemia, 69, 29 (1977), 57.

50.254   Peralta, Jaime. "España en tres poetas hispanoamericanos: Ne-
          ruda, Guillén y Vallejo." Atenea, Nos. 421-422 (1968),
          37-49.

50.255   Perdomo, Omar. "Guillén en un barco de papel de estraza."
          GdC, No. 163 (1978), 20-21.

50.256   Pereda Valdés, Ildefonso. "Nicolás Guillén." In his Lo negro
          y lo mulato en la poesía cubana (Montevideo?: Ciudadela,
          1970?), pp. 53-82.

50.257   _____. "Nicolás Guillén y el ritmo del son." In his Línea
          de color (Santiago de Chile: Ercilla, 1938), pp. 143-
          151.

50.258   Pichardo Loret de Mola, Luis. "Guillén, voz y acento de cuba-
          nía." In his Mi suma ideológica (Camagüey: El Camagüeya-
          no, 1956), pp. 167-168.

50.259 "Poesía cantada de Guillén en España." GdC, No. 168 (1978), 22.

50.260 "Los poetas jóvenes opinan sobre Guillén." RyC, No. 5 (1972), 32-35.

50.261 Polit, Carlos E. "Imagen inocente del negro en cuatro poetas antillanos." SinN, 5, 2 (1974), 43-60. Guillén inter alios.

50.262 Portal, Marta. "Nicolás Guillén, poeta de Cuba. En sus 70 años." CA, No. 197 (1974), 234-244.

50.263 Portogalo, José. "La poética de Nicolás Guillén." UH, 2, 23 (1952), 10.

50.264 Portuondo, José Antonio. "Canta a la revolución con toda la voz que tiene." In his Crítica de la época y otros ensayos (Santa Clara?: Universidad Central de Las Villas, 1965), pp. 188-196. Also in Nicolás Guillén, Tengo (H: Universidad Central de Las Villas, Consejo Nacional de Universidades, 1964), pp. 7-17. Also in Recopilación de textos sobre Nicolás Guillén, q.v., pp. 303-309.

50.265 _____. "Historia de un poema y su prólogo." GdC, No. 104 (1972), 6-8.

50.266 _____. "Sentido elegíaco de la poesía de Guillén." GdC, Nos. 8-9 (1962), 2-3.

50.267 Prats Sariol, José. "Los dientes de la rueda." RyC, No. 15 (1973), 64-67.

50.268 _____. "Novedad y sugerencia en el diario." GdC, No. 115 (1973), 14-16.

50.269 "Los primeros setenta de Guillén." CAm, No. 74 (1972), 177-178.

50.270 Quesada, Héctor Antón. "Poesía y música. El ritmo en la poesía de Nicolás Guillén." In his En busca de la poesía pura, esquiscio filosófico-literario (H: Ucar y García, 1960), pp. 26-30.

50.271 Rabanales, Ambrosio. "Relaciones asociativas en torno al 'Canto negro' de Nicolás Guillén." In Studia hispanica en honorem Rafael Lapesa (Madrid: Gredos, 1972), II, 469-491.

50.272 Rabassa, Gregory. "The gospel of Marx accoridng to Omolú and according to Jesus." Parnassus, 4, 2 (1976), 122-129.

50.273 Ramos, Sidroc. "Homenaje a Nicolás Guillén. Cuando se cumple vida bellamente." RBNJM, 3a serie, 14, 3 (1972), 5-31.

50.274 _____. "Presentación de Nicolás Guillén." Islas, 10, 1 (1968), 133-135.

50.275   "Recibe Nicolás Guillén alta condecoración antillana." GdC,
         No. 129 (1974), 21.

50.276   Rexach, Rosario. "La temporalidad en tres dimensiones poéti-
         cas: Unamuno, Guillén y José Martí." CHA, Nos. 289-290
         (1974), 86-119.

50.277   Rivera-Rodas, Oscar. "La imagen de los Estados Unidos en la
         poesía de Nicolás Guillén." CAm, No. 120 (1980), 154-160.

50.278   Rivero, Raúl. "Agua del recuerdo." RyC, No. 62 (1977), 4-6.

50.279   ____. "Entrevista [a Guillén]." CB, No. 126 (1978), 2-5.

50.280   ____. "Guillén regresa de España." Bohemia, 70, 43 (1978),
         58-61.

50.281   Rodríguez Feo, José. "Un estudio más de la obra de Nicolás
         Guillén." GdC, No. 152 (1977), 20.

50.282   Rodríguez Méndez, José. "Un son olvidado." GdC, No. 104
         (1972), 14.

50.283   Rodríguez Monegal, Emir. "Poesía de Nicolás Guillén." Mar-
         cha, 4-VII-1947, p. 14.

50.284   Rodríguez Rivera, Guillermo. "[El gran zoo]." CAm, No. 48
         (1968), 138-146.

50.285   Ruffinelli, Jorge. "Nuevos aportes a la poesía de Nicolás
         Guillén." RIL, 2a época, 1, 1 (1966), 95-102.

50.286   Ruscadella Bercedóniz, Jorge María. "Recuento poético de Ni-
         colás Guillén." SinN, 4, 2 (1973), 33-56.

50.287   Sáenz, Gerardo. "Nicolás Guillén, Langston Hughes y Luis Pa-
         lés Matos: Africa en tres tonos." In Homenaje a Lydia
         Cabrera (Miami: Universal, 1978), pp. 183-188.

50.288   Salomón, Noel. "A propos de El son entero." CSí, No. 12
         (1965), 3-12.

50.289   Sánchez, Juan. "Guillén en sus 75." Bohemia, 69, 28 (1977),
         58.

50.290   Sánchez-Rojas, Arturo. "Papá Montero: del son original al po-
         ema de Nicolás Guillén." Caribe, 1, 2 (1976), 49-56.

50.291   Sanclemente, Alvaro. "La poesía de Nicolás Guillén." RIn,
         28 (1946), 303-305.

50.292   Santana, Joaquín G. "Nicolás Guillén en Portugal 'Con uñas y
         con dientes defenderán su libertad los portugueses'."
         Bohemia, 67, 34 (1975), 22-23.

50.293 _____. "Nicolás Guillén. La poesía de América en la Gran
Bretaña." Bohemia, 67, 31 (1975), 24-25.

50.294 _____. "El periodista sigue librando." GdC, No. 106 (1972),
3.

50.295 Santos Moray, Mercedes. "Por ser el más joven de los poetas."
Unión, 17, 1 (1978), 99-103.

50.296 Sanzo, Nayda. "Que dure esa sonrisa siempre compañero Guillén." Bohemia, 66, 28 (1974), 63.

50.297 Sarusky, Jaime. "Nicolás Guillén habla de la 'Elegía a Jesús
Martínez'." Bohemia, 69, 3 (1977), 8-9.

50.298 "Los 70 de Nicolás Guillén." Unión, 11, 4 (1972), 180-192.

50.299 Simor, Adrás. "Algunas características comunes de un período
poético de Attlia József y de Nicolás Guillén." In Actas
del Simposio Internacional de Estudios Hispánicos (Budapest: Akademiai Kiadó, 1978), pp. 235-243. Also CAm, No.
100 (1977), 182-187.

50.300 Smart, Ian I. "Nicolás Guillén's Son poem: an African contribution to contemporary poetics." CLAJ, 23 (1980), 352-
363.

50.301 Stamate, Victor. "Nicolás Guillén: 'la 70 ani veiţii mele mă
simt puternic." RoLit, 20 (1972), 32.

50.302 Suárez, Adolfo. "La edad y la mariposa." VO, 14, 31 (1972),
21.

50.303 Suárez Solís, Rafael. "[Prosa de prisa]." Islas, 5, 1
(1962), 301-303.

50.304 Taboada Terán, Néstor. "Encuentro con Nicolás Guillén." In
his Cuba, paloma de vuelo popular (Oruro, Bolivia: Universitaria, 1964), pp. 136-142.

50.305 Tamayo Vargas, Augusto. "Tres poetas de América: César Vallejo, Pablo Neruda y Nicolás Guillén." MPer, No. 377
(1958), 483-503. Also RdL, 2, 7 (1957), 41-58.

50.306 Tcheho, Célestin. "Nicolás Guillén, the 'Cuban-Yoruba' poet."
Ngam, 1-2 (1979), 37-65.

50.307 Turull, Antoni. "Nicolás Guillén: people's poet." In Cuba:
the second decade (London: Writers & Readers, 1979), pp.
214-222.

50.308 Unamuno y Jugo, Miguel de. "Carta de don Miguel de Unamuno."
In Nicolás Guillén, Sóngoro cosongo, y otros poemas (H:
Páginas, 1942), pp. 9-11. 2. ed., 1943. Also in Nicolás
Guillén, El son entero; suma poética, 1929-1946 (BA:
Pleamar, 1947), pp. 9-12.

50.309 Uribe, Emilio. "La poesía de Nicolás Guillén." UH, 2, 23
        (1952), 11-37.

50.310 Val. "La defensa de lo cubano en Cantos para soldades y sones
        para turistas." Lotería, Nos. 293-294 (1980), 74-89.

50.311 Valdés-Cruz, Rosa E. "Nicolás Guillén." In her La poesía ne-
        groide en América (NY: Las Américas, 1970), pp. 63-77.

50.312 _____. "Tres poemas representativos de la poesía afro-cubana."
        Hispania, 54 (1970), 39-45. "Maracas" by Guillén inter
        alios.

50.313 Valdés Vivó, Raúl. "Guillén, periodista." GdC, Nos. 8-9
        (1962), 9.

50.314 Valle, Rafael Heliodoro. "Diálogo con Nicolás Guillén." UM,
        3 (1937), 21-27.

50.315 Van Praag-Chantraine, Jacqueline. "Touches blanches et noires
        à Cuba--Nicolás Guillén." Synthèses, Nos. 271-272 (1969),
        121-130.

50.316 Varela, José Luis. "Ensayo de una poesía mulata." In his
        Ensayos de poesía indígena en Cuba (Madrid: Cultura His-
        pánica, 1951), pp. 75-120.

50.317 Verhesen, Fernand. "Nicolás Guillén et Le grand zoo." JdP,
        37, 6 (1967), 3.

50.318 Vilar, Jean P. "Nicolás Guillén, journaliste de couleur."
        CSí, No. 12 (1965), 14-15.

50.319 Vitier, Cintio. "A Nicolás Guillén, en su día." GdC, No. 104
        (1972), 12.

50.320 _____. "Breve examen de la poesía 'social y negra'. La obra
        de Nicolás Guillén. Hallazgo del son." In his Lo cubano
        en la poesía (H: Universidad de Las Villas, 1958), pp.
        349-368. 2. ed., H: Instituto Cubano del Libro, 1970;
        pp. 412-434. Also in Recopilación de textos sobre Nico-
        lás Guillén, q.v., pp. 147-158.

50.321 Williams, Eric. "Four poets of the Greater Antilles." CarQ,
        2, 4 (1951-1952), 8-19. Guillén inter alios.

50.322 Williams, Lorna V. "The African presence in the poetry of Ni-
        colás Guillén." In Africa and the Caribbean: the legacy
        of a link (Baltiomre: Johns Hopkins University Press,
        1979), pp. 124-145.

50.323 Yanés, Mirta. "Cuatro ensayos en busca de Guillén." ULH,
        Nos. 196-197 (1972), 369-371. See item no. 51.22.

50.324 Yeatman, Edward D. "[Cuba libre]." RI, No. 29 (1949), 144-
        147.

50.325 Yudin, Florence L. "The great zoo. On Cuba's national poet, Nicolás Guillén." CarR, 5, 3 (1973), 30-34.

50.326 Zemoskov, V. B. "Sony Gil'en i nardonyi son." LatA, No. 3 (1970), 101-126.

51. GUIRAO, RAMON (1908-1949)

Critical Essays

51.1 Delgado Montejo, Alberto. "Evocación de Ramón Guirao." Crónica, (1949), 38-39.

51.2 Fernández, David. "Un color para esta canción." Unión, 5, 4 (1966), 157-159.

51.3 Fernández de la Vega, Oscar, and Alberto N. Pamies. "Ramón Guirao: biografía y bibliografía." In Iniciación a la poesía afro-americana (Miami: Universal, 1973), pp. 88-91.

51.4 Fernández Retamar, Roberto. "Ramón Guirao." In his La poesía contemporánea en Cuba (1927-1953) (H: Orígenes, 1954), pp. 53-54.

51.5 González y Contreras, Gilberto. "Bongó y el arte negro en Cuba." Grafos, No. 12 (1934), no pagination.

51.6 Jiménez, Max. "El poeta Ramón Guirao." RAm, 17 (1936), 248.

51.7 Labrador Ruiz, Enrique. "[Cuentos y leyendas negras de Cuba]." América, 24, 1-3 (1945), 93-94.

51.8 _____. "Guirao." In his El pan de los muertos (H: Universidad de Las Villas, Departamento de Relaciones Culturales, 1958), pp. 65-70.

51.9 Roa, Raúl. "[Orbita de la poesía afrocubana, 1928-37]." Grafos, No. 62 (1938), no pagination.

52.   HEREDIA, JOSE MARIA (1803-1839)

Bibliographies

52.1   Aparicio Laurencio, Angel. "Bibliografía de José María Heredia." RIB, 26 (1976), 177-196.

52.2   "Bibliografía de José María Heredia." BBIBA, Nos. 4-6 (1939), 37-41.

52.3   Fernández Robaina, Tomás. Bibliografía sobre José María Heredia. H: Biblioteca Nacional José Martí, 1970.

52.4   Pane, Remigio U. "Cuban poetry in English: a bibliography of English translations from Casal, Florit, Gómez de Avellaneda, Guillén, Heredia, Pedroso and 'Plácido'." BBDI, 18, 9 (1946), 199-201.

52.5   Toussaint, Manuel. Bibliografía mexicana de Heredia. M: Secretaría de Relaciones Exteriores, Departamento de Información para el Extranjero, 1953.

Critical Monographs and Dissertations

52.6   Aparicio Laurencio, Angel. Trabajos desconocidos y olvidados de José María Heredia. Miami: Universal, 1972.

52.7   Augier, Angel I. Reencuentro y afirmación del poeta Heredia. H: Molina, 1940. Same as item no. 52.51.

52.8   Balaguer, Joaquín. Heredia, verbo de la libertad. Santiago, República Dominicana: El Diario, 1939.

52.9   Bertot, L. Heredia, poeta del amor y de la naturaleza. Santiago de Cuba, 1922.

52.10 Casasús, Juan J. E. José María Heredia y Heredia, patriota, político y jurista. H: Imprenta Compañía Editora de Libros y Folletos, 1939.

52.11 Castellanos, Carlos A. La fiesta del poeta en casa de José María Heredia. H: La Propaganda, 1946.

52.12 Chacón y Calvo, José María. Estudios heredianos. H: Trópico, 1939.

52.13 _____. El horacianismo en la poesía de Heredia. H: Molina, 1939.

52.14   Díaz, Lomberto. Heredia, primer romántico hispanoamericano.
        Montevideo: Géminis, 1973. Orig. as "José María Heredia:
        vida y obra del primer romántico hispanoamericano." DAI,
        30 (1970), 5406A.

52.15   Esténger, Rafael. Hacia un Heredia genuino. Santiago de Cuba:
        "Renacimiento", 1939.

52.16   ____. Heredia, la incomprensión de sí mismo. H: Trópico,
        1938.

52.17   Garcerán de Vall y Sousa, Julio A. Heredia y la libertad. Mia-
        mi: Universal, 1978. Orig. as "Síntesis de dicotomía li-
        bertad-independencia en la poesía de Heredia." DAI, 37
        (1977), 6527A-6528A.

52.18   García Garófalo y Mesa, Manuel. Vida de José María Heredia en
        México, 1825-1839. M: Botas, 1945.

52.19   González, Manuel Pedro. José María Heredia, primogénito del ro-
        manticismo hispano; ensayo de rectificación histórica. M:
        Colegio de México, 1955.

52.20   González del Valle y Ramírez, Francisco. Cronología herediana
        (1803-1839). H: Montalbo y Cárdenas, 1938.

52.21   ____. Del epistolario de Heredia. Cartas a Silvestre Alfonso.
        H: Secretaría de Educación, Dirección de Cultura, 1937.

52.22   ____. Documentos para la vida de Heredia. H: Molina, 1938.

52.23   ____. Heredia en la Habana. H: Municipio de la Habana, 1939.

52.24   ____. Poesías de Heredia traducidas a otros idiomas. H: Moli-
        na, 1940.

52.25   Guiteras, Pedro José. Don José María Heredia. H: Imprenta Mi-
        litar de la Vda. de Soler, 1881.

52.26   Ibrovats, Miodrag. José María Heredia, sa vie, son oeuvre.
        Paris: Les Presses Françaises, 1923.

52.27   José María Heredia. Toluca, Méx.: Testimonios del Estado de
        México, 1979. Pertinent items are listed separately.

52.28   Lazo, Raimundo. Heredia, Zenea y Martí; poetas patrióticos.
        H: Imprenta del Ejército, 1929.

52.29   Lens y de Vera, Eduardo Félix. Heredia y Martí; dos grandes
        figuras de la lírica cubana. H: Selecta, 1954.

52.30   Lopes, Ernani. Heredia e herediólogos. Rio de Janeiro: Jornal
        de Comércio, 1959.

52.31   Mejía Ricart, Gustavo Adolfo. José María Heredia y sus obras.
        H: Molina, 1941.

52.32 Memoria de los trabajos realizados por la "Junta Heredia" desde
su fundación en el año 1889 hasta la entrega de la casa
donde nació el poeta José María Heredia. H?, 1903.

52.33 Páez, Alfonso E. Recordando a Heredia (estudio crítico). H:
Cultural, 1939.

52.34 Rangel, Nicolás. Nuevos datos para la biografía de José María
Heredia. H: El Universo, 1930.

52.35 Re, Achille del. José María Heredia, poeta e patriota cubano
(1803-1839). Roma, 1958.

52.36 Rodríguez Demorizi, Emilio. El cantor del Niágara en Santo Domingo. Ciudad Trujillo, República Dominicana: Montalvo,
1939.

52.37 Utrera, Cipriano de. Heredia. Ciudad Trujillo, República Dominicana: Franciscana, 1939.

Critical Essays

52.38 Aguiar, Ricardo J. "José María Heredia. Un poema inédito."
BBib, No. 444 (1970), 15-19.

52.39 ____. "José María Heredia y el manuscrito Arce." BBib, No.
440 (1970), 8-11.

52.40 ____. "Poemas inéditos de José María Heredia." BBib, 2a época, No. 454 (1971), 8-11.

52.41 ____. "La poesía amorosa de José María Heredia en el manuscrito Arce." BBib, No. 441 (1970), 6-9.

52.42 ____. "Sobre José María Heredia. Curioso manuscrito de la
primera mitad del siglo XIX." BBib, No. 439 (1970), 4-6.

52.43 Alonso, Amado. "Heredia crítico." In his Ensayo sobre la novela histórica. El modernismo en La gloria de don Ramiro
(BA: Instituto de Filología, 1942), pp. 75-78.

52.44 ____, and Julio Caillet-Bois. "Heredia como crítico literario." RevC, 15 (1941), 54-62.

52.45 Aparicio Laurencio, Angel. "Las cartas sobre la mitología..."
PHisp, 2a época, No. 237 (1972), 24-32.

52.46 ____. "Heredia: poeta patriótico." PEsp, No. 213 (1970), 13-
19.

52.47 ____. "Influencias poéticas en José M.ª Heredia." In José
María Heredia, Poesías completas (Miami: Universal, 1970),
pp. 11-66.

52.48 _____. "José María Heredia, redactor y editor de la Miscelá-
       nea." In José María Heredia, Trabajos desconocidos y ol-
       vidados (Miami: Universal, 1972), pp. 11-28.

52.49 Arias, Salvador. "Nuestro primer gran poema (estudio de 'En el
       Teocalli de Cholula' de Heredia)." In his Búsqueda y aná-
       lisis (H: Unión, 1974), pp. 15-58. Orig. L/L, Nos. 3-4
       (1972-1973), 87-134.

52.50 Arnáiz y Freg, Arturo. "El primer centenario de la muerte de
       Heredia." RI, No. 1 (1939), 117-120. Also in José María
       Heredia, q.v., pp. 85-90.

52.51 Augier, Angel I. "Reencuentro y afirmación del poeta Heredia."
       In José María Heredia, Poesías completas (H: Municipio de
       la Habana, 1940-1941), I, 53-77. Same as item no. 52.7.

52.52 Bachiller y Morales, Antonio. "Don José María Heredia." In
       his Galería de hombres útiles (H: Instituto Nacional de
       Cultura, 1955), pp. 183-193.

52.53 Bédarida, H. "De Foscolo a José María de Heredia: une adapta-
       tion cubaine des 'Sepolcri'." In Hommage à Ernest Marti-
       nenche (Paris: d'Artrey, 1939?), pp. 75-82.

53.54 Bello, Andrés. "[Comentario sobre la obra de Jouy, Sila, tra-
       ducida por Heredia]." RepAm, 4 (1827), 306.

53.55 _____. "Juicio sobre Heredia." RHab, No. 3 (1862), 246-250.

53.56 _____. "Juicio sobre las poesías de J. M. Heredia (Nueva York,
       1825)." RepAm, 4 (1827), 34-45.

53.57 Bernal, Emilia. "José María Heredia: su vida y su obra." In
       her Cuestiones cubanas para América (Madrid: Hernández y
       Galo Sáez, 1928), pp. 181-212.

53.58 "La biblioteca de Heredia." Romance, 1, 7 (1940), 22.

53.59 Blanchet, Emilio. "Heredia." CCont, 3 (1913), 221-242.

53.60 Blixen, Samuel. "Heredia y su oda al Niágara." In José María
       Heredia, Antología herediana (Montevideo: C. García,
       1945), pp. 57-65.

52.61 Boxhorn, Emilio. "El gran poeta José María Heredia." CCont,
       41 (1926), 113-133.

52.62 Bueno, Salvador. "Heredia otra vez." Unión, 5, 2 (1966), 169-
       171.

52.63 _____. "José María Heredia, el poeta romántico." In his Figu-
       ras cubanas del siglo XIX (H: Unión de Escritores y Artis-
       tas, 1980), pp. 95-105.

52.64 Cánovas del Castillo, Antonio. "Estudio sobre la literatura hispano-americana. Don José María Heredia." REAM, 1 (1853), 303-320, 393-414, 571-584.

52.65 Carilla, Celina E. C. de. "José María Heredia y 'Los conquistadores'." HumT, No. 9 (1958), 159-168.

52.66 Carilla, Emilio. "La lírica de Heredia. 'En el Teocali de Cholula'." In his Pedro Henríquez Ureña y otros estudios (BA: R. Medina, 1949), pp. 43-54.

52.67 _____. "La prosa de José María Heredia." BAAL, No. 53 (1945), 667-685. Also in his Pedro Henríquez Ureña y otros estudios (BA: R. Medina, 1949), pp. 69-86.

52.68 _____. "Los tres 'grandes': Bello, Olmedo, Heredia." In his La literatura de la Independencia hispanoamericana; 2. ed. (BA: EUDEBA, 1966), pp. 70-116. Orig. 1964.

52.69 Carlos, Alberto J. "José María Heredia y su visita al Niágara." In Instituto Internacional de Literatura Iberoamericana, La literatura iberoamericana del siglo XIX (Tucson: University de Arizona, 1974), pp. 73-80.

52.70 Carter, Boyd G. "Traducciones francesas de José María Heredia en la Revue des deux mondes." RI, No. 16 (1951-1952), 315-330.

52.71 Castellanos, Carlos A. "En la fiesta del poeta José María Heredia." RFLC, 36, 1-2 (1926), 23-39.

52.72 Castellanos, Jesús. "Heredia y el parnasianismo." In his Los optimistas (Madrid: Editorial-América, 1918), pp. 123-143. Also in his Colección póstuma (H: El Siglo XX de A. Miranda, 1914-1916), I, 177-194.

52.73 "Centenarios. Conmemoración del centenario de la muerte de José María Heredia en México." RI, No. 1 (1939), 487-488.

52.74 Chacón y Calvo, José María. "Un aspecto de la poesía de Heredia: su tonalidad religiosa." Noverim, 2, 6 (1957), 37-52. Also in Miscelánea de estudios dedicados a Fernando Ortiz (H, 1955), I, 473-487.

52.75 _____. "Las constantes de la vida de Heredia." RI, No. 3 (1940), 87-98.

52.76 _____. "La evolución literaria de Heredia. Su educación. Las influencias literarias sobre su obra y la esencia de su arte." CCont, 8 (1918), 154-163.

52.77 _____. "Heredia considerado como crítico." In José María Heredia, Revisiones literarias (H: Ministerio de Educación, 1947), pp. 9-34.

52.78 _____. "Heredia en.México." In José María Heredia, q.v., pp. 39-67. Also in his Ensayos sobre literatura cubana (Madrid: "Saturnino Calleja", 1932), pp. 221-276. Also RevC, 24 (1949), 225-229.

52.79 _____. "Heredia y su ensayo sobre la novela." AANAL, 29 (1949), 171-192. Also in Instituto Internacional de Literatura Iberoamericana, Memoria del Cuarto Congreso (H: Ministerio de Educación, Dirección de Cultura, 1949), pp. 177-198.

52.80 _____. "Heredia y su influjo en nuestro orígenes nacionales." CUA, No. 44 (1952), 101-123.

52.81 _____. "El horacianismo en la poesía de Heredia." AANAL, 20 (1938-1940), 139-183. Also UCB, 6 (1941), 233-262. Same as item no. 52.13.

52.82 _____. "José María Heredia." RevC, 24 (1949), 225-259.

52.83 _____. "Nueva vida de Heredia." In José María Heredia, Pequeña antología (H: J. Montero, 1939), pp. 7-89. Also in his Estudios heredianos, q.v., pp. 87-143.

52.84 _____. "La poesía de Heredia en su centenario." RevC, 8 (1937), 134-144.

52.85 _____. "El poeta Heredia y el sentido de la libertad." Lyceum, 3, 9-10 (1938), 3-12.

52.86 _____. "Proceso de la poesía de Heredia." ULH, Nos. 38-39 (1941), 134-149.

52.87 _____. "Vida universitaria de Heredia, papeles inéditos." CCont, 11 (1916), 200-212.

52.88 Chapin, Clara C. "Bryant and some of his Latin American friends." BUP, 83 (1944), 609-613. Heredia inter alios.

52.89 Chapman, Arnold. "Atala [de René Chateaubriand] and 'Niágara': futher comment." MLN, 68 (1953), 150-154.

52.90 _____. "Heredia's Ossian translations." HR, 23 (1955), 231-236.

52.91 _____. "Unos versos olvidados de José María Heredia." RI, No. 52 (1961), 357-365.

52.92 Coester, Alfred L. "Hallazgo de un regalo desconocido de Domingo del Monte a José María Heredia." RBC, 43 (1939), 354-357.

52.93 "Conmemoración del centenario de la muerte de José María Heredia en México." In José María Heredia, q.v., pp. 101-104.

52.94 Cossío, Adolfina. "Heredia, el primer romántico." Cultura, 1, 7 (1964), 6-9.

52.95 Cruz, Manuel de la. "José María Heredia." In his Cromitos cubanos (Madrid: Saturnino Calleja, 1926), pp. 245-256.

52.96 Cruz, Mary. "Osada modificación a un texto de José María Heredia." L/L, No. 1 (1970), 166-175.

52.97 _____. "Pushkin y Heredia." Unión, 10, 4 (1971), 15-30.

52.98 Cuervo, Rufino José. "Otra carta inédita." RSFB , 11 (1898), 178-180.

52.99 Defant, Alba. "José María Heredia y el romanticismo." HumT, No. 14 (1961), 171-178.

52.100 Del Monte y Aponte, Domingo. "Anuncio. Poesía de d. J. M. Heredia." RPL, No. 13 (1823), 31.

52.101 _____. "Cartas de Domingo del Monte a su amigo d. José María Heredia, a su hermano d. José y a d. José L. Alfonso." RCub, 8 (1888), 171-178.

52.102 _____. "Poesías de Heredia." RBC, 2, 5 (1832), 275.

52.103 _____. "Primeros versos de Heredia." RBNC , 2a serie, 4, 4 (1953), 9-12. Also in Cintio Vitier, La crítica literaria y estética en el siglo XIX cubano (H: Biblioteca Nacional "José Martí", Departamento Colección Cubana, 1968), I, 109-110.

52.104 _____. "Tres cartas inéditas de del Monte a Heredia." RevC, 10 (1937), 28-30.

52.105 Diego, Eliseo. "Encuentro con el joven Heredia." Unión, 12, 1 (1973), 39-45.

52.106 Diez Canedo, Enrique. "Heredia y Martí." RBC, 29 (1932), 179-183.

52.107 "Documentos sobre la declaración de Pablo Aranguren acusando como partidarios de la independencia de Cuba al poeta José María Heredia y otros." BAN, 43 (1944), 196-198.

52.108 "Don José María Heredia. Documentos para su vida." RdC, 9 (1881), 270-273.

52.109 Escoto, José Augusto. "Correspondencia de José María Heredia. Cartas del poeta a Domingo del Monte." RHCB, 1, 2 (1916), 157-169.

52.110 _____. "Ensayo de una biblioteca herediana." CyA, 14, 6 (1904), 148-149; 14, 10 (1904), 261-269.

52.111 _____. "Una nueva obra del teatro de José María Heredia."
        RHCB, 1, 4 (1917), 360-369.

52.112 _____. "Una obra inédita de teatro de Heredia." RHCB, 1, 1
        (1916), 49-58.

52.113 _____. "Los primeros estudios de Heredia." RHCB, 1, 3 (1916),
        258-266.

52.114 _____. "Los restos de José María Heredia." CyA, 13, 7 (1903),
        207-211.

52.115 Esténger, Rafael. "Esquema de Heredia." In José María Here-
        dia, Poesías completas (H: Municipio de la Habana, 1940-
        1941), II, 376-397.

52.116 _____. "Heredia en la Avellaneda." América, 1, 4 (1939), 12-
        13.

52.117 Feijóo, Samuel. "Cartas sin entereza revolucionaria del gran
        poeta cubano José María Heredia." Signos, No. 21 (1978),
        220-226.

52.118 Fernández, Aida E. "Rasgos psíquicos de Heredia." RBC, 43
        (1939), 419-420.

52.119 Fernández de Castro, José Antonio. "Domingo del Monte, editor
        y corrector de la poesía de Heredia." RevC, 12 (1938),
        91-144.

52.120 Fernández de la Vega, Oscar. "Rebeldía y nostalgia en el des-
        tierro: Heredia." In Guillermo Díaz Plaja, Historia gene-
        ral de las literaturas hispánicas (Barcelona: Barna,
        1949-), V, 459-463.

52.121 Fernández Morera, Anastasio. "Heredia lírico eminente." Amé-
        rica, 1 (1939), 43-48.

52.122 Fontanella, Lee. "J. M. Heredia: a case for critical inclu-
        siveness." RHM, 37 (1972-1973), 162-179.

52.123 Fornaris, José, and Joaquín Lorenzo Luaces. "José María Here-
        dia." In their Cuba poética (H: Imprenta y Papelería de
        la Vda. de Barcina, 1858), pp. 23-24.

52.124 García Marruz, Fina. "Martí y los críticos de Heredia del
        XIX (en torno a un ejemplar de Heredia anotado por Mar-
        tí)." In Cintio Vitier, and Fina García Marruz, Temas
        martianos (H: Biblioteca Nacional José Martí, 1969), pp.
        326-347.

52.125 García Tudurí, Mercedes. "Personalidad y nacionalidad en He-
        redia." RBC, 43 (1939), 421-427.

52.126 Garmendia, Miguel. "Bryant y Heredia." RHCB, 1, 2 (1916), 197-200.

52.127 Gay Calbó, Enrique. "Heredia." RBC, 43 (1939), 321-329.

52.128 ____. "Heredia. Apuntes para un estudio sobre su vida y su obra." In José María Heredia, Poesías completas (H: Municipio de la Habana, 1940-1941), I, 33-51.

52.129 Gicovate, Bernardo. "José María Heredia en el romanticismo hispánico." ALetM, 3 (1963), 300-308.

52.130 ____. "El yo poético y su significado." Asomante, 21, 3 (1965), 40-47. Heredia, Juan Ramón Jiménez, Rubén Darío.

52.131 Giusti, Roberto F. "José María Heredia." In his Lecciones de literatura argentina e hispanoamericana (BA: Angel Estrada, 1947), pp. 71-72.

52.132 Gómez de Avellaneda, Gertrudis. "A la muerte del célebre poeta cubano José María Heredia." RBC, 43 (1939), 439-441.

52.133 Gómez Vilá, Seida. "Heredia influido e influyente." RBC, 43 (1939), 432-436.

52.134 González, Manuel Pedro. "Bryant y Heredia, dos grandes pioneros de las relaciones culturales interamericanas." RNC, No. 155 (1962), 43-56. Also as "Two great pioneers of Inter-American cultural relations." Hispania, 42 (1959), 175-185.

52.135 ____. "Una influencia inexplorada en Ignacio Rodríguez Galván." BACL, 7, 3-4 (1958), 292-314.

52.136 González del Valle y Carbajal, Emilio Martín. "José María de Heredia." In his La poesía lírica en Cuba, apuntes para un libro de biografía y de crítica (Barcelona: Luis Tasso, 1900), pp. 67-93.

52.137 González del Valle y Ramírez, Francisco. "La carta acusatoria de Del Monte a Heredia." BAN, 35, 1-6 (1936), 5-11.

52.138 ____. "Cronología herediana (1803-1839)." RBC, 32 (1933), 50-67.

52.139 ____. "Del epistolario de Heredia. Cartas a Silvestre Alfonso." RBC, 40 (1937), 156-177.

52.140 ____. "La dignidad de Heredia como diputado." RBC, 43 (1939), 340-347.

52.141 ____. "José María Heredia, juez de Veracruz." RevC, 9 (1937), 318-345.

52.142 _____. "Mis trabajos heredianos." RBC, 46 (1940), 198-207.

52.143 _____. "El Niágara de Heredia y el de Brainard." Lyceum,
        Nos. 15-16 (1939), 6-18.

52.144 _____. "Poesías de Heredia traducidas a otros idiomas." RBC,
        44 (1939), 321-359. Same as item no. 52.24.

52.145 _____. "Tres cartas inéditas de Del Monte a Heredia." RevC,
        10 (1937), 246-255.

52.146 _____. "Vida política de José María Heredia." In José María
        Heredia, Prédicas de libertad (H: Cultural, 1936), pp.
        v-xxx. Signed Francisco G. del Valle.

52.147 _____, and Emilio Roig de Leuchsenring. "Días y hechos de Jo-
        sé María Heredia." In José María Heredia, Poesías comple-
        tas (H: Municipio de la Habana, 1940-1941), I, 19-31.

52.148 González Nuevo, Orosia. "Ambito universal y local que recibe
        Heredia." RBC, 43 (1939), 416-418.

52.149 Guiteras, Pedro José. "Don José María Heredia." RdC, 9
        (1881), 5-46.

52.150 Gutiérrez-Vega, Zenaida. "Estudios heredianos." In her José
        María Chacón y Calvo, hispanista cubano (Madrid: Cultura
        Hispánica, 1969), pp. 189-194.

52.151 Henríquez Ureña, Max. "Heredia." CCont, 34 (1924), 23-37.

52.152 _____. "Heredia y los pinos del Niágara." Social, 16, 6
        (1931), 45.

52.153 Henrírquez Ureña, Pedro. "La versificación de Heredia." RFH,
        4 (1942), 171-172.

52.154 _____. "Las 'nuevas estrellas' de Heredia." RR, 9 (1918),
        112-114.

52.155 Heredia, José María de. "A José María Heredia en su centena-
        rio." RBC, 43 (1939), 437-438.

52.156 Hills, Elijah Clarence. "¿Tradujo Bryant la oda de Heredia al
        'Niágara'?" Bohemia, 11, 12 (1920), 5, 31.

52.157 Iraizoz y de Villar, Antonio. "Un precursor olvidado: el ar-
        gentino José Antonio Miralla, su amistad y sus relaciones
        políticas con José María Heredia." CCont, 31 (1923),
        331-344. Also in his Lecturas cubanas; 2. ed. (H: "Her-
        mes", 1939), pp. 31-46.

52.158 Jiménez Pastrana, Juan. "Personalidad de José María Heredia
        y su influencia en los valores históricos de la naciona-
        lidad cubana." ULH, Nos. 24-25 (1939), 53-64.

52.159   "José María Heredia." Bohemia, 64, 52 (1972), 105.

52.160   Júlio, Sílvio. "José María Heredia." In his Escritores anti-
         lhanos (Rio de Janeiro: H. Antunes, 1944), pp. 57-92.

52.161   Lacoste de Arufe, María. "Biografía de José María Heredia."
         In José María Heredia, Poesías, discursos y cartas (H:
         Cultural, 1939), I, ix-cxcvi.

52.162   Larrondo y Maza, Enrique. "Una fábula de Heredia. El filóso-
         fo y el búho." Ideas, 3, 2 (1930), 66-69.

52.163   Leal, Rine. "El ángel caído." Santiago, No. 1 (1970), 147-
         160.

52.164   Leiva, Waldo. "Heredia, lira romántica y destierro terrible."
         Santiago, No. 7 (1972), 161-183.

52.165   Lezama Lima, José. "La poesía de José María Heredia." In
         José María Heredia, q.v., pp. 23-25.

52.166   Lista, Alberto. "Carta a Domingo del Monte." RdC, 6 (1879),
         192-194.

52.167   _____. "Juicios críticos de las poesías de don José María He-
         redia." RdC, 6 (1879), 190-194.

52.168   Mañach, Jorge. "Heredia y el romanticismo." CHA, No. 86
         (1957), 195-220.

52.169   Martí, José. "Heredia." In his Obras completas (H: Lex,
         1946), I, 762-777. Various other editions. Also in his
         Páginas selectas (BA: Angel Estrada, 1957), pp. 3-20.
         Also in Cintio Vitier, La crítica literaria y estética
         en el siglo XIX cubano (H: Biblioteca Nacional José Mar-
         tí, Departamento Colección Cubana, 1968), II, 445-463.
         Also in José María Heredia, Poesías, discursos y cartas
         (H: Cultural, 1939), II, 309-328. Also as "Martí sobre
         Heredia." In José María Heredia, q.v., pp. 33-38. Also
         as "Heredia: dos estudios." In José María Heredia, Anto-
         logía herediana (Montevideo: C. García, 1945), pp. 29-56.

52.170   Martí Rico, Dolores. "Las ideas de Heredia." RBC, 43 (1939),
         428-431.

52.171   Martínez Bello, Antonio. "José María Heredia: síntesis biográ-
         fica." Cuba, 2 (1946), 6-9, 26.

52.172   Martínez Echemendia, Luciano. "Informaciones. El centenario
         del poeta José María Heredia." RBC, 39 (1937), 457-459.

52.173   Mejía Ricart, Gustavo Adolfo. "José María Heredia y sus
         obras." RBC, 43 (1939), 360-414; 44 (1939), 62-128,
         249-290, 376-406; 45 (1940), 264-294, 410-440; 46 (1940),
         124-147, 279-303, 440-461. Same as item no. 52.31

52.174   Menéndez y Pelayo, Marcelino. "José María Heredia." In José
         María Heredia, Antología herediana (Montevideo: C. García,
         1945), pp. 5-28. Orig. in his Historia de la poesís his-
         pano-americana (Madrid: Victorino Suárez, 1911), I, 228-
         248.

52.175   Menton, Seymour. "Heredia, introductor del romanticismo."
         RI, No. 29 (1949), 83-90.

52.176   Mitjans, Aurelio. "Cartas de Domingo del Monte a su amigo
         d. José María Heredia, a su hermano d. José y a d. José
         L. Alfonso." RCub, 8 (1888), 171-178.

52.177   _____. "Luaces y Heredia." RCub, 7 (1888), 385-390.

52.178   _____. "Primeros versos de Heredia." RBNC, 2a serie, 4, 4
         (1953), 9-12.

52.179   _____. "Tres cartas inéditas de del Monte a Heredia." RevC,
         10 (1937), 28-30.

52.180   Monterde, Francisco. "Heredia y el enigma de 'Los últimos
         romanos'." In José María Heredia, q.v., pp. 91-99.
         Orig. RI, No. 2 (1939), 353-359.

52.181   Moore, Ernest R. "José María Heredia en Nueva York, 1824-
         1825." Symposium, 5 (1951), 256-291.

52.182   _____. "José María Heredia in the United States and Mexico."
         MLN, 65 (1950), 41-46.

52.183   Morales y Morales, Vidal. "José María Heredia." CyA, 14, 4
         (1904), 87-89.

52.184   Nadereau Maceo, Efraín. "José María Heredia: evocación y len-
         guaje." Santiago, No. 7 (1972), 184-204.

52.185   Nieto y Cartadella, Rafael. "Documentos sacramentales de al-
         gunos cubanos ilustres. 39. José María Heredia." RBNC,
         2a serie, 4, 4 (1953), 147-149.

52.186   Núñez, Estuardo. "José María de Heredia, cantos del Niágara."
         IPNA, No. 14 (1950), 27-29.

52.187   Núñez y Domínguez, José de Jesús. "En torno a la vida en Mé-
         xico de José María Heredia." AAHC, 13 (1931), 84-94.

52.188   Onís, José de. "The alleged acquaintance of William Cullen
         Bryant and José María Heredia." HR, 25 (1957), 217-220.

52.189   _____. "William Cullen Bryant y José María Heredia. Vieja y
         nueva polémica." CA, No. 98 (1958), 154-161.

52.190   Orjuela, Héctor H. "Revaloración de una vieja polémica: Wil-
         liam Cullen Bryant y la oda del Niágara de José María
         Heredia." Thesaurus, 19 (1964), 248-273.

52.191 Peraza Sarausa, Fermín. "Heredia en la Revista de Cuba."
AnBC, 1, 1 (1938), 1-3.

52.192 Pérez Blanco, Lucrecio. "Los conceptos de vida, amor, Dios y
muerte en tres poetas hispanoamericanos del siglo XIX."
REH, 12 (1978), 163-198. Heredia inter alios.

52.193 Pérez de Acevedo y Castillo, Luciano. "Un problema literario:
¿Bryant tradujo la 'Oda la Niágara', de Heredia?" CCont,
22 (1920), 210-212.

52.194 Piñeyro, Enrique. "José María de Heredia. La poesía cubana
y el Sr. Menéndez y Pelayo." In José María Heredia, Poesías, discursos y cartas (H: Cultural, 1939), II, 362-
375.

52.195 _____. "José María Heredia." BH, 9 (1907), 186-209.

52.196 _____. "José María Heredia." In his Cómo acabó la dominación
de España en América (Paris: Garnier, 1908), pp. 295-333.

52.197 _____. "José María Heredia y la antología de poetas hispanoamericanos de la Real Academia Española." In his Hombres
y glorias de América (Paris: Garnier, 1903), pp. 297-305.

52.198 _____. "Poetas líricos cubanos. I. José María Heredia." In
his Estudios y conferencias de historia y literatura (NY:
Thompson y Moreau, 1880), pp. 197-202.

52.199 Plasencia, Aleida. "Los manuscritos de José María Heredia en
la Biblioteca Nacional." RBNJM, 3a serie, 1, 1-4 (1959),
9-17.

52.200 "Poesías de don José María Heredia." In José María Heredia,
q.v., pp. 27-31.

52.201 Poncet y de Cárdenas, Carolina. "El centenario de José María
Heredia." Lyceum, No. 14 (1939), 62-65.

52.202 Potestad y Cordero, Ricardo. "Heredia y Plácido." PalL, 2,
5 (1878), 97-102. Signed Don Pascuale.

52.203 Puebla, Manuel de la. "Martí y Heredia." In Estudios martianos (Río Piedras, P.R.: Editorial Universitaria, Universidad de Puerto Rico, 1974), pp. 71-85.

52.204 Rangel, Nicolás. "Nuevos datos para la biografía de Heredia."
RBC, 25 (1930), 161-179, 355-379.

52.205 Roa, Raúl. "José María Heredia." In his Escaramuza en las
vísperas y otros engendros (H: Universidad Central de
Las Villas, 1966), pp. 296-298.

52.206 Roig de Leuchsenring, Emilio. "En el sesquicentenario del nacimiento de José María Heredia." Carteles, 35, 1
(1954), 68-70.

52.207 ____. "Introducción." In José María Heredia, Poesías completas (H: Municipio de la Habana, 1940-1941), I, 7-17.

52.208 Romera Navarro, Manuel. "Un soneto de Heredia atribuido a Bello." HR, 13 (1945), 197-203.

52.209 Saco, José Antonio. "Observaciones sobre el [']Juicio crítico
de las poesías de Heredia['] por d. Ramón de la Sagra."
In Cintio Vitier, La crítica literaria y estética en el
siglo XIX cubano (H: Biblioteca Nacional "José Martí",
Departamento Colección Cubana, 1968), I, 85-105. See
item no. 52.210.

52.210 Sagra, Ramón de la. "Variedades. Poesías de d. José María
Heredia..." ACACA, 2, 18 (1828), 178-182; 2, 19 (1829),
210-213; 2, 20 (1829), 239-243; 2, 21 (1829), 270-271.
Also as "Juicio crítico de las poesías de don José María
Heredia." In Cintio Vitier, La crítica literaria y esté-
tica en el siglo XIX cubano (H: Biblioteca Nacional "José
Martí", Departamento Colección Cubana, 1968), I, 69-82.
See also item 52.209.

52.211 Sainz, Enrique. "Apuntes acerca de un soneto de José María
Heredia ['A mi esposa']." L/L, No. 5 (1974), 130-138.

52.212 Sanguily y Garritte, Manuel. "Alrededor de Heredia." In his
Juicios literarios (H: Molina, 1930), I, 423-433.

52.213 ____. "Una estrofa sobre el Niágara en Heredia y dos poetas
yanquis." In his Literatura universal; páginas de crítica (H: Molina, 1930), I, 407-421.

52.214 ____. "José María Heredia..." In his Discursos y conferencias (H: Rambla, 1918), I, 213-235.

52.215 ____. "José María Heredia.--El poeta y el revolucionario cubano." In his Discursos y conferencias (H: Rambla, 1918),
I, 237-287. Also in José María Heredia, Poesías, discursos y cartas (H: Cultural, 1939), II, 329-361.

52.216 ____. "El soneto es de Heredia." In his Juicios literarios
(H: Molina, 1930), I, 435-446. Also in his Literatura
universal; páginas de crítica (Madrid: América, 1918),
pp. 261-272.

52.217 Santí, Enrico-Mario. "Más notas sobre un poeta olvidado de
Heredia." Dieciocho, 2 (1979), 43-54.

52.218 Sells, Lytton. "Heredia's Hellinism." MLR, 37 (1942), 241-
290.

52.219 Sierra y Rosso, Ignacio. "Biografía de d. José María Heredia."
AAHC, 13 (1932), 87-103.

52.220 Slingerland, Howard. "José María Heredia y José de Espronceda: ¿una conexión directa?" NRFH, 18 (1965-1966), 461-464.

52.221 Souza, Raymond D. "José María Heredia: the poet and the ideal of liberty." REH, 5 (1971), 31-38.

52.222 Spell, Jefferson Rea. "The Mexican periodicals of José María Heredia." Hispania, 20 (1939), 189-194.

52.223 Torriente, Loló de. "Sagrado dolor de Heredia." Santiago, No. 7 (1972), 149-160.

52.224 Toussaint, Manuel. "La importancia de Heredia en la literatura mexicana de su tiempo." REU, julio-septiembre 1939, pp. 105-113.

52.225 Valdés y de Latorre, Emilio. "Noticia biográfica." In José María Heredia, Antología herediana (H: "El Siglo XX", A. Muñiz, 1939), pp. ix-lxiii.

52.226 Valdespino, Andrés. "Orígenes de la crítica literaria en Hispanoamérica: la crítica antirromántica de José María Heredia." In Instituto Internacional de Literatura Iberoamericana, El ensayo y la crítica literaria en Iberoamérica (Toronto: Universidad de Toronto, 1970), pp. 123-129.

52.227 Valdespino, Luis. "El poema apócrifo de Heredia." BAHL, No. 23 (1979), 13-19. Also PPNWCFL, 28, 1 (1977), 149-151.

52.228 Valle, Rafael Heliodoro. "A cien años de Heredia." RBC, 46 (1940), 149-154.

52.229 _____. "Amigos mexicanos de Heredia." RBC, 43 (1959), 348-353.

52.230 Varona y Pera, Enrique José. "Heredia." In his Desde mi belvedere (Barcelona: Maucci, 1917), pp. 239-242.

52.231 Vera, Catherine. "Chocano y Heredia: la primera dedicatoria de Alma de América." AI.Hisp, No. 5 (1976), 365-369.

52.232 Villares, Ricardo. "Cuando Heredia nació." Bohemia, 62, 19 (1970), 18-25.

52.233 Vitier, Cintio. "El desterrado." In his Poetas cubanos del siglo XIX; semblanzas (H: Unión, 1969), pp. 9-12.

52.234 Vitier, Medardo. "José María Heredia." In his Estudios, notas, efigies cubanos (H: Minerva, 1944), pp. 212-215.

52.235 Zerolo, Elías. "Prólogo." In José María Heredia, Poesías líricas (Paris: Garnier, 1892), pp. ix-lxiii.

53. HERNANDEZ CATA, ALFONSO (1885-1940)

Critical Monographs and Dissertations

53.1 Barreras, Antonio, Jorge Mañach, and Juan Marinello. Recordación de Alfonso Catá. H: La Verónica, 1941.

53.2 Esténger, Rafael. Recordación de Hernández Catá. H, n.d.

53.3 Febles, Jorge Manuel. "Modalidades del cuento en la obra de Alfonso Hernández Catá." DAI, 36 (1975), 2241A.

53.4 Fernández de la Torriente, Gastón. La novela de Hernández-Catá: un estudio desde la psicología. Madrid: Playor, 1976.

53.5 Gutiérrez de la Solana, Alberto. Maneras de narrar: contraste de Lino Novás Calvo y Alfonso Hernández Catá. NY: Eliseo Torres, 1972. Orig. as "Lino Novás Calvo y Alfonso Hernández Catá: contraste de vida y obra." DAI, 29 (1968), 261A.

53.6 Insúa, Alberto. Evocación de Hernández Catá. BA: Ateneo Popular de la Boca, 1943.

53.7 Memoria de Alfonso Hernández Catá. H, 1953-54. 10 numbers. Pertinent items are listed separately with the abbreviation MAHC.

53.8 Mercado González, Anisia. Las novelas cortas de Alfonso Hernández Catá. Montevideo: Gémenis, 1973. Orig. DAI, 31 (1971), 4769A. Signed Anisia M. González.

53.9 Serpa, Enrique, and Fernando G. Campoamor. Recordación de Hernández Catá. H?: La Verónica, 1943.

Critical Essays

53.10 Aragón, Ernesto de. "Hernández Catá, el hombre." MAHC, No. 5 (1954), 123-125.

53.11 Baeza Flores, Alberto. "Hernández Catá." MAHC, No. 6 (1954), 191-192.

53.12 Balseiro, José A. "A. Hernández Catá y el sentido trágico de la vida." In his El vigía (Madrid: Mundo Latino, 1928), II, 273-384.

53.13 _____. "Alfonso Hernández-Catá." RI, No. 7 (1941), 37-48.

53.14 _____. "La casa de fieras." MAHC, No. 5 (1954), 126-128.

53.15 _____. "Introducción." In Alfonso Hernández Catá, Mitología de Martí (Miami: Mnemosyne, 1970), no pagination.

53.16 _____. "Notas acerca del arte de Hernández Catá." RBC, 23 (1928), 386-396.

53.17 _____. "Revisión de Hernández Catá." In Instituto Internacional de Literatura Iberoamericana, La novela en Iberoamérica (Albuquerque: University of New Mexico Press, 1952), pp. 105-122.

53.18 Barreras, Antonio. "Ideario de Alfonso Hernández Catá." MAHC No. 5 (1954), 117-122.

53.19 Barrios, Eduardo. "Seudoprólogo." In Alfonso Hernández Catá, Sus mejores cuentos (Santiago, Chile: Nascimento, 1936), pp. 5-15.

53.20 Blanco, Luis Amado. "Pasión de Catá." MAHC, No. 6 (1954), 168-169.

53.21 Bueno, Salvador. "El mensaje de Hernández Catá." MAHC, No. 6 (1954), 166-170.

53.22 Calmon, Pedro. "Despedida de Hernández Catá." RevC, 15 (1941), 283-285.

53.23 Campoamor, Fernando G. "Siembra de aniversario." MAHC, No. 5 (1954), 139-140.

53.24 Castellanos, Jesús. "[La juventud de Aurelio Zaldívar]." In his Colección póstuma (H: El Siglo XX de A. Miranda, 1914-1916), pp. 381-386.

53.25 _____. "Novela erótica." In his Colección póstuma (H: El Siglo XX de A. Miranda, 1914-1916), pp. 323-327.

53.26 Chacón y Calvo, José María. "Memoria de Alfonso Hernández Catá." MAHC, No. 8 (1954), 243-246.

53.27 _____. "La muerte de Alfonso Hernández Catá." RevC, 15 (1941), 276-277.

53.28 "Las conferencias de Hernández Catá en la Hispanoamericana de Cultura." Avance, No. 43 (1930), 61-62.

53.29 Esténger, Rafael. "Cubanidad de Alfonso Hernández Catá." MAHC, No. 7 (1954), 195-197.

53.30 Febles, Jorge M. "Configuración del símbolo en un cuento olvidado de Hernández Catá." ExTL, 9 (1980-1981), 61-66.

53.31 _____. "Hernández Catá y lo fantástico." Caribe, 2, 2 (1977), 17-34.

53.32   Fernández Flórez, Wenceslao. "Al amigo muerto." MAHC, No. 6
        (1954), 163-166.

53.33   Ferrer, Surama. "Hernández Catá en su décimo aniversario."
        RevC, 27 (1950), 263-265.

53.34   Francovich, Guillermo. "Hernández Catá." MAHC, No. 6 (1954),
        154-158.

53.35   Gay-Calbó, Enrique. "[La voluntad de Dios]." CCont, No. 109
        (1922), 84-85.

53.36   González Martínez, Enrique. "Carta a Alfonso Hernández Catá."
        Social, No. 1 (1927), 28.

53.37   Ichaso, Francisco. "[Mitología de Martí]." Avance, No. 44
        (1930), 90-92.

53.38   Iraizoz y de Villar, Antonio. "Apasionadamente hacia la muer-
        te." In his Libros y autores cubanos (Santa María de Ro-
        sario: Rosareña, 1956), pp. 94-98.

53.39   Latorre, Mariano. "Permanencia y sentido de Hernández Catá."
        Atenea, No. 187 (1941), 6-16.

53.40   Lazo, Raimundo. "Significación del homenaje a Hernández Catá."
        MAHC, No. 2 (1953), 24-27.

53.41   Lizaso y González, Félix. "Alfonso Hernández Catá." In his
        Ensayistas contemporáneos, 1900-1920 (H: Trópico, 1938),
        pp. 53-59.

53.42   _____. "Memoria de Alfonso Hernández Catá." MAHC, No. 5
        (1954), 145-147.

53.43   Marinello, Juan. "Nueva vida de Hernández Catá." RAm, 39
        (1942), 30-31. Also in his Contemporáneos; noticia y
        memoria (H: Universidad Central de Las Villas, 1964),
        pp. 15-22.

53.44   _____. "El último libro de Hernández Catá [Piedras preciosas]."
        Avance, No. 8 (1927), 204.

53.45   Mistral, Gabriela. "Despedida de Hernández Catá." RevC, 15
        (1941), 278-280. Also MAHC, No. 2 (1953), 17-21.

53.46   Montori, Arturo. "Libro de amor." Social, No. 8 (1924), 25,
        68.

53.47   Pedreira, A. S. "Alfonso Hernández Catá." REH-PR, No. 1
        (1928), 280-282.

53.48   Portuondo, Augusto A. "La novela cubana del exilio y Perro-
        mundo." In The Twenty-Seventh Annual Mountain Interstate
        Foreign Language Conference (Johnson City, TN: East Ten-

nessee State University, Research Council, 1978), pp. 207-212.

53.49 Portuondo, José Antonio. "Tarjetero: Cuba literaria." RBC, 52 (1943), 275-281.

53.50 Ramos, José Antonio. "Alfonso Hernández Catá." ULH, Nos. 70-72 (1947), 81-89.

53.51 Rodríguez Embil, Luis. "En la muerte de Alfonso Hernández Catá." MAHC, No. 7 (1954), 207-208.

53.52 Sáinz de Robles, Federico Carlos. "Alfonso Hernández Catá (Santiago de Cuba, 1885-Brazil, 1940)." EstLit, No. 448 (1970), 20.

53.53 Santovenia y Echaide, Emeterio Santiago. "Alfonso Hernández Catá." In his Vidas humanas (H: Librería Martí, 1956), pp. 481-483.

53.54 Serpa, Enrique. "Hernández Catá, cuentista." RI, No. 21 (1946), 69-74.

53.55 Suárez Solís, Rafael. "Los cuentos de Hernández Catá." Unión, 5, 5 (1966), 183-185.

53.56 _____. "Hernández Catá diplomático." RevC, 1 (1935), 320.

53.57 Torre, Miguel Angel de la. "[Los siete pecados]." In his Prosas varias (H: Editorial de la Universidad, 1966), pp. 325-329.

53.58 Zamacois, Eduardo. "¡Otro!..." MAHC, No. 5 (1954), 113-116.

53.59 Zweig, Stefan. "Despedida de Hernández Catá." RevC, 16 (1941), 281-283. Also MAHC, No. 1 (1953), 3-6.

54. JAMIS, FAYAD (1930-   )

Critical Essays

54.1   Augier, Angel I. "La poesía de Fayad Jamís." RBNJM, 3a serie, 12, 3 (1970), 139-146.

54.2   _____. "Por esta libertad, premio de poesía 1962." ULH, No. 159 (1963), 162-163.

54.3   Catá, Almayda. "Recuento sobre Fayad Jamís." Unión, 6, 2 (1967), 172-173.

54.4   Contreras, Félix. "Cara a cara con Fayad Jamís." Cuba, No. 77 (1968), 51.

54.5   Dalton, Roque. "[Por esta libertad]." CAm, Nos. 13-14 (1962), 61-63.

54.6   Feijóo, Samuel. "Fayad Jamís, libro y premio [Por esta libertad]." Islas, 6, 2 (1963), 399-403.

54.7   _____. "Los puentes universales [Los puentes]." Islas, 5, 1 (1962), 303-305.

54.8   Fernández, Pablo Armando. "[Los puentes]." CAm, No. 10 (1962), 140-148.

54.9   Ferré, Mariano. "Exposición de Fayad Jamís." GdC, No. 57 (1967), 6.

54.10   Lamadrid, Enrique R. "La poesía de Fayad Jamís y la revolución cubana; un estudio de cambio estético." Symposium, 33 (1979), 230-247.

54.11   Lihn, Enrique. "Un artista de doble oficio." GdC, No. 57 (1967), 6.

54.12   Medina, Richard. "Ante la puerta de Jamís." CAm, No. 87 (1974), 133-135.

54.13   Oráa, Francisco de. "A propósito de la segunda 'Pedrada'." Unión, 11, 2-3 (1972), 232-234.

54.14   _____. "Cuerpos, o de cuando Milosz recuperó la esperanza." GdC, No. 52 (1966), 10.

54.15   Rodríguez Rivera, Guillermo. "Trece años después." CAm, No. 43 (1967), 127-128.

54.16 Saínz, Enrique. "Notas a la poesía [Abrí la verja de hierro]." Unión, 13, 2 (1974), 190-193.

54.17 Selva, Maurcio de la. "[Cuerpos]." CA, No. 148 (1966), 268-270.

54.18 Slutsky, Boris. "Leyendo el libro de Fayad Jamís." LitS, No. 9 (1973), 186-187.

54.19 Suardíaz, Luis. "Sobre los puentes." Unión, 1, 2 (1962), 146-149.

54.20 Vidal, Manuel. "Fayad Jamís desde 'Las Antillas'." GdC, No. 57 (1967), 6.

KOZER, JOSE (1940-   )

Critical Essays

55.1   Alonso, Santos. "La intimidad narrativa de José Kozer." NE, (1979), 172-173.

55.2   Alvarez Cáccamo, José María. "Este judío de números y letras, palabra familiar y mitológica." Peñalabra, No. 17 (1975), 36-37.

55.3   Aranguren, Jorge G. "La poesía como cauterio." Kurpil, No. 5 (1975), 35-37.

55.4   Delgado, Bernardo. "[La rueca de los semblantes]." JcF, 10 (1980), 96-97.

55.5   Matamoro, Blas. "[La rueca de los semblantes]." CHA, No. 372 (1981), 703-704.

55.6   ____. "[Y así tomaron posesión en las ciudades]." CHA, No. 357 (1980), 748-749.

55.7   Minc, Rose S. "Convergencias judeo-cubanas en la poesía de José Kozer." CA, No. 240 (1980), 111-117.

55.8   ____. "Revelación y consagración de lo hebraico en la poesía de José Kozer." Chasqui, 10, 1 (1980), 26-35.

55.9   Morales, José Jurado. "[Este judío de números y letras]." Azor, No. 11 (n.d.), 58-59.

55.10   Pedemonte, Hugo Emilio. "[De Chepén a la Habana]." PHisp, No. 252 (1973), 92-93.

55.11   Plaza, Galvarino. "Isaac Goldemberg y José Kozer: De Chepén a la Habana." CHA, No. 301 (1975), 251-252.

55.12   Reis, Roberto. "Entrevista: José Kozer." Chasqui, 6, 1 (1976), 95-99.

55.13   Riosalido, Jesús. "José Kozer: Este judío de números y letras." AdF, No. 107 (1977), 20-21.

55.14   Rodríguez Padrón, Jorge. "La poesía de José Kozer." Eco, No. 223 (1980), 83-87. Also CulturaSS, No. 71 (1981), 39-43.

55.15   ____. "La rueca de los semblantes, de José Kozer." HdP, No. 13 (1980), 31-36.

55.16   Romero, Alberto.   "Padres y otras profesiones."   Envíos, No. 5
        (1973), 40.

55.17   Santos Betanzos, Manuel.   "De Chepen a la Habana y Poemas de
        Guadalupe."   Boreal, No. 2 (1974), 9-10.

55.18   Sheridan, Guillermo.   "[Y así tomaron posesión en las ciuda-
        des]."   Vuelta, No. 45 (1980), 43-44.

55.19   "Tres jóvenes poetas latinoamericanos en Nueva York."   Papeles,
        No. 16 (1972), 66-70.   Kozer inter alios.

56. LABRADOR RUIZ, ENRIQUE (1902-   )

Bibliographies

56.1 Febres Cordero G., Julio. "Enrique Labrador Ruiz, contribución a una bibliografía." RBNC, 3, 2 (1952), 93-135.

Critical Monographs and Dissertations

56.2 Bueno, Salvador. Trayectoria de Labrador Ruiz (a los 25 años de Laberinto). H: Librería Martí, 1958. Same as item no. 56.14

56.3 Molinero, Rita. La narrativa de Enrique Labrador Ruiz. Madrid: Playor, 1977.

56.4 Villarronda, Guillermo. Tres novelas distintas y... un solo autor verdadero. H: La Verónica, 1941.

Critical Essays

56.5 A. T. (Roncoso). "[Cresival]." Atenea, No. 140 (1937), 208-211.

56.6 Ardura, Ernesto. "[Trailer de sueños]." RevC, 25 (1949), 238-239.

56.7 Arenal, Humberto. "Prólog-entrevista con E. L. R." In Enrique Labrador Ruiz, Cuentos (H: Bolsilibros Unión, 1970), pp. 7-15.

56.8 Baciu, Stefan. "Enrique Labrador Ruiz." CulturaSS, No. 71 (1981), 85-90.

56.9 Baeza Flores, Alberto. "Expediente literario y humano de Enrique Labrador Ruiz." Atenea, No. 357 (1955), 257-266.

56.10 _____. "[El gallo en el espejo]." RBNC, 2a serie, 4, 4 (1953), 197-200.

56.11 Bueno, Salvador. "La cuentería criolla de Labrador Ruiz." Atenea, No. 345 (1954), 222-225.

56.12 _____. "Labrador Ruiz en su 'Laberinto'." CulturaSS, No. 13 (1958), 50-52.

56.13 _____. "El primer libro de Labrador Ruiz." Carteles, 8-VI-1958, p. 10.

56.14   ____. "Trayectoria de Labrador Ruiz. A los 25 años de La-
         berinto." RBC, 74 (1958), 195-218. Also in his Temas
         y personajes de la literatura cubana (H: Unión, 1964),
         pp. 251-275. Same as item no. 56.2.

56.15   ____. "El último libro de Labrador Ruiz: 'Yo no invento na-
         da'." IAL, No. 80 (1955), no pagination.

56.16   ____. "Los veinticinco años de Laberinto." ND, 38, 4 (1958),
         96-98.

56.17   Carrera, Julieta. "Carta abierta de Julieta Carrera a Labrador
         Ruiz." RAm, 36 (1938-1939), 358.

56.18   Carreras, Dino. "Labrador Ruiz en el cuento cubano." GdC, No.
         89 (1971), 30-31.

56.19   De León, Trigueros. "Enrique Labrador Ruiz." Centroamericana,
         7, 2 (1956), 30-31.

56.20   Diego Cuscoy, Luis. "Hallazgos canarios en un libro de cuentos
         cubanos [El gallo en el espejo]." RBNC, 2a serie, 6, 3
         (1955), 210-213.

56.21   Entralgo, Elías. "[Carne de quimera]." ULH, Nos. 70-72 (1947),
         369-370.

56.22   Febres Cordero G., Julio. "[La sangre hambrienta]." RBNC, 2a
         serie, 2, 1 (1951), 280-281.

56.23   Fernández, José B. "Conversation with Enrique Labrador Ruiz."
         LALR, No. 16 (1980), 266-272.

56.24   Fernández de Castro, José Antonio. "Nuevo avatar de Labrador
         Ruiz." UM, No. 57 (1951), 8-9.

56.25   Gallegos Valdés, Luis. "Escritores hispanoamericanos del siglo
         XX: Enrique Labrador Ruiz." CulturaSS, No. 71 (1981), 112-
         116.

56.26   Gerbasi, Vicente. "Enrique Labrador Ruiz, viajero de la angus-
         tia." RAm, 65 (1949), 168-169. Also RNC, No. 67 (1948),
         136-140.

56.27   Jamís, Fayad. "Comentarios sobre la aparición de un libro cu-
         bano [Cuentos]." Unión, 12, 1 (1973), 162-163.

56.28   Jiménez, Max. "Enrique Labrador Ruiz." RAm, 33 (1937), 103.

56.29   Lazo, Raimundo. "Labrador Ruiz, creador novelesco [La sangre
         hambrienta]." MALHC, 1, 5 (1950), 5.

56.30   Leante, César. "Cuentos de Labrador Ruiz." Santiago, No. 6
         (1972), 239-246. Also in his El espacio real (H: Unión
         de Escritores y Artistas de Cuba, 1975), pp. 71-78.

284 · CUBAN LITERATURE

56.31 Mata, G. H. "Dos escritores frente a un plagio." Cervantes, Nos. 10-11 (1940), 35.

56.32 Medina, José Ramón. "[La sangre hambrienta]." RNC, No. 60 (1950), 314.

56.33 Montes Huidobro, Matías. "Labrador Ruiz: estética del subconsciente en la narrativa cubana." ALHisp, No. 5 (1976), 209-219.

56.34 ____. "Labrador Ruiz. pruebas de galera del proceso creador." Chasqui, 7, 1 (1978), 5-16.

56.35 Navarro Montes de Oca, J. "Tendencias de la nueva narrativa cubana." RAm, 38 (1941), 40, 46-47.

56.36 Pita, Juana Rosa. "La palabra en el espejo: conversación con Enrique Labrador Ruiz." CulturaSS, No. 71 (1981), 91-111.

56.37 Pogolotti, Marcelo. "La república de Labrador Ruiz." In his La república de Cuba al través de sus escritores (H: Lex, 1958), pp. 180-182.

56.38 Remos y Rubio, Juan Nepomuceno José. "[Carne de quimera]." RevC, 21 (1946), 182-184.

56.39 Rodríguez Alemán, Mario A. "[El gallo en el espejo]." ULH, Nos. 115-117 (1954), 233-236.

56.40 Rojas, Manuel. "Peculiaridades de un escritor cubano." Crónica, 2, 15 (1952), 44-45.

56.41 Sánchez, Reinaldo. "Enrique Labrador Ruiz y la novela gaseiforme: una aproximación al texto narrativo." CH, 3, 1 (1981), 37-46.

56.42 Villaronda, Guillermo. "[Anteo]." Cervantes, Nos. 10-11 (1940), 28.

56.43 ____. "[Cresival]." RIn, No. 9 (1938), 58-59.

56.44 Wapnir, Salomón. "[El pan de los muertos]." USF, No. 39 (1959), 275.

57. LEANTE, CESAR (1928-   )

Critical Monographs and Dissertations

57.1   Luis, William. "César Leante: the politics of fiction." DAI,
        41 (1980), 270A-271A.

Critical Essays

57.2   "Algunas opiniones sobre César Leante." GdC, No. 173 (1978), 7.

57.3   Alvarez García, Imeldo. "Los esclavos insumisos [Los guerrille-
        ros negros]." Plural, No. 94 (1979), 63-66.

57.4   ____. "[Los guerrilleros negros]." Bohemia, 69, 26 (1977),
        24.

57.5   ____. "La obra narrativa de César Leante." CAm, No. 118
        (1980), 108-113.

57.6   Augier, Angel I. "[Con las milicias]." VU, No. 142 (1962),
        19-20.

57.7   Benítez Rojo, Antonio. "Otros padres, otros hijos [Padres e hi-
        jos]." CAm, No. 50 (1968), 183-184.

57.8   "Cinco preguntas a César Leante." GdC, No. 173 (1978), 5-6.

57.9   Contreras, Orlando. "[Con las milicias]." VO, 3, 18 (1962),
        62.

57.10   Deschamps Chapeaux, Pedro. "[Los guerrilleros negros]." GdC,
        No. 155 (1977), 20.

57.11   Díaz Martínez, Manuel. "Un reportaje a César Leante." VO, 3,
        19 (1962), 67.

57.12   Feijóo, Samuel. "[Con las milicias]." Islas, 5, 1 (1962), 303.

57.13   Fernández Retamar, Roberto. "Con César Leante." GdC, No. 2
        (1962), 6-7.

57.14   Lorenzo, José. "Una novela de César Leante." Bohemia, 57, 7
        (1965), 28.

57.15   Lucyga, Christine. "Traditionsbeziehungen in modernen kuban-
        ischen Roman: Manuel Cofiño López und César Leante." WB,
        26, 9 (1980), 159-163.

57.16   Luis, William. "Con César Leante." Bohemia, 70, 48 (1978), 10-
        13.

57.17   _____. "Myth and reality in César Leante's Muelle de caballe-
        ría." LALR, No. 16 (1980), 256-265.

57.18   Martínez Herrera, Alberto. "[Con las milicias]." Unión, 1, 2
        (1962), 143-145.

57.19   Mosquera, Gerardo. "Leante me dijo..." RyC, No. 57 (1977),
        21-23.

57.20   Piñeiro, Abelardo. "Un miliciano cuenta." GdC, No. 39 (1964),
        22.

57.21   Ruiz, Bertha. "Los guerrilleros negros, de César Leante: una
        novela diferente." Romance, 41, 2 (1978), 86-87.

58. LEZAMA LIMA, JOSE (1910-1976)

Bibliographies

58.1 Foster, David William. "A bibliography of the fiction of Carpentier, Cabrera Infante, and Lezama Lima." Abraxas, 1, 3 (1971), 305-310.

Critical Monographs and Dissertations

58.2 Casa de las Américas. Centro de Investigaciones Literarias. Interrogando a Lezama Lima. Barcelona: Anagrama, 1974?

58.3 Fernández Sosa, Luis Francisco. José Lezama Lima y la crítica anagógica. Miami: Universal, 1976. Orig. DAI, 36 (1975), 271A.

58.4 Gimbernat de González, Ester. "Paradiso: 'aventura sigilosa' de un sistema poético." DAI, 36 (1976), 6670A.

58.5 Junco Fazzolari, Margarita. Paradiso y el sistema poético de Lezama Lima. BA: Fernando García Cambeiro, 1979. Orig. DAI, 38 (1977), 1429A-1430A.

58.6 Lutz, Robyn R. "The poetry of José Lezama Lima." DAI, 41 (1980), 2135A-2136A.

58.7 Márquez, Enrique. "José Lezama Lima: una poética de la figuración." DAI, 40 (1980), 4006A-4007A.

58.8 Recopilación de textos sobre José Lezama Lima. H: Casa de las Américas, 1970. Pertinent items are listed separately.

58.9 Ríos-Avila, Rubén. The American gnosis of José Lezama Lima. Columbia: University of Missouri Press, 1984.

58.10 Ruiz Barrionuevo, Carmen. El Paradiso de Lezama Lima. Madrid: Insula, 1980.

58.11 Souza, Raymond D. The poetic fiction of José Lezama Lima. Columbia: University of Missouri Press, 1983.

58.12 Ulloa, Justo Celso. "La narrativa de Lezama Lima y Sarduy: entre la imagen visionaria y el juego verbal." DAI, 35 (1974), 1676A-1677A.

58.13 Valdivieso, Jaime. Bajo el signo de Orfeo: Lezama Lima y Proust. Madrid: Orígenes, 1980.

58.14   Villa, Alvaro de, and José Sánchez-Boudy. <u>Lezama Lima: peregri-</u>
        <u>no inmóvil</u> (Paradiso al desnudo); un <u>estudio crítico de</u>
        <u>Paradiso</u>. Miami: Universal, 1973.

58.15   Zaldívar, Gladys. <u>Novelística cubana de los años 60: Paradiso</u>.
        <u>El mundo alucinante</u>. Miami: Universal, 1977. <u>Lezama Lima</u>
        <u>and Reinaldo Arenas</u>.

Critical Essays

58.16   Achúgar Ferrari, Hugo. "Un primer asombro ante <u>Paradiso</u>." <u>Bre-</u>
        <u>chaM</u>, 1, 1 (1968), 41-42.

58.17   Aínsa, Fernando. "Imagen y la posibilidad de la utopía en <u>Pa-</u>
        <u>radiso</u>, de Lezama Lima." <u>RI</u>, Nos. 123-124 (1983), 263-277.

58.18   Aleixandre, Vicente. "Testimonio." In José Lezama Lima, <u>Orbita</u>
        (H: Unión Nacional de Escritores y Artistas de Cuba, 1966),
        pp. 49-50.

58.19   Alonso, J. M. "A sentimental realism." <u>Review</u>, No. 12 (1974),
        46-47.

58.20   Altamirano, Donaldo. "João Guimarães Rosa e José Lezama Lima:
        comandantes de guerrilha cultural do muito novo e muito an-
        tigo barroco americano." <u>MGSL</u>, 9-VI-1979, p. 4.

58.21   Alvarez Bravo, Armando. "Conversación con Lezama Lima." <u>MNu</u>,
        No. 24 (1968), 32-39.

58.22   _____. "Lezama Lima." In José Lezama Lima, <u>Lezama Lima</u> (BA:
        Jorge Alvarez, 1968), pp. 7-41.

58.23   _____. "Lezama Lima, una trayectoria de la inocencia." <u>GdC</u>,
        No. 67 (1968), 3.

58.24   _____. "El maestro antólogo." <u>GdC</u>, No. 45 (1965), 26.

58.25   _____. "Orbita de Lezama Lima." In <u>Recopilación de textos so-</u>
        <u>bre José Lezama Lima</u>, q.v., pp. 42-67. Also in José Lezama
        Lima, <u>Orbita</u> (H: Unión de Escritores y Artistas de Cuba,
        1966), pp. 9-47.

58.26   Amorós, Andrés. "José Lezama Lima." In his <u>Introducción a la</u>
        <u>novela hispanoamericana actual</u> (Salamanca: Anaya, 1971),
        pp. 99-108.

58.27   Aparicio, Raúl. "De una primera lectura de <u>Paradiso</u>." <u>GdC</u>,
        No. 51 (1966), 9.

58.28   Arcocha, José Antonio. "Dicotomías: Lezama Lima y Cabrera In-
        fante." <u>Aportes</u>, No. 11 (1969), 59-65.

58.29   Arroitia-Jáuregui, Marcelo. "Dos notas sobre <u>Analecta del re-</u>
        <u>loj</u>." <u>Orígenes</u>, No. 35 (1954), 61-64.

58.30 Arrom, José Juan. "Lo tradicional cubano en el mundo novelístico de José Lezama Lima." RI, Nos. 92-93 (1975), 469-477.

58.31 Augier, Angel I. "Tres siglos de poesía cubana [Antología de la poesía cubana]." Unión, 5, 2 (1966), 168-169.

58.32 Baeza Flores, Alberto. "[Analecta del reloj]." RBNC, 2a serie, 4, 4 (1953), 181-185.

58.33 Bejel, Emilio F. "Cultura, historia y escritura en Lezama Lima." In Rose S. Minc, Literatures in transition: the many voices of the Caribbean area (Gaithersburg, Md.: Hispamérica, 1982), pp. 117-122.

58.34 _____. "La dialéctica del deseo en Aventuras sigilosas." TC, No. 13 (1979), 135-145.

58.35 Benedetti, Mario. "Lezama Lima, más allá de los malentendidos." In his El recurso del supremo patriarca (M: Nueva Imagen, 1979), pp. 109-114.

58.36 Berg, Walter Bruno. "Die Provokation Lezama Limas: Aspekte gegenwärtiger Rezeption; Schriften aus dem Nachlass." Iberoamericana, No. 11 (1980), 29-49.

58.37 Bernáldez Bernáldez, José María. "La expresión americana de Lezama Lima." CHA, No. 318 (1976), 653-670.

58.38 Bueno, Salvador. "[La expresión americana]." GdC, No. 83 (1970), 27.

58.39 _____. "Intentos de captación de una poesía críptica [La fijeza]." MALHC, 1, 4 (1950), no pagination.

58.40 _____. "Sobre Paradiso." Bohemia, 58, 23 (1966), 17.

58.41 Cabrera, Lydia. "El sincretismo religioso de Cuba. Santos Orisha Ngangas. Lucumis y Congos." Orígenes, No. 36 (1954), 8-20.

58.42 Cabrera Infante, Guillermo. "Cabrera Infante habla de Lezama Lima." RLati, No. 20 (1976), 1, 7-8.

58.43 _____. "Encuentros y recuerdos con José Lezama Lima." Vuelta, No. 3 (1977), 46-48.

58.44 _____. "Vidas para leerlas." Vuelta, No. 41 (1980), 4-16.

58.45 Campos, Jorge. "Paradiso de José Lezama Lima." Insula, Nos. 260-261 (1980), 11, 28.

58.46 Cardenal, Ernesto. "Con Lezama Lima." In his En Cuba (BA/M: Lohlé, 1972), pp. 213-217.

58.47 Cardoza y Aragón, Luis. "[Paradiso]." Marcha, No. 1401 (1968), 29.

58.48   Cascardi, Anthony J. "Reference in Lezama Lima's 'Muerte de
        Narciso'." JSSTC, 5 (1977), 5-11.

58.49   Charry Lara, Fernando. "El mundo poético de Lezama Lima." El
        urogallo, No. 4 (1970), 66-68.

58.50   Collazos, Oscar. "La expresión americana." In Recopilación de
        textos sobre José Lezama Lima, q.v., pp. 130-137.

58.51   Conrad, Andrée. "An expanding imagination." Review, No. 12
        (1974), 48-51.

58.52   Conte, Rafael. "José Lezama Lima o el aerolito." In his Len-
        guaje y violencia (Madrid: Al-Borak, 1972), pp. 213-221.

58.53   Correa, Pedro. "José Lezama Lima, poeta." NTiem, No. 250
        (1975), 33-48.

58.54   Cortázar, Julio. "José Lezama Lima, 1910-1976: an ever-present
        beacon." Review, No. 18 (1976), 30.

58.55   _____. "Para llegar a Lezama Lima." Unión, 5, 4 (1966), 36-60.
        Also in his La vuelta al día en ochenta mundos (M: Siglo
        XXI, 1967), pp. 135-155. Also in Recopilación de textos
        sobre José Lezama Lima, q.v., pp. 146-168. Also as "An ap-
        proach to Lezama Lima." Review, No. 12 (1974), 20-25.

58.56   Cortázar, Mercedes. "Entering Paradiso." Review, No. 12
        (1974), 17-19.

58.57   Cuadra, Pablo Antonio. "Breve nota ante la muerte de Lezama
        Lima." RLati, No. 18 (1976), 4.

58.58   Díaz Martínez, Manuel. "Introducción a José Lezama Lima." In-
        dice, No. 232 (1968), 35-38.

58.59   _____. "Lezama, crítico de nuestra poesía." Bohemia, 58, 2
        (1966), 26-27.

58.60   Diego, Eliseo. "En la calzada de Jesús del Monte; el segundo
        discurso; el que pasa." Orígenes, No. 14 (1947), 23-24.

58.61   _____. "Recuento de José Lezama Lima." In Recopilación de
        textos sobre José Lezama Lima, q.v., pp. 289-290.

58.62   Domínguez Rey, Antonio. "Lezama Lima y su 'embriaguez miste-
        riosa'." NE, 8 (1979), 67-69.

58.63   Donoso Pareja, Miguel. "Paradiso: tres adolescentes excepcio-
        nales." CEm, No. 23 (1961), 147-148.

58.64   Echavarren Welker, Roberto. "Obertura de Paradiso." Eco, No.
        202 (1978), 1043-1073.

58.65 Fazzolari, Margarita. "Reader's guide to Paradiso." Review, No. 29 (1981), 47-54.

58.66 Fernández, Jesse. "Varias manifestaciones del simbolismo acuático en Paradiso." In Rose S. Minc, Requiem for the "Boom" --premature? A symposium (Upper Montclair, N.J.: Montclair State College, 1980), pp. 110-122.

58.67 Fernández Bonilla, Magali. "Hacia una elucidación del Capítulo I de Paradiso de José Lezama Lima." Románica, 12 (1975), 37-46.

58.68 Fernández Retamar, Roberto. "José Lezama Lima." In his La poesía contemporánea en Cuba (1927-1953) (H: Orígenes, 1954), pp. 89-99.

58.69 _____. "La poesía de José Lezama Lima." In Recopilación de textos sobre José Lezama Lima, q.v., pp. 90-99.

58.70 Fernández Sosa, Luis Francisco. "Northrup Frye y unos poemas anagógicos de Lezama Lima." Hispania, 61 (1978), 877-887.

58.71 Ferré, Rosario. "Oppiano Licario, o la resurrección por la imagen." Escritura, No. 2 (1976), 319-326.

58.72 Figueroa-Amaral, Esperanza. "Forma y estilo en Paradiso." RI, No. 72 (1970), 425-435.

58.73 Forastieri Braschi, Eduardo. "Aproximación al tiempo y a un pasaje de Paradiso." SinN, 5, 1 (1974), 57-61.

58.74 _____. "Nota al 'aspa volteando incesante oscuro' en la 'episodio para el mulo' de José Lezama Lima." RP, No. 2 (1973), 137-141.

58.75 Fossey, Jean Michel. "Antes de morir: Lezama Lima." Indice, Nos. 401-402 (1976), 45-49.

58.76 _____. "Entrevista con Lezama Lima." Imagen, 46 (1969), 8-17. Also as "José Lezama Lima." In his Galaxia latinoamericana (Las Palmas de Gran Canaria: Inventarios Provisionales, 1973), pp. 29-50.

58.77 Foxley, Carmen. "Paradiso, un espacio precario para la duración." RChL, No. 21 (1983), 5-45.

58.78 Franco, Jean. "Lezama Lima en el paraíso de la poesía." Vórtice, 1, 1 (1974), 30-48.

58.79 García Flores, Margarita. "José Lezama Lima." RUM, 21, 9 (1967), 14-16.

58.80 García Marruz, Fina. "Por Dador de José Lezama Lima." CUNESCO, No. 4 (1961), 258-277. Also in Recopilación de textos sobre Lezama Lima, q.v., pp. 278-288.

58.81   García Ponce, Juan. "Imagen posible de José Lezama Lima."
        Vuelta, No. 1 (1976), 18-21.

58.82   García Vega, Lorenzo. "Tierra en Jagüey." Orígenes, No. 25
        (1950), 50-53.

58.83   Gaztelu, Angel. "Muerte de Narciso. Rauda cetrería de metáfo-
        ras." Verbum, 1, 3 (1937), 49-52. Also in Recopilación
        de textos sobre José Lezama Lima, q.v., pp. 103-106.

58.84   Ghiano, Juan Carlos. "Introducción a Paradiso, de Lezama Lima."
        Sur, No. 314 (1968), 62-78. Also in Recopilación de textos
        sobre José Lezama Lima, q.v., pp. 250-266.

58.85   Gimbernat de González, Ester. "[Oppiano Licario]." Hispaméri-
        ca, No. 22 (1979), 110-114.

58.86   _____. "Paradiso: contracifra de un sistema poético." CHA, No.
        318 (1977), 671-686.

58.87   _____. "Paradiso: reino de la poesía." PCL, 5 (1979), 116-123.

58.88   _____. "El 'peldaño que falta' en un oscuro texto de Paradiso
        de J. Lezama Lima." In La Chispa '81: selected proceedings
        (New Orleans: Tulane University, 1981), pp. 125-132.

58.89   _____. "El regreso de Oppiano Licario." Eco, No. 222 (1980),
        648-664.

58.90   _____. "La transgresión, regla del juego en la novelística de
        Lezama Lima." In Rose S. Minc, Latin American fiction to-
        day (Takoma Park, Md.: Hispamérica; Upper Montclair, N.J.:
        Montclair State College, 1980), pp. 147-152.

58.91   González, Eduardo G. "Lezama póstumo: navegaciones y regresos."
        Escandalar, 3, 1 (1980), 73-79.

58.92   González, Reinaldo. "José Lezama Lima, el ingenuo culpable."
        In Recopilación de textos sobre José Lezama Lima, q.v.,
        pp. 219-248.

58.93   González Echevarría, Roberto. "Apetitos de Góngora y Lezama."
        RI, Nos. 92-93 (1975), 479-491. Also in his Relecturas;
        estudios de literatura cubana (Caracas: Monte Ávila, 1976),
        pp. 95-118. Also in Instituto Internacional de Literatura
        Iberoamericana, XVII Congreso (Madrid: Cultura Hispánica
        del Centro Iberoamericano de Cooperación, 1978), pp. 555-
        572.

58.94   González Montes, Yara. "José Lezama Lima: sentido humano de un
        poeta hermético." PPNWCFL, 23 (1972), 296-302.

58.95   Goytisolo, José Agustín. "La espiral milagrosa." In José Leza-
        ma Lima, Fragmentos a su imán (Barcelona: Imán, 1977), pp.
        7-21.

58.96   ____. "Introducción." In José Lezama Lima, Posible imagen
           de José Lezama Lima; 4. ed. (Barcelona: Llibres de Sine-
           ra, 1971), pp. 7-18. Orig. 1969.

58.97   Goytisolo, Juan. "La metáfora erótica: Góngora, Joaquín Belda
           y Lezama Lima." RI, No. 95 (1976), 157-175.

58.98   Guillermo, Edenia, and Juana A. Hernández. "Paradiso, culmina-
           ción del barroco cubano." PSA, No. 219 (1974), 223-248.

58.99   Hurtado, Oscar. "Lezama. Arte y literatura." Bohemia, 58, 2
           (1966), 24-25, 90.

58.100   ____. "Sobre ruiseñores." In Recopilación de textos sobre
           José Lezama Lima, q.v., pp. 298-304.

58.101   Ionescu, Andrei. "Recuperarea naturii prin imagine." RoLit,
           No. 24 (1972), 28-29.

58.102   Jiménez Emán, Gabriel. "Lezama Lima: la imagen para mí es la
           vida." Imagen, No. 109 (1976), 42-46.

58.103   Jitrik Noé. "A propos de Paradiso de J. Lezama Lima." In
           Littérature latino-americaine d'aujourd'hui; Colloque
           Cerisy (Paris: Union Générale d'Editions, 1980), pp. 256-
           271.

58.104   ____. "Paradiso entre desborde y ruptura." TC, No. 13
           (1979), 71-89.

58.105   "José Lezama Lima: el cable de la Habana." Plural, No. 12
           (1976), 41.

58.106   Josef, Bela. "A narrativa barroca de Lezama Lima." In Séptimo
           Congreso Brasileiro de Língua e Literatura (Rio de Janei-
           ro, 1975), pp. 157-163.

58.107   Juliosvaldo. "El infierno de Paradiso." Bohemia, 58, 27
           (1966), 40.

58.108   Kalicki, Rajmund. "Obrasy Lezamy Limy." Tw, 32, 12 (1976),
           49-54.

58.109   Koch, Dolores. "Lezama Lima: contradicción y júbilo de la poe-
           sía." Chasqui, 8, 3 (1979), 84-88.

58.110   Labrador Ruiz, Enrique. "Pistiner toma transferencia." Oríge-
           nes, No. 24 (1949), 11-20.

58.111   Lafourcade, Enrique. "Carpentier, Lezama Lima: la revolución
           puesta a prueba." Imagen, 90 (1971), 16-19.

58.112   Lavín Cerda, Hernán. "José Lezama Lima o la agonía verbal."
           TC, No. 13 (1979), 126-134.

58.113   Lázaro, Felipe. "José Lezama Lima: fundador de poesía." CHA,
         No. 318 (1976), 713-719.

58.114   Lezama Lima, Eloísa. "Introducción." In José Lezama Lima,
         Cartas (1939-1976) (Madrid: Orígenes, 1979), pp. 9-10.

58.115   _____. "José Lezama Lima, mi hermano." RevI, 8 (1978), 297-
         304.

58.116   Lezama Lima, José. "Carta a Fina García Marruz, sobre su crí-
         tica a Dador." Signos, No. 21 (1978), 272-273. See
         item no. 58.80.

58.117   _____. "Confluences." Review, No. 12 (1974), 6-16.

58.118   Lihn, Enrique. "Paradiso, novela y homosexualidad." Hispamé-
         rica, No. 22 (1979), 3-21.

58.119   Lope, Monique de. "Narcisse ailé: étude sur Muerte de Narci-
         so (1937) de J. Lezama Lima." Caravelle, No. 29
         (1977), 25-44.

58.120   López, César. "Una aproximación a Paradiso." Indice, No. 232
         (1968), 39-41.

58.121   _____. "Sobre Paradiso." Unión, 5, 2 (1966), 173-180. Also
         in Recopilación de textos sobre José Lezama Lima, q.v.,
         pp. 182-190.

58.122   López Delpecho, Luis. "El solitario de José Lezama Lima."
         IAL, No. 71 (1969), 1-2.

58.123   López Segrera, Francisco. "Lezama Lima, figura central del
         grupo Orígenes." Caravelle, No. 16 (1971), 87-97.

58.124   Luna, Norma. "Paradiso y El siglo de la luces: en torno a la
         dialéctica mitopoética." REH, 14, 1 (1980), 121-130.

58.125   Lutz, Robyn R. "The tribute to everyday reality in José Leza-
         ma Lima's Fragmentos a su imán." JSSTC, 8, 3 (1980),
         249-266.

58.126   Mac Adam, Alfred J. "Juan Carlos Onetti and José Lezama Lima,
         a double portrait of the artist." In his Modern Latin
         American narratives; the dreams of reason (Chicago: Uni-
         versity of Chicago Press, 1977), pp. 102-107.

58.127   Mañach, Jorge. "El arcano de cierta poesía nueva. Carta a-
         bierta al poeta José Lezama Lima." Bohemia, 41, 39
         (1949), 78, 90.

58.128   _____. "Reacciones a un diálogo literario (algo más sobre po-
         esía vieja y nueva)," Bohemia, 41, 42 (1949), 63, 107.

58.129   Mandell, Olga Karman. "Cuatro ficciones y una ficción: estu-
         dio del capítulo XII de Paradiso." RI, Nos. 123-124
         (1983), 279-291.

58.130   Martínez Laínez, Fernando. "Entrevista con José Lezama Lima."
         In his Palabra cubana (Madrid: Akal, 1975), pp. 49-81.

58.131   Matamoro, Blas. "Oppiano Licario: seis modelos en busca de
         una síntesis." TC, No. 13 (1979), 112-125.

58.132   Meneses, Carlos. "In memoriam: José Lezama Lima, 1916-1976."
         Hispamérica, No. 15 (1976), 119-120.

58.133   Mignolo, Walter. "Paradiso: derivación y red." TC, No. 13
         (1979), 90-111.

58.134   Monsiváis, Carlos. "La calle Trocadero como medio, José Leza-
         ma Lima como fin." RUM, 22, 12 (1968), ii-iii.

58.135   Montero, Oscar. "Maitreya: lama, Lezama, L.S.D." In Rose S.
         Minc, Literatures in transition: the many voices of the
         Caribbean area (Gaithersburg, Md.: Hispamérica, 1982),
         pp. 123-135.

58.136   Mora, Juan Miguel de. "Lezama Lima, autor de la novela Para-
         diso." VUM, No. 890 (1968), 12, 14.

58.137   Morales, Miguel Angel. "[Oppiano Licario]." RUM, 32, 5
         (1978), 38-39.

58.138   Moreno Fragináls, Manuel. "Lezama Lima y la revolución."
         Plural, No. 74 (1977), 15-18.

58.139   Moscoso-Góngora, Peter. "A Proust of the Caribbean." Nation,
         No. 218 (1974), 600-601.

58.140   Müller-Bergh, Klaus. "Lezama Lima y Paradiso." RO, No. 84
         (1970), 357-364. Also as "Lezama Lima and Paradiso."
         BA, 44 (1970), 36-40.

58.141   Neves, Eugenia. "Entrevista con José Lezama Lima." AdL, No.
         11 (1969), 20-21. Also Marcha, No. 1465 (1969), 12-13.

58.142   Novas, Benito. "Lezama, invitación al viaje." Bohemia, 63,
         1 (1971), 9-11.

58.143   Ortega, Julio. "La biblioteca de José Cemí." VidaL, No. 6
         (1974), 6-17. Also RI, Nos. 92-93 (1975), 509-521.

58.144   _____. "Una coherencia de la expansión poética." RBA, No.
         27 (1969), 81-95. Also as "Lezama Lima." In his Relato
         de la utopía (Barcelona: La Gaya Ciencia, 1973), pp. 51-
         97. Also as "Aproximaciones a Paradiso." In Recopila-
         ción de textos sobre José Lezama Lima, q.v., pp. 191-218.

58.145 _____. "Language as hero." Review, No. 12 (1974), 35-42.

58.146 _____. "Lezama Lima y la cultura hispanoamericana." Inti, Nos. 5-6 (1977), 72-78.

58.147 _____. "Paradiso." In his La contemplación y la fiesta (Caracas: Monte Avila, 1969), pp. 77-116. Also as "Paradiso, de Lezama Lima." In Angel Flores, and Raúl Silva Cáceres, La novela hispanoamericana actual (NY: Las Américas, 1971), pp. 39-71. Orig. as "Aproximaciones a Paradiso." Imagen, No. 40 (1969), 9-16.

58.148 Panebianco, Cándido. "Il Paradiso esoterico di Lezama Lima." SLI, 9 (1979), 71-112.

58.149 Parajón, Mario. "Delicia de proseguir." Orígenes, No. 29 (1951), 45-46.

58.150 Paternain, Alejandro. "Hylem (a propósito de Lezama Lima)." RNC, No. 204 (1972), 10-21.

58.151 Pelegrin, Benito. "Approches d'un continent vierges: José Lezama Lima." In Demarches linguistiques et poétiques (Sainte-Etienne: Centre Interdisciplinaire d'Etude et de Recherche sur l'Expression Contemporaine, 1977), pp. 277-295.

58.152 _____. "Tours, détours, contours d'un système poétique; José Lezama Lima." In Littérature latino-américaine d'aujourd'hui: Colloque de Cerisy (Paris: Union Générale d'Editions, 1980), pp. 335-351.

58.153 Pellón, Gustavo. "Paradiso: un fibroma de diecisiete libras." Hispamérica, Nos. 25-26 (1980), 147-151.

58.154 Pérez Firmat, Gustavo. "Descent into Paradiso: a study of heaven and homosexuality." Hispania, 59 (1976), 247-257.

58.155 Peri Rossi, Cristina. "Un banquete lujurioso." Marcha, No. 1510 (1970), 29.

58.156 _____. "Solamente para subdesarrollados." In Recopilación de textos sobre José Lezama Lima, q.v., pp. 267-277.

58.157 Persin, Margo. "Language as form and content in Paradiso." TAH, No. 8 (1976), 11-17.

58.158 Piñera, Virgilio. "Dos poetas, dos poemas, dos modos de poesía [Muerte de Narciso]." EdP, No. H (1941), 16-19.

58.159 _____. "Opciones de Lezama." In Recopilación de textos sobre José Lezama Lima, q.v., pp. 294-297.

58.160 Prieto, Abel E. "Poesía póstuma de José Lezama Lima." CAm, No. 112 (1979), 143-149.

58.161 Quintain, Alain. "Paradiso de José Lezama Lima, escritor neobarroco." In Instituto Internacional de Literatura Iberoamericana, XVII Congreso (Madrid: Cultura Hispánica del
Centro Iberoamericano de Cooperación, 1978), pp. 573-582.

58.162 "Recuerdo de José Lezama Lima." CHA, No. 318 (1976), 651-719.

58.163 Ribeyro, Julio Ramón. "Notas sobre Paradiso: Lezama Lima y
Marcel Proust." VP, No. 3 (1968), 53-55. Also in Recopilación de textos sobre José Lezama Lima, q.v., pp.
175-181.

58.164 _____. "Prólogo." In José Lezama Lima, Paradiso (Lima: Paradiso, 1968), I, no pagination.

58.165 Riccio, Alessandro. "José Lezama Lima." Belfagor, 32 (1977),
639-652.

58.166 _____. "Una nuova chiave di lettura per Paradiso: il surrealismo." AION-SR, 17 (1975), 141-158.

58.167 Ríos-Avila, Rubén. "The origin and the island: Lezama and Mal-
larmé." LALR, No. 16 (1980), 242-255.

58.168 Rodríguez Monegal, Emir. "Paradiso en su contexto." MNu, No.
24 (1968), 40-44. Also in his Narradores de esta América;
2. ed. (Montevideo: Alfa, 1969-1974), II, 130-155. Also
Imagen, No. 25 (1968), 4-5. Also as "The text in its context." Review, No. 12 (1974), 30-34.

58.169 _____. "Paradiso: una silogística de sobresalto." RI, Nos.
92-93 (1975), 523-533.

58.170 Rogman, Horst. "José Lezama Lima: Paradiso." Iberoromania,
3, 1 (1977), 78-96.

58.171 Ruiz Barrionuevo, Carmen. "Paradiso o la aventura de la imagen." AlHisp, No. 9 (1980), 221-234.

58.172 Sabatini, Arthur J. "On reading Paradiso." In Rose S. Minc,
Latin American fiction today (Takoma Park, Md.: Hispamérica; Upper Montclair, N.J.: Montclair State College,
1980), pp. 139-146.

58.173 Sánchez, Héctor. "José Lezama Lima. Paradiso, la corpografía
de una realidad caótica." RyFa, No. 15 (1969), 131-133.

58.174 Sánchez, Luis Alberto. "El ángel de la poesía [Poesías com-
pletas]." Inti, No. 4 (1976), 67-68.

58.175 Santana, Joaquín G. "Lezama Lima." Bohemia, 63, 1 (1971),
4-8.

58.176 Santí, Enrico-Mario. "Hacia Oppiano Licario." RI, Nos. 116-
117 (1981), 273-279.

298   CUBAN LITERATURE

58.177 _____. "Lezama, Vitier y la crítica de la razón reminiscente."
       RI, Nos. 92-93 (1975), 535-546.

58.178 _____. "Párridiso." MLN, 94 (1979), 343-365.

58.179 Sarduy, Severo. "A Cuban Proust." Review, No. 12 (1974), 43-
       45.

58.180 _____. "Dispersión/falsa notas. Homenaje a Lezama." MNu,
       No. 24 (1981), 5-17. Also as "Dispersión/falsas notas."
       In his Escrito sobre un cuerpo (BA: Sudamericana, 1969),
       pp. 61-89.

58.181 _____. "[Oppiano Licario]." Vuelta, No. 2 (1978), 32-35.

58.182 _____. "Página sobre Lezama Lima." RI, Nos. 92-93 (1975),
       467.

58.183 Schultze-Kraft, Peter. "Sobre el reconocimiento." Eco, No.
       217 (1979), 72-74.

58.184 Schwartz, Ronald. "Lezama Lima: Cuban sexual propensities."
       In his Nomads, exiles, and emigrés: the rebirth of the
       Latin American narrativa, 1960-80 (Metuchen, N.J.: Scare-
       crow Press, 1980), pp. 24-33.

58.185 Serra, Edelweis. "Paradiso: una aventura de la palabra." In
       Instituto Internacional de Literatura Iberoamericana,
       XVII Congreso (Madrid: Cultura Hispánica del Centro Ibe-
       roamericana de Cooperación, 1978), pp. 583-595.

58.186 Shaw, Donald L. "José Lezama Lima." In his Nueva narrativa
       hispanoamericana (Madrid: Cátedra, 1981), pp. 153-156.

58.187 Smith, Octavio. "Para llegar al mito amigo." In Recopilación
       de textos sobre José Lezama Lima, q.v., pp. 291-293.

58.188 Solís, Cleva. "José Lezama Lima." In Recopilación de textos
       sobre José Lezama Lima, q.v., pp. 305-307.

58.189 Souza, Raymond D. "The sensorial world of Lezama Lima." In
       his Major Cuban novelists (Columbia: University of Missou-
       ri Press, 1976), pp. 53-79.

58.190 Sucre, Guillermo. "[Fragmentos a su imán]." Vuelta, No. 28
       (1979), 37-39.

58.191 _____. "Lezama Lima: el logos de la imaginación." RI, Nos.
       92-93 (1976), 493-508. Also Eco, No. 175 (1975), 9-38.

58.192 Téllez, Freddy. "Lezama Lima o el juego de la escritura."
       Libre, No. 3 (1972), 22-27.

58.193 Torriente, Loló de la. "Epitafio para un poeta." CA, No.
       211 (1977), 211-217.

58.194 ____. "Fiesta de natalicio (en los 60 años de José Lezama
         Lima, en la Habana)." CA, No. 173 (1971), 158-166.

58.195 ____. "La imagen como fundamento poético del mundo." Bohe-
         mia, 55, 39 (1963), 84-87, 99.

58.196 ____. "Paradiso." Bohemia, 58, 27 (1966), 38-39.

58.197 Toti, Gianni. "José Lezama Lima. Il famoso capitolo ottavo,
         Paradiso." CSeg, 2, 7 (1968), 77-78.

58.198 Trajtenberg, Mario. "De Narciso a Fonesis: la condición del
         poeta." AdL, 11, 2 (1969), 15-17. Also Marcha, No. 1434
         (1969), 28-29.

58.199 Trigo, Pedro. "Paradiso. J. Lezama Lima." Reseña, No. 30
         (1969), 339-341.

58.200 Ulloa, Pedro Celso. "De involución a evolución: la transforma-
         ción órfica de Cemí en Paradiso de Lezama Lima." In The
         analysis of Hispanic texts: current trends in methodology
         (Jamaica, N.Y.: Bilingual Press/York College, 1976), pp.
         48-60.

58.201 Urondo, Francisco. "Paradiso, 'retumba como un metal', o toda
         la memoria del mundo." Indice, Nos. 251-252 (1969), 50-
         53.

58.202 Valdés, Adriana. "Paradiso de Lezama Lima." RNC, No. 234
         (1978), 23-44.

58.203 Valente, José Angel. "Carta abierta a José Lezama Lima." In-
         sula, No. 260 (1968), 30.

58.204 Varela Jácome, Benito. "Estructuras novelísticas de Lezama Li-
         ma." ALHisp, No. 6 (1977), 175-204.

58.205 Vargas Llosa, Mario. "Paradiso de José Lezama Lima." Amaru,
         No. 1 (1967), 72-75. Also Unión, 5, 4 (1966), 36-60.
         Also GdC, No. 58 (1967), 2. Also in Jorge Lafforgue,
         La nueva novela latinoamericana (BA: Paidós, 1969-1972),
         I, 131-141. Also as "Paradiso: una summa poética, una
         tentativa imposible." In Recopilación de textos sobre
         José Lezama Lima, q.v., pp. 169-174. Also as "Attempting
         the impossible." Review, No. 12 (1974), 26-29.

58.206 Vitier, Cintio. "Introducción a la obra de José Lezama Lima."
         In José Lezama Lima, Obras completas (Madrid: Aguilar,
         1975), pp. xi-lxiv.

58.207 ____. "Un libro maravilloso [Tratados en la Habana]." In
         Recopilación de textos sobre José Lezama Lima, q.v., pp.
         138-145. Also in his Crítica sucesiva (H: Contemporáne-
         os, UNEAC, 1971), pp. 252-266.

58.208 _____. "Nueva lectura de Lezama." In José Lezama Lima, Fragmentos a su imán (Barcelona: Imán, 1977), pp. 23-36.

58.209 Vitier, Medardo. "De José Lezama Lima." In his Valoraciones (H: Universidad Central de Las Villas, 1960), I, 248-252.

58.210 Waller, Claudia Joan. "José Lezama Lima's Paradiso. The theme of light and the resurrection." Hispania, 56 (1973), 275-282.

58.211 Wood, Michael. "[Paradiso]." NYRB, 21, 6 (1974), 14-16.

58.212 Xirau, Ramón. "José Lezama Lima: de la imagen y la semejanza." Plural, No. 1 (1971), 6-7. Also in his Poesía iberoamericana; doce ensayos (M: SepSetentas, 1971), pp. 97-111.

58.213 _____. "José Lezama Lima: el Eros relacionable o la imagen omnívodo y omnívora." Eco, No. 194 (1977), 212-213.

58.214 _____. "Lezama Lima o de la fe poética." In his Poesía y conocimiento (M: Joaquín Mortiz, 1978), pp. 66-91. Also as "Lezama Lima o del fidelismo poético." Diálogos, No. 73 (1977), 6-8.

58.215 Zambrano, María. "La Cuba secreta." Orígenes, No. 20 (1948), 3-9.

58.216 _____. "Cuba y la poesía de José Lezama Lima." Insula, Nos. 260-261 (1968), 4.

58.217 _____. "José Lezama Lima en la Habana." Indice, No. 232 (1968), 29-31. Also GdC, No. 67 (1968), 2-3.

58.218 Zoido, Antonio. "Ante Paradiso, de Lezama Lima (notas y atisbos de un lector)," CHA, No. 318 (1975),

59. LLES Y BERDAYES, FERNANDO (1883-1949)

Critical Monographs and Dissertations

59.1 Loveira y Chirino, Carlos. Un gran ensayista: Fernando Lles. H: "El Siglo XX", 1926.

59.2 Nodarse y Cabrera, José J. El pensamiento de Fernando Lles. H: Cultural, 1933.

Critical Essays

59.3 Acosta, Agustín. "Fernando Lles, poeta." RevC, 27 (1950), 82-87.

59.4 Grismer, Raymond L., and Manuel Rodríguez Saavedra. "Fernando Lles y Berdayes." In their Vida y obras de autores cubanos (H: "Alfa", 1940-), I, 113-115.

59.5 Lizaso y González, Félix. "Fernando Lles." In his Ensayistas contemporáneos, 1900-1920 (H: Trópico, 1938), pp. 102-105.

59.6 Martínez, Emilio. "[Sol de invierno]." Bohemia, 2, 27 (1911), 229-230.

59.7 Martínez Bosch, M. "[La higuera de Timón]." EspN, 2, 23 (1922), 8-9.

59.8 Nodarse y Cabrera, José J. "La filosofía social y política de Lles." RevC, 27 (1950), 89-101.

59.9 Páez, Alfonso E. "A propósito de la conferencia de Lles sobre individualismo, socialismo y comunismo." ULH, No. 4 (1934), 185-192.

59.10 Rodríguez Rivero, Luis. "Noticia bibliográfica de Fernando Lles y Berdayes." RevC, 27 (1950), 111-122.

59.11 Russinyol, José. "Fernando Lles: el hombre y el medio." RevC, 27 (1950), 102-110.

59.12 Varona y Pera, Enrique José. "Cartas de Enrique José Varona y a Fernando Lles y Berdayes." RevC, 27 (1950), 123-125.

59.13 Vitier, Medardo. "Fernando Lles." In his Apuntaciones literarias (H: Minerva, 1935), pp. 165-169.

59.14 ____. "Fernando Lles, escritor." RevC, 27 (1950), 75-81.

60. LOVEIRA Y CHIRINO, CARLOS (1882-1928)

Bibliographies

60.1 Gay Calbó, Enrique. "Bibliografía de Generales y doctores." CCont, 26 (1921), 183-185.

60.2 _____. "Bibliografía de Los ciegos." CCont, 30 (1922), 101-109.

60.3 _____. "Bibliografía de Los inmortales." CCont, 19 (1921), 183-185.

Critical Monographs and Dissertations

60.4 Agüero Vives, Eduardo. Carlos Loveira. Un activo trabajador social. Apuntes biográficos de Carlos Loveira. H: C. González, 1946.

60.5 Marqués, Sarah. Arte y sociedad en las novelas de Carlos Loveira. Miami: Universal, 1977. Orig. DAI. 37 (1976), 1583A.

60.6 Martínez, Miguel A. "Visión cubana de Carlos Loveira." DAI, 30 (1970), 3016A-3017A.

60.7 Ortúzar-Young, Ada. "Tres representaciones literarias de la vida política cubana." DAI, 40 (1979), 2711A-2712A. Loveira, L. F. Rodríguez, J. A. Ramos.

Critical Essays

60.8 Aguirre, Mirta. "Carlos Loveira. Generales y doctores." CSoc, No. 21 (1963), 132-139.

60.9 _____. "Las novelas de Loveira." Revolución, 1-IX-1965, p. 3.

60.10 Alba-Buffill, Elio. "Carlos Loveira y Chirino (1882-1928): sus obras." Círculo, 4 (1973-1974), 118-119.

60.11 _____. "Loveira y Zeno Gandía: representantes del naturalismo en las Antillas." In Estudios literarios sobre Hispanoamérica (homenaje a Carlos M. Raggi y Ageo) (San José, Costa Rica: Círculo de Cultura Panamericana, 1976), pp. 85-96.

60.12 _____. "El naturalismo en la obra de Carlos Loveira." Círculo, 4 (1973-1974), 106-117.

60.13 Branly, Roberto. "Carlos Loveira: imagen de un tiempo supera-do." PyC, No. 14 (1963), 19-23.

60.14 Bravet, Rogelio Luis. "Las viejas verdades [Generales y docto-res]." Bohemia, 55, 24 (1963), 58-59.

60.15 Bryant, Shasta M., and J. Riis Owre. "Introduction." In Carlos Loveira y Chirino, Generales y doctores (a novel of Cuban life) (NY: Oxford University Press, 1965), no pagination.

60.16 Bueno, Salvador. "Carlos Loveira. 1882-1929." CubaI, No. 60 (1974), 58.

60.17 ____. "Lo que se sabe de Carlos Loveira." Revolución, 1-XI-1965, p. 3.

60.18 Catalá, Ramón. "Divagaciones sobre la novela." AANAL, 10 (1926), 60-93.

60.19 Entralgo, Elías José. "Generales y doctores." In his Perfiles (apuntes críticos sobre literatura cubana contemporánea) (H: "Hermes", 1923), pp. 129-136.

60.20 Espinosa, Ciro. "Juicio sobre la novela Los ciegos." In his Indagación y crítica; novelistas cubanos (H: Cultural, 1940), pp. 49-118. See also "Datos biográficos de Carlos Loveira," pp. 47-48.

60.21 Fernández Retamar, Roberto. "De Generales y doctores a coman-dantes y licenciados." In his Papelería (Santa Clara: Uni-versidad Central de Las Villas, Dirección de Publicaciones, 1962), pp. 209-212.

60.22 Lavié, Nemesio. "Carlos Loveira." Archipiélago, No. 8 (1928), 130, 140.

60.23 Leante, César. "La república de Juan Criollo." RyC, 2a época, No. 1 (1972), 70-82. Also CA, No. 184 (1972), 139-150. Also in his El espacio real (H: Unión de Escritores y Ar-tistas de Cuba, 1975), pp. 43-57.

60.24 "Loveira, académico." CCont, 38 (1925), 210.

60.25 Marinello, Juan. "[Juan Criollo]." Avance, No. 22 (1928), 130.

60.26 Martínez, Miguel A. "Causa, tesis y tema en la novela de Carlos Loveira." Hispania, 54 (1971), 73-79.

60.27 ____. "The multiple meaning of 'Liborio' in the novels of Car-los Loveira." CarS, 12, 4 (1973), 92-95.

60.28 ____. "Los personajes secundarios en las novelas de Carlos Lo-veira." Hispania, 56 (1973), 1030-1039.

60.29 Martínez Márquez, Guillermo. "Carlos Loveira, su vida y su o-
       bra." RAm, 18 (1929), 249-250, 325-326. Also Social, 14,
       2 (1929), 38-40; 14, 3 (1929), 42; 14, 4 (1929), 26-30.

60.30 Montori, Arturo. "Las novelas de Carlos Loveira." CCont, 30
       (1922), 213-239.

60.31 "La muerte de Carlos Loveira." Avance, No. 29 (1928), 362.

60.32 Nieves, Dolores. "Juan Criollo y la novela picaresca." Bohe-
       mia, 66, 22 (1974), 10-13.

60.33 Owre, J. Riis. "Carlos Loveira, novelista cubano que previó la
       trageida." In Actas del Segundo Congreso Internacional de
       Hispanistas (Nijmegen: Universidad de Nimega, Instituto Es-
       pañol, 1967), pp. 457-465.

60.34 _____. "Carlos Loveira's Los inmorales." REH, 5 (1972), 321-
       332.

60.35 _____. "Generales y doctores after forty-five years." JIAS,
       8 (1966), 371-385.

60.36 _____. "Juan Criollo after forty years." JIAS, 9 (1967), 396-
       412.

60.37 Parajón, Mario. "Juan Criollo." Bohemia, 6, 26 (1969), 6-7.

60.38 Pogolotti, Marcelo. "[Loveira]." In his La república de Cuba
       al través de sus escritores (H: Lex, 1958), pp. 48-50, 60-
       62, 79-81.

60.39 Ripoll, Carlos. "Estudio preliminar." In Carlos Loveira y Chi-
       rino, Juan Criollo (NY: Las Américas, 1964), pp. v-xxviii.

60.40 Rodríguez, César. "[Los ciegos]." EspN, No. 43 (1922), 9-10.

60.41 Roig de Leuchsenring, Emilio. "Carlos Loveira." Social, 11, 1
       (1926), 7-8.

60.42 Spell, Jefferson Rea. "Carlos Loveira, advocate of a new moral-
       ity for Cuba." In his Contemporary Spanish American fic-
       tion (Chapel Hill, N.C.: University of North Carolina
       Press, 1944), pp. 101-134.

60.43 Torriente, Loló de la. "La Habana de Carlos Loveira." Carte-
       les, No. 18 (1960), 54-55, 70-71.

60.44 Ulloa, Rebeca. "La realidad nacional en tres novelistas de la
       república mediatizada." TallerC, No. 28 (1974), 26-29.

60.45 Verdecía, Luis Ernesto. "Introspección objetiva a una novela
       cubana [Juan Criollo]." TallerC, No. 22 (1971), 4-8.

61. LOYNAZ, DULCE MARIA (1903-   )

Critical Monographs and Dissertations

61.1   Boza Masvidal, Aurelio. Dulce María Loynaz: poesía, ensueño y
        silencio. H: Universidad de la Habana, 1948. Same as
        item no. 61.4

61.2   Carbonell y Rivero, Miguel Angel. Esquema de Dulce María Loy-
        naz de Alvarez Cañas. H: Academia Nacional de Artes y
        Letras, 1951.

61.3   Cuéllar de la Paz, Aída. Ala y raíz en el Jardin de Dulce Ma-
        ría Loynaz. H, 1950.

Critical Essays

61.4   Boza Masvidal, Aurelio. "Dulce María Loynaz: poesía, ensueño
        y silencio." ULH, Nos. 82-87 (1949), 87-108. Same as
        item no. 61.1

61.5   Bueno, Salvador. "Notas sobre la prosa poética de Dulce María
        Loynaz." CUNESCO, 3, 1 (1954), 1-3.

61.6   Conde, Carmen. "Poetisas de lengua española: Dulce María Loy-
        naz de Cuba." MHisp, No. 154 (1961), 29.

61.7   Fernández de la Vega, Oscar. "Nota bibliográfica al estudio de
        Aurelio Boza Masvidal." RFD, abril 1950, p. 78. See item
        no. 61.1.

61.8   González-Ruano, César. "[Dulce María Loynaz]." In his Litera-
        tura americana; ensayos de madrigal y de crítica (I. Poe-
        tisas modernas) (Madrid: Fernando Fe, 1924), pp. 134-139.

61.9   Jimenes Grullón, Juan Isidro. "Dulce María Loynaz." In his
        Seis poetas cubanos (ensayos apologéticos) (H: "Cromos",
        1954), pp. 113-142.

61.10   Jiménez, Juan Ramón. "Dulce María Loynaz (1937)." In his Espa-
        ñoles de tres mundos (BA: Losada, 1942), pp. 136-140.

61.11   Lombardo, Oscar. "Figulina de ensueño... Dulce María Loynaz
        y Muñoz. La poesía de unos ojos y el alma de un poema."
        Bohemia, 12, 30 (1921), 6, 21.

61.12 Marquina, Rafael. "Una poetisa cubana. Dulce María Loynaz."
       Lyceum, Nos. 11-12 (1938), 26-48.

61.13 _____. "[Versos. 1920-1938]." RevC, 19 (1945), 149-150.

61.14 Martínez Bello, Antonio. "[Carta de amor a Tut-Ank-Amen]."
       RBNC, 2a serie, 5, 2 (1954), 150-152.

61.15 _____. "Dulce María Loynaz. Jardín. Novela lírica." RBNC,
       2a serie, 3, 2 (1952), 314-319.

61.16 Sainz de Robles, Federico Carlos. "Dulce María Loynaz." In
       Dulce María Loynaz, Obra lírica (Madrid: Aguilar, 1955),
       pp. 11-14.

61.17 Valdés de la Paz, Osvaldo. "Gabriela Mistral y Dulce María
       Loynaz, las dos poetisas, se encuentran en Italia." Car-
       teles, No. 38 (1951), 78-80.

62. LUACES, JOAQUIN LORENZO (1826-1867)

Critical Monographs and Dissertations

62.1   Salazar y Roig, Salvador. Milanés, Luaces y la Avellaneda como poetas dramáticos. H: Miranda, 1916.

Critical Essays

62.2   Arrufat, Antón. "Aviso sobre el teatro de Luaces." Unión, 4, 3 (1965), 174-178.

62.3   Bielsa Vives, Manuel. "Los sonetos de Joaquín Lorenzo Luaces." In his Cosas de ayer (H: La Correspondencia, 1906), pp. 87-97.

62.4   Blanchet, Emilio. "Joaquín Lorenzo Luaces." RFLC, 16, 1 (1913), 23-45.

62.5   Bueno, Salvador. "El centenario de Joaquín Lorenzo Luaces." RBNJM, 3a serie, 10, 1 (1968), 100-108.

62.6   _____. "Joaquín Lorenzo Luaces, poeta y dramaturgo." In his Figuras cubanas del siglo XIX (H: Unión de Escritores y Artistas, 1980), pp. 129-133.

62.7   Chaple, Sergio. "Notas sobre la poesía de Joaquín Lorenzo Luaces." L/L, Nos. 3-4 (1972-1973), 150-171.

62.8   Doubon, Alvaro S. "Pequeñas biografías: Joaquín Lorenzo Luaces, poeta y dramaturgo." Carteles, 34, 26 (1953), 24.

62.9   Fornaris, José. "Con motivo de las anacreónticas de Joaquín Lorenzo Luaces." CubaL, No. 1 (1861), 268-274.

62.10   _____. "Poetas cubanos: Joaquín Lorenzo Luaces." RCub, 11 (1881), 561-567.

62.11   González del Valle y Carbajal, Emilio Martín. "Joaquín Lorenzo Luaces." In his La poesía lírica en Cuba (Barcelona: Luis Tasso, 1900), pp. 189-217.

62.12   González Freire, Natividad. "[El fantasmón de Aravaca]." Bohemia, 66, 16 (1974), 21; 66, 17 (1974), 27.

62.13   Leal, Rine. "Luaces, nuestro desconocido." Islas, No. 38 (1971), 89-93.

62.14 No item.

62.15 Montes Huidobro, Matías. "La reacción antijerárquica en el teatro cubano colonial [El becerro de oro]." CHA, No. 334 (1978), 5-19.

62.16 Nieto y Cortadellas, Rafael. "Documentos sacramentales de algunos cubanos ilustres." RBNC, 2a serie, 6, 3 (1955), 159-171.

62.17 _____. "Obras póstumas de Joaquín Lorenzo Luaces." RCub, 4 (1878), 441-448.

62.18 Piñeyro, Enrique. "Poesías de Luaces." RCub, 14 (1883), 564-572.

62.19 _____. "Una tragedia griega por un poeta cubano." In Joaquín Lorenzo Luaces, Aristodemo; tragedia (H: Comisión Cubana de Publicaciones, 1919), pp. v-xiii.

62.20 Poncet y de Cárdenas, Carolina. "Algunos aspectos de la poesía de Joaquín Lorenzo Luaces." In Miscelánea de estudios dedicados a Fernando Ortiz (H, 1955), pp. 1225-1233.

62.21 Sánchez de Bustamante y Sirvén, Antonio. "Discurso sobre Joaquín L. Luaces..." In his Discursos (H: El Siglo XX, 1923), V, 5-28.

62.22 Sanguily y Garritte, Manuel. "José María Heredia." In his Discursos y conferencias (H: Rambla, Bousa, 1918), I, 218-223. On Heredia and Luaces.

62.23 Vitier, Cintio. "El obrero." In his Poetas cubanos del siglo XIX; semblanzas (H: Unión, 1969), pp. 36-39.

62.24 Zambrana, Ramón. "[Luaces]." In his Soliloquios (H: La Intrépida, 1865), pp. 140-141.

63. LUZ Y CABALLERO, JOSE DE LA (1800-1862)

Bibliographies

63.1 Figarola-Caneda, Domingo. Bibliografía de Luz y Caballero.
H: El Siglo XX, 1915.

Critical Monographs and Dissertations

63.2 Agramonte y Pichardo, Roberto. Prédica y ejemplo de Luz y Caballero. H, 1950.

63.3 Entralgo, Elías. Dos arquetipos para una deontología cubana:
Don Pepe y el generalismo. H: Universidad de la Habana,
1952.

63.4 Esténger, Rafael. Don Pepe, retrato de un maestro de escuela.
H: Alfa, 1940.

63.5 González del Valle y Ramírez, Francisco. La conspiración de La
Escalera. I. José de la Luz y Caballero. H: El Siglo XX,
1925.

63.6 _____. Dos orientadores de la enseñanza: el padre José Agustín
Caballero y José de la Luz y Caballero. H: Molina, 1935.

63.7 _____. José de la Luz y los católicos españoles. H: Cuba Contemporánea, 1919.

63.8 Guerra, Ramiro. José de la Luz y Caballero como político. H:
Universidad Central de Las Villas, 1957.

63.9 Luz y Duarte, Francisco de la. Don José de la Luz y Caballero.
Datos biográficos, recopilación de escritos sobre su muerte, así como los aforismos, pensamientos y artículos más
interesantes del sabio maestro. H: Rambla, Bouza, 1913.

63.10 Mañach, Jorge. Luz y "El Salvador". H: Siglo XX, 1948.

63.11 Méndez, Manuel Isidoro. Notas para el estudio de las ideas éticas en Cuba (siglo XIX: José A. Caballero, Félix Varela y
José de la Luz y Caballero). H: Lex, 1947.

63.12 Mesa Rodríguez, Manuel I. Don José de la Luz y Caballero (biografía documental). H: La Logia Realidad No. 8, 1947.

63.13 _____. José de la Luz y Caballero, maestro de una gran generación. H: Oficina del Historiador de la Ciudad, 1956.

63.14 _____. Tres retratos de Luz y Caballero. H: El Siglo XX, 1950.

63.15 Páez, Alfonso E. Estudio sobre José de la Luz Caballero. H: Imprenta Cubana, 1914.

63.16 Pérez Cabrera, José Manuel. El texto de lectura de Luz y Caballero. H, 1937.

63.17 Rodríguez, Carlos Rafael. José de la Luz y Caballero. H: Revista Fundamentos, 1947.

63.18 Rodríguez, José Ignacio. Vida de don José de la Luz y Caballero. NY: El Mundo Nuevo-La América Ilustrada, 1874. 2. ed., aum. y corr., NY: N. Ponce de León, 1878.

63.19 Saíz de la Mora, Jesús. José de la Luz y Caballero; influencia social y política de su labor educativa. H: El Dante, 1929.

63.20 Sanguily y Garritte, Manuel. José de la Luz y Caballero. H: C. Blasco, 1913.

63.21 _____. José de la Luz y Caballero (estudio crítico). H: O'Reilly 9, 1890. Also H: A. Dorrbecker, 1926. Also H: Consejo Nacional de Cultura, 1962.

63.22 Soto Paz, Rafael. La falsa cubanidad de Saco, Luz y del Monte. H: Alfa, 1941.

63.23 Vitier, Medardo. José de la Luz y Caballero como educador. H: Universidad Central de Las Villas, 1956.

Critical Essays

63.24 Agramonte Simoni, Arístides. "Don José de la Luz en la Sociedad Económica." RBC, 26 (1930), 186-188.

63.25 Bueno, Salvador. "José de la Luz y Caballero, maestro y pensador." In his Figuras cubanas del siglo XIX (H: Unión de Escritores y Artistas, 1980), pp. 43-53.

63.26 Cabrera, Raimundo. "[Carta abierta ... sobre la estatua en bronce de José de la Luz y Caballero]." RBC, 7 (1912), 316-320.

63.27 Casas, Antonio. "Con ocasión de hacerse cargo José de la Luz y Caballero de la dirección del Colegio del Carraguao." RdC, 14 (1883), 193-200.

63.28 Chacón y Calvo, José María. "Maestro y discípulo: José de la Luz y Caballero y Manuel Sanguily." Abside, 27 (1963), 5-28.

63.29 "Corrigenda a la edición de los aforismos de Luz." ULH, Nos. 58-60 (1945), 1-2.

63.30 Cruz, Manuel de la. "José de la Luz y Caballero." In his <u>La literatura cubana</u> (H: Saturnino Calleja, 1924), pp. 149-154.

63.31 Delgado Fernández, Gregorio. "Los enlaces genealógicos cubanos del appelido Luz." <u>RBC</u>, 47 (1941), 232-243.

63.32 González del Valle y Ramírez, Francisco. "'José de la Luz y Caballero y la Biblioteca de la Sociedad Económica." <u>RBC</u>, 37 (1936), 77-83.

63.33 _____. "José de la Luz y los católicos españoles." <u>CCont</u>, 20 (1919), 165-219.

63.34 _____. "Páginas para la historia de Cuba: documentos para la biografía de José de la Luz y Caballero." <u>CCont</u>, 26 (1921), 139-157, 245-250, 389-395; 27 (1921), 173-182, 253-260, 357-364; 28 (1922), 230-240, 314-323; 29 (1922), 172-184, 368-373; 30 (1922), 86-96.

63.35 _____. "La personalidad de Luz y Caballero." <u>RevC</u>, 2, 4-6 (1935), 251-264.

63.36 _____. "El propuesto traslado de la estatua de José de la Luz y Caballero." <u>CCont</u>, 41 (1926), 275-280.

63.37 Gordillo G., Miguel Angel. "José de la Luz y Caballero, 1800-1862." <u>RevEG</u>, junio 1943, pp. 198-203.

63.38 Guardia, J. M. "Filósofos españoles de Cuba: Félix Varela y José de la Luz." <u>RCub</u>, 25 (1892), 233-247, 412-427, 493-502.

63.39 Guerra, Ramiro. "La preparación de los maestros: Luz Caballero y las Escuelas Normales." <u>CCont</u>, 12 (1916), 274-292.

63.40 López del Amo, Rolando. "José de la Luz y Caballero visto por Manuel Sanguily." <u>ULH</u>, No. 195 (1972), 179-182.

63.41 Mañach, Jorge. "'El Salvador', vivero de hombres." <u>Bohemia</u>, 40, (1948), 24, 56.

63.42 Martí, José. "Cartas inéditas y José de la Luz." In his <u>Obras completas</u> (H: Editorial Nacional de Cuba, 1963), V, 249-250.

63.43 _____. "José de la Luz." In his <u>Obras completas</u> (H: Editorial Nacional de Cuba, 1963), V, 271-273.

63.44 Maza, Piedad de la. "Ideas pedagógicas de d. José de la Luz y Caballero." <u>RFLC</u>, 34, 1-2 (1924), 111-139; 34, 3-4 (1924), 346-391; 35, 1-2 (1925), 74-108.

63.45 Medrano, Higinio J. "José de la Luz y Caballero, profesor de idealismo." <u>RevC</u>, 24 (1949), 103-143.

63.46   Merchán, Rafael María. "El espinar cubano y la segur barran-
        tina." In his Variedades (Bogotá: La Luz, 1894), pp. 169-
        177.

63.47   Mesa Rodríguez, Manuel I. "Don José de la Luz y Caballero."
        RBC, 37 (1937), 84-88.

63.48   _____. "José de la Luz y Caballero. Consideraciones en el cen-
        tenario de su muerte. 1862-1962." RBNJM, 3a serie, 2,
        1-4 (1960), 7-28.

63.49   _____. "Don José de la Luz y la mujer. Conversación para muje-
        res." Trimestre, 3, 3 (1949), 341-352.

63.50   Monal, Isabel. "Tres filósofos del centenario." ULH, No. 192
        (1968), 111-129. Luz y Caballero inter alios.

63.51   "Monumento a Luz y Caballero." RBNC, 1, 1-2 (1909), 48-51.

63.52   Moreno Davis, Julio César. "Esbozo biográfico y pensamiento fi-
        losófico de José de la Luz y Caballero." Lotería, No. 262
        (1977), 69-110.

63.53   Mouillaron, Adolphe. "José de la Luz y Caballero." RBNC, 1,
        1-2 (1909), 10.

63.54   Páez, Alfonso E. "José de la Luz y Caballero, desde el punto
        de vista científico." AAHC, 19 (1937), 107-121.

63.55   Pichardo, Hortensia. "Fundación e historia del Colegio de Ca-
        raguao." RevE, 3a época, 1, 8 (1924), 398-408.

63.56   _____. "El plan de estudios de Carraguao." RevE, 3a época, 1,
        9 (1924), 573-596.

63.57   Piñeyro, Enrique. "José de la Luz y Caballero." In his Hombres
        y glorias de América (Paris: Garnier, 1903), pp. 157-203.

63.58   Remos y Rubio, Juan Nepomuceno José. "El colegio de don Pepe."
        In his Micrófano (H: Molina, 1937), pp. 147-154.

63.59   Rodríguez, Manuel V. "José de la Luz y Caballero." RFLC, 10
        (1910), 225-243.

63.60   Roig de Leuschsenring, Emilio. "Don José de la Luz y Caballe-
        ro nunca poseyó esclavos." Carteles, 28, 27 (1947), 42-43.

63.61   _____. "José de la Luz y Caballero, decidido y valiente anti-
        esclavista." Carteles, 28, 26 (1947), 42-43.

63.62   _____. "José de la Luz y Caballero, fundador de la nación cuba-
        na." Carteles, 35, 27 (1954), 61-66.

63.63   _____. "El patriotismo cubanísimo de José de la Luz y Caballe-
        ro." Carteles, 28, 28 (1947), 42-43.

63.64 Sanguily y Garritte, Manuel. "José de la Luz y Caballero y su biografía." <u>RCub</u>, 2 (1885), 385-420.

63.65 Santovenia y Echaide, Emeterio Santiago. "La locura de Luz y Caballero." <u>Bohemia</u>, 42, 28 (1950), 40-41, 105.

63.66 ____. "Luz y Caballero y la revolución de Lincoln." <u>Carteles</u>, 27-VI-1948, p. 11.

63.67 Torriente, Loló de la. "Raíz y fronda." <u>Unión</u>, 4, 4 (1965), 128-146.

63.68 Valdés Rodríguez, José Manuel. "José de la Luz y Caballero. Discurso pronunciado en la Universidad." <u>RBC</u>, 8 (1913), 5-24.

63.69 Varona y Pera, Enrique José. "Lección inaugural." In his <u>Conferencias filosóficas (primera serie)</u>. <u>Lógica</u> (H: Soler, 1880), pp. 7-29.

63.70 ____. "Luz y Caballero." In his <u>Artículos y discursos (literatura--política--sociología)</u> (H: A. Alvarez, 1891), pp. 285-299.

63.71 ____. "Luz y Caballero; a propósito del libro del señor Sanguily." <u>RBC</u>, 12 (1890), 97-106. See item no. 63.21.

63.72 ____. "El padre Varela, los González del Valle, Luz y Caballero, Mestre, Bachiller y Morales." In <u>El libro de Cuba</u> (H: Molina, 1925), pp. 563-565.

63.73 Vitier, Medardo. "Las doctrinas filósoficas en Cuba (síntesis de un curso)." In his <u>Valoraciones</u> (H: Universidad Central de Las Villas, 1961), II, 28-62.

63.74 ____. "José de la Luz y Caballero." In his <u>Estudios, notas, efigies cubanas</u> (H: Minerva, 1944), pp. 228-234.

63.75 ____. "José de la Luz y Caballero; sus ideas filosóficas." In <u>Las ideas y la filosofía en Cuba</u> (H: Ciencias Sociales, 1970), pp. 373-390.

63.76 ____. "José de la Luz y Caballero: vida y escritos." In his <u>Las ideas y la filosofía en Cuba</u> (H: Ciencias Sociales, 1970), pp. 359-371.

63.77 ____. "¿Volver a José de la Luz." In his <u>Valoraciones</u> (H: Universidad Central de Las Villas, 1960), I, 331-334.

63.78 Zambrana, Ramón. "Elogio de d. José de la Luz." In his <u>Trabajos académicos</u> (H: La Intrépida, 1865), pp. 7-22.

63.79 Zayas y Alfonso, Alfredo. "Ante la estatua de Luz y Caballero." In his <u>Discursos y conferencias</u> (H: Molina, 1942), II, 54-58.

63.80 _____. "Don José de la Luz." <u>RdC</u>, 6 (1879), 78-94.

63.81 _____. "Un episodio de la vida de tres hombres célebres." <u>RCub</u>, 9 (1890), 367-378.

63.82 _____. "Por la gloria de Luz y Caballero." In his <u>Discursos y conferencias</u> (H: Molina, 1942), I, 152-157.

64. MAÑACH, JORGE (1898-1961)

Bibliographies

64.1 Gay Calbó, Enrique. "Bibliografía. Jorge Mañach." CCont, 15 (1927), 358-369.

Critical Monographs and Dissertations

64.2 Alvarez, Nicolás Emilio. La obra literaria de Jorge Mañach. Potomac, Md.: José Porrúa Turanzas, 1979.

64.3 Jorge Mañach (1898-1961): homenaje de la nación cubana. San Juan, P.R.: San Juan, 1972. Pertinent items are listed separately.

64.4 Martí, Jorge Luis. El periodismo literario de Jorge Mañach. Río Piedras, P.R.: Editorial Universitaria, Universidad de Puerto Rico, 1977.

64.5 O'Cherony, Rosalyn Krantzler. "The critical essays of Jorge Mañach." DAI, 31 (1971), 6067A.

64.6 Pinto Albiol, Angel César. El Dr. Mañach y el problema negro. H: Nuevos Rumbos, 1949.

64.7 Santovenia y Echaide, Emeterio Santiago. Discursos leídos en la recepción pública del Dr. Jorge Mañach y Robeto. H: El Siglo XX, 1943.

64.8 Sternlicht, Madeline. "Man or myth: José Martí in the biographies of Jorge Mañach, Alberto Baeza Flores, and Ezequiel Martínez Estrada." DAI, 37 (1977), 4390A-4391A.

64.9 Torre, Amalia María V. de la. Jorge Mañach, maestro del ensayo. Miami: Universal, 1978. Orig. DAI, 36 (1976), 5333A.

64.10 Valdespino, Andrés. Jorge Mañach y su generación en las letras cubanas. Miami: Universal, 1971. Orig. as "Significación literaria de Jorge Mañach." DAI, 30 (1969), 344A.

Critical Essays

64.11 Abela, Eduardo. "El futuro artista [La nueva estética]." Avance, No. 5 (1927), 104-105.

64.12   Acosta, Agustín. "Al Dr. Jorge Mañach, en la Habana." BACL,
        10 (1961), 14-18.

64.13   Agramonte y Pichardo, Roberto. "Recordando a Jorge Mañach."
        Círculo, 10 (1981), 41-46.

64.14   Alfonso Roselló, Arturo. "El Cuarto Salón de Humoristas, in-
        terview con un crítico." Carteles, 7-XII-1924, pp. 10, 22.

64.15   Alvarez, Nicolás Emilio. "Martí y Mañach: análisis estilístico
        de un panegírico." ExTL, 7, 1 (1978), 43-51.

64.16   Arias, Augusto. "Recuerdo de Jorge Mañach." LetE, No. 124
        (1961), 1, 13.

64.17   Arredondo, Alberto. "Veinticuatro horas de la vida de Jorge
        Mañach." Bohemia, 28, 21 (1946), 42-47, 49, 56-58, 64-66.

64.18   Baeza Flores, Alberto. "Hacia un humanismo: Jorge Mañach." In
        his Cuba, el laurel y la palma; ensayos literarios (Miami:
        Universal, 1977), pp. 117-142.

64.19   Baquero, Gastón. "Jorge Mañach o la tragedia de la inteligencia
        en la América hispana." CubaN, 1 (1962), 18-30.

64.20   Baralt, Luis. "Presentación del Dr. Jorge Mañach." Ultra, No.
        29 (1938), 470-471.

64.21   Boti, Regino E. "Baedeker ilusionado: Estampas de San Cristó-
        bal." Avance, No. 4 (1927), 88-89.

64.22   Braschi, Wilfredo. "Jorge Mañach y su paso por Puerto Rico."
        In Jorge Mañach, q.v., pp. 137-140.

64.23   Cano, José Luis. "Jorge Mañach." Insula, Nos. 176-177 (1961),
        2.

64.24   _____. "[Vistas españolas]." Insula, Nos. 164-165 (1960), 17.

64.25   Chacón y Calvo, José María. "Nota bibliográfica sobre Historia
        y estilo de Jorge Mañach." RevC, 18 (1944), 183-186.

64.26   Costa, Octavio Ramón. "Jorge Mañach." In his Diez cubanos (H:
        Ucar, García, 1944), pp. 83-98.

64.27   _____. "Mañach intuitivo." CyE, No. 26 (194?), 47.

64.28   "En recuerdo a Jorge Mañach." BACL, 10 (1961), 5-45.

64.29   García-Castro, Ramón. "[Vistas españolas]." CHA, No. 44
        (1960), 501-505.

64.30   Gómez Reinoso, Manuel. "Aspectos humanos de Jorge Mañach."
        In Homenaje a Humberto Piñero: estudios de literatura, ar-
        te e historia (Madrid: Playor, 1979), pp. 97-104.

64.31   González, Manuel Pedro.   "En torno a los nuevos." Hispania, 13
        (1930), 95-104. Also RBC, 35 (1930), 382-393. Mañach in-
        ter alios.

64.32   _____. "Jorge Mañach." Nosotros, No. 252 (1930), 282-284.

64.33   Grismer, Raymond L., and Manuel Rodríguez Saavedra. "Jorge Ma-
        ñach y Robato." In their Vida y obras de autores cubanos
        (H: "Alfa", 1940-), I, 13-16.

64.34   Gutiérrez Delgado, Luis. "Jorge Mañach, Cuban man of letters."
        Américas, 13, 11 (1961), 26-28. Also as "Jorge Mañach,
        hombre de letras." Américas [Spanish edition], 13, 12
        (1961), 26-28.

64.35   "Homenaje a Jorge Mañach." RevC, 15 (1941), 274-277.

64.36   "Jorge Mañach." Horizontes, No. 21 (1961), 5-7.

64.37   Lezama Lima, José. "Carta abierta a Jorge Mañach. Respuesta
        y nuevas interrogaciones." Bohemia,   (1949), 77.

64.38   Llés, Fernando. "La obra perdurable en un ensayista cubano,
        Estampas de San Cristóbal." Social, 12 (1927), 35, 66.

64.39   López Morales, Humberto. "Magister et amicus." BACL, 10
        (1961), 43-45.

64.40   Marinello, Juan. "Sobre Mañach y su Glosario." Social, 11
        (1924), 20, 70, 76.

64.41   Martí, Jorge Luis. "Mañach y su legado cívico." In Jorge Ma-
        ñach, q.v., pp. 21-33.

64.42   _____. "Mocedad de Jorge Mañach." Círculo, 7 (1978), 33-43.

64.43   Meléndez, Concha. "La inquietud cubana en la universal quie-
        tud." AtP, 2, 2 (1936), 94-107.

64.44   _____. "Jorge Mañach en su última frontera." La torre, No. 65
        (1969), 11-27.

64.45   _____. "Jorge Mañach y la inquietud cubana." In her Signos de
        Iberoamérica (M: Manuel León Sánchez, 1936), pp. 153-167.

64.46   Mercuelo, Otto. "Réplica lo que ayer sirvió a la dictadura y
        hoy combate la revolución." Bohemia, 44, 31 (1952), 88-91.

64.47   Mistral, Gabriela. "Algo sobre Jorge Mañach." AJM, 5 (1952),
        250-252. Also RdAm, No. 43 (1948), 33-36.

64.48   _____. "Prólogo." In Jorge Mañach, Martí, el apóstol (NY: Las
        Américas, 1963), pp. 7-10. Also as "On Mañach." In Jorge
        Mañach, Martí; apostol of freedom (NY: Devin-Adair, 1970),
        pp. xiii-xvi.

64.49   "Notas del Director Literario. Los nuevos. Jorge Mañach." So-
        cial, 10 (1925), 7-8.

64.50   Ortega, Antonio. "Raíz y ala de Jorge Mañach." In Jorge Mañach,
        q.v., pp. 129-136.

64.51   Pego, Aurelio. "Jorge Mañach, una pluma elegante." Horizontes,
        No. 21 (1961), 8, 32.

64.52   Rexach, Rosario. "La estructura de los ensayos de Jorge Mañach."
        Círculo, 7 (1978), 9-31.

64.53   Riaño Jauma, Ricardo. "Jorge Mañach." RevC, 20 (1945), 99-111.

64.54   Roa, Raúl. "Mañach y el choteo [Indagación del choteo]." Avan-
        ce, No. 27 (1928), 292-293.

64.55   _____. [Tiempo muerto]." Avance, No. 22 (1928), 131-132.

64.56   Sánchez, Luis Alberto. "Elogio de Jorge Mañach." ND, 41, 4
        (1961), 24-27.

64.57   _____. "Recuerdo de Jorge Mañach." In Jorge Mañach, q.v., pp.
        63-64.

64.58   Sánchez de Bustamante y Montoro, Antonio. "Contestación al dis-
        curso de ingreso del académico Dr. Jorge Mañach y Robato."
        AANAL, 25 (1944), 90-98.

64.59   _____. "Homenaje a Jorge Mañach." In his Ironía y generación;
        ensayos (H, 1937), pp. 147-157.

64.60   Santovenia y Echaide, Emeterio Santiago. "Jorge Mañach." In
        his Vidas humanas (H: Librería Martí, 1956), pp. 488-492.

64.61   Souvirón, José María. "Conversaciones con Jorge Mañach." CHA,
        No. 139 (1961), 79-81.

64.62   _____. "Palabras sobre Jorge Mañach." CHA, No. 93 (1957),
        409-411.

64.63   Tamargo, Agustín. "Mañach: una inteligencia que sirvió sin re-
        bajarse." In Jorge Mañach, q.v., pp. 121-127.

64.64   Unamuno y Jugo, Miguel de. "De Unamuno a Mañach [Indagación del
        choteo]." Avance, No. 30 (1929), 30.

64.65   Valdespino, Andrés. "Jorge Mañach y su contribución a la cultu-
        ra hispanoamericana." La torre, No. 68 (1970), 101-113.

64.66   Valle, Rafael Heliodoro. "Diálogo con Jorge Mañach." UM, No.
        48 (1950), 19-21.

64.67   Villoldo, Julio. "[Glosario]." CCont, 12 (1924), 357-358.

64.68 Vitier, Medardo. "Carta abierta a Jorge Mañach." <u>Bohemia</u>, 38,
       21 (1946), 20, 63.

64.69 _____. "Jorge Mañach." In his <u>Apuntaciones literarias</u> (H: Mi-
       nerva, 1935), pp. 159-164.

64.70 Zavala, Luis de. "La ilusión del Dr. Mañach." <u>Lectura</u>, 81-82,
       1 (1951), 50-60.

65. MANZANO, JUAN FRANCISCO (1797-1854)

Critical Essays

65.1 Bueno, Salvador. "La autobiografía de Manzano en húngaro. Crónica." RBNJM, 3a serie, 63, 2 (1972), 172-173.

65.2 Calcagno, Francisco. "Juan Francisco Manzano." In his Poetas de color (H: Soler, 1878), pp. 25-46.

65.3 _____. "Poetas cubanos: Juan Francisco Manzano." RdC, 4 (1878), 456-476.

65.4 Chang-Rodríguez, Raquel. "[Autobiografía de un esclavo]." RCLL, No. 3 (1970), 109-111.

65.5 Del Monte, Ricardo. "Paralelo entre Plácido y Manzano." RdC, 4 (1878), 476-477.

65.6 Franco, José Luciano. "Juan Francisco Manzano, el poeta esclavo y su tiempo." In Juan Francisco Manzano, Autobiografía, carta y versos (H: Municipio de la Habana, 1937), pp. 9-32.

65.7 Friol, Roberto. "Juan Francisco Manzano." Bohemia, 70, 3 (1978), 10-14.

65.8 Gallina, Annamaria. "[Autobiografía de un esclavo]." QIA, Nos. 49-50 (1977), 102-103.

65.9 García Marruz, Fina. "De Estudios delmontinos: el caso de Domingo Del Monte. Manzano y Del Monte." RBNJM, 3a serie, 11, 3 (1969), 23-49.

65.10 Gilard, Jacques. "[Autobiografía de un esclavo]." Caravelle, No. 25 (1975), 194-197.

65.11 Jackson, Richard L. "Slave poetry and slave narrative: Juan Francisco Mazano and black autobiography." In his Black writers in Latin America (Albuquerque: University of New Mexico Press, 1979), pp. 25-35.

65.12 Leante, César. "Dos obras antiesclavistas cubanas." CA, No. 207 (1976), 175-189. Manzano and Anselmo Suárez Romero.

65.13 Madden, R. R. "Preface." In Juan Francisco Manzano, Poems by a slave in the island of Cuba, recently liberated (London: T. Ward, 1840), pp. i-v.

65.14   Matas, Julio. "La Zafira de Manzano." Unión, 2, 7 (1963), 96-
        98.

65.15   Mullen, Edward J. "Introduction." In Juan Francisco Manzano,
        Life and poems of a Cuban slave (Hamden, Conn.: Shoe
        String Press, 1981), pp. 1-32.

65.16   Roig de Leuchsenring, Emilio. "Palabras." In Juan Francisco
        Manzano, Autobiografía, cartas y versos (H: Municipio de
        la Habana, 1937), pp. 5-7.

65.17   Vitier, Cintio. "Dos poetas cubanos del siglo XIX: Plácido y
        Manzano." Bohemia, 65, 50 (1973), 18-21.

65.18   _____. "El esclavo." In his Poetas cubanos del siglo XIX; sem-
        blanzas (H: Unión, 1969), pp. 18-23.

66. MARINELLO, JUAN (1898-1977)

Bibliographies

66.1 Alvarez Bravo, Armando. "Bibliografía de Juan Marinello."
GdC, No. 132 (1975), 30.

66.2 Antuña, María Luisa, and Josefina García Carranza. "Bibliografía de Juan Marinello." GdC, No. 117 (1973), 28-32.

66.3 _____. "Bibliografía de Juan Marinello." RBNJM, 3a serie, 16, 3 (1974), 25-473.

Critical Essays

66.4 Arias, Salvador. "Der Essay als Waffe im Kampf: Juan Marinello und sein 'Momento español'." WB, 24, 12 (1978), 156-165.

66.5 Armas, Emilio de. "Valoración de una poesía interrumpida." ULH, No. 201 (1974), 36-43.

66.6 Augier, Angel I. "Juan Marinello, ejemplo de escritores." Bohemia, 65, 44 (1973), 44-45.

66.7 _____. "Juan Marinello: un escritor militante." GdC, No. 117 (1973), 14.

66.8 _____. "Orbita de Juan Marinello." In Juan Marinello, Orbita de Juan Marinello (H: Colección Orbita, 1968), pp. 7-37.

66.9 Benedetti, Mario. "Contemporáneos y complementarios de Marinello." In his El recurso del supremo patriarca (M: Nueva Imagen, 1979), pp. 115-120.

66.10 Bueno, Salvador. "De recuerdos y en homenaje." GdC, No. 117 (1973), 18.

66.11 CAm, No. 103 (1977), entire issue.

66.12 Carpentier, Alejo. "Juan, tres veces joven." GdC, No. 117 (1973), 3.

66.13 Castellanos, Orlando. "Conversación a los 75." GdC, No. 117 (1973), 4-10.

66.14 _____. "Juan Marinello: a los 75 años de su vida." Bohemia, 65, 44 (1973), 4-15.

66.15   Corretjer, Juan Antonio. "Tres instantáneas de Juan Marinello."
        CAm, No. 118 (1980), 97-100.

66.16   Feijóo, Samuel. "Divagaciones sobre un libro martiano de Juan
        Marinello [José Martí, escritor americano]." Islas, 2, 1
        (1959), 295-297. See item no. 67.168.

66.17   Fernández de Castro, José Antonio. "Juan Marinello Vidaurreta."
        CCont, 41 (1926), 193-194.

66.18   Fernández Retamar, Roberto. "Para Juan Marinello." GdC, No.
        117 (1973), 12.

66.19   Ferrer Canales, José. "Marinello: relieves de su mensaje."
        CA, No. 217 (1978), 15-24.

66.20   Forné Farreres, José. "Las Españas de Juan Marinello." GdC,
        No. 117 (1973), 22-24.

66.21   González, Manuel Pedro. "En torno a los nuevos." RBC, 25
        (1930), 382-393. Marinello inter alios.

66.22   González, Omar. "Juan Marinello." CB, No. 94 (1975), 16-19.

66.23   Grismer, Raymond L., and Manuel Rodríguez Saavedra. "Juan Ma-
        rinello y Vidaurreta." In their Vida y obras de autores
        cubanos (H: "Alfa", 1940-), I, 33-37.

66.24   Grobart, Fabio. "Juan Marinello: el comunista." CAm, No. 103
        (1977), 45-49.

66.25   "Juan Marinello, ejemplo de intelectual revolucionario." VO,
        15, 45 (1973), 6-7.

66.26   Laurenza, Roque Javier. "A Don Juan Marinello que le ofreció
        una colección de estampas con imágenes de la fauna marina
        de Cuba y el Caribe." GdC, No. 117 (1973), 15.

66.27   Lazo, Raimundo. "Juan Marinello, ensayista hispanoamericano."
        ULH, Nos. 20-21 (1938), 60-71.

66.28   Leante, César. "Juan Marinello, hombre de acción e intelec-
        tual." GdC, No. 117 (1973), 21.

66.29   _____. "Presencia de Navarro Luna en Juan Marinello." Bohe-
        mia, 69, 38 (1977), 10-13.

66.30   Lizaso y González, Félix. "Juan Marinello Vidaurreta." CCont,
        41 (1926), 193-194.

66.31   Marinello, Juan. "Intermedio primero." In his Contemporáneos
        (H: Contemporáneos, 1975), pp. 115-139.

66.32   "Marinello a los setenticinco años..." CA, No. 79 (1973), 117-
        118.

66.33 Melon, Alfred. "Sobre tres discursos de Juan Marinello." CAm, No. 115 (1979), 46-59.

66.34 Méndez Capote, Renée. "Juan y Pepilla, un todo indisoluble." GdC, No. 117 (1973), 19-20.

66.35 Oráa, Pedro de. "Marinello: lírica y circunstancia social." Unión, 17, 3 (1978), 99-106.

66.36 Pavón Tamayo, Luis. "Creación y revolución en Juan Marinello." VO, No. 48 (1973), 13-15. Also RyC, No. 18 (1974), 3-6.

66.37 Polišenský, Josef. "Literatura y revolución: Juan Marinello: 1898-1973." PP, 16 (1973), 201-209.

66.38 Portuondo, José Antonio. "Juan Marienllo, poeta." GdC, No. 117 (1973), 11.

66.39 Prats Sariol, José. "Nota a Liberación." GdC, No. 117 (1973), 25.

66.40 Roca, Blas. "El compañero Juan." GdC, No. 117 (1973), 2.

66.41 Rodríguez Benthencourt, Miriam. "Juan Marinello." CubaI, No. 40 (1972), 44-46.

66.42 Sánchez Vázquez, Adolfo. "Marinello en tres tiempos." CAm, No. 109 (1978), 113-116.

66.43 Tallet, José Zacarías. "Marinello el amigo." GdC, No. 117 (1973), 13.

67. MARTI, JOSE (1953-1895)

Bibliographies

67.1   Aportes para una bibliografía de José Martí. Montevideo: Universidad de la República, Facultad de Humanidades y Ciencias, 1954.

67.2   Blanch y Blanco, Celestino. "Bibliografía martiana." AMart, No. 1 (1969), 361-372; No. 2 (1970), 587-626; No. 3 (1971), 341-384; No. 4 (1971), 401-444.

67.3   _____. Bibliografía martiana, 1954-1963. H: Biblioteca Nacional "José Martí", Departamento de Colección Cubana, 1965.

67.4   Blondet Tudisco, Olga. "José Martí: bibliografía selecta." RHM, 18 (1952), 151-161. Also in José Martí, q.v., pp. 163-173.

67.5   García Carranza, Araceli. "Bibliografía martiana." AMart, No. 7 (1977), 423-490.

67.6   _____. "Bibliografía martiana (1976 y 1977)." AMart, No. 1 (1978), 346-402.

67.7   _____. "Bibliografía martiana (septiembre de 1968-agosto de 1969)." AMart, No. 2 (1970), 587-626.

67.8   González, Manuel Pedro. Fuentes para el estudio de José Martí; ensayo de bibliografía clasificada. H: Ministerio de Educación, 1950.

67.9   Guía bibliográfica sobre José Martí. H: Biblioteca Municipal, Dirección de Cultura, 1937.

67.10 Klein, Linda B. "De bibliografía martiana." CA, No. 188 (1973), 206-210.

67.11 Lizaso y González, Félix. "Una bibliografía y una obra inédita; ensayo de bibliografía martiana." RAm, 26 (1933), 339-341.

67.12 Peraza Sarausa, Fermín. Bibliografía de José Martí. H: Biblioteca Nacional,1941-1956? Publisher varies.

67.13 _____. Bibliografía martiana, 1853-1953. H: Comisión Nacional Organizadora de los Actos y Ediciones del Centenario y del Monumento de Martí, 1954.

67.14 _____. Bibliografía martiana, 1853-1955. H: Anuario Bibliográfico Cubano, 1956.

67.15 _____. Bibliografía martiana, 1942-1943. H: Biblioteca Municipal de la Habana, 1944.

67.16 _____. Bibliografía martiana, 1945. H: Biblioteca Municipal de la Habana, 1946.

67.17 _____. Bibliografía martiana (1946). H: Municipio de la Habana, 1948.

67.18 _____. Bibliografía martiana, 1955. H: Departamento de Educación, 1956.

67.19 _____. "Bibliografía martiana 1956-1968." RevCu, 1, 2 (1968), 485-499.

67.20 _____. Bibliografía martiana 1956-1957. H: Municipio de la Habana, Departamento de Educación, 1958.

67.21 _____. Cronología de la obra martiana. H: Anuario Bibliográfico Cubano, 1955.

67.22 Quintana, Jorge. Cronología bibliográfica de José Martí. Caracas: Delta, 1964.

67.23 Ripoll, Carlos. Archivo José Martí; repertorio crítico. Medio siglo de estudios martianos. NY: Eliseo Torres, 1971.

67.24 _____. Indice universal de la obra de José Martí. NY: Eliseo Torres, 1971.

67.25 Valle, Rafael Heliodoro. "Bibliografía de Martí en México." LyP, 10, 9 (1932), 28-31.

Critical Books and Monographs

67.26 A la memoria de Martí. La república cubana con todos y para todos. Ofrenda consagrada a Martí. H, 1901.

67.27 Agramonte y Pichardo, Roberto. Martí y su concepción del mundo. Río Piedras, P.R.: Editorial Universitaria, Universidad de Puerto Rico, 1971.

67.28 Almendras, Herminio. A propósito de La edad de oro de José Martí; notas sobre literatura infantil. Santiago de Cuba: Universidad de Oriente, Departamento de Relaciones Culturales, 1956. Also H: Instituto Cubano del Libro, 1972.

67.29 _____. Martí; 2. ed. M: Oasis, 1969.

67.30 Alonso, Luis Ricardo. "Hostos y Martí: novelistas." DAI, 36 (1975), 1546A.

67.31 Alvarez y Juan, Aurelio. <u>Martí y Barbarrosa. Cuatro cartas inéditas.</u> Caracas, 1975.

67.32 Amador Sánchez, Luis. <u>Cuatro estudios: Hostos, Martí, Rodó, Blanco-Fombona.</u> São Paulo: Universidad de São Paulo, 1958.

67.33 Andino, Alberto. <u>Martí y España.</u> Madrid: Playor, 1973. Orig. "España en la obra de Martí." <u>DAI</u>, 34 (1971), 7697A.

67.34 <u>Archivo José Martí.</u> H: Ministerio de Educación, Dirección de Cultura, 1940-1953.

67.35 Archivo Nacional de Cuba. <u>El Archivo Nacional en la conmemoración del centenario del natalicio de José Martí y Pérez 1853-1953.</u> H, 1953.

67.36 Argilados, Rafael G. <u>Martí: infancia, juventud y muerte.</u> Santiago de Cuba: Departamento de Cultura del Municipio de Santiago de Cuba, 1956.

67.37 <u>Así vieron a Martí.</u> H: Ciencias Sociales, Instituto Cubano del Libro, 1971. Since this volume is composed of generally brief sketches, its contents are not listed separately.

67.38 Avila, Francisco J. <u>Martí y el periodismo caraqueño. El estilo prospectivo de un maestro de la comunicación social.</u> Caracas: Secretaría General, 1968.

67.39 Baeza Flores, Alberto. <u>¿Quién fue José Martí?</u> M: Novaro, 1958.

67.40 _____. <u>Vida de Martí: el hombre íntimo y el hombre público.</u> H: Comisión Nacional Organizadora de los Actos y Ediciones del Centenario y del Monumento de Martí, 1954.

67.41 Bazil, Osvaldo. <u>Vidas de iluminación. La huella de Martí en Rubén Darío. Cómo era Rubén Darío.</u> H: Julio Arroyo, 1932.

67.42 Béguez, César J. A. <u>Martí y el krausismo.</u> H: Cía. Editora de Libros y Folletos, 1944.

67.43 Benvenuto, Ofelia M. B. de. <u>José Martí.</u> Montevideo: González Panizza, 1942.

67.44 Bernal, Emilia. <u>Martí, por sí mismo.</u> H: Molina, 1934.

67.45 Blomberg, Héctor Pedro. <u>Martí, el último libertador.</u> BA: La Universidad, 1945.

67.46 Boix y Comas, Alberto. <u>La ruta de la gloria.</u> H: El Siglo XX, 1955.

67.47 Boti, Regino Eladio. <u>Martí en Darío.</u> H: El Siglo XX, 1925.

67.48 Briceño Perozo, Mario. <u>La popularidad de Martí en Venezuela.</u> Caracas: Italgráfica, 1971.

67.49 Brodermann, Ramón E. "El pensamiento literario de José Martí: sus mocedades." DAI, 33 (1972), 1136A.

67.50 Cabral, Alexandre. José Martí e a revolução cubana. Lisboa: Avante, 1976.

67.51 Camacho, Pánfilo Daniel. Martí, un genio creador. H: El Siglo XX, 1956.

67.52 ____. Martí, una vida en perenne angustia. H: El Siglo XX, 1948.

67.53 ____. Martí y el Partido Revolucionario Cubano. H: "El Siglo XX", 1953.

67.54 Cantón Navarro, José. Algunas ideas de José Martí en relación con la clase obrera y el socialismo. H: Dirección Política de las FAR, 1970.

67.55 Capuano, Isaac. "El desdoblamiento del 'yo' en la poesía de José Martí, Miguel de Unamuno, Antonio Machado y Juan Ramón Jiménez." DAI, 37 (1976), 1586A.

67.56 ____. Martí: sus últimos días. H: "El Siglo XX", 1950.

67.57 Caraballo y Sotolongo, Francisco. José Martí. Matanzas: T. González, 1916.

67.58 ____. José Martí, poeta, pensador y revolucionario (estudio crítico). Matanzas: T. González, 1916.

67.59 Carbonell, Néstor. José Martí: apóstol, héroe y mártir. BA: J. Suárez, 1933.

67.60 ____. Martí, carne y espíritu. H:Seoane, Fernández, 1952.

67.61 ____. Martí: su vida y su obra. H: Rambla y Bouza, 1911. Also H: El Siglo XX, 1923.

67.62 ____. Martí: su vida y su obra. II. El poeta. H: Seoane y Alvarez, 1913.

67.63 ____. Presencia de Martí en la guerra. H: "El Siglo XX", 1958.

67.64 Carrancá y Trujillo, Camilo. Acerca de Martí en México (de una polémica). M: Mundial, 1934.

67.65 ____. Martí. Traductor de Víctor Hugo. M: Talleres Gráficos de la Nación, 1933.

67.66 ____. Las polémicas de José Martí en México. Los cubanos en el centenario americano. M: Bloque de Obreros Intelectuales de México, 1931.

67.67 Carricarte, Arturo R. de. La cubanidad negativa del apóstol Martí. H: M. I. Mesa Rodríguez, 1934.

67.68 Carrillo, José. El verdadero José Martí (3 ensayos críticos). M: Bayo Libros, 1953.

67.69 Casals, Jorge. La epopeya de Martí, desde Paula hasta Dos Ríos. Matanzas: Pedro P. Solés, 1953.

67.70 Catalá, Raquel. Vida y pensamiento de Martí. H: Molina, 1947.

67.71 Conangia Fontanillos, José. Martí y Cataluña; examen retrospectivo de unos conceptos inverosímiles, atribuidos al gran apóstol cubano. H: Mundial, 1954.

67.72 Conte Agüero, Luis. José Martí y la oratoria cubana. BA: El Sol, 1959.

67.73 Corbitt, Roberta Day. "The colossal theater: the United States interpreted by José Martí." DA, 20 (1960), 4109.

67.74 Córdova y de Quesada, Federico de. Martí, líder de la independencia cubana. H: "El Siglo XX", 1947.

67.75 Cortina, José Manuel. Apología de José Martí. H: Rampla, Bouza, 1935. Also as Apologie de José Martí. Paris: Messein, 1938.

67.76 Cue Cánovas, A. Martí, el escritor y su época. M: Centenario, 1961.

67.77 Cuesta Gonsenheim, Sylvia. Literatura y periodismo en José Martí. M: Universidad Femenina de México, 1953.

67.78 Daireaux, Max. José Martí (1853-1895). Paris: France-Amérique, 1939. Same as item no. 67.462.

67.79 Davison, Ned J. Sound patterns in a poem of José Martí; an examination of phonemic structures and poetic musicality. Salt Lake City: Damuir Press, 1975. On "Yo soy un hombre sincero."

67.80 Díaz Plaja, Guillermo. Martí desde España. H: Selecta, 1956.

67.81 Dill, Hans-Otto. El ideario literario y estético de José Martí. H: Casa de las Américas, 1975.

67.82 Dougé, Joubert. Essai sur José Martí. Port-au-Prince: Telhomme, 1943.

67.83 Douglas, Frances. José Martí of Cuba. Washington, D.C.: The Pan American Union, 1935?

67.84 Embajada de Venezuela en Cuba. Venezuela a Martí. H, 1953.

67.85   Espina García, Antonio. Martí; estudio y antología. Madrid:
        Compañía Bibliográfica Española, 1969.

67.86   Esténger, Rafael. Martí frente al comunismo. Glosas de contra-
        punto entre el hombre libre y el autómata marxista. Miami:
        AIP, 1966.

67.87   Estrada, Domingo. José Martí. Guatemala: A. Síguere, 1899.
        2. ed., H: "El Mundo", 1901.

67.88   Estudios martianos. Río Piedras, P.R.: Editorial Universitaria,
        Universidad de Puerto Rico, 1974. Pertinent items are
        listed separately.

67.88   Estudios sobre Martí. H: Ciencias Sociales, 1975. Pertinent
        items are listed separately.

67.90   Fernández, Wilfredo. Martí y la filosofía. Miami: Universal,
        1974.

67.91   Fernández Concheso, Aurelio. José Martí, filósofo. Berlin:
        Fred Dümmler, 1937. Same as item no. 67.

67.92   Fernández Retamar, Roberto. Introducción a José Martí. H:
        Casa de las Américas, Centro de Estudios Martianos, 1978.

67.93   _____. Lectura de Martí. M: Nuestro Tiempo, 1972.

67.94   _____. Martí. Montevideo: Biblioteca de Marcha, 1970.

67.95   _____. Sobre la crítica de Martí. Santiago de Chile: Andrés
        Bello, 1973.

67.96   Ferrara, Oreste. Martí y la elocuencia. H: C. López Bustaman-
        te, 1926.

67.97   Fountain, Anne Owen. "José Martí and North American authors."
        DAI, 34 (1974), 5169A.

67.98   Franchella, Quirino. José Martí. L'uomo d'azione e di pensie-
        ro. Parma/Roma: Madcari, 1955. Also 1967.

67.99   Franco, Luis. Sarmiento y Martí. BA: Lautaro, 1958.

67.100 Galindo, Isis Molina de. "La modalidad impresionista en la
        obra de José Martí." DA, 27 (1966), 1816A.

67.101 García Consuegra, M. Conozca a José Martí como maestro, como
        filósofo y como espiritista. Santa Clara, 1955.

67.102 García Martí, Raúl. Martí. Biografía familiar. H: Cárdenas,
        1938.

67.103 Gay-Calbó, Enrique. Martí y la conducta humana. H: "El Siglo
        XX", Muñiz, 1949.

67.104 Ghiano, Juan Carlos. José Martí. BA: Centro Editor de América Latina, 1967.

67.105 Gimena Corbo, Angela. José Martí: poemas. Breve ensayo sobre su vida. Montevideo, 1954.

67.106 Godoy, Armando. La lengua de Martí. H: Secretaría de Educación, 1934.

67.107 González, Manuel Pedro. Antología crítica de José Martí. M: Cultura, 1960. Petinent items are listed separately.

67.108 _____. Indagaciones martianas. Santa Clara: Universidad Central de Las Villas, Departamento de Relaciones Culturales, 1961.

67.109 _____. José Martí en el octogésimo aniversario de la iniciación modernista 1882-1962. Caracas: Ministerio de Educación, Dirección de Cultura y Bellas Artes, Departamento de Publicaciones, 1962.

67.110 _____. José Martí, epic chronicler of the United States in the eighties. Chapel Hill: University of North Carolina Press, 1953. 2. ed., H: Center of Studies on Martí, 1961.

67.111 _____. La revaloración de Martí (acotaciones en torno a su bibliografía). H: Cultural, 1936. Same as item no. 67.623.

67.112 _____. Variaciones en torno a la epistolografía de José Martí. San José, Costa Rica: Repertorio Americano, 1948.

67.113 _____, and Ivan A. Schulman. José Martí, esquema ideológico. M: Cvltvra, 1961. Also Santiago de Cuba: Universidad de Oriente, 1961.

67.114 González Gutiérrez, Diego. La continuidad revolucionaria de Varela en las ideas de Martí. H: "El Siglo XX", Muñiz, 1953.

67.115 González Veranes, Pedro N. ¿Quién fué el progenitor espiritual de Martí? H: Luz-Hilo, 1942.

67.116 Gray, Richard Butler. José Martí, Cuban patriot. Gainesville: University of Florida Press, 1962.

67.117 Guerra Sánchez, Ramiro. Martí en las primeras décadas de la Escuela Primaria Republicana. H: "El Siglo XX", Muñiz, 1952.

67.118 Guevara, Ernesto. José Martí, Antonio Guiteras, Antonio Maceo, Camilo Cienfuegos. H: Ciencias Sociales, 1977.

67.119   Havana. Biblioteca Nacional. Relación de las obras de y sobre
         José Martí que posee la Biblioteca Nacional. H, 1953.

67.120   Henríquez, Fernando Abel. Primer viaje de Martí a la República
         Dominicana. H, 1956.

67.121   Henríquez i Carvajal, Federico. Martí; próceres, héroes i már-
         tires de la Independencia de Cuba. Ciudad Trujillo: Quis-
         queya, 1945.

67.122   Henríquez Ureña, Camila et al. El periodismo en José Martí.
         H: Orbe, 1977.

67.123   Heredia, Nicolás, and N. Bolet Peraza. Homenaje a José Martí.
         NY: América, 1898.

67.124   Hernández Catá, Alfonso. Mitología de Martí. Madrid: Renaci-
         miento, 1929. 2. ed., BA: Club del Libro Amigos del Li-
         bro Americano, 1939. Also Miami: Mnemosyne, 1970.

67.125   Hernández-Chiroldes, Juan Alberto. "Análisis crítico de los
         Versos sencillos de José Martí." DAI, 39 (1978), 6792A.

67.126   Herrera Franyutti, Alfonso. Martí en México; recuerdos de una
         época. M: A. Mijares, 1969.

67.127   Homenaje a José Martí, 1853-1895. Santiago de Cuba: "Pini-
         llos", 1954.

67.128   Homenaje a Martí en el cincuentenario de la fundación del Par-
         tido Revolucionario Cubano, 1892-1942. H: Municipio de
         la Habana, 1942.

67.129   Homenaje al apóstol José Martí en el centenario de su natali-
         cio. H: Universidad de la Habana, 1953.

67.130   Ibáñez, Roberto. José Martí; introducción al estudio de su
         obra lírica. Montevideo: Organización Taquigráfica Me-
         dina, 1946.

67.131   Iduarte, Andrés. Martí escritor. M: Cuadernos Americanos,
         1945. 2. ed., H: Ministerio de Educación, Dirección de
         Cultura, 1951.

67.132   _____. Sarmiento, Martí y Rodó. H: Siglo XX, 1955.

67.133   Instituto Internacional de Literatura Iberoamericana. Homenaje
         a Hidalgo, Díaz Mirón y Martí. M: Universitaria, 1954.

67.134   Iraizoz y de Villar, Antonio. La estética acrática de José
         Martí. H: El Siglo XX, 1924. Same as item no. 67.722.

67.135   _____. Las ideas pedagógicas de Martí. H: El Siglo XX, 1920.
         Same as item no. 67.724.

67.136 _____. Ideología de José Martí. Lisboa: La Bécarre, 1926.

67.137 Jinesta, Carlos. José Martí en Costa Rica. San José, Costa Rica: Alsina, Josef Sauter, 1933.

67.138 José Martí (1853-1895): vida y obra--bibliografía--antología. NY: Hispanic Institute in the United States, 1953. Also Río Piedras, P.R.: Universidad de Puerto Rico, Departamento de Estudios Hispánicos, 1953. Pertinent items are listed separately.

67.139 Jústiz y del Valle, Tomás de. Mayo 19 de 1895. H: "El Siglo XX", Muñiz, 1953.

67.140 Kirk, John M. "The socio-political thought of José Martí: his plans for the liberated patria." DAI, 38 (1977), 2826A.

67.141 Langhorst, Frederick Hart. "Three Latin Americans look at us; the United States as seen in the essays of José Martí, José Enrique Rodó, and José Vasconcelos." DAI, 36 (1976), 8046A-8047A.

67.142 Lazo, Raimundo. Martí y su obra literaria. H: "La Propagandista", 1929.

67.143 Leber, Gisela. Die Bedeutung von José Martí für die Ausprägung des kubanischen Nationalbewusstseins. Rostock: Universität Rostock, Philosophische Fakultät, 1965.

67.144 Lemus, José María. Apuntes y reflexiones sobre la vida y obra de José Martí. San Salvador: Imprenta Nacional, 1957.

67.145 Lens y de Vera, Eduardo Félix. Heredia y Martí; dos grandes figuras de la lírica cubana. H: Selecta, 1954.

67.146 Lizaso y González, Félix. José Martí, apuntes inéditos. H: Archivo Nacional de Cuba, 1951.

67.147 _____. José Martí; recuento de centenario. H: Ucar García; P. Fernández, 1953.

67.148 _____. Martí, espíritu de la guerra justa. H: Ucar, García, 1944.

67.149 _____. Martí, místico del deber. BA: Losada, 1940. Also as Martí. Martyr of Cuban independence. Albuquerque: University of New Mexico Press, 1953.

67.150 _____. Martí y la utopía de América. H: Ucar, García, 1942.

67.151 _____. Pasión de Martí. H: Ucar, García, 1938.

67.152 _____. Posibilidades filosóficas en Martí. H: Molina, 1935.

67.153 _____. Proyección humana de Martí. BA: Raigal, 1953.

67.154 ____, and Ernesto Ardura. Personalidad e ideas de José Martí.
        H: Ucar, García, 1954.

67.155 Llaverías y Martínez, Joaquín. Martí en el Archivo Nacional.
        H: El Siglo XX, 1945. Same as item no. 67.813.

67.156 ____. Los periódicos de Martí. H: Pérez, Sierra, 1929. Same
        as item no. 67.814.

67.157 López Blanco, Mariano. Perennidad de Martí. H: Lex, 1956.

67.158 Machado Bonet de Benvenuto, Ofelia. José Martí. Montevideo:
        González Panizza, 1942.

67.159 Magdaleno, Mauricio. José Martí (fulgor de Martí). M: Botas,
        1941.

67.160 Mañach, Jorge. El espíritu de Martí. Curso de 1951. H:
        Cooperativa Estudiantil, n.d.

67.161 ____. Martí, el apóstol. Madrid-Barcelona: Espasa-Calpe,
        1933. 2. ed., BA: Espasa-Calpe, 1942? 3. ed., NY: Las
        Américas, 1963.

67.162 ____. El pensamiento político y social de Martí (discurso en
        el Senado). H: Edición Oficial del Senado, 1941.

67.163 ____. Significación del centenario martiano. H: Lex, 1953.
        Same as item no. 67.838.

67.164 Marinello, Juan. Actualidad americana de José Martí. H: Ar-
        row Press, 1945.

67.165 ____. El caso literario de José Martí: motivos de centenario.
        H, 1954.

67.166 ____. Ensayos martianos. H: Universidad Central de Las Vi-
        llas, 1961.

67.167 ____. José Martí. Madrid: Júcar, 1972.

67.168 ____. José Martí, escritor americano; Martí y el modernismo.
        M: Grijalbo, 1958. 2. ed., H, 1962.

67.169 ____. Once ensayos martianos. H: Comisión Nacional Cubana
        de la UNESCO, 1964.

67.170 Márquez Sterling, Carlos. Martí, ciudadano de América. NY:
        Las Américas, 1965.

67.171 ____. Martí, maestro y apóstol. H: Seoane, Fernández, 1942.

67.172 Martí Llorente, Francisco. Martí y los negros. H: "Arquim-
        bau", 1947. Signed Armando Guerra.

67.173 Martí; valoraciones críticas. Montevideo: Fundación Cultura
Universitaria, 1973. Partinent items are listed separately.

67.174 Martínez Bello, Antonio. Ideas sociales y económicas de José
Martí. H: La Verónica, 1940.

67.175 Martínez Estrada, Ezequiel. Familia de Martí. H: Nacional,
1962.

67.176 ____. Martí; el héroe y su acción revolucionaria. M: Siglo
XXI, 1966.

67.177 ____. Martí revolucionario. H: Casa de las Américas, 1967.

67.178 Martínez Rendón, Miguel D. En torno a la poesía de Martí.
M: B.O.I., 1933. Same as item no. 67.880.

67.179 Mas, José L. "Perspectiva ideológica de José Martí en sus
crónicas sobre los Estados Unidos." DAI, 35 (1974),
1111A-1112A.

67.180 Massuh, Víctor. El activismo creador de Martí. Montevideo?:
Fundación de Cultura Universitaria, n.d.

67.181 Memoria del Congreso de Escritores Martianos. H: Comisión
Nacional Organizadora de los Actos y Ediciones del Centenario y del Monumento de Martí, 1953. Pertinent items
are listed separately.

67.182 Méndez, Manuel Isidro. Martí; estudio crítico-biográfico. H,
1941.

67.183 Meo Zilio, Giovanni. De Martí a Sábat Ercasty. Montevideo:
El Siglo Ilustrado, 1967.

67.184 Mistral, Gabriela. La lengua de Martí. H: Secretaría de Educación, 1934. Same as item no. 67.917.

67.185 Montaner, Carlos Alberto. Martí y Puerto Rico. San Juan,
P.R.: Editorial Puerto Rico, 1970.

67.186 ____. El pensamiento de José Martí. Madrid: Plaza Mayor,
1971.

67.187 Nolasco, Sócrates. Martí, el modernismo y la poesía tradicional. Santiago de Cuba: Universidad de Oriente, Departamento de Extensión y Relaciones Culturales, 1955.

67.188 Núñez y Domínguez, José de Jesús. Martí en México. M: Secretaría de Relaciones Exteriores, 1933.

67.189 Opatrný, Josef. José Martí. Praha: Horizont, 1975.

67.190 Oria, Tomás G. "Martí, el moralista del krausismo." DAI, 40
(1980), 6300A.

67.191   Ortega, Luis. El suelo y la distancia. M: Ganivet, 1968.

67.192   Pensamiento y acción de José Martí. Santiago de Cuba: Universidad de Oriente, Departamento de Extensión y Relaciones Culturales, 1953.

67.193   Pérez Cabrera, José Manuel. La Academia de la Historia y el centenario de Martí. H: "El Siglo XX" Muñiz, 1954.

67.194   Piedra-Bueno, Andrés de. Evocación de Byrne y Martí americanista. H: Institución Inclán, 1942.

67.195   _____. Martí. Mensaje biográfico; 2. ed. H: Ministerio de Educación, Instituto Cívico-Militar, 1953. 3. ed., 1955.

67.196   Pinto Albiol, Angel César. El pensamiento filosófico de José Martí y la revolución cubana. H: "Jaidy", 1946.

67.197   Pitchón, Marco. José Martí y la comprensión humana 1853-1953. H: P. Fernández, 1957.

67.198   Ponte Domínguez, Francisco. Pensamiento laico de José Martí. H: Modas Magazine, 1956.

67.199   Portuondo, José Antonio. José Martí, crítico literario. Washington, D.C.: Unión Panamericana, 1953.

67.200   Quesada, Luis Manuel. "José Martí: cuentos de La edad de oro: edición estudiantil con introducción, vocabulario y notas." DAI, 29 (1969), 2274A-2275A.

67.201   Quesada y Miranda, Gonzalo de. Anecdotario martiano: nuevas facetas de Martí. H: Seoane, Fernández, 1948.

67.202   _____. Facetas de Martí. H: Trópico, 1939.

67.203   _____. Guía para las obras completas de Martí. H: Trópico, 1947.

67.204   _____. Juventud de Martí. H: "El Siglo XX" Muñiz, 1943.

67.205   _____. Martí, hombre. H: Seoane, Fernández, 1940. 2. ed., 1944.

67.206   _____. Martí, periodista. H: Rambla, Bouza, 1929.

67.207   Ríos, Fernando de los. Martí y el fascismo. H: Ucar, García, 1937. Same as item no. 67.

67.208   Ripoll, Carlos. La doctrina de Martí. Elizabeth, N.J.: La Voz, 1976.

67.209   _____. José Martí; letras y huellas desconocidas. NY: Eliseo Torres, 1976.

67.210 _____. Patria: el periódico de José Martí; registro general (1892-1895). NY: Eliseo Torres, 1971.

67.211 Rodríguez, Pedro Pablo. La idea de liberación nacional en José Martí. Santiago de Chile: Quimantú, 1973.

67.212 Rodríguez Demorizi, Emilio. Martí y Máximo Gómez en la poesía dominicana. Ciudad Trujillo: Montalvo, 1953.

67.213 Rodríguez-Embil, Luis. José Martí, el santo de América; estudio crítico-biográfico. H: P. Fernández, 1941.

67.214 Rodríguez y Expósito, César. Médicos en la vida de Martí. H: Ministerio de Salubridad y Asistencia Social, 1955.

67.215 Roig de Leuchsenring, Emilio. La España de Martí. H: Páginas, 1938.

67.216 _____. Martí, antimperialista; 2. ed. aum. H: Ministerio de Relaciones Exteriores, 1961. Also as Martí, anti-imperialist. H: Book Institute, 1967.

67.217 _____. Martí, síntesis de su vida. H: Oficina del Historiador de la Ciudad de la Habana, 1961.

67.218 Salazar y Roig, Salvador. El dolor en la lírica cubana. H: El Siglo XX, 1925.

67.219 Santovenia y Echaide, Emeterio Santiago. Bolívar y Martí. H: El Siglo XX, 1934.

67.220 _____. Dos creadores, Mazzini y Martí. H: Trópico, 1936.

67.221 _____. Genio y acción, Sarmiento y Martí. H: Trópico, 1938.

67.222 _____. Lincoln en Martí. H: Trópico, 1948.

67.223 _____. Política de Martí; 2. ed. H: Lex, 1944.

67.224 _____, and Raúl M. Shelton. Martí y su obra. Miami: Educational Publishing Co., 1970.

67.225 Schulman, Ivan A. Génesis del modernismo. Martí, Nájera, Silva, Casal. M: El Colegio de México; St. Louis: Washington University Press, 1966. 2. ed., 1967. Pertinent items are listed separately.

67.226 _____. Símbolo y color en la obra de José Martí. Madrid: Gredos, 1960.

67.227 _____, and Manuel Pedro González. Martí, Darío y el modernismo. Madrid: Gredos, 1969.

67.228 Schultz de Mantovani, Fryda. Genio y figura de José Martí. BA: EUDEBA, 1968.

67.229 Šiškina, Valentina Ivanovna. Social'no-političeskie vsgljady
        Chose Marti. Moskva: Izd. Moskovskgo Univ., 1969.

67.230 Sneary, Eugene Chester. "José Martí in translation." DA, 20
        (1959), 1795-1796.

67.231 Sociedad Cubana de Filosofía. Conversaciones filosóficas in-
        teramericanas: homenaje de centenario al apóstol José
        Martí. H: Comisión Nacional Organizadora de los Actos y
        Ediciones del Centenario y del Monumento de Martí, 1955.

67.232 Soto-Hall, Máximo. La niña de Guatemala: el idilio trágico de
        José Martí. Guatemala: Nacional, 1942.

67.233 Sternlicht, Madeline. "Man or myth: José Martí in the biogra-
        phies of Jorge Mañach, Alberto Baeza Flores, and Ezequiel
        Martínez Estrada." DAI, 37 (1977), 4390A-4391A.

67.234 Ternovoj, Oleg J. Chose Marti. Moskva: Izd. "Mysl", 1966.

67.235 Torriente y Peraza, Cosme de la. Martí y su guerra 24 de fe-
        brero de 1895. H: "El Siglo" Muñiz, 1953.

67.236 Vásquez, Mari. José Martí; vida y obra. Montevideo?: Libre-
        ría Técnica, n.d.

67.237 Vela, David. Martí en Guatemala. Guatemala: Ministerio de
        Educación Pública, 1954.

67.238 Verdaguer, Roberto. José Martí, peregrino de una idea. H,
        1955.

67.239 Vida y pensamiento de Martí. Homenaje de la ciudad de la Ha-
        bana en el cincuentenario de la fundación del Partido
        Revolucionario Cubano, 1892-1942. H, 1942.

67.240 Vitier, Cintio. Temas martianos; segunda serie. H: Centro
        de Estudios Martianos; Letras, 1982. Pertinent items are
        listed separately.

67.241 _____, and Fina García Marruz. Temas martianos. H: Biblioteca
        Nacional José Martí, Departamento Colección Cubana, 1969.
        Also Río Piedras, P.R.: Huracán, 1981. Pertinent items
        are listed separately.

67.242 Vitier, Medardo. Martí; estudio integral. H: Comisión Nacio-
        nal Organizadora de los Actos y Ediciones del Centenario
        y del Monumento de Martí, 1954.

67.243 _____. Martí; su obra política y literaria. Matanzas: La Plu-
        ma de Oro, 1911.

67.244 _____. La ruta del sembrador; motivos de literatura y filoso-
        fía. Matanzas, 1921.

67.245 Vizen, L. Khose Marti: chronika žizni povstanca. Moskva: Izd.
"Molodaja Gvardija", 1964.

67.246 Wilson, Charles Kendall. "Imagery in the poetry of José Martí." DAI, 36 (1975), 2816A-2817A.

67.247 Zéndegui, Guillermo de. Ambito de Martí. H: Comisión Nacional
Organizadora del Centenario y del Monumento de Martí,
1953.

Critical Essays

67.248 Abellán, José Luis. "José Martí y el actual pensamiento cubano." Insula, Nos. 260-261 (1968), 10.

67.249 Abreu Licairac, Rafael. "José Martí." In his Mi óbolo a Cuba
(NY: "Patria", 1897), pp. 11-15.

67.250 Acevedo Escobedo, Antonio. "Huellas de Martí en México."
RAm, 26 (1933), 296, 301-302.

67.251 Achúgar Ferreri, Hugo. "José Martí y nuestra América." AMart,
No. 1 (1978), 41-411.

67.252 Acosta, Agustín. "Ya sería un viejo." BACL, 1 (1952), 776-
778.

67.253 Acosta, Alberto. "Martí y la vagancia." Bohemia, 63, 11
(1971), 100.

67.254 Acosta, Leonardo. "La concepción histórica de Martí." CAm,
No. 67 (1971), 13-36.

67.255 _____. "Martí descolonizador. Apuntes sobre el simbolismo
nahuatl en la poesía de Martí." CAm, No. 73 (1972), 29-
43.

67.256 _____. "Una tragedia simbólica de los tiempos presentes."
GdC, No. 105 (1972), 22-23.

67.257 Acosta Medina, Reinaldo. "Algunas ideas de Martí y la pedagogía revolucionaria de hoy." In Estudios sobre Martí, q.
v., pp. 133-145.

67.258 Agramonte y Pichardo, Roberto. "Martí y el mundo de lo colec-
tivo." ULH, Nos. 38-39 (1941), 16-43. Also RMS, 3, 4
(1941), 7-34. Also AJM, 3, 1 (1943), 126-143.

67.259 _____. "Martí y su concepción de la sociedad: primicias del
libro de este título, en prensa en la Editorial Universitaria de Puerto Rico." Círculo, 8 (1979), 47-60.

67.260 _____. "Origen y desarrollo de la conciencia filosófica cubana." RMS, 25 (1963), 1073-1093.

67.261 _____. "Persona y prójimo, patria y humanidad en el pensamiento de José Martí." RMS, 22 (1960), 801-822.

67.262 Aguirre, Mirta. "La edad de oro y las ideas martianas sobre educación infantil." Lyceum, Nos. 33-34 (1953), 33-58.

67.263 _____. "Los principios estéticos e ideológicos de José Martí." AMart, No. 1 (1978), 133-152.

67.264 Alazraki, Jaime. "El indigenismo de Martí y el antindigenismo de Sarmiento." CA, No. 140 (1965), 135-157.

67.265 Alba, Pedro de. "Martí, amigo del indio." In his Del nuevo humanismo y otros ensayos (M: Universidad Nacional, 1937), pp. 209-213. Also RBC, 41 (1938), 200-201. Also AJM, 2, 2 (1941), 150-154.

67.266 _____. "Martí and his pilgrimage. Tribute on the fiftieth anniversary of his death." BUP, 79 (1945), 265-269.

67.267 _____. "La ruta de Martí." AANAL, 14 (1930), 315-318.

67.268 _____. "Semblanza y ruta de José Martí." AJM, 3, 1 (1945), 57-62.

67.269 Alba-Buffill, Elio. "José Martí y Enrique José Varona: pasión y razón en la agomá cubana." In Homenaje a Humberto Piñera (Madrid: Playor, 1979), pp. 11-20.

67.270 Albornoz, Alvaro de. "Homenaje de un español a José Martí." Humanismo, 3, 13 (1953), 10-17.

67.271 Aldao, Carlso. "Martí." RevC, 29 (1951-1952), 202-206.

67.272 Alegría, Ciro. "Whitman y Martí." Islas, 4, 1 (1961), 103-106.

67.273 Alegría, Fernando. "El Whitman de José Martí." Humanismo, 3, 24 (1953), 239-247. Also in his Walt Whitman en Hispanoamérica (M: de Andrea, 1954), pp. 22-34.

67.274 Almendras, Herminio. "Notas sobre Martí, innovador en el idioma." CAm, No. 41 (1967), 31-44.

67.275 Alonso Sánchez, Andrés. "Los libros editados por Martí." CBib, 2a época, 5, 1-2 (1960), 106-108.

67.276 Alpízar, Sergio Po. "Martí, el Partido y la revolución." VO, 17, 46 (1975), 30-33.

67.277 Alvarado García, Ernesto. "José Martí, Adolfo Zúñiga y Jerónimo Zelaya." AJM, 4, 4 (1949), 456-460.

67.278 Alvarado Sánchez, José. "Sobre José Martí y su viva lección." RBC, 47 (1941), 381-394.

67.279 Alvarez, Nicolás Emilio. "Martí y Mañach: análisis estilístico de un panegírico." ExTL, 7, 1 (1978), 43-51.

67.280 Anderson Imbert, Enrique. "Comienzos del modernismo en la novela [Amistad funesta]." NRFH, 7 (1953), 515-525. Also as "La prosa poética de José Martí. A propósito de Amistad funesta." In Memoria del Congreso de Escritores Martianos, q.v., pp. 570-616. Also in Manuel Pedro González, Antología crítica de José Martí, q.v., pp. 93-131. Also Ars, 9, 3 (1953), 13-20. Also in his Crítica interna (Madrid: Taurus, 1960), pp. 93-135. Also in his Estudios sobre escritores de América (BA: Raigal, 1954), pp. 125-165.

67.281 Andino, Alberto. "Conceptismo: una faceta del barroco en Martí." In Instituto Internacional de Literatura Iberoamericana, XVII Congreso (Madrid: Cultura Hispánica del Centro Iberoamericano de Cooperación, 1978), pp. 409-416.

67.282 _____. "Reflejos teresianos en la prosa de José Martí." DHR, 4, 3 (1965), 135-151.

67.283 Anton, Karl-Heinz. "'Dulce consuelo'." In Francisco E. Porrata, and Jorge A. Santana, Antología comentada del modernismo (Sacramento: California State University, Department of Spanish and Portuguese, 1974), pp. 39-47. ExTL, Anexo I.

67.284 Aparicio, Raúl. "Martí y Maceo." Bohemia, 64, 23 (1972), 94-95.

67.285 Araquistáin, Luis. "Martí." RAm, 14 (1927), 328.

67.286 Arce de Vázquez, Margot. "'La niña de Guatemala'." REH-PR, 1, 3-4 (1971), 5-17.

67.287 Arciniegas, Germán. "José Martí, símbolo de América." CCLC, No. 2 (1953), 3-5.

67.288 Ardura, Ernesto. "Ideas básicas de José Martí." In his Prédica ingenua; ensayos y comentarios de interpretación nacional (H: Ucar García, 1954), pp. 9-38.

67.289 _____. "José Martí: Latin America's U.S. correspondent." Américas, 32, 11-12 (1980), 38-42.

67.290 _____. "Martí y la libertad." AJM, 5, 1 (1950), 90-95.

67.291 Argilagos, Rafael G. "Estampas martianas: con guante blanco." AJM, 5, 2 (1950), 266.

67.292 _____. "¿Qué entiende usted por patria?" AJM, 5, 3 (1951), 402-406.

67.293   Argüello, Santiago. "José Martí." RAm, 17 (1928), 120, 127,
         143-144, 326-327.

67.294   _____. "El Martí poeta." AANAL, 13, 1 (1929), 30-52.

67.295   Arias, Augusto. "José Martí." AméricaQ, 12 (1938), 157-168.

67.296   _____. "Martí en Venezuela." Política, No. 7 (1960), 53-61.

67.297   _____. "Martí siempre." In Memoria del Congreso de Escrito-
         res Martianos, q.v., pp. 162-188.

67.298   _____. "Prosa y estilística de José Martí." UAnt, No. 113
         (1953), 73-80.

67.299   _____. "'Sueño con claustros de mármol...' de Martí." In
         Estudios martianos, q.v., pp. 57-69.

67.300   Arias, Salvador. "Estudio de 'Los dos príncipes' de José Mar-
         tí." ULH, No. 178 (1966), 37-157.

67.301   _____. "Martí como escritor para niños. A través del análi-
         sis de 'Tres héroes' de la Edad de oro." Unión, 12, 1
         (1973), 49-59. Also in his Búsqueda y análisis (H: Unión,
         1974), pp. 58-88.

67.302   Armas, Emilio de. "Escrito en la realidad: nuevas ediciones
         de Ismaelillo." AMart, No. 1 (1978), 443-447.

67.303   Armas, Ramón de. "Apuntes sobre la presencia en Martí del Mé-
         xico de Benito Juárez." CAm, No. 115 (1979), 10-19.

67.304   _____. "La revolución pospuesta: destino de la revolución mar-
         tiana de 1895." PCr, Nos. 49-50 (1971), 7-119. Also
         AMart, 4, 4 (1972), 215-325.

67.305   _____. "Siete voces marxistas hablan de José Martí." AMart,
         No. 1 (1978), 325-330.

67.306   Armas y Cárdenas, José de. "Martí." In his Ensayos críticos
         de literatura inglesa y española (Madrid: Suárez, 1910),
         pp. 207-214. Also AJM, 4, 2 (1943), 361-364. Also BACL,
         1 (1952), 483-487. Also RevC, 29 (1951-1952), 170-175.

67.307   Arrom, José Juan. "Martí y el problema de las generaciones."
         Thesaurus, 28 (1973), 29-45. Also as "Martí and the prob-
         lem of generations." LALR, No. 1 (1972), 25-38.

67.308   _____. "Raíz popular de los Versos sencillos de José Martí."
         In Instituto Internacional de Literatura Iberoamericana,
         Homenaje a Hidalgo, Díaz Mirón y Martí, q.v., pp. 155-
         168. ALso in Manuel Pedro González, Antología crítica
         de José Martí, q.v., pp. 411-426. Also in his Certidum-
         bre de América (H: Anuario Bibliográfico Cubano, 1959),
         pp. 61-81. 2. ed., M: Gredos, 1971; pp. 77-96.

67.309 Arroyo, Anita. "Hostos y Martí, universales." RICP, No. 24 (1964), 4-11.

67.310 Artiles, Freddy. "Patria y libertad: germen de un teatro americano." Conjunto, No. 45 (1980), 93-102.

67.311 Assardo, M. Roberto. "'La rosa blanca'." In Francisco E. Porrata, and Jorge A. Santana, Antología comentada del modernismo (Sacramento: California State University, Department of Spanish and Portuguese, 1974), pp. 51-54. ExTL, Anexo I.

67.312 Aubrun, Charles V. "'Homagno', un poema de José Martí: ensayo de un nuevo método de crítica literaria." CCLC, No. 75 (1963), 51-59.

67.313 _____. "José Martí, poète et martyr de l'indépendence cubaine." LNL, No. 130 (1954), 16-27.

67.314 Augier, Angel I. "Martí como pretexto de difamación." GdC, No. 105 (1972), 2-3. See item no. 67.1185.

67.315 _____. "Martí, poeta, y su influencia innnovadora en la poesía de América." In Vida y pensamiento de Martí, q.v., II, 265-333.

67.316 _____. "Martí: tesis antimperialista en la cuna del panamericanismo." CAm, No. 82 (1974), 52-64.

67.317 _____. "Notas sobre el proceso de creación poética en Martí." L/L, No. 6 (1975), 13-34.

67.318 _____. "Sobre una edición española de los Versos libres." L/L, Nos. 3-4 (1972-1973), 172-187.

67.319 Avila, Julio Enrique. "Exaltación de José Martí." AJM, 3, 1 (1945), 47-52.

67.320 Avilés Ramírez, Eduardo. "Influencia de Martí en Darío." AJM, 6, 1-4 (1952), 436-437.

67.321 Ayón, María. "Martí y los trabajadores." CB, No. 52 (1972), 9-11.

67.322 Baeza Flores, Alberto. "Agonía y deber en José Martí." Atenea, 69 (1942), 90-101.

67.323 _____. "De país en país. Martí en Darío." RNC, No. 178 (1966), 37-45.

67.324 _____. "José Martí, el poeta de su apostolado." Atenea, 72 (1943), 26-46.

67.325 _____. "Martí, el poeta de la muerte suya." Atenea, 79 (1945), 44-63. Also AJM, 5, 2 (1945), 188-198.

67.326 _____. "El 'otro' José Martí." In his Cuba, el laurel y la palma (Miami: Universal, 1977), pp. 79-116.

67.327 Ballagas, Emilio. "'Lalla Rookh', el poema que Martí tradujo." AJM, 6, 1-4 (1952), 201-202.

67.328 Ballón Aguirre, José. "'Mi caballero' de José Martí." Vórtice, 2, 2-3 (1979), 161-181.

67.329 Balseiro, José A. "Cuatro enamorados de la muerte en la lírica hispanoamericana." In his Expresión de Hispanoamérica (San Juan, P.R.: Instituto de Cultura Puertorriqueña, 1960), I, 121-137. Martí inter alios.

67.330 _____. "Lección de cultura martiana." RevCu, 1, 2 (1968), 333-338.

67.331 _____. "El sentido de la justicia en José Martí." In his Expresión de Hispanoamérica (San Juan, P.R.: Instituto de Cultura Puertorriqueña, 1960), I, 139-151.

67.332 Bar-Lewaw, Itzhak. "La prosa de José Martí y Julián del Casal." In his Temas literarios latinoamericanos (M: Costa-Amic, 1961), pp. 33-46.

67.333 Baralt, Luis. "Martí y el teatro." ULH, Nos. 38-39 (1941), 182-210.

67.334 Barbieri, Lázaro. "Martí y la utopía de América." HumT, No. 15 (1962), 167-182.

67.335 Barrial Domínguez, José. "Relación de lo publicado, durante 50 años, por don Federico Henríquez y Carvajal sobre José Martí." RBNC, 2a serie, 4, 3 (1953), 88-95.

67.336 Barrios, Gilberto. "Martí, Darío y el modernismo." Educación, No. 20 (1962), 43-47. Also in his Nuestro Rubén (León, Nicaragua: Hospicio, 1965), pp. 56-63.

67.337 Barros, Silvia A. "La literatura para niños de José Martí en su época." In Estudios críticos sobre la prosa modernista hispanoamericana (NY: Eliseo Torres, 1975), pp. 107-119.

67.338 Bazil, Osvaldo. "La huella de Martí en Rubén Darío." AJM, 4, 4 (1949), 481-494. Also in Manuel Pedro González, Antología crítica de José Martí, q.v., pp. 237-245. Also in Emilio Rodríguez Demorizi, Rubén Darío y sus amigos dominicanos (Bogotá: Espiral, 1948), pp. 294-319.

67.339 Becali, Ramón. "Martí, precursos del Poliecran." LyP, No. 64 (1970), 6-10.

67.340 _____. "La Revista ilustrada de Nueva York." Bohemia, 63, 2 (1971), 40-41.

p. 345 follows p. 348

67.409 Carrancá y Trujillo, Camilo. "El americanismo de Martí." RAm, 26 (1933), 300-301.

67.410 Carrillo, José. "En la huella de Martí." In his Ensayos literarios y didácticos (M: Mercantil, 1949), pp. 105-121.

67.411 Carrillo, Pedro. "¿Quién mató a Martí?" Bohemia, 61, 20 (1969), 4-11.

67.412 Carsuzán, María Emma. "José Martí, el precursor americano." In his La creación en la prosa de España e Hispanoamérica (BA: Raigal, 1955), pp. 63-68.

67.413 Carteles, 34, 5 (1953), entire issue.

67.414 Carter, Boyd G. "Gutiérrez Nájera y Martí como iniciadores del modernismo." RI, No. 54 (1962), 295-310.

67.415 _____. "Martí en las revistas del modernismo antes de su muerte." RI, No. 73 (1970), 547-558. Also AMart, 4, 4 (1972), 335-347.

67.416 _____. "Martí en México: 1894. Un escrito de Puck." LyP, No. 61 (1970), 9-12. Also AMart, 4, 4 (1972), 354-358.

67.417 _____. "Martí y las hijas de Gutiérrez Nájera." SAm, No. 220 (1970), 10-14.

67.418 Casanova Guzmán, Manuel Alberto. "José Martí y la integración." CAn, 2, 2 (1980), 82-88.

67.419 Casaus, Víctor. "El Diario de José Martí: rescate y vigencia de nuestra literatura de campaña." AMart, No. 1 (1978), 189-206.

67.420 Caso, Quino. "El sentimiento amoroso en la obra libertadora de Martí." CulturaSS, No. 12 (1958), 133-139.

67.421 Castelar, Emilio. "Murmuraciones europeas." AJM, 4, 1 (1947), 31-34.

67.422 Castellanos, Jesús. "La estela de Martí." In his Colección póstuma (H: El Siglo XX de A. Miranda, 1914-1916), pp. 267-271.

67.423 Castillo, Andrés. "La primera canción de Martí." Bohemia, 64, 19 (1972), 103-104.

67.424 Castro, José R. "El centenario de José Martí en Guatemala." AJM, 6, 1-4 (1952), 414-417.

67.425 Castro de Morales, Lilia. "Proemio." In José Martí, Diccionario del pensamiento de José Martí (H: Selecta, 1952), pp. 7-29.

67.356 Blanco-Fombona, Rufino. "José Martí." AJM, 6, 1-4 (1952),
        130-132.

67.357 Bohemia, 45, 5 (1953), entire issue.

67.358 Boix Comas, Alberto. "Diario de un ideal. Siguiendo a Martí
        de 'Playitas a Dos Ríos, 1895-1947'." RBNC, 2a serie, 8,
        3 (1957), 39-79.

67.359 Bolet Peraza, N. "José Martí como literato." AJM, 5, 2
        (1950), 199-209.

67.360 Bonilla, Juan. "Impresiones de una velada." RevC, 29 (1951-
        1952), 418-421.

67.361 Bordoli, Domingo L. "Ubicación literaria de Martí." In Martí;
        valoraciones críticas, q.v., pp. 37-43.

67.362 Borrero de Luján, Dulce María. "Martí, poeta." CCont, 32
        (1923), 293-307.

67.363 Borroto Mora, Thomas. "José Martí." Claridad, No. 312 (1937),
        no pagination.

67.364 Boti, Regino Eladio. "De re martiana." RevC, Nos. 31-33
        (1938), 175-186.

67.365 _____. "Martí en Darío." CCont, 37 (1925), 112-124. Also
        AJM, 4, 2 (1943), 378-388. Also BACL, 1 (1952), 584-596.
        Same as item no. 67.47.

67.366 _____. "La obra poética de José Martí: su cronología y anto-
        logía." ROr, Nos. 20-21 (1930), 6-7, 9.

67.367 Boydston, Jo Ann Harrison. "José Martí y Oklahoma." RAm, 43
        (1948), 373-375. Also AJM, 4, 2 (1948), 195-201.

67.368 Boza Masvidal, Eduardo. "Martí, sembrador de ideas." In
        Festschrift José Cid Pérez (NY: Senda Nueva, 1981), pp.
        307-315.

67.369 Brenes-Mesén, Roberto. "José Martí, poeta." In his Crítica
        americana (San José, Costa Riva: Convivio, 1936), pp.
        13-27. Also AJM, 4, 2 (1944), 368-375.

67.370 _____. "Martí en México." RAm, 30 (1953), 3.

67.371 Briceño Perozo, Mario. "La popularidad de Martí en Venezuela."
        BHist, No. 26 (1971), 186-190.

67.372 Brown, Dolores. "The poetic world of José Martí seen in Ver-
        sos sencillos." RomN, 10 (1969), 292-295.

67.373 Bueno, Salvador. "El apóstol José Martí." In his Figuras cu-
        banas del siglo XIX (H: Unión de Escritores y Artistas,
        1980), pp. 205-209.

67.374 _____. "Huella y mensaje de José Martí." In his La letra como
testigo (H: Universidad Central de las Villas, 1957), pp.
209-236.

67.375 _____. "Introducción a la lectura de José Martí." CHA, No.
285 (1974), 602-616.

67.376 _____. "Martí al filo de novecientos. Estudios de intercomu-
nicación hispánica de Guillermo Díaz Plaja." GdC, No. 99
(1972), 31.

67.377 _____. "El pintor húngaro: Munkacsy y José Martí." Bohemia,
64, 26 (1972), 94-95.

67.378 _____. "La única novela que escribió Martí: Lucía Jerez o a-
mistad funesta." Bohemia, 61, 47 (1969), 26-31, 112.
Also as "La única novela que escribió Martí." Unión, 17,
3 (1978), 60-74.

67.379 Cabral, Alexandre. "José Martí: inspirador teórico da revolução cubana." Vértice, 36 (1976), 125-137.

67.380 Cabrera, Rosa M. "Las ideas estéticas de Martí y Varona."
Ceiba, 3, 5 (1975), 60-66.

67.381 _____. "El sentido del color y del sonido en la poesía de
Casal y Martí." PLit, No. 22 (1966), 16.

67.382 Caillet-Bois, Julio. "José Martí." CyC, 28 (1946), 277-299.
Also AJM, 6 (1946), 314-322.

67.383 _____. "Martí y el modernismo literario." In Memoria del Congreso de Escritores Martianos, q.v., pp. 474-489.

67.384 Campillo, J. F. "El maestro; sus versos: su biografía."
RFLC, 16 (1913), 98-111.

67.385 Campoamor, Fernando G. "Martí, cronista de su tiempo." Bohemia, 61, 24 (1969), 32-39.

67.386 _____. "Martí, líder revolucionario." Bohemia, 61, 14 (1969),
12-19.

67.387 Campos, Jorge. "Gavidia, Rubén, Martí y el modernismo." Insula, No. 192 (1962), 11.

67.388 _____. "José Martí y su novela Lucía Jérez." Insula, Nos.
275-276 (1969), 11. Also AMart, 3 (1971), 311-317.

67.389 _____. "La obra renovadora de José Martí." Insula, No. 287
(1970), 11.

67.390 Cañas, Salvador. "Plenitud de José Martí." Síntesis, No. 20
(1955), 25-27.

67.391   Cantón Navarro, José. "Martí, la república y la revolución."
         VO, 14, 3 (1972), 20-27.

67.392   _____. "Martí y el anarquismo." Bohemia, 63, 8 (1970), 20-25.

67.393   _____. "Rusia en Martí." VO, 13, 46 (1971), 20-25.

67.394   Capote, Lincoln. "Textos para la facultad obrera campesina."
         AMart, No. 7 (1977), 405-407.

67.395   Carbonell, Néstor. "Martí y el Uruguay." RABA, No. 77 (1930),
         121-129. Also AANAL, 15 (1930), 391-399.

67.396   _____. "Martí y la Argentina." RABA, No. 66 (1929), 136-155.
         Also AANAL, 13 (1929), 438-460. Also AJM, 4, 2 (1948),
         151-166.

67.397   _____. "Un trabajo de Martí desconocido." AANAL, 11 (1927),
         5-27.

67.398   Carbonell, Reyes. "José Martí y sus versos libres." Estudios,
         Nos. 6-7 (1953), 39-44.

67.399   Carbonell y Rivero, José Manuel. "Las ideas americanistas de
         Martí." Atenea, 17 (1931), 499-503.

67.400   _____. "José Martí." RevC, 29 (1951-1952), 317-324.

67.401   _____. "José Martí." In his La poesía lírica en Cuba (H:
         El Siglo XX, 1928), IV, 160-167.

67.402   _____. "El primer homenaje de la República a su libertador
         José Martí." RBNC, 2a serie, 4, 4 (1953), 71-82.

67.403   Carbonell y Rivero, Miguel Angel. "Martí: su obra literaria
         y su obra política." BACL, 1 (1952), 763-775. Also CPro,
         5 (1953), 94-96.

67.404   Carew, Jan. "José Martí y el Caribe de habla inglesa." AMart,
         No. 1 (1978), 411.

67.405   Carilla, Emilio. "Carlos Rumagosa y José Martí: sobre Martí
         en la Argentina." In Instituto Internacional de Litera-
         tura Iberoamericana, La literatura iberoamericana del si-
         glo XIX (Tucson: Universidad de Arizona, 1974), pp. 221-
         227.

67.406   _____. "Perfil moral de José Martí." HumT, 1 (1953), 317-335.

67.407   Carneado, José Felipe. "Discurso en la clausura del VII Semi-
         nario." AMart, No. 1 (1978), 284-299.

67.408   Carpentier, Alejo. "Martí y Francia." CubaI, No. 107 (1978),
         14-21.

p. 349 follows p. 344

67.341 Bellini, Giuseppe. "L'Italia di José Martí." In his Storia
        delle relazioni letterarie tra l'Italia e l'America di
        lingua spagnola (Milano: Istituto Editoriale Cisalpino-
        La Goliardica, 1977), pp. 185-195.

67.342 Benedetti, Mario. "Martí y el Uruguay." In his El recurso
        del supremo patriarca (M: Nueva Imagen, 1979), pp. 121-
        133.

67.343 Benítez Fleites, Augusto. "Martí y el Partido Revolucionario
        Cubano." In Estudios sobre Martí, q.v., pp. 69-86.

67.344 Bennett, John M. "'Estoy en el baile extraño'." In Francisco
        E. Porrata, and Jorge A. Santana, Antología comentada del
        modernismo (Sacramento: California State University, De-
        partment of Spanish and Portuguese, 1974), pp. 36-39.
        ExTL, Anexo I.

67.345 _____. "'Yo sé de Egipto y Niágara'." In Francisco E. Porra-
        ta, and Jorge A. Santana, Antología comentada del moder-
        nismo (Sacramento: California State University, Department
        of Spanish and Portuguese, 1974), pp. 31-36. ExTL, Anexo
        I.

67.346 Bermúdez, Néstor. "José Martí." In his Mensajeros del ideal
        (H: F. Verdugo, 1940), pp. 73-82.

67.347 Bernal, Emilia. "Martí, por sí mismo." RBC, 33 (1934), 445-
        473; 34 (1934), 125-144. Same as item no. 67.44.

67.348 Bernal del Riesgo, Alfonso. "Estampa psíquica de Martí."
        RBC, 41 (1938), 233-242.

67.349 Berríos Martínez, Rubén. "Martí ante la autonomía." CA, No.
        181 (1972), 141-147.

67.350 Betancourt, Lino. "María Granados, amiga de Martí." Bohemia,
        63, 6 (1971), 55.

67.351 Bianchi Ross, Ciro. "Martí: Coloquio Internacional de Burde-
        os." GdC, No. 99 (1972), 30.

67.352 Billone, Vicente Atilio. "El futuro histórico de José Martí."
        HumT, No. 21 (1968-1969), 77-82.

67.353 Bisbé, Manuel. "Martí, los clásicos y la enseñanza humanísti-
        ca." In Vida y pensamiento de Martí, q.v., I, 253-273.

67.354 _____. "El sentido del deber en la obra de José Martí." RBC,
        37 (1936), 330-341.

67.355 Blanck, Willy de. "José Martí, el gran político cubano que
        se adelantó a su tiempo." AJM, 5, 2 (1950), 219-228.

67.426 Castro Herrero, Guillermo. "Martí en el Moncada." Plural,
        2a época, No. 98 (1979), 16-24.

67.427 Castro Leal, Antonio. "Prólogo." In José Martí, Los cien me-
        jores poemas de José Martí (M: Aguilar, 1974), pp. 1-28.

67.428 Catalá, Raquel. "Martí y el espiritualismo." In Vida y pensa-
        miento de Martí, q.v., I, 297-339. Same as item no.
        67.70.

67.429 Cepeda, Rafael. "La raza de Martí." ND, 37, 1 (1957), 32-36.

67.430 Céspedes Pantoja, Rubén. "La noticia de la muerte de Martí."
        Bohemia, 64, 19 (1972), 96-98.

67.431 Céspedes Ponce, Silvia M. "Recuerdos de un curso martiano."
        AJM, 5, 3 (1951), 381-383.

67.432 Chacón, Francisco. "Martí en la vida social." RevC, 29
        (1951-1952), 430-434.

67.433 Chacón Nari, Rafaela. "Martí y algunos famosos cuadros de Go-
        ya." Bohemia, 70, 42 (1978), 10-13.

67.434 Chacón y Calvo, José María. "Una figura continental." AJM,
        1, 1 (1940), 28-31. Also BACL, 1 (1952), 634-639.

67.435 Cid Pérez, José, and Dolores Martí de Cid. "Hacia una inter-
        pretación del teatro martiano." In Homenaje a Humberto
        Pinera (Madrid: Playor, 1979), pp. 41-52.

67.436 Cimorra, Clemente. "Cómo amaban los grandes." AJM, 5, 3
        (1951), 398-401.

67.437 Cisneros, Florencio J. "José Martí y la pintura moderna."
        Círculo, 4 (1973-1974), 125-128.

67.438 Clavijo Tisseur, Arturo. "Honrar, honra." AJM, 5, 3 (1951),
        396-397.

67.439 Cobb, Carl W. "José Martí's influence on Unamuno's blank
        verse." KFLQ, 11 (1964), 71-78.

67.440 Coleman, Alexander. "Martí y Martínez Estrada." RI, Nos. 92-
        93 (1975), 629-645.

67.441 Contreras, Félix. "Viene mi José Martí." GdC, No. 97 (1971),
        23.

67.442 Cordero Amador, Raúl. "América y Martí." AJM, 6, 1-4 (1952),
        426-432.

67.443 _____. "José Martí." RBC, 41 (1938), 212-215.

67.444 _____. "Martí y la prensa." In Memoria del Congreso de Escritores Martianos, q.v., pp. 729-734.

67.445 Córdova y de Quesada, Federico de. "Martí americanista." ULH, Nos. 46-48 (1943), 83-102.

67.446 _____. "Martí escritor." ULH, Nos. 50-51 (1943), 114-132.

67.447 _____. "Martí idealista." ULH, No. 49 (1943), 23-42.

67.448 _____. "Martí orador." ULH, Nos. 52-54 (1944), 97-114.

67.449 "Corona a José Martí." CA, No. 21 (1945), 157-214.

67.450 Cortina, José Manuel. "Apología de José Martí." AJM, 6, 1-4 (1952), 87-105. Same as item no. 67.75.

67.451 Costa, Octavio R. "José Martí." In his Diez cubanos (H: Ucar, García, 1944), pp. 15-27.

67.452 _____. "El sentimiento de la amistad en José Martí." AJM, 4, 2 (1942), 167-175.

67.453 _____. "Visión americanista de Martí." RevH, 7 (1946), 534-544.

67.454 Cova, Jesús A. "Venezuela y los venezolanos en la prosa de José Martí." In Memoria del Congreso de Escritores Martianos, q.v., pp. 735-743.

67.455 Cox, Carlos Manuel. "Marx, Martí y Marinello." Claridad, No. 289 (1935), no pagination.

67.456 "¿Una crónica desconocida?" AMart, No. 1 (1978), 22-23.

67.457 Cruz, Manuel de la. "José Martí." In his Literatura cubana (Madrid: "Saturnino Calleja", 1924), pp. 409-424.

67.458 Cruz, Mary. "Alegoría viva: Martí." L/L, No. 2 (1971), 25-46. Also CB, No. 54 (1972), 16-18.

67.459 "Cuba: July 26, 1953. Centennial of the birth of José Martí." Tricontinental, No. 40 (1969), 3-26.

67.460 Cueto, Mario G. del. "Martí en la ruta de Girón." Bohemia, 64, 16 (1972), 14-23.

67.461 D'Estetano del Día, Miguel A. "Ho Chi Minh y José Martí, revolucionarios anticolonialistas." CAm, No. 90 (1975), 59-67.

67.462 Daireaux, Max. "José Martí (1853-1895)." AJM, 2, 2 (1941), 123-140. Same as item no. 67.78.

67.463 Darío, Rubén. "José Martí." In his Los raros (Barcelona: Maucci, 1905), pp. 217-228. Various subsequent editions.

67.464 _____. "José Martí, poeta." In Manuel Pedro González, Antología crítica de José Martí, q.v., pp. 267-295.

67.465 Dávalos, Isidro. "Los diarios de Martí." Ciclón, 2, 2 (1956), 86-87.

67.466 Debicki, Andrew. "José Martí: el empleo artístico de una anécdota ['La niña de Guatemala']." RI, No. 69 (1970), 491-504.

67.467 _____. "Punto de vista y experiencia en los Versos sencillos de José Martí." In his Poetas hispanoamericanos contemporáneos (Madrid: Gredos, 1976), pp. 17-37.

67.468 Delfín Avila, Germán. "Sobre un poema inédito de Martí." AJM, 5, 4 (1951), 517-530.

67.469 Delgado, Manuel Patricio. "Martí en Cayo Hueso." RBC, 31 (1933), 353-359.

67.470 Deschamps Chapeaux, Pedro. "José Martí, maestro de obreros." In Estudios sobre Martí (H: Ciencias Sociales, 1975), pp. 147-168.

67.471 Desnoes, Edmundo. "José Martí, intelectual revolucionario y hombre nuevo." CAm, No. 54 (1969), 115-121.

67.472 _____. "Martí en Fidel." SCRI, 1967, pp. 43-49. Also in his Puntos de vista (H: Instituto del Libro, 1967), pp. 21-33.

67.473 Dessau, Adalbert. "Stellung und Bedeutung José Martís in der Entwicklung der lateinamerikanischen Literatur." BRP, 11, 2 (1972), 185-207.

67.474 Dey, Susnigdha. "José Martí in today's developing world." IndH, 26, 4-27, 1 (1977-1978), 41-44.

67.475 Díaz Abreu, Antonio. "Reflexiones martianas." AJM, 6, 1-4 (1952), 219-221.

67.476 Díaz Arrieta, Hernán. "Gabriel Mistral y José Martí." IndiceH, 5, 3 (1940), 11-13.

67.477 Díaz de Arce, Omar. "Martí y la revolución latinoamericana." Islas, No. 15 (1964), 23-31.

67.478 Díaz Ortega, Enrique. "Humanismo y amor en José Martí." AJM, 5, 3 (1951), 331-340.

67.479 _____. "El sentimiento de la amistad en José Martí." AJM, 4, 2 (1948), 176-185.

67.480 _____. "Los valores educacionales en José Martí." AJM, 5, 1 (1950), 77-89.

67.481 Díaz Plaja, Guillermo. "Lenguaje, verso y poesía en José Martí." CHA, No. 39 (1953), 312-322. Also in Memoria del Congreso de Escritores Martianos, q.v., pp. 617-631.

67.482 _____. "Martí." In his Modernismo frente a noventa y ocho (Madrid: Espasa-Calpe, 1951), pp. 305-307. Also AJM, 6, 1-4 (1952), 441-442. Also BACL, 1 (1952), 542-544. Also in Manuel Pedro González, Antología crítica de José Martí, q.v., pp. 247-249.

67.483 _____. "Martí, admirador de Goya." In Miscelánea de estudios a Fernando Ortiz (H, 1955), pp. 489-493.

67.484 Díaz Pozzoto, Jaime. "Nuestra América, la plena libertad y José Martí." CA, No. 200 (1975), 77-87.

67.485 Díez Canedo, Enrique. "Heredia y Martí." RBC, 29 (1932), 179-183. Also in his Letras de América (M: El Colegio de México, 1944), pp. 179-183.

67.486 _____. "Martí en edición española." In his Letras de América (M: El Colegio de México, 1944), pp. 184-186.

67.487 Domenech, Camilo. "Guanabacoa. Presencia de Martí." VO, 17, 22 (1975), 30-33.

67.488 Domínguez, Luis Orlando. "Discurso." In Estudios sobre Martí, q.v., pp. 331-344.

67.489 Dominici, Pedro César. "José Martí." In his Tronos vacantes (BA: "La Facultad", Juan Roldán, 1924), pp. 123-136.

67.490 "El donativo de Néstor Carbonell (carta autógrafas de José Martí)." RBNJM, 3a serie, 3, 1-4 (1961), 50-87.

67.491 Dorr, Nicolás. "José Martí, dramaturgo." Bohemia, 69, 4 (1977), 10-13. Also Conjunto, No. 33 (1977), 112-119.

67.492 _____. "José Martí y sus críticas teatrales mexicanas." Conjunto, No. 41 (1979), 3-6.

67.493 Dougé, Joubert. "José Martí, crítico literario." In Memoria del Congreso de Escritores Martianos, q.v., pp. 691-705.

67.494 Doumont, Monique. "Notas para un estudio del "Whitman' de José Martí." AnuarioF, 8-9 (1969-1970), 199-212.

67.495 Echagüe, Juan Pablo. "José Martí, personalidad de América." AJM, 5, 1 (1950), 19-28.

67.496 Echevarría, Israel. "Repertorios para el trabajo de consulta y referencia con la obra martiana." Bibliotecas, 6, 6 (1968), 1-11.

67.497   Entralgo, Elías. "El centenario de Martí." AJM, 5, 2 (1950),
         253-256.

67.498   Eremberg, Ilya. "Homenaje de la URSS a José Martí en el cente-
         nario de su nacimiento." CSov, No. 102 (1953), 36-37.

67.499   Escala, Víctor Hugo. "Evocación de Martí en el primer centena-
         rio de su muerte." AméricaQ, Nos. 81-82 (1945), 416-433.

67.500   Escudero, Alfonso M. "Martí. I. Los 42 años de José Martí.
         II. Más trazos para su retrato espiritual. III. El escri-
         tor y los géneros literarios. IV. El intelectual y el ar-
         tista. V. Al cabo de los años." Atenea, 110 (1953), 16-
         54.

67.501   _____. "Prólogo." In José Martí, Páginas escogidas (BA: Es-
         pasa-Calpe Argentina, 1953), pp. 9-41.

67.502   Esténger, Rafael. "Esbozo de Martí." In Memoria del Congreso
         de Escritores Martianos, q.v., pp. 90-119.

67.503   _____. "Guía en la poética de Martí." In José Martí, Poesías
         completas (Madrid: Aguilar; H: Librería Económica, 1953),
         pp. 9-46.

67.504   Estrada, Domingo. "José Martí." AJM, 5, 2 (1950), 201-218.
         Also RevC, 29 (1952), 108-118. Also ASGHG, 31, 1-4
         (1958), 286-295.

67.505   Estrade, Paul. "Martien, martiste ou martinien?..." Cara-
         velle, No. 35 (1980), 135-137.

67.506   _____. "La Pinkerton contra Martí." AMart, No. 1 (1978),
         207-221.

67.507   _____. "Un 'socialista' mexicano: José Martí." CAm, No. 82
         (1974), 40-50.

67.508   Estrella Gutiérrez, Fermín, and Emilio Suárez Calimano. "José
         Martí." BACL, 1 (1952), 557-560.

67.509   F. M. Z. "El magisterio de Martí." AJM, 5, 4 (1951), 541.

67.510   Fabbiani Ruiz, José. "Martí y nosotros." AJM, 5, 3 (1951),
         393-395.

67.511   Febres Cordero G., Julio. "Glosas martianas." RNC, No. 86
         (1951), 88-109.

67.512   FedE, enero-febrero 1953, entire issue.

67.513   Feijóo, Samuel. "Algunos antecedentes de los Versos sencillos
         de José Martí." CB, No. 124 (1978), 25-27.

67.514 _____. "La cuarteta y la décima folklórica en la poesía de José Martí." Bohemia, 66, 46 (1974), 8-11.

67.515 Fernández, Gastón J. "La presencia del negro en los Versos sencillos de Martí." In Homenaje a Lydia Cabrera (Miami: Universal, 1978), pp. 123-129.

67.516 _____. "El tema de la esclavitud en los Versos sencillos de José Martí." In Studies in Language and Literature (Richmond, Ken.: Eastern Kentucky University, Department of Foreign Languages, 1976), pp. 153-158.

67.517 Fernández, José R. "[Discurso]." EduciaciónH, No. 16 (1975), 49-63.

67.518 Fernández, Justino. "Política y arte en la crítica de Martí." In Memoria del Congreso de Escritores Martianos, q.v., pp. 714-717.

67.519 Fernández Concheso, Aurelio. "José Martí, filósofo." IAA, 11 (1973), 107-121. Same as item no. 67.91.

67.520 Fernández de Castro, José Antonio. "José Martí." CCont, 35 (1924), 281-289.

67.521 Fernández de la Vega, Oscar. "Martí y [José] White." Círculo, 8 (1979), 61-70.

67.522 Fernández Marcané, Luis. "Maura y Martí." BAN, 39 (1940), 311-317.

67.523 Fernández Retamar, Roberto. "Algunos problemas de una biografía ideológica de José Martí." Latinoamérica, 12 (1979), 141-167.

67.524 _____. "La crítica de Martí." In his Para una teoría de la literatura hispanoamericana; 2. ed. (M: Nuestro Tiempo, 1977), pp. 11-29. Orig. H: Casa de las Américas, 1976.

67.525 _____. "Introducción a Martí." In José Martí, Cuba, nuestra América, los Estados Unidos (M: Siglo XXI, 1973), pp. ix-lxiii. A fragment appeared in CAm, No. 93 (1975), 33-47.

67.526 _____. "Lectura de José Martí." In his Papelería (Santa Clara: Universidad Central de Las Villas, Dirección de Publicaciones, 1962), pp. 257-263.

67.527 _____. "Las letras fieras de José Martí." TC, No. 14 (1979), 28-43.

67.528 _____. "Martí en su (tercer) mundo." In José Martí, Páginas escogidas (H: Universitaria, 1965), I, 5-62. Also 1974. Also SCRI, 1967, pp. 3-26. Also in his Ensayo de otro mundo (Santiago de Chile: Universitaria, 1969), pp. 19-51. Also in Martí; valoraciones críticas, q.v., pp. 1-35.

Also in José Martí, José Martí (San José, Costa Rica: Ministerio de Cultura, 1976), pp. 19-68. Also as "Préface: Martí en son (tiers) monde." In José Martí, Nôtre Amérique (Paris: Máspero, 1968). Contains "... Chronologie et notes d'André Joucla-Ruau."

67.529 _____. "Martí y Ho Chi Minh, dirigentes coloniales." AMart, No. 3 (1971), 180-189. Also as "Sobre Martí y Ho Chi Minh, dirigentes coloniales." CAm, No. 63 (1970), 48-53.

67.530 _____. "Martí y la revolución de nuestra América." Crisis, No. 5 (1973), 52-55.

67.531 _____. "Notas sobre Martí, Lenin y la revolución anticolonial." CAm, No. 59 (1970), 116-130. Also AMart, No. 3 (1971), 161-180.

67.532 _____. "Sobre Ramona de Helen Hunt Jackson y José Martí." In Mélanges à la mémoire d'André Joucla-Ruau (Aix-en-Provence: Université de Provence, 1978), pp. 699-705.

67.533 _____. "El 26 de julio y los 'compañeros desconocidos' de José Martí." Indice, No. 333 (1973), 43-46.

67.534 Ferrer-Canales, José. "José Martí y Betances." In Actas del Quinto Congreso Internacional de Hispanistas (Bordeaux: Presses Universitaires de Bordeaux, 1977), pp. 385-392. Also as "Martí y Betances." CA, No. 200 (1975), 130-137.

67.535 _____. "José Martí y José de Diego." Asomante, 22, 3 (1966), 53-80.

67.536 _____. "Martí en Varona." RIB, 15 (1966), 251-256.

67.537 _____. "Martí y Puerto Rico." CA, No. 80 (1955), 141-169.

67.538 _____. "El negro en José Martí." In Estudios martianos, q. v., pp. 109-118.

67.539 _____. "Palabras a José Martí." CCLC, No. 19 (1956), 175-177.

67.540 _____. "Rousseau y Martí en Roa." In Instituto Internacional de Literatura Iberoamericana, Literatura iberoamericana; influjos locales (M, 1965), pp. 165-182.

67.541 Figueredo, Bernardo. "Recuerdos de Martí." AMart, No. 3 (1971), 137-160.

67.542 Figueroa, Pedro Pablo. "José Martí." RevC, 20 (1951-1952), 180-191.

67.543 Flores, Saúl. "José Martí, educador." AJM, 6, 1-4 (1952), 443-447.

67.544 Florit, Eugenio. "Bécquer en Martí." La torre, No. 10 (1955), 131-140.

67.545 _____. "José Martí: vida y obra. 2. Versos." RHM, 18 (1952), 20-71. Also in José Martí (1953-1895), q.v., pp. 27-78. Also in Manuel Pedro González, Antología crítica de José Martí, q.v., pp. 297-342.

67.546 _____. "Mi Martí." Orígenes, No. 33 (1953), 47-48. Also in his Poesía casi siempre (ensayos literarios) (Madrid/NY: Mensaje, 1978), pp. 79-80.

67.547 _____. "Notas sobre la poesía en Martí." AJM, 2, 2 (1941), 15-27. Also RI, No. 8 (1942), 253-266. Also BACL, 1 (1952), 605-619. Also AUC, No. 89 (1953), 82-96.

67.548 _____. "La poesía de Martí." AJM, 6, 1-4 (1952), 106-117.

67.549 _____. "Los versos de Martí." In José Martí, Versos (NY: Las Américas, 1967), pp. 7-63.

67.550 Foncueva, José Antonio. "Novísimo retrato de José Martí." AMart, No. 1 (1978), 300-309.

67.551 Forne Farreres, José. "Martí, admirador de Goya." Cuba, No. 21 (1964), 26-29.

67.552 _____. "Martí y la Primera República Española." VO, 14, 4 (1972), 24-29.

67.553 Franco, Luis. "Martí, escritor." AJM, 5, 3 (1951), 325-330. Also BACL, 1 (1952), 597-604.

67.554 Freire, Joaquín. "José Martí: el maestro del deber." Educación, 13, 12 (1964), 99-107.

67.555 Fundora, Osvaldo. "Martí político, revolucionario." Bohemia, 64, 6 (1972), 98-100.

67.556 Galich, Manuel. "Acotaciones a Nuestra América." CAm, No. 68 (1971), 50-58.

67.557 _____. "Agradecimiento a Martí y a Cuba." RBC, 57 (1945), 201-208.

67.558 Gamboa, Emma. "Americanismo de José Martí." In Actas del XXXIII Congreso Internacional de Americanistas (San José, Costa Rica, 1959), III, 59-65.

67.559 Garasino, Ana María. "Trayectoria laicista de José Martí." ULH, Nos. 130-132 (1957), 41-119.

67.560 García Agüero, Salvador. "Martí orador." In Vida y pensamiento de Martí, q.v., II, 249-263.

67.561 _____. "Secuencias martinianas." RBC, 37 (1936), 206-217.

67.562 García Calderón, Ventura. "José Martí." CCont, 34 (1924), 93-96.

67.563 García Cantú, Gastón. "México en Martí." AMart, No. 1 (1978), 222-228.

67.564 García del Cueto, Mario. "Martí pasó la luna de miel en Acapulco." Bohemia, 61, 11 (1969), 4-9.

67.565 García del Pino, César. "El Laborante: Carlos Sauvalle y José Martí." RBNJM, 3a época, 11, 2 (1969), 165-201.

67.566 García Espinosa, Juan M. "En torno a la novela del apóstol [Amistad funesta]." ULH, No. 171 (1965), 7-99.

67.567 García Galló, Gaspar Jorge. "El humanismo martiano y sus raíces." AMart, No. 1 (1978), 265-280.

67.568 _____. "José Martí y la educación." Islas, No. 41 (1972), 33-44.

67.569 _____. "Martí y los tabaqueros." Islas, 3, 3 (1961), 63-69.

67.570 García Godoy, Federico. "José Martí." In his Americanismo literario (Madrid: América, 1917), pp. 25-72.

67.571 García Kohly, Mario. "Homenaje a José Martí." AJM, 6, 1-4 (1952), 163-168.

67.572 García Marruz, Fina. "Amistad funesta." CB, No. 45 (1971), 5-8. Also in Cintio Vitier, and Fina García Marruz, Temas martianos, q.v., pp. 282-291.

67.573 _____. "Una carta de Juana Borrero sobre Martí." AMart, 4, 4 (1972), 359-363.

67.574 _____. "Gracián y Martí." Islas, 3, 1 (1960), 161-168.

67.575 _____. "José Martí." Lyceum, No. 30 (1952), 5-41. Also AJM, 6, 1-4 (1952), 52-86. Also in Manuel Pedro González, Antología crítica de José Martí, q.v., pp. 193-213. Also in José Martí, Diarios (H: Libro Cubano, 1956), pp. 5-69.

67.576 _____. "Los versos de Martí." RBNJM, 3a serie, 10, 1 (1968), 15-51. Also in Cintio Vitier, and Fina García Marruz, Temas martianos, q.v., pp. 240-267.

67.577 García-Marruz, Graciella. "El expresionismo en la prosa de José Martí." In Estudios críticos sobre la prosa modernista hispanoamericana (NY: Eliseo Torres, 1975), pp. 35-55.

67.578 García Monge, J. "José Martí en Costa Rica." RAm, 39 (1942), 97-98. Also AJM, 4, 2 (1944), 410-412.

67.579 García Pascual, Luis. "Por la senda del apóstol." AMart, No. 3 (1971), 249-307.

67.580 García Pons, César. "Ezequiel Martínez Estrada. Martí revolucionario. La personalidad. El hombre." RevCu, 1, 2 (1968), 470-475. See item no. 67.177.

67.581 _____. "Martí y los días del obispo Espada." RBC, 59 (1947), 212-216.

67.582 García Ronda, Dania. "Tanteos para una tabla de valores en la correspondencia de José Martí." In Estudios sobre Martí, q.v., pp. 259-330.

67.583 García Tuduri, Mercedes. "Las conversaciones filosóficas interamericanas y el centenario de Martí." CPro, 5 (1953), 38.

67.584 Gay Calbó, Enrique. "Americanismo en Martí." In Vida y pensamiento de Martí, q.v., I, 27-59.

67.585 _____. "Martí americano." RBC, 58 (1946), 145-154. Also AJM, 4, 2 (1948), 202-211.

67.586 _____. "Martí y la conducta humana." AJM, 6, 1-4 (1952), 338-349.

67.587 _____. "La serenidad de Martí." RBNC, 2a serie, 4, 4 (1953), 90-94.

67.588 Ghiano, Juan Carlos. "Martí poeta." In José Martí, Poesías (BA: Raigal, 1952), pp. 7-52. Also in Manuel Pedro González, Antología crítica de José Martí, q.v., pp. 343-365.

67.589 Ghiraldo, Alberto. "José Martí, su personalidad." In José Martí, Lira guerrera (Madrid: Atlántida, 1925), I, 11-84.

67.590 Gicovate, Bernardo. "Aprendizaje y plenitud de José Martí." In his Conceptos fundamentales de literatura comparada (San Juan, P.R.: Asomante, 1962), pp. 79-103.

67.591 _____. "Hallazgo lingüístico en José Martí." RI, No. 39 (1955), 13-17.

67.592 Gilabert, Juan. "José Martí, cronista de España." Hispanófila, No. 43 (1971), 45-61.

67.593 Gimeno, Patricio. "Reminiscencias de José Martí." RBC, 29 (1932), 321-326.

67.594 Ginsberg, Judith. "From anger to action: the avenging female
        in two Lucías [Martí and Humberto Solas]." REH, 14, 1
        (1980), 131-138.

67.595 _____. "Los juicios de José Martí acerca de la inmigración a
        los Estados Unidos." BR/RB, 1 (1974), 185-192.

67.596 Giusti, Roberto F. "José Martí." AJM, 3, 1 (1945), 23-28.

67.597 Godoy, Armando. "José Martí, poète et libérateur." ND, 34, 1
        (1954), 86-90.

67.598 Godoy, Gustavo J. "José Martí en Jacksonville." Círculo, 7
        (1978), 55-61.

67.599 Goldarás, Roberto L. "La ruta de Martí." CPro, No. 5 (1953),
        11-15.

67.600 Gómez, Máximo. "José Martí." Bohemia, 64, 20 (1972), 100.

67.601 Gómez Ferrer, Juan Gualberto. "Martí y yo. La última visita.
        La última carta." RBC, 31 (1933), 5-11.

67.602 Gómez Haedo, Juan Carlos. "Hombre y letras." RNM, 6 (1939),
        419-428. Martí inter alios.

67.603 González, Manuel J. "El maestro." RevC, 29 (1951-1952), 121-
        125.

67.604 González, Manuel Pedro. "Aclaraciones en torno a la génesis
        del modernismo." CCLC, No. 75 (1963), 41-50.

67.605 _____. "Aforismos y definiciones, o la capacidad sintética de
        Martí." AMart, 4, 4 (1972), 27-50.

67.606 _____. "Al margen de una polémica.martiana." CA, No. 188
        (1973), 165-183.

67.607 _____. "Aspectos inexplorados en la obra de José Martí."
        CyC, 45 (1954), 313-325. Also Islas, 2, 1 (1959), 49-61.

67.608 _____. "Crecimiento y revelación de José Martí." CA, No.
        172 (1970), 158-173.

67.609 _____. "El culto a Martí en la Argentina." RBNC, 2a serie,
        5, 2 (1954), 45-57.

67.610 _____. "En el centenario de Rubén Darío. (Deslindes inde-
        clinables)." CAm, No. 42 (1967), 36-51.

67.611 _____. "Evolución de la estimativa martiana." In Antología
        crítica de José Martí, q.v., pp. xi-xxix.

67.612 _____. "La exégesis estilística de la obra martiana." Unión,
        6, 1 (1968), 56-60.

67.613   . "Las formas sintácticas en el período de mayor madurez de la prosa martiana (1880-1895)." In Estudios martianos, q.v., pp. 15-27.

67.614   . "Fuentes para el estudio de José Martí: I. por José I. Mantecón. II. por Antonio Martínez Bello. III. por Salvador Bueno." AJM, 5, 2 (1950), 276-288.

67.615   . "I. Iniciación de Rubén Darío en el culto a Martí. II. Resonancias de la prosa martiana en la de Darío (1886-1900)." In Memoria del Congreso de Escritores Martianos, q.v., pp. 503-569. Also in Juan Loveluck, Diez estudios sobre Rubén Darío (Santiago de Chile: Zig-Zag, 1967), pp. 73-122.

67.616   . "Intemperancia y arbitrariedad de un sofista." Unión, 3, 4 (1964), 137-144.

67.617   . "José Martí, anticlerical irreductible." CA, No. 73 (1954), 170-197.

67.618   . "José Martí en Rusia." RBC, 73 (1957), 77-84. Also Humanismo, No. 45 (1957), 19-27.

67.619   . "José Martí, epistológrafo." RI, No. 25 (1947), 23-37. Also AJM, 4, 4 (1949), 465-476.

67.620   . "José Martí: jerarca del modernismo." In Miscelánea de estudios dedicados a Fernando Ortiz (H: Sociedad Económica de Amigos del País, 1955), pp. 727-762.

67.621   . "José Martí, su circunstancia y su tiempo." Islas, 2, 2-3 (1960), 357-378.

67.622   . Prefacio a la edición española de Lucía Jerez." In José Martí, Lucía Jerez (Madrid: Gredos, 1969), pp. 7-58.

67.623   . "La revaloración de Martí (acotaciones en torno a su bibliografía)." ULH, Nos. 11-12 (1935), 5-22. Also in his Estudios sobre literaturas hispanoamericanas (M: Cultura, 1951), pp. 133-150.

67.624   . "Semblanza de José Martí: glosa del centenario." Hispania, 36 (1953), 43-51.

67.625 González Blanco, Edmundo. "Martí y su obra." AJM, 6, 1-4 (1952), 175-177.

67.626 González Bolaños, Aimée. "Algunas consideraciones sobre los motivos poéticos de 'Ismaelillo'." Islas, No. 46 (1973), 45-52.

67.627 González Calzada, Manuel. "Apologética de Martí." RevC, 26 (1950), 112-179.

67.628   González Freire, Natividad. "Sentir y decir a Martí." Bohe-
         mia, 63, 42 (1971), 28-29.

67.629   González Guerrero, Francisco. "Martí, escritor." AJM, 3, 1
         (1945), 108-110. Also BACL, 1 (1952), 628-631.

67.630   González Jiménez, Omar. "De la prosa martiana." Bohemia, 64,
         7 (1972), 104.

67.631   González Palacios, Carlos. "Exaltación a la fe: intimidad de
         Martí." AJM, 6, 1-4 (1952), 145-160.

67.632   _____. "Valoración de Martí." AJM, 6, 1-4 (1952), 16-51.

67.633   González Rodríguez, José. "Martí en la caricatura." AMart,
         No. 7 (1977), 127-162.

67.634   Grass, Roland. "A sincere man views boomers, sooners, and the
         land run." CimR, 28 (1974), 19-24.

67.635   Gray, Richard Butler. "José Martí and social revolution in
         Cuba." JIAS, 5 (1963), 249-256.

67.636   _____. "The Quesadas of Cuba: biographers and editors of José
         Martí." RIB, 16 (1966), 369-382.

67.637   Gregori, Nuria. "Correcciones a las ediciones del Diario de
         campaña de Martí." L/L, No. 1 (1970), 3-102.

67.638   _____. "Los cubanismos de Martí en su Diario de campaña."
         L/L, No. 2 (1971), 47-55.

67.639   Guandique, José Salvador. "José Martí, vocación humana." AJM,
         4, 4 (1949), 497-501.

67.640   Guerra de la Piedra, Agustín. "El sentimiento de la amistad
         en José Martí." AJM, 4, 2 (1948), 186-194.

67.641   Guerra Iñiguez, Daniel. "José Martí y su ideal de patria."
         RNC, No. 98 (1953), 93-98.

67.642   Guevara, Ernesto. "Apología de Martí." Humanismo, Nos. 58-59
         (1959-1960), 35-40.

67.643   Guillén, Nicolás. "Martí en Azul [Argentina]." In his Prosa
         de prisa, crónicas (Santa Clara: Universidad Central de
         Las Villas, Dirección de Publicaciones, 1962), pp. 69-77.

67.644   Guiral Moreno, Mario. "La autenticidad de un grupo histórico."
         RBNC, 2a serie, 6, 4 (1955), 103-119.

67.645   Gutiérrez Corrales, Miguel. "Martí y el americanismo." In
         Memoria del Congreso de Escritores Martianos, q.v., pp.
         348-361.

67.646 Gutiérrez de la Solana, Alberto. "El arte de Alfonso Hernández Catá en la Mitología de Martí." In Homenaje a Humberto Piñera (Madrid: Playor, 1979), pp. 105-110. See item no. 67.124.

67.647 _____. "José Martí: prefiguración de su vida en Abdala y Patria y libertad." LATR, 11, 2 (1978), 17-23.

67.648 _____. "José Martí visto por Rubén Darío." Círculo, 3 (1972), 10-24.

67.649 _____. "Martí: teatro, ética y estética." In Instituto Internacional de Literatura Iberoamericana, XVII Congreso (Madrid: Cultura Hispánica del Centro Iberoamericano de Cooperación, 1978), pp. 1219-1228.

67.650 _____. "Marx, Engels, Martí y las razas y nacionalidades." Abdala, No. 17 [sic, for No. 18] (1973), 5-6.

67.651 _____. "La piel: novela antirracista psicológica." In Homenaje a Lydia Cabrera (Miami: Universal, 1978), pp. 201-209.

67.652 _____. "Vigencia del pensamiento martiano." In Estudios sobre Hispanoamérica (homenaje a Carlos M. Raggi y Ageo) (San José, Costa Rica: Círculo de Cultura Panamericana, 1976), pp. 49-66.

67.653 Gutiérrez Nájera, Manuel. "Carta inconclusa de Gutiérrez Nájera a Martí." RBNJM, 3a serie, 4, 1-4 (1962), 82-87.

67.654 _____. "La edad de oro, de José Martí." RyC, No. 3 (1972), 5-8.

67.655 Halperin, Renata Donghi de. "Nuestra América y su vocero: José Martí." CyC, 30 (1947), 329-346. Also AJM, 4, 1 (1947), 93-105.

67.656 Halperin Donghi, Tulio. "Martí, novelista del fin de siglo." AJM, 6, 1-4 (1952), 400-402.

67.657 Hammitt, Gene M. "Función y símbolo del hijo en el Ismaelillo de Martí." RI, No. 59 (1965), 71-81.

67.658 Hart Dávalos, Armando. "Discurso." AMart, No. 7 (1977), 25-28.

67.659 _____. "Mensaje al VI Seminario Juvenil Nacional de Estudios Martianos." AMart, No. 1 (1978), 11-12.

67.660 Hedberg, Nils. "José Martí y el artista Norrman. Comentario sobre su retrato." ULH, No. 172 (1965), 77-127.

67.661 Hedman Marrero, Humberto. "Martí por España: incursión bibliográfica." VU, No. 214 (1969), 2-6.

67.662 Henríquez Ureña, Max. "José Martí." CCont, 2 (1913), 5-10.

67.663 _____. "José Martí." In his Breve historia del modernismo;
        2. ed. (M/BA: Fondo de Cultura Económica, 1962), pp. 53-
        66. Orig. 1954.

67.664 _____. "José Martí y su personalidad genial." Bohemia, 64,
        20 (1972), 101.

67.665 _____. "Martí en Santo Domingo." CCont, 2 (1913), 177-203.
        Also AJM, 4, 3 (1948), 245-264.

67.666 _____. "Martí, iniciador del modernismo." In Memoria del Con-
        greso de Escritores Martianos, q.v., pp. 447-465. Also in
        Manuel Pedro González, Antología crítica de José Martí, q.
        v., pp. 167-186.

67.667 Henríquez Ureña, Pedro. "José Martí." BACL, 1 (1952), 506-
        507.

67.668 _____. "Martí." RAm, 23 (1931), 33-34. Also RBC, 27 (1931),
        371-373. Also Sur, No. 1 (1931), 220-223. Also AJM, 6,
        1-4 (1952), 483-485.

67.669 _____. "Martí, escritor." AJM, 4, 2 (1944), 358-360.

67.670 Henríquez y Carvajal, Federico. "Martí en la prensa." AAHC,
        12 (1929), 310-314. Also RBC, 25 (1930), 321-327. Also
        BAN, 39 (1940), 228-233.

67.671 Heredia, Nicolás. "La obra de José Martí." AJM, 5, 2 (1950),
        193-198.

67.672 Heredia Rojas, Israel Ordenal. "La elegía en la obra de José
        Martí." Islas, No. 46 (1973), 25-33.

67.673 _____. "Liberación, patria y pueblo en el pensamiento martia-
        no." Islas, No. 66 (1980), 31-45.

67.674 Henrández Catá, Alfonso. "Martí en portugués." BACL, 1
        (1952), 545-548.

67.675 _____. "Mitología de Martí. (Estampas de nacimiento). Be-
        lén." Crónica, 3, 20 (1953), 15.

67.676 Hernández Novas, Raúl. "José Martí, crítico de la poesía fran-
        cesa del siglo XIX." In Estudios sobre Martí, q.v., pp.
        219-257.

67.677 Hernández Otero, Ricardo L. "Colaboración martiana en La o-
        frenda de oro (notas sobre un artículo desconocido de Jo-
        sé Martí)." L/L, Nos. 7-8 (1976-1977), 38-67.

67.678 Hernández Pardo, Héctor. "Raíz martiana de nuestra pedagogía."
        AMart, No. 1 (1978), 240-248.

67.679 Herrera, Darío. "Crítica literaria: Martí, iniciador del modernismo americano." Lotería, No. 59 (1960), 56-58.

67.680 Herrera, Enrique. "José Martí: orador y político." Abside, 43, 2 (1979), 165-194.

67.681 Herrera Franyutti, Alfonso. "Actualidades de José Martí." AMart, No. 7 (1977), 275-288.

67.682 _____. "Martí en tierra de Mayab." RUY, No. 109 (1977), 78-97.

67.683 _____. "Una poesía desconocida de José Martí ['De noche, en la imprenta']." CAm, No. 93 (1975), 87-89.

67.684 _____. "Tras las huellas de Martí en México. Martí en Veracruz." AMart, 4, 4 (1972), 349-353.

67.685 Hidalgo, Ariel. "El canal de Panamá en las proyecciones políticas de José Martí." AMart, No. 1 (1978), 229-239.

67.686 _____. "José Martí y los antecedentes del neocolonialismo yanqui en Nicaragua." CAm, No. 117 (1979), 48-54.

67.687 _____. "Martí y el neocolonialismo imperialista." CAm, No. 84 (1974), 89-95.

67.688 "Homenaje a José Martí." RevC, 29 (1951-1952), 7-517.

67.689 "Homenaje a Martí en Washington." AJM, 6, 1-4 (1952), 418-425.

67.690 "Homenajes a Martí en Francia." CUNESCO, No. 41 (1972), 2-11.

67.691 Hostos y Bonilla, Eugenio María de. "El testamento de Martí." In his Obras completas (H: Cultural, 1939), IX, 483-484. His Temas cubanos.

67.692 House, Laraine R. "José Martí en el ansia del amor puro." CA, No. 239 (1981), 134-152.

67.693 Huré, Claude. "Les dernières notes de voyage de José Martí." LNL, No. 161 (1962), 62-81.

67.694 Ibáñez, Roberto. "Imágenes del mundo y del trasmundo en los Versos sencillos." In Manuel Pedro González, Antología crítica de José Martí, q.v., pp. 367-380. Also Pórtico, 2, 4 (1964), 161-181.

67.695 Ibarbourou, Juana de. "La poesía de Martí." In Memoria del Congreso de Escritores Martianos, q.v., pp. 632-637.

67.696 Ichaso, Francisco. "Conocimiento de Martí." In his Defensa del hombre (H: Trópico, 1937), pp. 44-64.

67.697 _____ . "Lo español y lo europeo en Martí." In Memoria del Congreso de Escritores Martianos, q.v., pp. 276-284.

67.698 _____ . "Martí y el teatro." In Vida y pensamiento de Martí, q.v., II, 63-90. Also BACL, 1 (1952), 734-762.

67.699 Iduarte, Andrés. "Cuba, Varona y Martín." RAm, 46 (1950), 153-154.

67.700 _____ . "De cómo honrar a José Martí." AJM, 6, 1-4 (1952), 11-15.

67.701 _____ . "Ideas económicas de José Martí." ND, 26, 9 (1945), 10-12, 29.

67.702 _____ . "Ideas filosóficas." In Manuel Pedro González, Antología crítica de José Martí, q.v., pp. 513-526.

67.703 _____ . "Ideas pedagógicas de Martí." ND, 26, 8 (1945), 3-5.

67.704 _____ . "Las ideas políticas de José Martí (capítulos de un libro inédito)." CA, No. 14 (1944), 155-177.

67.705 _____ . "Ideas religiosas, morales y filosóficas de Martí." ND, 25, 2 (1944), 3-7, 26-32.

67.706 _____ . "José Martí." UM, No. 20 (1932), 160-177.

67.707 _____ . "José Martí: vida y obra. 3. Prosa." RHM, 18 (1952), 71-83. Also in José Martí (1853-1895), q.v., pp. 79-91.

67.708 _____ . "José Martí: vida y obra. 4. América." RHM, 18 (1952), 83-113. Also in José Martí (1853-1895), q.v., pp. 92-122.

67.709 _____ . "Martí." RHM, 8 (1942), 193-204.

67.710 _____ . "Martí en el mural del Prado." ND, 38, 4 (1958), 41-43.

67.711 _____ . "Martí en las letras hispánicas." Bolívar, No. 17 (1953), 279-295.

67.712 _____ . "México y América en el centenario de Martí." AJM, 6, 1-4 (1952), 409-413.

67.713 _____ . "Sobre el americanismo de José Martí." In Instituto Internacional de Literatura Iberoamericana, Homenaje a Hidalgo, Díaz Mirón y Martí (M: Universitaria, 1954), pp. 149-154.

67.714 _____ . "Sobre José Martí." RUM, 21, 6 (1967), 3-5.

67.715 _____ . "Valoración literaria de Martí." BACL, 1 (1952), 529-535. Also in his Martí escritor, q.v., pp. 287-293.

67.716 Indžov, Nikola. "Xristo Botev; Xose Martí: edin simvol na dva naroda." Plamăk, 20, 7 (1976), 299-201.

67.717 "Informe de la Comisión Nacional Permanente a la plenaria inicial del IV Seminario de Estudios Martianos." AMart, No. 7 (1977), 175-182.

67.718 "La intervención norteamericana en la guerra de Cuba tuvo el definido propósito de frustrar el más profundo de los ideales martianos." RyC, No. 8 (1973), 3-11.

67.719 Ionescu, Andrei. "José Martí, omul cel mai pur al Americii." SXX, 15, 10-12 (1972), 217-218.

67.720 Iraizoz y de Villar, Antonio. "Aspectos paradójicos de José Martí." In his Lecturas cubanas; 2. ed. (H: "Hermes", 1939), pp. 169-177.

67.721 _____. "Comentarios sobre José Martí." In Libros y autores cubanos (Santa María de Rosario: Rosareña, 1956), pp. 129-175.

67.722 _____. "La estética acrática de José Martí." In his Pnys (Madrid: Mundo Latino, 1926), pp. 151-181.

67.723 _____. "La evolución artística de Martí." BACL, 1 (1952), 662-675.

67.724 _____. "Las ideas pedagógicas de Martí." CCont, 23 (1920), 5-30. Same as item no. 67.135. Also as "Martí's ideas upon education." Inter-America, 3 (1920), 350-363.

67.725 _____. "Las siete palabras de Martí." AJM, 6, 1-4 (1952), 187-189.

67.726 _____. "Sobre un brindis de Martí." In his Penumbras del recuerdo (H, 1948), pp. 121-126.

67.727 _____. "El suspiro de Martí." In his Penumbras del recuerdo (H, 1948), pp. 127-130.

67.728 _____. "Tres notas martianas." AJM, 4, 2 (1948), 225-230. Also in his Penumbras del recuerdo (H, 1948), pp. 116-130.

67.729 Isaacson, William D. "Un análisis de la crítica de José Martí del ensayo La naturaleza de Ralph Waldo Emerson." In Memoria del Congreso de Escritores Martianos, q.v., pp. 706-713.

67.730 _____. "José Martí y el 'Club Crepúsculo'." AJM, 5, 1 (1950), 112-118.

67.731 Izaguirre, José María. "Martí en Guatemala." RevC, 29 (1951-1952), 332-342.

67.732 Jarnés, Benjamín. "Martí y las razas." CA, No. 188 (1973), 155-164.

67.733 _____. "La prosa heroica de Martí." RAm, 18 (1929), 344.

67.734 Jiménez, Gildardo. "Martí, un precursor." UAnt, No. 110 (1953), 404-406.

67.735 Jiménez, José Olivio. "Una aproximación existencial al Prólogo al 'Poema del Niágara', de José Martí." ALHisp, 2-3 (1973-1974), 407-441. Also in Estudios críticos sobre la prosa modernista hispanoamericana (NY: Eliseo Torres, 1975), pp. 11-33.

67.736 _____. "Una contribución importante a la bibliografía de Martí." La voz, 7, 4 (1963), 16-17.

67.737 _____. "Dos símbolos existenciales en la obra de José Martí." Románica, 15 (1978-1979), 112-125.

67.738 _____. "Un ensayo de ordenación trascendente en los Versos libres de Martí." RHM, 34 (1968), 671-684.

67.739 _____. "Poesía y existencia en José Martí." LLM, 2, 1 (1983), 8-9.

67.740 Jiménez, Juan Ramón. "José Martí." RAm, 37 (1940), 129-130. Also BACL, 1 (1952), 536-539. Also AUC, 111 (1953), 42-45. Also Islas, 7, 3 (1965), 129-131. Also in Manuel Pedro González, Antología crítica de José Martí, q.v., pp. 215-217.

67.741 Jiménez Monge, E. "Homenaje a la memoria del apóstol." AJM, 3, 1 (1945), 39-40.

67.742 Jones, Willis Knapp. "José Martí dramaturgo." In Memoria del Congreso de Escritores Martianos, q.v., pp. 718-728.

67.743 _____. "The Martí centenary." MLJ, 37 (1953), 398-402.

67.744 Jorge, Elena. "Notas sobre la función en La edad de oro." ULH, Nos. 198-199 (1973), 39-56.

67.745 Jorrín, Miguel. "Ideas filosóficas de Martí." RBC, 47 (1941), 41-61. Also AJM, 4, 1 (1947), 35-49. Also in Manuel Pedro González, Antología crítica de José Martí, q.v., pp. 479-496.

67.746 _____. "Martí y la filosofía." In Vida y pensamiento de Martí, q.v., I, 61-81. Also in Manuel Pedro González, Antología crítica de José Martí, q.v., pp. 459-478.

67.747 "José Martí." RBC, 41 (1938), 161-303.

67.748 "José Martí: su mundo." RyC, No. 8 (1973), 12-92.

67.749 Júlio, Sílvio. "José Martí." In his Escritores antilhanos
(Rio de Janeiro: H. Antunes, 1944), pp. 92-146.

67.750 Karras, Bill J. "José Martí and the Pan American Conference,
1889-1891." RHA, Nos. 77-78 (1974), 77-99.

67.751 Kelin, Fedor. "José Martí y los estudios latino-americanos en
la Unión Soviética." AJM, 6 (1946), 376-377. Also LitS,
No. 3 (1946), pagination unknown.

67.752 Key-Ayala, Santiago. "Caracas en Martí." RNC, No. 96 (1953),
9-17.

67.753 _____. "Martí, las rosas, la guerra y la muerte." AJM, 6,
1-4 (1952), 222-224.

67.754 Khumu, Henry. "El hombre de acción en José Martí." In Estudios sobre Martí, q.v., pp. 87-96.

67.755 Kirk, John M. "El aprendizaje de Martí revolucionario: una
aproximación psico-histórica." CA, No. 210 (1977), 109-
122.

67.756 _____. "From apóstol to revolutionary: the changing image of
José Martí." NS/N, 4, 7 (1979), 89-106.

67.757 _____. "From 'inadaptado sublime; to 'líder revolucionario':
some further thoughts on the presentation of José Martí."
LARR, 15, 3 (1980), 127-147.

67.758 Klein, Linda B. "Ficción y magisterio en la narrativa de José
Martí: 'La muñeca negra'." QIA, Nos. 47-48 (1975-1976),
372-377.

67.759 _____. "Martí y la creación literaria." La torre, Nos. 75-76
(1973), 37-52.

67.760 Lagos Lisboa, Jerónimo. "José Martí." Atenea, 110 (1953), 12-
15.

67.761 Laguado, Jaime F. "La diestra de Martí." RAm, 14 (1927), 328.

67.762 Lamothe, Louis. "José Martí." In his Los mayores poetas latinoamericanos de 1850 a 1950 (M: Libro Mex, 1959), pp. 31-
37.

67.763 Landa, Rubén. "Martí como maestro." CA, No. 71 (1953), 77-96.

67.764 Lara, Elvira de. "Divulgando una novela de Martí, Amistad funesta." Panorama, 1, 4 (1953), 16-17.

67.765 Larrea, Elba M. "José Martí, insigne maestro de literatura
infantil." CA, No. 163 (1969), 238-251.

67.766 _____. "La prosa de José Martí en La edad de oro." CCLC, No. 61 (1962), 3-10.

67.767 Lavín, Pablo F. "Martí, filósofo." CPro, No. 5 (1953), 21, 100.

67.768 Lázaro, Angel. "Los Versos sencillos de Martí." AJM, 2, 1 (1941), 68-80. Also BACL, 1 (1952), 567-583.

67.769 Lazo, Raimundo. "Martí y su obra literaria." RFLC, 38 (1928), 241-365. Same as item no. 67.142.

67.770 _____. "La personalidad de Martí en el estudio de su estilo." BACL, 1 (1952), 657-661.

67.771 _____. "La personalidad y el mensaje de Martí." In Pensamiento y acción de José Martí, q.v., pp. 31-48.

67.772 _____. "Prólogo." In José Martí, Obras (M: Porrúa, 1973), pp. xi-xvii. Each section is also preceded by a critical introduction.

67.773 _____. "Reseña cultural." In José Martí, Escritos de un patriota (BA: W. M. Jackson, 1946), pp. vii-xli.

67.774 Le Riverand, Julio. "Martí: del 19 de mayo de 1895 al 20 de mayo de 1902." VO, 14, 21 (1972), 24-31.

67.775 _____. "Martí en la revolución de 1868." CAm, No. 51 (1968), 95-110.

67.776 _____. "Martí: ética y acción revolucionaria." AMart, No. 2 (1970), 123-144.

67.777 _____. "Martí y el derecho." In Vida y pensamiento de Martí, q.v., II, 7-34.

67.778 _____. "Martí y Lenin." PolI, No. 27 (1970), 57-71.

67.779 _____. "La Sociedad Económica en el centenario de Martí." RBC, 69 (1952), 27-35.

67.780 _____. "Teoría martiana del partido político." In Vida y pensamiento de Martí, q.v., I, 83-110.

67.781 Leal, Rine. "De Abdala a Chac-Mool." AMart, No. 7 (1977), 69-102.

67.782 Leber, Gisela. "Die Bedeutung von José Martí für die Auspräng des kubanischen Nationalbewussteins." Lateinamerika, 1966, pp. 61-72. Same as item no. 67.143.

67.783 Lemus, José María. "Apuntes y reflexiones sobre la vida y la obra de José Martí." Ateneo, No. 197 (1953), 26-37. Same as item no. 67.144.

67.784 León, José de la Luz. "El narcisismo en la vida y en la obra de Martí." In Homenaje a Enrique José Varona (H: Secretaría de Educación, Dirección de Cultura, 1935), pp. 245-253.

67.785 León de la Barba, Luis. "El canto a Cuba en tres poetas del siglo pasado: Martí, Sanacilia y de la Barra." In Memoria del Congreso de Escritores Martianos, q.v., pp. 744-753.

67.786 LeRoy y Gálvez, Luis F. "Martí, Valdés Domínguez y el 27 de noviembre de 1871." AMart, No. 2 (1970), 449-477.

67.787 Lewis, Bart L. "Sarmiento, Martí, and Rodó: three views of the United States in the Latin American essay." In Portrayal of America in various literatures (Lubbock: Texas Tech University, Interdepartmental Committee on Comparative Literature, 1978), pp. 29-40.

67.788 Lewis, Julie Howe. "La poesía en José Martí." Abside, 34 (1970), 431-458.

67.789 Lezama Lima, José. "José Martí poeta." Bohemia, 63, 1 (1971), 13.

67.790 Lida, Raimundo. "José Martí. Su vida. Su obra." BACL, 1 (1952), 549-556. Also AUC, 111 (1953), 35-41.

67.791 _____. "José Martí (1853-1895)." In José Martí, Páginas selectas (BA: Angel Estrada, 1957), pp. vii-xxx.

67.792 Lizaso y González, Félix. "Bajo el signo de Martí." Avance, No. 46 (1930), 144-145.

67.793 _____. "Busca y hallazgo del hombre en Martí." CA, No. 21 (1945), 170-184. Also AANAL, 26 (1945-1946), 61-75. Also AJM, 6, 1-4 (1952), 225-236.

67.794 _____. "Hombre de servicio y de pensamiento." RAm, 26 (1933), 289-291.

67.795 _____. "La intimidad literaria de Martí." RevC, 5 (1936), 306-328. Also BACL, 1 (1952), 715-733.

67.796 _____. "José Martí." CCont, 35 (1924), 281-289.

67.797 _____. "José Martí, precursor de la UNESCO." CPro, No. 5 (1953), 89-91, 102.

67.798 _____. "Labor americanista de Martí." RBC, 24 (1929), 641-653.

67.799 _____. "Los que conocieron a Martí." RBC, 28 (1931), 321-322.

67.800 _____. "Martí, crítico de arte." In Vida y pensamiento de Martí, q.v., I, 275-295.

67.801 _____. "Martí en la Argentina." AJM, 5, 4 (1951), 542-548.

67.802 _____. "Martí en los Estados Unidos." RBNC, 2a serie, 4, 4 (1953), 61-69.

67.803 _____. "Martí en México (especial para 'América')." América, 5, 2-3 (1940), 28-30.

67.804 _____. "Martí, espíritu de la nueva guerra." RevH, No. 2 (1942), 123-146.

67.805 _____. "Martí, ó, la vida del espíritu; fragmentos." Avance, No. 31 (1929), 38-39.

67.806 _____. "Martí y el libro." RBC, 37 (1936), 53-60.

67.807 _____. "Normas periodísticas de José Martí." RI, No. 56 (1963), 227-249.

67.808 _____. "Nuestro Martí." Política, No. 34 (1964), 31-52.

67.809 _____. "Un poema desconocido de Martí." RBC, 29 (1932), 332-342.

67.810 _____. "Posibilidades filosóficas en Martí." In Homenaje a José Varona (H: Secretaría de Educación, Dirección de Cultura, 1935), pp. 121-139.

67.811 _____. "Primera lección martiana." RBC, 49 (1942), 307-311.

67.812 _____, and José Antonio Fernández de Castro. "José Martí." CCont, 35 (1924), 281-289.

67.813 Llaverías y Martínez, Joaquín. "Martí en el Archivo Nacional." AJM, 6, 1-4 (1952), 237-271. Same as item no. 67.155.

67.814 _____. "Los periódicos de Martí." BAN, 39 (1940), 59-227. Same as item no. 67.156.

67.815 López Dórticos, Pedro. "Intimidad de Martí en sus cartas a Manuel A. Mercado." AJM, 5, 1 (1950), 44-76.

67.816 López Morales, Eduardo E. "Apuntes para un estudio de la lucha armada en Ho Chi Minh y José Martí." CAm, No. 63 (1970), 54-63.

67.817 _____. "Un aspecto olvidado del Martí literario." CHA, No. 145 (1962), 53-60.

67.818 López-Muñoz y Larraz, Gustavo A. "Influencia de Martí en Rubén Darío." InsulaH, 1, 1 (1957), 53-59.

67.819 López Oliva, Manuel. "Presencia de una imagen." CubaI, No. 33 (1972), 14-17.

67.820 López Pellón, Nivio. "Martí y la mujer." RBNC, 2a serie, 4, 2 (1953), 5-19.

67.821 Losada, Juan. "Generación: pensamiento, personalidad e historia en José Martí." CB, No. 39 (1970), 19-24.

67.822 Loveluck, Juan. "Un símbolo persistente en la lírica de Martí." La torre, No. 59 (1968), 173-193.

67.823 Lugo, Américo. "José Martí." AJM, 4, 3 (1948), 354-371. Partially reproduced as "José Martí. El orador. El escritor. El poeta." BACL, 1 (1952), 488-493.

67.824 Madrigal, Luis Iñigo. "Martí novelista (acerca de Amistad funesta)." In Lengua, literatura, folklore. Estudios dedicados a Rodolfo Oroz (Santiago de Chile, 1967), pp. 233-243.

67.825 Maestri, Aníbal. "El hombre José Martí." BAN, 63 (1963), 121-128.

67.826 Magdaleno, Mauricio. "Prólogo." In José Martí, Martí (M: Secretaría de Educación Pública, 1942), pp. v-xxxix.

67.827 Maharg, James. "Fructiferous exile: Martínez Estrada and the encounter with Martí." Los ensayistas, 1, 2 (1976), 25-33. Also EIA, 2, 2 (1976), 227-234.

67.828 Maldonado-Denis, Manuel. "La América de Martí." La torre, No. 53 (1966), 196-203.

67.829 _____. "Martí y Fanon." CA, No. 185 (1973), 189-202. Also CAm, No. 73 (1972), 17-27.

67.830 _____. "Martí y su concepto de la revolución." RICP, No. 45 (1969), 32-37. Also CAm, No. 67 (1971), 3-11. Also Desarrollo, No. 14 (1970), 16-20.

67.831 _____. "Vigencia de Martí en el Puerto Rico de hoy." CA, No. 152 (1967), 131-146.

67.832 Mañach, Jorge. "Espiritú de Martí." RevCu, 1, 2 (1968), 289-305.

67.833 _____. "Fundamentación del pensamiento martiano." In Manuel Pedro González, Antología crítica de José Martí, q.v., pp. 443-457.

67.834 _____. "José Martí." AANAL, 29 (1949), 109-129.

67.835 _____. "Martí en 'The hour'." AJM, 1, 1 (1940), 34-39.

67.836 _____. "El pensador en Martí." Avance, No. 31 (1929), 40-42.

67.837 _____. "Perfil de Martí." BACL, 1 (1952), 640-656. Also AUC, 111 (1953), 55-71.

67.838 _____. "Significación del centenario martiano." Lyceum, Nos. 33-34 (1953), 5-31. Same as item no. 67.163.

67.839 _____. "Vida y letra de Martí." In José Martí, Sus mejores páginas (H: Primer Festival del Libro Cubano, 1950), pp. 7-16.

67.840 Manrique Cabrera, F. "La compañía de José Martí." In Estudios martianos, q.v., pp. 99-107.

67.841 Marichal, Juan. "De Martí a Rodó: el idealismo democrático (1870-1910)." In his Cuatro fases de la historia intelectual latinoamericana, 1810-1970 (Madrid: Fundación Juan March/Cátedra, 1978), pp. 69-90.

67.842 Marinello, Juan. "El antimperialismo de Martí. Darío y Rodó en la Agresida Francesa." AMart, 4, 4 (1972), 365-369.

67.843 _____. "Caminos en la lengua de Martí." In Manuel Pedro González, Antología crítica de José Martí, q.v., pp. 219-236. Also in Miscelánea de estudios dedicados a Fernando Ortiz (H: Sociedad Económica de Amigos del País, 1955), pp. 969-986.

67.844 _____. "El caso literario de José Martí." In Pensamiento y acción de José Martí, q.v., pp. 103-124. Also as "Sobre el caso literario de José Martí." RAm, 48 (1954), 257-262. Also in Salvador Bueno, Los mejores ensayistas cubanos (H: Organización Continental de los Festivales del Libro, 1959), pp. 90-102.

67.845 _____. "Discurso." AMart, No. 7 (1977), 11-24.

67.846 _____. "La españolidad literaria de José Martí." AJM, 2, 2 (1942), 42-66. Also in Vida y pensamiento de José Martí, q.v., I, 159-186. Also in his Orbita de Juan Marinello (H: Colección Orbita, 1968), pp. 126-158.

67.847 _____. "Francia en Martí--Martí en Francia. El verso creciente de José Martí." Bohemia, 62, 4 (1970), 4-13.

67.848 _____. "Gabriela Mistral y José Martí." Sur, No. 4 (1931), 156-163. Also RAm, 24 (1932), 49-51. Also RBC, 30 (1932), 232-238. Also in his Literatura hispanoamericana; hombres, meditaciones (M: Universidad Nacional de México, 1937), pp. 23-32.

67.849 _____. "Homenaje a José Martí en el 38 aniversario de su muerte." RAm, 26 (1933), 290-295.

67.850 _____. "José Martí." RevG, 6, 6 (1953), 59-83.

67.851 _____. "José Martí, artista." RAm, 26 (1933), 292-295. Also Atenea, 33 (1936), 191-205.

67.852 _____. "Martí en la revolución." VO, 13, 5 (1971), 21-24.

67.853 _____. "Martí, escritor americano." In his Literatura hispanoamericana; hombres, meditaciones (M: Universidad Nacional de México, 1937), pp. 33-43.

67.854 _____. "Martí: poesía." Bohemia, 61, 17 (1969), 28-35.

67.855 _____. "Martí político." Bohemia, 63, 11 (1971), 18.

67.856 _____. "Martí y el mar." Bohemia, 64, 2 (1972), 64-65.

67.857 _____. "Martí y México." LyP, 11, 5 (1933), 183-186.

67.858 _____. "El pensamiento de Martí y nuestra revolución socialista." PenP, No. 76 (1975), 517-524. Also in his Orbita de Juan Marinello (H: Colección Orbita, 1968), pp. 360-386.

67.859 _____. "El poeta José Martí." RAm, 18 (1929), 232, 236-237, 245-246, 263, 267-269. Also Avance, No. 31 (1929), 44-46. Also in José Martí, Poesías (H: Cultural, 1928), pp. xv-xlv.

67.860 _____. "Sobre la filiación filosófica de José Martí." RAm, 38 (1941), 225-226.

67.861 _____. "Sobre la interpretación y el entendimiento de la obra de José Martí." AMart, No. 1 (1978), 7-10.

67.862 _____. "Sobre la poesía de Martí." VO, 14, 15 (1972), 19.

67.863 _____. "Ultima conferencia. Sobre las raíces antimperialistas de José Martí." CAm, No. 103 (1977), 124-131.

67.864 Márquez, Narciso. "Martí, peregrino de la libertad." NRRP, Nos. 3-4 (1953), 37-41.

67.865 Márquez Sterling, Carlos. "El universo de Martí." Centro, No. 1 (1965), 38-40.

67.866 Martínez, José Luis. "Palabras para José Martí." CA, No. 21 (1945), 160-161. Also BACL, 1 (1952), 626-627.

67.867 Martínez Bello, Antonio. "Cartas inéditas de Martí frente a la tesis del 'suicidio'." RBNC, 2a serie, 6, 3 (1955), 69-79.

67.868 _____. "Objetividad del pensamiento de Martí." In Memoria del Congreso de Escritores Martianos, q.v., pp. 763-768.

67.869 _____. "El pensamiento de Julio Antonio Mella en relación
con las ideas sociales de José Martí." ULH, No. 165
(1964), 35-55.

67.870 _____. "El temperamento de Martí." RBNC, 2a serie, 5, 7
(1954), 61-106.

67.871 Martínez Estrada, Ezequiel. "Apostolado de José Martí: el noviciado." CA, No. 134 (1964), 65-84.

67.872 _____. "El diario de campaña de Martí como documento caracte-
rológico." RBNJM, 3a serie, 3, 1-4 (1963), 5-49.

67.873 _____. "Doña Leonor, mater dolorosa." Cuba, 1, 6 (1962), 46-
49.

67.874 _____. "Dos capítulos sobre Martí." Sur, No. 329 (1972), 256-
267.

67.875 _____. "Juristas y justos." Islas, 3, 3 (1961), 31-37.

67.876 _____. "Por una alta cultura popular y socialista cubana."
Unión, 1, 1 (1962), 43-74.

67.877 _____. "Sarmiento y Martí." CA, No. 28 (1946), 197-214.
Also NRC, 1962, pp. 13-33.

67.878 Martínez-Fortún y Foyo, Carlos A. "Algunas facetas de Martí
jurista." RBNC, 2a serie, 4, 4 (1953), 83-94.

67.879 Martínez Gómez, Yolanda. "Algunas consideraciones sobre el
Martí crítico." AJM, 5, 3 (1951), 374-380.

67.880 Martínez Rendón, Miguel D. "En torno a la poesía de Martí."
In José Martí, La clara voz de México (M: B.O.I., 1933),
I, 21-56. Same as item no. 67.178.

67.881 Mas, José L. "En torno a la ideología de José Martí (su iden-
tificación con F. R. Lamennais y el romanticismo social)."
CA, No. 199 (1975), 82-114.

67.882 _____. "La huella de José Martí en Ariel [de Enrique José
Rodó]." Hispania, 62 (1979), 275-281.

67.883 _____. "José Martí y el romanticismo social (F. R. Lammenais:
una posible influencia en el joven José Martí)." CA, No.
193 (1974), 160-181.

67.884 Masó y Vásquez, Calixto. "Ideas de José Martí sobre las universidades." RMS, 26, 2 (1964), 451-456.

67.885 Massuh, Víctor. "El activismo creador de José Martí." AJM,
6, 1-4 (1952), 403-408.

67.886 Maza Rodríguez, Emilio. "Significación de José Martí." RBC, 41 (1938), 272-281.

67.887 Mazzei, Angel. "José Martí." In his Lecciones de literatura americana y argentina; 3. ed. (BA: Ciordia, 1958), pp. 315-318.

67.888 Medina, Waldo. "Martí, capitán de arcángeles." AJM, 5, 3 (1951), 347-349.

67.889 Medrano, Higinio J. "Martí: maestro de niños y de hombres." CCont, 28 (1922), 97-102.

67.890 Mejía Sánchez, Ernesto. "El caso Martí-Whitman-Darío. Las relaciones literarias interamericanas." CAm, No. 42 (1967), 52-57. Also as "Las relaciones literarias inter-americanas: el caso Martí-Whitman-Darío." ZF, No. 41 (1967), 12-15.

67.891 _____. "José Martí en el Partido Liberal (1886-1892)." AMart, No. 7 (1977), 299-379.

67.892 _____. "Los últimos días de José Martí." HumM, 4 (1963), 343-355. Also RNC, No. 153 (1962), 52-64.

67.893 Meléndez, Concha. "El crecer de la poesía de Martí." In Memoria del Congreso de Escritores Martianos, q.v., pp. 638-657.

67.894 _____. "Versos libres de José Martí." Rueca, 1, 3 (1942), 5-7.

67.895 Melis, Antonio. "Lucha antimperialista y lucha de clases en José Martí." CAm, No. 54 (1969), 126-133.

67.896 Mella, Julio Antonio. "Glosando los pensamientos de José Martí." In his La lucha revolucionaria contra el imperia-lismo (H: Sociales, 1940), pp. 53-59. Also Xilote, 9, 2-42 (1975), 2-7.

67.897 Mencía, Mario. "Concepción de la guerra en Martí." Bohemia, 67, 8 (1975), 4-9.

67.898 Méndez, Manuel Isidro. "Entraña y forma de Versos sencillos." RBNC, 2a serie, 7, 1 (1956), 125-131.

67.899 _____. "Humanidad de Martí." In Vida y pensamiento de Martí, q.v., I, 9-25.

67.900 _____. "Por qué vino Martí a la guerra." RBNC, 2a serie, 7, 1 (1956), 125-131.

67.901 _____. "Sugerencias martianas. Los versos a sus hermanos." RBNC, 2a serie, 8, 1 (1957), 121-123.

67.902 Méndez Pereira, Octavio. "La prosa de Martí a la luz de Mar-
        tí." In Memoria del Congreso de Escritores Martianos,
        q.v., pp. 672-679.

67.903 Meo Zilio, Giovanni. L'iterazione nella prosa de José Martí."
        LSt, 14, 4 (1965), 3-12. Also as "Iteración y estructura
        en el esilo de Martí." In his De Martí a Sabat Ercasty,
        q.v., pp. 9-74.

67.904 _____. "Note di fonologia letteraria in torno a un testo cu-
        bano." QIG, 5 (1960), 119-124. Also as "Notas de fono-
        logía en torno a un texto cubano." In his De Martí a Sa-
        bat Ercasty, q.v., pp. 95-102.

67.905 _____. "Prolepsis, imágenes e ideología en un texto martiano."
        ALetM, 5 (1965), 141-160. Also in his De Martí a Sabat
        Ercasty, q.v., pp. 75-94.

67.906 Mercado, Alfonso. "Martí en casa de Mercado." ULH, No. 159
        (1963), 61-69.

67.907 _____. "Mis recuerdos de José Martí." RBC, 29 (1932), 161-
        167.

67.908 Meruelo, Otto. "Estampa de José Martí." Bohemia, 44, 4
        (1952), 34-36, 76-78.

67.909 Mesa Rodríguez, Manuel I. "Letra y espíritu de Martí a través
        de su epistolario." AJM, 6, 1-4 (1952), 315-337.

67.910 Meyer-Minneman, Klaus. "José Martí, Amistad funesta. Zur Vor-
        geschichte des modernistischen Romans im Lateinamerika."
        RJ, 22 (1971), 306-318. Also as "Die Vorgeschichte des
        spanischamerikanischen Fin de siècle-Romans. (I): José
        Martí, Amistad funesta." In his Der spanischamerikanische
        Roman des Fin de siècle (Tübingen: Max Niemeyer, 1979),
        pp. 110-127.

67.911 Meza Fuentes, Roberto. "El creador de una patria." In his
        De Díaz Mirón a Rubén Darío; 2. ed. (Santiago de Chile:
        Andrés Bello, 1964), pp. 53-68.

67.912 Mijares, Augusto. "Martí, utopía y realidad de América." CA,
        No. 6 (1942), 164-168.

67.913 Mikulski, Richard M. "Martí en tierra yanqui." AJM, 4, 4
        (1949), 428-443.

67.914 Miranda, Wenceslao. "Comentarios a la ideología filosófica
        y social de José Martí." In his Ensayos (Lugo, Spain:
        "Celta", 1972), pp. 133-150.

67.915 Miró, Ricardo. "Cuba, Martí y nosotros." Lotería, 2a época,
        No. 135 (1967), 9-13.

67.916 Mistral, Gabriela. "La condición mágica de José Martí." CPro, No. 5 (1953), 20, 92-93.

67.917 _____. "La lengua de Martí." AJM, 5, 2 (1950), 139-152. Also RO, 2a época, No. 38 (1966), 133-105. Also BACL, 1 (1952), 508-527. Also AUC, 111 (1953), 97-116. Also RBNC, 2a serie, 8, 1 (1957), 141-164. Also in Manuel Pedro González, Antología crítica de José Martí, q.v., pp. 23-39. Same as item no. 67.184.

67.918 _____. "Los Versos sencillos de José Martí." RBC, 41 (1938), 161-175. Also AJM, 5, 2 (1950), 153-163. Also Islas, No. 43 (1972), 7-23. Also Bohemia, 61, 9 (1969), 4-9. Also in Manuel Pedro González, Antología crítica de José Martí, q.v., pp. 253-265.

67.919 Molina de Galindo, Isis. "El diálogo creador de José Martí." RBNC, 63, 2 (1972), 37-44.

67.920 _____. "La modalidad impresionista en la obra de José Martí." AMart, 4, 4 (1972), 51-115.

67.921 _____. "'El presidio político en Cuba', de José Martí (1871). Intento de un análisis estilístico." RI, No. 54 (1962), 311-336.

67.922 Montaner, Carlos Alberto. "El pensamiento de José Martí." HBA, 15, 2 (1971), 227-246.

67.923 Monterde, Francisco. "Amigos mexicanos de Martí en el modernismo." In Memoria del Congreso de Escritores Martianos, q.v., pp. 490-502.

67.924 _____. "La poesía de Martí en México." In Instituto Internacional de Literatura Iberoamericana, Homenaje a Hidalgo, Díaz Mirón y Martí, q.v., pp. 143-148.

67.925 Montero, Marco Arturo. "Primer centenario de José Martí." AJM, 6, 1-4 (1952), 438-440.

67.926 Montillaro, Gaspar. "Martí, poeta del aula." In Memoria del Congreso de Escritores Martianos, q.v., pp. 781-800.

67.927 Montori de Gutiérrez, Violeta. "El modernismo en la oratoria de José Martí." Caribe, 2, 2 (1977), 97-104.

67.928 Mora y Varona, Gastón. "Martí." RevC, 29 (1951-1952), 232-236.

67.929 Morales, Angel Luis. "Presentación [del Seminario José Martí]." In Estudios martianos, q.v., pp. 11-13.

67.930 Morales, Ernesto. "Martí y La edad de oro." RBC, 41 (1938), 224-232. Also in his Los niños y la poesía en América (Santiago de Chile: Ercilla, 1936), pp. 44-50.

67.931 Morales, Salvador. "Así fue Martí." Bohemia, 69, 13 (1977),
        26.

67.932 _____. "'Guatemala', de José Martí." Bohemia, 70, 20 (1978),
        10-13.

67.933 _____. "Ideas de Martí sobre la economía y el desarrollo en
        el caso de México." AMart, No. 7 (1977), 289-298. Also
        CB, No. 86 (1975), 14-15.

67.934 _____. "Martí en inglés." AMart, No. 7 (1977), 389-391.

67.935 _____. "Martí en el Partido Revolucionario Cubano." RyC, No.
        4 (1972), 82-89.

67.936 _____. "Martí en la génesis de la solidaridad antillana."
        CAm, No. 90 (1975), 43-57.

67.937 _____. "El partido que fundó Martí." VO, 17, 4 (1975), 18-23.

67.938 Moreno Pla, Enrique H. "Reflexiones sobre la muerte de Martí."
        AMart, No. 3 (1971), 201-227.

67.939 Munilla, Alberto. "Martí, el poeta de la libertad." AJM, 5,
        1 (1945), 135-136.

67.940 Nassif, Ricardo. "Aproximación a José Martí como pedagogo y
        educador." HumT, 1 (1953), 379-400.

67.941 Navarro, Noel. "Ese hombre de La edad de oro." RyC, No. 2
        (1972), 14-22.

67.942 Nieto, Severo. "José Martí y el ajedrez." VO, 18, 6 (1977),
        51-52.

67.943 Novas, Benito. "Tributo a Martí." AMart, 4, 4 (1972), 143-
        168.

67.944 Novas Calvo, Lino. "El estilo que falta." AJM, 6 (1946),
        392-394. BACL, 1 (1952), 620-623.

67.945 Nuiry, Nuria. "Las independencias de José Martí." VO, 13, 39
        (1971), 22-24.

67.946 Núñez, Ana Rosa. "Atlas poético de Martí en el destierro."
        RevCu, 1, 2 (1968), 355-361.

67.947 Núñez Jiménez, Antonio. "Martí, la historia y la revolución."
        Bohemia, 64, 5 (1972), 36-43.

67.948 Núñez Machín, Ana. "La raíz y el ala." Islas, 6, 2 (1964),
        88-90.

67.949 Núñez Mata, Efren. "Presencia de Martí en América." AJM, 4,
        4 (1949), 421-427.

67.950   Núñez Ponte, J. M. "Palabras de clausura del acto académico
         en honor de Martí." BAVC, No. 77 (1953), 19-24.

67.951   Núñez y Domínguez, José de J. "Los familiares de Martí en Mé-
         xico." RBC, 31 (1933), 28-33.

67.952   _____. "José Martí y Gutiérrez Nájera." RAm, 26 (1933), 240.

67.953   _____. "El mexicanismo de José Martí." AJM, 5, 1 (1945),
         119-123. Also CA, No. 21 (1945), 199-204.

67.954   Núñez y Domínguez, R. "Martí y México." AJM, 3, 1 (1945),
         95-96.

67.955   Oliva Pulgarón, Luis. "19 de mayo." RBC, 41 (1938), 301-303.

67.956   Olivera, Otto. "José Martí y la expresión paralela de prosa y
         verso." RI, No. 43 (1957), 71-82.

67.957   _____. "José Martí y la polémica sobre el modernismo." RAmer,
         5, 2 (1979), 16-19.

67.958   Onís, Federico de. "José Martí, 1953-1895." In his España en
         América (Río Piedras, P.R.: Ediciones de la Universidad
         de Puerto Rico, 1955), pp. 193-194.

67.959   _____. "José Martí: vida y obra. 5[i.e., 6]. Valorización."
         RHM, 18 (1952), 145-150. Also in José Martí (1853-1895),
         q.v., pp. 154-159. Also in his España en América (Rio
         Piedras, P.R.: Ediciones de la Universidad de Puerto Rico,
         1955), pp. 615-621. Also in Manuel Pedro González, Anto-
         logía de José Martí, q.v., pp. 13-21.

67.960   _____. "Martí and the Caribbean theatre." In The Caribbean:
         its culture (Gainesville: University of Florida Press,
         1955), pp. 74-84.

67.961   _____. "Martí y el modernismo." In Memoria del Congreso de
         Escritores Martianos, q.v., pp. 431-446. Also in Manuel
         Pedro González, Antología crítica de José Martí, q.v.,
         pp. 155-166. Also in his España en América (Río Piedras,
         P.R.: Ediciones de la Universidad de Puerto Rico, 1955),
         pp. 622-632.

67.962   _____. "Valor actual de José Martí. Tiene que hacer todavía
         en América." CPro, No. 5 (1953), 17, 93.

67.963   _____. "Valoración de Martí." ND, 36, 2 (1956), 64-71.

67.964   Onís, José de. "José Martí in the United States." Los ensa-
         yistas, Nos. 10-11 (1981), 129-138.

67.965   _____. "Martí y los Estados Unidos." In Instituto Internacio-
         nal de Literatura Iberoamericana, Homenaje a Hidalgo, Díaz
         Mirón y Martí, q.v., pp. 135-141.

67.966 _____. "Una página blanca: poesía inédita de José Martí."
RI, No. 40 (1955), 225-233.

67.967 Orbón, Julián. "José Martí: poesía y realidad." Exilio, 4,
4-5, 1 (1971), 4-40.

67.968 Orillion, Juliette. "La discriminación racial en los Estados
Unidos vista por José Martí." AMart, No. 3 (1971), 9-94.

67.969 Orovio, Helio. "Munkacsy, el pintor que vio Martí." GdC,
No. 101 (1972), 16.

67.970 Ortiz, Even Fontaine, Pedro Suárez, and Matías Chapeaux. "Martí: breve estudio político." In Estudios sobre Martí, q.
v., pp. 37-54.

67.971 Ortiz, Fernando. "'Cañales', dijo Martí." RBC, 44 (1939),
291-295.

67.972 _____. "Cuba, Martí and the race problem." Phylon, 3 (1942),
253-276.

67.973 _____. "La fama póstuma de José Martí." RBC, 73 (1957), 5-28.

67.974 _____. "Martí y las razas." RBC, 48 (1941), 203-233. Also
in Vida y pensamiento de Martí, q.v., II, 335-367.

67.975 _____. "Martí y las 'razas de librería'." CA, No. 21 (1945),
185-198. Also AJM, 5, 2 (1945), 166-174. Also AUC, 111
(1953), 117-130.

67.976 _____. "Oración a Martí." RBC, 70 (1955), 236-248.

67.977 _____. "La religión de Martí." ND, 38, 2 (1958), 52-57.

67.978 Ossandrón Buljevic, Carlos A. "Nuestra América de José Martí." ACh, No. 10 (1980), 23-32.

67.979 Pabón Núñez, Lucio. "El cincuentenario de Martí." AJM, 3, 1
(1945), 31-36.

67.980 Pagés Larraya, Antonio. "Nueva visión de Martí." Nosotros,
2a época, No. 74 (1942), 177-186. Also RBC, 50 (1942),
310-316.

67.981 Paladini, María Delia. "José Martí, vida y literatura." HumT,
1 (1953), 337-350.

67.982 _____. "Literatura en José Martí." Sarmiento, No. 24 (1953),
1-3.

67.983 Palcos, Alberto. "Goya, Sarmiento, y José Martí." AJM, 4, 4
(1949), 449-452.

67.984 Paltsits, Víctor Hugo. "José Martí, maestro y caballero."
        RBC, 30 (1932), 321-325.

67.985 "Para la biografía de José Martí." RBNC, 1, 5-6 (1909), 131-
        160.

67.986 Paravich Sarhan, Jasna. "Temática y expresión en la poesía
        de José Martí." RLet, 8-9 (1966), 155-170.

67.987 Pavón Tamayo, Luis. "Contra la falsificación de nuestra his-
        toria y la adulteración del pensamiento martiano." In
        Estudios sobre Martí, q.v., pp. 15-34.

67.988 Pazos y Roque, Felipe de. "Las ideas económicas de Martí."
        In Vida y pensamiento de Martí, q.v., II, 177-209.

67.989 Pedemonte, Hugo Emilio. "La influencia del Libertador en la
        prosa de José Martí." RSBV, No. 54 (1958), 9-14.

67.990 Pedreira, A. S. "Hostos y Martí." RBC, 26 (1930), 249-253.

67.991 Pedroso, Regino. "Presencia de Martí en la revolución cuba-
        na." In his Regino Pedroso (H: Unión de Escritores y
        Artistas de Cuba, 1975), pp. 391-399.

67.992 Peñalver Moral, Reinaldo. "Un periodista legó a la posteri-
        dad los más destacados discursos de José Martí." Bohe-
        mia, 67, 5 (1975), 32-34.

67.993 Peñate, Florencia. "Martí y su contexto latinoamericano."
        VO, 18, 4 (1977), 30-33.

67.994 Peraza Sarausa, Fermín. "Martí, los libros y sus libros."
        RIB, 3 (1953), 245-251.

67.995 Pereira, Armando, and Carlos Muciño. "Para un estudio de José
        Martí." Alero, No. 16 (1976), 123-137.

67.996 Pérez, Dionisio. "La mitología de Martí en la historia de Es-
        paña." RBC, 41 (1938), 191-193. Also AJM, 4, 1 (1947),
        110-111. See item no. 67.124.

67.997 Pérez Guzmán, Francisco. "En torno al VI Seminario de Estu-
        dios Martianos." VO, 18, 7 (1977), 58-59.

67.998 Pérez Martín, Ezequiel. "El lirismo en la prosa martiana."
        CB, No. 132 (1978), 15.

67.999 Pérez-Rolo, Marta. "Martí líder político." PCr, No. 48
        (1971), 252-262.

67.1000 Perus, Françoise. "Martí y el modernismo." I&L, No. 11
        (1980), 97-115.

67.1001   Phillips, Allen W. "Naturaleza y metáfora en algunos poemas
          de José Martí." In his Temas del modernismo hispánico
          y otros estudios (Madrid: Gredos, 1974), pp. 241-260.

67.1002   _____. "Sobre una prosa de José Martí: 'El terremoto de
          Charleston'." In Instituto Internacional de Literatura
          Iberoamericana, Influencias extranjeras en la literatura
          iberoamericana (M, 1962), pp. 99-111. Also in his Estu-
          dios y notas sobre literatura hispanoamericana (M: Cul-
          tura, 1965), pp. 5-18.

67.1003   Pichardo, Hortensia. "Martí y la naturaleza." EducaciónH,
          3, 10 (1973), 9-15.

67.1004   Picón-Salas, Mariano. "Arte y virtud en José Martí." Cróni-
          ca, No. 20 (1953), 13-14. Also in Memoria del Congreso
          de Estudios Martianos, q.v., pp. 150-156. Also Cordi-
          llera, 1, 1 (1956), 20-23. Also ND, 40, 1 (1960), 40-
          41.

67.1005   Piedra-Bueno, Andrés de. "Martí americanista." AJM, 3, 1
          (1942), 104-125.

67.1006   _____. "Palabras de un profesor." RBNC, 2a serie, 4, 1
          (1953), 101-105.

67.1007   Pillepich, Pietro. "El último libertador de América." RBC,
          41 (1938), 194-199.

67.1008   Pineda Barnet, Enrique. "Páginas del Diario de José Martí."
          CubaI, No. 29 (1972), 36-37.

67.1009   Piñera, Humberto. "Martí, pensador." In Pensamiento y ac-
          ción de José Martí, q.v., pp. 167-188. Also in Manuel
          Pedro González, Antología crítica de José Martí, q.v.,
          pp. 527-537.

67.1010   Plasencia Azucena, Isabel. "Los cien mejores poemas de José
          Martí." AMart, No. 7 (1977), 383-387.

67.1011   _____. "José Martí: el pensamiento revolucionario cubano."
          AMart, No. 7 (1977), 401-404.

67.1012   Plochet, Alberto. "Los ojos de Martí." RBC, 30 (1932), 162-
          165.

67.1013   Ponce de León y Aymé, Antonio. "La oruga que nombró Martí."
          RBNC, 2a serie, 2, 3 (1951), 16-19.

67.1014   Ponte Rodríguez, Francisco J. "Pensamiento laicista de Mar-
          tí." Liberalis, No. 27 (1954), 4-16.

67.1015   Portuondo, Fernando. "Martí en la preparación de la guerra
          necesaria." VO, 14, 9 (1972), 22-29.

67.1016 _____. "Martí, Gómez y el alzamiento del 95 en Camagüey." ULH, Nos. 196-197 (1972), 158-169.

67.1017 Portuondo, José Antonio. "Abordaje numismático de José Martí." AMart, No. 1 (1978), 408-409.

67.1018 _____. "Aspectos de la crítica literaria en Martí." In Vida y pensamiento de Martí, q.v., I, 233-252.

67.1019 _____. "Dos héroes [Martí y Jristo Botev]." Santiago, No. 6 (1972), 225-238. Also Bohemia, 64, 21 (1972), 4-12.

67.1020 _____. "Dos vidas paralelas: Martí y Lenin." Unión, 9, 2 (1970), 69-79.

67.1021 _____. "Hidalgo y Martí." In Instituto Internacional de Literatura Iberoamericana, Homenaje a Hidalgo, Díaz Mirón y Martí, q.v., pp. 129-134.

67.1022 _____. "Introducción al estudio de las ideas sociales de Martí." In Vida y pensamiento de Martí, q.v., II, 227-248.

67.1023 _____. "José Martí: vida y obra. 5. Crítica." RHM, 18 (1952), 114-144. Also in José Martí (1853-1895), q.v., pp. 123-153.

67.1024 _____. "Martí, escritor." CA, No. 21 (1945), 205-214.

67.1025 _____. "Martí y Darío, polos del modernismo." CAm, No. 42 (1967), 68-72. Also as "Martí și Darío, poli ai modernismului." SXX, 16, 8-9 (1973), 203-205.

67.1026 _____. "Martí y el Partido Revolucionario Cubano." Islas, 10, 4 (1968), 171-174.

67.1027 _____. "El periodista José Martí." Santiago, No. 15 (1974), 7-29.

67.1028 _____. "Retratos infieles de José Martí." RBNJM, 3a serie, 10, 1 (1968), 5-14.

67.1029 _____. "Teoría martiana del Partido Revolucionario." CAm, No. 90 (1975), 14-23.

67.1030 _____. "La voluntad de estilo en José Martí." In Pensamiento y acción de José Martí, q.v., pp. 285-310.

67.1031 Poumier, María. "Aspectos del realismo martiano." AMart, No. 1 (1978), 153-188.

67.1032 Poveda, José Manuel. "Martí y Maceo en la mejorana." In his José Manuel Poveda (H: Instituto de Literatura y Lingüística de la Academia de Ciencias de Cuba, 1975), pp. 430-436.

67.1033   Prats Sariol, José. "Martí, Rilke y la bailarina española."
          GdC, No. 139 (1975), 13-15.

67.1034   "Preocupaciones de Martí por la fiebre amarilla." Finlay,
          No. 5 (1965), 59-62.

67.1035   "Presencia de Martí en el VIII Salón de Propaganda Gráfica
          '26 de julio'." AMart, No. 7 (1977), 417-420.

67.1036   Prío Socarrás, Carlos. "Martí, arquetipo de lo cubano."
          AJM, 6 (1946), 380-391.

67.1037   Prjevalinsky Ferrer, Olga. "Al margen de la explicación de
          texto: 'La luminosidad de la prosa de José Martí' y 'Una
          experiencia poética de Darío en torno al no ser'." His-
          panólfila, No. 9 (1960), 45-48.

67.1038   Promis, José M. "Martí escribe una novela [Lucía Jerez]."
          RI, Nos. 112-113 (1980), 413-425.

67.1039   Puebla, Manuel de la. "Martí y Heredia." In Estudios mar-
          tianos, q.v., pp. 71-85.

67.1040   Quesada, Luis Manuel. "Estructura teatral de la novela mar-
          tiana." Prisma, 1, 1 (1971), 35-43.

67.1041   _____. "Teoría martiana de la novela." DHR, 7, 2 (1968),
          29-36.

67.1042   _____. "La única novela martiana." REH, 4 (1970), 27-34.

67.1043   Quesada y Miranda, Gonzalo de. "Martí: flores del desierto."
          RBC, 30 (1932), 326-342; 31 (1933), 12-27, 161-182.

67.1044   _____. "Martí periodista." In Vida y pensamiento de Martí,
          q.v., II, 35-61.

67.1045   _____. "Martí visto por una norteamericana." RBC, 40 (1937),
          256-258.

67.1046   _____. "Martí y su amor a los libros." RBNC, 2a serie, 4,
          3 (1953), 38-43.

67.1047   Quijano, Alejandro. "Conferencia sobre José Martí." RBNC,
          2a serie, 7, 4 (1956), 21-31.

67.1048   Quintana, Jorge. "Algunas indagaciones en torno a José Mar-
          tí." AJM, 5, 2 (1950), 259-265.

67.1049   _____. "Prólogo. Cronolía biobibliográfica." In José Mar-
          tí, Obras completas (Caracas, 1964), I-1, v-xv, xvii-
          cclxxiv.

67.1050   Quinteros, Alberto (hijo). "El pensamiento vivo en José Mar-
          tí." AJM, 3, 1 (1945), 53-54.

67.1051 Quiroz, Alberto. "José Martí." LyP, 16, 6 (1954), 23-25.

67.1052 Rabassa, Gregory. "Walt Whitman visto por José Martí." ND, 39, 4 (1959), 88-93.

67.1053 Raggi, Ana H. "José Martí y las mujeres que lo amaron." Círculo, 6 (1977), 97-111.

67.1054 Rama, Angel. "Análisis de 'La niña de Guatemala'." In Martí; valoraciones críticas, q.v., pp. 65-84.

67.1055 _____. "La dialéctica de la modernidad en José Martí." In Estudios martianos, q.v., pp. 129-197.

67.1056 _____. "Indagación en la ideología de la poesía: los dípticos seriados de los Versos sencillos." RI, Nos. 112-113 (1980), 353-400.

67.1057 _____. "Luz y sombra en la poesía de Martí." In Martí; valoraciones críticas, q.v., pp. 45-63.

67.1058 _____. "Martí, poeta visionario." ELic, 2a época, Nos. 1-2 (1953), 157-160.

67.1059 Ramírez Rausee, J. A. "José Martí o la pasión por un ideal de libertad y de justicia." RUZ, 2a época, No. 33 (1966), 165-171.

67.1060 Ramón, Ramón. "Discurso." AMart, No. 1 (1978), 259-264.

67.1061 Redondo de Feldman, Susana. "José Martí: vida y obra. Vida." RHM, 18 (1952), 1-20. Also in José Martí (1853-1895), q.v., pp. 7-26.

67.1062 Regato, J. A. del. "José Martí, rebelde sin odios." Américas, 19, 2 (1967), 29-35. Also as "José Martí: rebel without hatred." Américas [English edition], 19, 1 (1977), 29-35.

67.1063 Rego, Oscar F. "A la sombra de un ala." Bohemia, 69, 7 (1977), 32-33.

67.1064 Remos y Rubio, Juan Nepomuceno José. "La emoción histórica en la prosa de José Martí." AJM, 6, 1-4 (1952), 380-399. Also BACL, 1 (1952), 685-706.

67.1065 _____. "Martí, el Paraguay y la independencia de Cuba." RBNC, 2a serie, 4, 4 (1953), 45-60.

67.1066 Rey-Barreau, José Luis. "Ecos de Martí en 'Marcha triunfal' de Darío." In Studies in language and literature (Richmond: Eastern Kentucky University, Department of Foreign Language, 1976), pp. 501-506.

67.1067   Reyes, Alfonso. "José Martí." CA, No. 21 (1945), 162-163.

67.1068   _____. "Martí a la luz de la nueva física." BACL, 7 (1958),
          221-222.

67.1069   Reyes Trejo, Alfredo. "Martí periodista." VO, 12, 2 (1971),
          4-8.

67.1070   Ríos, Fernando de los. "Ofrenda en torno al sentido de la
          vida en Martí." REH-PR, 1 (1928), 345-360. Also as
          "Reflexiones en torno al sentido de la vida en Martí."
          MIHC, 1, 2 (1928), 89-109. Also RBC, 41 (1938), 176-190.
          Also AJM, 4, 1 (1947), 21-30. Also in Manuel Pedro Gon-
          zález, Antología crítica de José Martí. q.v., pp. 429-
          441.

67.1071   _____. "Significación de lo humano en José Martí." ULH, Nos.
          38-39 (1941), 97-109.

67.1072   Ripoll, Carlos. "Crónicas desconocidas de José Martí."
          RevCu, 1, 2 (1968), 409-445.

67.1073   _____. "Dos cartas inéditas de José Martí." In Homenaje a
          Humberto Piñera (Madrid: Playor, 1979), pp. 221-230.

67.1074   _____. "Martí, profesor de español." RevCu, 1, 2 (1968),
          447-456.

67.1075   _____. "Martí: romanticismo e idioma." Círculo, 9 (1980),
          7-16.

67.1076   _____. "Martí y el romanticismo: lenguaje y literatura."
          REH-PR, 6 (1979), 183-204.

67.1077   _____. "Prólogo." In José Martí, Estudios desconocidos de
          José Martí (NY: Eliseo Torres, 1971), pp. 9-20.

67.1078   Rivera, Arelys, and Georgina Castellanos. "Martí revolucio-
          nario cubano." In Estudios sobre Martí, q.v., pp. 55-
          68.

67.1079   Rivera-Rodas, Oscar. "José Martí: estilo y concepción de la
          vida y el hombre." Plural, No. 64 (1977), 67-70.

67.1080   Rivero Muñiz, José. "Martí y los tabaqueros." RBNC, 2a se-
          rie, 4, 1 (1953), 81-99.

67.1081   Roa, Raúl. "La ética política de José Martí." Humanismo,
          No. 27 (1955), 62-68.

67.1082   _____. "Martí y el fascismo." Claridad, No. 312 (1937), no
          pagination.

67.1083   _____. "Rescate y proyección de Martí." AJM, 5, 3 (1951),
          307-318.

67.1084   Roa García, Raúl. "Martí, poeta nuevo." Avance, No. 10
          (1927), 254-255, 269.

67.1085   Roberts, W. Adolphe. "José Martí. Great man of the Caribbe-
          an." CarQ, 1, 4 (1950), 4-6.

67.1086   Rodríguez, Carlos Rafael. "Discurso." AMart, No. 7 (1977),
          261-266.

67.1087   _____. "José Martí." Unión, 2, 5-6 (1963), 5-18.

67.1088   _____. "José Martí, contemporáneo y compañero." ULH, Nos.
          196-197 (1972), 3-29.

67.1089   _____. "Martí, guía de su tiempo y anticipador del nuestro."
          AMart, No. 1 (1970), 310-323.

67.1090   Rodríguez, Emilio Jorge. "Un martiano de la república demo-
          crática alemana." CAm, No. 92 (1975), 102-104.

67.1091   Rodríguez, Pedro Pablo. "La idea de liberación nacional en
          José Martí." PCr, Nos. 49-50 (1971), 120-220. Also
          AMart, 4, 4 (1972), 169-213.

67.1092   _____. "Papelería martiana." Bohemia, 70, 37 (1978), 30.

67.1093   _____. "El primer discurso cubano de Martí." RBNC, 21, 3
          (1979), 69-78.

67.1094   Rodríguez, Rafael. "Una lectura krausista de la poesía de
          José Martí." ALHisp, No. 6 (1977), 65-85.

67.1095   Rodríguez Acosta, Hortensia. "Grandeza. A José Martí."
          RBNC, 2a serie, 4, 1 (1953), 73-78.

67.1096   Rodríguez-Cáceres, Armantina. "Martí y su labor periodísti-
          ca." AJM, 5, 3 (1951), 366-373.

67.1097   Rodríguez Demorizi, Emilio. "Entrevista Darío-Martí." ND,
          42, 1 (1962), 74-76.

67.1098   _____. "Henríquez y Carvajal y el culto de Martí en Santo
          Domingo." AJM, 4, 3 (1948), 265-268.

67.1099   _____. "Martí y Enriquillo." In Memoria del Congreso de Es-
          critores Martianos, q.v., pp. 257-275.

67.1100   _____. "El último traje de Martí." Bohemia, 64, 20 (1972),
          98-99.

67.1101   Rodríguez-Embil, Luis. "Breve apunte inédito de exégesis mar-
          tiana. Los primeros años." RBNC, 2a serie, 4, 1 (1953),
          79-80.

67.1102   ____. "Coloquio de los héroes." RBNC, 2a serie, 5, 1 (1954), 115-122.

67.1103   ____. "Martí y el presente." América, 14, 3-4 (1942), 10-12.

67.1104   Rodríguez y Expósito, César. "Médicos en la vida de Martí." TMC, Nos. 487-492 (1963), 73-83.

67.1105   Rodríguez Feo, José. "Martí y la revolución cubana." In his Notas críticas (primera serie) (H: Unión, 1962), pp. 7-19.

67.1106   Rodríguez Hidalgo, Alfonso. "La Biblia en el pensamiento de Martí." ND, 41, 1 (1961), 20-26.

67.1107   Rodríguez López, Pedro Pablo. "Un compromiso indeclinable." Bohemia, 69, 31 (1977), 30-31.

67.1108   ____. "Estudios sobre Martí." AMart, No. 7 (1977), 395-397.

67.1109   ____. "José Martí y el conocimiento de la especificidad latinoamericana." AMart, No. 7 (1977), 103-126.

67.1110   Rodríguez Monegal, Emir. "La poesía de Martí y el modernismo." Número, 5 (1953), 38-67.

67.1111   Rodríguez Núñez, Víctor. "Para leer realmente a José Martí." CAm, No. 115 (1979), 141-146.

67.1112   Roggiano, Alfredo A. "Acción y libertad en la poética de José Martí." RI, Nos. 112-113 (1980), 401-412.

67.1113   ____. "Poética y estilo de José Martí." HumT, 1 (1953), 351-378. Also in Manuel Pedro González, Antología crítica de José Martí, q.v., pp. 41-69.

67.1114   Roig de Leuchsenring, Emilio. "La benemérita labor de los escritores martistas." AJM, 6, 1-4 (1952), 178-184.

67.1115   ____. "Las dos Españas de Martí." RBNC, 2a serie, 4, 1 (1953), 37-57.

67.1116   ____. "Los dos primeros periódicos de Martí y los únicos publicados en la Habana." Carteles, 34, 4 (1953), 90-92.

67.1117   ____. "Un español, martista y martilatra [Isidro Méndez]." Bohemia, 63, 11 (1971), 20-21.

67.1118   ____. "Hostos y Martí, dos ideologías antillanas concordantes." RBC, 43 (1939), 5-19.

67.1119   ____. "El internacionalismo antimperialista en la obra política revolucionaria de José Martí." In Homenaje a Enrique José Varona (H: Secretaría de Educación, Dirección de Cultura, 1935), pp. 331-396.

67.1120 _____. "Martí en los Liceos de Guanabacoa y Regla." AJM, 5, 4 (1951), 499-516.

67.1121 _____. "Martí en los trágicos sucesos ocurridos en La Habana el mes de enero de 1869." Bohemia, 61, 9 (1969), 100-104.

67.1122 _____. "Martí vuelve a Guatemala." RBC, 57 (1945), 193-200.

67.1123 _____. "Martí y las religiones." In Vida y pensamiento de Martí, q.v., I, 111-158.

67.1124 _____. "Martí y los niños." In José Martí, La edad de oro (H: Cultural, 1958), pp. 7-89.

67.1125 _____. "Nacionalismo e internacionalismo de Martí." CCont, 44 (1927), 5-21.

67.1126 _____. "Propaganda y organización en la revolución de Martí." Bohemia, 62 (1970), 98-105.

67.1127 _____. "La república de Martí." In Vida y pensamiento de Martí, q.v., II, 369-433. Also as "Algunos conceptos martianos de la república." AJM, 3, 1 (1942), 60-79.

67.1128 Rojas, Manuel. "José Martí." AUC, 111 (1953), 5-9.

67.1129 _____. "José Martí y el espíritu revolucionario de los pueblos." In his De la poesía a la revolución (Santiago de Chile: Ercilla, 1958), pp. 195-204. Orig. RBC, 41 (1938), 216-223.

67.1130 Rojas Jiménez, Oscar. "La huella del peregrino: José Martí, el viajero." RNC, No. 96 (1953), 22-31.

67.1131 _____. "La huella del peregrino. José Martí en Caracas, monólogo nocturno." Shell, No. 44 (1962), 29-40.

67.1132 Romagosa, Carlos. "Darío y Martí." AJM, 4, 2 (1943), 357.

67.1133 Román Hernández, Jorge. "Consideraciones sobre la obra unificadora de Martí y el Partido Revolucionario Cubano." AMart, No. 7 (1977), 241-257.

67.1134 Romera, Antonio R. "José Martí y la pintura española." Atenea, 114 (1954), 74-84.

67.1135 Rosenblat, Angel. "Los venezolanismos de Martí." RNC, No. 96 (1953), 32-53.

67.1136 Roviera, Rosalinda. "'Pecho herido'." In Francisco E. Porrata, and Jorge A. Santana, Antología comentada del modernismo (Sacramento: California State University, Department of Spanish and Portuguese, 1974), pp. 48-50. ExTL, Anexo I.

67.1137   Sabat Ercasty, Carlos. "Habla Sabat Ercasty sobre las efemé-
          rides de Martí." AJM, 6, 1-4 (1952), 126-129.

67.1138   Sabella, Andrés. "José Martí en la huella de su gloria."
          Atenea, 110 (1953), 66-79.

67.1139   Sabourín Gornaris, Jesús. "José Martí: letra y servicio."
          Santiago, No.1 (1970), 4-15. Also AMart, No. 3 (1971),
          191-200.

67.1140   _____. "Martí en el Che [Guevara]." CAm, No. 73 (1972), 5-
          15.

67.1141   _____. "Martí: literatura y política." CAm, No. 54 (1969),
          122-125.

67.1142   Sacoto, Antonio. "El indio en la obra literaria de Sarmiento
          y Martí." CA, No. 156 (1968), 149-163.

67.1143   _____. "José Martí." In his El indio en el ensayo de la
          América española (Cuenca, 1981), pp. 68-85.

67.1144   _____. "'Nuestra América' de José Martí." CA, No. 215
          (1977), 96-105.

67.1145   Sáenz, Vicente. "Raíz y ala de José Martí." CA, No. 68
          (1953), 7-62.

67.1146   Salado, Minerva. "Sala Martí." CubaI, No. 33 (1972), 10-13.

67.1147   Salas, Argeo. "Raíces, proyección y vigencia de la obra mar-
          tiana." Santiago, No. 12 (1973), 181-192.

67.1148   Salazar y Roig, Salvador. "Martí." CCont, 17 (1918), 5-16.

67.1149   Salinas de Aguilar, Norberto. "José Martí: la cristalización
          del ritmo de nuestra América." In Memoria del Congreso
          de Escritores Martianos, q.v., pp. 658-671.

67.1150   Salinas Quiroga, Genaro. "Martí, el cubano inmortal." AJM,
          5, 3 (1951), 362-365.

67.1151   Salomon, Noël. "En torno al idealismo de José Martí." AMart,
          No. 1 (1978), 41-58.

67.1152   _____. "José Martí y la toma de conciencia latinoamericana."
          AMart, 4, 4 (1972), 9-25.

67.1153   _____. "Nación y unidad continental en la obra de José Mar-
          tí." Bohemia, 69, 3 (1977), 25.

67.1154   Sánchez, Luis Alberto. "Dos notas sobre Martí." Atenea, 110
          (1953), 55-65.

67.1155 _____. "José Martí." In his Escritores representativos de América; primera serie; 2. ed. (Madrid: Gredos, 1963), II, 189-202.

67.1156 _____. "Perenne actualidad de Martí." AJM, 5, 1 (1950), 123-124.

67.1157 _____. "Sobre el pensamiento americano de José Martí." Bolívar, No. 23 (1953), 483-496.

67.1158 Sánchez, Myriam F. "Interpretación y análisis de 'Pollice verso' de José Martí." Hispania, 57 (1974), 40-42.

67.1159 Sánchez, Reinaldo. "Ideología y ética del héroe martiano en Amistad funesta." CA, No. 203 (1975), 194-203.

67.1160 Sánchez-Trincado, J. L. "En el cincuentenario de José Martí." AJM, 5, 1 (1945), 139-143.

67.1161 Santos Moray, Mercedes. "Empresa del corazón y no de mero negocio [La edad de oro]." CAm, No. 116 (1979), 3-13.

67.1162 _____. "Lucía Jerez." In Estudios sobre Martí, q.v., pp. 203-217.

67.1163 _____. "Prólogo." In José Martí, Lucía Jerez y otras narraciones (H: Arte y Literatura, 1975), pp. 7-16.

67.1164 Santovenia y Echaide, Emeterio Santiago. "Alabanza de Martí por una autoridad licolniana." AJM, 5, 3 (1951), 341-344.

67.1165 _____. "Dos centenarios." AJM, 6, 1-4 (1952), 456-457.

67.1166 _____. "José Martí y Zayas Bazán." In his Vidas humanas (H: Librería Martí, 1956), pp. 220-224.

67.1167 _____. "Juicios de Sarmiento sobre el estilo de Martí." BACL, 1 (1952), 676-684.

67.1168 _____. "Martí en francés e inglés." AJM, 6, 1-4 (1952), 185-186.

67.1169 _____. "Martí, hombre de estado." CPro, No. 5 (1953), 98, 101.

67.1170 _____. "El primer retrato de Martí." RBNC, 2a serie, 3, 2 (1952), 11-20.

67.1171 _____. "Universalidad de dos americanos [Martí y Benjamin Franklin]." JIAS, 4 (1962), 33-51.

67.1172 Sarabia, Nydia. "Martí y la Avellaneda." Bohemia, 63, 28 (1971), 100-102.

67.1173   ____. "Por las huellas de Martí." Bohemia, 68, 33 (1976),
           88-93.

67.1174   Sautié Mederos, Félix. "Campaña de Martí contra el reformis-
           mo, el autonomismo, el anexionismo y la discriminación
           del negro." CB, No. 52 (1972), 3-8.

67.1175   Schnelle, Kurt. "José Martí. Leben und Dichtung." SuF, 14,
           3 (1962), 332-370.

67.1176   Schnoll, Kurt. "Observaciones sobre la significación de la
           obra de José Martí para la investigación histórica marx-
           ista." ULH, No. 158 (1962), 39-56.

67.1177   Schulman, Ivan A. "Bécquer y Martí: coincidencias en su teo-
           ría literaria." DHR, 3, 2 (1964), 57-87. Also in his
           Génesis del modernismo (M: El Colegio de México; St.
           Louis: Washington University Press, 1966), pp. 66-94.

67.1178   ____. "Darío y Martí: 'Marcha triunfal', 'El centenario de
           Calderón' y 'Castelar'." Atenea, Nos. 415-416 (1967),
           421-430.

67.1179   ____. "Desde los Estados Unidos: Martí y las minorías étni-
           cas y culturales." Los ensayistas, Nos. 10-11 (1981),
           139-152.

67.1180   ____. "En torno al texto y la fuente de 'Pollice verso'."
           In Estudios de literatura hispanoamericana en honor a
           José J. Arrom (Chapel Hill: University of North Carolina,
           Department of Romance Languages, 1974), pp. 125-142.

67.1181   ____. "La 'Estrofa nueva' y la dialéctica del mundo y tras-
           mundo de los Versos libres." In Homenaje a Sherman H.
           Eoff (Madrid: Castalia, 1970), pp. 259-272.

67.1182   ____. "Las estructuras polares en la obra de José Martí y
           Julián del Casal." RI, No. 56 (1963), 251-282. Also in
           his Génesis del modernismo (M: El Colegio de México; St.
           Louis: Washington University Press, 1966), pp. 153-187.

67.1183   ____. "Génesis del azul modernista." RI, No. 50 (1960),
           251-271. Also in his Génesis del modernismo (M: El Co-
           legio de México; St. Louis: Washington University Press,
           1966), pp. 115-138.

67.1184   ____. "La influencia de Martí en la prosa madura de Darío
           (1896-1913)." RBNJM, 3a serie, 11, 2 (1969), 109-144.

67.1185   ____. "Introducción." In José Martí, Versos libres (Barce-
           lona: Labor, 1970), pp. 11-48.

67.1186   ____. "José Martí and Mark Twain: a study of literary spon-
           sorship." Symposium, 15 (1961), 104-113.

67.1187 _____ . "José Martí y el Sun de Nueva York: nuevos escritos desconocidos." AUC, 124 (1966), 30-49.

67.1188 _____ . "José Martí y La revista ilustrada de Nueva York." CA, No. 159 (1968), 141-153.

67.1189 _____ . "José Martí y Manuel Gutiérrez Nájera: iniciadores del modernismo." RI, No. 57 (1964), 9-50. Also in his Génesis del modernismo (M: El Colegio de México; St. Louis: Washington University Press, 1966), pp. 21-65.

67.1190 _____ . "Martí y Darío frente a Centroamérica: perspectivas de realidad y ensueño." RI, No. 66 (1968), 201-236.

67.1191 _____ . "Martí y el modernismo." Nivel, No. 91 (1970), 5, 10-11.

67.1192 _____ . "Modernismo, revolución y pitagorismo en Martí." CAm, No. 73 (1972), 45-55.

67.1193 _____ . "¿Poseemos los textos auténticos de Martí? El caso de los versos libres." AMart, No. 3 (1971), 101-113.

67.1194 _____ . "Resonancias martianas en la prosa de Rubén Darío (1898-1916). 'El pobre y grande José Martí'." In Diez estudios sobre Rubén Darío (Santiago de Chile: Zig-Zag, 1967), pp. 123-154.

67.1195 _____ . "El simbolismo de José Martí: teoría y lenguaje." Inti, 8 (1980), 7-28.

67.1196 _____ . "Textos y contextos martianos: variaciones en torno a 'Pollice verso'." In Estudios martianos, q.v., pp. 29-55.

67.1197 Schultz de Mantovani, Fryda. "Dimensión íntima de Martí." RevC, 27 (1950), 5-22. Also AJM, 6, 1-4 (1952), 133-144.

67.1198 _____ . "La edad de oro de José Martí." CA, No. 67 (1953), 217-235.

67.1199 Schwartz, Kessel. "José Martí, The New York Herald and President Garfield's assassin." Hispania, 56 (1973), 335-342.

67.1200 "Secularidad de José Martí." Orígenes, No. 33 (1953), 3-4.

67.1201 Serra Badué, Daniel. "José Martí y los pintores de Cuba." RevCu, 1, 2 (1968), 339-353.

67.1202 Shuler, Esther Elise. "José Martí. Su crítica de algunos autores norteamericanos." AUC, 111 (1953), 131-153. Also AJM, 5, 2 (1950), 164-192.

67.1203   Silva, Josefina, Martha Marcos, and Angel Diez. "Las concepciones martianas sobre la escuela y la educación." San-tiago, No. 12 (1973), 171-179.

67.1204   Sirkó, Okasana María. "La crónica modernista en sus inicios: José Martí y Manuel Gutiérrez Nájera." In Estudios críticos sobre la prosa modernista hispanoamericana (NY: Eliseo Torres, 1975), pp. 57-73.

67.1205   Sneary, Eugene Chester. "Cecil Charles, traductor de Martí." RI, No. 45 (1958), 155-162.

67.1206   _____. "José Martí in Russian translatior." FurmS, 21, 4 (1974), 1-6.

67.1207   Solá, María Mercedes. "Presencia de Puerto Rico y los puertorriqueños en Martí (un aspecto del desarrollo de su pensamiento antillano)." In Estudios martianos, q.v., pp. 87-97.

67.1208   Solá Hernández, Ramón M. "Martí en la Comisión Monetaria Internacional Americana de 1895." In Estudios sobre Martí, q.v., pp. 97-129.

67.1209   Soler, Ricaurte. "De nuestra América de Blaine a nuestra América de Martí." CAm, No. 119 (1980), 9-61.

67.1210   Solís, Carlos A. (hijo). "La libertad en el pensamiento de Martí." RUT, 16, 12 (1953), 13-15.

67.1211   Sosa de Quesada, Arístides. "Presencia de Agramonte y de Varona en la vida de Martí." RBNC, 2a serie, 4, 2 (1953), 40-48.

67.1212   Stabb, Martin S. "Martí and the racists." Hispania, 40 (1957), 434-439. Also as "Martí y los racistas." RBC, 75 (1958), 179-189.

67.1213   Stolbov, V. S. "José Martí, patriota, revolucionario y poeta cubano." ULH, No. 175 (1965), 7-52.

67.1214   Suchlicki, Jaime. "The political ideology of José Martí." CarS, 6, 1 (1966), 25-36.

67.1215   Tamargo, María Isabel. "Amistad funesta: una teoría del personaje novelesco." ExTL, 10 (1981), 117-123. Signed Maribel Tamargo.

67.1216   Tijerino Rojas, Agustín. "Martí y Justo Rufino Barrios." RANCR, 23, 7-12 (1959), 341-343.

67.1217   Tirado, Modesto A. "Vacilaciones." RBC, 32 (1933), 226-234. Also RevC, 29 (1951-1952), 81-91.

67.1218 Toledo Sande, Luis. "Anticlericalismo, idealimso, religiosi-dad y práctica en José Martí." AMart, No. 1 (1978), 79-132.

67.1219 _____. "José Martí hacia la emancipación de la mujer." CAm, No. 90 (1975), 25-41. Also AMart, No. 7 (1977), 207-239.

67.1220 Torre, José R. de la. "Consideraciones socio-literarias sobre un texto martiano." In Estudios martianos, q.v., pp. 119-127.

67.1221 Torres Bodet, Jaime. "Conmemoración de José Martí en México. Discurso." RBC, 55 (1945), 283-286.

67.1222 Torres Cuevas, Eduardo. "La revolución necesaria." Bohemia, 69, 4 (1977), 84-87.

67.1223 Torres-Morales, José A. "Bécquer y Martí." La torre, No. 39 (1962), 127-142.

67.1224 Torres-Ríoseco, Arturo. "Estudios literarios: José Martí. El hombre." Hispania, 5 (1922), 282-285.

67.1225 _____. "Estudios literarios: José Martí, el poeta." Hispa-nia, 6 (1923), 323-327. This and previous item as "José Martí (1853-1895)." In his Precursores del modernismo (Madrid: Calpe, 1925), pp. 75-92.

67.1226 _____. "José Martí, poeta (1853-1895)." CCLC, No. 36 (1959), 22-29.

67.1227 Torriente, Loló de la. "Ambito de José Martí." Bohemia, 64, 3 (1972), 98-101.

67.1228 _____. "Carta sin nombre." Bohemia, 63, 11 (1971), 19.

67.1229 _____. "Las flechas de odiseo y los pretendientes martianos." CA, No. 190 (1973), 146-155.

67.1230 _____. "El pensamiento de Bolívar y Martí flota sobre Améri-ca." Bohemia, 64, 4 (1972), 94-99.

67.1231 Unamuno y Jugo, Miguel de. "Desde Salamanca: sobre los Ver-sos libres de Martí." AJM, 4, 1 (1947), 7-9.

67.1232 _____. "Notas de estética. Cartas de poeta." AJM, 4, 1 (1947), 16-18.

67.1233 _____. "Sobre el estilo de Martí." Germinal, 1, 2 (1921), 2-4. Also AJM, 4, 1 (1947), 11-14. Also BACL, 1 (1952), 500-502. Also in Manuel Pedro González, Anto-logía crítica de José Martí, q.v., pp. 187-191.

67.1234 _____. "Los versos libres de Martí." AUC, 111 (1953), 72-81.

67.1235   Urmeneta, Fermín de. "Sobre lo estético en José Martí."
          RIE, 33 (1975), 55-58.

67.1236   Valdés, Gemma. "Martí y el modernismo." In Estudios sobre
          Martí, q.v., pp. 171-181.

67.1237   Valdés, Miguel Angel. "Martí, masón." RBC, 41 (1938), 243-
          271.

67.1238   Valdés Gilbert, Eduardo. "La revolución necesaria." Bohemia,
          69, 4 (1972), 84-87.

67.1239   Valdespino, Andrés. "Imagen de Martí en las letras cubanas."
          RevCu, 1, 2 (1968), 307-331.

67.1240   Valle, Rafael Heliodoro. "Honduras en Martí." RUT, 16, 12
          (1953), 4-6.

67.1241   _____. "Martí en México." ND, 15, 5 (1934), 13-14.

67.1242   _____. "Martí modernista." Ateneo, No. 197 (1953), 50-54.
          Also in Memoria del Congreso de Escritores Martianos,
          q.v., pp. 466-473.

67.1243   _____. "Mexicanos que conocieron a Martí." RBC, 34 (1934),
          161-163.

67.1244   _____. "Poemas desconocidos de Martí." RHM, 13 (1947), 305-
          309. Also RAm, 45 (1949), 369-370. Also AJM, 4, 4
          (1949), 444-448.

67.1245   Varela, José Luis. "Ensayo de una poesía criolla: Martí."
          In his Ensayos de poesía indígena en Cuba (Madrid?:
          Cultura Hispánica, 1951), pp. 15-74.

67.1246   Varona y Pera, Enrique José. "Hombre de América: Martí."
          MEC, No. 926 (1959), 33-44.

67.1247   _____. "Martí y su obra poética." In his De la colonia a
          la república (H: Sociedad Editorial Cuba Contemporánea,
          1919), pp. 83-94.

67.1248   _____. "Mis recuerdos de Martí." RBC, 30 (1932), 5-8.

67.1249   Vasconcelos, José. "El genio en Ibero-América." RAm, 17
          (1928), 8-9.

67.1250   Velazco Aragón, Luis. "Rodó y Martí." RBC, 22 (1927), 231-
          232.

67.1251   Vélez, Román. "José Martí." RevC, 29 (1951-1952), 217-223.

67.1252   Vergara Leonard, Alejandro. "La obra político-revolucionaria
          de Martí (análisis dialéctico-materialista)." RMC, 71,
          1 (1960), 1-18.

67.1253 Vian, Francesco. "José Martí (1853-1895)." In his Il "moder-
         nismo" nella poesia ispanica (Milano: La Goliardica,
         1955), pp. 55-69.

67.1254 Vicente Hercia, Walfredo R. "Martí en Dos Ríos." RBC, 41
         (1938), 282-300.

67.1255 Victoria, Marcos. "Martí y los niños." GLite, 1, 3 (1956),
         5, 7.

67.1256 Vignier, Enrique. "Acechanzas a Martí." RyC, Nos. 30-31
         (1975), 57-59.

67.1257 Villalba Villalba, Luis, and Pedro Sotillo. "Martí y la edu-
         cación fundamental." AJM, 5, 3 (1951), 409-412.

67.1258 Villanar Cusidó, Manuel. "Discurso." AMart, No. 7 (1977),
         165-173.

67.1259 Villares, Ricardo. "Martí y el pintor nuevo de Cuba." Bohe-
         mia, 69, 44 (1977), 30-31.

67.1260 Vitier, Cintio. "Algo más sobre el apóstol." CA, No. 134
         (1964), 85-94.

67.1261 _____. "El arca de nuestra alianza." AMart, 4, 4 (1972),
         381-389.

67.1262 _____. "Casal como antítesis de Martí. Hastío, forma, belle-
         za, asimilación y originalidad." Nuevos rasgos de lo cu-
         bano. 'El frío' y 'Lo otro'." In his Lo cubano en la
         poesía (Santa Clara: Universidad Central de Las Villas,
         Departamento de Relaciones Culturales, 1958), pp. 242-
         268.

67.1263 _____. "Los discursos de Martí." LyP, No. 56 (1969), 22-25.
         Also Bohemia, 61, 22 (1969), 19-27. Also in Cintio Vi-
         tier, and Fina García Marruz, Temas martianos, q.v., pp.
         67-91.

67.1264 _____. "En la mina martiana." In Ivan A. Schulman, and Ma-
         nuel Pedro González, Martí, Darío y el modernismo (Ma-
         drid: Gredos, 1969), pp. 9-21.

67.1265 _____. "Una fuente venezolana de José Martí." CA, No. 210
         (1977), 150-171. Also in his Temas martianos; segunda
         serie, q.v., pp. 105-142.

67.1266 _____. "Imagen de José Martí." AMart, No. 3 (1971), 231-248.

67.1267 _____. "Lava, espada, alas." ULH, No. 195 (1972), 29-33.
         Also as "Lava, espada, alas (en torno a la poética de
         los Versos libres)." In his Temas martianos; segunda
         serie, q.v., pp. 48-74.

67.1268 ____. "Lucía Jerez." Diálogos, No. 87 (1979), 3-8.

67.1269 ____. "Manuel Pedro González y la Sala Martí: de un discurso inaugural." RBNJM, 3a serie, 10, 1 (1968), 93-100.

67.1270 ____. "Martí como crítico." RBNJM, 3a serie, 10, 3 (1968), 19-38. Also in Cintio Vitier, and Fina García Marruz, Temas martianos, q.v., pp. 174-191.

67.1271 ____. "Martí futuro." CA, No. 156 (1968), 217-237. Also in Cintio Vitier, and Fina García Marruz, Temas martianos, q.v., pp. 121-140.

67.1272 ____. "Música y razón." AMart, 4, 4 (1972), 372-376.

67.1273 ____. "Notas críticas." AMart, No. 3 (1971), 325-330.

67.1274 ____. "Noticias y comentarios." AMart, No. 3 (1971), 331-339.

67.1275 ____. "El poeta." In his Poetas cubanos del siglo XIX; semblanzas (H: Unión, 1969), pp. 53-57.

67.1276 ____. "Prólogo." In José Martí, Obra literaria (Caracas: Biblioteca Ayacucho, 1978), pp. ix-xxi.

67.1277 ____. "Prologue: Martí et 'notre Amérique'." In José Martí, La guerre de Cuba et le destin de l'Amérique latine (Paris" Aubier-Montaigne, 1973), pp. 25-36.

67.1278 ____. "Sobre Lucía Jerez." Diálogos, No. 87 (1979), 3-8.

67.1279 ____. "Sor Juana, Meza, Martí." In his Crítica sucesiva (H: Contemporáneos, UNEAC, 1971), pp. 267-275.

67.1280 ____. "Vallejo y Martí." RCLL, No. 13 (1981), 98-104.

67.1281 ____. "Los Versos libres de Martí." Lyceum, Nos. 33-34 (1953), 59-69. Also in Manuel Pedro González, Antología crítica de José Martí, q.v., pp. 381-390. Also as "Los Versos libres." In Cintio Vitier, and Fina García Marruz, Temas martianos, q.v, pp. 152-162.

67.1282 ____. "Versos sencillos." CB, No. 45 (1971), 9-13.

67.1283 ____. "Visión del maestro." CubaI, No. 33 (1972), 4-9.

67.1284 Vitier, Medardo. "Aspectos en la figura de Martí." RevC, 5 (1936), 48-53.

67.1285 ____. "La capacidad de magisterio en Martí." In Vida y pensamiento de Martí, q.v., II, 211-225.

67.1286 ____. "Dimensión filosófica, sobre todo en su sentido de la vida." In Manuel Pedro González, Antología crítica de José Martí, q.v., pp. 497-512.

67.1287 _____. "Estudio técnico de su estilo en prosa." In Manuel Pedro González, Antología crítica de José Martí, q.v., pp. 133-153.

67.1288 _____. "Influencias en Martí." Avance, No. 38 (1929), 268-269, 284.

67.1289 _____. "José Martí." In his Estudios, notas, efigies cubanas (H: Minerva, 1944), pp. 245-247.

67.1290 _____. "Sobre el estilo de Martí." BACL, 1 (1952), 713-714.

67.1291 Weber, Fryda. "Martí en La nación de Buenos Aires (1885-1890)." RevC, 10 (1937), 71-105. Also AJM, 6, 1-4 (1952), 458-482.

67.1292 Wiegman, Neal A. "'Sueño despierto'." In Francisco E. Porrata, and Jorge A. Santana, Antología comentada del modernismo (Sacramento: California State University, Department of Spanish and Portuguese, 1974), pp. 28-30. ExtL, Anexo I.

67.1293 Winocur, Marcos. "José Martí: anexión o independencia." In Mélanges à la mémoire d'André Joucla-Ruau (Aix-en-Provence: Université de Provence, 1978), pp. 383-388.

67.1294 Yáñez, Agustín. "Discurso." AMart, No. 7 (1977), 267-273.

67.1295 Yépez, Luis. "Martí, arquetipo moral." RNC, No. 96 (1953), 18-21.

67.1296 Yoskowitz, Marcia. "El arte de síntesis e interpretación: un estudio de 'El terremoto de Charleston' de José Martí." CA, No. 161 (1968), 135-148.

67.1297 Zacharie de Baralt, Blanche. "José Martí, caballero." RBC, 28 (1931), 323-333.

67.1298 Zamora, Juan Clemente. "Martí y Echegaray, nota rectificatoria." RomN, 18 (1977), 73-75.

67.1299 Zayas, Lincoln de. "La apoteosis de Martí." RevC, 29 (1951-1952), 143-150.

67.1300 Zdenek, Joseph W. "Un estudio de la poética de Ismaelillo de José Martí." ExTL, 4 (1975), 87-91.

67.1301 Zell, Rosa Hilda. "Notas al margen de una página del Diario de Martí de Cabo Hatiano a Dos Ríos." AMart, 4, 4 (1972), 327-334.

67.1302 _____. "Roncaral, çmucarai?" AMart, No. 3 (1971), 225-230.

67.1303 Zéndegui, Guillermo de. "La dimensión heroica en Martí." RevC, 30 (1956), 97-109.

67.1304 _____ . "Martí en México." Américas, 15, 7 (1963), 12-16.
Also as "Martí in México." Américas [English edition],
15, 6 (1963), 12-16.

67.1305 _____ . "Martí en Nueva York." Américas, 25, 1 (1973), 7-12.
Also as "Martí in New York." Américas [English edition],
5, 1 (1973), 7-12.

67.1306 _____ . "Martí, the hero and his time." Américas, 27, 6-7
suppl. (1975), S1-S16. Also as "José Martí." Américas
[Spanish edition], 27, 6-7 suppl. (1975), S1-S16.

67.1307 Zulueta, Luis de. "Martí, el luchador sin odio." RBC, 43
(1939), 161-177.

68. MILANES, JOSE JACINTO (1814-1863)

Critical Essays

68.1   Abdo, Ada. "El siglo XIX a la escena [El conde Alarcos]."
        GdC, No. 35 (1964), 22.

68.2   Arias, Salvador. "El diminutivo en Milanés." RBNJM, 3a serie,
        8, 2 (1966), 76-84.

68.3   Barreda-Tomás, Pedro M. "El teatro de José Jacinto Milanés."
        In Instituto Internacional de Literatura Iberoamericana,
        Literatura de la emancipación hispanoamericana y otros
        ensayos (Lima: Universidad de San Marcos, 1972), pp. 319-
        345.

68.4   Boudet, Rosa Ileana. "La ciudad de Milanés." RyC, No. 18
        (1974), 48-51.

68.5   Bueno, Salvador. "Imagen del poeta Milanés." RBNJM, 3a serie,
        6, 3-4 (1966), 5-14. Also in his Temas y personajes de la
        literatura cubana (H: Unión, 1964), pp. 41-50.

68.6   _____. "José Jacinto Milanés." In his Figuras cubanas del si-
        glo XIX (H: Unión de Escritores y Artistas, 1980), pp. 109-
        119.

68.7   Castañeda, James A. "Renacimiento romántico en Cuba del tema
        del conde Alarcos." In Estudios de literatura hispanoame-
        ricana en honor a José J. Arrom (Chapel Hill, N.C.: Uni-
        versity of North Carolina, Department of Romance Languages,
        1974), pp. 99-108.

68.8   Chamberlin, Vernon A. "Schlegel y Milanés: dos dramas románti-
        cos sobre el tema del conde Alarcos." Hispanófila, No. 3
        (1959), 27-38.

68.9   Fernández de Castro, José Antonio. "Milanés y Plácido." CCont,
        5 (1914), 425-457.

68.10   González del Valle y Carbajal, Emilio Martín. "José Jacinto Mi-
        lanés." In his La poesía lírica en Cuba, apuntes para un
        libro de biografía y de crítica (Barcelona: Luis Tasso,
        1900), pp. 143-170.

68.11   Harzenbusch, Juan Eugenio. "Crítica literaria: El conde Alar-
        cos, de José Jacinto Milanés." RdC, 8 (1880), 337-339.

68.12   Iraizoz y de Villar, Antonio. "Milanés incomprendido." In his
        Libros y autores cubanos (Santa María de Rosario: Rosareña,
        1956), pp. 17-20.

68.13   Martínez Bello, Antonio. "Glorias de Cuba: José Jacinto Mila-
        nés." Carteles, 21-XI-1948, pp. 27, 58.

68.14   Mitjans, Aurelio. "Estudio sobre J. J. Milanés." In Cintio
        Vitier, La crítica literaria y estética en el siglo XIX
        cubano (H: Biblioteca Nacional "José Martí", Departamento
        Colección Cubana, 1968), III, 155-175.

68.15   Montes Huidobro, Matías. "El teatro de Milanés y la formación
        de la conciencia cubana." AlHisp, Nos. 2-3 (1973-1974),
        223-240.

68.16   Poncet y de Cárdenas, Carolina. "José Jacinto Milanés y su o-
        bra poética." CCont, 31 (1923), 117-154.

68.17   Roig de Leuchsenring, Emilio. "José Jacinto Milanés." In his
        La literatura costumbrista cubana de los siglos XVIII y
        XIX (H: Oficina del Historiador de la Ciudad de la Habana,
        1962-), III, 151-153.

68.18   Suárez y Romero, Anselmo. "Dos cartas a José Jacinto Milanés."
        RBNC, 2a serie, 5, 1 (1954), 45-49.

68.19   Vitier, Cintio. "El obseso." In his Poetas cubanos del siglo
        XIX; semblanzas (H: Unión, 1969), pp. 25-27.

69. MONTANER, CARLOS ALBERTO (1943-   )

Bibliographies

69.1   Goodyear, Russell Howard. "Bibliografía de la narrativa de
         Carlos Alberto Montaner." In La narrativa de Carlos Al-
         berto Montaner, q.v., pp. 253-260.

Critical Monographs and Dissertations

69.2   La narrativa de Carlos Alberto Montaner. Madrid: CUPSA, 1978.
         Pertinent items are listed separately.

Critical Essays

69.3   Arciniegas, Germán. "Montaner y el informe 'secreto'." In La
         narrativa de Carlos Alberto Montaner, q.v., pp. 247-251.

69.4   Baeza Flores, Alberto. "Notas sobre Perromundo y la novela de
         nuestro tiempo." In La narrativa de Carlos Alberto Monta-
         ner, q.v., pp. 91-148. Also as "Perromundo, de Carlos Al-
         berto Montaner y la novela de nuestro tiempo." In his Cu-
         ba, el laurel y la palma; ensayos literarios (Miami: Uni-
         versla, 1977), pp. 229-293.

69.5   Chang-Rodríguez, Raquel. "El tema de la locura en un narrador
         cubano." NNH, 2, 1 (1972), 209-211.

69.6   Cohen, J. M. "On Castro's blacklist." TLS, 6-VIII-1976, pp.
         982-983.

69.7   Diez Borque, José María. "Deshumanización y degradación del en-
         torno: claves de Perromundo." In La narrativa de Carlos
         Alberto Montaner, q.v., pp. 205-213.

69.8   Fernández de la Torriente, Gastón. "200 aos de gringos y el
         tema de nuestro tiempo." In La narrativa de Carlos Alberto
         Montaner, q.v., pp. 217-246.

69.9   _____. "Prólogo." In Carlos Alberto Montaner, Poker de brujas
         (Bilbao: Vasco-Americana, 1968), pp. 7-11.

69.10   Fernández-Vázquez, Antonio A. "Perromundo: novela de la para-
         doja de la revolución cubana." KRQ, 28 (1981), 267-278.

69.11 Hernández-Miyares, Julio. "Los cuentos de Carlos Alberto Monta-
          ner." In La narrativa de Carlos Alberto Montaner, q.v.,
          pp. 19-39.

69.12 Labrador Ruiz, Enrique. "Pañuelo de piedra." In La narrativa
          de Carlos Alberto Montaner, q.v., pp. 197-203.

69.13 Mocega-González, Esther Po. "En torno al tiempo en Perromundo,
          de Carlos Alberto Montaner." In La narrativa de Carlos Al-
          berto Montaner, q.v., 155-180. Orig. Yelmo, No. 21 (1974-
          1975), 26-32.

69.14 Rodríguez, Israel. "Perromundo: ficción y realidad." In La
          narrativa de Carlos Alberto Montaner, q.v., pp. 181-196.

69.15 Rodríguez Dod, Gladys. "Carlos Alberto Montaner nos habla de
          sus libros y de la guerra de Angola." Pueblo, 1, 12
          (1977), 30-33.

69.16 Souza, Raymond D. "El humor en los cuentos de Carlos Alberto
          Montaner." In La narrativa de Carlos Alberto Montaner,
          q.v., pp. 41-55.

69.17 Suárez-Galbán, Eugenio. "Literatura, ideología e historia: el
          caso de Perromundo." SinN, 8, 4 (1977), 47-48.

69.18 Suárez Rivero, Eliana. "El estilo literario de Perromundo: aná-
          lisis de una novela de Carlos Alberto Montaner." ALHisp,
          Nos. 2-3 (1973-1974), 593-615.

69.19 Zayas-Bazán, Eduardo. "Póker de brujas." In La narrativa de
          Carlos Alberto Montaner, q.v., pp. 11-18.

70. MONTES HUIDOBRO, MATIAS (1931-   )

Critical Essays

70.1 Colecchia, Francesca. "Matías Montes Huidobro: his theater." LATR, 13, 2 suppl. (1980), 77-80.

70.2 E. M. G. "Los cuentos y el autor." In Matías Montes Huidobro, La anunciación y otros cuentos cubanos (Madrid: Clemares, 1967), pp. 9-13.

70.3 González-Cruz, Luis F. "Matías Montes Huidobro, the poet: selected poems and an interview." LALR, No. 4 (1974), 163-170.

70.4 Jaimes-Freyre, Mireya. "[Desterrados al fuego]." LALR, No. 9 (1976), 96-98.

70.5 Pérez-Montaner, Jaime. "[Desterrados al fuego]." Chasqui, 6, 2 (1977), 87-89.

70.6 Raggi, Carlos M. "[La vaca de los ojos largos]." Círculo, 2 (1970), 135-136.

70.7 Roberts, Gemma. "[Desterrados al fuego]." RI, Nos. 96-97 (1976), 642-644.

70.8 Siemens, William L. "Parallel transformations in Desterrados al fuego." Término, No. 6 (1984), 17-18.

70.9 Torres Fierro, Danubio. "El libro de las metamorfosis [Desterrados al fuego]." Plural, No. 54 (1976), 63-65.

71. MORUA DELGADO, MARTIN (1856-1910)

Critical Monographs and Dissertations

71.1 Canales Carazo, Juan. Amarguras y realidades. Recopilación de datos relativos a la labor del ilustre cubano desaparecido Martín Morúa Delgado. H: O'Reilly, 1910.

71.2 González, Julián. Martín Morúa Delgado, impresiones sobre su última novela. H: Rambla y Bouza, 1902.

71.3 Horrego Estuch, Leopoldo. Martín Morúa Delgado. Vida y mensaje. H: Sánchez, 1957.

71.4 Meza Rodríguez, Manuel I. Martín Morúa Delgado. H: El Siglo XX, 1956.

71.5 Pérez Landa, Rufino. Vida pública de Martín Morúa Delgado. H: Carlos Romero, 1957.

71.6 Romaní, Salvador, and Joaquín Texidor. Iconografía de Martín Morúa Delgado. H: Nosotros, 1956.

Critical Essays

71.7 Alvarez García, Imeldo. "Prólogo." In Martín Morúa Delgado, Sofía (H: Instituto Cubano del Libro, 1972), pp. vii-xii.

71.8 Cobb, Martha K. "Bibliographical essay: an appraisal of Latin American slavery through literature." LNH, 58 (1973), 460-469. Morúa Delgado inter alios.

71.9 _____. "Martín Morúa Delgado." NHB, 36 (1973), 12.

71.10 Hernández-Miyares, Julio. "El tema del negro en las novelas naturalistas de Martín Morúa Delgado." In Homenaje a Lydia Cabrera (Miami: Universal, 1978), pp. 211-219.

71.11 Jackson, Richard L. "From antislavery to antiracism: Martín Morúa Delgado, black novelist, politician and critic of post-abolitionist Cuba." In his Black writers in Latin America (Albuquerque: University of New Mexico Press, 1979), pp. 45-52.

71.12 Portuondo, Aleida T. "Vigencia política y literaria de Martín Morúa Delgado." Círculo, 9 (1980), 101-111.

71.13 Rodríguez Figueroa, Iraida. "Sofía." ULH, Nos. 198-199 (1973),
210-215.

72. NAVARRO LUNA, MANUEL (1894-   )

Critical Monographs and Dissertations

72.1   Santana, Joaquín G. Furia y fuego en Manuel Navarro Luna. H: Unión de Escritores y Artistas de Cuba, 1975.

Critical Essays

72.2   Arango Arias, Arturo. "Homenaje a Navarro Luna." Bohemia, 70, 27 (1978), 24-25.

72.3   Bianchi Ross, Ciro, and Sonia Díaz. "Yo vengo de esta tierra." RyC, No. 20 (1974), 32-35.

72.4   Branly, Roberto. "Vigencia y actualidad de Navarro Luna." GdC, No. 109 (1973), 27-28.

72.5   C. P. S. "[La tierra herida]." Atenea, No. 158 (1938), 332-334.

72.6   "Cartas al poeta." GdC, No. 109 (1973), 28-32.

72.7   Catalá, Rafael. "La evolución del pensamiento en tres poetas del Caribe: Manuel Navarro Luna, Clemente Soto Vélez y Pedro Mir." In Rose S. Minc, Literatures in transition: the many voices of the Caribbean area (Gaithersburg, Md.: Hispamérica, 1982), pp. 97-106.

72.8   Daskevitch, Yuri. "El poeta de la revolución cubana: Manuel Navarro Luna." In Manuel Navarro Luna, Poemas (H: Unión de Escritores y Artistas de Cuba, 1963), pp. 199-206.

72.9   Delebro, J. F. "Homenaje a Manuel Navarro Luna." VO, 14, 29 (1972), 61.

72.10   Fernández Retamar, Roberto. "Manuel Navarro Luna." In his La poesía contemporánea en Cuba (1927-1935) (H: Orígenes, 1954), pp. 67-69.

72.11   ____. "Rebelión de la poesía." RyC, No. 14 (1973), 57-59.

72.12   Ferrer, Raúl. "Navarro Luna: una conciencia anhelante." GdC, No. 109 (1973), 6-8.

72.13   Forné Farreres, José. "Evocación de Manuel Navarro Luna." GdC, No. 109 (1973), 22-23.

72.14 Guillén, Nicolás. "A Manuel Navarro Luna." <u>GdC</u>, No. 109
       (1973), 16-17.

72.15 ____. "Un poeta de su tiempo, el tiempo nuestro." <u>GdC</u>, No.
       109 (1973), 26-27.

72.16 Ichaso, Francisco. "<u>Surco</u>, por Manuel Navarro Luna." <u>Avance</u>,
       No. 30 (1929), 26-27.

72.17 Iznaga, Alcides. "Manual Navarro Luna." <u>Bohemia</u>, 66, 24
       (1974), 93.

72.18 Jimenes Grullón, Juan Isidro. "Manuel Navarro Luna." In his
       <u>Seis poetas cubanos (ensayos apologéticos)</u> (H: "Cromos",
       1954), pp. 59-84.

72.19 Leante, César. "Presencia de Navarro Luna en Juan Marinello."
       <u>Bohemia</u>, 69, 38 (1977), 10-13.

72.20 "Manuel Navarro Luna, poeta de la lucha y de la vida." <u>CB</u>, No.
       68 (1973), 11-13.

72.21 Marinello, Juan. "Las cartas de Navarro Luna." <u>GdC</u>, No. 52
       (1966), 2.

72.22 ____. "Margen apasionado." In Manuel Navarro Luna, <u>Pulso y
       onda</u> (H: Hermes?, 1933?), pp. 5-15. Also in his <u>Orbita de
       Juan Marinello</u> (H: Colección Orbita, 1968), pp. 114-125.
       Also in his <u>Poética; ensayos en entusiasmo</u> (Madrid: Espasa-
       Calpe, 1933), pp. 63-98.

72.23 ____. "Navarro Luna en tres tiempos." <u>GdC</u>, No. 109 (1973),
       2-4. Also in his <u>Contemporáneos</u> (H: Contemporáneos, 1975),
       pp. 141-154.

72.24 ____. "Tierra y canto." In Manuel Navarro Luna, <u>La tierra
       herida</u> (Manzanillo: Sariol, 1938?), pp. [7-10].

72.25 Más, Oscar. "Manuel Navarro Luna, hombre y poeta." <u>GdC</u>, No.
       109 (1973), 24-25.

72.26 Nadereau Maceo, Efraín. "La poesía de Manuel Navarro Luna."
       <u>TallerC</u>, No. 26 (1973), 26-29. Also <u>GdC</u>, No. 109 (1973),
       18-20.

72.27 "Navarro Luna: VIII aniversario." <u>GdC</u>, No. 125 (1974), 13.

72.28 Padilla, Heberto. "Introducción." In Manuel Navarro Luna,
       Surco, 1963), pagination unknown.

72.29 ____. "Prólogo." In Manuel Navarro Luna, <u>Poemas</u> (H: Unión de
       Escritores y Artistas de Cuba, 1963), pp. 5-8.

72.30 Pita Rodríguez, Félix. "Manuel Navarro Luna y las virtudes re-
       volucionarias." <u>GdC</u>, No. 109 (1973), 12-13.

72.31   Roa, Raúl. "Mongo Paneque [pseud. de Navarro Luna]." GdC, No.
        109 (1973), 4-6.

72.32   Santana, Joaquín G. "La poesía civil y patriótica de Manuel Na-
        varro Luna." GdC, No. 109 (1973), 13-15.

72.33   Suárez, Adolfo. "Imagen del poeta en la memoria." GdC, No. 109
        (1973), 21.

72.34   Vignier, Marta. "Manuel Navarro Luna, arma y bandera." RBNJM,
        3a serie, 17, 2 (1975), 127-133.

73. NOVAS CALVO, LINO (1905-   )

Critical Monographs and Dissertations

73.1   Gutiérrez de la Solana, Alberto. Maneras de narrar: contraste de Lino Novás Calvo y Alfonso Hernández Catá. NY: Eliseo Torres, 1972. Orig. as "Lino Novás Calvo y Alfonso Hernández Catá: contraste de vida y obra." DAI, 29 (1968), 261A.

73.2   Souza, Raymond D. Lino Novás Calvo. Boston: Twayne/G. K. Hall, 1981.

73.3   _____. "The literary world of Lino Novás Calvo." DA, 25 (1964), 1926.

Critical Essays

73.4   Anderson Imbert, Enrique. "La originalidad de Lino Novás Calvo." Symposium, 29 (1975), 212-219.

73.5   Ben-Ur, Lorraine. "La época española de Novás Calvo: 1931-1939." Chasqui, 6, 3 (1977), 69-76.

73.6   _____. "Lino Novás Calvo: a sense of the preternatural." Symposium, 29 (1975), 220-228.

73.7   Bueno, Salvador. "Un cuentista cubano." Américas, 3, 3 (1951), 10-12, 41, 44-45. Also as "Cuban storyteller." Américas [English edition], 3, 2 (1951), 10-12, 39, 41.

73.8   _____. "Semblanza biográfica y crítica de Lino Novás Calvo." Lyceum, No. 28 (1951), 36-49. Also in his Medio siglo de literatura cubana (1902-1952) (H: Comisión Cubana de la UNESCO, 1953), pp. 211-234.

73.9   Clinton, Stephen. "The scapegoat archetype as a principle of composition in Novás Calvo's 'Un dedo encima'." Hispania, 62 (1979), 56-61.

73.10 "10 preguntas a Lino Novás Calvo." AA, 1, 2 (1971), 106-107.

73.11 Fernández, Sergio. "Lino Novás Calvo, hechizador de negros." Universidad, Nos. 14-15 (1957), 47-55.

73.12 _____. "'El otro cayó': vía de redención." In his Cinco escritores hispanoamericanos (M: Universidad Autónoma de México, Dirección General de Publicaciones, 1958), pagination unknown.

73.13 Ferrán, James. "Lino Novás Calvo." Symposium, 29 (1975), 189-
       192.

73.14 Galbis, Ignacio R. M. "Tanatología en la narrativa de Novás
       Calvo." Symposium, 29 (1975), 229-242.

73.15 Gutiérrez de la Solana, Alberto. "Lino Novás Calvo: literatura
       y experiencia." Caribe, 2, 1 (1977), 61-75.

73.16 _____. "Novás Calvo: precursor y renovador." Symposium, 29
       (1975), 243-254.

73.17 Homs, Ernesto. "Novás Calvo, su cachima y su cuchitril." Orbe,
       No. 36 (1931), 12, 38.

73.18 Irby, James E. "Lino Novás Calvo (1905)." In his La influencia
       de William Faulkner en cuatro narradores hispanoamericanos
       (M, 1956), pp. 45-73.

73.19 Leal, Luis. "The pursued hero: 'La noche de Ramón Yendía'."
       Symposium, 29 (1975), 255-260.

73.20 Lichtblau, Myron I. "Reality and unreality in 'La vaca en la
       azotea'." Symposium, 29 (1975), 261-265.

73.21 _____. "Técnica narrativa de El negrero de Lino Novás Calvo."
       In Homenaje a Lydia Cabrera (Miami: Universal, 1978), pp.
       221-227.

73.22 _____. "Visión irónica en tres cuentos de Lino Novás Calvo."
       Caribe, 1, 2 (1976), 21-27.

73.23 Pogolotti, Marcelo. "El coche y el automóvil." In his La
       república de Cuba al través de sus escritores (H: Lex,
       1958), pp. 72-75.

73.24 Portuondo, José Antonio. "Four Cuban novelists." BA, 18
       (1944), 235-238. Novás Calvo inter alios.

73.25 _____. "Lino Novás Calvo y el cuento hispanoamericano." CA,
       No. 55 (1947), 245-263.

73.26 Rodríguez Feo, José. "Los cuentos cubanos de Novás Calvo."
       Orígenes, No. 12 (1946), 25-30.

73.27 Rodríguez-Luis, Julio. "Lino Novás Calvo y la historia de Cu-
       ba." Symposium, 29 (1975), 281-293.

73.28 Romeu, Raquel. "Lo negro cubano y Lino Novás Calvo." Sympo-
       sium, 29 (1975), 266-277.

73.29 Saz, Agustín del. "Lino Novás Calvo y la novela de protesta
       social." RevC, 26, 1-2 (1950), 320-323.

73.30 Souza, Raymond D. "The early stories of Lino Novás Calvo (1929-
       32): genesis and aftermath." KRQ, 26 (1979), 221-229.

73.31 _____. "Lino Novás Calvo and the Revista de avance." JIAS, 10 (1968), 233-243.

73.32 _____. "On Lino Novás Calvo and his Maneras de contar." IFR, 2 (1975), 67-68.

73.33 _____. "Time and terror in the stories of Lino Novás Calvo." Symposium, 29 (1975), 294-299.

73.34 _____. "Two 'lost' stories of Lino Novás Calvo." RomN, 9 (1967), 49-52.

73.35 Valverde, José María. "Dos narradores de Hispanoamérica: Jorge Icaza (ecuatoriano), Lino Novás Calvo (cubano)." LetE, 9, 2 (1954), 24-23 [sic].

74. ORTIZ, FERNANDO (1881-1969)

Bibliographies

74.1   Barnet, Miguel. "Bibliografía de Fernando Ortiz." GdC, No. 42 (1965), 19-20.

74.2   Becerra Bonet, Berta. "Bibliografía de Fernando Ortiz." In Miscelánea de estudios, q.v., pp. 1589-1621. Also RBC, 74 (1958), 141-165.

74.3   García-Carranza, Araceli. Bio-bibliografía de don Fernando Ortiz. H: Biblioteca Nacional José Martí, 1970.

Critical Monographs and Dissertations

74.4   Miscelánea de estudios dedicados a Fernando Ortiz por sus discípulos, colegas y amigos. H, 1955. Pertinent items are listed separately.

Critical Essays

74.5   Ardura, Ernesto. "Fernando Ortiz: su mejor día." ND, 35, 1 (1955), 114-115.

74.6   Arenas, Reinaldo. "Elogio a una bio-bibliografía." RBNJM, 62, 2 (1971), 174-176. See item no. 74.3.

74.7   Barnet, Miguel. "Don Fernando, no me trate de usted." CAm, No. 5 (1969), 10-11.

74.8   _____. "La segunda agricanía [Africanía de la música folklórica de Cuba]." Unión, 5, 3 (1966), 108-119.

74.9   _____. "Visión de Ortiz." GdC, No. 42 (1965), 17-18.

74.10   Becerra Bonet, Berta. "El doctor Ortiz, periodista." In Miscelánea de estudios, q.v., pp. 155-160.

74.11   Bueno, Salvador. "Aproximaciones a la vida y la obra de Fernando Ortiz." CAm, No. 113 (1979), 119-128.

74.12   _____. "Don Fernando Ortiz: al servicio de la ciencia y de Cuba." In his Temas y personajes de la literatura cubana (H: Unión, 1964), pp. 209-218.

74.13 _____. "En la muerte de don Fernando Ortiz." Asomante, 25, 3
(1969), 31-37. Also as "En la muerte del sabio cubano Fernando Ortiz." RBNJM, 3a época, 11, 1 (1969), 195-197.

74.14 _____. "Una pelea cubana contra los demonios [Historia de una
pelea cubana contra los demonios]." GdC, No. 42 (1965),
15-16.

74.15 Campoamor, Fernando G. "Don Fernando Ortiz, el maestro fuerte."
Crónica, 2, 5 (1951), 28-29.

74.16 Castellanos, Isabel. "Fernando Ortiz en las ciencias criminólo-
gicas." In Miscelánea de estudios, q.v., pp. 298-322.

74.17 Céspedes, Miguel Angel. "Justo homenaje a Fernando Ortiz."
RBC, 51 (1943), 248-255.

74.18 Comas, Juan. "Fernando Ortiz." AAntr, No. 7 (1970), 285-289.

74.19 _____. "La obra científica de Fernando Ortiz." RBC, 70 (1955),
17-28.

74.20 _____. "La obra escrita de don Fernando Ortiz." RIB, 7 (1957),
347-371.

74.21 Deschamps Chapeaux, Pedro. "[Contrapunteo cubano del tabaco y
el azúcar]." GdC, No. 42 (1965), 14-15.

74.22 Dollero, Adolfo. "Las simpatías de Cuba por Italia. Con motivo
de la reimpresión del folleto del Dr. Fernando Ortiz, Los
mambises italianos." RBC, 12 (1917), 327-331.

74.23 Echavarri, Luis. "Ni racismo ni xenofobias." RBC, 14 (1919),
571-575.

74.24 Espinosa Domínguez, Carlos. "Una obra fundamental es imprescin-
dible." GdC, No. 152 (1977), 14-15.

74.25 _____. "Ortiz y sus contrapunteos." In Fernando Ortiz, Contra-
punteo cubano del tabaco y el azúcar (Caracas: Biblioteca
Ayacucho, 1978?), pp. ix-xxxii.

74.26 Franco, José Luciano. "Mis recuerdos de don Fernando." CAm,
No. 55 (1969), 6-8.

74.27 González, Manuel Pedro. "Cuba's Fernando Ortiz." BA, 20
(1946), 9-13.

74.28 Guillén, Nicolás. "Ortiz: misión cumplida." CAm, No. 55
(1969), 5-6.

74.29 Guiteras Holmes, Calixta. "Fernando Ortiz: palparlo todo, oler-
lo todo, saborearlo todo." GdC, No. 42 (1965), 4-8.

74.30 Gutiérrez de la Solana, Alberto. "En torno a Fernando Ortiz,
       lo afrocubano y otros ensayos." In Instituto Internacio-
       nal de Literatura Iberoamericana, El ensayo y la crítica
       en Iberoamérica (Toronto: Universidad de Toronto, 1970),
       pp. 81-87.

74.31 Hernández Travieso, Antonio. "Fernando Ortiz y la Hispanocuba-
       na de la Cultura." In Miscelánea de estudios, q.v., pp.
       817-827.

74.32 Le Riverend, Julio. "Fernando Ortiz." AmerI, 29 (1969), 892-
       898.

74.33 ____. "Fernando Ortiz y su obra cubana." Unión, 11, 4 (1972),
       119-147.

74.34 ____. "Nota sobre la obra de Fernando Ortiz." GdC, No. 42
       (1965), 11-13.

74.35 ____. "Palabras de apertura." RBC, 70 (1955), 15-16.

74.36 León, Argeliers. "El aporte de Fernando Ortiz a la etnomusico-
       logía." GdC, No. 42 (1965), 9-10.

74.37 Lizaso y González, Félix. "Fernando Ortiz." In his Ensayistas
       contemporáneos, 1900-1920 (H: Trópico, 1938), pp. 31-33.

74.38 Malinowski, Bronislaw. "La 'transculturación', su vocablo y su
       concepto." RBC, 46 (1940), 220-228.

74.39 Marinello, Juan. "En la muerte de otro descubridor de Cuba."
       In his Contemporáneos (H: Contemporáneos, 1975), pp. 103-
       114.

74.40 Martínez, Luciano R. "Dr. Fernando Ortiz en la Sociedad Econó-
       mica." In Miscelánea de estudios, q.v., pp. 1007-1020.

74.41 Martínez Furé, Rogelio. "Don Fernando Ortiz: un maestro de la
       cubanía." CubaI, No. 55 (1974), 48-51.

74.42 Mintz, Sidney Wilfred. "La obra etnomusicológica de Fernando
       Ortiz." RBC, 71 (1956), 282-284.

74.43 Novás Calvo, Lino. "Cubano de tres mundos." In Miscelánea de
       estudios, q.v., pp. 113-141. Orig. Américas, 2, 7 (1950),
       6-8, 44. Also as "Mister Cuba." Américas [English edi-
       tion], 2, 6 (1950), 6-8, 46.

74.44 Portuondo, José Antonio. "Fernando Ortiz: humanismo y raciona-
       lismo científico." CAm, No. 55 (1969), 8-10.

74.45 Price-Mars, Jean. "Hommage à Fernando Ortiz." In Miscelánea
       de estudios, q.v., pp. 1249-1252. Also as "Homenaje a Fer-
       nando Ortiz." GdC, No. 42 (1965), 12-13.

74.46 Romero, Fernando. "Los Estudios afrocubanos y el negro en la patria de Martí." RBC, 47 (1941), 395-401.

74.47 Sánchez, Luis Alberto. "Fernando Ortiz y Fernando." In his Escritores respresentativos de América; segunda serie (Madrid: Gredos, 1972), II, 133-144.

74.48 Santovenia y Echaide, Emeterio Santiago. "Fernando Ortiz." In his Vidas humanas (H: Librería Martí, 1956), pp. 449-454.

74.49 Selva, Juan B. "Plausible obra del doctor Ortiz." In Miscelánea de estudios, q.v., pp. 1375-1379.

74.50 Stingl, Miloslav. "Los negros esclavos de Fernando Ortiz." GdC, No. 42 (1965), 11.

74.51 Vitier, Medardo. "El aliento cubano y el espíritu científico en la obra de Fernando Ortiz." RBC, 70 (1955), 29-42.

75. OTERO, LISANDRO (1932-   )

Critical Essays

75.1   Alvarez, Federico. "Lisandro Otero: La situación." GdC, No. 39 (1964), 2.

75.2   Arrufat, Antón. "La burguesía en busca de la seguridad perdida [La situación]." GdC, No. 29 (1963), 2-3.

75.3   Benítez Rojo, Antonio. "[En ciudad semejante]." CAm, Nos. 65-66 (1971), 160-163.

75.4   Bueno, Salvador. "[En ciudad semejante]." SinN, 2, 1 (1971), 89-91. Also Unión, 10, 1 (1971), 152-154.

75.5   Carballo, Emmanuel. "Hemingway de cuerpo entero [Hemingway]." GdC, No. 18 (1963), 13.

75.6   Carpentier, Alejo. "Un jurado opina [La situación]." GdC, No. 14 (1963), 3.

75.7   Dalton, Roque. "La situación, un ejemplo de literatura revolucionaria." Bohemia, 55, 44 (1963), 10-11.

75.8   Depestre, René. "La situación: una novela revolucionaria." GdC, No. 29 (1963), 4.

75.9   Desnoes, Edmundo. "[La situación]." CAm, Nos. 20-21 (1963), 77-80.

75.10 Fornet, Ambrosio. "Entrevista con Lisandro Otero." GdC, No. 14 (1963), 4-5.

75.11 "Lo que ha dicho la crítica [La situación]." GdC, No. 29 (1963), 5.

75.12 Martí, Agenor. "Cara a cara con Lisandro Otero." CubaI, No. 102 (1978), 32-35.

75.13 Martínez Bello, Antonio. "[Tabaco para un jueves santo y otros cuentos cubanos]." RBNC, 2a serie, 6, 4 (1955), 177-178.

75.14 Morbán, Jorge A. "Social realism in a Cuban novel: La situación by Lisandro Otero." IFR, 2, 1 (1975), 58-61.

75.15 Nadereau Maceo, Efraín. "[En ciudad semejante]." RyC, marzo 1972, pp. 67-69.

75.16 Otero, Lisandro. "Conversación sobre el arte y la literatura."
CAm, Nos. 22-23 (1964), 130-138.

75.17 Schulman, Ivan A. "La situación y Gestos [Severo Sarduy]: dos
técnicas y dos visiones de la realidad cubana." DHR, 5
(1967), 121-133. Also as "La situación y Gestos: dos visiones de la experiencia histórica cubana." NNH, 4 (1974),
345-352.

75.18 Vázquez, Antonio. "[En ciudad semejante: crónica o epopeya]."
Santiago, Nos. 2-3 (1971), 223-225.

76. PADILLA, HEBERTO (1932-   )

Critical Monographs and Dissertations

76.1   Casal, Lourdes. El caso Padilla: literatura y revolución en
       Cuba; documentos. Miami: Universal; NY: Nueva Atlántida,
       n.d. [1971?].

Critical Essays

76.2   "El 'affaire' Padilla. ¿Por qué se exilan los escritores lati-
       noamericanos?" Indice, Nos. 292-295 (1971), 41-77.

76.3   Avila, Leopoldo. "Las provocaciones de Padilla." VO, 9, 45.
       (1968), 17-18. Also as "Le provocazioni di Padilla." In
       his Cuba: letteratura e rivoluzione. Le correnti della
       critica e della letteratura cubana (Milano: Libreria Fel-
       trinelli, 1969), pp. 5-14.

76.4   Benedetti, Mario. "Las prioridades del escritor." CAm, No.
       68 (1971), 70-79.

76.5   "El 'caso Padilla'." Mensaje, No. 199 (1971), 229-239.

76.6   "El caso Padilla. Documentos." Libre, No. 1 (1971), 95-145.

76.7   Cohen, J. M. "Introduction." In Heberto Padilla, Sent off the
       field (London: Ardré Deutsch, 1972), pp. 9-14.

76.8   _____. "Prophet [Legacies: selected poems]." NYRB, 30, 11
       (1983), 32-35.

76.9   Droguett, Carlos. "El escritor y su pasión necesaria." CAm,
       No. 68 (1971), 60-68.

76.10 "'Der Fall' Padilla und die Intellektuellen." LatH, No. 5
       (1970), 97-104.

76.11 "O la revolución o nada." Indice, Nos. 288-289 (1971), 19-36.

76.12 Otero, Lisandro. "Del otro lado del Atlántico: una actitud."
       CB, No. 21 (1968), pagination unknown.

76.13 Quesada, Luis Manuel. "Fuera del juego: a poet's appraisal of
       the Cuban revolution." LALR, No. 6 (1975), 89-98.

76.14 _____ . "Temas y estilo en Fuera del juego." In Instituto Inter-
          nacional de Literatura Iberoamericana, Otros mundos otros
          fuegos: fantasía y realismo mágico en Iberoamérica (East
          Lansing: Michigan State University, Latin American Studies
          Center, 1975), pp. 409-416.

76.15 Simó, Ana María. "El justo tiempo humano." Unión, 4, 1 (1965),
          143-148.

76.16 Skytte, Göran. "Fallit Heberto Padilla: en påminnelse om en ak-
          tuell debatt." OB, 82 (1973), 292-296.

76.17 Yglesias, José. "The case of Heberto Padilla." NYRB, 16, 10
          (1971), 3-8.

77. PEDROSO, REGINO (1898-   )

Bibliographies

77.1   Pane, Remigio U. "Cuban poetry in English: a bibliography of English translations from Casal, Florit, Gómez de Avellaneda, Guillén, Heredia, Pedroso and 'Plácido'." BBDI, 18, 9 (1946), 199-201.

Critical Essays

77.2   Bianchi Ross, Ciro. "Regino Pedroso, el poeta proletario." CubaI, No. 70 (1975), 50-53.

77.3   Casaus, Víctor. "Regino Pedroso: tirar la primera piedra." Unión, 5, 2 (1966), 188-191.

77.4   Díaz Martínez, Manuel. "Regino Pedroso." GdC, No. 57 (1967), 12.

77.5   Fernández Retamar, Roberto. "Regino Pedroso." In his La poesía contemporánea en Cuba (1927-1935) (H: Orígenes, 1954), pp. 65-67.

77.6   Florit, Eugenio. "Regino Pedroso, poeta cubano." RHM, 11 (1945), 237-239.

77.7   González I., Waldo. "Regino Pedroso poeta militante." Bohemia, 67, 28 (1975), 25.

77.8   "Homenaje a Regino Pedroso. Presentación y testimonios." RBNJM, 3a serie, 14, 3 (1972), 33-53.

77.9   Navarro, Osvaldo. "[Prólogo]." In Regino Pedroso, Regino Pedroso (H: Unión de Escritores y Artistas de Cuba, 1975), pp. 7-34. Cover title: Orbita de Regino Pedroso.

77.10   _____. "Regino Pedroso poeta de nosotros." CB, No. 71 (1973), 11-14.

77.11   Pereda Valdez, Ildefonso. "Regino Pedroso." In Lo negro y lo mulato en la poesía cubana (Montevideo?: Ciudadela, 1970?), pp. 32-44.

77.12   Pita Rodríguez, Félix. "Regino Pedroso, pionero de una nueva poesía." RyC, No. 17 (1974), 3-8.

77.13 "Regino Pedroso." <u>Bohemia</u>, 62, 32 (1970), 4-10.

77.14 "Regino Pedroso." <u>VO</u>, 16, 9 (1974), 18.

77.15 Rodríguez, Rafael. "Regino Pedroso y la poesía social." <u>VO</u>, 14, 23 (1972), 60.

77.16 Rodríguez Sosa, Fernando. "Regino Pedroso, yunque y verso." <u>Bohemia</u>, 68, 33 (1976), 10-13.

77.17 Santos, Romualdo. "Entrevista a Regino Pedroso." <u>Bohemia</u>, 69, 21 (1977), 26-27.

78. PIÑERA, VIRGILIO (1914-   )

Critical Monographs and Dissertations

78.1   Flynn, Susan Kingston. "The alienated hero in contemporary Spanish American drama." DAI, 38 (1977), 299A. Piñera inter alios.

Critical Essays

78.2   Bianco, José. "Prólogo: Piñera, narrador." In Virgilio Piñera, El que vino a salvarme (BA: Sudamericana, 1970), pp. 7-19.

78.3   Cabrera Infante, Guillermo. "Vidas para leerlas." Vuelta, No. 41 (1980), 4-16. Piñera and José Lezama Lima.

78.4   Casey, Calvert. "Una segunda mirada de Aire frío," GdC, No. 16 (1963), 14.

78.5   "Dos viejos pánicos en Colombia." Conjunto, No. 7 (no date), 69-71.

78.6   Fernández Retamar, Roberto. "Virgilio Piñera." In his La poesía contemporánea en Cuba (1927-1935) (H: Orígenes, 1954), pp. 99-101.

78.7   Fornet, Ambrosio. "Anatomía de una cucaracha [Pequeñas maniobras]." In his En tres y dos (H: R, 1964), pp. 73-78.

78.8   Gilgen, Read G. "Virgilio Piñera and the short story of the absurd." Hispania, 63 (1980), 348-355.

78.9   González-Cruz, Luis F. "Arte y situación de Virgilio Piñera." Caribe, 2, 2 (1977), 77-86.

78.10   ____. "Virgilio Piñera y el teatro del absurdo en Cuba." Mester, 5, 1 (1974), 52-58.

78.11   Leal, Rine. "Dos farsas cubanas del absurdo." Ciclón, 3, 2 (1957), 65-67. Virgilio Piñera, Falsa alarma, and Antón Arrufat, El caso se investiga.

78.12   ____. "Virgilio Piñera o el teatro como ejercicio mental." GdC, No. 34 (1964), 2-3.

78.13   Llopis, Rogelio. "[Pequeñas maniobras]." CAm, No. 24 (1964), 106-107.

78.14 López, César. "El aire en el remolino [Aire frío]." GdC, No. 58 (1967), 11, 15.

78.15 _____. "Chiclets, canasta, presiones y diamantes [Presiones y diamantes]." Unión, 6, 3 (1967), 131-134.

78.16 McLees, Ainslee Armstrong. "Elements of Sartrian philosophy in Electra Garrigó." LATR, 7, 1 (1973), 5-11.

78.17 Malaret, Niso. "Cuentos fríos [Cuentos fríos]." Ciclón, 3, 1 (1957), 62-65.

78.18 Martin, Eleanor Jean. "Dos viejos pánicos: a political inter- pretation of the Cuban theater of the absurd." RInter, 9 (1979), 50-56.

78.19 Méndez y Soto, E. "Piñera y el tema del absurdo." CHA, No. 299 (1975), 448-453.

78.20 Morello-Frosch, Marta. "La anatomía: mundo fantástico de Virgi- lio Piñera." Hispamérica, Nos. 23-24 (1979), 19-34.

78.21 Moro, Lilliam. "Los cuentos de Virgilio." Unión, 4, 1 (1965), 148-152.

78.22 Narváez, Carlos R. "Lo fantástico en cuatro relatos de Virgilio Piñera." Románica, 13 (1976), 77-86.

78.23 Novoa, Mario E. "Virgilio Piñera: premio al pánico [Dos viejos pánicos]." Exilio, 4, 4-5, 1 (1971), 127-141.

78.24 Ortega, Julio. "El que vino a salvarme, de Virgilio Piñera." In his Relato de la utopía (Barcelona: La Gaya Ciencia, 1973), pp. 99-113.

78.25 Rodríguez Feo, José. "Una alegoría de la carne [Pequeñas manio- bras]." In his Notas críticas (primera serie) (H: Unión, 1962), pp. 165-167. Orig. Ciclón, 1, 1 (1955), 43.

78.26 _____. "En los infiernos [Electra Garrigó]." In his Crítica sucesiva (H: Contemporáneos, UNEAC, 1971), pp. 411-421.

78.27 _____. "Hablando de Piñera." In his Notas crítica (primera se- rie) (H: Unión, 1962), pp. 41-62.

78.28 Vitier, Cintio. "Virgilio Piñera: poesía y prosa." Orígenes, No. 5 (1945), 47-50.

78.29 Zalacaín, Daniel. "Falsa alarma: vanguardia del absurdo." RomN, 21 (1980), 28-32.

79. PIÑEYRO, ENRIQUE (1839-1911)

Bibliographies

79.1   "Bibliografía de Enrique Piñeyro." In Enrique Piñeyro, Vida y escritos de Juan Clemente Zenea (H: Consejo Nacional de Cultura, 1964), pp. 217-321.

Critical Monographs and Dissertations

79.2   Bueno, Salvador. Enrique Piñeyro y la crítica literaria. H: Ministerio de Educación, Instituto Nacional de Cultura, 1956?

79.3   Iraizoz y de Villar, Antonio. Enrique Piñeyro; su vida y sus obras. H: "El Siglo XX", 1922.

Critical Essays

79.4   Bueno, Salvador. "Enrique Piñeyro, patriota y escritor." In his Figuras cubanas del siglo XIX (H: Unión de Escritores y Artistas, 1980), pp. 261-265.

79.5   _____. "Enrique Piñeyro y la crítica literaria." RBC, 69 (1952), 242-325.

79.6   _____. "Pequeñas biografías. Enrique Piñeyro, patriota y escritor." Carteles, 34, 28 (1953), 89, 102.

79.7   _____. "La tumba de un patriota cubano en París." Carteles, 32, 8 (1951), 50.

79.8   Castellanos, Jesús. "Piñeyro en su casa." In his Los optimistas (Madrid: Editorial-América, 1918), pp. 175-180. Also in his Colección póstuma (H: El Siglo XX de A. Miranda, 1914-1916), I, 255-259.

79.9   Caturla, Victoria de. "Caracteres de Enrique Piñeyro como historiógrafo." ULH, No. 49 (1943), 81-95.

79.10 Cruz, Manuel de la. "Enrique Piñeyro." In his Cromitos cubanos (H: Arte y Literatura, 1975), pp. 139-145.

79.11 "Enrique Piñeyro." RBNC, 5, 1-6 (1911), 107-116.

79.12 González del Valle y Carbajal, Emilio Martín. "[Piñeyro]." In his La poesía lírica en Cuba; apuntes para un libro de biografía y de crítica (Barcelona: Luis Tasso, 1900), pp. 319-333.

79.13 Rodríguez Alemán, Mario A. "Enrique Piñeyro." RevC, 24 (1949), 375-398.

79.14 Sanguily y Garritte, Manuel. "Enrique Piñeyro (con un grabado)." RFLC, 12 (1911), 237-244.

79.15 _____. "Piñeyro y Scherer." CCont, 37 (1925), 201-217.

79.16 Tejera, Diego Vicente. "Enrique Piñeyro." In his Prosa literaria (H: Rambla, Bouza, 1936), II, 175-179.

79.17 Varona y Pera, Enrique José. "Bibliografía [Estudios y conferencias de historia y literatura]." RdC, 8 (1880), 562-565.

79.18 _____. "Una conferencia del señor don Enrique Piñeyro." RdC, 7 (1880), 69-73.

79.19 _____. "Leyendo á Piñeyro (el romanticismo de España)." In his Violetas y ortigas; notas críticas (Madrid: Editorial-América, n.d.), pp. 196-199.

79.20 Vitier, Cintio. "Enrique Piñeyro." RBNJM, 3a serie, 63, 3 (1972), 163-166.

79.21 Vitier, Medardo. "Enrique Piñeyro." In his Apuntaciones literarias (H: Minerva, 1935), pp. 137-143.

79.22 _____. "Enrique Piñeyro." In his Estudios, notas, efigies cubanas (H: Minerva, 1944), pp. 238-240.

79.23 _____. "Enrique Piñeyro." MALHC, 1, 1 (1949), 2.

80. PITA RODRIGUEZ, FELIX (1909-   )

Critical Essays

80.1   Abalat, Antonio. "Conversando con Félix Pita Rodríguez." Is-
        las, No. 62 (1979), 75-81.

80.2   Alvarez Bravo, Armando. "[Poemas y cuentos]." Unión, 4, 4
        (1965), 169-171.

80.3   Armas, Mirta de. "Esa forma de recordar." RyC, No. 55 (1977),
        4-11.

80.4   Baeza, Francisco. "Elogio de un elogio apasionado." Unión, 14,
        1 (1975), 149-152.

80.5   Bianchi Ross, Ciro. "Cara a cara con Félix Pita." CubaI, No.
        50 (1973), 48-49.

80.6   Chericián, David. "Crónica de un testigo apasionado." GdC, No.
        155 (1977), 5-6.

80.7   "Crítica: la fabulosa realidad [Elogio de Marco Polo]." GdC,
        No. 125 (1974), 29.

80.8   Depestre, René. "La bella voz de Félix Pita Rodríguez." Bohe-
        mia, 61, 31 (1969), 11.

80.9   Díaz Martínez, Manuel. "Las crónicas [Las crónicas, poesía ba-
        jo consigna]." Unión, 1, 1 (1962), 136-137.

80.10   Escobar Linares, Rafael. "Félix Pita Rodríguez, un narrador an-
        tológico." Cuba, No. 17 (1963), 36-39.

80.11   Garzón Céspedes, Francisco. "Lo que va más allá de todos los
        sueños. Entrevista a Félix Pita Rodríguez." Islas, No.
        38 (1971), 47-57.

80.12   González Bolaños, Aimée. "Acerca de los cuentos tempranos de
        Félix Pita Rodríguez." Islas, No. 61 (1978), 65-85.

80.13   _____. "Los cuentos de Montecallado [San Abdul de Montecalla-
        do]." Islas, No. 50 (1975), 107-152.

80.14   _____. "La maravilla poliana [Elogio de Marco Polo]." Islas,
        No. 60 (1978), 63-72.

80.15 González Jiménez, Omar. "Una manera de mirar el mundo." CB, No. 85 (1974), 16-18.

80.16 González López, Waldo. "Félix Pita Rodríguez." Bohemia, 68, 53 (1976), 10-13.

80.17 _____. "Sábado con Félix Pita Rodríguez." Bohemia, 69, 13 (1977), 24.

80.18 Gorrín, José. "Esbozo biográfico y artístico de la obra de Félix Pita Rodríguez." Islas, No. 45 (1973), 3-56.

80.19 Iznaga, Alcides. "Importante ensayo [Literatura comprometida, detritus y buenos sentimientos]." Islas, 4, 2 (1962), 337-338.

80.20 Martínez Laínez, Fernando. "Entrevista con Félix Pita Rodríguez." In her Palabra cubana (Madrid: Akal, 1975), pp. 223-255.

80.21 Navarro, Desiderio. "Quiere decir olvido [Historia tan natural]." GdC, No. 94 (1971), 31.

80.22 Nieves, Dolores. "Félix Pita Rodríguez: Ludovico Amaro, temponauta." CubaI, No. 97 (1977), 42-43.

80.23 Núñez Lemus, H. "Félix Pita y el testimonio policial." Bohemia, 67, 42 (1975), 26.

80.24 Rodríguez Hernández, Luis M., and Aimée González Bolaños. "Cronología de la vida y obra de Félix Pita Rodríguez." Islas, No. 62 (1979), 3-73.

80.25 Santos Moray, Mercedes. "[Elogio de Marco Polo]." CB, No. 82 (1974), 28.

80.26 Victori, María del Carmen. "Elogio elusivo para Félix Pita." RyC, Nos. 52-54 (1977), 68-69.

81. PORTUONDO, JOSE ANTONIO (1911-   )

Critical Essays

81.1 Arias, Salvador. "[La emancipación literaria de Hispanoaméri-
ca]." CAm, No. 100 (1977), 195-197.

81.2 Fernández, Olga. "José Antonio Portuondo." CubaI, No. 68
(1975), 24-25.

81.3 Fernández Retamar, Roberto. "El compañero crítico José Antonio
Portuondo." RCLL, No. 16 (1982), 103-115.

81.4 _____. "Lecciones de Portuondo." In his Para una teoría de la
literatura hispanoamericana; 2. ed. (M: Nuestro Tiempo,
1977), pp. 30-38.

81.5 González Montes, Antonio. "[La emancipación literaria de Hispa-
noamérica]." RCLL, No. 6 (1977), 168-171.

81.6 Martínez Laínez, Fernando. "Entrevista con José Antonio Portuondo." In his Palabra cubana (Madrid: Akal, 1975), pp. 173-
196.

81.7 Rodríguez Feo, José. "Los afanes escolares de José Antonio Portuondo." Orígenes, No. 7 (1945), 38-39.

81.8 _____. "La dialéctica de José Antonio Portuondo." Ciclón, 1, 3
(1955), 55-63.

82. POVEDA, JOSE MANUEL (1888-1926)

Critical Essays

82.1 Chaple, Sergio. "El epistolario Boti-Poveda." L/L, No. 6 (1975), 89-113.

82.2 Esténger, Rafael. "Evocación de Poveda." In José Manuel Poveda, Proemios de cenáculo (H: Ministerio de Educación, Dirección de Cultura, 1948), pp. 5-27.

82.3 Godoy, Gustavo J. "En el cincuentenario de José Manuel Poveda, poeta ancestral." In Homenaje a Lydia Cabrera (Miami: Universal, 1978), pp. 139-147.

82.4 Hurtado, Rogelio Fabio. "La poesía invisible de Poveda." GdC, No. 102 (1972), 14.

82.5 Lizaso y González, Félix. "José Manuel Poveda." In his Ensayistas contemporáneos, 1900-1920 (H: Trópico, 1938), pp. 72-76.

82.6 Pogolotti, Marcelo. "Poveda prosista." In his La república de Cuba al través de sus escritores (H: Lex, 1958), pp. 58-60.

82.7 Rocasolano, Alberto. "El caso de Alma Rubens." L/L, No. 2 (1971), 57-90.

82.8 _____. "Nota biográfica. Introducción." In José Manuel Poveda, José Manuel Poveda (H: Instituto de Literatura y Lingüística de la Academia de Ciencias de Cuba, 1975), pp. 7-37, 39-81.

82.9 _____. "Poveda visto a través de el [sic] Pencil y Renacimiento; 1909-1910." Unión, 9, 1 (1970), 141-151.

82.10 Torriente, Loló de la. "Boti y Poveda: el provincialismo literario." GdC, No. 173 (1978), 26-27.

83. RAMOS, JOSE ANTONIO (1885-1946)

Bibliographies

83.1   Peraza Sarausa, Fermín. "Bibliografía de José Antonio Ramos."
       RI, No. 24 (1947), 335-400. Also H: Anuario Bibliográfico
       Cubano, 1947. 2. ed., 1956.

Critical Monographs and Dissertations

83.2   Ortúzar-Young, Ada. "Tres representaciones literarias de la
       vida política cubana [Ramos, Carlos Loveira y Chirino,
       Luis Felipe Rodríguez]." DAI, 40 (1979), 2711A-2712A.

Critical Essays

83.3   Alvárez Bravo, Armando. "[Caniquí]." GdC, No. 34 (1964), 22.

83.4   Alvárez García, Imeldo. "Coaybay...o la constante esencial de
       José A. Ramos." Unión, 14, 3 (1975), 41-51.

83.5   _____. "Prólogo." In José Antonio Ramos, Coaybay (H: Arte y
       Literatura, 1975), pp. 9-25.

83.6   Alvárez Morales, Manuel. "Inadaptación, rebeldía y pasión de
       Antonio Ramos." ULH, Nos. 70-72 (1947), 218-220.

83.7   Arrom, José Juan. "El teatro de José Antonio Ramos." RI, No.
       24 (1947), 263-271. Also RevC, 23 (1948), 164-175. Also
       in his Estudios de literatura hispanoamericana (H: Ucar
       García, 1950), pp. 147-159.

83.8   Barros y Gómez, Bernardo G. "El teatro de Ramos." CCont, No.
       86 (1920), 201-209.

83.9   Benavente, Jacinto. "Carta-Prólogo." In José Antonio Ramos,
       Liberta (Madrid: Médica Casa Vidal, 1911), no pagination.

83.10 Bueno, Salvador. "[Caniquí]." RBNJM, 3a serie, 6, 2 (1954),
       93-95.

83.11 Carrasquilla Mallarino, Eduardo. "[Liberta]." Letras, 2a épo-
       ca, 7 (1911), pagination unknown.

83.12 Castellanos García, Gerardo. "[José Antonio Ramos]." In his
       Panorama histórico (H, 1934), pp. 909-920.

83.13 Chacón y Calvo, José María. "José Antonio Ramos y su teatro." RevC, 15 (1941), 231-234.

83.14 "Cómo ven las nuevas generaciones a José Antonio Ramos." ULH, Nos. 70-72 (1947), 205-225.

83.15 Díaz Roque, José, and Francisco Rodríguez Alemán. "José Antonio Ramos: su teatro y su ideología." Islas, No. 63 (1979), 91-150.

83.16 Dorr, Nicolás. "Acercamiento al teatro de José Antonio Ramos." Unión, 16, 2 (1977), 48-77.

83.17 Echevarría, Israel. "José Antonio Ramos y la Biblioteca Nacional." RBNJM, 3a serie, 20, 2 (1978), 117-147.

83.18 "En la muerte de José Antonio Ramos." RevC, 21 (1946), 119-145.

83.19 Englekirk, John E. "[Caniquí]." Cervantes, Nos. 11-12 (1937), 8. Orig. RHM, 3 (1937), 85.

83.20 Espinosa, Enrique. "José Antonio Ramos." InC, julio-agosto 1947, pp. 30-31.

83.21 García Vega, Lorenzo. "José Antonio Ramos en el ensayo." Exilio, 4, 4-5, 1 (1971), 113-123.

83.22 Garzón Céspedes, Francisco. "José Antonio Ramos: una línea ascendente de rebeldía." LATR, 14, 2 (1981), 5-10. Also GdC, No. 141 (1975), 20-21.

83.23 González, Manuel Pedro. "Letras cubanas: José Antonio Ramos." In José Antonio Ramos, Las impurezas de la realidad (Barcelona: Cosmos, 1929), pp. 5-10.

83.24 _____. "Razón de este homenaje." RI, No. 24 (1947), 211-214.

83.25 González Freire, Natividad. "Tembladera." Bohemia, 69, 11 (1977), 28-29.

83.26 Gutiérrez y Sánchez, Gustavo. "José Antonio Ramos." RevH, 4, 10 (1930), 1-11.

83.27 Henríquez Ureña, Max. "[Entreactos]." CCont, 1, 4 (1913), 308-311.

83.28 _____. "Evocación de José Antonio Ramos." RI, No. 24 (1947), 251-261.

83.29 _____. "[Satanás]." CCont, 2, 4 (1913), 232-234.

83.30 Inerárity Romero, Zaida. "José Antonio Ramos: un escritor actual." CB, No. 85 (1974), 14.

83.31 Iraizoz y de Villar, Antonio. "José Antonio Ramos." AANAL, 19, 4 (1937), 193-226.

83.32 Leal, Rine. "Ramos dramaturgo o la república municipal y espe-
       sa." Islas, No. 36 (1970), 73-91.

83.33 Lizaso y González, Félix. "José Antonio Ramos." RevC, 21
       (1946), 141-145.

83.34 _____. "José Antonio Ramos; el inútil vidente." In his Ensa-
       yistas contemporáneos, 1900-1920 (H: Trópico, 1938), pp.
       42-48.

83.35 Llaguno, Oscar A. "Tembladera." CB, No. 113 (1977), 9.

83.36 Mañach, Jorge. "Duelo de José Antonio Ramos." Bohemia, 38,
       36 (1946), 35, 38. Also RAm, 42 (1946), 321-324.

83.37 Montes Huidobro, Matías. "Técnica dramática de José Antonio
       Ramos." JIAS, 12 (1970), 229-241.

83.38 Ocampo, María Luisa. "Recuerdo de José Antonio Ramos." RI,
       No. 24 (1947), 301-308.

83.39 Olguín, Manuel. "La filosofía de José Antonio Ramos y su afini-
       dad con la del pueblo y los pensadores de los Estados Uni-
       dos." RI, No. 24 (1947), 291-299.

83.40 Pogolotti, Marcelo. "La cuestión del adulterio." In his La
       república de Cuba al través de sus escritores (H: Lex,
       1958), pp. 52-56.

83.41 _____. "El perfecto fulanista [Manual del perfecto fulanista]."
       In his La república de Cuba al través de sus escritores
       (H: Lex, 1958), pp. 86-88.

83.42 Portuondo, José Antonio. "El contenido político y social de
       las obras de José Antonio Ramos." RI, No. 24 (1947), 215-
       250. Also RBNJM, 3a serie, 11, 1 (1969), 5-58.

83.43 _____. "José Antonio Ramos y la primera generación republicana
       de escritores cubanos." RBC, 62 (1948), 56-68.

83.44 _____. "Una perspectiva a distancia de José Antonio Ramos."
       ULH, Nos. 70-72 (1947), 207-210.

83.45 Reid, John T. "José Antonio Ramos y la literatura norteamerica-
       na." RI, No. 24 (1947), 273-277.

83.46 Remos y Rubio, Juan Nepomuceno José. "En torno a José Antonio
       Ramos y su labor como novelista." RI, No. 24 (1947), 279-
       289. Also RevC, 21 (1946), 119-131.

83.47 Rodríguez, Luis Felipe. "Ficción y sensibilidad de José Anto-
       nio Ramos." ULH, Nos. 70-72 (1947), 184-193.

83.48 Sánchez-Grey Alba, Esther. "Clasicismo e historicidad de La re-
       curva de José Antonio Ramos." Círculo, 9 (1980), 63-69.

83.49 _____. "Presencia de Ibsen en Calibán Rex de José Antonio Ramos." In Festschrift José Cid Pérez (NY: Senda Nueva, 1981), pp. 95-101.

83.50 Smith, Octavio. "Travesía por José Antonio Ramos." RBNJM, 3a serie, 66, 3 (1975), 17-31.

83.51 Torre, Miguel Angel de la. "[Tembladera]." In his Prosas varias (H: Editorial de la Universidad, 1966), pp. 309-312.

83.52 Troncoso, Arturo. "[Caniquí]." Atenea, No. 137 (1936), 218-221.

83.53 _____. "[Panorama de la literatura norteamericana]." RevC, 3, 7 (1935), 133-137.

83.54 Valdés Rodríguez, José Manuel. "José Antonio Ramos y el teatro en Cuba." ULH, Nos. 70-72 (1947), 194-203.

83.55 Valle y Costa, Adrián. "[Almas rebeldes. Una bala perdida]." CyA, 23, 20 (1907), 350.

83.56 Vasconcelos, Ramón. "José Antonio Ramos nunca fue humillado." Bohemia, 38, 40 (1946), 53.

83.57 Villagómez, Alberto. "El concepto de patria en José A. Ramos." Conjunto, No. 34 (1977), 125.

84. RODRIGUEZ, LUIS FELIPE (1888-1947)

Critical Monographs and Dissertations

84.1   Marinello, Juan. Americanismo y cubanismo literarios: ensayo
       en Marcos Antilla, cuentos de cañaveral por Luis Felipe
       Rodríguez. H: Hermes, 1932? Same as item no. 84.15.

84.2   Ortúzar-Young, Ada. "Tres representaciones literarias de la
       vida política cubana." DAI, 40 (1979), 2711A. Rodríguez,
       Carlos Loveira, José Antonio Ramos.

Critical Essays

84.3   Ducazal (pseud.). "Humorismo y folklorismo en la novela cubana.
       Luis Felipe Rodríguez y su labor." RAm, 35 (1938), 53.

84.4   Fernández Montes de Oca, Estrella. "Luis Felipe Rodríguez, un
       escritor comprometido." Bohemia, 67, 36 (1975), 10-13.

84.5   González y Contreras, Gilberto. "La sátira y el humorismo en
       Luis Felipe Rodríguez." RevC, 6, 2 (1936), 255-267.

84.6   Grismer, Raymond L., and Manuel Rodríguez Saavedra. "Luis Feli-
       pe Rodríguez." In their Vida y obras de autores cubanos
       (H: "Alfa", 1940-), I, 91-93.

84.7   Iznaga, Alcides. "Luis Felipe, un precedente." Bohemia, 69,
       31 (1977), 25-26.

84.8   Labrador Ruiz, Enrique. "Luis Felipe Rodríguez (1888-1947)."
       Atenea, 109 (1953), 227-235. Also in his El pan de los
       muertos (Santa Clara: Universidad Central de Las Villas,
       1958), pp. 19-24.

84.9   Latcham, Ricardo A. "Dos novelas cubanas." Atenea, 57 (1939),
       506-514. Also in his Doce ensayos (Santiago de Chile:
       La Semana Literaria, 1944), pp. 73-82. Ciénaga by Rodrí-
       guez, and Contrabando by Enrique Serpa.

84.10 Lázaro, Angel. "La muerte de Luis Felipe Rodríguez." RevC, 22
       (1947), 240-242.

84.11 Leante, César. "Ciénaga; visión de la república en la novela
       de Luis Felipe Rodríguez." Bohemia, 66, 12 (1974), 10-13.
       Also as "Ciénaga." In his El espacio real (H: Unión de
       Escritores y Artistas de Cuba, 1975), pp. 59-69.

84.12 ____. "Prólogo." In Luis Felipe Rodríguez, Ciénaga (H: Arte
       y Literatura, 1975), pp. 9-20.

84.13 Lizaso y González, Félix. "Luis Felipe Rodríguez." In his En-
       sayistas contemporáneos, 1900-1920 (H: Trópico, 1938), pp.
       92-96.

84.14 Maestri Arredondo, Raoul. "[La pascua de la tierra natal]."
       Avance, No. 23 (1928), 160-161.

84.15 Marinello, Juan. "Americanismo y cubanismo literarios." LyP,
       11, 8 (1933), 286-299. Also in Luis Felipe Rodríguez, Re-
       latos de Marcos Antilla; la tragedia del cañaveral (H:
       Impresora Cubana, 1932?), pp. i-xvii. Same as item no.
       88.1

84.16 ____. "Comentario chaplinesco de Luis Felipe Rodríguez." In
       his Literatura hispanoamericana. Hombres. Meditaciones
       (M: Universidad Nacional de México, 1937), pp. 65-74.

84.17 Muiños, René. "Notas para una sociología del cuento de Luis
       Felipe Rodríguez." Santiago, No. 17 (1975), 203-212.

84.18 Nieves, Dolores. "Luis Felipe Rodríguez." CubaI, No. 91
       (1977), 46.

84.19 Novás Calvo, Lino. "Palabras sobre nosotros." ND, 28, 2
       (1948), 65-69.

84.20 Pogolotti, Marcelo. "La vida rural." In his La república de
       Cuba al través de sus escritores (H: Lex, 1958), pp. 62-
       66.

84.21 Portuondo, José Antonio. "Four Cuban novelists." BA, 18
       (1944), 235-238. Rodríguez inter alios.

84.22 Rocasolano, Alberto. "Luis Felipe Rodríguez entre el querer y
       el poder." Unión, 10, 1-2 (1971), 123-127.

84.23 Sánchez Quesada, E. "Luis Felipe Rodríguez." Orto, 36, 8
       (1947), 1-8.

84.24 Tejera, José Luis de. "Sociología de la cuentística de Luis
       Felipe Rodríguez." Santiago, No. 28 (1977), 75-115.

85. ROIG DE LEUCHSENRING, EMILIO (1889-1964)

Critical Essays

85.1 "Emilio Roig de Leuchsenring." Bohemia, 62, 37 (1970), 4-13.

85.2 Gay-Calbó, Enrique. "El caballero que perdió su señora." RBNC, 2a serie, 8, 4 (1957), 123-125.

85.3 Grismer, Raymond L., and Manuel Rodríguez Saavedra. "Emilio Roig Leuchsenring." In their Vida y obras de autores cubanos (H: "Alfa", 1940-), I, 151-159.

85.4 Le Riverend, Julio. "Semblanza biográfica de Emilio Roig de Leuchsenring." ULH, Nos. 184-185 (1967), 191-205.

85.5 Lizaso y González, Félix. "Emilio Roig." In his Ensayistas contemporáneos, 1900-1950 (H: Trópico, 1938), pp. 166-172.

85.6 Pogolotti, Marcelo. "Más en torno a la enmienda Platt." In his La república de Cuba al través de sus escritores (H: Lex, 1958), pp. 145-149.

85.7 Vignier, Enrique. "Nunca se arrió tu bandera; a propósito de una semblanza biográfica de Emilio Roig de Leuchsenring." RyC, No. 33 (1975), 54-57.

86. SANCHEZ BOUDY, JOSE (1927-   )

Critical Essays

86.1 Alba-Buffill, Elio. "Prólogo." In José Sánchez-Boudy, El Picúo, el fisto, el barrio y otras costumbres cubanas (Miami: Universal, 1977), pp. 5-10.

86.2 Fernández-Marcané, Leonardo. "Prólogo." In José Sánchez-Boudy, Aché, babalú ayé (retablo afrocubano) (Miami: Universal, 1975), pp. 9-13.

86.3 Fernández Vázquez, Antonio A. "Orbus terrarum: análisis de una anatomía apocalíptica." In The Twenty-Seventh Annual Mountain Interstate Foreign Language Conference (Johnson City, Tenn.: East Tennessee State University, Research Council, 1978), pp. 193-198.

86.4 Gutiérrez de la Solana, Alberto. "Palabras preliminares." In José Sánchez-Boudy, Ekué abankué akué (Miami: Universal, 1977), pp. 13-25.

86.5 Landa Triolet, René. "Prólogo." In José Sánchez-Boudy, La soledad de la Playa Larga (mañana, mariposa) (Miami: Universal, 1975), pp. 9-10.

86.6 León, Julio A. "[Aché, babalú ayé]." ExTL, 5, 2 (1976), 231-232.

86.7 Raggi, Carlos M. "[Crocante de maní]." Círculo, 4 (1973-1974), 193-194.

86.8 Sánchez, Reinaldo. "Algunas consideraciones sobre las estructuras temporales y simbólicas en Los cruzados de la aurora." Círculo, 9 (1980), 87-92.

87. SANTA CRUZ, MARIA MERCEDES, Condesa de Merlín (1789-1852)

Critical Monographs and Dissertations

87.1   Bacardí Moreau, Emilio. La condesa de Merlín. Santiago de Cuba: Oriente, 1922.

87.2   Figarola-Caneda, Domingo. La condesa de Merlín; estudio biográfico e iconográfico. Paris: Excelsior, 1928.

87.3   Figueroa, Agustín de. La condesa de Merlín, musa del romanticismo. Madrid, 1934.

87.4   Jiménez, Dora. La condesa de Merlín. H: Empresa Editora de Publicaciones, 1938.

Critical Essays

87.5   Agüero, Pedro. "Cubanos distinguidos: la condesa de Merlín." RdC, 5 (1879), 251-263.

87.6   Boxhorn, Emilia. "Prólogo." In María Marcedes Santa Cruz, Correspondencia íntima (Madrid: Paris, 1928), pp. v-vii.

87.7   Bueno, Salvador. "Un libro polémico: El viaje a la Habana de la condesa de Merlín." CA, No. 199 (1975), 161-177.

87.8   Calcagno, Francisco. "[Introducción]." In María Mercedes Santa Cruz, Mis doce primeros años (H: "El Siglo XX", 1922), pagination unknown.

87.9   Cuza Malé, Belkis. "Viaje a la Habana: la condesa de Merlín." LLM, 2, 1 (1983), 11-12.

87.10 Flouret, Michèle. "Notice biographique. María de las Mercedes de Santa Cruz y Montalvo, condesa de Jaruco, comtesse Merlin." In Hommage à André Joucla-Ruau (Aix-en-Provence, Université de Provence, Département d'Etudes Hispaniques, 1974), pp. 84-120.

87.11 García de Coronado, Domitila. "Condesa de Merlín." In her Album poético-fotográfico de escritoras y poetisas cubanas escrito en 1868 para la señora doña Gertrudis Gómez de Avellaneda (H: El Fígaro, 1926), pp. 13-21.

87.12 Gómez de Avellaneda, Gertrudis. "Apuntes biográficos de la condesa de Merlín." CyA, 6 (1902), 158-160.

87.13   Hernández de Norman, Isabel. "María Mercedes Santa Cruz, conde-
        sa de Merlín (1789-1852)." In her La novela criolla en las
        Antillas (NY: Plus Ultra, 1977), pp. 107-110.

87.14   _____. "María Mercedes Santa Cruz, condesa de Merlín (1789-
        1852)." In her La novela romántica en las Antillas (NY:
        Ateneo Puertorriqueño de Nueva York, 1969), pp. 107-110.

87.15   Luz y Caballero, José de la. "La señora condesa de Merlín."
        In his Escritos literarios (H: Editorial de la Universidad,
        1946), pp. 99-116, 247-262.

87.16   Ramírez, Serafín. "La condesa de Merlín." In his La Habana ar-
        tística (H: E. M. de la Capitanía General, 1891), pp. 35-
        55.

87.17   Sand, George. "Souvenirs de Madame Merlin." In her Questions
        d'art et de littérature (Paris: Calmann Lévy, 1878), pp.
        53-60. Dated 1836.

87.18   Suárez-Murias, Marguerite C. "The countess of Merlin: her so-
        cial vantage and editorial dilemmas." In her Essays on
        Hispanic literature; ensayos de literatura hispana; a bi-
        lingual anthology (Washington, D.C.: University Press of
        America, 1982), pp. 195-207.

87.19   _____. "La primera novela cubana." La voz, 4, 9 (1960), 16.
        Also as "Curiosidades literarias: la primera novela cuba-
        na [Mes douze premières années]." In her Essays on Hispan-
        ic literature; ensayos de literatura hispana; a bilingual
        anthology (Washington, D.C.: University Press of America,
        1982), pp. 67-70.

87.20   Villa Urrutia, Marqués de. "La condesa de Merlín." RBC, 27
        (1931), 262-270.

88. SARDUY, SEVERO (1937-   )

Bibliographies

88.1   González Echevarría, Roberto. "Para una bibliografía de y sobre Severo Sarduy (1955-1971)." RI, No. 79 (1972), 333-343. Also as "Para una bibliografía de y sobre Severo Sarduy (1955-1974)." In Severo Sarduy, q.v., pp. 177-192.

Critical Monographs and Dissertations

88.2   Incledon, John Scott. "The fearful sphere: difference and repetition in the writing of Jorge Luis Borges, Julio Cortázar and Severo Sarduy." DAI, 40 (1980), 4583A.

88.3   Montero, Oscar. "The French interext of De donde son los cantantes." DAI, 39 (1979), 4227A-4228A.

88.4   Orrantia, Dagoberto. "The situation of the narrator as a formal principle in four representative works of the Spanish-American new novel." DAI, 38 (1977), 3535A. Sarduy's De donde son los cantantes inter alias.

88.5   Severo Sarduy. Madrid: Fundamentos, 1976. Pertinent items are listed separately.

88.6   Ulloa, Justo Celso. "La narrativa de Lezama Lima y Sarduy: entre la imagen visionaria y el juego verbal." DAI, 35 (1974), 1676A-1677A.

Critical Essays

88.7   Aguilar Mora, Jorge. "Cobra, cobra, la boca obra, recobra barroco." In Severo Sarduy, q.v., pp. 25-33.

88.8   Alzola, Concepción Teresa. "Verba cubanorum." In Cinco aproximaciones a la narrativa hispanoamericana contemporánea (Madrid: Playor, 1977), pp. 11-81.

88.9   Barrenechea, Ana María. "Severo Sarduy o la aventura textual." In Narradores hispanoamericanos de hoy (Chapel Hill: University of North Carolina, Department of Romance Languages, 1973), pp. 89-100.

88.10 Barthes, Roland. "Sarduy: la faz barroca." MNu, No. 14 (1967), 70-71. Also as "The baroque face." Review, No. 6 (1972),

31-32. Orig. as "Sarduy, la face baroque." QL, No. 28 (1967), pagination unknown.

88.11 Bejel, Emilio F. "[Barroco]." TC, No. 7 (1977), 191-193.

88.12 Bravo, Víctor A. "Notas crítica sobre dos novelas de Sarduy." CUn, No. 101 (1975), 211-221.

88.13 Burgos, Fernando. "Sarduy: una escritura en movimiento [Gestos]." In La Chispa '81: selected proceedings (New Orleans: Tulane University, 1981), pp. 43-50.

88.14 Bush, Andrew. "Literature, history, and literary history: a Cuban family romance [Gestos]." LALR, No. 16 (1980), 161-172.

88.15 Cabrera, Vicente. "Diálogo de Tres tristes tigres [de Guillermo Cabrera Infante] y una Cobra con Cervantes y Góngora." CA, No. 228 (1980), 114-123.

88.16 Campos, Julieta. "[Maitreya]." Vuelta, No. 29 (1979), 35-36.

88.17 Carrera, Arturo. "El juego de las simpatías." Hispamérica, No. 2 (1973), 19-26.

88.18 Christ, Ronald. "Emergency essay." Review, No. 6 (1972), 33-36.

88.19 ____. "The new Latin American novel." PR, 42 (1975), 459-463.

88.20 Conte, Rafael. "Severo Sarduy o la experimentación lingüística." In his Lenguaje y violencia (Madrid: Al-Borak, 1972), pp. 247-252.

88.21 Couffon, Claude. "Severo Sarduy et la réalité cubaine." LetF, 22-V-1967, pp. 9-10. Also as "Severo Sarduy y la realidad cubana." MNu, No. 22 (1968), 87-88.

88.22 Cozarinski, Edgardo. "Un espacio verbal llamado Cuba." Sur, No. 22 (1968), 69-70.

88.23 Estange, Luc. "Gestes, romain cubain sur rhythme de cha-cha-cha." FigL, 22-VI-1963, p. 5.

88.24 Feito, Francisco E. "Severo Sarduy en la actual narrativa hispanoamericana." El urogallo, No. 8 (1971), 94-97.

88.25 Fossey, Jean-Michel. "Entrevista con Severo Sarduy." Imagen, Nos. 94-95 (1971), 28-29.

88.26 ____. "Severo Sarduy." In his Galaxia latinoamericana (Las Palmas de Gran Canario: Inventarios Provisionales, 1973), pp. 221-252.

88.27 ____. "Severo Sarduy: del 'boom' al 'bing-bang'." Indice, No. 333 (1973), 55-59.

88.28   _____. "Severo Sarduy: máquina barroca revolucionaria." In Severo Sarduy, q.v., pp. 15-24.

88.29   _____. "Severo Sarduy par lui même." Coromán, No. 6 (1970), 4-5.

88.30   Chertman, Sharon. "Language as protagonist in Sarduy's De donde son los cantantes: a linguistic approach to narrative structure." In The analysis of literary texts: current trends in methodology; 3rd & 4th York College Colloquia (Ypsilanti, Mich.: Bilingual Press, 1980), pp. 145-152.

88.31   González, Eduardo G. "Baroque endings: Carpentier, Sarduy and some textual commentaries." MLN, 92 (1977), 169-195.

88.32   González Echevarría, Roberto. "Guapacha barroca. Conversación con Severo Sarduy." Papeles, No. 16 (1972), 24-48.

88.33   _____. "In search of the lost center." Review, No. 6 (1972), 28-31.

88.34   _____. "Interview/Severo Sarduy." Diacritics, 2, 2 (1972), 27-34.

88.35   _____. "Memoria de apariencias y ensayo de Cobra." Eco, No. 171 (1975), 240-258. Also in his Relecturas; estudios de literatura cubana (Caracas: Monte Avila, 1976), pp. 129-152. Also in Severo Sarduy, q.v., pp. 63-86.

88.36   _____. "El primer relato de Severo Sarduy." RI, Nos. 118-119 (1952), 73-90.

88.37   _____. "Sarduy en traducción." In Instituto Internacional de Literatura Iberoamericana, Otros mundos otros fuegos: fantasía y realismo mágico en Iberoamérica (East Lansing: Michigan State University, Latin American Studies Center, 1975), pp. 277-280. Also in his Relecturas; estudios de literatura cubana (Caracas: Monte Avila, 1976), pp. 119-127.

88.38   _____. "Son de la Habana: ruta de Severo Sarduy." RI, Nos. 76-77 (1971), 725-740.

88.39   Goytisolo, Juan. "Severo Sarduy: el lenguaje del cuerpo." Triunfo, No. 719 (1976), 58-60.

88.40   Henric, Jacques. "Cuba, l'île lue." FrN, 16-VIII-1967, p. 13.

88.41   Hurtado, Efraín. "Entrevista con Severo Sarudy." Actual, 2, 5 (1969), 123-128.

88.42   Johndrow, Donald R. "'Total' reality in Severo Sarduy's search for lo cubano." RomN, 13 (1972), 445-452.

88.43   Johnston, Craig P. "Irony and the double in short fiction by Julio Cortázar and Severo Sarduy." JSSTC, 5 (1977), 111-122.

88.44   Josef, Bela. "A máscara da literatura: Severo Sarduy." MGSL, 18-X-1975, p. 10.

88.45   Levine, Suzanne Jill. "Borges a Cobra es barroco exégesis: un estudio de la intertextualidad." In Severo Sarduy, q.v., pp. 87-105.

88.46   _____. "Cobra: el discurso como bricolage." In Severo Sarduy, q.v., pp. 123-134.

88.47   _____. "La escritura como traducción: Tres tristes tigres [de Guillermo Cabrera Infante] y Cobra." RI, Nos. 92-93 (1975), 557-567. Also as "Writing as translation: Three trapped tigers and a Cobra." MLN, 90 (1975), 265-277.

88.48   _____. "Jorge Luis Borges and Severo Sarduy: two writers of the neo-baroque." LALR, No. 4 (1974), 25-37.

88.49   _____. "On translating Severo Sarduy's Cobra." In Instituto Internacional de Literatura Iberoamericana, Otros mundos otros fuegos: fantasía y realismo mágico en Iberoamérica (East Lansing: Michigan State University, Latin American Studies Center, 1975), pp. 271-275.

88.50   Libertella, Héctor. "Severo Sarduy: Cobra." In his Nueva escritura en Latinoamérica (Caracas: Monte Avila, 1977), pp. 83-85.

88.51   Mac Adam, Alfred J. "Severo Sarduy, vital signs." In his Modern Latin American narratives; the dreams of reason (Chicago: The University of Chicago Press, 1977), pp. 44-50.

88.52   Mace, Marie-Anne. "La face française de Severo Sarduy." RECIFS, 3 (1981), 87-93.

88.53   Méndez, Adriana. "Erotismo, cultura y sujeto en De donde son los cantantes." RI, Nos. 102-103 (1978), 45-63.

88.54   Meneses, Perla. "De Gestos a Cobra (fragmentarismo 'in crescento')." Románica, 13 (1976), 96-104.

88.55   Miranda, Julio E. "Escrito en cubano." Imagen, No. 74 (1970), 10.

88.56   _____. "El nuevo pensamiento cubano." El urogallo, No. 8 (1971), 84-93.

88.57   Monteiro, Oscar. "Maitreya: lama, Lezama, L.S.D." In Rose S. Minc, Literatures in transition: the many voices of the Caribbean (Gaithersburg, Md.: Hispamérica, 1982), pp. 123-135.

88.58 _____. "The word made flesh and other problems: Severo Sarduy's La plage and France-Soir." RomN, 18 (1978), 415-419.

88.59 Murena, Héctor A. "Un romancier jeune, plein de sensibilité et de vigueur." LetN, 13 (1970), 139-142.

88.60 Ortega, Julio. "De donde son los cantantes." In Severo Sarduy, q.v., pp. 193-202.

88.61 _____. "Notas sobre Sarduy." In his La contemplación y la fiesta (Caracas: Monte Avila, 1969), pp. 205-210. Also as "Severo Sarduy." In his Relato de la utopía (Barcelona: La Gaya Ciencia, 1973), pp. 161-172.

88.62 Pagés Larraya, Antonio. "Una novela de Severo Sarduy [Gestos]." Comentario, No. 65 (1969), 55-57.

88.63 Papastamatiu, Basilia. "Entrevista con Severo Sarduy. Una nueva interpretación del barroco." Imagen, Nos. 14-15 (1967), 3.

88.64 Peña, Margarita. "[De donde son los cantantes]." Diálogos, No. 21 (1968), 36-37.

88.65 Pérez Rivera, Francisco. "Budismo y barroco en Severo Sarduy." LLM, 2, 1 (1983), 6.

88.66 Rivera, Carlos. "Tres escrituras: Cobra, El mundo alucinante [de Reinaldo Arenas] y Sebregondi retrocede [de Osvaldo Lamborghini]." Románica, 2 (1975), 55-62.

88.67 Rivero Potter, Alicia. "Algunas metáforas somáticas--erótico-escripturales--en De dónde son los cantantes." RI, Nos. 123-124 (1983), 497-507.

88.68 Rodríguez-Luis, Julio. "Sobre los cantantes de Severo Sarduy." Insula, No. 303 (1972), 4-5.

88.69 Rodríguez Monegal, Emir. "Entrevista con Severo Sarduy." RO, No. 93 (1970), 315-343.

88.70 _____. "Sarduy: las metamorfosis del éxito." In his Narradores de esta América; 2. ed. (Montevideo: Alfa, 1969-1974), II, 421-445. Also in Severo Sarduy, q.v., pp. 35-61.

88.71 _____. "Severo Sarduy." In his El arte de narrar (Caracas: Monte Avila, 1968), pp. 269-292. Orig. as "Las estructuras de la narración. Diálogo." MNu, No. 2 (1966), 15-26.

88.72 Rosa, Nicolás. "[Escrito sobre un cuerpo]." Los libros, No. 2 (1969), 5.

88.73 Rozencvaig, Perla. "El Big bang de Severo Sarduy o la explosión poética." Chasqui, 10, 1 (1980), 36-42.

88.74   Rumazo, Lupe. "Discurso del estructuralismo americano." RyFa,
        No. 11 (1969), 54-60.

88.75   Santí, Enrico-Mario. "Textual politics: Severo Sarduy." LALR,
        No. 16 (1980), 152-160.

88.76   Sarduy, Severo. "Chronology." Review, No. 6 (1972), 24-27.

88.77   Schulman, Ivan A. "Severo Sarduy." In Narrativa y crítica de
        nuestra América (Madrid: Castalia, 1978), pp. 387-404.

88.78   ____. "Severo Sarduy y la metamorfosis narrativa." El uroga-
        llo, Nos. 35-36 (1975), 108-114.

88.79   ____. "La situación [de Lisandro Otero] y Gestos: dos visiones
        de la experiencia histórica cubana." NNH, 4 (1974), 345-
        352. Also DHR, 5, 3 (1966), 121-133.

88.80   Schwartz, Ronald. "Cobra meets the spiderwoman: two examples
        of Cuban and Argentinian 'camp'." In Rose S. Minc, Re-
        quiem for the "boom'--premature? A symposium (Montclair,
        N.J.: Montclair State College, 1980), pp. 137-149.

88.81   ____. "Sarduy: Cuban 'camp'." In his Nomads, exiles, and emi-
        grés: the rebirth of the Latin American narrative, 1960-80
        (Metuchen, N.J.: Scarecrow Press, 1980), pp. 92-99.

88.82   Seager, Dennis. "Conversation with Severo Sarduy: a dialogue."
        Dispositio, Nos. 15-16 (1980-1981), 129-142.

88.83   Shaw, Donald L. "Severo Sarduy." In his Nueva narrativa hispa-
        noamericana (Madrid: Cátedra, 1981), pp. 174-179.

88.84   Sollers, Phillippe. "La boca obra." TelQ, No. 42 (1970), 35-
        36.

88.85   Sucre, Guillermo. "Severo Sarduy: los plenos poderes de la re-
        tórica." Imagen, No. 20 (1968), 24.

88.86   Torres Fierro, Danubio. "Severo Sarduy: lluvia fresca, bajo el
        flamboyant." Escandalar, 1, 3 (1978), 65-70.

88.87   Ulloa, Justo Celso. "Contenido y forma yoruba en 'La Dolores
        Rendón' de Severo Sarduy." In Homenaje a Lydia Cabrera
        (Miami: Universal, 1978), pp. 241-250.

88.88   ____. "Severo Sarduy: por un arte urbano." In The Twenty-
        Seventh Annual Mountain Interstate Foreign Language Con-
        ference (Johnson City, Tenn.: East Tennessee State Univer-
        sity, Research Council, 1978), pp. 232-237.

88.89   ____, and Leonor A. de Ulloa. "Leyendo las huellas de Auxilio
        y Socorro." Hispamérica, No. 10 (1975), 9-24.

88.90 _____. "Proyecciones y ramificaciones del deseo en 'Junto al río de Cenizas de Rosa'." RI, Nos. 92-93 (1975), 569-578.

88.91 Valdesueiro, Luis. "El orbe poético de Severo Sarduy." CHA, No. 312 (1976), 739-742.

88.92 Vázquez-Ayora, Gerardo. "Estudio estilístico de Cobra de Severo Sarduy." Hispamérica, Nos. 23-24 (1979), 35-42.

88.93 Weiss, Judith A. "On the trail of the (un)holy serpent: Cobra, by Severo Sarduy." JSSTC, 5 (1977), 57-69.

89. SOLER PUIG, JOSE (1916-   )

Critical Essays

89.1   Alvarez Baragaño, José. "'El maestro' entre los tabaqueros."
        Unión, 1, 1 (1962), 109-113.

89.2   Benedetti, Mario. "La hazaña de un provinciano [El pan dormi-
        do]." Santiago, No. 28 (1977), 55-62. Also RCLL, Nos.
        7-8 (1978), 199-204.

89.3   Benítez Rojo, Antonio. "El pan dormido: hacia una nueva per-
        ceptiva." CAm, No. 112 (1979), 150-162.

89.4   Campa, Román V. de la. "El pan dormido: 'una aventura narrati-
        va ante la farándula machadista'." Hispamérica, No. 31
        (1982), 85-92.

89.5   Cardoso, Onelio Jorge. "Palabras en los sesenta de Soler."
        GdC, No. 152 (1977), 3-4.

89.6   Fornet, Ambrosio. "De provinciano a provinciano [El derrumbe]."
        GdC, No. 39 (1964), 9-11.

89.7   Greiding, Yuri. "José Soler Puig: '...sin la revolución no hu-
        biera podido llegar a ser escritor...'." ALat, No. 4
        (1979), 149-153.

89.8   Márquez, Bernardo. "Sí a Soler Puig." Bohemia, 69, 23 (1977),
        29.

89.9   Pokal'chuk, Iuriĭ. "Pered bureiu." Vsesvit, 9 (1980), 63-64.

89.10   Portuondo, José Antonio. "José Soler Puig y la novela de la re-
        volución cubana." In his Crítica de la época y otros ensa-
        yos (Santa Clara?: Universidad Central de Las Villas,
        1965), pp. 197-208. Also as "Prólogo." In José Soler
        Puig, El derrumbe (Santiago: Consejo Nacional de Univer-
        sidades, 1964), pp. v-xiii. Orig. GdC, No. 39 (1964), 6-
        8.

89.11   _____. ‹"Prólogo." In José Soler Puig, El pan dormido (H: Unión
        de Escritores y Artistas de Cuba, 1975), pp. 5-6.

89.12   Repilado, Ricardo. "Algunos caminos para llegar a El pan dor-
        mido." Santiago, No. 20 (1975), 280-282.

89.13   _____. "En los sesenta años de José Soler Puig." Unión, 16, 1
        (1977), 116-131.

89.14   Rivero García, José. "El caserón, un buen experimento en la
        obra de Soler Puig." CB, No. 111 (1977), 25.

89.15   Rodríguez Sosa, Fernando. "Lo último de Soler Puig [El case-
        rón]." Bohemia, 69, 19 (1977), 25.

89.16   Romero, Cira. "José Soler Puig o la imagen real. A propósito
        de El caserón." GdC, No. 166 (1978), 18-19.

89.17   Sarusky, Jaime. "José Soler Puig." Bohemia, 69, 35 (1977),
        86-87.

89.18   Sass, U., and C. Holz. "Die kubanische Revolution in den Werken
        von José Soler Puig." Lateinamerika, Fall 1978, pp. 25-34.

90. SUAREZ Y ROMERO, ANSELMO (1818-1878)

Bibliographies

90.1 Moreno Fraginǎls, Manuel. "Indice de los manuscritos de Anselmo
Suárez y Romero que se conservan en la Biblioteca Nacional." RBNC, 2a serie, 1, 2 (1950), 73-116.

Critical Monographs and Dissertations

90.2 Cepero, Elodia. Anselmo Suárez y Romero y su obra literaria.
H: Universidad de la Habana, 1943.

Critical Essays

90.3 "Anselmo Suárez Romero." RBNC, 2a serie, 1, 2 (1950), 61.

90.4 Barnet, Miguel. "Yaguas y naranjos para la historia [Colección
de artículos, trabajos periodísticos]." GdC, No. 26
(1963), 14-15.

90.5 Bueno, Salvador. "Anselmo Suárez y Romero, el autor de Francisco." In his Figuras cubanas del siglo XIX (H: Unión
de Escritores y Artistas, 1980), pp. 253-257.

90.6 _____. "En el centenario de la muerte de Anselmo Suárez y Romero." Bohemia, 70, 8 (1978), 10-13.

90.7 _____. "Pequeñas biografías: Anselmo Suárez y Romero, el autor
de Francisco." Carteles, 34, 47 (1953), 24.

90.8 Caballero Ríos, Norberto. "Crónica de la esclavitud [Francis-
co]." TLit, 5, 5-6 (1975), 13-17.

90.9 Cabrera Saqui, Mario. "Vida, pasión y gloria de Anselmo Suárez
y Romero." In Anselmo Suárez y Romero, Francisco; el inge-
nio o las delicias del campo; novela cubana (H: Ministerio
de Educación, Dirección de Cultura, 1947), pp. 5-36.

90.10 Cobb, Martha K. "Bibliographical essay: an appraisal of Latin
American slavery through literature." JNH, 58 (1973),
460-469. Suárez Romero inter alios.

90.11 Cuza Malé, Belkis. "¿Esclavista o defensor de esclavos?" GdC,
No. 166 (1978), 12-14.

90.12 Díaz González, Enrique. "'Las delicias del campo cubano' durante la primera mitad del siglo XIX." TLit, 5, 5-6
(1975), 33-35.

90.13 González del Valle, José Zacarías. "Cartas inéditas: a d. Anselmo Suárez y Romero." RdC, 5 (1879), 236-250, 323-342,
482-489, 569-580.

90.14 Gutiérrez de la Solana, Alberto. "Ideas morales, políticas y
sociales en dos novelas cubanas del siglo XIX." In Instituto Internacional de Literatura Iberoamericana, La literatura iberoamericana del siglo XIX (Tucson: Universidad
de Tucson, 1974), pp. 191-201.

90.15 _____. "Sab [de Gertrudis Gómez de Avellaneda] y Francisco:
paralelo y contraste." In Homenaje a Gertrudis Gómez de
Avellaneda (Miami: Universal, 1981), pp. 301-317.

90.16 Hernández de Norman, Isabel. "Anselmo Suárez y Romero (1818-
1878)." In her La novela criolla en las Antillas (NY:
Plus Ultra, 1977), pp. 173-185.

90.17 _____. "Anselmo Suárez y Romero (1818-1878)." In her La novela romántica en las Antillas (NY: Ateneo Puertorriqueño de
Nueva York, 1969), pp. 173-185.

90.18 Leante, César. "Dos obras antiesclavistas cubanas." CA, No.
207 (1976), 175-188. Suárez Romero and Juan Francisco
Manzano.

90.19 _____. "Francisco y Juan Francisco. Coincidencias que no son
casuales. Dos estremecedoras denuncias." CB, No. 95
(1975), 4-5, 28-29.

90.20 Masiello, Francine Rose. "The other Francisco: film lessons
on novel reading [Francisco, el ingenio]." I&L, No. 5
(1978), 19-27.

90.21 Mesa Rodríguez, Manuel I. "Anselmo Suárez y Romero, el cantor
de la naturaleza guajira." In Conferencias de historia
habanera. I. Habaneros ilustres (H: Municipio de la Habana, 1937), pp. 95-110.

90.22 Morales y Morales, Vidal. "Escritores cubanos. Anselmo Suárez
y Romero." RdC, 3, 2-3 (1878), 113-131, 210-231. Also in
his 3 biografías (H: Ministerio de Educación, 1949), pp.
33-112.

90.23 _____. "La novela Francisco." CyA, No. 108 (1902), 213-217.

90.24 Moreno Franginάls, Manuel. "Anselmo Suárez y Romero (1818-
1878)." RBNC, 2a serie, 1, 2 (1950), 59-72.

90.25 Peña, Rafael Esteban. "Francisco: la fantasía al servicio de
la verdad." TLit, 5, 5-6 (1975), 21-25.

90.26 Roig de Leuchsenring, Emilio. "Anselmo Suárez y Romero." In
his La literatura costumbrista cubana de los siglos XVIII
y XIX (H: Oficina del Historiador de la Ciudad de la Habana, 1962-), III, 169-183.

91. TALLET, JOSE Z. (1893-   )

Critical Essays

91.1 Augier, Angel I. "Tallet: 85." GdC, No. 173 (1978), 3-4.

91.2 Bueno, Salvador. "El poeta José Zeta Tallet." In his Temas y personajes de la literatura cubana (H: Unión, 1964), pp. 219-228.

91.3 Carrera, Dino. "Tallet, el periodista." UPC, Nos. 17-18 (1972), 38-41.

91.4 Chericián, David. "Conversación con Tallet." GdC, No. 116 (1973), 2-6.

91.5 David, José Z. "Tallet, caricatura." CubaI, No. 54 (1974), 50.

91.6 "José Z. Tallet." CubaI, No. 54 (1974), 50-51.

91.7 Martínez Bello, Antonio. "[Versos]." RBNC, 2a serie, 6, 3 (1955), 195-196.

91.8 Núñez Machín, Ana. "Tallet en el regreso." GdC, No. 122 (1974), 20.

91.9 "Los 85 de Tallet. Homenaje conjunto." GdC, No. 173 (1978), 3.

91.10 Orovio, Helio. "Desde la nebulosa hasta José Tallet." In José Z. Tallet, Orbita (H: UNEAC, 1969), pp. 7-20.

91.11 _____. "Tallet y la antipoesía." Unión, 5, 1 (1966), 157-160.

91.12 Pérez Martín, Ezequiel. "Así so yo." Bohemia, 70, 43 (1978), 90-91.

91.13 Rodríguez, Pedro Pablo. "En sus 85 años." Bohemia, 70, 43 (1978), 54-55.

91.14 Suardíaz, Luis. "Hay poesía en los 85 años de Tallet." RyC, No. 75 (1978), 2-7.

91.15 Vitier, Cintio. "Palabra, Tallet." In his Crítica sucesiva (H: Contemporáneos, UNEAC, 1971), pp. 422-424.

92. TORRIENTE-BRAU, PABLO DE LA (1901-1936)

Critical Essays

92.1 Abad, Diana. "Nota." CAm, No. 106 (1978), 78-79.

92.2 Aldereguía, Gustavo. "Prólogo." In Pablo de Torriente-Brau, Realengo 18 (H: Nuevo Mundo, 1962), pp. 9-63.

92.3 Dumpierre, Erasmo. "Evocación de Pablo de la Torriente Brau." Islas, 10, 4 (1968), 211-220.

92.4 Fabal, Gustavo. "Mis recuerdos de Pablo." Bohemia, 63, 51 (1971), 98-101.

92.5 Frutos Redondo, Justino. "Sobre la muerte de Pablo de la Torriente-Brau." Unión, 5, 3 (1966), 188-193.

92.6 González, Reinaldo. "Torriente-Brau, el héroe 'anti-héroe'." Unión, 8, 3 (1969), 16-45.

92.7 González Carbajal, Ladislao. "Pablo de la Torriente Brau." BAN, 63 (1963), 135-148.

92.8 Marinello, Juan. "Pablo de la Torriente. Héroe de Cuba y de España." In his Contemporáneos: noticia y memoria (Santa Clara: Universidad Central de Las Villas, Consejo Nacional de Universidades, 1964), pp. 241-263.

92.9 Martínez Márquez, Guillermo. "Semblanza." In Pablo de la Torriente-Brau, Pluma en ristre (H: Ministerio de Educación, Dirección de Cultura, 1949), pp. xvii-lxiv.

92.10 "Pablo de la Torriente-Brau. 40 aniversario." Santiago, No. 23 (1976), 9-107.

92.11 Prío Socarrás, Carlos. "Prólogo." In Pablo de la Torriente-Brau, Pluma en ristre (H: Ministerio de Educación, Dirección de Cultura, 1949), pp. ix-xv.

92.12 Roa, Raúl. "Inicial." In Pablo de la Torriente-Brau, Aventuras del soldado desconocido cubano (novela) (H: Nuevo Mundo, 1962), pp. 7-13. Various other editions.

93. TRIANA, JOSE (1933-   )

Critical Monographs and Dissertations

93.1   Campa, Román V. de la. José Triana: ritualización de la socie-
        dad cubana. Minneapolis: Institute for the Study of Ide-
        ologies and Literature, 1979. Orig. as "El teatro criollo
        de José Triana: rito y sociedad cubana." DAI, 37 (1976),
        37A.

Critical Essays

93.2   Brownell, Virginia A. "The eucharistic image as a symbol of
        the downfall of moden man." LATR, 10, 1 (1976), 37-43.
        Triana inter alios.

93.3   Dauster, Frank N. "The game of chance: the theater of José
        Triana." In Dramatists in revolt: the new Latin American
        theater (Austin: University of Texas Press, 1976), pp. 167-
        189. Orig. LATR, 3, 1 (1969), 3-8.

93.4   Estorino, Abelardo. "Destruir los fantasmas, los mitos de las
        relaciones familiares. Entrevista a Revuelta y Triana [La
        noche de los asesinos]." Conjunto, No. 4 (1967), 6-14.
        Also as "Détruits les fantasmes: les mythes des rélations
        familiales." CRB, 75 (1971), 9-22.

93.5   Fernández-Fernández, Ramiro. "José Triana habla de su teatro."
        Romanica, 15 (1978-1979), 33-45.

93.6   Hurtado, Oscar. "Triana musical." GdC, No. 42 (1965), 25.

93.7   "José Triana, Premio Casa de las Américas 1965." GdC, No. 43
        (1965), 18-19.

93.8   Justina, Ana. "Los asesinos a juicio internacional." GdC, No.
        57 (1967), 10.

93.9   Leal, Rine. "De la nada al infinito." GdC, No. 5 (1962), 3.

93.10   López, César. "La noche no tiene asesinos ante el espajo [No-
        che de los asesinos]." GdC, No. 55 (1967), 11.

93.11   Miranda, Julio E. "José Triana o el conflicto." CHA, No. 230
        (1969), 439-444.

93.12 Moretta, Eugene L. "Spanish American theatre of the 50's and 60's: critical perspectives on role playing." LATR, 13, 3 (1980), 5-30. Triana inter alios.

93.13 Murch, Anne C. "Genet-Triana-Kopit: ritual as 'danse macabre' [La noche de los asesinos]." MD, 15 (1973), 369-381.

93.14 Nigro, Kirsten F. "La noche de los asesinos: playscript and stage enactment." LATR, 11, 1 (1977), 45-57.

93.15 O'Nan, Martha. "The 1967 French critical reception of José Triana's La noche de los asesinos." In Festschrift José Cid Pérez (NY: Senda Nueva, 1981), pp. 119-124.

93.16 Ortega, Julio. "La noche de los asesinos." CA, No. 164 (1969), 262-267.

93.17 Piñera, Virgilio. "[La noche de los asesinos]." GdC, No. 47 (1965), 25.

93.18 Revuelta, Vicente. "Un théâtre d'imprécation." CRB, 75 (1971), 3-8.

93.19 Río, Marcela del. "La noche de los asesinos puesta por Juan José Gurrola." RBA, No. 18 (1967), 85-86.

94. VALDES, GABRIEL DE LA CONCEPCION ("Plácido," 1809-1844)

Bibliographies

94.1 Bar-Lewaw, Itzhak. "Bibliografía esquemática de Plácido (según Itzhak Bar-Lewaw)." RBNJM, 6, 3-4 (1964), 125-129.

94.2 Cervantes, Carlos A. "Bibliografía placidiana." RevC, Nos. 22-24 (1937), 155-186.

94.3 Pane, Remigio U. "Cuban poetry in English: a bibliography of English translations from Casal, Florit, Gómez de Avellaneda, Guillén, Heredia, Pedroso and 'Plácido'." BBDI, 18, 9 (1946), 199-201.

94.4 "Plácido. Bibliografía pasiva (selección)." RBNJM, 3a serie, 6, 3-4 (1964), 117-124.

94.5 Plascencia, Aleida. "Bibliografía activa de Gabriel de la Concepción Valdés, Plácido." RBNJM, 6, 3-4 (1964), 77-116.

Critical Monographs and Dissertations

94.6 Bar-Lewaw, Itzhak. Plácido: vida y obra. M: Botas, 1960.

94.7 Carruthers, Ben F. The life, work and death of Plácido. Unpublished Ph.D. dissertation, University of Illinois, 1941.

94.8 Casals, Jorge. Plácido como poeta cubano; ensayo biográfico crítico. H: Ministerio de Educación, Dirección de Cultura, 1944.

94.9 Figarola-Caneda, Domingo. Plácido, poeta cubano. Contribución histórico-literaria. H: Siglo XX, 1922.

94.10 García Garófalo y Mesa, Manuel. Plácido, poeta y mártir. M: Botas, 1938.

94.11 González del Valle y Ramírez, Francisco. Discurso leído en la recepción pública del doctor Francisco González y Ramírez. [Es de Plácido La plegaria a Dios?]. H: "El Siglo XX", 1923.

94.12 Horrego Estuch, Leopoldo. Plácido, el poeta infortunado. H: Luz-Hilo, 1944. 2. ed., 1949. Ed. definitiva, aum. y corr., H: Dirección de Cultura, Ministerio de Educación, 1960.

94.13 Sagua la Grande. Instituto de Segunda Enseñanza. Homenaje a Plácido en el centenario de su muerte, 1844-1944. Sagua la Grande: "El Porvenir", 1944.

94.14 Saíz de la Mora, J. Plácido: su popularidad, su obra, sus críticos. H, 1919.

94.15 Stimson, Frederick S. Cuba's romantic poet; the story of Plácido. Chapel Hill: University of North Carolina Press, 1964.

Critical Essays

94.16 Arias, Salvador. "Intento por fijar un texto poético: La 'Plegaria a Dios', de Plácido." L/L, No. 6 (1975), 123-142.

94.17 Armas y Cárdenas, José de. "El poeta envilecido." In his Ensayos críticos de literatura inglesa y española (Madrid: V. Suárez, 1910), pp. 215-220.

94.18 Augier, Angel I. "Realidad y poesteridad de Plácido o una defensa sin lugar." Bohemia, 40, 37 (1948), 12, 114-116.

94.19 _____. "Silueta de Plácido." Bohemia, 40, 28 (1948), 50, 82.

94.20 Bachiller y Morales, Antonio. "Plácido." RCub, 2 (1885), 547-561.

94.21 Barr, Amelia E. "Plácido: slave, poet, and martyr." ChU, 8 (1873), 62-63.

94.22 Bernal, Emilia. "Gabriel de la Concepción Valdés: su vida y su obra." In her Cuestiones cubanas para América (Madrid: Hernández y Galo Sánz, 1928), pp. 213-241. Also as "Gabriel de la Concepción Valdés, his life and works." Inter-America, 8 (1924), 152-165.

94.23 _____. "Los poetas mártires: Gabriel de la Concepción Valdés: su vida y su obra." CCont, 35 (1924), 216-232.

94.24 Bueno, Salvador. "Plácido, el poeta mártir." In his Figuras cubanas del siglo XIX (H: Unión de Escritores y Artistas, 1980), pp. 123-126.

94.25 Calcagno, Francisco. "Plácido." In his Poetas de color (H: Soler, 1878), pp. 5-24.

94.26 _____. "Poetas cubanos: Plácido." RdC, 4 (1878), 594-613.

94.27 Castellanos, Jesús. "La sombra de Plácido." In his Colección póstuma (H: El Siglo XX de A. Miranda, 1914-1916), I, 315-318. Also in his Los optimistas (Madrid: Editorial-América, 1918), pp. 171-174.

94.28   Castellanos, Jorge. "Plácido, poeta social." Exilio, 5, 2
        (1971), 63-96.

94.29   _____. "Plácido: ¿víctima o mártir?" Exilio, 7, 2-3 (1973),
        31-48.

94.30   Chapin, Clara Cutler. "Plácido, centenary of a Cuban poet."
        BUP, 78 (1944), 318-320. In Spanish, pp. 376-377.

94.31   Chapman, Maria Weston. "Plácido." LB, 1845, pp. 67-71.

94.32   Concha Arenas, Rubén Enrique. "Plácido o el poeta trágico de
        la revolución cubana." CdG, No. 17 (1958), 14-15.

94.33   Del Monte y Aponte, Domingo. "Paralelo entre Plácido y Manza-
        no." RdC, 5 (1878), 476-477.

94.34   Eligio de la Puente, A. M. "Introducción." In Gabriel de la
        Concepción Valdés, Poesías selectas (H: Cultural, 1930),
        pp. vii-xl.

94.35   Esténger, Rafael. "Plácido." RBC, 52 (1943), 18-34.

94.36   Feijóo, Samuel. "Un paralelo satírico: Plácido y Nicolás Gui-
        llén." Unión, 16, 3 (1977), 150-155.

94.37   Fernández de Castro, José Antonio. "Milanés y Plácido." CCont,
        5 (1914), 425-457.

94.38   Franco, José Luciano. "Plácido, una polémica que tiene cien a-
        ños." GdC, No. 4 (1962), 11-12.

94.39   González del Valle y Carbajal, Martín. "Gabriel de la Concep-
        ción Valdés." In his La poesía lírica en Cuba, apuntes
        para un libro de biografía y de crítica (Barcelona: Tasso,
        1900), pp. 111-136.

94.40   Horrego, Leopoldo. "En defensa de Plácido, réplica y esclareci-
        miento." Bohemia, 40, 32 (1948), 30, 93.

94.41   _____. "Evocación de aniversario: Plácido, improvisador."
        Carteles, 31, 27 (1950), 34-35.

94.42   _____. "Plácido y la conspiración." MALHC, 1, 7 (1950), 6,
        19.

94.43   Hostos y Bonilla, Eugenio María de. "Plácido." In his Obras
        completas (H: Cultural, 1939), IX, 7-109. His Temas cu-
        banos. Also ULH, Nos. 17-18 (1938), 34-68. Also in Clau-
        dio Santos González, Poetas y críticos de América (Paris:
        Casa Editorial Garnier Hermanos, 1912?), pp. 251-292.

94.44   "Iconografía. Sobre un retrato de 'Plácido'." RBNC, 1, 3-4
        (1909), 75-87.

94.45 Iraizoz y de Villar, Antonio. "¿Quién descubrió a Plácido como poeta?" In his Penumbras del recuerdo (H, 1948), pp. 70-74.

94.46 Jackson, Richard L. "Slave societies and the free black writer: José Manuel Valdés and 'Plácido'." In his Black writers in Latin America (Albuquerque: University of New Mexico Press, 1979), pp. 36-44.

94.47 Ortiz, Pedro. "Notas sobre Plácido." TallerC, No. 25 (1973), 6-11.

94.48 Osiek, Betty Tyree. "Plácido: critic of the vice-ridden masters and abuses of the enslaved black." SECOLASA, 9 (1978), 62-67.

94.49 Pérez Cabrera, José Manuel. "Plácido y la conspiración de 1844." RevH, agosto 1944, pp. 530-539.

94.50 Pérez de la Riva, Juan. "En el ciento veinte aniversario del fusilamiento de Plácido." RBNJM, 3a serie, 6, 3-4 (1964), 73-76.

94.51 Piñeyro, Enrique. "Gabriel de la Concepción Valdés (Plácido)." In his Biografías americanas (Paris: Garnier, 1906), pp. 329-359.

94.52 Portuondo, José Antonio. "Miseria y soledad de Plácido el mulato." Mediodía, No. 2 (1936), 9-10.

94.53 Ramírez Pellerano, Juan. "Un gram amor de Plácido." TLit, 1, 1 (1971), 7.

94.54 Remos y Rubio, Juan Nepomuceno José. "Valores poéticos de Plácido." RevC, 18 (1944), 86-104.

94.55 Rivera, Guillermo. "El ensayo de Hostos sobre Plácido." Hispania, 22 (1939), 145-152. See item no. 94.43.

94.56 Saíz de la Mora, Jesús. "El poeta Plácido." RevH, No. 22 (1944), 322-345.

94.57 Sánchez, E. "Un episodio de la vida de Plácido." Hero, enero-febrero 1944, pp. 21-25.

94.58 Sanguily y Garritte, Manuel. "Un improvisador cubano." In his Juicios literarios (H: Molina, 1930), I, 215-236. His Obras, VII.

94.59 _____. "Otra vez Plácido y Menéndez Pelayo." In his Juicios literarios (H: Molina, 1930), I, 237-257. His Obras, VIII.

94.60 _____. "El poema perdido de Plácido." In his Literatura universal; páginas de crítica (Madrid: América, 1918), pp. 273-281. Also in his Juicios literarios (H: Molina, 1930), I, 275-283. His Obras, VIII.

94.61   Schomberg, Arthur Alfonso. "Plácido, a Cuban martyr." NCent,
        25-XII-1909, pagination unknown.

94.62   Stimson, Frederick S. "Botanists and romantic poets in Cuba:
        Humboldt and Plácido." In Homage to Irving A. Leonard
        (East Lansing: Michigan State University, Latin American
        Studies Center, 1977), pp. 131-136.

94.63   _____. "Un poesía desconocida de Plácido." RI, No. 48 (1959),
        363-366.

94.64   _____, and Humberto E. Robles. "Introducción." In Gabriel de
        la Concepción Valdés, Los poemas más representativos de
        Plácido (edición crítica) (Chapel Hill, N.C.: Estudios de
        Hispanófila, 1976), pp. 9-27.

94.65   Varona y Pera, Enrique José. "Una nueva edición de Plácido."
        In his Artículos y discursos (literatura--política--socio-
        logía) (H: A. Alvarez, 1891), pp. 53-56.

94.66   Vitier, Cintio. "Dos poetas cubanos del siglo XIX: Plácido y
        Manzano." Bohemia, 65, 50 (1973), 18-21.

94.67   _____. "El juglar." In his Poetas cubanos del siglo XIX; sem-
        blanzas (H: Unión, 1969), pp. 13-17.

95. VARONA Y PERA, ENRIQUE JOSE (1849-1933)

Bibliographies

95.1 Peraza Sarausa, Fermín. "Bibliografía de Enrique José Varona."
RBC, 26 (1930), 161-177; 27 (1931), 100-116, 226-250, 427-
454; 28 (1931), 94-131, 278-315, 459-473; 29 (1932), 130-
157, 306-313, 425-474; 30 (1932), 120-158, 302-307; 39
(1937), 240-272, 460-476; 40 (1937), 133-146, 310-319; 41
(1938), 304-316; 42 (1938), 304-316. Partially published
also as a monograph, H: Molina, 1932.

95.2 _____. "Bibliografía del Primer Centenario del Nacimiento de
Enrique José Varona." In Homenaje a Enrique José Varona,
1951, q.v., II, 177-189. Also H: Anuario Bibliográfico Cubano, 1949.

95.3 _____. "La muerte de Varona: fichas bibliográficas." In Homenaje a Enrique José Varona, 1951, q.v., II, 394-402.

95.4 Trelles, Carlos M. "Bibliografía de Varona." In Homenaje a Enrique José Varona, 1935, q.v., pp. 495-518.

Critical Monographs and Dissertations

95.5 Agramonte y Pichardo, Roberto. El pensamiento filosófico de Varona. H: Universidad de la Habana, 1935.

95.6 _____. Varona, el filósofo del escepticismo creador. Exégesis
de centenario (1849-1949). H: J. Montero, 1949.

95.7 Alba-Buffill, Elio. Enrique José Varona, crítica y creación literaria. Madrid: Hispanova, 1976. Orig. DAI, 35 (1974),
1083A.

95.8 _____. Los estudios cervantinos de Enrique José Varona. NY:
Senda Nueva, 1979.

95.9 Arce, Luis A. Varona, destino sin frustración. H: Selecta,
1954.

95.10 Cabrera, Francisco de Asís. Razón contra razón; refutación de
los conceptos filosóficos, metafísicos o científicos de
Enrique José Varona. H: Herederos de S. S. Spencer, 1889.

95.11   Camacho, Pánfilo Daniel. <u>Varona, un escéptico creador.</u> H: So-
        ciedad Lyceum, 1949.

95.12   Carbonell Villalón, Walterio. <u>Biografía sintética de Enrique
        José Varona.</u> H: Lex, 1949.

95.13   Carbonell y Rivero, Miguel Angel. <u>El Varona que yo conocí.</u> H:
        "El Siglo XX", 1950. Same as item no. 95.66.

95.14   Cueva Zequeira, Sergio. <u>Discurso pronunciado ... en la sesión
        solemne de la Universidad de la Habana confiriendo al Dr.
        Enrique José Varona el título de catedrático honorario.</u>
        2. ed., H: "Tipografía Moderna" de A. Dorrbecker, 1923.

95.15   Dihigo, Juan Manuel. <u>Elogio del Dr. Enrique José Varona y Pera.</u>
        H: "El Siglo XX", 1935.

95.16   Entralgo, Elías. <u>Algunas facetas de Varona.</u> H: Comisión Nacio-
        nal Cubana de la UNESCO, 1965.

95.17   ____. <u>Dos apelativos continentales. Enrique José y José Enri-
        que.</u> H, 1947. Varona y Rodó, respectively.

95.18   ____. <u>La genuina labor periodística de Enrique José Varona.</u>
        H: Selecta, 1949.

95.19   ____. <u>El ideario de Varona en la filosofía social.</u> H: Biblio-
        teca Municipal de la Habana, 1937.

95.20   ____, Medardo Vitier, and Roberto Agramonte y Pichardo. <u>Enri-
        que José Varona: su vida, su obra y su influencia.</u> H,
        1937. Three essays, separately signed.

95.21   Fernández de Castro, José Antonio. <u>Varona, recuerdos persona-
        les.</u> H: Lex, 1949.

95.22   Ferrer Canales, José. <u>Imagen de Varona.</u> Santiago de Cuba: Uni-
        versidad de Oriente, 1964.

95.23   ____. <u>Varona, escritor.</u> Unpublished doctoral thesis, Univer-
        sidad Nacional Autónoma de México, 1952.

95.24   <u>Homenaje a Enrique José Varona en el centenario de su natalicio.</u>
        H: Ministerio de Educación, 1951. Pertinent essays are
        listed separately.

95.25   <u>Homenaje a Enrique José Varona en el cintenario de su primer
        curso filosófico (1880-1930).</u> Miscelánea de estudios li-
        terarios, históricos y filosóficos. H: Secretaría de Edu-
        cación, Dirección de Cultura, 1935. Pertinent items are
        listed separately.

95.26   Lizaso y González, Félix. <u>El pensamiento vivo de Varona.</u> BA:
        Losada, 1940. Also Lima: Torres Aguirre, 1964?

95.27   Mañach, Jorge. Semblante histórico de Varona. H: "El Siglo
        XX", Muñiz, 1949.

95.28   Martínez, Oscar. "Vida y obras de Enrique José Varona, ensayis-
        ta cubano." DAI, 33 (1972), 3656A.

95.29   Peraza Sarausa, Fermín. Iconografía de Enrique José Varona. H:
        Municipio de la Habana, Departamento de Cultura, 1942.

95.30   Pérez, Emma. Cómo ser fieles a Varona. H: Lex, 1949.

95.31   Sánchez Reulet, Aníbal. Centenario de Varona. Washington,
        D.C.: Unión Panamericana, 1950.

95.32   Vitier, Medardo. Enrique José Varona. H: Molina, 1935.

95.33   _____. Enrique José Varona, su pensamiento representativo;
        2. ed. H: Lex, 1949.

95.34   _____. La lección de Varona. M: El Colegio de México, 1945.

95.35   _____. Varona, maestro de juventudes. H: Trópico, 1937.

Critical Essays

95.36   Agramonte y Pichardo, Roberto. "Enrique José Varona." CUA,
        1950, pp. 57-68.

95.37   _____. "Legado del maestro." ULH, Nos. 97-99 (1951), 123-142.

95.38   _____. "La obra filosófica." In Enrique José Varona y Pera,
        Obras (H: Ministerio de Educación, 1936), I, 73-188.

95.39   _____. "La obra político-social." In Enrique José Varona y
        Pera, Obras (H: Ministerio de Educación, 1936), I, 239-270.

95.40   _____. "Varona, filósofo del escepticismo creador." CA, No.
        44 (1949), 193-208. Same as item no. 95.6.

95.41   Aguayo, Alfredo M. "La pedagogía del Dr. Varona." In Homenaje
        a Enrique José Varona, 1951, q.v., II, 342-353.

95.42   Aguilar León, Luis Enrique. "El pensamiento de Enrique José
        Varona." Trimestre, 3, 1 (1949), 55-66.

95.43   Alba-Buffill, Elio. "La Avellaneda a la luz de la crítica de
        Enrique José Varona." In Homenaje a Gertrudis Gómez de
        Avellaneda (Miami: Universal, 1981), pp. 213-223.

95.44   _____. "La conferencia sobre Cervantes de Enrique José Varona."
        Círculo, 7 (1977), 73-79.

95.45   Antuña, Vicentina. "Ideas de Varona sobre la mujer." ULH, Nos.
        97-99 (1951), 168-192. Also in Homenaje a Enrique José
        Varona, 1951, q.v., I, 235-250.

95.46   No item.

95.47   Arce, Luis A. "En torno a un epistolario de Varona ." <u>ULH</u>, Nos.
        168-169 (1964), 69-95.

95.48   Arciniegas, Germán. "Cien mil estudiantes en busca de un maes-
        tro." In <u>Homenaje a Enrique José Varona</u>, 1951, q.v., II,
        200-203.

95.49   Ardura, Ernesto. "El ejemplo de Varona." <u>InC</u>, marzo-abril,
        1947, pp. 18-19.

95.50   _____. "Enrique José Varona: deber y devoción." <u>MALHC</u>, 1, 1
        (1949), 4.

95.51   _____. "El ideario de Varona." In <u>Homenaje a Enrique José Va-
        rona</u>, 1951, q.v., I, 127-164.

95.52   Aróstegui, Gonzalo. "Cómo conocí a Enrique José Varona." In
        <u>Homenaje a Enrique José Varona</u>, 1935, pp. 491-493.

95.53   Augier, Angel I. "El magisterio literario de Varona." In <u>Home-
        naje a Enrique José Varona</u>, 1951, q.v., II, 44-48.

95.54   Baeza Flores, Alberto. "Enrique José Varona y la poesía." In
        <u>Homenaje a Enrique José Varona</u>, 1951, q.v., II, 135-167.

95.55   Baeza Flores, Angel. "En el gran centenario. Lección, pasión
        y espacio de Varona." <u>Carteles</u>, 30, 16 (1949), 46-47.

95.56   Baquero, Gastón. "Enrique José Varona." <u>RevH</u>, No. 14 (1944),
        33-35. Also in <u>Homenaje a Enrique José Varona</u>, 1951, q.v.,
        II, 62-64.

95.57   Baralt, Luis. "Las ideas estéticas de Varona." <u>ULH</u>, Nos. 97-
        99 (1951), 143-167. Also <u>RCF</u>, 1, 4 (1949), 19-26. Also
        in <u>Homenaje a Enrique José Varona</u>, 1951, q.v., I, 326-341.

95.58   Bernal del Riesgo, Alfonso. "Psicología de E. J. Varona." In
        <u>Homenaje a Enrique José Varona</u>, 1951, q.v., pp. 74-84.

95.59   Bisbé, Manuel. "Varona y los clásicos." <u>ULH</u>, Nos. 94-96
        (1951), 56-81.

95.60   Blanco, Alberto. "Varona y la ley." <u>Crónica</u>, 1, 4 (1949), 14.

95.61   Bueno, Salvador. "Enrique José Varona." <u>Santiago</u>, Nos. 13-14
        (1973-1974), 201-219.

95.62   _____. "Enrique José Varona, filósofo." In his <u>Figuras cubanas
        del siglo XIX</u> (H: Unión de Escritores y Artistas, 1980),
        pp. 87-92.

95.63   _____. "Notas al margen del centenario." In <u>Homenaje a Enrique
        José Varona</u>, 1951, q.v., II, 65-72.

95.64 Cabrera, Rosa M. "Las ideas estéticas de Martí y Varona." Ceiba, 3, 5 (1975), 60-66.

95.65 Carbonell, Néstor. "Enrique José Varona." BAAL, No. 4 (1933), 379-381.

95.66 Carbonell y Rivero, Miguel Angel. "El Varona que yo conocí." AANAL, 28 (1949), 55-88. Same as item no. 95.13.

95.67 Casal, Julián del. "Enrique José Varona." In Homenaje a Enrique José Varona, 1951, q.v., II, 271-274.

95.68 Caso, Antonio. "Enrique José Varona." In Homenaje a Enrique José Varona, 1951, q.v., II, 314-315.

95.69 Castañón R., Jesús. "El maestro Antonio Caso y Enrique José Varona." BBib, No. 81 (1956), 1.

95.70 Castro, Octavio Ramón. "Ante el centenario, actualidad de Varona." Crónica, 1, 2 (1949), 7-8.

95.71 _____. "Varona y su influencia en la juventud." Crónica, 1, 5 (1949), 11.

95.72 Castro Leal, Antonio. "Enrique José Varona y el espíritu americano." In Homenaje a Enrique José Varona, 1951, q.v., II, 217-223.

95.73 Castro Turbiano, Máximo. "Varona y el positivismo." RCF, 1, 4 (1949), 9-13. Also in Homenaje a Enrique José Varona, 1951, q.v., I, 109-126.

95.74 Chacón y Calvo, José María. "La iniciación cervántica de don Enrique José Varona." BACL, 4, 1-2 (1955), 77-102.

95.75 _____. "La iniciación filológica de un clásico de América." BACL, 4, 3-4 (1955), 145-153.

95.76 _____. "La poesía de don Enrique José Varona." In Homenaje a Enrique José Varona, 1951, q.v., II, 13-23.

95.77 _____. "Varona en la cultura nacional." RBC, 37 (1936), 49-52.

95.78 Crawford, William Rex. "Enrique José Varona." IPNA, No. 16 (1951), 50-55. Also in Homenaje a Enrique José Varona, 1951, q.v., II, 476-482.

95.79 Cruz, Manuel de la. "Enrique José Varona." In Homenaje a Enrique José Varona, 1951, q.v., II, 278-296.

95.80 _____. "Enrique José Varona." In his Literatura cubana (Madrid: Calleja, 1924), pp. 253-281.

95.81 _____. "Enrique José Varona." In his Cromitos cubanos (H: Arte y Literatura, 1975), pp. 269-293. Various other editions.

95.82   De la Luz León, José. "Enrique José Varona, su olvidada doctri-
         na." In Homenaje a Enrique José Varona, 1951, q.v., II,
         403-427.

95.83   Entralgo, Elías José. "Los conceptos libertadores de Enrique
         José Varona." ULH, Nos. 112-114 (1954), 104-167.

95.84   _____. "La genuina labor periodística de Enrique José Varona."
         In Homenaje a Enrique José Varona, 1951, q.v., I, 41-64.
         Also in Enrique José Varona, Artículos (H: Ministerio de
         Educación, Dirección de Cultura, 1949), pp. 5-42.

95.85   _____. "El ideario de Varona en la filosofía social." RBC, 39
         (1937), 273-320. Same as item no. 95.18.

95.86   _____. "El período esenciador en las ideas de Varona." In Ho-
         menaje a Enrique José Varona, 1951, q.v., I, 167-221.

95.87   _____. "Varona y los libros." Bohemia, 42, 3 (1950), 140-141.
         Also MALHC, 1, 7 (1950), 5, 22.

95.88   _____. "Varona y su proyección sobre la Cuba de hoy." CUA, 4
         (1949), 15-21. Also in Homenaje a Enrique José Varona,
         1951, q.v., I, 354-359.

95.89   _____. "Una vida sin prisa pero sin tregua." In Enrique José
         Varona y Pera, Obras (H: Ministerio de Educación, 1936),
         I, 9-20.

95.90   "Los estudios universitarios de Varona." VU, No. 219 (1970),
         49-51.

95.91   Fernández Arrondo, Ernesto. "Nuestras relaciones epistolares
         con Varona." In Homenaje a Enrique José Varona, 1951, q.
         v., II, 103-109.

95.92   Fernández de Castro, José Antonio. "Mis recuerdos de Varona."
         Bohemia, 61, 21 (1969), 6-9, 113. Also in Homenaje a En-
         rique José Varona, 1951, q.v., I, 85-96.

95.93   _____. "Prólogo." In Enrique José Varona y Pera, Varona (M:
         Secretaría de Educación Pública, 1934), pp. v-xxxvi.

95.94   _____. "Ubicación de Varona." ULH, No. 49 (1943), 43-80.

95.95   _____. "Varona, recuerdos personales." AANAL, 31 (1950), 111-
         126.

95.96   Ferrer Canales, José. "Martí en Varona." RIB, 15 (1966), 251-
         256.

95.97   _____. "Varona, Roa y Puerto Rico." ULH, Nos. 97-99 (1951),
         193-220.

95.98   García Alzola, Ernesto. "Varona y la cultura revolucionaria."
         Unión, 16, 4 (1977), 119-139.

95.99   García Calderón, Francisco. "Enrique José Varona." In Enrique
         José Varona y Pera, Desde mi belvedere (Barcelona: Maucci,
         1917), pp. 5-9.

95.100   García Hernández, Antonio. "Varona, autonomista." RBC, 65
         (1950), 5-20.

95.101   García Tudurí, Mercedes. "Vocación íntima de Varona." In Ho-
         menaje a Enrique José Varona, 1951, q.v., II, 89-95.

95.102   García Tudurí, Rosaura. "Presencia de Varona." In Homenaje a
         Enrique José Varona, 1951, q.v., II, 96-102.

95.103   Gay-Calbo, Enrique. "Enrique José Varona." RBC, 35 (1935),
         198-206.

95.104   _____. "Homenaje a Varona." AANAL, 25 (1944), 177-193.

95.105   _____. "Varona, hombre de fe." In Homenaje a Enrique José
         Varona, 1951, q.v., I, 314-325.

95.106   Giusti, Roberto F. "Enrique José Varona, escritor." In Home-
         naje a Enrique José Varona, 1951, q.v., II, 230-238.

95.107   González, Miguel. "Varona y el arte." In Homenaje a Enrique
         José Varona, 1951, q.v., I, 276-280.

95.108   González del Valle y Carbajal, Martín. "Enrique José Varona."
         In his La poesía lírica en Cuba, apuntes para un libro de
         biografía y de crítica (Barcelona: Luis Tasso, 1900), pp.
         279-299.

95.109   Gracia, Jorge J. E. "Antropología positivista en América lati-
         na. Enrique José Varona y José Ingenieros." CA, No. 193
         (1974), 93-106.

95.110   Guadarrama González, Pablo M. "El ateísmo y el anticlericalis-
         mo de Enrique José Varona." Islas, No. 59 (1978), 163-
         182.

95.111   _____. "Enrique José Varona y el positivismo." Islas, No. 54
         (1976), 3-25.

95.112   _____. "Las ideas éticas de E. J. Varona." Islas, Nos. 55-56
         (1976-1977), 171-202.

95.113   _____. "Las ideas sociopolíticas de Enrique José Varona."
         Islas, No. 57 (1977), 51-110.

95.114   _____. "La sociología en el pensamiento filosófico de Enrique
         José Varona." Islas, No. 60 (1978), 83-125.

95.115   Guerra Castañeda, Armando. "Varona en la cultura cubana."
         RAm, 46 (1950), 17-19. Also in Homenaje a Enrique José
         Varona, 1951, q.v., II, 168-176.

95.116   Guerra Sánchez, Ramiro. "Tributo a Enrique José Varona." In
         Homenaje a Enrique José Varona, 1951, q.v., I, 399-415.

95.117   Henríquez Ureña, Max. "Enrique José Varona." In Homenaje a
         Enrique José Varona, 1951, q.v., II, 302-313. Orig.
         CCont, 4 (1914), 229-240.

95.118   _____. "Mi último recuerdo de Varona." In Homenaje a Enrique
         José Varona, 1951, q.v., II, 428-429.

95.119   Henríquez Ureña, Pablo. "El maestro de Cuba." In Homenaje a
         Enrique José Varona, 1951, q.v., II, 471-475. Orig.
         MAHLC, 1, 1 (1949), 22-23.

95.120   Heredia, Nicolás. "Enrique José Varona." In Homenaje a Enri-
         que José Varona, 1951, q.v., II, 275-277.

95.121   Hernández Catá, Alfonso. "Enrique José Varona." In Homenaje
         a Enrique José Varona, q.v., II, 316-327.

95.122   _____. "Prólogo." In Enrique José Varona y Pera, Violetas y
         ortigas; notas críticas (Madrid: Editorial-América, n.d.),
         pp. 7-26.

95.123   Hernández Figueroa, José R. "La perennidad de Varona." In
         Enrique José Varona, 1951, q.v., II, 53-56.

95.124   Hernández-Travieso, Antonio. "Varona, el filósofo de Cuba."
         ND, 26, 10 (1945), 12-13.

95.125   Hershey, John. "Enrique José Varona, Cuban positivist." Hu-
         manist, 3 (1943-1944), 164.

95.126   "Homenaje a Varona." AANAL, 28 (1949), 3-88.

95.127   Ichaso, Francisco. "El 'Año de Varona' debe ser el 'año de
         la cultura cubana'." In Homenaje a Enrique José Varona,
         1951, q.v., II, 7-12.

95.128   Iduarte, Andrés. "Cuba, Varona y Martí." In Homenaje a Enri-
         que José Varona, 1951, q.v., II, 210-213. Orig. RAm, 46
         (1950), 153-154.

95.129   Iglesias Trauler, María. "Ideario social de Enrique José Va-
         rona." In Homenaje a Enrique José Varona, 1951, q.v.,
         I, 269-275.

95.130   Iraizoz y de Villar, Antonio. "Anacreonte en Camagüey." In
         his Libros y autores cubanos (Santa María de Rosario: Ro-
         sareña, 1956), pp. 47-51.

95.131 Jiménez Rueda, Julio. "En el centenario de Varona." In Homenaje a Enrique José Varona, 1951, q.v., II, 204-205.

95.132 Lazo, Raimundo. "La crítica literaria de Varona." AANAL, 28
(1949), 17-30.

95.133 _____. "Interpretación de Varona." In Enrique José Varona y
Pera, Textos escogidos (M: Porrúa, 1968), pp. vii-xxv.

95.134 _____. "Los temas literarios de Varona." In Homenaje a Enrique José Varona, 1951, q.v., I, 65-73.

95.135 _____. "Varona en la historia literaria de Cuba." In Homenaje
a Enrique José Varona, 1951, q.v., I, 231-234.

95.136 Leal, Eusebio. "Raúl Roa: evocando a Varona." Bohemia, 69, 25
(1977), 41.

95.137 Lizaso y González, Félix. "Varona: culminación y síntesis de
los anhelos de Cuba." In Homenaje a Enrique José Varona,
1951, q.v., I, 360-379.

95.138 _____. "Varona y los valores humanos." In Homenaje a Enrique
José Varona, 1951, q.v., I, 97-108. Also CA, No. 50
(1950), 141-155.

95.139 Llaverías y Martínez, Joaquín. "Cómo pensaba Varona sobre Cuba en 1878 y 1879." In Homenaje a Enrique José Varona,
1935, q.v., pp. 105-110.

95.140 López Pellón, Nivio. "El lenguaje de Varona." In Homenaje a
Enrique José Varona, 1951, q.v., II, 73-75.

95.141 Mañach, Jorge. "El filosofar de Varona." AANAL, 35 (1949),
31-53. Also in Homenaje a Enrique José Varona, 1951, q.
v., I, 380-398. Also Bohemia, 41, 15 (1949), 49, 90; 41,
16 (1949), 50, 94.

95.142 Marinello, Juan. "Enrique José Varona y el imperialismo." In
his Contemporáneos: noticia y memoria (Santa Clara: Universidad Central de Las Villas, Consejo Nacional de Universidades, 1964), pp. 109-126.

95.143 Márquez Sterling, Manuel. "Enrique José Varona." BUP, 68
(1934), 431-436. In Spanish, pp. 487-493. Also in Homenaje a Enrique José Varona, 1951, q.v., II, 430-435.

95.144 Martí, Jorge Luis. "Varona: maestro de la democracia." In
Homenaje a Enrique José Varona, 1951, q.v., II, 57-59.

95.145 Martí, José. "El poeta anónimo de Polognia de Enrique José
Varona." In Homenaje a Enrique José Varona, 1951, q.v.,
II, 270.

95.146 _____. "Seis conferencias de Enrique José Varona." In Homenaje a Enrique José Varona, 1951, q.v., II, 266-269.

95.147 Martínez, Luis. "Varona y el arte." In Homenaje a Enrique José Varona, 1951, q.v., I, 341-353.

95.148 Martínez Bello, Antonio. "¿Fue Varona un filósofo?" In Homenaje a Enrique José Varona, 1951, q.v., II, 126-134.

95.149 Martínez de Cabrera, Rosa. "Ideas estéticas de Varona." In
Homenaje a Enrique José Varona, 1951, q.v., I, 303-313.

95.150 Martínez Márquez, Guillermo. "Recuerdo de Varona." In Homenaje a Enrique José Varona, 1951, q.v., II, 60-61.

95.151 Méndez, Manuel Isidro. "Sugerencias martianas. Varona, Martí
y Cervantes." Crónica, 1, 5 (1949), 13.

95.152 Montoro, Rafael. "Varona." In Homenaje a Enrique José Varona,
1935, q.v., pp. 13-18. Also in Homenaje a Enrique José
Varona, 1951, q.v., II, 436-440.

95.153 "Nuestro homenaje a Enrique José Varona." RBNC, 2a serie, 1,
1 (1949), 3-8.

95.154 Ortiz, Fernando. "¿Qué pensaría Varona?" In Homenaje a Enrique José Varona, 1951, q.v., II, 24-26.

95.155 Peraza Sarausa, Fermín. "Iconografía de Enrique José Varona."
RBC, 44 (1939), 129-143, 223-247, 445-460; 45 (1940), 113-
128, 241-256, 441-456; 46 (1940), 41-56, 227-244; 47
(1941), 150-153, 295-297, 427-430; 48 (1941), 115-123,
450-453; 49 (1942), 137-141, 296-305; 50 (1942), 140-142,
303-306, 444-456.

95.156 Pérez, Bernardo. "Enrique José Varona." In Homenaje a Enrique
José Varona, 1951, q.v., II, 263-265.

95.157 Pérez Téllez, Emma. "Alrededor del ideal educativo de Varona."
ULH, Nos. 55-57 (1944), 145-164.

95.158 Picón Salas, Mariano. "El ejemplo de Varona." In Homenaje a
Enrique José Varona, 1951, q.v., II, 214-216.

95.159 _____. "Palabras." In Enrique José Varona y Pera, Por la patria en la colonia y en la república (H: Municipio de la
Habana, Oficina del Historiador de la Ciudad, 1949), pp.
xli-xliii.

95.160 Piedra-Bueno, Andrés de. "Perfil del maestro." In Homenaje a
Enrique José Varona, 1951, q.v., II, 115-125.

95.161 Piñera Llera, Humberto. "Ideas del hombre y de la cultura en
Varona." In Homenaje a Enrique José Varona, 1951, q.v.,
II, 80-88.

95.162 Plana, Juan F. "Enrique José Varona y la Sociedad Popular de Santa Cecilia." In Homenaje a Enrique José Varona, 1951, q.v., II, 110-114.

95.163 Pogolotti, Marcelo. "Varona y la colonia." In his La república de Cuba al través de sus escritores (H: Lex, 1958), pp. 9-11.

95.164 Prío Socarrás, Carlos. "Mi homenaje a Varona." Bohemia, 41, 16 (1959), 56-57, 74. Also in Homenaje a Enrique José Varona, 1951, q.v., I, 19-25.

95.165 Rego, Oscar F. "La influencia de Varona en la cultura cubana." In Homenaje a Enrique José Varona, 1951, q.v., II, 76-79.

95.166 Remos y Rubio, Juan Nepomuceno José. "Enrique José Varona." In his Los poetas de "Arpas amigas" (H: Cárdenas, 1943), pp. 125-174.

95.167 _____. "El Ramillete poético de Varona." In Homenaje a Enrique José Varona, 1951, q.v., II, 41-43.

95.168 Roa, Raúl. "Adios al maestro." In Homenaje a Enrique José Varona, 1951, q.v., II, 331-335.

95.169 _____. "Discurso [sobre Varona]." Bohemia, 69, 17 (1977), 50-56.

95.170 _____. "Enrique José Varona." CA, No. 213 (1977), 190-205.

95.171 _____. "Enrique José Varona y nuestra generación." In Homenaje a Enrique José Varona, 1951, q.v., I, 251-263.

95.172 _____. "Evocación y homenaje." In Homenaje a Enrique José Varona, 1951, q.v., I, 267-268.

95.173 _____. "Palabras en la tumba de Enrique José Varona." RAm, 28 (1934), 233-234.

95.174 _____. "Varona y nuestra generación." Unión, 6, 4 (1967), 35-52.

95.175 Rodó, José Enrique. "Carta a Enrique José Varona." In Homenaje a Enrique José Varona, 1951, q.v., II, 297.

95.176 Rodríguez, Carlos Rafael. "Varona y la trayectoria del pensamiento cubano." In Enrique José Varona y Pera, Por la patria en la colonia y en la república (H: Municipio de la Habana, Oficina del Historiador de la Ciudad, 1949), pp. xxiii-xl.

95.177 Rodríguez Loeches, Enrique. "Varona y la revolución." In Homenaje a Enrique José Varona, 1951, q.v., I, 295-300.

95.178 Roig de Leuchsenring, Emilio. "Enrique José Varona, forjador
        de la república." In Enrique José Varona y Pera, Por la
        patria en la colonia y en la república (H: Municipio de
        la Habana, Oficina del Historiador de la Ciudad, 1949),
        pp. ix-xxi.

95.179 _____. "Maestros de ciudadanía: Sanguily y Varona." Humanis-
        mo, Nos. 53-54 (1959), 53-54.

95.180 _____. "Proyección de Enrique José Varona en nuestra histo-
        ria." In Homenaje a Enrique José Varona, 1951, q.v., II,
        32-34.

95.181 _____. "Vigencia de la obra patriótica de Enrique José Varo-
        na." ULH, Nos. 55-57 (1944), 332-345.

95.182 Romero, Francisco. "Enrique José Varona." CyC, Nos. 131-132
        (1943), 415-436. Also in Homenaje a Enrique José Varona,
        1951, q.v., II, 454-470.

95.183 _____. "Varona como filósofo." Américas, 20, 1 (1968), 13-18.
        Also as "Varona as a philosopher." Américas [English edi-
        tion], 19, 12 (1967), 13-18.

95.184 Russo Delgado, José. "Varona, el humanista y el hombre." USC,
        18 (1950), 53-69. Also in Homenaje a Enrique José Varona,
        1951, q.v., II, 239-249.

95.185 Salazar y Roig, Salvador. "Una vida paralela." In Homenaje a
        Enrique José Varona, 1951, q.v., II, 354-360.

95.186 Sánchez, Luis Alberto. "El centenario de Varona." In Homenaje
        a Enrique José Varona, 1951, q.v., II, 206-209.

95.187 Sánchez Arango, Aureliano. "Varona y la educación." In Home-
        naje a Enrique José Varona, 1951, q.v., I, 29-40.

95.188 Sánchez de Bustamante y Montoro, Antonio. "El pensamiento de
        Varona." In his Ironía y generación; ensayos (H, 1937),
        pp. 85-100.

95.189 _____. "El sentido de Varona en el pensamiento cubano." In
        Homenaje a Enrique José Varona, 1951, q.v., II, 360-365.

95.190 _____. "Varona." In his Ironía y generación; ensayos (H,
        1937), pp. 203-208.

95.191 Sánchez Reulet, Aníbal. "Enrique José Varona." In Homenaje a
        Enrique José Varona, 1951, q.v., II, 250-260.

95.192 Sanguily y Garritte, Manuel. "Enrique José Varona (su libro
        Desde mi belvedere)." In Homenaje a Enrique José Varona,
        1951, q.v., II, 298-301. Also as "El libro de Varona."
        In his Juicios literarios (H: Molina, 1930), I, 397-405.
        His Obras, VIII. Also as "E. J. Varona (su libro Desde

mi belvedere)." In his Literatura universal; páginas de
crítica (Madrid: América, 1918), pp. 291-299.

95.193 _____. "Una opinión asendereada." In his Juicios literarios
(H: Molina, 1930), I, 259-273. His Obras, VIII.

95.194 Sanín Cano, Baldomero. "Un grande americano." In Homenaje a
Enrique José Varona, 1951, q.v., II, 193-199.

95.195 _____. "Un rayo de luz en las tinieblas." In Homenaje a Enrique José Varona, 1935, q.v., pp. 19-22.

95.196 Santovenia y Echaide, Emeterio Santiago. "Enrique José Varona." In his Vidas humanas (H: Librería Martí, 1956), pp.
351-356.

95.197 _____. "Enrique José Varona, personalidad suma." Crónica, 1,
5 (1949), 4-5. Also in Homenaje a Enrique José Varona,
1951, q.v., II, 27-31.

95.198 Sardiña Sánchez, Rafael. "¿Corresponde esta universidad al
pensamiento de Varona?" In Homenaje a Enrique José Varona, 1951, q.v., I, 281-288.

95.199 Sosa de Quesada, Arístides. "Presencia de Agramonte y de Varona en la vida de Martí." RBNC, 2a serie, 4, 2 (1953), 40-
48.

95.200 Tejera, Humberto. "Enrique José Varona." In Homenaje a Enrique José Varona, 1935, pp. 73-76.

95.201 Torre, Roberto de la. "¿Cuándo se hará el museo Varona?" Carteles, 30, 29 (1949), 70-72.

95.202 Torriente y Peraza, Cosme de la. "Varona en la política cubana." In Homenaje a Enrique José Varona, 1951, q.v., II,
35-40.

95.203 _____. "Varona: un gran estadista." In Homenaje a Enrique José Varona, 1951, q.v., II, 49-52.

95.204 _____. "Varona y la política." RevH, No. 39 (1945), 224-234.

95.205 Valle, Raquel del. "Varona y la juventud." In Homenaje a Enrique José Varona, 1951, q.v., I, 289-294.

95.206 Varela Zequeira, José. "La figura de Enrique José Varona, su
influencia y su escepticismo." In Homenaje a Enrique
José Varona, 1951, q.v., II, 441-453.

95.207 _____. "La personalidad de Enrique José Varona." In Homenaje
a Enrique José Varona, 1951, q.v., II, 336-341.

95.208 Villoldo, Julio. "El busto de Varona." RBC, 51 (1943), 151-
157.

95.209 Vitier, Medardo. "Enrique José Varona." AANAL, 22 (1945), 67-81.

95.210 _____. "Enrique José Varona." RevC, 15 (1941), 79-96.

95.211 _____. "Enrique José Varona." In El libro de Cuba (H: Molina, 1925), pp. 565-567.

95.212 _____. "Enrique José Varona." In his Estudios, notas, efigies cubanos (H: Minerva, 1944), pp. 9-25, 248-253.

95.213 _____. "Enrique José Varona." In his Las ideas y la filosofía en Cuba (H: Ciencias Sociales, 1970), pp. 417-442.

95.214 _____. "Enrique José Varona." In his Apuntaciones literarias (H: Minerva, 1935), pp. 113-120.

95.215 _____. "La influencia de Varona." In Enrique José Varona y Pera, Obras (H: Ministerio de Educación, 1936), I, 271-284.

95.216 _____. No item.

95.217 _____. "El magisterio de Varona." Islas, 1, 1 (1958), 37-43.

95.218 _____. "La obra literaria de Enrique José Varona." In Enrique José Varona y Pera, Obras (H: Ministerio de Educación, 1936), I, 21-72.

95.219 _____. "La obra políticosocial." In Enrique José Varona y Pera, Obras (H: Ministerio de Educación, 1936), I, 189-238.

95.220 _____. "La personalidad de Enrique José Varona." In Homenaje a Enrique José Varona, 1951, q.v., I, 222-230.

95.221 _____. "Las preocupaciones de Enrique José Varona." RI, No. 1 (1939), 29-32.

95.222 _____. "La significación de Varona en nuestra cultura." In Homenaje a Enrique José Varona, 1951, q.v., II, 366-388.

95.223 _____. "Varona como maestro de cultura cubana." Anales, enero-junio 1944, pp. 83-102.

95.224 Weinberg, Gregorio. "El escepticismo de Varona." In Homenaje a Enrique José Varona, 1951, q.v., II, 224-229.

96. VILLAVERDE, CIRILO (1812-1894)

Bibliographies

96.1 Blondet Tudisco, Olga, and Antonio Tudisco. "Cirilo Villaverde, bibliografía." In Cirilo Villaverde, Cecilia Valdés o La Loma del Angel (NY: Anaya, 1971), I, 45-54.

96.2 Ximeno, J. Manuel de. "Papeletas bibliográficas de Cirilo Villaverde." RBNC, 2a serie, 4, 2 (1953), 133-153.

Critical Monographs and Dissertations

96.3 Farinas, Lucila. "Las dos versiones de Cecilia Valdés: evolución temático-literaria." DAI, 40 (1979), 1494A-1495A.

96.4 Geada y Fernández, Juan J. Un novelista pinareño: Cirilo Villaverde. H, 1929.

96.5 Gómez y Martínez, Luis. Cirilo Villaverde. Reflexiones a propósito de su personalidad literaria, resumida en su inmortal novela Cecilia Valdés. H: Rambla y Bouza, 1927.

96.6 Karras, M. Elizabeth. "Tragedy and illicit love: a study of the incest motif in Cecilia Valdés and Os Maias [by José María Eça de Queiroz]." DAI, 34 (1973), 1961A-1917A.

96.7 Morúa Delgado, Martín. Impresiones literarias: las novelas del Sr. Villaverde. H: A. Alvarez, 1892.

96.8 Padrón, Elsie Corbero. "Un estudio sobre la mujer y el ambiente en Cecilia Valdés de Cirilo Villaverde." DAI, 41 (1980), 1074A-1075A.

96.9 Sánchez, Julio C. La obra novelística de Cirilo Villaverde. H, 1955.

96.10 Santovenia y Echaide, Emeterio Santiago. Cirilo Villaverde. Madrid: De Orbe Novo, 1973.

96.11 _____. Personajes y paisaje de Villaverde. H: Cubana, 1911.

96.12 Torriente, Loló de la. La Habana de Cecilia Valdés. H: J. Montero, 1946.

96.13 Young, Robert J. La novela costumbrista de Cirilo Villaverde. M: Universidad Nacional Autónoma de México, 1949.

Critical Essays

96.14   Arrufat, Antón. "Cirilo Villaverde: excursión a Vueltabajo."
        CAm, No. 10 (1962), 133-140.

96.15   Baraona, Javier. "Itinerario de Cecilia Valdés." Carteles,
        31, 18 (1950), 14-17; 31, 19 (1950), 25-28.

96.16   Barreda-Tomás, Pedro M. "La visión conflictiva en la sociedad
        cubana: tema y estructura de Cecilia Valdés." ALHisp, No.
        5 (1976), 131-153.

96.17   Blondet Tudisco, Olga, and Antonio Tudisco. "Cirilo Villaver-
        de. Vida y obra." In Cirilo Villaverde, Cecilia Valdés
        (NY: Anaya, 1971), I, 7-44.

96.18   Bueno, Salvador. "Cirilo Villaverde." Bohemia, 69, 42 (1977),
        10-13.

96.19   _____. "Cirilo Villaverde, creador de Cecilia Valdés." In his
        Figuras cubanas del siglo XIX (H: Unión de Escritores y
        Artistas, 1980), pp. 225-235. Orig. as "El creador de Ce-
        cilia Valdés." Bohemia, 40, 51 (1948), 12-14, 210-211.

96.20   _____. "Cirilo Villaverde y su novela máxima [Cecilia Valdés]."
        RBNJM, 3a serie, 17, 1 (1975), 145-150.

96.21   Castellanos, Jesús. "Cecilia Valdés." RevH, 10 (1947), 307-
        321.

96.22   Cortina, Alvaro. "Novela cubana de la 'Flecha de oro'." Exi-
        lio, 6, 3 (1972), 27-34.

96.23   Cruz, Manuel de la. "Cecilia Valdés." ICub, 3, 17 (1887), 186-
        188.

96.24   _____. "Cecilia Valdés." Islas, No. 66 (1980), 65-80.

96.25   _____. "Cecilia Valdés (impresión)." In his Literatura cubana
        (Madrid: Calleja, 1924), pp. 193-200.

96.26   _____. "Cirilo Villaverde." In his Cromitos cubanos (H: La Lu-
        cha, 1892), pp. 189-211. Various other editions. Orig.
        RCub, 11, 10 (1890), 541-548.

96.27   _____. "Dos amores, novela cubana de Cirilo Villaverde." In
        his Literatura cubana (Madrid: Calleja, 1924), pp. 189-192.
        Various other editions. Cruz's notes were all reprinted,
        CUNESCO, Nos. 3-5 (1964), 73-89.

96.28   Deschamps Chapeaux, Pedro. "Autenticidad de algunos negros y
        mulatos de Cecilia Valdés." GdC, No. 81 (1970), 24-27.

96.29   Dorr, Nicolás. "Cecilia Valdés: ¿novela costumbrista o novela
        histórica?" Unión, 9, 1 (1970), 157-162.

96.30 Eligio de la Puente, Antonio. "Introducción." In Cirilo Villa-
       verde, Dos amores (H: Cultural, 1930), pp. v-xxxiv. Also
       as "Prólogo a Dos amores." CUNESCO, Nos. 3-5 (1964), 136-
       150.

96.31 Fernández de la Vega, Oscar. "La nueva traducción de Cecilia
       Valdés." RIB, 14 (1964), 415-422.

96.32 Fernández Villa-Urrutia, Rafael. "Para una lectura de Cecilia
       Valdés." RevC, 31 (1957), 31-43.

96.33 González Manet, Enrique. "Una incursión por Cecilia." ULH,
       No. 158 (1962), 171-179.

96.34 Gutiérrez de la Solana, Alberto. "Ideas morales, políticas y
       sociales en dos novelas cubanas del siglo XIX." In Insti-
       tuto Internacional de Literatura Iberoamericana, La litera-
       tura iberoamericana del siglo XIX (Tucson: Universidad de
       Arizona, 1974), pp. 191-201.

96.35 Hernández de Norman, Isabel. "Cirilo Villaverde (1812-1894)."
       In her La novela criolla en las Antillas (NY: Plus Ultra,
       1977), pp. 27-52, 119-131.

96.36 _____. "Cirilo Villaverde (1812-1894)." In her La novela ro-
       mántica en las Antillas (NY: Ateneo Puertorriqueño de Nue-
       va York, 1969), pp. 27-52, 119-131.

96.37 "Homenaje a Cirilo Villaverde." CUNESCO, Nos. 3-5 (1964), en-
       tire issue.

96.38 Jackson, Shirley M. "Fact from fiction: another look at slavery
       in three Spanish-American novels." In Miriam DeCosta,
       Blacks in Hispanic literature: critical essays (Port Wash-
       ington, N.Y.: Kennikat, 1977), pp. 83-89. Cecilia Valdés
       inter alias.

96.39 Lamore, Jean. "Cecilia Valdés: realidades económicas y compor-
       tamientos sociales en la Cuba esclavista de 1830." CAm,
       No. 110 (1978), 41-53.

96.40 _____. "Le thème de la traite negrière dans Cecilia Valdés de
       Cirilo Villaverde." In Hommage des hispanistes français
       à Noël Salomon (Barcelona: LAIA, 1979), pp. 455-463.

96.41 Lazo, Raimundo. "Estudio crítico." In Cirilo Villaverde, Ce-
       cilia Valdés (M: Porrúa, 1972), pp. vii-xli.

96.42 Leante, César. "Cecilia Valdés: espejo de la esclavitud."
       CAm, No. 89 (1975), 19-25. Also in his El espacio real
       (H: Unión de Escritores y Artistas de Cuba, 1975), pp.
       27-42.

96.43 Martí, José. "Cirilo Villaverde." In his Obras completas (H:
       Lex, 1946), I, 833-835. Also in his Hombres de Cuba (H:

Publicaciones de la Secretaría de Educación, 1936), pp.
32-36. Also CUNESCO, Nos. 3-5 (1964), 114-115.

96.44   Martínez Bello, Antonio. "Cirilo Villaverde y la novela cuba-
        na." Carteles, 31-X-1948, pp. 25-58.

96.45   Meza y Suárez Inclán, Ramón. "Cirilo Villaverde." RFLC, 12
        (1911), 210-217.

96.46   Mitjans, Aurelio. "Una opinion de Mitjans sobre Villaverde."
        CUNESCO, Nos. 3-5 (1964), 97-99.

96.47   Montero de Bascom, Berta. "Cecilia Valdés." FA, 21-22, 17
        (1972), 182-188.

96.48   Morúa Delgado, Martín. "Impresiones literarias: las novelas
        del señor Villaverde." CUNESCO, Nos. 3-5 (1964), 116-135.

96.49   "Nota biográfica." REsp, No. 403 (1884), 475-477.

96.50   "Noticia biográfica." In Cirilo Villaverde, Cecilia Valdés
        (H: Cultural, 1941), pp. v-viii.

96.51   Nunn, Marshall E. "Las obras menores de Cirilo Villaverde."
        RI, No. 28 (1948), 255-262.

96.52   _____. "La primera novela cubana." The Americas, 39 (1953),
        30-34.

96.53   _____. "Some notes on the Cuban novel Cecilia Valdés." BHS,
        24 (1947), 184-186.

96.54   Palma, Ramón de. "El espetón de oro." El album, 4 (1838), 5-
        11. Also in Cirilo Villaverde, El espetón de oro (H: Bo-
        loña, 1939), pagination unknown. Also as "Crítica del
        Espetón de oro." CUNESCO, Nos. 3-5 (1964), 103-113.

96.55   Parajón, Mario. "Prólogo a La joven de la flecha de oro."
        CUNESCO, Nos. 3-5 (1964), 151-161. Orig. in Cirilo Villa-
        verde, La joven de la flecha de oro (H: Comisión Nacional
        Cubana de la UNESCO, 1962), pp. 5-30.

96.56   Peñalver Moral, Reinaldo. "Leonardo Gamboa (el verdadero) no
        murió asesinado." Bohemia, 67, 9 (1975), 4-9.

96.57   _____. "¿Será esta la tumba de Cecilia Valdés." Bohemia, 66,
        50 (1974), 30-33.

96.58   Rodríguez, Ileana. "Cecilia Valdés de Villaverde: raza, clase
        y estructura familiar." Areito, No. 18 (1979), 30-36.

96.59   Rodríguez Herrera, Esteban. "Prólogo." In Cirilo Villaverde,
        Cecilia Valdés o La Loma del Angel (H: Lex, 1953), pp.
        vii-lxviii.

96.60 Ruiz, Gervasio F. "La navidad cubana en 1930 [Cecilia Valdés]." Carteles, 36, 51 (1955), 8-10, 182-183.

96.61 Sánchez, Guillermo. "Crónica." RBNJM, 66, 1 (1975), 145-151.

96.62 Sánchez, Julio C. "La sociedad cubana del siglo XIX a través de Cecilia Valdés." CA, No. 175 (1971), 123-134.

96.63 Santiesteban, Elder. "Estampas de Cecilia Valdés." VO, 14, 19 (1972), 57.

96.64 Tejera, Diego Vicente. "Juicio crítico sobre Cecilia." RCub, 4 (1886), 534-541. Also as "Una novela cubana" In his Prosa literaria (H: Rambla Bouza, 1936), II, 41-49.

96.65 _____. "Una moda cubana." CUNESCO, Nos. 3-5 (1964), 90-96.

96.66 Torriente, Loló de la. "Cirilo Villaverde y la novela cubana." ULH, Nos. 91-93 (1950), 179-194.

96.67 Varona y Pera, Enrique José. "El autor de Cecilia Valdés." CUNESCO, Nos. 3-5 (1964), 100-102.

96.68 _____. "Dos amores." RCub, 7 (1888), 84-92.

96.69 Villaverde, Cirilo. "Prólogo." In his Cecilia Valdés (NY: Anaya, 1971), I, 55-60. Dated 1879.

97. VITIER, CINTIO (1921-   )

Critical Monographs and Dissertations

97.1   _Homenaje a Cintio Vitier, 30 años con la poesía._ H: Biblioteca
        Nacional "José Martí", 1968.

Critical Essays

97.2   Aponte, Samuel A. "[Ese sol del mundo moral]." _Latino América_,
        9 (1976), 341-344.

97.3   Arrufat, Antón. "El fruto después de las vísperas [Canto lla-
        no]." _Ciclón_, 2, 3 (1956), 53-55.

97.4   Barradas, Efraín. "[Ese sol del mundo moral]." _SinN_, 8, 3
        (1977), 82-85.

97.5   Bejel, Emilio F. "Entretien avec Cintio Vitier." _Caravelle_,
        No. 38 (1982), 187-192.

97.6   Campuzano, Luisa. "Autografía por la crítica." _ULH_, No. 198
        (1972), 186-188.

97.7   Catalá, Rafael. "A propósito de Ese sol del mundo moral."
        CUG, 5 (1979), 173-174.

97.8   Chacón y Calvo, José María. "Un libro de Cintio Vitier: Lo
        cubano en la poesía." _BACL_, 8, 1-4 (1959), 246-252.

97.9   Diego, Eliseo. "Homenaje a Cintio Vitier." _Unión_, 6, 4 (1968),
        50-53.

97.10   Feijóo, Samuel. "[Escrito y cantado]." _Islas_, 2, 2-3 (1960),
        810-811.

97.11   Fernández Retamar, Roberto. "Cintio Vitier." In his _La poesía_
        contemporánea en Cuba (1927-1935) (H: Orígenes, 1954), pp.
        105-110.

97.12   Garganigo, John F. "Cintio Vitier: de la conciencia de la poe-
        sía a la poesía de la conciencia." _REH_, 14, 1 (1980),
        93-100.

97.13   _____. "Cintio Vitier: encarnación de una poética." _ALHisp_,
        No. 4 (1975), 207-230.

97.14 Méndez, Adriana. "Historia y poesía [De Peña Pobre]." Plural,
       No. 89 (1979), 67.

97.15 Pérez de la Riva, Juan. "Treinta años con la poesía: homenaje
       a Cintio Vitier." RBNJM, 3a serie, 10, 3 (1968), 162-169.

97.16 "Refutación a Vitier." Ciclón, 4, 1 (1959), 51-68.

97.17 Rosales, César. "Cintio Vitier o la poesía del deseo." RevC,
       31 (1957), 45-55.

97.18 Santi, Enrico-Mario. "Lezama, Vitier y la crítica de la razón
       reminiscente." RI, Nos. 92-93 (1975), 535-546.

98. ZENEA, JUAN CLEMENTE (1832-1871)

Critical Monographs and Dissertations

98.1 Carbonell y Rivero, José Manuel. Juan Clemente Zenea, poeta y mártir. H: Avisador Comercial, 1929.

98.2 Chacón y Calvo, José María. Juan Clemente Zenea, poeta elegíaco. H: El Siglo XX, 1951.

98.3 Gómez Carbonell, María. Estudio crítico biográfico de Juan Clemente Zenea. H: Caras, 1926.

98.4 Piñeyro, Enrique. Vida y escritos de Juan Clemente Zenea. Paris: Garnier, 1901. Also H: Consejo Nacional de Cultura, 1964.

98.5 Valverde y Maruri, Antonio L. La poesía de Juan Clemente Zenea, "A una golondrina"; estudio crítico. H: "Hermes", 1924.

Critical Essays

98.6 Aparicio Laurencio, Angel. "Juan Clemente Zenea." Yelmo, No. 8 (1972), 50-52.

98.7 _____. "Juan Clemente Zenea y el Diario de un mártir." In Juan Clemente Zenea, Diario de un mártir y otros poemas (Miami: Universal, 1972), pp. 11-28.

98.8 Bernal, Emilia. "Juan Clemente Zenea: su vida y su obra." In her Cuestiones cubanas para América (Madrid: Hernández y Galo Sanz, 1928), pp. 243-272.

98.9 Brull, Mariano. "Juan Clemente Zenea y Alfredo de Musset (diálogo romántico entre Cuba y Francia)." RevH, No. 26 (1944), 141-159.

98.10 Bueno, Salvador. "Juan Clemente Zenea, el poeta infortunado." In his Figuras cubanas del siglo XIX (H: Unión de Escritores y Artistas, 1980), pp. 137-141.

98.11 _____. "La obra poética de Zenea." Unión, 5, 4 (1966), 171-173.

98.12 Carbonell y Rivero, José Manuel. "Juan Clemente Zenea, poeta y mártir." In his Los poetas de "El laúd del desterrado" (H: "Avisador Comercial", 1930), pp. 137-193.

98.13 Chacón y Calvo, José María. "Los comienzos literarios de Ze-
        nea." RBC, 23 (1928), 700-709.

98.14 Chaple, Sergio. "Para una comprensión mejor de Zenea." L/L,
        Nos. 7-8 (1976-1977), 68-99.

98.15 Cruz, Mary. "Zenea o la traición." GdC, No. 95 (1971), 24.

98.16 Estevañez, Nicolás. "Juan Clemenete Zenea." RdC, 14 (1883),
        557-563.

98.17 Estrade, Paul. "El puñado de oro de la traición de Zenea."
        RBNJM, 3a serie, 20, 1 (1978), 93-100.

98.18 Feito, Francisco E. "Manuscritos desconocidos de Juan Clemente
        Zenea." Envíos, 1, 2 (1971), 38-47.

98.19 Florit, Eugenio. "Juan Clemente Zenea (márgenes al centenario
        de su nacimiento)." RBC, 29 (1932), 168-173.

98.20 _____. "Zenea: último y primero." In Instituto Internacional
        de Literatura Iberoamericana, La literatura iberoamericana
        del siglo XIX (Tucson: Universidad de Arizona, 1974), pp.
        183-190. Also in his Poesía, casi siempre (ensayos lite-
        rarios) (Madrid/NY: Mensaje, 1978), pp. 211-217.

98.21 Garrigó, Roque E. "Juan Clemente Zenea." CCont, 42 (1926),
        57-82, 150-212.

98.22 González del Valle y Carbajal, Emilio Martín. "Juan Clemente
        Zenea." In his La poesía lírica en Cuba, apuntes para un
        libro de biografía y de crítica (Barcelona: Luis Tasso,
        1900), pp. 243-257.

98.23 Hernández Miyares, Julio. "Juan Clemente Zenea: patria y poe-
        sía." El habanero, No. 18 (1971), 7.

98.24 Inclán, Josefina. "Juan Clemente Zenea: el desterrado de ayer."
        Envíos, 1, 2 (1971), 30-36.

98.25 Iraizoz y de Villar, Antonio. "Unos amores de Zenea." In his
        Lecturas cubanas; 2. ed. (H: "Hermes", 1939), pp. 115-118.

98.26 _____. "Homenaje a Juan Clemente Zenea." In his Pnys (Madrid:
        Mundo Latino, 1926), pp. 101-108.

98.27 _____. "El poeta mártir." In his Lecturas cubanas; 2. ed.
        (H: "Hermes", 1939), pp. 197-201.

98.28 Lezama Lima, José. "Prólogo." In Juan Clemente Zenea, Poesía
        (H: Academia de Ciencias de Cuba, 1966), no pagination.

98.29 Martí de Cid, Dolores. "Comparación estilística de Fidelia y
        La vuelta al bosque (de Juan Clemente Zenea y Luisa Pérez
        de Zambrana)." Círculo, 10 (1981), 57-67.

98.30 Martínez Bello, Antonio. "Juan Clemente Zenea (síntesis biográ-
       fico)." Cuba, 3, 4 (1947), 8-12.

98.31 Merchán, Rafael María. "Poesías de Juan Clemente Zenea." In
       his Estudios críticos (Madrid: Editorial-América, n.d.),
       pp. 187-232. Also in Cintio Vitier, La crítica literaria
       y estética en el siglo XIX cubano (H: Biblioteca Nacional
       José Martí, Departamento Colección Cubana, 1968), II, 161-
       192.

98.32 Morro, Juan del (pseud.). "Documentos relativos a Juan Clemente
       Zenea." RBC, 21 (1926), 676-680.

98.33 Piñeyro, Enrique. "Vida y escritos de Juan Clemente Zenea."
       In Cintio Vitier, La crítica literaria y estética en el
       siglo XIX cubano (H: Biblioteca Nacional José Martí, De-
       partamento Colección Cubana, 1968), II, 142-157.

INDEX OF CRITICS
(Alphabetization follows the norms of the Library of Congress.)